FRUIT GROWING IN INDIA

FRUIT GROWING IN INDIA

By

W.B. Hayes

GYAN

Published by

GYAN

Gyan Publishing House
5, Ansari Road
Daryaganj, New Delhi-110002
Phone: 011-47034999, 9811692060
E-mail: books@gyanbooks.com

Distribution Network
gyanbooks.com
India, USA, Canada, UK, Australia, France

ISBN : 978-81-212-9919-0 (PB)
First Published, 1945

2nd Impression 2021

Printed at: Gyan Press, Delhi.

FRUIT GROWING IN INDIA
Author: **W.B. Hayes**

FRUIT GROWING
IN
INDIA

By

The Late **W. B. HAYES**

Horticulturist, Allahabad Agricultural Institute

PREFACE TO THE THIRD EDITION

Because of the rapid progress of horticulture in India, it is fortunate that a third edition of this book is now needed. This makes it possible to incorporate much of the information which has become available since the second edition went to the press.

It was planned that the author would read the proof before leaving India on furlough in May, 1956, but unforeseen difficulties in printing prevented this. Thus the task of proof reading fell to Mr. James N. Warner, of the staff of the Allahabad Agricultural Institute. That he was willing to undertake this heavy work in a field not his own puts me deeply in his debt. The many errors which mar these pages are largely due to the very imperfect manuscript which I left behind and, in some cases, to the failure of the press to exercise the extreme care necessary to produce a book free from error. I am very grateful to Mr. Warner for his careful and thorough work under difficult circumstances.

In spite of the delay in publication and the errors which have crept in, it is the hope of the author that this edition, to a greater extent than former ones, will serve college students, workers in the great and expanding extension service, and those who through the production of more and better fruit are contributing to the well-being of their country.

Berkeley, California, U. S. A.
March 1, 1957

W. B. HAYES

PREFACE TO THE SECOND EDITION

The kind reception given to this book, and the exhaustion of the first edition within a few years are evidence of the need for such a publication. The author welcomes the opportunity for revision, not only to remove some of the faults of the fast edition, but in particular to bring the work more nearly up to date. It is probable that at least as much has been published in India regarding fruit growing since the first edition was sent to the press as in all the years before that time. It is hoped that the incorporation of much of the information published in this period will make this edition more useful to the fruit grower and the student of pomology. There are still many phases of the subject of which little is known, and it is fortunate that research is continuing, although one inevitable result is that in some respects this edition is out of date even before it is published.

A note of explanation and apology is due to the public. It was hoped that a new edition would be available very soon after the old one ceased to be, and the text was turned over to the publishers early in 1951. For reasons beyond the control of the author, and not understood by him, publication has taken more than two years. In an attempt to incorporate new facts as they became known, additions have been made after the original text was in type. This has meant the insertion of new paragraphs when the purpose would have been better served by the revision of old ones. In some cases the new may partially contradict the old. The patience of the reader is requested with regard to this and the large number of typographical errors which have crept in.

Allahabad
February 4, 1953

W. B. HAYES

PREFACE TO THE FIRST EDITION

In a country as rich in fascinating horticultural plants as is India, it is not surprising that there have been, and are, many keen and skilful gardeners. A number of books have been written on gardening, mostly by amateurs whose love for their hobby is apparent. Many of these works contain sections on fruit, but the main emphasis has been on ornamental gardening. The growing of fruit for the market has been left largely in the hands of poor and uneducated men who have been content to continue the practices of their ancestors, and where these have failed, to accept failure.

In the early days of the modern development of agriculture in this country, attention was, not unnaturally, given almost exclusively to the crops occupying the largest areas : the cereals, legumes, oilseeds, and fibres. The potential importance of the fruit industry, and its great value to the country, were largely overlooked. When the author started practising and teaching fruit growing in India, the lack of any satisfactory text-book, and the scarcity of scientific reports on the subject proved great difficulties. Scientific investiagtion of the problems of pomology has increased markedly in recent years, particularly under the stimulus of the Imperial Council of Agricultural Research. Not only is much more being published on the subject, but the quality is, on the whole much higher. The need for a book in which the knowledge gained is gathered together and interpreted, remains.

The present attempt to meet that need was begun more than ten years ago. The material has been gathered and organized a chapter or two at a time, and published unbound, primarily for the use of students of Allahabad Agricultural Institute. It is now being published in a more permanent form, after thorough revision. The kind permission of the Imperial Council of Agricultural Research, the Department of Agriculture, Bombay, and the Indian Journal of Horticulture, to reproduce illustrations is thankfully acknowledged. The author is grateful to several generations of students for their kindly criticism which has helped him to remove inaccuracies and to make the language as clear as possible. His thanks are also due to several colleagues on the staff of the Agricultural Institute for reading much of the manuscript and for helpful suggestions and especially to Mr. A. N. Singh for drawings illustrating methods of vegetative reproduction. His indebtedness to the wise men who have taught him, and to the hundreds of scientists from whose work he has profited, is beyond expression.

Allahabad
May 15, 1944

W. B. HAYES

"One cannot have beautiful trees without loving them. Neither goodness of soil, nor rich manure, nor favourable situations will alone make them thrive, but it is the gardener's affection which make them strong and vigorous."

—LeGendre, Superintendent of the Royal Gardens
under Louis XIII in 1652.

CONTENTS

PART I

CHAPTER I

OPPORTUNITIES IN FRUIT GROWING

FRUIT has been grown in India for thousands of years, and occupies today a position of considerable importance. This importance has not been sufficiently recognized in the past by either government agencies or the public. Fruit has not had its fair share of the effort which has been made to develop agriculture along modern lines. The industry remains in a rather primitive condition, and contributes far too little to the prosperity of the people. Since 1930, a number of fruit research stations have been established in different States. State governments, universities, and other institutions are also making contributions to the development of the industry. Much of this work is partly financed by the Indian Council of Agricultural Research. But much more effort is needed.

Before the division of India, the total area under fruits had been estimated as two million acres (Anonymous, 1943a), whereas a total of such provincial statistics as were available at about that time amounted to nearly two and a half million acres, although large areas were not included. Rao (1946) gives the estimated acreage of a number of fruits but omits the papaya, litchi, and date, as well as some fruits of less importance. His total of 1,830,800 acres is thus obviously low. Some published estimates are misleading. For instance, the U. P. Agricultural Pocket Book for 1943 gives the area under fruits and vegetables in that province as 582,623 acres and fails to point out that mangoes and some other fruits have been omitted. According to one estimate, there were nearly a million acres of mangoes in the State at that time.

This illustrates one of the difficulties in securing satisfactory statistics. Mango trees occur to a limited extent in jungles; commonly along roadsides, in compounds, and as isolated trees in fields; and in groves, some of which are cultivated and yield commercial crops, and some of which are neglected and of value mainly for their wood. The dividing line between the last two groups is not always clear, and it is questionable which of the categories should be included in statistics of the acreage under fruit. Certainly figures which included all of these would give a false impression of the fruit industry.

Nevertheless, much better statistics are possible than are now available for the country. Bombay has published fairly accurate figures for the acreage of its principal fruits for a number of years, as have some other areas. It is highly desirable that statistics be published annually for all parts of the country, preferably prepared in a uniform way. This would greatly facilitate intelligent planning for the development of fruit growing and related industries. Accurate figures on yields would be more difficult to secure, but are also highly desirable.

Such statistics of the acreage of fruits in different States as are available are given in Table I. Although all State governments were requested to supply statistics for this purpose, only 13 responded including one from which the figures were not usable. For other States, figures were secured from other sources where possible, but none have been secured for Delhi, Manipur, Rajasthan, or Vindhya Pradesh. The coconut has been excluded from these statistics although it is a very important crop, as its culture is very different from that of most fruits

Table I.—Area under fruit in some parts of India

State	*Area in acres*	*Source of statistics*
Ajmer	1,821	Agricultural Officer, Ajmer, 1955.
Andaman Islands	385	Agricultural Officer, Andaman and Nicobar Islands, 1955.
Andhra	223,406	Rao, 1954a.
Assam	111,390	Horticultural Development Officer, Assam, for 1954.
Bhopal	4,070	Director of Agriculture, Bhopal, 1955.
Bihar	329,400	Horticultural Diary.*
Bombay	134,650	Horticultural Diary.*
Coorg	24,546	Horticulturist, Coorg, 1955.
Himachal Pradesh	1,848	Horticultural Officer, Himachal Pradesh, 1955.
Hyderabad	44,878	Bureau of Economics and Statistics, Hyderabad.**
Jammu and Kashmir	18,500	L. Singh and Singh, 1939.
Kutch	2;578	Agricultural Officer, Kutch, for 1953-54.
Madhya Bharat	14,800	Horticultural Development Officer, M. B., 1955.
Madhya Pradesh	98,643	Horticultural Diary.*
Madras	346,048	Horticultural Diary.*
Mysore	71,100	Lal and others, 1952.
Orissa	172,799	Director of Agriculture, Orissa, for 1955.
PEPSU	8,549	Fruit Specialist, PEPSU, for 1951-52.
Punjab	54,250	Bajwa and Jawanda, 1953.
Saurashtra	2,553	Horticultural Diary.*
Travancore-Cochin	61,512	Director of Agriculture, Travancore-Cochin, for 1954.
Uttar. Pradesh	1,458,890	Horticultural Diary.*
West Bengal	213,715	Horticultural Diary.*
Total	3,400,531	

*Horticultural Diary, 1956, published by the Agri-Horticultural Society, Hyderabad.

**Exclusive of about 100,000 acres of wild custard apples.

and is not discussed in this book. The data provided by the Government of Travancore-Cochin do not include the cashew, which, according to one estimate, occupies 88,000 acres in that State. Another estimate includes 65,637 acres of cashews out of a total of 141,239 acres of fruit in that State. Comparison with the acreages under the various fruits given in later chapters will indicate other variations in estimates from different sources.

A striking feature of Indian orchards is the small size of the individual holding. In 1928 the Punjab had 3,194 gardens of more than three acres, but only 413 of more than 10 acres, and but nine of over 50 acres. The situation in other States is similar, with perhaps a still lower proportion of large orchards. Chand (1943) gives information about the size of gardens in many districts of Uttar Pradesh. The average size on the plains varied from 0.8 to 3.1 acres; while in Naini Tal the average orchard was of nearly 6 acres. The predominance of very small orchards increases the difficulty of introducing better methods of culture and marketing.

It is easy to find fault with the present condition of Indian orchards, and the methods in vogue. Probably the greatest mistake of the fruit grower is the use of inferior varieties. It is true that the grower is forced to depend upon seedlings in growing some fruits, but in others vegetative propagation is possible, and in a few, like the mango, many excellent varieties are available. Yet many seedlings are still planted by preference, producing fruits of very inferior quality, with few exceptions. Another fault which is almost universal is the crowding of trees, making it impossible for them to develop normally. Insufficient manuring, and poor methods of irrigation, cultivation and pruning are also common. Marketing is chaotic. These problems will be treated in some detail in later chapters.

The difficulty of introducing improved methods is increased by the fact that gardening is largely in the hands of specialized castes of poor economic status and very little education. These gardeners cannot afford to experiment, and are slow to depart from traditional methods.

This situation is in striking contrast with that in those countries where fruit growing is most advanced. There the fruit growers form one of the most progressive groups of farmers. As Williams (1926) has pointed out, 'Successful fruit growing requires unusual knowledge, skill, accuracy and thoroughness in production and marketing.' 'Fruit growing enlists many unusually intelligent young farmers and this intelligence is developed by the practice of their vocation.' The industry appeals to intelligent young men because the work is pleasant, because the problems challenge their ability, because of the leisure at certain periods of the year, and because it is more profitable than general agriculture.

The same appeal is made by fruit growing in this country, and is beginning to find a response. The industry is expanding rapidly in some sections. In the Punjab the area under fruit increased from 68,290 acres in 1938 to 100,339 acres in 1942, an increase of about 47% in four years. By 1947 it was about 110,000 acres. In Bombay the area was only 57,662 acres in 1930-31 and by 1939-40 had increased to 84,407 acres, or by more than 46% (Anonymous, 1941c). By 1948 there was another increase of about 31%, to 110,402 acres, nearly 5,000 acres having been added in the last year. Similarly in Baroda there was an increase of 45% in the ten years ending in 1939-40. Darling (1930) refers frequently to the increased number of fruit and vegetable gardens in the Punjab, remarking in one place, 'The striking feature of today's march was the large number of mango groves, many of them new. These show the landlord at his best.' Uttar Pradesh is somewhat behind the Punjab in this respect. Mr. Allan, the Director of Agriculture, in an article in the press in October, 1932, observes, 'A tour through the province shows a number of gardens of which the owners may be justly proud, a far vaster number of gardens which are far from effectively managed, either in the way the trees are tended or in the character of the fruit tree which is being grown, and finally many areas on which fruit cultivation could be developed effectively, were they to be laid out in a systematic fashion with the right varieties. . . Another aspect which strikes the wanderer interested in fruit expansion and specially in that of the mango, is the apparent dominance of old orchards and the comparative scarcity of new or recent plantings.' However, a number of more progressive landlords and farmers are now developing orchards on more modern lines, and the interest which is being shown promises a brighter future for this branch of agriculture. There is need for young men with a sound knowledge of horticulture to provide technical leadership for the industry. That all their abilities will be needed is indicated by an experienced writer ('Kisan', 1942) who states, 'Having developed the largest commercial fruit farm and probably the largest preservation factory in India, we can now say that fruit farming is the most difficult branch of agriculture to take up and that the manufacture of its by-products is equally difficult'.

The extent to which the Government should encourage the expansion of the fruit industry is debatable. It should certainly include research on the problems involved, and advice to growers. It may well include the strict supervision of commercial nurseries, and perhaps such service as the production and distribution of nursery plants, as is done in some States. Kashmir formerly gave budded and grafted plants to the public, but by 1947 charged four annas a plant, which was said to cover the cost. Some growers felt it would be better to increase the price and supply more reliable plants. Raina (1944) reports that the Government was unable to meet the demand for two million plants. The Punjab has set apart 13,000 acres for co-operative garden colonies, according to J. Singh (1949). In each colony of 500 to 1,500 acres, the farmers must form a co-operative society for all horticultural operations from the nursery to the processing and selling of the fruit, and each farmer must devote at least three-fourths of his allotment to fruit, under the instructions of the Department of Agriculture. Whether such material aid and regimentation is desirable is questionable. Certainly the profit bleness of the industry should make such measures unnecessary.

Large Development Possible

Soil and climatic conditions in India are very favourable to a large number of fruits. There is a considerable variety of soil types, but deep loam soils, suitable to most fruits, are very common. The mango and most of the subtropical fruits grow well on the plains, while in Kashmir, the Kulu valley, the Kumaun hills, elsewhere in the Himalayas, and in the hills of South India apples, pears and other temperate fruits can be grown successfully. In the submontane tracts, especially in the Punjab, Pepsu, and the districts of Dehra Dun, Saharanpur, Muzaffarnagar and Meerut, peaches, plums, berries and other fruits of the milder temperate zone do very well. The Himalayan districts are faced with a very difficult problem in transporting their fruits to the centres of population, but the fruit growing districts of the plains have a good present market, and an enormous potential market.

While conditions are thus favourable, it must be recognized that irrigation is essential, and that profitable fruit growing depends on an economic source of irrigation water. This is undoubtedly a limiting factor at present. However the acreage under fruit shown in Table I represents only about 6.6% of the irrigated area of India and about 1.15 % of the area under cultivation in 1955. With the increasing development of water power and cheap electricity the use of tube-wells makes irrigation economical over large areas. With the increase in irrigation should come an increase in fruit growing.

The present demand for fruit fully justifies such an increase. This market is almost entirely in the cities, but as Allan points out, in the article mentioned above 'The fruit supply in these centres of population is far from adequate. Without considering the possibilities of extra-provincial markets as the development of fruit sales in the Punjab, we have within our own boundaries, markets which with better and more economical methods of growing and care, better transport and better placing of our fruit...would be able to absorb two or three times the fruit they now do.' The present price of fruit is so high, except during market gluts, as to put fresh fruit out of the reach of a large part of the population. With more efficient production and marketing, the price could be so reduced as to encourage a tremendous increase in consumption and still provide a good profit for the grower. It is significant that citrus fruits, apples and other fruits from Palestine, Japan, and the United States until recently competed with Indian fruit, even in inland cities. With labour costs and other expenses per tree greater than those of India, these foreign growers can pay heavy freight charges and compete in India only by growing larger crops of high quality fruit. According to Wallschlaeger (1933) the average cost of producing oranges, up to picking, for the five years, 1928-32, was $245 per acre, in California. At normal exhange at that time this amounts to Rs. 673. Exactly comparable figures are not available for India. Cheema and Dani (1928) give the costs of maintaining orchards of figs, pomegranates, papayas, and bananas for five years, the average for all being Rs. 281 per acre. It is doubtful if the actual cost of growing oranges in India was more than this, if as much. The cost of production, both in America and in India has greatly increased in recent years. If Indian growers can produce as large crops of good fruit, there should be no need of a protective tariff.

The present demand for fruit justifies increased production, but the potential market is much greater. The dietetic value of fruit has been definitely proved only in the present century, and the public is only beginning to realize the necessity of including fresh fruits and vegetables in the regular diet. The demand for fruit is thus increasing among the educated classes, and will continue to increase as knowledge of its value spreads. Even in a city like Bombay, the sale of fruits and vegetables amounted to only half an ounce per day per head, according to Cheema (1933) as compared with 4½ oz. in London and one pound in New York. Gadgil and Gadgil (1933) estimated the consumption of fruit in Poona at one ounce per person per day. The average consumption of fruit and vegetables in the United States in 1951 was 436 lb. per capita, which means that perhaps 13 oz. per day was actually eaten. Experts have stated that for a balanced diet this figure should be raised to 564 lb., and that 620 lb. would be better.

Not only may the city market be greatly expanded, but the rural market, potentially much larger, remains almost untouched. Seedling mangoes are eaten by practically the entire population during the season, but many villagers eat no other fruit. This is largely because fruit is not available in the villages, or if available, is beyond the means of the people. The village market cannot be developed until the price of fruit is lowered, or the purchasing power of the people is increased. As stated above, it will be possible to lower the price considerably when the yield per acre is increased. A general rise in the standard of living is essential to the welfare of India, and is an object of all rural extension programmes. There is therefore reason to expect that as fruit growing develops, the rural market will absorb an increasing proportion, at profitable rates.

However, neither city nor village markets may be expected to develop automatically. The public needs to be educated to think of fruit as a staple and important food, rather than as a luxury. Much of this educative work will have to be carried on by the fruit growers and marketing organizations. The consumption of citrus fruits in the United States was only 7 lb. per capita per annum in 1908, when Sunkist Growers, the famous citrus co-operative in California started to advertise. By 1944 it was 68 lb. Production has doubled in each of the last four decades and would have resulted in uneconomic returns had not the market expanded also, largely because of advertising. This had cost this co-operative more than $60,000,000 by 1952, in which year about $4,000,000 was spent. This amounted to only 2-3% of the sale value of the fruit at the point of shipping. India cannot now send comparable amounts, but needs more educative effort than is now made. Marketing facilities also need to be greatly improved. As will be seen in a later chapter, the markets of the larger cities are very inefficient, and fail to serve much of the population. The rural marketing of fruit is a different problem, and one which will have to engage the attention of growers more and more in the future.

The development of motor bus service is a factor of great importance in the problem of marketing. Through it the area within reach of local markets is being rapidly expanded. Up till the present, a large part of the fruit coming into all but the largest cities has been produced close enough to be carried to market in carts or in head-loads. Railway transportation necessitates the use of packages not easily opened by pilferers and strong enough to stand rough usage. The sending of railway receipts often causes delay. On the other hand, fruit sent by motor bus is in charge of the driver from the time it leaves the producer until it reaches his agent in the city. The driver can therefore be held responsible for safe delivery, without delay.

Increased Fruit Production Desirable

The development of fruit growing which seems possible, and which is now beginning, will be of great benefit to the country. The consumption of more fruit will doubtless have a beneficial effect on the health of the people. The use of the land for fruit instead of less valuable crops is an economic advantage to the country.

The health-giving character of some fruits has been rather widely recognized, but many people still regard fruit as a luxury rather than a food which should form part of the daily diet. During the second world war, it became widely recognized that India was not producing enough food for its people, even on the basis of the low standard of nutrition prevailing. Strenuous efforts have been made to increase the production of food, particularly in the 'Grow More Food' campaign. One of the basic needs of the body is foods producing heat and energy, measured in calories. Food grains are a very important source of calories, but even from this restricted point of view, some fruits and vegetables compare favourably. It is difficult to make an entirely satisfactory comparison, partly because of the lack of accurate statistics regarding yields. It is obviously unfair to compare the calories produced on a given area by one crop grown on rich land with irrigation with those produced by another crop on poor land without irrigation,

Table II.—Estimated number of calories provided by one acre each of certain crops

Crop	*Calories per ounce**	*Yield*	*Calories per acre*	*Remarks*
Wheat	98	660 lb.	1,034,880	Average, India.
		5,822 lb.	9,128,896	Record productions, India, 1952.
Banana	43	10 tons.	15,411,200	Average, India, Rao (1946).
		5.4 tons.	8,128,512	Average, S. India, Naik (1949).
Guava	19	2.2 tons.	1,511,532	Average, India, Rao (1946).
		23,048 lb.	7,006,592	Average, Allahabad, Prasad (1936).
Mango	14-16	5 tons.	2,688,000	Average, India, Rao (1946).
		3.4 tons.	1,827,840	Average, Madras, Naik (1949).
Papaya	11	48 tons.	18,923,520	Maximum, Trinidad, Simmonds (1946).
		30,000 lb.	5,280,000	Estimate, Madras, Naik (1949).
		60,000 lb.	10,560,000	Estimate, Madras, Naik (1949).

* According to Aykroyd (1951).

or to compare the maximum yield of one crop with the average of another. Also, it is difficult to make a fair comparison between a perennial fruit and a grain which occupies the ground only part of the year, whether another crop is grown in another season or not. However, certain significant calculations can be made. From Table II it will be seen that the production of calories per acre by certain fruits compares well with that of a single crop of wheat.

Most fruits contain considerable amounts of sugar or starch or both, and it is largely these which furnish the calories. Nuts, and the olive and avocado are important sources of fat, a concentrated energy-producing food. Protein is found in very small amounts. But it is now recognized that a diet of protein, fat and carbohydrate is incomplete, and that for the maintenance of health certain minerals and vitamins are required. Fruits are a very important source of mineral salts. These are especially necessary for the production of bones and teeth, and should therefore be supplied to children in adequate quantities. Vitamins are food factors discovered comparatively recently, and still imperfectly understood. There are a number of these, and the complete absence of any one from the diet results in sickness or imperfect development. There are certain 'deficiency' diseases which occur when the diet contains insufficient amounts. Most fruits are valuable sources of several vitamins, as are also tomatoes and green and yellow vegetables. It is reported that in 1952, fruits and vegetables accounted for 93% of the ascorbic acid in the diet of the American people, 63% of the vitamin A, 22% of the iron, substantial percentages of the B vitamins, 18% of the carbohydrates, and 7% of the protein.

Since fruits are such an important source of ascorbic acid or vitamin C, a brief glance at the history of this vitamin may be of interest. Scurvy, the disease caused by a lack of asçorbic acid, has played an important part in the history of the world. It is said to have been the main factor in the failure of the European nations to capture Palestine in the Crusades, and to have contributed largely to the defeat of the Russians by Japan, half of the 17,000 troops who surrendered at Port Arthur being disabled by scurvy. It has been estimated that from the 15th to the 19th century, about a million seamen died of this disease. It is said that the idea of using lime juice to prevent scurvy was put forward as early as the time of Hawkins, who crossed the Atlantic in 1575 (Anonymous, 1946). In the next century the famous British physician, Sir John Colbatch, stated that he had been told by seamen and ships' surgeons that the disease was cured by drinking orange or lemon juice (Lorenz, 1939). This was scientifically proved by James Lind, who published his results in 'A Treatise of the Scurvy' in 1753 (Roddis, 1953). Those who become impatient with the slow action of government agencies may derive some consolation from the fact that it was nearly half a century later, in 1795, that an administrative order required that each British sailor and marine be issued orange or lemon juice daily, thus ending scurvy in the Royal Navy and establishing the term 'lime juicer' for a sailor in the British Navy. The discovery that the effect of citrus juice was dependent on its ascorbic acid content came, of course, very much later.

It seems that the first 'lime' juice was extracted from Mediterranean lemons, perhaps mixed with sweet limes. Toward the end of the 19th century the juice of West Indian limes (the type commonly grown in India) was tried, but failed to protect sailors from scurvy. It is said that the fresh juice contains ascorbic acid, but that it soon deteriorates, and that the preserved lime juice is of no value for preventing or curing scurvy.

Later investigations have shown that the guava and *aonla* are much richer sources of vitamin C than the citrus fruits, while the Barbados cherry, a minor fruit almost unknown in India, perhaps heads the list. The *bael,* according to Leme (1951), compares well with the citrus fruits in this respect. Kamat and others (1952) report on the ascorbic acid content of a number of fruits found in the Poona market, and show that the mango, jujube, and papaya are good sources of this vitamin; the fig, sapota, pomegranate, *jamun*, wood-apple, and custard-apple are fair; while the banana, jackfruit, European grape, and pear are rather poor.

Often associated with ascorbic acid are the bioflavonoids, sometimes grouped together as vitamin P. Their absence may lead to bleeding from very small blood vessels. They and ascorbic acid together seem to increase the effectiveness of each other. The solid tissues of citrus fruits, especially sweet oranges, are perhaps the richest dietary source, according to Baier (1955), though one is found only in lemons. Carotene and other pigments from which the body manufactures vitamin A, are found in great abundance in the mango, to a considerable extent in papayas and persimmons, and in smaller amounts in oranges, particularly the loose-skinned type, and in a number of other fruits. Rege and Devadatta (1943) report thiamin (B) in the banana, orange, and sapodilla.

The amount of any vitamin present in any particular fruit depends on many factors. Murneek and Wittwe (1948) mention as factors affecting the ascorbic acid content of apples, varietal differences, stage of maturity, speed of ripening, duration and temperature of storage, the condition of the tree, the nitrogen supply, the size of the crop, the size of the fruit, and exposure of the fruit to light. The last seems to be of major importance. Jones and Parker (1947) consider climate or light and nitrogen the important factors in determining ascorbic acid in orange juice. In California, where there is a large degree of light, they found an inverse correlation between nitrogen applied as fertilizer and the percentage of ascorbic acid in the juice.

Fruits are also valuable because they provide bulk. This, together with the mineral salts which they contain, makes them useful in preventing constipation. It is now recognized that for all these reasons, fruit should be very generally eaton, especially by children. Fortunately, fruit is not a medicine which has to be forced down unwilling patients, but because of its attractive appearance and delicious flavour, it is readily eaten by both children and adults.

It is generally considered that changed food habits in the United States and some other countries are a major factor in the improvement in health and the lengthening of the average life. Clark and others (1947) state that, 'The most notable change in food consumption in the United States between 1909 and

1945 has been the upward trend for dairy products (except butter), citrus fruit, and leafy, green and yellow vegetables and the downward trend in potatoes and grain products.'

The need for a great increase in the production of fruits and vegetables in India is becoming widely recognized, and it is commonly suggested that the area should be doubled. An editorial in Indian Farming (Anonymous, 1948) points out that there were 3,078,000 acres of fruits and vegetables in the Indian Union provinces. On the basis of the 1942 population 233,148,000, taking 80% of this as the adult equivalent, and assuming an average yield of 47 maunds per acre, it suggested that to provide the minimum of four ounces a day per capita, India needed 4,400,000 acres of fruit alone. Of course, many persons will use more than four ounces, and it was recommended that the country should aim at a total of 6,000,000 acres. This would be only about 2.0% of the cultivated area. If this amount of land were devoted to the production of fruit, using the best varieties and the most efficient methods, the health of the people would benefit tremendously. Even this, however, would provide far less fruit than is desirable in the diet.

As it is in the interest of the country that the production of fruit be increased, it is fortunate that fruit growing is more profitable than most forms of agriculture. It may not be possible for a family to secure an adequate income from an average holding by growing most farm crops, but the growing of fruits makes this possible. According to Naik (1949), fruits occupy roughly 1.1% of the total cropped area of Madras, and produce 7. 4% of the crop wealth. He states that, 'Receipts exceeding Rs.10,000 per year per acre from some well kept orchards are not uncommon in South India.' Papayas are easily grown and should yield three crops in about four years. The crop has been sold on the trees at Allahabad for about Rs. 4,000 per acre. Expenses in growing fruits vary, but do not justify any such high returns. Bajwa (1953) reports on the first five years of a mixed orchard in the Punjab, with vegetables and field crops grown between the young trees. Non-recurring expenses amounted to Rs. 5,715 and recurring expenses averaged Rs. 6,300 a year. The total income was Rs. 46,200, so that in this period before most of the fruit was producing more than small crops, the capital charges had been paid and there was a net profit of Rs. 9,000.

Production should be increased until the price of fruit falls to a level at which a progressive grower can still make a satisfactory profit and all the people can afford to eat the fruit which is necessary for their health. The more this is done by increasing the production per acre, the better for all concerned. Not all orchards are now very profitable, and a fall in prices will compel some growers to improve their practices.

With the increased industrialization of the country, the pressure of population on the land may decrease, especially if the population ceases to increase. Nevertheless, it seems probable that for many years the average holding will remain small, making desirable an intensive type of agriculture, such as the growing of fruits and vegetables. The more food can be grown per acre, the more land can be released for non-food crops, such as fibres.

It is thus seen that by developing the fruit industry, India stands to gain both physically and economically. But such development will be possible only as intelligent men enter the industry, determined to apply themselves to its many problems with energy and persistence. Only thus can fruit do its full part in making this a land of healthy and prosperous people.

CHAPTER II

PLANNING THE ORCHARD

THE response of fruit trees to their environment is a very complicated subject. Differences of soil and climate which seem relatively small, may determine the success or failure of a venture. One must either choose the site of his orchard to suit the fruits he wishes to grow, or choose crops suited to his land. This factor is, however, frequently over-emphasized. There has been a tendency to accept too readily the impossibility of growing a certain fruit in a given locality, when it grows well under very similar conditions in a neighbouring district. Thus it was formerly held that papayas would not grow well in Allahabad, where they are now very commonly and successfully grown. It may well be that the present common belief that mandarins do not succeed in that district has no better basis.

There is frequently a marked difference in climatic requirements among varieties of the same species. The varieties of mango which do very well in Bombay or Madras are likely to fail completely in northern India, and the northern Langra has failed in Bombay. Many fruits do very well over wide areas, if a little care is exercised in selecting the site, and good cultural methods are used. In most sections of India, the grower has his choice of several excellent fruits.

In choosing which fruit or fruits to grow, of those which are known to do well in the district, a number of factors may be considered. Market conditions will naturally be an important consideration, as there is no use growing a fruit for which there is no demand, or one of which the supply is greater than the demand. A fruit which is increasingly popular, or one being supplied from a distance, offers a favourable opportunity. If a district has a reputation for fruits of a certain kind, advantage may be taken of this, and the export market may compensate for a flooded local market. The previous experience of the grower and his personal preference may also be considered.

Climatic Factors

Climate is, more often than soil, a limiting factor in the growing of fruits. In this respect, fruits are commonly grouped as temperate, subtropical, and tropicol. However, these classes are not very definite, and some fruits may be grown in more than one of these regions. Thus mangoes are both tropical and subtropical, and peaches do well in the milder sections of both temperate and subtropical regions.

Climate limits the growth of fruits in several ways. Broad-leafed evergreen trees, including most tropical and subtropical fruits, are severely damaged or killed if the temperature falls much below the freezing point, and therefore cannot be grown in regions of severe winters. Deciduous trees are able to stand great cold during the months when they are dormant, though even they are sometimes damaged by extreme cold. More frequently, however, the northern limit of commercial production of temperate fruits is determined by the likelihood of frost in the spring when the trees are blossoming. On the other hand, there is limit to the amount of heat which many trees will tolerate. Some are killed outright by high temperatures, and others fail to produce well. A peculiar condition is found in certain varieties of the peach in subtropical regions. The buds seem to require a certain degree of cold to break their dormancy, and after unusually mild winters, may fail to open until mid-summer. Most Indian peaches do not seem to suffer from this difficulty. Similarly, many other deciduous fruits and nuts require more or less chilling in the winter.

A somewhat similar problem is found in India, and particularly in central and southern India where there is little difference between summer and winter temperatures. Under such conditions, some trees seem to tend to continue in vigorous vegetative growth throughout the year. In order to induce fruitfulness, it is considered necessary by some to force the trees into dormancy by withholding water, or by exposing or pruning the roots. When growth is again encouraged, the trees blossom freely.

The amount of heat during the growing season often determines the time of ripening, and may determine the quality of the fruit. Not only the temperature, but, according to Harding and others (1954), the rainfall, wind, light, and air pollutants are known to influence the size of fruit. The last act both by a direct toxic effect and by decreasing radiation. The date-palm can endure temperatures well below freezing, but produces well only in regions of hot summers, preferably where the temperature stays above 100° F. for many days.

The control of the temperature is possible to a limited extent. Orchard heating is practicable only where valuable crops can be saved by slight changes in temperature for short times. Little can be done to reduce the temperature, though when high temperature is accompanied by strong wind, the damage may be decreased by the use of windbreaks. Strong wind by itself is frequently an important factor causing the breaking of trees, the loss of leaves, and the scarring or loss of fruit. The use of shade for certain tropical and subtropical crops is probably effective in reducing excessive light rather than in lowering the temperature. Smith, Kinnison and Carns (1931) believe that frequent irrigation of grapefruit in Arizona is beneficial in reducing soil temperature during the hot season. The use of straw mulch was found still better, reducing the temperature 7 to 9 degrees F. at a depth of one foot (Anonymous, 1934a).

Moisture relationships are also extremely important, but are more subject to control than is the temperature. The amount of moisture needed to produce a crop of fruit depends upon the kind and upon atmospheric conditions. During hot, dry weather enormous amounts of water are transpired through the leaves. If the air is humid, even though hot, the amount is much smaller. Much of the moisture added to the soil, either as rain or by irrigation, is wasted, by surface run-off, by seepage below the root zone, by evaporation, or by transpiration by weeds. Heavy soils retain more water than light soils. The distribution of rainfall throughout the year is also important. An annual rainfall of 40 inches may be quite adequate, if well distributed, but if it comes within a rainy season of two or three months, much of it will be wasted, and trees may suffer during the dry season. At the other extreme, frequent light showers may be evaporated before reaching the lower roots. If the water supply is scant trees may be planted at great distances and will then send out roots and draw water from a larger area. Kearney (1908) reports olive orchards in Tunis with trees planted sixty or eighty feet apart in order to use the scant rainfall.

In most parts of northern India, successful orcharding is possible only with irrigation. Many mature trees receive no irrigation, and yet bear large crops. This is possible because their roots extend far into the soil. Young trees require irrigation, at least during the first year, and for satisfactory growth and bearing, this must be continued. Some fruits are more resistant to drouth than others, and vary in the amounts of irrigation required.

A source of irrigation water is therefore a very important consideration in choosing an orchard site. This may be either a well or canal, or for small orchards, a tank. The point is that plentiful supplies of good water should be available at a reasonable cost. Very deep wells are apt to mean expensive water, except where cheap electric power is available. If canal water is depended upon, the grower should make sure that it will not be shut off at seasons when it is needed.

Soils for Fruit Growing

The soil is the basis of fruit production, as well as of other forms of agriculture. It is therefore extremely important that a suitable soil be chosen. Fortunately, many fruits may be grown on a wide variety of soil types. Extremes are to be avoided, for very heavy soils are difficult to handle, and sandy soils do not hold moisture well, and are likely to be infertile. A loam or sandy loam soil is good for most fruits, and such soils are common throughout India. The more fertile the soil is, the less manuring will be necessary, but in any case manure will be needed to maintain the fertility during the life of the orchard.

Shallow soils should be avoided. Fruit trees send their roots deep into the ground, and while young trees sometimes appear to be doing well on shallow soil, they soon become sickly and die. Good drainage is also essential, for trees cannot thrive with water standing around their roots. Mangoes seem to be particularly resistant to this condition, as they are often found growing on the banks of tanks, or even in the middle of them, with scarcely any dry ground beneath them. In heavy soils it is sometimes necessary to provide artificial drainage.

Producing fine fruit brings great satisfaction, but it does not keep the wolf from the door unless the fruit can also be sold at a profit. The prospective market is thus a very important factor in selecting the site for an orchard. Under present conditions the grower must depend primarily upon the city market. He may therefore select land very close to a city, or land connected with one or more cities by good means of communication. This may be either a good road or a railroad. The former is of especial value if there is motor-lorry service to the city. A railroad makes it possible to ship fruit to markets several hundred miles distant.

Co-operation has been of great importance in the fruit industry of some countries, and is being developed in India. This is possible only in regions where a good deal of fruit is grown. It is therefore an advantage to choose a site in a section where fruit growing is popular. Even if organized co-operative societies do not exist, one can learn much from the experience of other growers. It should also be remembered that fruit growing, like other forms of agriculture, is not only a science, an art, and a business, but also a way of living. The grower's home should be on or near his orchard. Medical, educational, social, and religious facilities should therefore be kept in mind.

Preliminary Operations

After selecting the site, and before planting any trees, it may be desirable to carry out one or more preliminary operations. This will depend on the state of the land, and the grower's plans. It may be necessary to grade and manure the land, to provide water, to build fences, and to plan for buildings. Any of these operations, if delayed, may cause a considerable loss.

It must be remembered that orchards require irrigation, and that this is ordinarily feasible only where the slope of the land is moderate and fairly uniform. The slope may be in two or more directions, provided there is a central high spot or ridge where water is available. If the land is very uneven, grading may be essential. If the slope is too great, irrigation becomes difficult and may cause washing of the soil. Erosion during the rainy season is also likely to be a great economic loss on such soil. On the other hand, soil which is too level is also difficult to irrigate. On the plains, however, it is gênerally possible to choose land which can be given a gentle slope with little grading. If any grading is done, it should be remembered that the sub-soil is often less fertile than the surface soil. Sometimes orchards are seen in which some trees are much less vigorous than others, because the surface soil had been removed from high spots. This difficulty can be largely overcome by a very liberal application of manure to such spots, before planting.

The irrigation system should be planned, and sometimes installed, before the trees are planted. If a well is to be dug, this should be done at a very early stage, for there is always the possibility that it will be a failure. It may be desirable to put in the permanent water channels before planting, and at least they should be planned.

Protection of the trees from animal pests and the prevention of stealing ordinarily require fencing of some kind, and this may often be done to advantage before planting. The fencing should be such as to exclude cattle, goats, deer, wild pigs, and monkeys, as well as human thieves. Many types of fencing are used, with more or less satisfaction.

Temporary fences may be made of brush and thorns, but they are not very satisfactory, and require frequent repair and replacement. Their only advantage is the low initial cost, and in the long run they are more expensive than more permanent types. Mud walls are frequently used, the earth being dug from the outside of the base of the wall, thus increasing its effective height. These are quite effective against the larger animals, but offer a slight obstacle to thieves. Cactus is often grown on top to increase their efficiency. High brick walls are permanent and very effective, but involve such a large initial expense as to be beyond the means of the ordinary grower, except for very small gardens.

Wire fences of various types are used, and in general vary in effectiveness with the cost. A strong woven wire fence, with a little barbed wire at the top, is effective against practically all animals and man, but is also very expensive. Cheaper wire fences, if properly erected, are effective against animals, but are more easily climbed, cut, or broken down by men. A well-kept wire fence is neat, occupies very little space, and neither shades the soil nor takes anything from it.

Hedges offer a more promising solution, being both cheap and effective if the proper material is used and the hedge is properly treated. They require a certain amount of labour from year to year, but this can be done at times when work is slack. Their worst feature is that, being living plants, they draw water and food from the soil, and may come into competition with the fruit trees. Unless properly pruned, many hedges tend to spread and occupy much ground. Hedges may also harbour insect and fungous pests which spread from them to fruit trees. These objections may be overcome, however, by careful planning and care. By cutting the roots which extend toward the trees within two feet of the surface, harmful competition may be largely avoided. Species should be used which are not subject to the same diseases and insect pests as the fruit. Thus a lime hedge should not be used around a garden of any of the citrus fruits, but would cause no damage around mangoes.

Many plants are commonly used for hedges. Some of these are useful in flower gardens, where the purpose is to form an artistic border or division, but are not strong enough to protect an orchard. These, such as *mehndi* (*Lawsonia alba*), are not here considered. Strong thorny hedges are desired. Griessen (1924) lists a number of such, including species of *Acacia* and *Citrus*. The karanda (*Carissa carandas*) is one of the best, as it is strong, well armed, attractive in appearance throughout the year, and may be pruned to any desired height. It has the additional advantage of bearing a valuable fruit if not pruned too closely. It requires a good deal of pruning if it is not to grow high and also spread somewhat. Its main disadvantage is that it takes a long time to reach an effective height. However, by applying manure in the trench in which it is planted, a good hedge may be secured in three or four years.

Inga dulcis is another strong hedge which is commonly used. Cactus (*nagphani*, *Opuntia sp.*), *thor* (*Euphorbia royleana*) and some species of *Agave* are also commonly planted. They are fairly effective, but are difficult to control, dirty, and give protection to weeds and snakes. *Parkinsonia aculeata* is very useful where a fast-growing hedge is desired. This will make a fairly good hedge in one year from seed. If properly pruned and trained it makes quite an effective barrier, but unless special care is taken the lower branches will not develop, and small animals will pass through it easily. It may well be used while a more permanent hedge is being grown.

If windbreaks are to be used, they should be planted at least as soon as the fruit trees, and it may be an advantage to plant them first, so they will provide some protection for the young trees. They are considered further in Chapter VI.

The treatment of the soil before planting will, of course, depend on its condition and previous history. If the land has been under cultivation and has been well manured, nothing further may be necessary. On the other hand, if the land has been uncultivated, it is likely to be both poor and hard. It is very difficult to give such soil effective treatment after the trees have been planted. Deep ploughing and a fairly heavy manuring are necessary. A green manure crop, in addition to the use of farmyard manure, is often the most economic means of increasing the organic matter in the soil. If these preliminary operations are begun in the monsoon season, it will be possible to set out the trees in the very early spring, but in most cases it will be better to wait a full year. In order to have the soil in good condition when the trees are planted, it is often desirable to grow vegetables or field crops for two or three years before planting the trees. In the case of land already under cultivation, such thorough treatment is not required, but a good manuring will generally be worth while.

Any buildings which are to be in the orchard should be planned before planting, though construction may be delayed. A garden affords a very pleasant site for a dwelling, and many owners who take very little active interest in the trees maintain residences in their gardens. This is very desirable in the case of those who intend to manage the orchard personally. Other buildings, such as a tool and implement store, a shed for oxen, and quarters for labourers, may also be desirable. These should all be near the road, and fairly central in the orchard, if it is a large one. Unless the site for buildings is selected before the trees are planted, some trees will be in the way and will have to be removed. In large orchards it is desirable to plan roads also, at least to the extent of leaving certain rows farther apart.

CHAPTER III

PROPAGATION

Growth, in all nature, results from the division of cells to form more similar cells. This may cause the individual to increase in size, or it may form new individuals. Thus bacteria reproduce by simple division, one of these one-celled plants being exactly like another. In higher plants and animals, a new individual is generally formed only when cell division follows the fusion of two cells. This is known as sexual reproduction, and in plants is the process by which seeds are formed. The new individuals formed in this way are more or less unlike their parents and unlike each other.

There are thus two ways of producing new plants, sexual and asexual, or vegetative, reproduction. Vegetative propagation avoids genetic variation and the differences between plants vegetatively reproduced are ordinarily so small as to be negligible. Those between sexually reproduced plants, seedlings, may be very small, or they may be very great. The more highly developed a plant is, and the more difference there is between the two parents, the greater is the probable variation in the seedlings. This is sometimes an advantage and sometimes a disadvantage. The history of agriculture is very largely the history of the improvement of plants and animals so that they more nearly meet man's needs. This is possible in animals, and with minor exceptions in plants, only through sexual reproduction. No one ever produced a new type of plant by budding, grafting, or other vegetative means of reproduction.

A certain amount of variation occurs among seedling plants, whether growing wild or under cultivation, and man has long taken advantage of this by selecting the best for propagation. Larger variations result from hybridization and from mutations. By controlled cross-pollination, man has sometimes been able to combine the best qualities of two or more varieties or species. Hybridization sometimes results in an increase in the number of chromosomes present in each cell. Darrow (1949) points out the importance of this factor in plant breeding, stating that, "The effects most often obtained through polyploidy are broader, thicker leaves, larger flowers, larger fruits and fertility of hybrids not fertile as diploids." It has been suggested that plants with basic chromosome numbers of 10 or higher may be of polyploid derivation, and Darrow says that if this is the case, only the peach, apricot, sweet cherry, raspberry, and a few blackberry varieties are not of polyploid origin. In nature, changes in the chromosome number have come largely through hybridization, but it is now known that ployploidy can be induced by treating plants with colchicine or certain other chemicals. This gives the plant breeder another tool, along with hybridization, to secure the changes he desires.

While some very valuable varieties have been produced by plant breeders, it must be recognized that most of the important varieties of fruit have come from chance seedlings or mutations, not controlled by man. This is true of practically all Indian varieties of mango and banana. In some cases the original seedling is known; often the origin of the variety is very obscure or unknown. There is doubt as to whether the grapefruit originated as a mutation or as a hybrid, but it is known that mutants occur frequently in this and other species of citrus fruits. The famous Washington Navel orange appears to have been propagated from a mutant by a Portuguese in Brazil between 1810 and 1820, but gained its name and reputation after being taken to the United States at about the end of the century. The Ruby grapefruit originated as a bud-sport (mutation) of the Thompson Seedless which had come in the same way from the Marsh which started about 1860 as a seedling or a bud-sport.

Plant and animal breeding is a slow and difficult process. Many thousands of individuals must be produced in order to find one having the desired characteristics. And when one desirable individual is found, the task is only begun, unless the new type can be reproduced indefinitely without variation. It is here that vegetative propagation is of great value. In breeding animals, and most vegetable and field crops, the process must be continued until the new strain breeds fairly true to type, that is, until the variation between sexual offspring is so small that it can be neglected. Even then, there is often the danger of cross-breeding with other strains, or other species, often resulting in the loss of the valuable characteristics which were secured with such great effort. But in working with plants which can be reproduced by vegetative means, this difficulty disappears. As soon as one plant with the desired characteristics is produced, it can be multiplied indefinitely. Most fruit trees can be propagated in this way.

Vegetative propagation is therefore of great importance to the nurseryman and fruit-grower, primarily because it makes possible the production of trees of uniformly high quality. It perpetuates and multiplies desirable trees. The use of such trees makes fruit growing much less of a gamble, for the grower knows at the time of planting, what kind of fruit the trees will bear. Uniformity is also a very desirable feature in harvesting and marketing. It is more economical to handle an orchard in which the fruit on all trees in a block ripens at the same time than it is where one tree may be several weeks ahead of the next. On the market, uniformity is of great importance. When the public learns that all fruit of a certain variety is of good quality, it naturally prefers to buy such fruit rather than that from seedling trees which may be good or poor. In pomology, the term 'variety' is properly restricted to plants propagated by vegetative means from one original ancestor. (In this definition, 'vegetative means' includes the use of apogamic seedlings, which are explained later in this chapter.) The term 'clone' is used to convey this meaning more accurately. Such varieties establish reputations which are of great value to the grower. In species grown only from seed, the term 'variety' has a less exact meaning. Unfortunately, most so-called varieties in Indian horticulture are not varieties in the strict sense. In most cases they represent a type. The variation within the 'variety' may be considerable, as in the case of 'Red Fleshed' or 'Allahabad' guavas; or minor, as in the case of 'Langra' mangoes.

It should be remembered that the use of vegetative propagation does not, of itself, insure trees of desirable characteristics. If the parent tree is of poor quality, then those propagated from it will be uniformly poor. The selection of the parent tree is therefore of utmost importance.

There are other advantages of vegetative propagation only less important than the perpetuation of desirable individuals. In certain cases, seed is not formed, and only vegetative means can be used. This is true of all the superior varieties of banana, and with some varieties of grapes and oranges. In other cases germination is very poor or very slow, and it is frequently more convenient to use vegetative methods.

It often happens that certain varieties or species which are otherwise desirable, are susceptible to some insect or disease, while others may be entirely or largely immune. If the pest is one which attacks only the roots, it can be overcome by the use of resistant varieties as rootstock. The classic example of this is the saving of the European grape industry. Grapes had flourished in France and other warmer parts of Europe for centuries before the discovery of America, and the subsequent discovery of American species of grapes. When the American grape was taken to France, it carried with it an insect, known as phylloxera. This insect soon began to attack the European grapes, and caused great damage. For a time it seemed as if the grape industry might be wiped out of Europe. But the American grapes, through long association with this insect, had developed great resistance to it. By grafting the European grapes on American roots, it was found that they could be grown without danger. The somewhat more costly form of propagation is much more than justified.

Similarly, some varieties of citrus fruits suffer from diseases of the collar or trunk, while others are immune. The use of the immune or resistant varieties as rootstock for those which are susceptible is consequently of great value.

In much the same way, budding or grafting may be used to adapt certain fruits to unfavourable environment. In temperate regions this is often done to secure hardiness against cold. If the roots of one variety are likely to be killed by freezing, this variety may be grafted on the roots of some more resistant type. Oranges grown in regions where there is danger of severe cold are sometimes budded on seedlings of the trifoliate orange, a deciduous tree which is not damaged by temperatures which would kill ordinary oranges. This may not make the oranges any more resistant except as it decreases growth during winter, and thus reduces the amount of tender wood and foliage, but in any case the tree itself will not be killed. At the worst, it would only be necessary for new shoots to come out after the freeze. Buds set on these would be producing fruit again in a few years, somewhat earlier than would be the case if the old trees had been killed and new ones planted.

In most cases the results of propagation on more suitable rootstock are not spectacular, but frequently some rootstock will prove somewhat better adapted to the environment than the roots of the variety desired.

The dwarfing of fruit trees is commonly practised in Europe, and may be of advantage under certain conditions in this country. If it is desired to have a large variety of fruits in a limited area, the advantage of dwarf plants is obvious. In Europe trees are often trained against walls, or otherwise severely pruned in order to secure a maximum of sunshine and warmth for the fruit. Such severe pruning is likely to interfere with fruiting on standard trees, but not on dwarf trees. In some cases orchards of dwarf trees produce about as much per acre as those of standard trees, and are more conveniently pruned, sprayed, and harvested. Certain rootstocks are known to cause dwarfing and are regularly used for this purpose. For instance, pear trees grown on quince roots are dwarfed

Another minor use of grafting is found in the case of dioecious plants, or those in which cross-pollination is necessary. Instead of planting occasional stammate (male) trees, or trees of a variety suitable for pollination, single branches of these may be grafted into occasional pistillate trees or trees of the main variety.

Citrus trees and some others are naturally thorny. It has been observed that when these are propagated by vegetative means, the size of the thorns is greatly reduced in many cases. This is a great advantage, as large thorns often damage the fruit.

Finally, an important use of grafting and budding is the correction of mistakes. Even in carefully conducted nurseries, plants are sometimes wrongly labelled, and the mistake may not be discovered until the trees begin to bear. Unscrupulous nurserymen deliberately supply cheap plants in the place of more expensive ones, or ones which are out of stock. The grower may also make a mistake and choose a variety of little value. Frequently market conditions change, making desirable a change of variety or even species. In all of these cases, it would mean a long delay and a great expense to remove the trees and plant new ones. By 'top-working' the trees to desired varieties the expense may be greatly lessened, and the trees may be bearing in two or three years.

While the advantages of vegetative propagation are so great that it should unquestionably be used with most fruits, there are certain advantages in the use of seedling trees. In a few species, no successful method of vegetative propagation has yet been discovered, and in others this is a difficult and expensive operation. Seedlings are ordinarily comparatively cheap. They often produce somewhat larger trees than are obtained vegetatively, and frequently bear heavy crops. While they do not ordinarily come into bearing quite as soon as grafted plants, they are commonly supposed to live longer. In many cases, grafted plants are short-lived, but this is probably due to imperfect compatibility between rootstock and scion. Some grafted plants probably live as long as do seedlings of the same species.

A great deal of work has been done in different parts of the world on the methods of propagation. Much of this has been summed up in books, such as the thorough and well-illustrated one by Kains and McQuesten (1944). Less work has been done on tropical plants than on those of temperate regions, but Feilden and Garner (1936) give information on a large number of tropical and subtropical plants. A review of the methods used with 14 fruits commonly grown in north India is given by Bajpai (1947).

Types of Vegetative Propagation

Before proceeding further with a discussion of propagation, it may be well to define certain terms. Considerable differences in terminology exist, and are sometimes confusing. Suggestions for clear and standardized terms have been made by Tukey (1938). The difference between the growth of seedling plants, on the one hand, and vegetative propagation on the other, has already been considered. Vegetative methods of propagation may be divided into three groups, division, rootage, and graftage. Division or separation involves only the removing from the parent plant of a part which would grow into a complete plant without man's intervention. This is a common method of propagating herbaceous perennials, but is used in the case of the banana and date only among the important fruits.

Rootage, or the propagation of trees on their own roots, covers a number of methods in which a complete plant is grown from one part, such as a stem, leaf, or root. Graftage includes the various forms of budding and grafting, in which a part of the stem of one plant, known as the scion, is joined to a rooted plant, or root, known as the rootstock, in such a way that the scion grows to form the fruit-bearing part of the tree.

The most common forms of rootage are stem cuttings and layering, in both of which the growth of roots from portions of the stem is induced. In the simplest type, stems are cut into pieces which are planted in the soil, where they develop roots and grow. Certain plants, such as the rose, grow so readily in this way that very little care is necessary. Of the fruits, the plum, fig, grape, and lemon are frequently grown in this way in India. In other countries, however, graftage is generally preferred for most fruits. Cuttings are very commonly used in propagating ornamental shrubs.

While leaves are sometimes used as cuttings, stems are the most common material used. These may be from herbaceous plants, or if from woody plants, may be either 'hard-wood' or 'soft-wood' cuttings. For fruits, hard-wood cuttings are ordinarily used, that is, stems which have become mature and hard. Cuttings of deciduous trees are made during the dormant period. In cold climates they are generally cut in early winter and planted in the spring. The callus which forms when the cuttings are stored in cool moist soil, sawdust, or other material, is an advantage, as it protects the cutting from decay organisms. Cuttings of evergreen trees, such as the lemon, may be made at any time, but are most likely to succeed during the rains or in early spring. The best results are obtained with branches of about the diameter of a lead pencil. They may vary from about four inches to a foot in length. The presence of leaves on the cuttings causes them to dry out more quickly, but in some cases the hormones in the leaves seem to be an important aid in the production of roots. Zimmerman and Hitchcock (1946) report that the age of the stem tissue is sometimes of importance. Cuttings of lilac in May formed roots, but the capacity declined and was gone by July. The apple is comparatively difficult to root, but they found that by applying growth substances to cuttings in early May, but not in June, they were successful. In species hard to root, cuttings from young seedlings (the value of which would not be known) form roots, whereas those from old trees rarely do, even when treated.

Ordinary soil, and particularly sandy soil is often used for rooting cuttings. Under some conditions pure sand is preferable. Peat moss and other materials have been used with some success. Gardner (1932), in summing up the results of several experimenters, indicates that while some species do best in peat moss and some in sand, a mixture of these two media is generally very satisfactory.

With species which do not root readily, special physical conditions may be helpful. The provision of 'bottom heat', that is heat in the soil beneath the cuttings, while the air above remains relatively cool, is often desirable. This was formerly done by placing a layer of fresh horse manure beneath the bed, which fermented and generated heat. Now it is more common to heat the soil with pipes in which warm water is circulated, or with electric cables. Especially for leafy cuttings, it may be necessary to keep the air about the cuttings saturated, which is possible when a spray of water is provided within a glass propagating case. A more simple method which is said to be successful with some leafless cuttings is the dipping of the portion of the cutting which is to remain above the soil in liquid paraffin wax of a low melting point (G. C. S., 1949).

In recent years a number of experiments have been made on the effect of chemical treatments on the rooting of cuttings. In many cases chemical treatment has increased the percentage of cuttings forming roots, but no one treatment has proved uniformly helpful. Potassium permanganate, manganese sulphate, acid, and sugar solutions have all seemed to give good results with certain species under certain conditions. May (1929) reported striking results with sugarcane and a number of other species from the use of a saturated solution of air-slaked lime. More recently attention has been centred on the plant hormones, or growth substances, chemicals which, in very dilute solutions or mixtures, affect the growth of plants. It has been shown that a large number of these compounds promote the growth of roots. Among those commonly used are indoleacetic, indolepropionic, indolebutyric, and naphthaleneacetic acids, and naphthalene acetamide. The most common form of treatment is placing the basal end of the cutting in an aqueous solution for about 24 hours. Solutions of about .01% are generally satisfactory. Other methods of applying the hormone are in irrigating water, as a dust, or in lanolin. These treatments frequently result in earlier rooting and in the production of more roots. Little success has accompanied attempts to produce roots on species which cannot be rooted by other means. Some interesting results have also been secured with vitamin B_1 (thiamin), but this seems to increase the growth of roots, rather than causing rooting, and in some experiments no effect has been observed. Murneek (1941) found that thiamin at the rate of .025 to 5.0 milligrams per gallon produced conspicuously beneficial results on esveral plants, but that a layer of half to three-fourths of an inch of leaf mould on the surface gave as good or better results. Leaf mould is known to contain thiamin and other stimulants.

Much of the work on plant hormones has been done in respect to deciduous plants, and Garner (1944) reviews this and other work on cuttings and layers. Considerable attention has also been given to fruits of warmer regions, and Cooper and Knowlton (1940) used aqueous solutions of indoleacetic acid successfully on 16 varieties of citrus fruits and the litchi, Natal plum, sapodilla, guava, and other fruits A thorough review of the use of growth substances in propagating tropical plants is given by Cooper and Stoutmyer (1945).

Layering differs from the use of cuttings only in that rooting is induced before the stem is severed from the parent plant. This has the advantage of keeping the stem growing for as long a time as is necessary for roots to grow and establish the new plant in the soil. It may thus be used for many species which cannot readily be grown by cuttings. By using a large branch, a much larger tree can be secured in the first instance. In fact, it is possible to have the tree bearing fruit within a few months, or even at the time it is separated from the parent tree. This fact is of little actual importance, but is used by nurserymen in advertising, and appeals to certain buyers.

Some plants, such as some of the berries, root naturally when their branches touch the ground. In layering, man encourages this natural tendency. In the simplest form, branches are drawn to the soil, firmly fastened, and covered with moist earth. The soil is kept moist until roots have developed and the new plant can be removed without danger. In order to encourage rooting, a ring of bark about half an inch wide is often removed from the part of the branch which is to be covered. Instead of this, the branch may be notched or slit. Plant hormones may also be used to stimulate rooting.

Mound layering and trench layering are forms not commonly used in India. The former is of interest as one method which has been successful in the vegetative production of apple stock, ordinary layering and cuttings being largely unsuccessful. In this method the plant is headed back close to the ground, and soil is mounded up around the shoots as they appear. Each shoot forms roots, and may be removed after several months. Trench layering is sometimes used with small plants having no branch which can be bent to the ground. A shallow trench is dug on one side of the tree, and the tree is bent over and pegged down in this trench and the new shoots are covered with soil. In both of these forms of layering, rooting is obtained in some species only by covering the plant entirely, so that the new shoots have to force their way through the soil. The portion of the shoot which is formed under the soil is white, or etiolated, and the method is referred to as etiolation. Lambourne (1935) has reported experiments with 27 fruits in Malaya. The method proved satisfactory with the carambola, citron, lemon, lime, mandarin orange, grapefruit, guava, jackfruit, karanda, rose-apple, and a few other species. Some success was also reported with the avocado, sapodilla, sweet orange, pummelo, and tamarind, but not with the mango.

Air layering differs from ordinary layering mainly in that instead of bringing a branch to the soil, soil is taken to the branch. The principle is exactly the same. In both cases a branch is encouraged to put out roots by contact with moist soil or other material, often aided by wounding. Air layering has the advantage of being applicable to any branch, but it requires more work, both in the first instance and until the layer is removed. The soil is held in place in several ways. One of the easiest methods, and one commonly used in India, is to wrap the soil with gunny or other cheap stout cloth. Or a small flower pot may be split and tied around the branch, and then filled with soil. Clay is preferred, as it holds water better than other soils. Moss may be substituted for soil. It is important that the soil or moss be kept moist at all times, which ordinarily requires daily watering. A device used to good effect is a small earthen pot, through the bottom of which a tiny hole is made. The pot is tied above the layer, and a string is run through the bottom to the layer. By filling the pot once a day, a constant water supply is secured. M. P. Singh (1954) describes a cylindrical container made of sheet metal which is assembled on the branch to be rooted and tied together with wire, and which can be used repeatedly.

To avoid the expense of frequent watering, at the cost of somewhat more expensive material, plastic wraps have been successfully used. Grove (1946) reports good results on the litchi, although rooting takes somewhat longer, using material such as Vitafilm, which holds water but allows the passage of gases. The wrap is twisted tightly around the soil or moss and tied top and bottom, preferably with rubber bands. A piece of paper is sometimes tied loosely over the plastic wrap to prevent birds from damaging it, and also to keep the layer from becoming too hot. Bajpai and Chand (1955) repor success using ordinary plasitc sheeting bought in the bazaar to cover a moist mixture, one-fourth leaf mold and the rest sawdust, tied around a treated branch. On the other hand, Hamner and Rai (1953) recommend special plastic material coated with root-inducing hormones, insecticides, and fungicides, and sold under the name of 'Airwrap'. This can also be used in preparing layered plants, and in potting.

Air layering is commonly used in propagating a number of fruits, including limes, pummeloes, litchis, and pomegranates. It is also known as marcottage, pot layering, aerial layering, Chinese layering, and in India, gootee.

In the methods described thus far, new plants are formed by causing roots to grow from a stem. The opposite process, the forming of leaves and stems from portions of root, is also used in some cases. It is likely to be easy in such plants as produce suckers freely. This is the case with the guava, and this fruit is sometimes propagated by root cuttings. It is obvious, however, that this method would be of value only in propagating seedling trees, or those grown by rootage, or in growing stock for budding or grafting. Root cuttings are made from roots of about the size of stems used in stem cuttings, and are treated in much the same way. A variation, on the analogy of layering, is the cutting of roots loose from the tree without removing them from the soil. The cut end is exposed to the light, and after a shoot has grown, it is removed with a portion of the root.

Graftage includes budding and grafting, which are the same in object and principle. In grafting the scion which is joined to the rootstock, is a stem, whereas in budding the scion is bud, an undeveloped stem. Various methods are used to encourage the union of the rootstock and scion, and some are more successful with some species, others with others. Some of the more common methods are here described.

Budding

The most common form of budding is called shield or **T** budding. This is the form used in budding oranges and other citrus fruits, as well as other fruits, and the rose among flowers. The scion wood should be mature and rounded, but not old. It is desirable, but not necessary, that the leaves should still be present. The blade of the leaf should be cut off, leaving the petiole as a handle. Special budding knives are on the market, but any very sharp knife with a rounded point may be used. Sharpness is essential. Budding knives often have blunt bone blades at one end, but these are not necessary, and are scorned by some professional budders. A vertical cut is made, just through the bark, 1 to 1½ inches long, on the stock. At the top of this a horizontal cut, about half an inch long, is made. If necessary, the bark is then loosened from the wood, using the back of the blade or the bone blade. The bud is then cut by passing the blade of the knife under it, so as to remove a shield-shaped patch of bark about 1 or 1½ inches long, and just slightly wider than the bud. This will include a small amount of the wood, which some budders claim should be removed. Others are just as emphatic that it should be allowed to remain. The bud should immediately be inserted under the bark of the stock, in the **T**-shaped cut. It should then be wrapped, in order to hold it firmly in position and to exclude air and water. This may be done with waxed tape, plastic tape, string, raffia, or even banana fibre. If the bud remains green for two weeks, this is evidence that it has united with the stock.

Variations of this type of budding are the placing of the horizontal cut at the base of the vertical cut, in which case it may be known as inverted **T** budding, and the omission of the horizontal cut. In the latter case the stock is bent toward the side on which the cut is made, in order to loosen the bark.

Ring budding is a form sometimes used in this country, particularly on the jujube. A ring of bark ½ or ¾ of an inch long, and containing a good bud, is loosened from the scion wood, and slipped off one end of the branch. The top of the stock is removed, and a portion of the bark is peeled off. The ring containing the bud is slipped down over the stock until it reaches the bark. If it does not now fit tightly, more bark is removed, and the ring is lowered. This is continued until a snug fit is secured. The bud is then wrapped.

Patch budding is similar to shield budding but in it the section of bark containing the bud is rectangular, and the bark of the stock is removed from an area the same size and shape. The bud is carefully tied in this place. Patch budding is not commonly used.

The Forkert method, particularly in its modified form, is almost exclusively used in Indonesia, and has been advocated for such fruits as the mango in India. It is similar to patch budding, with the patch about an inch long and a third as wide, but a flap of bark is left at the bottom. In one modified form, the bark is peeled off after making the initial transverse incision, instead of being cut. The patch of bark containing the bud is inserted under the flap, and covers the stripped section of the stock. It is tied as in other forms of budding.

In all forms of budding, it is essential that the bark be easily separated from the wood. This is the condition when the stock is growing vigorously. In northern India budding is most successful in the very early spring, just as growth starts, or during the early part of the rainy season. Buds should be plump, and ready to grow, but in no case should they have commenced growth. Bud wood may be kept for some time if packed in moist sawdust or moss, so that it does not dry out. In this way buds have been successfully sent by post from England and America to India.

When the bud begins to grow, or after a couple of weeks if it is still green, but has not begun to grow, the stock should be cut off a short distance about the bud.

Two tissues can unite, or grow together, only when the growing portion of one is in intimate contact with the growing portion of the other. The growing portion of a stem, aside from its tip, is limited to the cambium layer, just beneath the bark. It is therefore essential in all graftage that the cambium layers of rootstock and scion be brought together. This is easy in the case of budding, as the bud rests entirely on the cambium of the stock. There are various types of grafting, and in each it is necessary that care be taken to bring the cambium layers together.

Grafting

Ordinary grafting is used commonly with deciduous plants, and is practised while they are dormant. There is thus time for the union to form before the scion has any need of receiving water and nutrients from the root. In the simplest form of grafting, the scion and top of the rootstock are stems of the same size, generally $\frac{1}{4}$ to $\frac{1}{2}$ inch in diameter. Similar diagonal cuts, about $1\frac{1}{2}$ inches long, are made in the stock and scion, and the two are tied together tightly, and waxed. This is known as splice or whip grafting. The first term is to be preferred, as it is descriptive and as the second is also used for another type, tongue grafting. The latter which is also called whip-and-tongue grafting is started in the same way, but after making the diagonal cuts, both stock and scion are slit carefully about half an inch from the end, and to distance of about one half an inch. The two are then forced together so that the tongues enter into the slits. The graft is then waxed, with or without tying. The advantages of this type, as compared with splice grafting, are greater strength and a greater length of cambium in contact. Both types are used in root grafting, in which case, the root of a seedling, or part of a root, is used as the stock.

The saddle graft is another type sometimes used, particularly with plants with thick fleshy tissue, such as the papaya. The top of the stock is cut from both sides, to form a wedge and a corresponding cut is made in the scion, so that it will fit tightly over the stock. It is bound in this position, and may be waxed.

Patch Budding

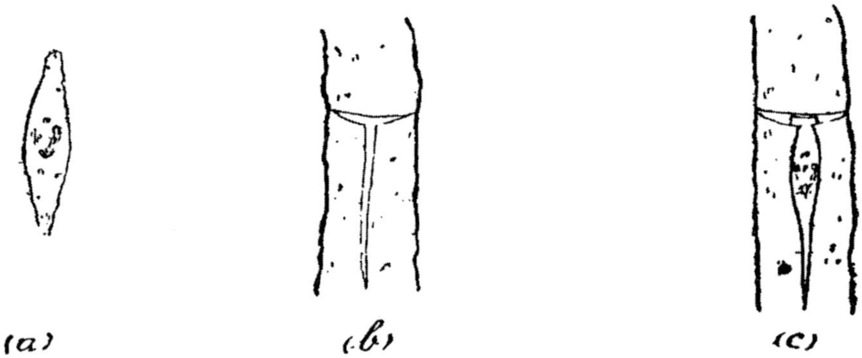

Shield Budding

Ring Budding

Three types of budding. In each, (a) represents the bud, (b) the rootstock, and (c) the rootstock with the bud in place.

The wedge or cleft graft is sometimes used when the stock is a section of root. The lower end of the scion is cut to form a wedge, and this is inserted in a cut in the top of the stock so that the cambium layers will coincide, at least on one side. The graft is then tied and waxed.

Side grafting is done without removing the top of the rootstock, which may be considerably larger than the scion. The base of the scion is cut to form a wedge with one side slightly longer than the other. An incision is made in the side of the rootstock at an angle of about 20 degrees, deep enough so that the wedge of the scion may be inserted. Tying may not be necessary, but waxing is In the side tongue graft, the wedge is made with one side much longer than the other. A tongue is cut on this long side. A long, sloping cut is made above the incision on the rootstock, and this is also slit to form a tongue which interlocks with the tongue of the scion when the latter is slipped into place.

When old trees are to be 'top-worked', that is, budded or grafted to some other variety, this may be done in several ways. The main branches may be cut back to within a few feet of the trunk. It was formerly common to bud or graft some of the shoots which were forced out by this severe pruning but it is probably better to place the buds or grafts directly in the old wood. In budding, it may be necessary first to thin the bark. For grafting, each branch, after being headed back, may be split. Scions, the size of a pencil, are cut wedge-shaped at the base and are inserted in the split, one on each side, care being taken that one cambium layer of the scion comes in contact with the cambium layer of the stock. This also is known as cleft grafting. Sometimes the tree is cut off a foot or two from the ground. If the trunk is not more than two or three inches in diameter, cleft grafting may then be used. Otherwise it is better to use bark grafting, in which the scions are cut on the diagonal as for splice grafting, and are inserted between the bark and the wood. This is also called rind or crown grafting.

Instead of ordinary top-working, a method developed in Australia and called frame-working may be used. This involves more work, but has the advantage that the tree gives some fruit in the second season and is in full bearing again from the third. The smaller branches and side shoots are removed, and most of the side shoots replaced by scions of the desired variety. Stub grafting and side grafting are the most common methods. In stub grafting, a scion about six inches long is cut in wedge form and inserted in a slanting incision on the upper side of the side shoot to be replaced, which is pressed down to allow the scion to be inserted and released to hold it fast. The shoot is then cut off just above the point of union, and the wound sealed with grafting wax.

None of these forms of grafting is easily applied to evergreen trees, especially in a dry atmosphere, and in consequence, they are of comparatively little importance on the plains of India. The form which is commonly used is known as inarching, or grafting by approach. Almost all of the grafted mangees are prepared in this way, and the method is often used for guavas, oranges, and other fruits. Inarching differs from ordinary grafting much as layering differs from propagation by cuttings. In it the scion from a good tree is grafted on to a seedling

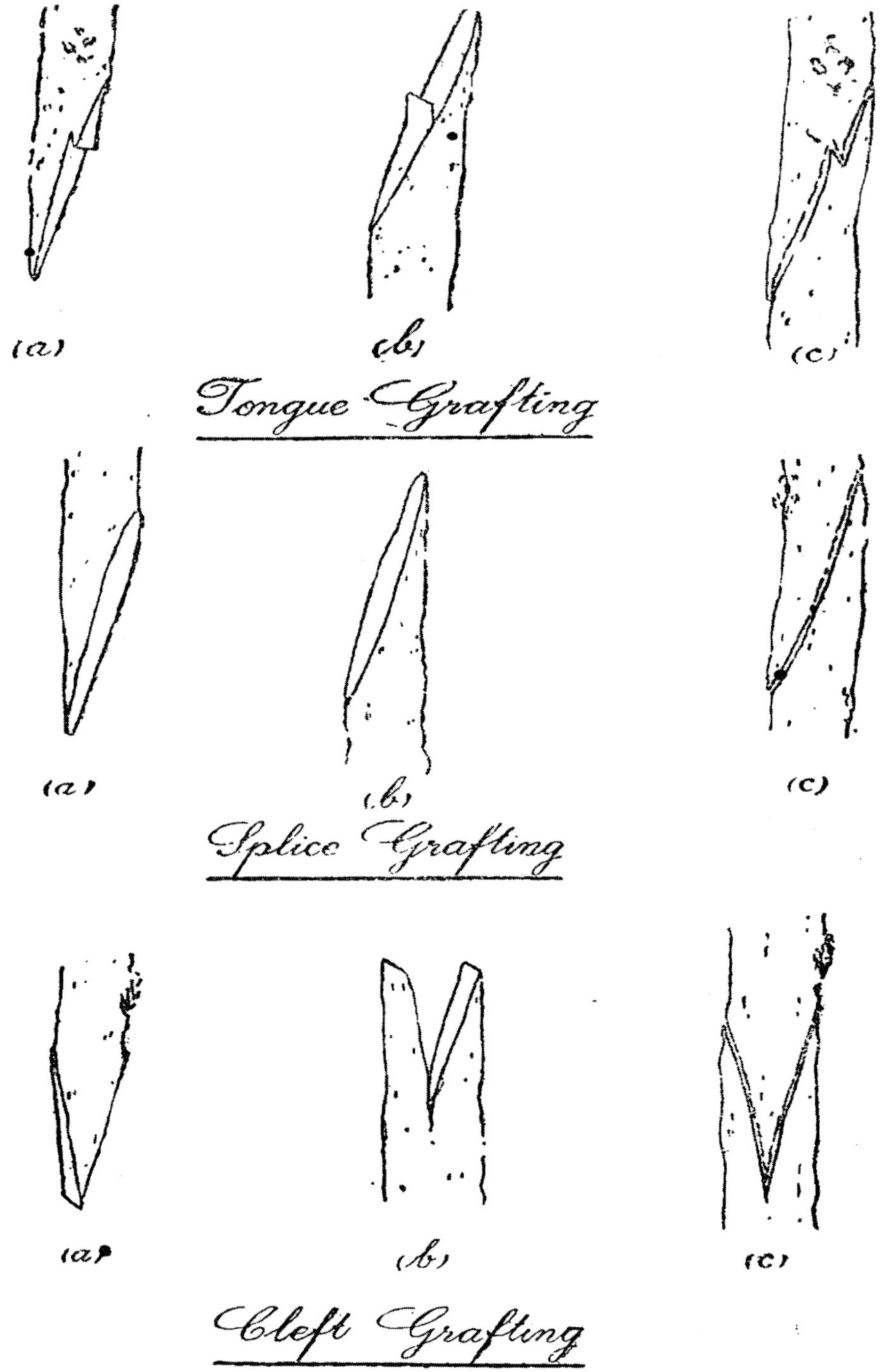

Three types of grafting. In each, (a) represents the scion, (b) the rootstock, and (c) the scion and rootstock joined.

stock, but in such a way that the scion is supported by the parent tree during the process of union. As union requires several weeks, the scion would dry out and die in the process, could it not draw water from the parent tree.

The process is very simple. A seedling plant is placed alongside a tree of the desired variety, in such a way that a branch of about the same size as the stem of the seedling may be brought in contact with it, running parallel to it. The end of the branch should be pointing upward, though careless gardeners often graft the other way around. Such plants grow, and are said to make fairly satisfactory trees eventually, but at best, their development is delayed a year. If there are branches coming to the ground, the seedlings may be planted in the ground, or they may be kept in pots on the ground. If there are no such branches, the seedlings must be in pots placed on platforms. With a sharp knife remove a thin slice of bark and wood an inch and a half or two inches long from one side of the stock, extending no deeper than a third of the diameter. Make a similar cut on the scion, so that the two can be drawn together and forced to meet the full length of the cut. If stock and scion are not of the same size, the smaller should be sliced deeper, so that the cambium layers will meet. The scion is carefully and tightly bound in place, so that there is no space between it and the stock. This is left for several weeks, or sometimes two or three months, the only care being to see that the seedling does not dry out. This means regular watering, especially if the plants are in pots. When time has been allowed for the union to take place, the scion is cut loose from the parent tree, just below the union, and the top of the stock is removed. It is well to make both cuts in three or four stages, at intervals of about a week. When the scion is finally severed from the parent tree, the young graft should be kept in the shade for several days, after which it may be planted in the nursery. It should be ready to plant out in from three months to a year.

A method is sometimes used in commercial nurseries which makes possible the inarching of a large number of plants on a small area. The parent trees are planted close together, headed low, and pruned heavily, while the ground is kept very fertile. The result is a large number of shoots suitable for grafting, near the ground. The roots of the seedlings, with small balls of earth, are frequently wrapped in grass instead of being put in pots, as they are then easier to handle. One disadvantage of this method is that the parent trees bear little or no fruit, so there is no check on the inherent capacity of the strain.

While inarching is not a difficult method, and a high percentage of success is secured by ordinary gardeners, it is not to be recommended if other methods can be used. It is cumbersome method and therefore expensive. The number of grafts which can be taken from one tree is much less than the number of buds which can be secured. The union is at first rather weak, and for several months the scion is in danger of being broken off. Because of this danger, the tie is often left on too long, causing an uneven growth at the point of union. Nevertheless, it is a very valuable method in that it can be used where all other forms of vegetative propagation fail or succeed so rarely as to be uneconomical.

When the root or lower part of the trunk of a tree becomes diseased or is damaged by rodents, it is sometimes possible to save its life by inarching one or

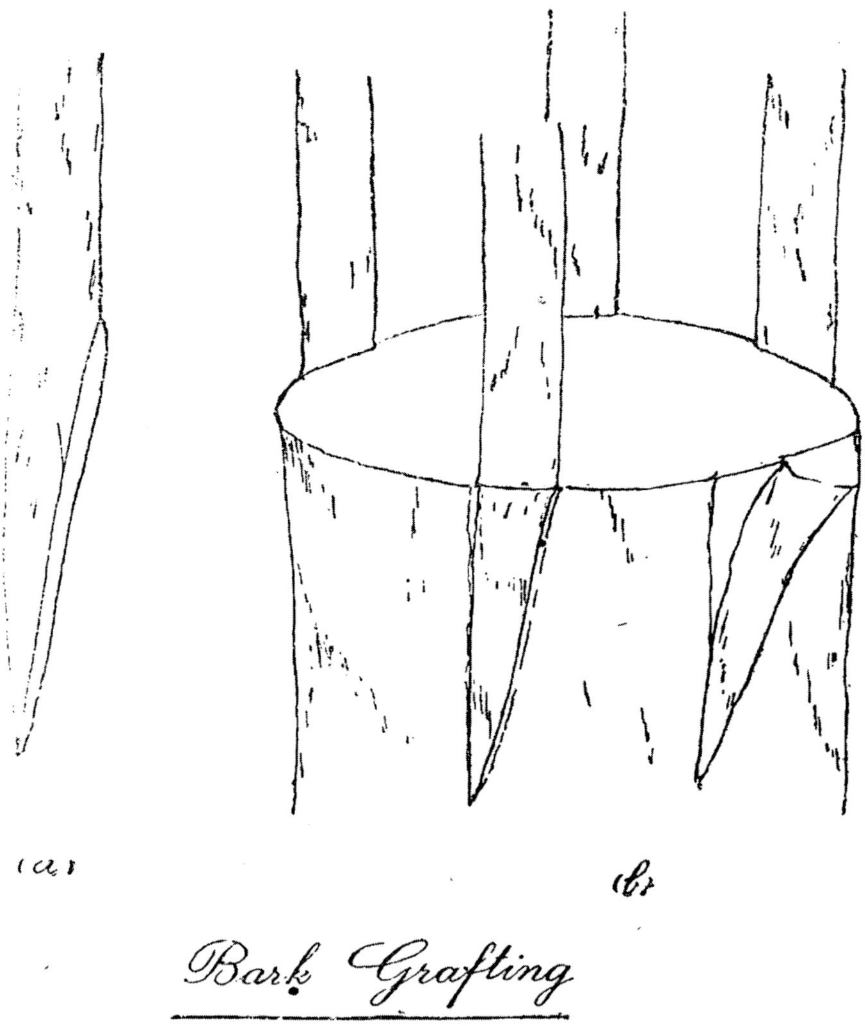

Bark, rind, or crown grafting. (a) scion, (b) rootstock with four scions inserted and a place prepared for another.

more seedlings into the trunk above the place where the damage has occurred. In such cases the seedlings are planted close to the trunk, and when established are grafted by one of several methods. They may be grafted as in ordinary inarching, when the top of the seedling is left on it until after union has taken place. Or the top may be removed with a slanting cut and inserted under the bark of the older tree which is prepared as for inverted **T** budding. In some cases it is desirable to fasten the rootstock firmly in place by means of a tack, as well as tying it in the normal way. Gandhi (1950A) points out that the seedlings should be inarched into the scion and not into the upper part of the rootstock of a grafted tree, and that it is useless to try to increase the vigour of a tree in this way unless the reason for the lack of vigour is an unsatisfactory rootstock.

Influence of Stock and Scion

Will oranges grown on lemon or *khatta* stock be sour ? This is a question which is often asked. Popular opinion often answers this and similar questions in the affirmative, but the evidence is in the negative. The question of the influence of the stock on the scion, and *vice versa*, has been discussed ever since graftage was first practised. It is now agreed that such influences exist, but that they are not nearly as important as has often been supposed. Gardner and others (1927) state in this regard, 'Differences in the character of the fruit produced, depending on the kind of stock used, are generally negligible or wholly absent, judged by commercial standards.' In selecting stock, therefore, one need not fear a stock bearing sour fruit. What is important is that the stock be one which experience has shown to be successful with the fruit concerned.

The stock influences the scion by the amount of water and nutrients which it supplies. A vigorous stock is obviously able to absorb more from the soil than a weak stock. This difference is sufficient to explain the variations ordinarily observed, but some other factor may be involved. Smith and others (1949) analyzed the leaves of Valencia oranges grown on six rootstocks and found highly significant differences in the percentage of nitrogen, potassium, calcium, magnesium, manganese, copper, boron, zinc, and iron, but not of sodium. The concentration of the minor elements varied more than that of the major elements but the absolute amount of nitrogen per leaf appeared to be correlated with tree size, suggesting a large difference in the ability of the rootstocks to supply nitrogen, which in turn contributes toward producing different growth rates. Hass (1948c) reports similar findings. Similarly, Cooper and Peynado (1955) found that with irrigation water containing from 0.2 to 6 ppm of boron, the concentration of boron in the leaves of grapefruit trees on different rootstocks varied from 61 to 880 ppm. Trees on sweet lime and sweet lemon had a high boron content, those on Cleopatra mandarin, sour orange, sweet orange, and rough lemon had less, and those on *Severina buxifolia* the least. Where the boron content of the soil or water is high, the choice of rootstock might make the difference between success and failure. Orange trees contained practically the same amount of boron as grapefruit trees on the same rootstock with the same kind of irrigation water.

Certain Russian biologists have reported remarkable effects of rootstocks and other factors in the environment, in some cases heritable effects. Scientists in other countries have not been able to confirm these experiments.

The changes in the scion induced by the rootstock may concern the size, shape, and longevity of the tree, the time of flowering, and the amount, time of maturity, size, colour, and quality of the fruit. In a similar way, the scion seems to influence the stock, although the evidence is not so often noticed, the root being out of sight. If the scion is vigorous, it probably supplies the roots with more food material, and thus encourages faster root growth. There is also evidence that the branching habit of the tree is reflected in the root system. The combination of rootstock and scion is called a stion, and the effect of one on the other may be referred to as a stionic effect.

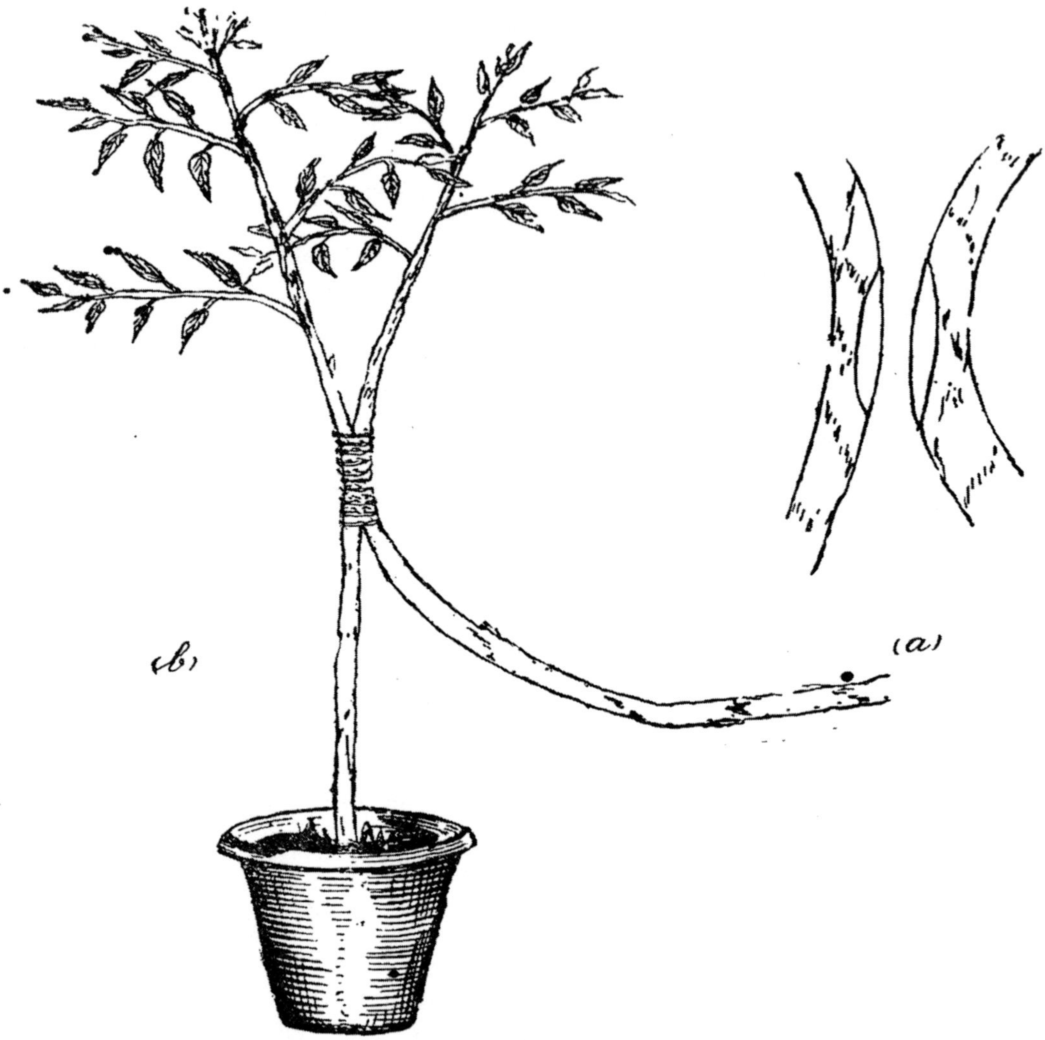

Inarching. (a) rootstock and scion prepared for grafting, (b) rootstock growing in a flower pot and joined to the scion, which is a branch of the tree to be propagated.

Of more practical importance is the question of compatibility of the stock and scion. By this is meant whether a particular rootstock and a particular scion may be united with permanent success. Budding and grafting are commonly possible between varieties in a species, or between the species of a genus, and sometimes between different genera of a family. Different families are considered incompatible, and the statement of Naik (1949) that inarching the rose-apple, a member of the *Myrtaceae*, on the star-apple, of the family *Sapotaceae*, and *vice versa* had been found easy, was based on a mistaken identification. Sometimes graftage is seemingly successful but the union is not satisfactory and after a few years the tree is dwarfed and unhealthy, or dies. In some cases the stem above the union becomes larger than that below the union. The reverse also occurs. Such differences generally indicate a difference in the relative vigour of stock and scion, but not always. Nor are such unions always unsatisfactory.

There is no limit to the number of buds or grafts which may be made on one tree. As curiosities, trees are sometimes prepared which bear fruits of a number of different varieties or species. These are seldom of any practical importance. Double working, however, is often of real value. If the fruit to be grown is not compatible with the rootstock which is best suited to the locality, it is sometimes possible to make a first graft with a variety which is compatible with both, and then graft the desired variety on this. In the same way, a trunk may be grown from a variety which is more resistant to trunk diseases than either the root or the top. In a review of the literature, Katyal (1949) deals with the effect of the intermediate stem-piece on size, yield, hardiness, disease resistance, fruit setting, size and quality of the fruit, and the physiology and chemistry of the plant. The effect on the root system is often greater than on the top.

The causes of incompatibility are not understood. In some cases it may be the formation of an imperfect union between rootstock and scion, or some inhibition of the transport of materials across the union in the phloem. That these are not the causes in all cases has been pointed out by Sax (1954) who found that in certain plums, pears, and apples, the use of an interstock compatible with both scion and rootstock did not always prevent failure if the scion and rootstock were mutually incompatible. On the other hand, an incompatible rootstock may be compatible as an interstock between scion and rootstock which are themselves compatible.

Practice must therefore be based on experience. Fortunately, there is a vast body of recorded experience on the question of suitable stocks for the different fruits. An excellent summary of this material was published by Argles (1937). But comparatively little of this relates to India. As a stock which is suitable under one set of conditions may fail in a different environment, it is necessary to test stocks locally. Many more carefully controlled stock trials are needed in India. A complicating factor is the fact that two species may be compatible when one is the stock and the other the scion, but not when the second is the stock and the first is the scion.

It was formerly thought that all scions of a given variety were equally good for propagation. The falsity of this idea was first noticed in the citrus orchards of California, where some trees were observed to be very poor producers. It was found that these trees came from buds taken from low yielding branches. Shamel and others who investigated, explained the phenomenon as being caused by bud variation. Certain buds, for no known reason, develop into branches which differ from the rest of the tree. Not only are there differences in yield, but the nature of the fruit is also often affected. In later reports, Shamel has shown that similar variations occur in many fruits, though not often as marked as in citrus fruits.

As L. Singh (1932) has pointed out, there is much variation in the fruit trees grown in India. It is therefore very important that scions be very carefully selected from the best trees. In order to be safe, it is necessary to select scions from branches which are bearing fruit at the time.

The production of rootstock for propagation is often given only casual consideration by nurserymen and fruit-growers. Seedlings are used, and one seedling of the species is regarded as being as good as another. As a matter of fact, there is much variation among seedlings and not all are suitable for stock. Nevertheless, seedlings make the best rootstock in most cases. Clonal stock, such as cuttings, is sometimes desirable, especially for experimental work, where the greatest possible uniformity in plants is needed. If seedlings are used, only those making a fairly uniform, vigorous growth should be selected. If seedlings are given a fair chance in the nursery, those which are stunted at the age of six months or a year are likely to remain small throughout life. Scions grafted on such stock are also likely to make a poor growth.

While it is true that in most cases seedling fruit trees are likely to be unsatisfactory, there are a few exceptions. Much fine citrus fruit in India is borne on seedling trees, and in some other countries, seedling mangoes are excellent. This is explained by a condition known as polyembryony, which is common among citrus fruits, and occurs in mangoes and some other fruits also. One seed contains two or more embryos, only one of which is sexual, the result of the union of male and female cells. The others arise from the tissue of the mother plant, and are genetically just like it. Not all of the embryos develop, and a polyembryonic seed may give rise to only one plant. As the asexual (apogamic or, preferably, apomictic) embryos are frequently more vigorous than the sexual ones, the percentage of apomictic seedlings is likely to be rather high. In some cases, particularly in hybrids, only apomictic seedlings develop. When, as in the case of the citrus fruits, the extra embryos arise in the nucellus, they are called nucellar embryos and become nucellar seedlings.

The question arises whether or not one is justified in using vegetative propagation in the case of varieties with a large degree of polyembryony. The apomictic seedlings will bear fruit like that of the female parent, although Swingle (1948) reports that of 40 or more apomictic seedlings of navel oranges, none showed a true navel, and there may be other slight changes. As a group of budded or grafted trees propagated from a single plant have rootstocks which may vary considerably, apomictic seedlings may actually show more uniformity. Like ordinary seedlings, however, the trees tend to be tall and slender, and to come into bearing later than budded or grafted trees. In the case of citrus trees, they are likely to be thorny. So it is frequently desirable to use vegetative means of propagation, even where there is a high degree of ployembryony.

The value of apomictic seedlings as rootstocks is obvious, for they are likely to be more vigorous and more uniform than sexual seedlings. Sometimes varieties which have been propagated vegetatively for many generations become somewhat lacking in vigour. Hodgson and Cameron (1938) and Frost (1938) have pointed out that such varieties may have their vigour restored by being grown once from apomictic seedlings. For this process of rejuvenation, Swingle in 1932 coined the term 'neophyosis', from the Greek meaning, 'causing to grow anew'. In the case of thorny citrus seedlings, by taking buds only from branches arising after three or four years, excessive thorniness may be avoided. The loss of vigour in old clones may, at least in some cases, be caused by a gradual accumulation of mild virus diseases. Because viruses are ordinarily not transmitted through seed, as they are by vegetative propagation, the apomictic seedling are free from them. Swingle (1948) states that nucellar seedlings of citrus are entirely free from virus, apparently because the embryo sac and immediately adjoining tissues are impregnated at flowering time with some substance, believed to be desoxyribose nucleic acid, which destroys all the virus present.

While polyembryony is often an advantage, it increases the difficulties of the plant breeder who wishes to produce hybrids. By laborious hand pollination, he may secure a large number of seed, but because many of the seedlings resulting are apomictic he may have few actual hybrids.

In growing seedlings, either for rootstock or for the growing of seedling trees, an effort should be made to provide favourable conditions for germination and growth. This involves a well-prepared seed-bed, and provision for an adequate water supply. Weeding and cultivation are also necessary. Nursery practice differs in different places and with different fruits. Ordinarily the seed is either broadcast or sowed rather close together in rows. When the seedlings are large enough to transplant readily, they are set out in nursery rows. They should be ready for budding or grafting in about one year. After budding or grafting they are ordinarily kept in the nursery for at least a year. With most sorts, it is best to plant the trees in their permanent positions between one and two years after graftage. Many ignorant growers consider it an advantage to get very large plants, and nurserymen take advantage of this to dispose of stock which has been in the nursery four or five years, or even longer. The initial advantage which such stock seems to have is more than counterbalanced by the slow growth such plants make. In selecting trees in the nursery, attention should be paid to both the size and the age. One or two-year old trees which are large for their age are desirable. Dishonest nurserymen sometimes put slow-growing older trees in with normal younger ones, to the great disadvantage of the buyer.

CHAPTER IV

PLANTING

The actual planting of the trees in the orchard is an operation of great importance. Mistakes made at this time are likely to cause loss throughout the life of the orchard, and it is very difficult or impossible to correct them. Comparatively simple though the operation is, it should be carefully planned and executed. Well-grown trees of the best kinds, properly planted on soil that has been wisely chosen and thoroughly prepared, form the foundation of flourishing and profitable orchard.

The season of planting is a large factor in the successful establishment of the orchard. This will vary with different fruits and under different local conditions. In India the most common seasons for planting are the monsoon and the middle of the winter, the former being the most popular. This is probably the best time for most evergreen trees. If these are planted early in the rainy season, they soon establish themselves, and grow vigorously. By the end of the rains the roots have spread to a considerable extent and frequent irrigation is not necessary. Such trees are in excellent condition to withstand the heat and drying winds of summer. Some authorities, however, prefer to transplant trees in the month of January, and where irrigation is easy and inexpensive, this may be desirable. The trees at that time are not growing as rapidly as in the rains, and suffer less shock. They start growing as the weather begins to warm up, and by the rains are well established and ready to take full advantage of the excellent growing conditions which exist at that time.

Deciduous trees may be transplanted during the winter while they are dormant, without shock. Except under unusual conditions, this is the best time, although such plants may often be transplanted during the rains with little loss. During the dormant period plants may be handled with bare roots resulting in a considerable saving in packing and railway costs, if the trees are shipped any distance. It is important that dormant planting be not delayed until too late in the season. If growth starts before transplanting, the trees are likely to suffer severely and be in poor condition for the hot weather.

Planting Plans

In planting an orchard, a well-considered plan should be followed. This should provide for the maximum number of trees per acre consistent with sufficient space for the proper development of each tree and convenience in orchard operations. If more than one kind of fruit is to be planted, each kind should ordinarily be in a block by itself. It is obvious that large trees cannot be mixed with small ones in an orderly fashion without waste space. Fruits ripening at the same season should be grouped together for convenience in protection and harvesting. If there is variation in the soil, the blocks should be so planned as to suit the different species to the soil, as far as possible. In some fruits, as the cherry, certain varieties are self-sterile, and occasional trees, at least, of a different variety known to pollinate these should be planted in the blocks.

A number of planting plans are in use, the most important being the rectangular (including the square), the hexagonal, the quincunx, and in hilly country, the contour.

Some form of the rectangular plan is probably used in a majority of cases, all over the world. In this the trees are planted in straight rows running at right angles. This is a very neat system, easy to understand, and easy to lay out. If the distance from tree to tree in the row is the same as from row to row, this is known as the square system. This allows for cultivation and irrigation in two directions, and is the most popular of all plans. Some growers, however, prefer to plant the trees closer together in the row, thus getting more trees per acre, while leaving more space between the rows for cultural operations.

The hexagonal system is also known as the equilateral triangle, as the trees are planted in the corners of equilateral triangles. Six trees thus form a hexagon, with another tree at its centre. The main advantage of this system is that by using it about 15% more trees can be planted per acre at any given distance, than by the square system. Thus, by the square system, about 109 trees

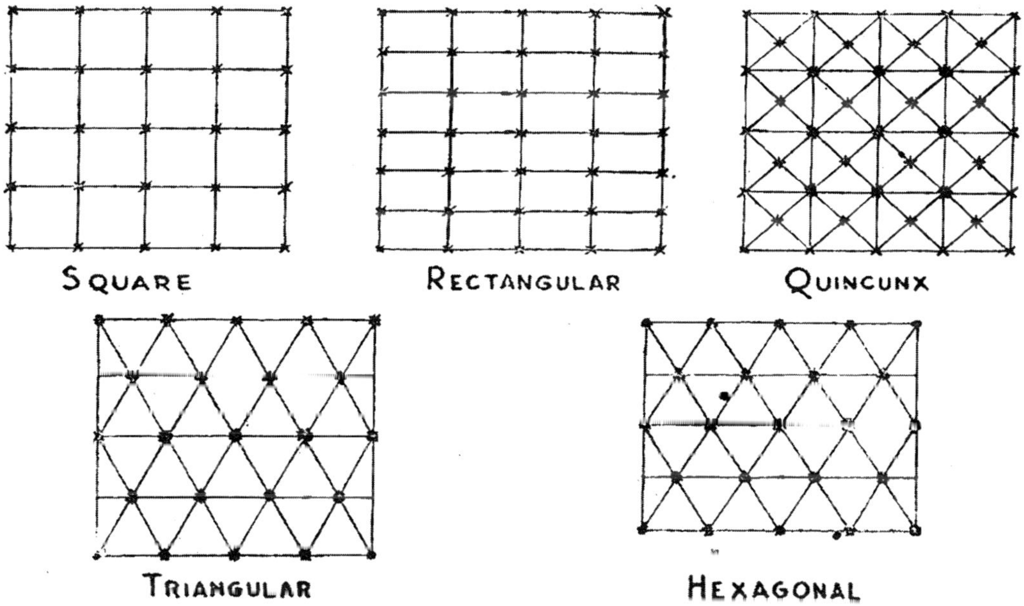

Figure 1. Diagrams of common planting plans

can be planted per acre if the distance between trees is 20 feet, but by the hexagonal system the number is 125. Cultivation may be carried on in three directions, but the distance between rows is not quite as great, although the distance between trees is. There is less 'waste' space between the trees. The branches of a tree spread in a more or less circular manner, and the hexagon more nearly approximates the circle than does the square. However, this advantage is not as large as it appears, for the roots of the tree extend in any direction in which they find moisture and food. They enter and exploit the soil in the centre as well as that beneath the branches. Where land is expensive and adequate manure and moisture can be applied the advantage of the hexagonal system is considerable. Inasmuch as it is easy to lay out an orchard by this plan and it has no real drawbacks, it should probably be preferred under most conditions.

The hexagonal system should not be confused with the so-called triangular system. In the latter, the trees are planted as in the square system, except that those in the even-numbered rows are midway between, instead of opposite to, those in the odd. This system bears the same relation to the hexagonal as the rectangular does to the square. Somewhat fewer trees per acre may be planted than in the square system with the rows the same distance apart.

The quincunx system is the same as the square, with the addition of a tree in the centre of each square. In this way the number of trees is almost doubled but the distance between the central and corner trees is greatly reduced. This results in eventual crowding, with no clear space for cultivation. This system is therefore used mainly where it is desired to have temporary trees along with the permanent ones. The temporary trees, known as fillers, are planted in the centres and the permanent trees in the corners of the squares.

All of the systems thus far described involve planting trees in straight lines. This is very desirable, but is not always practicable in hilly country, especially if irrigation is necessary. The ground may be too steep to allow irrigation or cultivation in straight lines without undue erosion. Under such circumstances the trees may well be planted in lines following the contour of the soil, with only a slight slope. Irrigation and cultivation are then practised only along the tree row, not across it. The trees will not be equidistant, and the number per acre will generally be less than by the other systems, but the advantages outweigh these defects. If the land is very steep, each contour may become a terrace. This system of planting is known as the contour system.

Contour planting should be adopted wherever runoff occurs and the surface is not too irregular to permit it, according to Bregger and Brown (1945), but perhaps they were not thinking of areas subject to torrential rains, where there is runoff from land almost level. Bench terraces are used where the slope is greater than 10%, and detailed instructions are given by these authors for both contour planting and terraces. LaRue and Rounds (1948) advocate contour planting where the slope exceeds 3%, unless sprinkler irrigation is to be used. On comparatively steep slopes, terraces are likely to develop gradually with cultivation along the contours, and while not as satisfactory as 'performed' terraces, are much less expensive.

The calculation of the number of trees per acre when planted by the rectangular system is easy. Each tree occupies a plot of land equal to the multiple of the distances from tree to tree and row to row. One acre contains

43,560 square feet. By dividing this number by the number of square feet occupied by each tree, the approximate number of trees per acre is found. Whether this will be entirely accurate or not will depend on the shape of the field. If this is such that at the given distance there is some waste space at the end of the row, the actual number of trees will be slightly less than the theoretical. A plot of land 660 feet by 66 feet contains one acre, and would theoretically contain 69 trees planted 25 feet apart. Actually, if 12½ feet is allowed between the trees and the boundary, there will be only two rows of 26 trees each, or a total of 52 trees. In practice, the distance between trees would be altered slightly in such cases, so as to avoid waste spaces. If the trees in this plot are planted 22 feet by 25 feet 4 inches, there will be room for 78. In larger fields, the percentage difference between the theoretical number and the actual number possible will be less.

When trees are planted by the hexagonal system, the distance between rows is equal to the altitude of the equilateral triangle, the base of which is the distance between trees. Each tree occupies a space equivalent to the distance between trees times the distance between rows. This means that the area is about 86% of the square of the distance between trees, and that the number of trees per acre is about 15% more than could be planted at the same distance by the square system. The number of trees per acre may also be found by dividing 50,299 by the square of the distance between trees.

The triangular system allows the same number of trees and the quincunx twice the number of trees, as the square system, except that in each case there is one less tree in every second row, and in the quincunx system there is one less row.

Spacing of Trees

The distance to be allowed between trees depends on a balance between several factors, and is a question on which there is much disagreement. Most authorities agree that most orchards in India are actually planted too closely for the best results, but they frequently disagree as to the space that should be allowed.

The maximum development of the individual tree requires that it be planted where it will come into competition with no other tree. The roots of the trees extend much further than do the branches, several times as far under certain conditions. To avoid all competition, therefore, would require such wide spacing that it is obvious that the yield per acre would be greatly reduced. Only in very exceptional cases would this be justifiable. Ordinarily it is more profitable to plant the trees closer together and supply the needed water and food materials.

If the trees are too close together, however, no amount of irrigation and manuring will produce as good crops as are borne by properly spaced trees. On the other hand, the closer the trees are planted, the more there are per acre. The maximum yield per acre will be had by placing the trees somewhat closer, in most cases, than the distance at which the maximum yield per tree is found.

Most growers seem to space their trees with a mental picture of the tree as it will be in the first few years in which it bears, rather than as a mature tree. The great bulk of the fruit borne in the lifetime of an orchard will be borne after the tree attains nearly its full size. Close planting results in a greater yield per acre during the early life of the tree, but less in the more important later years. The use of fillers avoids the early loss from adequate spacing.

Many Indian orchards are planted so closely that long before the trees reach maturity they interfere with each other. This causes them to grow tall, increasing the difficulty of pruning, spraying, guarding the fruit, harvesting and other cultural operations. The trees shade each other, resulting in little fruit being borne on the lower branches. Cultivation between the trees becomes very difficult. In many cases the lower branches, which secure insufficient light, die.

No definite rule can be laid down which will apply in all cases. In general, sufficient space should be allowed so that the branches will barely touch when the trees are mature. Under favourable conditions trees grow larger and therefore need more space. The size also depends somewhat on the variety of both the scion and the stock. Under certain conditions; with some fruits, the orchardist may be justified in planting his trees rather close together and then keeping the branches from interfering by severe pruning. It should be remembered, however, that the roots will still be in competition.

As a basis of judgment, it may be said that such trees as the papaya may be planted 10 ft. apart, the grafted guava 25 and the grafted mango 40 to 60.

It is customary to lay out the orchard by first placing pegs where the trees are to be. The first row is located, ordinarily parallel to the edge of the field and half as far from it as the distance between trees. Pegs are placed the desired distance apart along this line, beginning at half the distance from the edge of the field. In all systems except the hexagonal, it is desirable to lay out lines at either end of the field, perpendicular to the base line, and on these also place pegs at the required distances. The next step may be taken in different ways. For accurate work it is well to have a wire the length of the field, with markers soldered on at the required distances. This is stretched between each pair of pegs, and other pegs driven in at the markers. By placing tall stakes at the marks on the four edges of the field, the other pegs can be fixed by sighting across both ways. Fields are also marked in some cases by ploughing furrows between such stakes, setting the trees where the furrows cross. This is not accurate, and can only be used in case the animals have been trained to walk in a straight line or with a tractor.

In laying out a field by the hexagonal system, two chains should be used, each the length of the distance between trees. Both chains are fastened at one end to a common ring, and each has a ring at the other end. The rings are just large enough to slip easily over the pegs used to mark the places where the trees are to be. After laying out the first row, the two free rings are placed over adjacent pegs, and the chains are drawn taut and a peg driven through the common ring. This is repeated until the entire field is laid out. One man with two helpers forms an efficient team for this work. It is well to test the accuracy of the work by occasionally sighting along the lines in three directions, to see that they are straight. Where the spacing is not more than about 20 ft. two bamboos of the required length may be used instead of the chains.

In digging the hole for the tree, it is obviously necessary to remove the peg. When the tree is placed in the hole, it may not come exactly where the peg was. If care is taken in digging the hole, outlining the circumference before removing the peg, this inaccuracy may be kept within a few inches, which is ordinarily satisfactory. For more accurate work, however, a planting board may be used. This is a plank eight inches to a foot wide and four to six feet long. At the centre a notch is cut in one side, and similar notches are made in or near each end, equidistant from the central notch. This planting board is placed with the central notch against the peg, and other pegs are driven in the end notches. The board is removed and the hole dug. When the tree is planted, the board is replaced, and the tree is so placed that it comes in the central notch, exactly where the original peg had been.

Digging the Hole

Regarding the digging of the hole in which the tree is to be planted, there is much difference of opinion. The amateur often makes the mistake of planting in holes barely large enough to receive the roots. There is more danger of this being done when the tree is dug with bare roots than when they are balled. The hole should be large enough to allow the roots to extend naturally, or at least not to be twisted around each other. There should also be ample room to work, so that soil may be filled in around the roots, leaving no air pockets.

On the other hand, the digging of very large holes is very commonly advocated in this country, and sometimes in other countries also. Firminger's Manual (Burns, 1930) recommends a hole three feet each way for fruit trees, while others have frequently preferred four-or even five-foot holes. Such recommendations, however, seem to rest on a fallacy and an undesirable assumption. They assume that the soil of the field is too poor and hard to form a good medium for root development. They therefore conceive of the hole as a sort of pot in which to grow the tree. If this is the case, and unfortunately it sometimes is, then the larger the hole, the better the growth of the tree. But it is questionable whether it is ever economical to plant trees in such poor soil. Certainly, in most cases it will be advantageous to bring the whole field into good condition before planting the trees. It was a wise gardener who, when asked how large the hole in which to plant a fruit tree should be, answered, 'As large as the field.'

Where the soil is in fairly good condition, the digging of very large holes is not only an expensive and unnecessary operation, but it may actually interfere with the subsequent growth of the trees. Chandler (1925) mentions a number of experiments in England and America with deep holes or deep trenching, which indicate that these methods are of no advantage, and in some cases seem to have reduced the yield. In arid regions dynamite is sometimes used to break up an impervious layer near the surface, and under such conditions may be beneficial.

An exceptional case, in which the digging of very large holes was justified, is reported by Hinrichs and Cross (1948). Peach trees growing in loose topsoil over compact subsoil frequently blew over bacause of the shallow nature of their root system. Planting trees in holes five feet in diameter and four feet deep, filled with topsoil, resulted in a more fibrous root system, penetrating further, and giving better anchorage. In the first year the roots reached a depth of seven and a half feet and spread six feet, while trees planted in small holes had roots limited largely to the top two feet. The trunk and shoot growth were correspondingly larger. Dynamiting produced some improvement, but less than that from large holes. Hamilton (1954) reports an attempt to grow papayas in a layer of clay loam 6 to 14 in. thick over hardpan which effectively restricted root penetration and drainage. Satisfactory growth was secured only by digging holes 3 ft. cube and filling them with a mixture of equal parts of the soil removed and well-rotted Napier grass compost. Similar pits filled with the same soil, with or without lime, were little better than small pits, while blasting the soil was only slightly better.

In spite of strong recommendations that holes be dug weeks or months before the trees are to be planted, this is probably a matter of very little importance. The advantages are said to be the weathering of the exposed soil and the aeration of the soil around the hole. The effect of weathering is negligible and may involve the loss of nitrogen and organic matter from the soil. Some growers are convinced that if a hole is left for some time, a hard surface is formed, and that before planting, the walls of the hole should be scraped. On the whole, the best time to dig the holes is when it is most convenient and economical.

A similar question, on which there is difference of opinion, is as to the desirability of adding manure to the hole at the time of planting. Especially in poor soil, the use of well-rotted manure makes for more vigorous early growth. Perhaps the same amount of manure worked into the top soil around the plant would be as effective or more so. If the soil is rich, this is not necessary. Only a moderate amount should be used in any case, and it should be well mixed with the soil. In no case should fresh manure be allowed to come near the roots. The use of other fertilizers such as bone meal and ashes, is sometimes advocated. The need for applying such fertilizers will be discussed in a later chapter. Suffice it to say here that there seems to be no justification for making it a rule to apply these.

In the nursery, trees are sometimes kept in pots until they are planted in their permanent positions, or sold. This is ordinarily a bad practice, for while it is very easy to handle such trees, they are almost sure to become root-bound. The roots reach the wall of the pot, and grow along it. This results in a mass of matted roots, which never develop properly. Such trees are likely to remain stunted throughout their life.

It is therefore better to plant the trees out in the nursery, although this inevitably results in some of the roots being cut when the plant is dug. If the nursery trees are transplanted about twice a year, both before and after graftage, the roots do not penetrate as deeply or widely as they do when left undisturbed, and there is less shock when they are finally removed.

Transplanting

In digging trees in the nursery, it is convenient to dig a trench along each side of the row, with a spade or a *pharua*. This should be about four inches from the row, and about a foot deep. The plants may then be easily removed with a ball of earth around the roots, the *khurpi* being an excellent tool for this operation. The size and shape of the ball will depend on the size of the plant, the nature of its root system, and the distance it is to be moved. The larger the plant is, the larger the ball of earth should be. If, however, the plant is to be shipped some distance, it will be wise to decrease the size of the ball, and prune the top more heavily. The shape of the ball depends on whether the plant has a tap root or several spreading roots. For an ordinary tree with roots two or three years old, a ball of earth 6 to 8 in. in diameter and 8 to 10 in. deep is sufficient.

When trees are handled with bare roots, the soil is loosened with a spade or fork, and the trees are gently pulled out. Care should then be taken to prevent the smaller roots from drying out, though no harm is done if the fibrous roots become dry, or are broken off entirely. The roots are sometimes coated with clay, by dipping them in a heavy suspension, in order to prevent them from drying out. If the trees are to be shipped, or kept any time before planting, the roots should be packed in moist moss or other material.

Great care in the treatment of roots is often advocated, but experiments seem to show that this subject has been over-emphasized. It is said that all broken roots should be cut off leaving a clean cut, and it is sometimes added that this should be flat against the ground. Chandler (1925) has pointed out that from various experiments it is evident that there is no advantage in pruning the roots unless they are twisted around each other. In the latter case they should be separated, or one root should be removed. Nor does there seem to be any serious harm from the bending and bruising of roots.

Whenever trees are transplanted, whether with balled or bare roots, part of the roots are left in the soil, and those which are not left are somewhat disturbed. This means that the amount of moisture which the tree can absorb is considerably reduced. Under normal conditions the amount of moisture absorbed and the amount transpired through the leaves is equal; when transpiration is greater than absorption, the plant wilts. When absorption is decreased, the amount of transpiration is also decreased to a certain extent, in an attempt to restore the balance. But when the reduction is as great as it is when a tree is transplanted, this balance can be maintained only by reducing the number of leaves. Even then temporary wilting generally occurs. Tender shoots are likely to be killed. It is therefore customary to reduce transpiration by pruning the tops of the trees.

The severity of the pruning at the time of transplanting depends on the species, on the condition of the plant, and on the extent of the disturbance to the root system. When evergreen trees are moved with bare roots, it is customary to remove all or practically all of the leaves, and often all branches, leaving only one bare stem. When the roots are balled, such severe pruning is not customary. Experience affords a basis for estimating the amount of pruning necessary. Only enough pruning should be done to prevent wilting which lasts more than a couple of days. The more leaves remain on the tree in good condition, the sooner growth will start. In pruning at the time of transplanting, the shaping of the tree should also be kept in mind. This is dealt with in Chapter VII. The pruning may be done just before or just after transplanting, but it is ordinarily more convenient to prune first.

Evergreen trees, including most of the common fruits of the plains, should be planted out as soon after digging from the nursery as possible. In transplanting deciduous trees while they are dormant, there is, of course, no harm in delay.

The trees should be planted approximately where the original pegs were placed. If a planting board has been used in digging the holes, this should be replaced at the time of planting, and the tree so placed as to come in the central notch. It should be held with the trunk erect, or leaning slightly toward the south or toward the prevailing wind. One of the most common mistakes is that of planting the tree too deep. Gardeners often leave the trees in holes or depressions, which makes irrigation easy. It also causes water to collect around the tree during the rainy season. This damages the tree, and frequently causes death. It is also harmful to plant the trees deeper than they were in the nursery, in most cases. Some plants may be put an inch or two deeper, while a few may be planted much deeper. These are those which easily put out new roots from the stem. On the other hand, the roots should not be left uncovered. However, it is frequently good practice to plant the trees slightly higher than the level of the field, and leave a slight mound of earth around each tree.

If the hole has been dug deeper than is necessary, part of the earth may be returned, and pressed down firmly. The tree is then held in position, and the earth filled in around it. More care is necessary in the case of trees with bare roots, to make sure that the roots are well spaced, and that no air-pockets are left. As the earth is filled in, it is tamped down firmly, but not in such a way as to make it very hard. If it is not tamped, or only the top layer is tamped, it is likely to settle when the tree is watered, and leave the tree slanting and in a depression. It is generally considered desirable to replace the top soil first, using the subsoil as a top layer.

As soon as the tree is planted, it should be irrigated sufficiently to wet all of the soil which was removed in digging. This consolidates the soil and helps the roots to establish contact with it, and to secure a supply of water quickly. A small basin may be made around the tree for this purpose, but if planting takes place during the rains this basin should be demolished within a day or two, so that water will not collect around the tree. This is more dangerous on heavy than on light soils.

Some young trees are subject to considerable injury from sunburn, particularly if they have been trained to a single stem, with no branches for 18 inches or more from the ground. Such trunks can be protected by wrapping them with paper or other material, or by painting them with whitewash. The latter is probably best, as most materials wrapped around the trunks would be subject to termite attack.

Chapter V

ORCHARD SOIL MANAGEMENT

The importance of choosing a good soil was stressed in an earlier chapter. It is equally important that the soil be intelligently managed, in order that it be maintained in a condition suitable to the needs of the tree, without undue expense. This involves questions of the physical condition of the soil and its moisture and nutrient content. These depend largely on the practices of cultivation, irrigation, and manuring.

Under certain conditions fruit may be grown without cultivation, but these conditions do not exist on the plains of India. In the cooler, moist regions of Europe and America, trees are often grown under sod. Grass is planted, or the natural grass is allowed to grow, beneath and between the trees, and the soil is not stirred in any way. The grass is mowed from time to time, and preferably left on the ground. This practice is contrasted with the method known as 'clean cultivation', which is increasingly popular, and in which the soil is cultivated, and the growth of weeds prevented at least part of the year. A cover crop or green manure may be grown during part of the year.

The effects of sod are imperfectly understood, but seem to be mainly a reduction in soil moisture and available nitrogen. It is known that grass and other vegetation draws much water from the soil and gives it off into the atmosphere in the process of transpiration. Careful measurements have shown that the amount of moisture in the soil under sod is much less than in soil of a similar nature where clean cultivation is practised, unless large amounts are added by rain or irrigation. It has also been shown that the amount of available nitrogen is also decreased. This decrease can be explained only in part by the amount used by the vegetation. It is known that the addition of non-nitrogenous organic matter, such as wheat straw, reduces the amount of available nitrogen, perhaps by encouraging the growth of bacteria which use nitrate as a source of nitrogen. Chandler (1925) suggests that the reduction of available nitrogen under sod may be due to the activities of bacteria which are encouraged by the organic matter secreted by the roots. It has also been suggested by Pickering (1911) that part of the observed injury to trees under sod is caused by a toxic material secreted by the grass roots.

Under conditions of ample rainfall it may be possible to get good crops by applying nitrogen to the soil, and this may be less expensive than clean cultivation. While the amount of fruit is likely to be somewhat reduced, and the growth of the trees somewhat less, this may be more than made up by the decreased expenditure. With such trees as the apple, better colour is often secured by the use of sod, as the vigorous vegetative growth under clean cultivation shades the fruit and prevents bright coloration. There is also a great advantage in having sod in hilly country, as it prevents erosion.

Need of Cultivation

On the plains of India sod should never be used in the orchard. Both water and available nitrogen are scarce during much of the year. Experiments at Pusa have indicated very clearly the desirability of clean culture. Early in this century limited experiments were reported by Howard (1906, 1910) which showed that sod was definitely injurious, and that lack of cultivation caused poor growth as compared with clean cultivation. Further work was reported by Howard in 1925. In an experimental plot of 24 trees each of eight species of fruit trees, a strip containing nine trees of each kind was sodded with *dub* grass. The effect on young trees was striking. Those of custardapple were all dead in two years, whereas loquats lived five years, plums seven and limes eight. Guavas proved most resistant, but at the time of the report they were only half as tall as those under clean cultivation.

Mature trees did not suffer to the same extent, but in no case did they make as good growth as similar trees under clean cultivation. The order of susceptibility was the same as with the young trees. Accidental aeration by rat holes seemed to be of marked benefit to certain trees, and it was found that trenches dug between the rows also decreased the damage. This indicates that at least part of the effect of the grass was due to changes in the soil atmosphere. It was suggested by Howard that the damage may have been caused by an excess of carbon dioxide in the soil.

It seems clear that under most Indian conditions, sod in the orchard is harmful. The question remains as to how much cultivation is needed, the best time for it, and the best methods. These questions can be answered intelligently only after a consideration of the purposes of cultivation in the orchard.

Many advantages of cultivation have been suggested. Undoubtedly the most important, under most conditions, is the killing of weeds. It has been seen that vegetation removes large quantities of moisture from the soil and also ties up nitrogen so that it is not available to the trees at the time, though it may be returned later when the weeds die. Weeds also harbour insect pests and diseases. When they become large they interfere with orchard operations, and some of them climb up on the trees and by shading the leaves cause great damage.

Cultivation is also necessary to keep the surface soil from becoming hard. Hard soil greatly adds to the difficulty of irrigation. It is frequently said that hard soil interferes with the growth of roots. This is true, but ordinary cultivation does not soften the soil below the depth of tillage, and to this depth the roots are broken with each cultivation. In the main root zone, the hardness of the soil ordinarily depends on the amount of moisture present. A very compact layer of soil within a few feet of the surface may prevent the penetration of both roots and water. It should be broken up before the orchard is planted and the soil so managed as to prevent compaction. Manures, fertilizers, green manure, and other organic matter are covered and mixed with the soil by means of cultivation, and their value is thus conserved. A soil which has been cultivated before the monsoon absorbs more water, at least in the early stages, than a hard soil. Cultivation, especially ploughing in the hot weather, kills a number of insects.

Aeration is also thought to be affected by cultivation, but the exact importance of this factor has not been determined. It is probably not very great. In fact, Subbayya (1954) denies that cultivation aids aeration or conserves moisture except as it prevents its loss through weeds. He points out that while tillage may be necessary, it has some harmful effects, including damage to soil structure, the depletion of fertility in some cases, the cutting of roots, and an increase in erosion.

It was formerly believed that cultivation, and the maintenance of a soil mulch were important as a means of preventing the evaporation of moisture. It is true that cultivated soil dries out much more slowly than uncultivated soil, but only if there are weeds growing in the uncultivated field. Experiments have shown that moisture rises to the surface by capillary action only if the water table is very close to the surface. If weeds are removed without disturbing the surface of the soil, very little water is lost by evaporation. If a mulch is created and maintained, evaporation may be somewhat reduced, but the amount lost in any case is not significant in an orchard. D. Singh and Nijhawan (1944) report an experiment at Rohtak where the surface was a medium loam and the subsoil a silty clay. A soil mulch conserved moisture, in comparison with the removal of weeds without mulching, significantly only in the first foot, and mainly in the first six inches. The difference remained for two or three months. In the check plot where the weeds were allowed to grow, there was a great loss of moisture from the top six feet. The important point is to prevent the growth of weeds, and this can ordinarily be done most efficiently by cultivation.

Since 1938, a programme of non-cultivation and the killing of weeds by spraying has been tried by a number of growers of citrus fruits in California, where the rainfall is less than in most parts of India, and water conservation is important. Moore (1946) points out some of the advantages which have led to the spread of this programme to several thousand acres. He states that cultivation sole is largely eliminated, leading to better water penetration; that most cultural and harvesting operations are made more easy; and that costs are reduced, after the first year or two. In comparison with a cost of $15 to $20 an acre for conventional tillage and furrowing, the average cost for weed control under non-cultivation was about $25 the first year, but fell to as low as $5 by the fifth year. Kimball and others (1950) report that by 1905 about 60,000 acres, or one-fifth of the citrus acreage of California was under non-tillage and that the practice was extending to avocadoes and deciduous fruits. A preliminary study was made of a Valencia orange orchard planted in 1929, which was given somewhat less than the usual amount of tillage until 1941, when tillage was discontinued in part. By 1945 furrow irrigation was no longer satisfactory in this part because of more rapid water penetration, and from that year sprinklers were used. Studies made in 1948 to 1950 showed that in comparison with the part of the orchard which was still tilled, there were twice the weight of feeder roots in the first five feet of untilled soil, with a higher percentage in the upper levels, but more at all levels.

Because of the larger number of feeder roots the soil dried out more rapidly and more irrigations were needed each season. There was slightly more organic matter in the top six inches, and a correspondingly lower pH value. The water penetration was much more rapid. Trees in this section bore larger crops (partly because the branches were allowed to grow to the ground) of larger fruit containing juice with more soluble solids and slightly less acid, indicating earlier maturity. In other experiments, Lombard (1950b) found that the amount of nitrate nitrogen in the soil which was not tilled was very much greater than in similar cultivated soil given the same amount or more nitrogen as fertilizer. He suggests that the difference may be explained by the tying up of the nitrogen by cover crops and the destruction of nitrogen-fixing bacteria by cultivation. It is still possible that after further trial harmful results may appear.

The practice of non-tillage is being tried in other countries also. In spite of the rather high cost of oil for weed killing in Israel, it is reported to be successful with bananas, citrus fruits, and the avocado. In Australia experiments begun somewhat later than in California also show a tendency for the trees to produce more when the weeds are controlled by spraying than when tillage is used. Weeds are killed mainly by the use of oil sprays, and until oil, or some other satisfactory herbicide is cheaply available in India, the method will probably not be practicable here. Recent investigations in California (Day, 1955) indicate that certain urea weed killers, notably CMU and DCMU may be used to prevent the growth of annual weeds at an initial cost of about half that of oil sprays. Similar results may be achieved by frequent light hoeing or other means of preventing the growth of weeds without greatly disturbing the soil. The economics of such operations remain to be studied. But the fact that orchards tend to be in better condition and yield more fruit after years without cultivation at least raises questions about the values attributed to cultivation, and the necessity for adding other organic material than that contributed by the trees themselves.

The use of a green manure or cover crop is common in many parts of the world, and is sometimes found in India. Quite frequently weeds are allowed to grow during the rainy season. This has the double advantage of adding organic matter to the soil and preventing erosion. If clean cultivation is attempted during the rains, considerable erosion is almost sure to occur. It is probably best to plant a green manure crop between the trees early in the rains, and plough it into the soil toward the end. It is generally wise to use a leguminous green manure, although Batchelor (1948b) states that nitrogen fixation by bacteria associated with legumes may be negligible when the nitrate in the soil is as plentiful as it should be in a mature citrus orchard. If a non-legume will provide a larger amount of organic matter, it may be preferable. In India, however, there are a number of legumes which are satisfactory. Sunn-hemp is commonly used, but if it is allowed to grow throughout the rains, it is likely to become woody and be slow in rotting, whereas if it is ploughed under earlier, erosion may result. It can, however, be knocked down at the right stage and ploughed in later. Or some less woody legume may be grown, such as the cowpea.

Where irrigation water is available in plenty and not expensive, it may be desirable to grow a cover crop in the winter also. L. B. Singh and Nauriyal (1953) report on an experiment in an 18-year old sweet orange orchard at Saharanpur in which berseem in two cuttings yielded at the rate of 12,495 lb. per acre and raised the nitrogen in the soil from 98 to 434 ppm, on an air-dry basis. Lucerne and *methi* (fenugreek) made a smaller contribution to the soil nitrogen as well as having a lower yield. Marloth (1954) reports that in South Africa a permanent cover crop of the legume, *Glycine javanica*, gave as good results as clean cultivation, which was much better than sod.

Whether green manure is used or not, it is desirable that the orchard be ploughed at least once during the year, with a soil-inverting plough. The depth need not be very great, and with many trees should not be greater than is necessary to turn under the green manure or weeds. It is, of course, possible to remove the weeds and grass before ploughing, using them as fodder, but this robs the soil of a valuable manure, and is not ordinarily a desirable practice. Because of the trees, it is impossible to plough all of the land in one direction. A second ploughing in another direction is therefore necessary, but this should be delayed until the vegetation turned under by the first ploughing has decayed. In a very young orchard, the strip left unploughed may be so narrow that it is more economical to have it dug by hand in place of the second ploughing. In small gardens all ploughing may be replaced by digging with a *pharua*, but where a plough can be used this will ordinarily be more satisfactory.

In large orchards, where tractors are used for power, ploughing may be replaced by the use of a heavy disc harrow. This is not practicable where oxen are used.

The soil may also be ploughed at other times of the year if manure is applied, or if the weeds become so large or numerous that they cannot otherwise be conveniently killed. Ordinarily, however, it will be more economical to kill the weeds before they become large, by means of a harrow or cultivator. In the same way the soil may be kept soft. During the dry season it may be desirable to cultivate after each irrigation, but often it will be more economical to cultivate less frequently.

The time of cultivation is of some importance. If the soil is worked while wet, the physical condition is likely to be damaged, plough sole often being formed. Frequent cultivation, especially when the soil is damp, sometimes lessens the ability of water to penetrate to the lower levels. These dangers are more serious on heavy than on light soil. However, as a general rule, cultivation should be practised when the soil is as dry as possible without having it turn up in large clods.

Intercropping

In young orchards, the question of the use of the soil between the trees arises. If the trees are properly spaced, there is considerable land which will not be used by the permanent trees for several years. It naturally appeals to the grower to get some return from this land, especially when he is getting no return

Brinjal growing between rows of mango trees at the Allahabad Agricultural Institute.

Chillies growing between rows of tangelo trees at the Allahabad Agricultural Institute.

A healthy guava tree.

A guava tree, showing part of its root system.

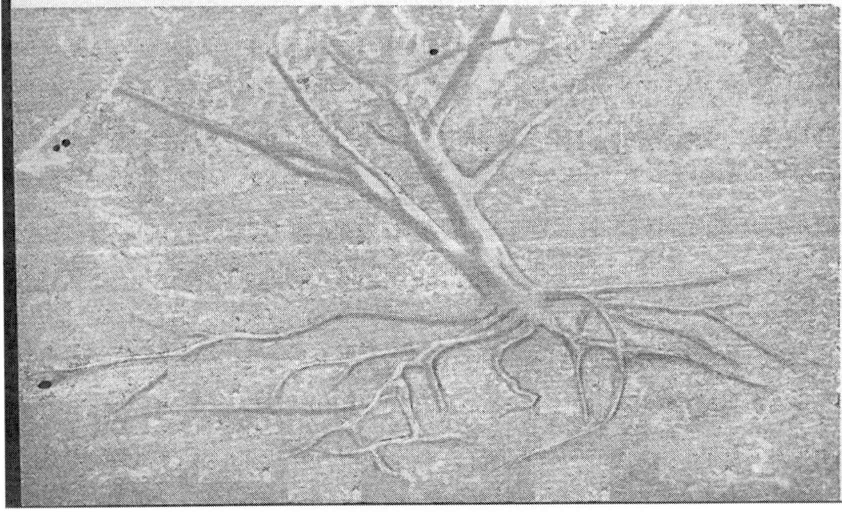

from his young trees. Merely to neglect this land means its deterioration and the growth of weed seed which will infect the area around the trees and also adjoining fields. If the land must be cultivated in any case, to control weeds, why should not the grower secure some return for his labour ? Nevertheless, some authorities are opposed to the planting of any crop between the permanent trees, feeling that the temporary gain is likely to be more than off-set by permanent damage to the trees. If damage to the trees were inevitable, there would be much to say for this point of view. Carefully controlled, however, with primary consideration always given to the permanent trees, there is no reason why intercropping should damage the trees. On the other hand, it may be an advantage to them.

The crop grown between the permanent trees may be some other fruit or it may be a vegetable or field crop. Two or more of these types may be grown in the same orchard at first when the space is large.

Many growers prefer some quick-growing fruit, as being in line with the permanent planting, and affording valuable experience in culture and marketing. A number of satisfactory fruits are available for the purpose. In temperate climates, peaches are often grown between such trees as the apple. In a properly spaced mango orchard there is room for guava trees, which begin to bear after two or three years, and will produce a number of crops before it is necessary to remove them. Among smaller trees, such fruits as the papaya, banana or phalsa may well be grown. Allen (1934) advises against bananas as fillers in citrus groves because they require more water than is good for the citrus fruits, and against papayas because they are tall and shade the trees. This argument is of little weight, however, if the fillers are kept well away from the permanent trees. In no case should the roots of the intercrop occupy the soil where the roots of the permanent trees are concentrated.

The danger in using fillers is that they will be allowed to remain in the orchard too long. Growers frequently fail to realize that the root systems extend more rapidly than the branches, and that the roots of the permanent trees come in contact with the roots of the fillers before there is any crowding above ground. Even when the branches begin to interfere, there is always the temptation to allow the fillers to remain and produce one more crop. In this way the permanent trees may be hindered. The only safe rule is to make definite plans to remove the fillers after a certain number of years, varying with the fruit concerned, and act accordingly, even when that means taking out beautiful trees when there is no apparent danger of competition between them and the permanent trees.

There is much less of this danger in the growing of annual crops, whether vegetables or field crops. The choice between the two will depend on the available labour, manure, and water and on market conditions. Where these are favourable, a larger return can be secured from vegetables. Bajwa and Jawanda (1954) recommend a large number of vegetables and a few leguminous field crops for growing in orchards in the Punjab, but point out that canal concessions were not available for four of the vegetables recommended. In any case, but especially if vegetables or other exhaustive crops are grown it must be remembered that the soil fertility must be maintained or improved. It is a very shortsighted policy to deplete the fertility of the soil in the years when the fruit trees are coming to maturity. Again it must be remembered that the intercrop should be kept well away from the permanent trees, and irrigated independently of them. The intercrop may require an irrigation at a time when it would be detrimental to the trees. Care should be taken to see that the water is then limited to the area of the crop. At other times it may be economical to irrigate trees and crop at the same time.

Irrigation

The water relations of the plant are of extreme importance, both for vegetative growth, and for fruit production. In regions having a well-distributed rainfall, it is customary to depend on this. The grower accepts an occasional loss due to drought or insufficient rain, in consideration of the saving of the cost of irrigation. This condition prevails in the fruit-growing districts in the Himalayas. On the plains, however, irrigation is the rule. This increases the cost, but adds to the grower's independence, and makes fruit growing less of a gamble and more of a business.

Some fruit is grown on the plains without irrigation, and in the case of such deep-rooted trees as the mango, fair crops may be produced by the mature trees. From a commercial point of view, however, irrigation is a necessity in order to secure rapid growth of young trees and satisfactory crops. In places where the water level is close to the surface, the need for irrigation is much less. Howard studied the root systems of the various fruits in the experiments at Pusa, where the water table is about 16 feet below the surface. He found that all had similar systems, with one set of spreading roots in the upper 18 inches of soil. From the lower surface of these roots, others drop vertically and spread out at lower levels. In the plum, peach, custardapple, mango, and loquat, the second layer of roots was just above the water table. As the surface soil dries out in the winter, the upper set of roots ceases to function, and the rootlets die. If unirrigated, these roots are dormant from March to June and the tree depends on the lower set. Within 30 hours of heavy rain or irrigation, the upper roots break into activity. As the water level rises during the rains, the lower rootlets are killed and the tree depends on the upper roots. Even under such circumstances, however, irrigation is an advantage, as it keeps the roots active in the upper layers where nutrients are more plentiful.

Irrigation water may come from canals or wells. Water containing large amounts of salts is to be avoided, especially if there is any tendency for the soil to be alkali. Very rarely water is found containing amounts of boron which, while very small, are still sufficient to damage an orchard. Most sources of water, however, are quite satisfactory.

The methods of applying water commonly used in India are very inefficient. Water is generally given in a small basin around the trunk of the tree, or in a ring of small diameter. A little consideration of the way in which water is absorbed by the tree will show the foolishness of this method. Absorption is largely through the root hairs, which are found near the growing tips of the roots. The roots of fruit trees are found extending to some depth in the soil, but mainly in the top two feet, and often extending horizontally far beyond the spread of the branches. Roots are likely to be deeper on light than on heavy soils and the depth is also influenced by the rootstock. Ford (1954) reports that in the sandy soils of Florida, roots of rough lemon may penetrate more than 17 ft. below the surface, as well as extending horizontally for 25 ft. from the trunk. Sour orange and Cleopatra mandarin roots went as deep, and sweet orange almost as deep, whereas grapefruit roots seemed not to go more than 8 ft. below the surface. With some of these rootstocks, half or more of the feeder roots may be in the zone 30 to 60 in. from the surface. In a mature orchard, even if the distance between trees is liberal, the roots will ordinarily occupy all of the soil. If irrigation is given only around the trunk of the tree, it is obvious that this will reach only a small proportion of the growing ends. Irrigation in this manner tends to discourage the spreading of roots and thus to limit the area from which nutrients are drawn. Some trees, particularly the citrus fruits, are subject to diseases attacking the collar and trunk, when water is allowed to touch them.

A good irrigation system should reduce to the minimum the loss of water. This loss may take place through surface run-off, deep percolation, surface evaporation, or the use of the water by weeds. Surface evaporation is inevitable, but is greater where the entire surface is wetted than where the area wetted is restricted. The loss through deep percolation is often great, and much of it is unnecessary. Once water gets below the region where the roots are, it is lost, and it may carry with it nutrients of great value. Surface run-off and the loss through weeds should be very largely eliminated.

When trees are small, some system of irrigation in rings is desirable. These should be so planned as to irrigate the soil at least as far as the roots extend. The rings may be connected with each other in series, and the water run down the tree row, or each ring may be connected with a channel running between the tree rows. If water is expensive it may be carried in buckets or in a tank wagon to the rings. As the trees grow the diameter of the ring increases.

Some modification of the furrow system is one of the best ways to irrigate mature trees. There is some evidence that production is sometimes greater if all of the soil occupied by roots is kept well supplied with water, but little damage is done if part of it becomes dry. Furrows can be made in two directions in an orchard, so that all of the soil between the trees is irrigated, but this involves more hand labour. Many growers find it satisfactory to use straight furrows in one direction, though some will alternate the direction from one irrigation to the next. Where there is not enough water to irrigate each row every time and have the water wet the root zone, it may be better to wet only the alternate 'middles'. Under ordinary conditions, the trees seem to be able to absorb all the water they need from the side where the soil is moist, and there is no difficulty in its distribution to all branches. Under certain conditions, such as with heavy clay or where there is lime-induced chlorosis, it may even be an advantage to let part of the soil dry out. Where straight furrows are used there should be one furrow as close to the 'skirt' of the tree as it can be conveniently made, and it is well to have other furrows at distances of from one and a half to three feet until the skirt of the next tree is reached. Broad, shallow furrows are generally best, as they provide better distribution of the water than narrow ones, and cause less erosion. The length of the furrow should depend on the slope, and on the nature of the soil. In heavy soil percolation is more slow, and the furrow may be longer. The furrow should not be so long that there is much waste of water by seepage in the upper part before the lower end secures sufficient water. Taylor (1941) recommends furrows 200 to 400 feet long. Some inequality in amounts is hard to avoid. A certain amount of run-off at the bottom of the furrows is also a common fault in this type of irrigation.

Irrigation in basins is also practised, and has the advantage of providing a more equal distribution. It involves more labour and is difficult to use unless the slope is very gentle. It wets more of the surface and results in more loss by evaporation, and also in the necessity for more cultivation. Irrigation with sprinklers is increasingly popular in the United States and in some other countries. Oppenheimer (1953) states that in the important citrus district of Jaffa in Israel, furrows were not satisfactory and basins were formerly used, but that by 1951, sprinklers had been installed in 70% of the orchards. Sprinklers placed above the trees have been tried, but the preference is for those placed under the trees. The initial cost is high, but there is a considerable saving of labour. Erosion is largely eliminated, which makes this almost the only suitable system for steep unterraced land. In India, sprinklers are used on tea and coffee estates, but have not yet seemed economical for fruits.

The amount of water required varies with so many factors that it is not possible to form a general rule. There is danger in over-irrigation as well as in under-irrigation. The rapidity with which water is withdrawn from the soil depends on the size and nature of the trees, the nature of the soil, and the climatic conditions. The amount of water which can be stored in the soil depends on the nature of the soil. A heavy soil requires more water at one time than does a light soil, but irrigations may be much less frequent. More water should not be applied than will wet the soil to the depth to which the roots extend. An exception to this rule may be made when salts tend to accumulate in the root zone and may be removed to lower levels by very heavy irrigation.

Except where it is necessary to check the trees to induce fruitfulness, the leaves should be kept from wilting, as far as possible. As Magness (1935) has pointed out in his excellent summary of investigations, there is a rapid recovery in trees after wilting, if the leaves do not fall, but the size of any fruit growing at the time is permanently reduced. In periods of dry heat, especially if there is also considerable wind, the tree may not be able to bring to the leaves sufficient moisture to prevent wilting, or even desiccation, no matter how much moisture there may be in the soil. Under less severe conditions, if there is fruit on the tree, moisture may be withdrawn from it in order to make good the deficiency in the leaves. This results in slow growth of the fruit. Even under favourable climatic conditions, the tree may suffer if the supply of moisture in the soil becomes too scant. On the other hand, it seems to be better for the trees to have the water supply fluctuate from field capacity to a point safely above the wilting point than to have it maintained near field capacity by very frequent irrigation. As the soil loses moisture, its pH becomes lower, with the result that minerals are dissolved and become available to the trees.

Intelligent irrigation practice will therefore depend upon observation of the condition of the trees, and of the soil. Instruments are now available which can be placed in the soil and which indicate the amount of moisture present. With much less expense for equipment, but with more labour, the state of the soil may be observed by means of a soil auger. If samples from different depths are taken, and the percentage of moisture determined, the point at which wilting occurs can be found out, and thereafter water applied just as it is needed. If an auger is not available, a better understanding of soil moisture conditions may be had by digging a hole a couple of feet deep with a shovel or other tool, than by looking at the surface. If there are weeds growing, their condition is also an indication of the state of the soil. As the great majority of the roots are in the top soil, this will dry out much more quickly than that at lower levels. It may therefore be desirable to give one or more light irrigations between heavy irrigations. At times when transpiration is likely to be very great, it is well to keep the soil moisture well above the wilting point. Frequent irrigation during very hot weather may also be beneficial in reducing the temperature of the soil.

Manures and Fertilizers

The nutrition of the tree is a matter of supreme importance and has been discussed thoroughly by a number of American authorities under the editorship of Childers (1955). Fruits remove larger amounts of nutrients from the soil than most other crops. An orchard can be maintained in commercial bearing only by adequate manuring. The general principles of manuring are very well known; nevertheless, much is written on the subject which is inaccurate, to say the least. This may be blamed in part on the propaganda of firms dealing in commercial fertilizers, who are sometimes more interested in sales than in profitable orcharding. Also, some ideas seem to gain credulity by virtue of being often repeated. As maintaining fertility is likely to be one of the more expensive parts of fruit growing, it will repay the grower to base his programme on known principles and careful experiments, and if further manuring seems needed, to make his own experiments on a small scale before adopting any practice.

Fruit trees, in common with other plants, require for their growth a number of minerals, most of which are found in ordinary soils in adequate amounts. The amounts which are soluble and available to the tree may be much less. Chemical analysis of the soil is ordinarily of little value in showing what elements are needed. The more soils are studied, the more difficult and complicated the problems of nutrition appear. The ability of the plant to secure for itself the necessary amount of an element depends not only on the amount of the element present in a soluble form, but also on the reaction (pH) of the soil, and the amounts of various other elements. As Shear and others (1946) state, 'All other factors being constant, plant growth is a function of the two variables of nutrition, intensity and balance, as they are reflected in the composition of leaves when the plants are in the same stages of growth and development.' All of the mineral elements in the leaves must be considered in determining the balance, including those not required for normal growth.

The complexity of the situation is illustrated by Wallace and Hewitt (1946) with regard to iron. They state that a simple deficiency of this element probably does not occur in the field, but that the deficiencies found in plants may be classified as lime-induced, those resulting from deficiencies of other elements, and those resulting from excesses or toxicities of other minerals. An iron deficiency may be caused by a deficiency of potassium, by an excess of cobalt, on neutral or slightly alkaline soils by an excess of phosphorus, or on an acid soil by an excess of zinc. Another illustration is given by Beyers (1955) who worked with grapes in South Africa. He found that the application of ammonium sulphate markedly increased the uptake by the vines of manganese, and to a less degree of nitrogen and magnesium, but reduced that of potassium. Superphosphate had no effect except a slight increase in the phosphorus absorbed. Potassium sulphate increased the absorption of potassium, manganese and iron but reduced that of nitrogen, calcium, and magnesium, causing chlorosis as a result of deficiency of magnesium.

Early attempts to judge fertilizer needs by analyzing the plants also failed but later more refined methods have proved of value. Bathurst (1943) reports on several years' experience in South Africa on citrus fruits. Leaves were taken from the fruit stems in May or June, when they were 10 or 11 months old. The amounts of the different elements present in the leaves of healthy trees were determined. In many cases, where the leaves showed much less than the normal amount of an element, the application of that element as a fertilizer produced good results. In one case, where the amount of nitrogen was above normal, the addition of nitrogenous fertilizer reduced the yield. Chapman (1949) has done much analysis of citrus leaves as a measure of potassium nutrition. On the basis of this and of work by others on other elements, he presents a table showing the minimum range in good orchards in California, average and maximum percentages of N, P, S, Ca, Mg, K, Fe, Mn, Zn, Cu, Mo, Na and Cl, and the effect, as far as it is known, of a deficiency of each on all the others except Na and Cl, which are not essential. Caution is still needed in selecting leaves for analysis and interpreting the results. Not only does the age of the leaf affect its mineral content, but, as Monselise and Heymann-Herschberg (1953) found with the Shamouti orange in Israel, the exposure of the leaf to the sun. They found that the greater the intensity of the light reaching the leaf, the smaller it was and the greater the dry weight of a given area. The amount of nitrogen and phosphorus decreased with decreasing light. Cain (1953), on the basis of evidence which he considers inconclusive, questions the belief that one ion in the nutrient solution has much effect on the absorption of another, except that if it increases the dry weight of the plant it tends to increase the absorption of all nutrients. He found that in one variety of apple fertilized with nitrogen and potassium for five years, differences in the mineral contents of the leaves did not correspond with differences in the entire tree. He considered the differences in phosphorus and potassium in the leaf of a tree which had been given nitrogenous fertilizer to be caused by dilution (dividing the amount absorbed among the larger number of leaves) and changes in distribution within the plant. Also working with the apple, Titus and Boynton (1953) found correlations between leaf and soil analysis ranging from none to excellent. They consider the use of the two measurements together more meaningful than either by itself. Ramamoorthy and Desai (1946) have reported preliminary studies of nutritional deficiencies in India by the spectroscopic examination of both leaves and soil.

Many crops react favourably to the addition of three elements, nitrogen, phosphorus, and potassium, on many soils. Deficiencies in other elements have been recognized much less frequently. Fruit growers have therefore paid most attention to these elements, and some have assumed that all three should be applied. Analysis of fruits and leaves of a number of fruit trees has shown that large amounts of nitrogen, even larger amounts of potassium, and small amounts of phosphorus are removed. On the basis of this analysis, potassium has been regarded as having special importance for fruit trees.

Extensive field experiments with deciduous fruits have been carried out in Europe and America, and while the results are not conclusive in all cases, much valuable information has been secured. Chandler (1925), after a very thorough review of the literature, comes to the conclusion that fruits often fail to respond to fertilizers in soils in which field crops show a decided response. Fruits respond to all three elements only in soils unusually deficient in them, but many trees will respond to nitrogen on any soils where field crops respond. Citrus trees seem to require more nitrogen than deciduous fruits or most field crops. None of the fruits tested make any response to the application of phosphorus on soils deficient in this element for field crops, unless the deficiency is extreme. Lileland and others (1942) report that on a clay loam with a very low content of available phosphorus, 18 annual crops failed to make satisfactory growth without additional phosphorus, and the adding of the element to the holes in which nursery trees were planted was helpful. But established trees of eight species showed no response to a heavy application on the surface or injected to a depth of three feet. All grew well and bore satisfactory crops whether phosphorus was added or not. Where potassium is exceptionally low, fruit trees may make a marked response to additions; otherwise the response is not measurable. There seems to be an indication of a very slight response in many soils, even though they are rich in this element naturally. However, this response does not justify expenditure on potash fertilizers.

Experiments with citrus fruits are likely to have more meaning for India than those with deciduous fruits. The most thorough experiments with citrus fruits have undoubtedly been carried on in California, and the results achieved there are very striking. In one report, Batchelor (1933) states that nitrogen is needed, but that, 'The total absence of any effect from phosphate or potash has been observed with regard to the growth of weeds, cover crops, and trees, and fruit tonnage and quality.' The possibility exists that the supply of other elements may gradually be used up. Parker and Jones (1950a, b) report on a fertilizer experiment begun in 1927 in the same state. In the early years there was no significant effect from the use of potassium, but later the potassium apparently caused a small average increase in the size of the fruit, and, as there was no reduction in numbers, in the yield. The increase was considerable only in the years when the fruit on the trees receiving no potassium was unusually small. The effect was more pronounced when the potassium was applied in bulky organic manures than when chemical forms were used. There was a correlation between large size and the concentration of potassium in the leaves. Aldrich and Cooney (1951) report a deficiency of phosphorus in certain lemon orchards in California.

It has long been known that plants required a number of elements in addition to nitrogen, phosphorus, and potassium, but it has generally been assumed that these were present in sufficient quantities in practically all soils. It is now known that plants suffer from deficiencies in these elements quite commonly, even though the amount required may be very small. Camp and Fudge (1939) report that in Florida, symptoms resulting from deficiencies in copper, zinc, manganese, magnesium, iron, and boron occur in citrus orchards. As Camp and others (1949) and Bain (1941) have pointed out, symptoms of the lack of most of these elements have been observed in other parts of the world. The list of elements which have been found deficient in orchards of deciduous fruits is not as long but, according to Davidson (1949), contains calcium as well as magnesium, boron, and zinc. Certain deficiencies cause rather definite patterns in the leaves which can generally be recognized by those familiar with them. However, symptoms resulting from different causes may be very similar, and at times more than one element may be deficient, making the cause difficult to identify. In fact, Shear and others (1946) state that there are no deficiency symptoms which may be accurately diagnosed visually.

The degree of damage caused by these deficiencies varies. It may be severe, as in the case of magnesium in Florida where, according to Cowart (1942), a deficiency of this element causes a decline in both tree growth and yield in oranges and grapefruit. The application of magnesium not only increases the crop, but increases the content of sugar and vitamin C, and improves the taste of the juice. It is thought that the improvement is brought about by increasing the area and efficiency of the leaves. On the other hand, Parker and Southwick (1941) state that although symptoms of manganese deficiency are widespread in California, its control by means of suitable sprays seems to make no difference in the general health or yield of the trees except in severe cases.

Most deficiencies may be rather readily controlled by applying salts of the elements to the soil, or in some cases, by spraying them on the foliage. Zinc, copper, manganese and magnesium salts are commonly applied as sprays. Injecting the elements into the trees has also been tried with some success. In alkaline soils, these elements may be present but because they are relatively unavailable, symptoms of deficiency may occur. The use of bulky organic fertilizers may be useful in such cases not only because of the elements contained, but also because of their influence on the reaction of the soil. It is possible that at least part of the advantage of organic sources of nitrogen over inorganic is the presence of small amounts of these elements.

A deficiency of iron is fairly commonly found in orchards, and is one of the more difficult to correct. Iron added to many soils almost immediately becomes unavailable to the tree, and while application of suitable salts to the leaves may have some effect, sprays have generally been found unsatisfactory. Since the middle of this century, there has been much experimentation with what are called chelating agents or chelates, these terms coming from the Greek word for claw. A chelate (pronounced 'keelate') is defined by Haertl (1955) as 'Any compound which will inactivate a metallic ion with the formation of an inner ring structure in the molecule, the metallic ion becoming a member of the ring.' A fairly full statement on the chelates is given by Stewart and Leonard (1955). Many salts of organic acids in the soil are chelating agents, but are broken down by micro-organisms, but those which are used are not. The first one used commonly was ethylenediamine tetraacetic acid (EDTA) (Stewart and Leonard, 1952 a). This seems to be very effective on acid soils, where Ford and others (1954) report that when combined with iron it eliminates leaf symptoms, increases shoot growth and significantly increases the growth of feeder roots of citrus trees suffering from a deficiency of iron. Haertl (1955) claims that this combination maintains the iron in a form available to the trees even in soil with a pH as high as 9, but that in highly alkaline soils the response may appear after several months. He also says that such treatment sometimes improves the yield even where the leaves had shown no deficiency symptoms. Bould (1955) reported the cure of lime-induced chlorosis in some fruit trees in soil of pH 7.8 by applying 8 oz. per tree of this chelated iron, followed by thorough watering, and suggested that the success of soil applications may depend on using enough of the material and its transport to the roots by water. Leonard and Stewart (1954) found that on calcareous soil, the application of 4—5 lb. of technical grade sulphuric acid before small applications of Fe-EDTA gave good results.

Several other chelates appear promising. Wallace and others (1953) report two of these to be definitely superior to EDTA in alkaline and calcareous soils : hydroxyethylethylenediamine triacetic acid (HEEDTA, EEDTA, or EDTA-OH) and diethylenetriamine pentaacetic acid(DTPA). Leonard and Stewart(1954) report that 25—100 g. per tree of Fe-HEEDTA resulted in excellent recovery in lime-induced chlorosis, whereas 300 g. of Fe-EDTA was required. The same authors (1953) found 20 g. of Fe-EDTA effective in causing a greening of the leaves within six weeks, on acid soil.

Foliage sprays with chelates have also been used, generally with unsatisfactory results. Bould (1955), however, reports success with several chelated iron compounds in treating chlorosis of plums and peaches, and considers this cheaper than treating the soil. One of these compounds, 0.1% ferric diethyltriamine pentaacetate, cured extremely chlorotic peach trees in one application.

Cases of burning of the foliage and fruits from chelate sprays have been reported.

Other minerals may also be chelated, but less attention has been paid to them because they are either less commonly deficient, or easily applied as ordinary salts. Zinc sulphate and Bordeaux mixture are commonly sprayed to provide zinc and copper, or the latter may be added to the soil as copper oxide.

Interesting possibilities are opened up by the report of Haas and Brusca (1954a, b) that rooted cuttings and larger trees of the avocado were greatly stimulated by the addition to the nutrient solution on three occasions of 0.005, 0.010, and 0.015 ppm of the growth substance, 2, 4-D. Similar treatment or soaking seed over night in a solution of 0.0075 ppm of 2, 4-D increased the germination and growth of citrus seed. This may be effective as a hormone, promoting the growth of roots, rather than as a nutrient.

While comparatively little work has been done on the so-called minor or trace elements in India, it is apparent that deficiencies do occur here. Choudhury (1936) claimed to have controlled chlorosis of citrus trees in the Punjab by spraying with iron salts. Marudarajan (1949) reports a deficiency of zinc in oranges in several districts of Madras, and while soil applications did not correct the condition, spraying with zinc sulphate twice a year proved effective. He states that a deficiency of copper in Batavian oranges in the Northern Circars was improved by spraying with Bordeaux mixture. A decline of citrus trees in the submontane tracts of the Shevaroys, Kotagiri, and Coorg did not respond to initial treatment, and leaf analysis showed deficiencies of phosphorus, magnesium, manganese, and boron, though phosphorus was the only element found to be deficient in the soil. Elements present in the soil may have been unavailable because the soil had a pH value of 7. Either the citrus fruits are especially susceptible to such deficiencies, or the symptoms are more frequently recognized on them. Further reports will be considered in the chapter on these fruits.

Fertilizer Fallacies

It is frequently argued with considerable plausibility that trees should be given a 'balanced ration' of nitrogen, phosphorus, and potassium, just as men and animals require a balanced diet. The fallacy lies in disregarding the fact that the tree gets its food from the soil, and that the aim of manuring is only to make good any deficiencies. Only if all three elements are deficient is it logical to supply such a balanced ration.

Another fallacy which may be encouraged by fertilizer propaganda is the idea that dung or farmyard manure supplies only nitrogen. It is true that such manure is ordinarily applied primarily for its nitrogen and organic matter, but it also contains considerable amounts of both phosphorus and potassium. Batchelor and Parker (1934) analyzed numerous lots of dairy manure, and found them to contain nitrogen, phosphorus, and potassium in the proportion 10 : 7 : 20. They report that water-soluble phosphate and potash gradually increased in the root zone of citrus trees fertilized with dairy manure, as well as where the minerals were applied.

It has been found in numerous experiments that, irrespective of the amount of nitrogen available, trees do not flourish unless the supply of organic matter in the soil is maintained at a fairly high standard. This can be supplied in part by the use of green manures, but where farmyard manure is available, it is highly desirable that it be used. In California citrus groves, it is commonly recommended that in addition to green manuring, about half of the nitrogen added be in the form of farmyard manure, and the remainder in whatever form is cheapest.

There seems to be little difference in the effectiveness of the different chemical nitrogenous fertilizers. Sulphate of ammonia tends to make the soil reaction more acid, while nitrate of soda may result in the accumulation of sodium in the soil, if used in liberal quantities over a period of years. Wander (1954) found that ammonium nitrogen lowered the pH in the subsoil when applied to a fine sand in Florida, even when the topsoil was maintained at pH 5.5—5.8 by adding ground limestone. He also reports that as a result of sulphur sprays, the soil became more acid to a depth of at least 6 ft.

There have been a number of manurial experiments conducted in India, but few have dealt with the requirements of fruit trees. Sahasrabuddhe (1934), in reviewing manurial experiments in Bombay up to 1931, mentions experiments with four fruits, but with the doubtful exception of a one-year experiment on the fig, none gave any significant result. It is therefore difficult to understand the assurance with which many authorities advocate complicated and exact manurial treatment. It is desirable that careful experiments be carried out with the different fruits and under different conditions of soil and climate. Until this is done, the grower must base his programme on common experience, on the results of experiments with other crops in India, and on the experiments on fruits in other countries.

The use of nitrogen, particularly in bulky organic forms, is justified by experiments in other countries, as has been seen; by experiments with other crops in this country; and by common experience. It is generally recognized that most Indian soil are lacking in nitrogen, and particularly in organic matter. Nitrogenous manures are commonly used in orchards, often without other fertilizers, with obviously profitable results. Both nitrogen and phosphorus, generally in the form of super-phosphate, increased the yields of many crops in trials in various parts of India, according to Vaidyanathan (1934). As has been seen, such experiments do not indicate that fruit trees would respond to applications of phosphorus. There seem to have been very few experiments with potash, as most Indian soils are said to be well supplied, and there is no evidence of the value of applying it. In the Punjab, the manurial experiments of 20 years were statistically studied, and the results have been summed up by Johnston (1934). He reports that green manuring has invariably given good results; that artificial nitrogenous manures, alone and in conjunction with farmyard manure, have generally given good results; and that farmyard manure has almost always given better financial results than artificials, being the cheapest and most common means of adding organic matter and nitrogen to the soil.

The use of phosphorus and potassium, except as they are provided by farmyard manure, is not very common in Indian orchards, and there seems to be no clear indication that they are commonly needed. Superphosphate is reported to cause a positive response when applied to temperate fruit trees in Podsols and Brown Forest soils of Kumaun, as well as with sugarcane in leached calcium soils in three districts, but is not recommended elsewhere in Uttar Pradesh. Johnston, in the report referred to above, states that, 'the application of phosphatic and potassic fertilizers has almost always resulted in a financial loss.' If this is true of field crops, experiments in other countries would indicate that it would be even more true of fruits.

Importance of Nitrogen

It would seem, therefore, that the most important element in a manurial programme for Indian orchards, and pending further experiments, the only element to be generally recommended, is the supply of nitrogen and organic matter. It must be remembered that soils differ, and that no general recommendation will be universally applicable. Under certain conditions the use of other fertilizers will be economical.

The amount of nitrogen per tree or per acre which can be profitably applied is a question on which there is even less evidence. It is not known what the optimum amount, from the point of veiw of yield, is and this will obviously vary with the soil. The most profitable amount will ordinarily be less, as the law of diminishing returns is applicable. The most profitable amount may also vary from year to year, as it depends on the market value of the fruit, and the cost of the fertilizer, both of which fluctuate. Under some circumstances as much as three pounds of nitrogen per tree may be profitable. This would be supplied by about 300 pounds of farmyard manure of high quality or by 150 pounds of farmyard manure and 7½ pounds of ammonium sulphate. Batchelor (1948a) states, that, 'The experience of many successful citrus growers in California seems to justify applying annually 180 to 250 pounds of nitrogen per acre.'

When trees are young, and it is desired to maintain them in vigorous growth, there is little danger of providing too much nitrogen. When trees reach the stage at which they should produce fruit, it is commonly believed that the amount of nitrogen applied should be decreased. It seems probable that under some conditions, certain fruits are kept in vegetative growth, and fruitfulness is inhibited, by the application of nitrogenous manures. In cases of vigorous trees failing to fruit satisfactorily it may be well to reduce or omit the application of nitrogen. On the other hand, it may be better to limit vegetative growth by reducing the water supply, or to increase the proportion of carbohydrates in the branches by ringing or root pruning. It should be remembered that nitrogen is needed for the formation of fruit buds and fruit, as well as for vegetative growth. Also, vigorous growth means more leaves, and consequently the formation of more carbohydrate. A mature tree, producing large crops of fruit, require more nitrogen than a young growing tree.

Bulky organic manures should be spread over as much of the soil occupied by tree roots as is feasible, and mixed with the surface soil. The same method may be used for chemical fertilizers, but these are sometimes dissolved in the irrigation water, or applied in the furrows just before irrigation. An experiment was conducted in California on the effect of the placement of fertilizers on sweet orange and grapefruit trees. Each tree received 3 lb. of nitrogen each year, half from manure and half from anmonium sulphate and calcium nitrate. In some blocks this was applied to the cultivated zone and in others to the soil under the skirts of the trees. Jones and Cree (1953) point out that after this different placement had been continued for 20 years, the records showed no differonce in production due to placement. However, Haas (1950) points out the desirability of placing manure so that it is available to all major roots. Experimental citrus trees were grown with half of the roots in one container and half in another. After only one container had been irrigated for about two years, there was no indication of lack of water in any of the branches. But when the amount of nitrogen in the otherwise-balanced nutrient solution was varied, the branch above the root receiving more nitrogen grew and produced better than the other. Investigations with other plants have also indicated that there is no appreciable cross-transfer of nutrients, though there is of water.

As has been seen, the so-called minor elements are frequently supplied as sprays on the foliage. Under some conditions applications to the soil are useless, as the material immediately becomes insoluble. More recently, the application of nitrogen and, to a small extent, phosphorus and potash, as foliage sprays has received some consideration. Fisher and others (1948) were among the first to report on spraying apple leaves with urea, which seems to be the safest nitrogen-carrier for the purpose. As is so often the case, different varieties may react differently, and Beattie (1952) found urea sprays satisfactory for the Rome Beauty whereas it reduced the yields and terminal growth of the Jonathan. Crowe and others (1954) found the yield greater when nitrogen is applied in this way than when applied to the soil or by a combination of the two methods, in the case of three varieties, but in some other cases the combination proved best, and with one variety soil application alone was best. A little work has been done on other deciduous fruits, and Benson (1953) found that while it was safe to apply spray containing 5-6 lb. of urea per 100 gal. to apples, it was likely to injure peaches and sweet cherries and was not absorbed by the leaves of pears and apricots. Walker (1955) found urea sprays about as satisfactory as soil applications with the sour cherry.

Considerable work with urea sprays on citrus fruits has also been done. Jones and Parker (1949 b) found that it was possible to increase the nitrogen content of the leaves more quickly in this way than through soil applica ions, and Jones and Steinacker (1953) report that while more nitrogen is absorbed from more concentrated solutions, more than 10 lb. per 100 gal. seemed dangerous. The damage to the leaves is apparently caused by biuret, which occurs in urea which has been formed into pellets for ease in handling, but not in the crystalline form, according to Jones and Embleton (1954). Not more than 0.25 per cent. of biuret should be present in spray material, according to Jones and others (1955), although up to 2.5 per cent. is safe for soil applications of urea. Chen, (1954), working in Florida, found that another way to avoid injury was to apply on three or more occasions a spray containing 5 lb. of urea per 100 gal. He found that the percentage of the nitrogen which reached the leaves was about the same in spray and soil applications, but that the spray caused some increase in leaf nitrogen within one hour, and was more effective than soil application for two weeks.

The possible use of combined sprays on pineapples in Malaya has been suggested (Anon., 1954a). It was found that solutions as concentrated as 40 per cent., made from urea, mono-ammonium phosphate, and potassium nitrate could be sprayed on the plants in the evening with no harmful results, and as the pineapples grown on peat soils were commonly sprayed to provide copper, the addition of the other elements might prove economical. Sato and others (1954) sprayed seedlings grown on land deficient in phosphorus with mono-ammonium phosphate and increased the growth. The most effective concentrations were found to be 0.5—1.0 per cent. with the persimmon and grape, and 1.0 per cent. with the peach, pear, and Satsuma orange. Eggert and Kardos (1954), however, report that foliage sprays do not provide all the phosphorus needed by apple trees, though they may be useful in cases in which the trees get less than the optimum amount from the soil.

Chapter VI

PROTECTION FROM ADVERSE WEATHER CONDITIONS

No matter how favourable the climate may be for fruit production, there are in all regions occasional extremes which damage the fruit or the trees. Man has little control over the climate, but can in some cases decrease the amount of damage.

Extremes of temperature are the most common sources of damage. In temperate countries, and to a certain extent in subtropical regions, cold is a serious danger. Even the most hardy deciduous trees may be killed by extremely cold winters, though some can stand temperatures as low as 50 degrees below zero, Fahrenheit. There is little which can be done to protect trees from such cold, though the trunks may be protected by piling earth around them.

A more common form of cold injury to temperate fruits is the killing of buds, flowers, and young fruits by frost in the spring. In such frosts the temperature may go only a few degrees below the danger point, and ordinarily stays low only a few hours. Similarly, subtropical and tropical trees may be damaged by frost in winter or very early spring. In the case of some fruits, like the mango, the flowers may be damaged, while in others, like the citrus fruits, the fruits may be injured. Damage to the foliage, and even the wood, also occurs. In a study of the most severe freeze on record in northern California, Hodgson (1934, 1935) records several types of injury to the wood. The bark was in some cases killed, and in others merely discoloured. The cambium was sometimes killed outright and sometimes so damaged that normal growth was not resumed in the two seasons following. In the more tender species, there was much killing of the wood. Young guava trees in Allahabad have also had the cambium so damaged that they died up to more than a year after the frost, while others have been killed or killed to the ground at the time of the frost.

The ways in which low temperatures damage plant tissues are not completely understood, and as Chandler (1954) points out in a review of the subject, no simple theory is satisfactory. He notes that some plants, particularly tropical ones, are damaged or even killed by temperatures above the freezing point of water. On the other hand, the formation of ice crystals is frequently blamed, and some tissues which are killed when ice is formed in them are not seriously injured by supercooling to 3-4 degrees Centigrade below freezing if they are warmed to the freezing point without ice formation. Nor is the effect of spraying with the plant hormone 2, 4, 5-T, reported by Crane (1954b, c) entirely clear. He reports that spraying two varieties of apricots with this hormone 15 hours before frost occurred increased the resistance of the fruit to low temperatures, as the sprayed branches dropped 83.9 per cent. less fruit than the unsprayed. This substance is known to promote parthenocarpy, but this does not explain the results entirely, for the sprayed branches produced 69.7 per cent. more fruits with normal embryos. When another variety was sprayed after frost which caused the fall of all fruits on unsprayed branches, only 3 per cent. of the fruit fell before maturity and the rest was of normal size and flavour, though somewhat mis-shapen.

The most common type of frost is that which occurs on clear calm nights, when much heat is lost by radiation. "Temperature inversion" occurs, there being a layer of warmer air above the layer of cold air near the ground. The period of lowest temperature is ordinarily very short, just before dawn. On the other hand, in most subtropical regions there are occasional invasions of large masses of cold air, commonly referred to as freezes. In this case the cold is likely to last longer, and to be accompanied by wind. While freezes are not as common as the other type of frost, they are likely to be more severe.

Cold waves in northern India are associated with the western depressions which enter the country at intervals of about a week, as has been pointed out by Ramdas (1940). These depressions cross the plains toward the north-east frontier, and are at first warm and moist, then cool and dry, with wind from the north and north-west. If an anticyclone over Tibet and Mongolia drifts toward Europe as one of these depressions is starting, the cold in northern India is likely to be severe.

The severity of the damage caused by frost depends not only on actual temperature, and the duration of the frost, but also on the condition of the plants. Young plants are more susceptible to damage than old ones, and new growth is more likely to be injured than that which has had time to mature. In the freeze in California referred to above, the damage was the more severe because it came early in the winter, following unusually warm weather which had prevented the trees from hardening. On the other hand, damage done by the freeze in Florida in 1940 was less than the temperatures caused growers to expect, because of the very cool, but not freezing, weather which preceded it. The nutrition of the tree seems to be another important factor. In the Florida freeze, many orchards which had been suffering from deficiencies in certain elements in the soil, and had been given these elements, stood the frost better than those which had not been treated. Trees bearing heavy crops, particularly of the varieties having seed, suffered more than those with light crops, probably because the crop had reduced the mineral content of the leaves and twigs. It has also been recorded (Anonymous) that in a severe frost in the Punjab in 1929, weak and diseased trees suffered more than those in good health.

Hodgson and others (1950) report similar findings with regard to a number of subtropical and tropical fruit plants. Citrus trees on rough lemon rootstock suffered more than the same varieties on other rootstocks, and trees on their own roots suffered more than budded ones, even when the rootstock was rough lemon. Lack of vigour, often caused by lack of compatibility with the rootstock, always increased the damage. In the case of frosts caused by radiation, taller trees or anything which interfered with radiation helped much, and when damage was confined to a layer near the ground, close planting proved a protection.

Protection of orchards from frosts on still nights is often practicable, although the most effective methods may seldom be economical in this country. In other countries orchard heating by means of many small fires is sometimes used in deciduous orchards, and more often in subtropical orchards where the nearly mature crop, on which considerable money and effort has been spent, may be in danger. Probably the most efficient heaters are those which burn oil, but coal, wood, and even old automobile tyres are also used as fuel. There is a considerable expense involved in making preparations for heating, even if the fires are not lit. Heating of vineyards at Nasik by means of 400 cowdung and litter fires per acre is reported by Banerji and Ramdas (1946) to have raised the temperature as much as 10 degrees F. if the area was well enclosed by wind-breaks.

Another method involving a large capital expenditure is the use of 'wind machines', large fans on towers, which raise the temperature of the air around the trees, by mixing the warmer air higher up with the cold air near the ground.

Brooks and others (1950) state that the combination of wind machines and orchard heaters gave a gain in temperatures 20 to 30 % greater than the sum of the separate responses, and attributed this to the horizontal dispersal of the heater stack convection heat. Brooks and others (1951) state that while it is often necessary to fire from 25 to 50 heaters per acre when used alone, in combination with wind machine 8 to 15 are usually sufficient. They say that this is now the accepted system for economical frost protection in California. Actual expenditure for frost protection in Los Angeles country is given as 83.60 per acre per hour with heaters, $0.55 with wind machines, and $0.67 (about Rs. 3) with a combination of heaters and wind machines.

The use of infra-red radiation has also been tried, and, according to Farrall and others (1946), is a promising method of protecting low crops such as straw-berries and vegetables, having the advantage of being almost as effective on a windy night as on a still one. This method is not applicable to orchards, as the air is not heated, but only those portions of the plant struck by the radiations. An oil-heated apparatus proved much more economical than an electrical one.

The value of irrigating an orchard as a means of avoiding frost is questionable. In the Punjab publication referred to above, it is stated that by heavy irrigation it has been possible to raise the temperature two to five degrees above that of an adjacent unirrigated plot. It is not said at what height the temperature was measured. Ordinarily such differences could be secured only within a few feet of the ground. It is said that in the frost of 1929, in the freshly irrigated orchards there was less damage than in unirrigated ones, but this may have been because of the better condition of the trees. On the other hand, Hodgson found instances where the recently irrigated citrus trees suffered more severely. Ramdas suggests that irrigation is helpful in the case of a crop like wheat, if the frost is of short duration, but points out that in case of a frost lasting several days, this causes the loss of heat from the sun during the day.

Moist, fairly compact soil without a cover crop, it has been pointed out (A. E. S. 1949), absorbs heat during the day and gives it off at night. Because of evaporation, a wet soil has little heat to give off during the first week after a rain or irrigation. On the other hand, well-stirred soil does not absorb much heat because of the insulation of the air spaces.

As young plants are much more subject to damage than old ones, it is fortunate that it is much easier to protect them. Nursery stock is often grown under large trees, or is covered over during the period of danger. Young mango trees, and other tender trees in the cooler parts of northern India are often protected by covering them with stalks of fodder, or with gunny sacking.

Heat and Wind

The same trees which are injured by cold in the winter may be injured by heat in the summer. Branches, leaves, and fruits exposed to the sun become much hotter than the atmosphere. Heat is generally more harmful when accompanied by low humidity and by strong wind. This condition leads to very rapid transpiration and may desiccate the leaves and twigs. During the hot weather in northern India, conditions are often such as to cause the maximum transpiration. The ability of plants to withstand such conditions varies greatly with the species. Again, young trees are less hardy than old ones. This is a limiting factor in the case of certain fruits.

Young trees can be fairly easily protected by erecting light thatches over them, or by erecting temporary mud walls around them, or both. The same means used to protect young trees from the frost may be kept through the following hot weather. The provision of adequate irrigation is essential, but desiccation may take place in spite of plentiful soil moisture, and the plant may be unable to carry the water to the leaves as rapidly as it is transpired. Certain tropical crops are interplanted with tall trees which provide partial shade, but this is probably more important in reducing the intensity of the light than in reducing the temperature. Windbreaks are often important in avoiding damage done by hot winds.

Sunburn of the leaves, fruits, and bark is sometimes a serious factor. Permanent or temporary shade trees afford some protection against damage of this sort. The stems of young trees are often exposed, and branches may be in the case of extremely severe pruning, as is done in top-working. The bark may be shaded by wrapping paper around the limb. Or whitewash may be applied, which causes much of the light to be reflected and thus prevents the bark from becoming as hot as it otherwise would.

Lack of sufficient cold weather in the winter sometimes causes delayed foliation (prolonged rest, prolonged dormancy) in certain deciduous fruits grown in subtropical regions. These trees seem to require a certain amount of cool weather to break their rest period. Lacking this, there may be an excessive shedding of flower buds, delayed and protracted blossoming and foliation, poor setting (perhaps because it occurs when the weather has become too warm), and poor quality of fruit, especially its keeping quality. The deficiency in leaf surface and unbalanced growth which result may reduce the production of new wood and thus the capacity of the tree to bear in the following year also. The ultimate solution of the problem, as has been pointed out by Hill and Campbell (1949) and Black (1953) in reviews of the subject, is likely to be through the breeding of varieties with little need for winter cold. Considerable progress has been made in such breeding. Meanwhile, chemical treatments to break the rest period may be used. Reinecke (1936) found raw linseed oil and certain mineral oils effective. Rao and others (1952) found spraying with 3% raw linseed oil 6—13 weeks before the normal time of flowering hastened flowering, increased vegetative growth to a less extent, and increased the yield of apple trees in the Nilgiris. As the trees were sprayed only once each year and at different times on different years, their evidence on the best time of spraying is inconclusive. The same emulsion used on the Winterstein apple at Coonoor was reported to have had no effect. Various 'dinitro' compounds, such as dinitrophenol and dinitrocresol, added to a mineral oil have been found very effective by Chandler and others (1937), Weinberger (1940), Van Horn (1941), Samisch (1945) who found that early spraying had a forcing effect and later spraying increased the crop in the current and ensuing years, and Jeffery (1949). Guthrie (1941) tried 40 substances, and was successful in breaking the rest period of peach buds with three of them applied as sprays : $CH_3C_6H_4SH$, $C_6H_5CIC_6H_3OH$, and $CIOH_7NO_2$. Another type of treatment is reported by Kriel (1943) who injected a 2½% solution of sodium thiosulphate in an acid medium into the branches of various deciduous trees, causing flower and leaf buds to emerge about 4 to 6 weeks after the injection. Black (1953) states that dinitro-ortho-cresol sprays in petroleum oil have given good results with apples, pears, and plums, but less good with peaches and apricots. He points out the importance of timing and of the strength of the emulsion, as the optimum rate is near that which is lethal. With the Winterstein apple at Coonoor, the use of dinitro-ortho-cresol, 0.25% (Sandolin A) broke the rest period and resulted in a yield 120% more than that of untreated trees.

Strong winds not only increase the damage done by high or low temperatures, but are likely to cause damage of themselves, particularly to bearing trees. The branches are broken, the fruit is blown off or scarred, particularly if the tree is thorny, and even the leaves may be whipped off. Windbreaks are very useful in lessening the force of the wind and minimizing the damage. These are rows of tall trees planted close together. Height is more important than thickness, but a tree with a dense head is more effective than one of the same height with few branches. A windbreak ordinarily has its maximum effectiveness for a distance about four times as great as its height, but has some effect over about twice that distance. Where as complete protection as possible is desired, windbreaks should be planted at intervals in the orchard, as well as along the windward side. In many cases, however, the orchard trees themselves offer considerable resistance to the wind, and only one windbreak is necessary.

The most effective windbreak is a double row of tall trees, alternately placed. Allen (1934) recommends a third row of low trees, but this means the use of extra soil with little additional protection. He suggests the use of eucalyptus, *shesham*, carambola (*kamrakh*), jambolan (*jaman*), and paper mulberry. On the basis of experience at Attari in the Punjab in which trees of various kinds were planted as windbreaks in 1938, Bajwa and Kaura (1951) recommend *Terminalia arjuna*. They considered the *semal*, *Bombax malabaricum* second best, and *Eucalyptus rudis* and the *jaman* also very good. As low trees to alternate with the tall ones, they recommend the camphor and jujube. The *nim* and bamboo are also sometimes used. Several of these are spreading trees, and therefore require a good deal of room.

In northern India protection is needed primarily from the *loo*, and so the windbreak should be on the western border of the garden. It should ordinarily be planted at the same time as the orchard, or sooner, and it should be given favourable conditions for rapid growth. This may include both manuring and irrigation. There should be at least as much space between the windbreak and the first row of trees as between the fruit trees. In order to prevent competition between the windbreak and the orchard, a trench may be dug about three feet deep, not more than ten feet from the windbreak, and all roots cut. This trench may be filled in and the process repeated after about three years.

The danger of damage from windbreaks unless they are very carefully handled is illustrated by Lombard (1950 a). Production records were kept for five years in a 25-year-old lemon orchard in California, protected by a windbreak of eucalyptus which had been allowed to grow uncontrolled, without root pruning. Roots of the eucalyptus were found as far as the sixth row, approximately 160 feet from the windbreak. None of the first six rows produced as much as the poorest of the next six, and the average production per acre for the first six rows was 28,535 pounds, compared with 38,257 pounds for rows 7 to 12. There is some difference in the ability of fruit trees to stand the competition of windbreaks, and it is said that the mango and loquat are among those which are not much affected, whereas the avocado is very sensitive.

Hail occasionally causes damage in many fruit-growing regions, and India is no exception. Hail is one of the greatest hazards in the apple-growing regions in the Himalayas, and fruits on the plains also suffer. The papaya is particularly liable to damage, as the fruits are ripening at a season when hail is not uncommon, and the thin skins of the fruits are easily injured. The large leaves are also likely to be torn. Severe storms in early spring may knock off many of the leaves and fruits of the mango, and pit the fruits which are left. There is no way of protecting the trees from hail. The grower may protect himself by insuring his orchard against hail damage, but this is seldom done. For most fruit growers, as well as other farmers, this is just one of the many factors which make their occupation so much of a gamble.

CHAPTER VII

PRUNING

Pruning is one of the most ancient of horticultural practices, and it has had an honourable but varied history. Old Testament writers, probably in the eighth century B.C., speak of a coming age of peace, when men shall beat their swords into ploughshares, and their spears into pruning-hooks. Christ referred to the pruning of the vine, and it is interesting to note that of all the fruits, few respond favourably to as heavy pruning as does the vine. The pruning of the vine is also referred to in an old Greek legend, according to which Silenus learned the value of pruning when he observed that the vines bore more fruit which had been browsed by his faithful ass. Many later teachers of pruning have been less wise in their practice than this first instructor.

By pruning is meant the removal of any part of the plant, in order that the remaining parts may more nearly conform to the pruner's desire. The object in view may be beauty, strength, health, or the quantity or quality of the fruit borne. The parts most commonly removed are branches and leaves. The removal of young fruits is known as thinning, and will be considered in the next chapter. Root pruning is also very different in method and effect from ordinary pruning, and will be considered later in connection with problems of fruitfulness.

In pruning fruit trees artistic considerations must take a secondary place. The object of the grower is to produce large amounts of marketable fruit, and to do so without excessive expenditure. Pruning must therefore help to produce as soon as possible a tree capable of bearing large crops of fruit of a desirable size and good quality, and at the same time a tree which can be economically cared for. In all pruning operations, the objective must be kept in view. And while the immediate effects of pruning must not be ignored, the pruner must be able to see how his action will affect the tree in future years.

It is equally important that the pruner should understand how the tree will react to his work. 'It is better to understand principles and to be ignorant of rules of practice, than to be familiar with the latter and unacquainted with the former.' This statement of John Lindley, made with reference to one form of pruning in the middle of the last century, is true of all forms, and is as true today as when he made it. Yet it must be admitted that after all these years, there is much with regard to the principles of pruning which is still very imperfectly understood. Some basic facts, however, are quite clear and should be thoroughly understood by all who would prune intelligently.

A live tree is a growing tree. In the case of deciduous trees, the life of a leaf is less than one year, and in the case of most evergreen trees it is but little longer. Leaves are formed only on new growth, so it is obvious that if a tree ceased to form new branches for a few years it would be bare and leafless, and therefore unable to maintain life. Moisture and mineral nutrients are absorbed largely through the root hairs which are found just back of the growing tips of the roots. Only as the roots continue to grow can they perform their function of absorption. The absorbed material is conveyed to the leaves, where by the process of photosynthesis it is combined with carbon taken in from the air, to form the materials from which the growing parts are made. The branches and leaves depend on the roots for water and minerals, and the roots depend on the leaves for elaborated food. It is thus obvious that anything which affects one part of the tree affects all the parts.

In a normal tree there is a balance between the top and the root. When any part is removed, that balance is disturbed. If part of the root is removed, the supply of water is decreased and growth is slowed down until new roots grow to replace the part lost. On the other hand, if part of the top is removed, root growth seems to be inhibited until new branches take the place of those removed. The invigorating effect of pruning has often been noticed, and is mostly limited to the region of the cut. This vigorous growth, however, does not ordinarily make up for the loss sustained in the pruning. By reducing the amount of leaf surface, it decreases the amount of food which is elaborated with the result that the growth of the whole tree is somewhat checked. Pruning is therefore seen to be a dwarfing process, whether the part removed is above or below ground.

This dwarfing effect is noted not only on the tree as a whole, but particularly on the part pruned. If two branches are of equal size, and one is pruned more heavily than the other, the lightly pruned branch will become the larger, both in length and in diameter.

When a tree bears a heavy crop of fruit, this uses up large amounts of food material, and may so exhaust the reserves as to interfere with growth. If by pruning, a considerable part of the bearing area is removed, the crop of fruit is reduced and the dwarfing effect of the heavy crop may be avoided. In such cases the net effect of pruning may be to dwarf the tree little if at all.

Pruning may affect fruitfulness in another way. For either growth or fruit production, an adequate supply of both carbohydrates and nitrogen is necessary. If the proportion of nitrogen is relatively high, vegetative growth tends to follow; if carbohydrate is relatively high, fruitfulness may be expected. Pruning, by removing leaves in which carbohydrate is photosynthesized, decreases the relative amount of carbohydrate, and thus tends toward a vegetative condition. If the pruning is severe it may, for the time being, prevent the formation of flower buds. If, for any reason, a bearing tree is very severely pruned, it is likely to bear no fruit for several years. Such severe pruning is not, however, commonly practised on mature trees. It is probable, however, that some growers delay the bearing of young trees by unnecessarily severe pruning.

It would seem, then, that pruning is a dangerous, if not a harmful, practice. On the other hand, a certain amount of pruning is necessary in order to form a strong tree, capable of bearing heavy crops, and to keep the tree in a shape which prevents orchard operations from becoming too difficult. In some cases, if the tree is not pruned, it prunes itself by shading certain branches to the extent that they die. Judicious pruning may increase the size of the fruit, and in the case of highly coloured fruits, improve the colour by allowing more sunlight to reach the fruit. Pruning should be looked upon as a necessary evil, and should be kept to the minimum which experience has shown will produce the desired results.

Pruning may be divided into two parts, the training of young trees and the maintenance of mature trees. The objects sought at the two stages are different, and the methods used naturally vary.

Training the Young Tree

The training of the young tree may frequently be begun in the nursery, though some sorts are ordinarily not pruned until the time of transplanting. This will depend on the nature of the tree, and on the age at which it is planted in its permanent position. It is probably desirable in most cases to train the tree to a single stem, at least for a short distance above the ground. Some fruits tend to send up a number of stems, all but one of which should be removed as soon as they appear.

The distance from the ground at which the lowest branch should be allowed is a point on which there has been and is much difference of opinion. The present tendency is toward the 'lowheaded' tree, with the first branch about a foot and a half from the ground. It is still quite common, however, for the first branch to be three or four feet from the ground. Rarely trees are pruned so high that animals may be driven under the branches. Forming such high heads involves cutting off many branches, and thus has a distinctly dwarfing effect. High-headed trees also make such operations as pruning and harvesting more difficult.

Some young trees tend to grow quite tall before beginning to branch, in which case it is necessary to 'head them back' in order to force branching. When the top of the shoot is removed, several buds just below the cut are likely to begin to grow, the topmost of which generally straightens up and takes the place of the part removed. On the other hand, some trees naturally begin to branch very low, and it is only necessary to select the branches it is desired to keep.

The formation of the main framework of the tree is the most important part of training. This can well consist of from three to five branches. These should extend in different directions, so as to form a well-balanced tree. It is extremely important that the framework be strong, so that when heavily loaded with fruit the tree may not break to pieces. Especially in some species, there is a tendency for branches to split away from the trunk, or from larger branches. This causes wounds which are difficult to heal, as well as leaving large open spaces in the trees. This can be largely avoided by careful training of the main branches. Splitting is especially likely where several branches arise at or near one place. By spacing the branches six inches or more apart, vertically, the framework is greatly strengthened. Another danger-point is a crotch formed by two branches of equal size. If one branch is distinctly larger than the other, it tends to grow out around the smaller branch, holding it firmly in place. The wider the angle of the crotch, the stronger it will be, and extremely narrow angles are therefore to be avoided.

In many unpruned trees, the largest branch grows upward, smaller ones growing out from it in various directions. Such a tree is physically strong, but as an orchard tree it has disadvantages. It is likely to become so tall as to make pruning, spraying, and particularly harvesting, very difficult and expensive. The lower branches are sometimes so shaded that they die. In certain fruits, such as some apples, bright coloured fruit is desired, and this develops only when sunshine can reach it. Much of the fruit on such trees is borne in the shade, and fails to develop a good colour. This type of tree, known as the central leader type, was formerly common in orchards, but on account of its disadvantages, it has been largely given up.

For a time, orchardists went to the opposite extreme, and developed a type of tree known as the open centre or vase shaped. As the name indicates, no branch was allowed to grow vertically above the point where the tree was headed. A number of branches arose from this point, and were trained to form a large bowl or vase. This type of tree allows a maximum of sunshine to reach each branch, but it can be maintained only by rather heavy pruning, and it has the fatal disadvantage of structural weakness.

The present tendency is toward a type of tree which is a compromise between the above types, and which is called the modified central leader, or modified open centre. In this the framework branches are well spaced, and the uppermost one, while being allowed to grow more or less vertically, is not allowed to become much larger than the others. This produces a strong, moderately spreading tree, which still allows plenty of light to reach all parts. A large amount of pruning is not necessary to train a tree into this shape.

If a tree branches freely naturally, or upon being headed back, the framework branches may be selected, and all others removed. If, on heading back only the top few buds grow, it may be necessary to let one of these grow vertically, and after some months head it back so that more buds will grow. If necessary this process can be repeated again. In heading species which react in this way, the first cut should be lower than with those in which a large number of buds grow.

After the framework branches are started, comparatively little pruning is needed. If two branches forming a crotch tend to be equal, one may be removed entirely, or may be pruned back. This will allow the unpruned branch to grow more rapidly and become permanently the larger. In vigorously growing young trees, branches may grow long and thin. If left alone such branches later bend or break. They should therefore be headed back and forced to branch. If this is done by nipping off the end of the growing branch, very little wood is sacrificed. The main limbs may be allowed to branch naturally, except that equal crotches are to be avoided, and branches which would cross others should not be allowed to grow.

It has generally been considered best to form the framework as early as possible, but experiments indicate that in some cases at least this may well be left until later. Bioletti (1922) found that young olive trees left unpruned until they came into commercial bearing at five or six years of age not only grew more rapidly and bore fruit earlier, but also had a more desirable form, as compared with trees pruned according to common practice. Much more experimental work on Indian fruits is necessary before definite recommendations can be made with any assurance.

The amount of pruning which is desirable for mature trees differs in different species. The minimum which is common to all is the removal of broken or badly diseased branches, and of those which rub against others in such a way as to wear the bark of both. The jagged ends of broken branches cannot heal over, and sooner or later decay, allowing the decay organisms to enter the unbroken branches also. A diseased branch left in the tree may be a perennial source of infection and should be removed. But in some cases so many branches are diseased that to remove them all would ruin the tree. In addition, it is often desirable to thin out the branches in order to allow more light to enter the heart of the tree. If the secondary branches are numerous, they may grow long and straight, with no twigs until near the end, in which case fruit bearing is limited to the extremities. In order to let light into the tree, it is better to remove a few of the larger branches entirely, so that those which are left may be allowed to branch naturally. If trees are kept fairly open, in many kinds fruit will set in the centre of the tree as well as on the outside, and this inner fruit is protected from sunburn and the attack of birds.

Some species seem to require a larger amount of pruning, or at least to bear well in spite of heavy pruning. This is particularly true in the case of fruits which bear near the ends of branches of the current season's growth. Unless pruned rather severely, such trees tend to bear at the end of long branches which are therefore likely to bend or break. Where trees can be pruned heavily without reducing the amount of fruit, it is sometimes an advantage to prune off the higher branches, so as to keep the tree low and easily handled.

In other cases, annual pruning may well be very light, but after some years it may become necessary to prune heavily. Otherwise the trees may lack vegetative vigour, and make very little growth. The size of the fruit is likely to become small, and eventually the tree may practically cease bearing. In such cases, heavy 'renewal pruning' is desirable. Often only the main framework branches are left, all others being removed, but generally somewhat less drastic action is sufficient. For a year or two after severe pruning there is vigorous vegetative growth, and then another period of satisfactory bearing may be expected.

Pruning Tools

Many tools have been devised for pruning but the ordinary grower can get along well with a very few. Pruning tools may be divided into knives, shears and saws. The standard pruning knife is of fairly heavy construction, with a curved blade. It should be made of high-grade steel, and for convenience should have a folding blade. The pruning hook, used mainly for bramble fruits, is a modification of the pruning knife, having a long handle.

The hand shear or secateur may be had in a variety of forms. Simple construction, a good spring not likely to fall out and be lost, and good material, are the most important points on which to base selection. The lopping shear, or lopper, has handles about two feet long, of wood, with a heavy blade which in the better patterns is shaped much like that of the hand shear. It is designed for pruning larger branches than the hand shear. The blades should be fastened together with a bolt and locknut, to allow adjustment, rather than with a rivet. Unless the steel is very good, such shears 'spring' so that the blades do not come together closely, and the shanks bend so that the handles come too nearly together, causing the operator to knock his knuckles together. Pole shears, with a sharp blade fitting into a curved guard, are opened and closed by means of a heavy wire or cord leading from the blade to a lever on the handle, the length of which varies.

Many types of saws are on the market, several of which are highly desirable. One useful type, especially for large branches, closely resembles the carpenter's saw. For lighter work, a narrower saw is satisfactory. Those with curved blades are especially convenient. A tapered saw with an adjustable and replaceable blade, makes it possible to cut in a plane different from the one in which the saw is held, and is particularly desirable for work in narrow crotches. The teeth of pruning saws are set to cut as the saw is drawn toward the operator. Double-edged saws are sold to those who are so foolish as to buy implements which are likely to injure both the tree and the pruner. Less dangerous, but equally useless is the pole saw, for it is impossible to make a good cut with such an instrument.

A number of combination instruments are offered by manufacturers, such as combined saws and shears. These and other fancy instruments are designed for sale rather than for use. They have no place in the orchard.

The ordinary fruit grower will not wish to buy all even of the desirable types of pruning tools. While there are occasions on which the grower may well use both hand shears and pruning knife, he can get along with one or the other. An ordinary pocket-knife makes a fairly satisfactory substitute for the pruning knife. The work done by lopping shears may be done with hand shears plus a saw. In fact, some pruners prefer not to use loppers, feeling that better work can be done with a saw on branches too large to be pruned with hand shears. On the other hand, the use of loppers greatly increases the speed of pruning, and if they are kept sharp and used carefully, satisfactory work is done. They are especially convenient in pruning thorny trees. The temptation to use them for larger branches than they are intended for should be shunned. Most loppers are intended for branches of not more than one inch diameter. At least one saw is necessary in any set of pruning tools. If the pruning programme calls for the heading back of small branches which cannot be reached from the ground with hand shears, pole shears are desirable, as they save much time. Otherwise the use of a ladder is necessary.

Several general rules should be observed in pruning. If a branch is cut back, but not entirely removed, several buds near the end of the part remaining are likely to grow, whereas if the branch is removed entirely at the point where it leaves another branch, the stimulus to growth is transferred to the other branch, at least very largely. If it is desired to open up a tree, therefore, branches should be thinned out rather than headed back. Short stubs should never be left, as these do not heal, and eventually they decay, and allow decay to enter the rest of the tree. Healing is most rapid if the cut is parallel to the branch which remains, but the smallest cut is that at right-angles to the direction of the branch removed. The best results are generally secured by a compromise, in which the cut starts next to the remaining branch and finishes a little further from it. All cuts should be straight and smooth, in order to encourage rapid healing.

The removal of large branches is sometimes difficult. If one begins sawing from the bottom, the saw soon binds; but if the cut is made from above, the branch will nearly always break before the cut is finished, often tearing the bark off for some distance below the cut. To avoid this, the cut should be started on the under side, and finished from the top. In the case of heavy limbs, it may be necessary to make a preliminary cut, a foot or two from the final cut, and on the under side. Next the limb is cut from above, a few inches beyond, until it breaks. This leaves a stub which is then cut off in the ordinary manner.

In using hand shears, and particularly with loppers, the shears should be so held that the heavy blade is away from the part of the branch which is to remain. The heavy blade bruises the bark against which it presses, and it also prevents the cut from being close to the limb which is being left.

A pruning wound is a possible opening for disease organisms and the fungi which cause decay. The tree protects itself by growing bark over the wound, but this is a process which takes time, and horticulturists have long tried to protect the tree from infection until healing is completed. These efforts have met with only partial success. Most coverings which have been used give only partial, or temporary protection. Most paints soon crack and allow the entrance of organisms which find favourable conditions for growth at the bottom of the cracks.

Ordinarily there is little danger from pathogenic organisms entering pruning wounds, but where certain diseases are present, it is advisable to disinfect the wound. Bordeaux paste is commonly used for this purpose. It needs to be renewed frequently or followed by some more permanent covering. When, as is more common, only saprophytic organisms are present, there is no danger for a year or more. During this time small wounds will ordinarily heal. The common practice of neglecting such wounds is thus justified. It is, however, probably a good practice to paint wounds more than two inches in diameter. This painting can safely be delayed a year after pruning, and is probably more effective after the wound has dried out. Most substances used delay the process of healing if applied before the bark has started to cover the wound. In the case of large wounds, it may be necessary to repaint after a few years. Grafting wax is a fairly satisfactory covering, and certain commercial preparations are even better. Of the various paints, white lead is perhaps the best.

Chapter VIII

PROBLEMS OF FRUITFULNESS

Among the most perplexing problems confronting the fruit grower are those dealing with fruitfulness. Why does one tree fail to bear, while another tree of the same kind, under similar conditions and with similar treatment, produces a heavy crop ? What are the fundamental conditions within the plant which make it bloom and bear fruit ? Much study has been devoted to these questions, but no clear and definite answer can yet be given.

In many plants, vigorous vegetative growth and fruitfulness seem to be antogonistic. It is a common observation that young plants grow much more rapidly before they begin to bear fruit than they do afterward. On the other hand, an extreme lack of vigour is also accompanied by a failure to produce fruit, though a sudden severe check to a tree which has been vigorous may cause it to bear a very heavy crop It is sometimes seen that a plant bears an unusually large number of fruits just before it dies.

Chemical studies of plant tissue, as well as fertilizer experiments, have shown the close relationship of abundant nitrogen with vegetative growth. In the same way, the presence of large amounts of carbohydrate in the tissues of the plant accompanies fruitfulness. In a well-known experiment with the tomato, Kraus and Kraybill (1918) found that plants deficient in either nitrogen or carbohydrate were weak in growth and unfruitful, those with an abundance of both were vigorous but unfruitful, while those with an abundance of carbohydrate and a smaller amount of nitrogen were fruitful, but less vegetative. Other work has established the importance of the amounts of carbohydrate and nitrogen present to the bearing of fruit trees. Some writers have reduced this to a question of the carbohydrate-nitrogen ratio, but the total amounts are also important. It would seem that for fruit bud formation it is necessary to have present in the tissues of the plant a fair amount of nitrogen, and a relatively larger amount of carbohydrate. It is possible that the actual factors causing fruit bud formation may be some particular carbohydrate or nitrogen compounds, or other substances, but the total carbohydrate and nitrogen seem to be a fair measure of the factors, whatever they may be. It should be remembered, however, that carbohydrate is manufactured in the leaves, and a plentiful supply depends on ample healthy leaves, which, in turn, depend on a sufficient supply of nitrogen. It is probable that failure to bear well because of too much nitrogen is very rare in India.

If a tree fails to bear a satisfactory crop, this may be due to lack of flowers, or it may be caused by the failure of the flowers to develop into fruits. The physiological condition of the tree may affect both. It is thus clear that fruit production may be controlled at the time fruit buds are differentiated from vegetative buds, as well as when the flowers and young fruits are on the tree. It is, then, of interest to know when fruit-bud differentiation takes place, but unfortunately this knowledge has not been secured for all fruits. In the apple, and many other temperate fruits, it is known to occur early in the summer previous to the opening of the buds. Ullah (1954) reports that in the C. O. Smith peach at Palampur, differentiation took place in the first three weeks of July, while in a double-flowering peach at Lyallpur it occurred throughout August and September. He attributes the difference to the climate, but it is also possible that there is a difference between the two varieties. If conditions are unfavourable at the time of differentiation, no amount of effort in the autumn or early spring will secure a good crop. On the other hand, in some tropical and sub-tropical fruits, flowering may be affected by treatment immediately preceding it, as bud differentiation does not cease, at least, until just before the buds open.

In the case of the Langra mango in Bihar, Sen and Mallik (1941) found that differentiation began late in September or October, when there is a sharp reduction in the temperature, and continued until the middle of November. Chemical conditions favouring flower bud differentiation must be present somewhat earlier, for it is frequently noticed that the first growth made by mangoes grafted in the monsoon season is an inflorescence. Sen (1942 c) reports that in a year of very heavy flowering, out of 1,102 grafts on two year-old rootstock, 20 produced panicles from the stock as well as from the scion, and four set fruit. Panicles arising from the scion have also been observed at Allahabad. As seedling plants never flower at such a young age the stimulus must come from the scion. A hormone may be involved. Sen (1945) failed to induce any flowering on seedlings by ringing, or by inarching one seedling on another. Fifty seedlings were inarched in each case with ringed and unringed branches of the Fazli variety in its 'on' year, and of Langra in its 'off' year. All of the ringed Fazli scions flowered, and 32 of the rootstocks, while of the unringed scions 27 flowered, and four of the rootstocks. Of the Langra, 32 ringed scions and 10 rootstocks flowered, and 10 of the unringed scions, but no rootstock. Musahib-ud-din (1946 a) found that in the Punjab differentiation was somewhat earlier, taking place from the middle of August until the end of October for all flushes except that of July, in which case it extended into November.

On the other hand, Abbott (1935) states that in citrus trees differentiation occurs at the initiation of growth in the spring or the resumption of growth following a period favourable to the accumulation of reserve food. Randhawa and Densa (1947 b) found that at Lyallpur differentiation in the case of the sweet orange and sweet lime began with the advent of growth in the spring. In the orange but not the lime, more flower buds differentiated on the early flushes than on late ones. Ahmad and Khan (1950) found that in the sour lime also, more flower buds differentiated on the earlier flushes in the spring. Ahmad and Khan (1951) found that in the grapefruit, differentiation takes place along with growth, in the latter half of February in the Punjab. In more detail, West and Barnard (1935) state that in two varieties of the sweet orange, the terminal flower primordia differentiate when the shoot is about to emerge, while axillary flowers differentiate when the shoot is about a fourth of an inch long.

During the part of the year when the leaves are on the tree, but growth is not active, carbohydrate is either used in the formation of fruit, or is stored. When nitrogen is present in abundance, and other conditions are favourable, continued growth may take place instead of storage. This in turn may result in conditions unfavourable to flowering.

Efforts to induce fruitfulness, in addition to those which make for the general health of the tree, are mainly intended to increase the amount of carbohydrate present in the tissues, in so far as these are reasoned and not merely rule-of-thumb practices. They fall into two classes, those which tend to diminish growth, and those which interfere with the passage of organic compounds into the roots of the tree, and thus result in a concentration of them in the top.

Root pruning is the method of inducing fruitfulness, or determining the time of flowering, most commonly used in India. The practice varies in different parts of the country, and with different fruits, but the general effect is much the same. The operation is generally accompanied by the drying out of the soil. From two to four months before the trees are expected to flower, irrigation is withheld. The soil often dries out to the extent that part or all of the leaves drop. About a month before the flowering season, certain of the larger roots are exposed, and the smaller roots are removed. In some cases this is done in a circle with a radius of about two feet, around the trunk of the tree, the earth being removed to a depth of from four to six inches. Sometimes the section dug is a band around and just beyond the tips of the branches. Some writers seem to recommend the removal of several inches of soil from the trunk right out to the skirt of the tree. Another type of pruning involves the digging of a trench two and a half to three feet deep at the skirt of the tree, and cutting all roots which cross it. The most severe type of pruning advocated in the literature is that recommended by Davies (1918) for citrus fruits in Uttar Pradesh. His recommendation that one-third of the thicker descending roots be cut can scarcely be taken seriously. Aside from the severe nature of the pruning, the difficulty of accomplishing it makes it impracticable. At the other extreme, ploughing results in a certain amount of pruning of the smaller roots.

Some weeks after the exposure and pruning of the roots, fresh soil, or the old soil mixed with manure, is put around the roots, and they are irrigated, lightly at first, and after a few days, more heavily. Or where irrigation is not practised, the covering of the roots is done shortly before rain is expected at the beginning of the monsoon. The trees respond by putting out new leaves, and blossoming freely.

Theory of Root Pruning

Little attempt has been made to explain the effect of root pruning in the literature on the subject. It would seem that for the most part it is practised in India because it is the custom, and gains the desired end, without questioning whether it is the best way of gaining that end. The nearest to an explanation which is ordinarily attempted is the statement that it allows the tree to rest, and that this rest period must precede fruiting. As it is admitted by a number of writers that root pruning has a harmful effect on the tree, it would seem wise to consider the exact effect, and whether this could be accomplished in some other way. If root pruning is the best way of accomplishing the object, then it should be known what degree of pruning is sufficient. More severe treatment than is needed should certainly be avoided.

When vegetative growth is stopped by root pruning, it seems certain that the amount of carbohydrate in the tree increases, for the process of photosynthesis continues and very little material is used up in growth. The amount of nitrogen absorbed by the root is also decreased. Thus conditions are brought about which are known to accompany fruitfulness. A light irrigation then provides a sufficient stimulus to cause the tree to burst into bloom, whereas a heavy irrigation might be expected to cause such a sudden increase in nitrogen as to produce more vegetative growth than bloom. Just prior to the fall of the leaves, most of the carbohydrate in them may be transferred to the stem, thus further increasing the concentration around the buds. This theory does not explain the supposed advantage of pruning the roots after the leaves have fallen, or of causing leaf-fall much before the new growth starts. It is, of course, possible that some chemical change takes place after the falling of the leaves, which favours fruitfulness. Some would argue from the analogy that deciduous fruits blossom immediately after the dormant period, but it must be remembered that the flower buds differentiate during the previous summer, when the leaves are on the tree, though after active growth has ceased.

In some cases, at least, vegetative growth can be sufficiently checked by allowing the soil to dry out, and this is probably less harmful to the tree than root pruning. Even drying out will cause the death of many of the smaller roots, but the loss will be less than with pruning. In either case there is both the direct loss of roots, and the slowing down of growth. If practised on young trees, the decreased size of the tree may be of some importance. In most cases, however, the damage is greater. Cheema and Bhat (1928) state that roots are frequently torn, that they begin to rot, and that this, combined with the alternation of drought and waterlogged conditions of the soil, damages the health of the trees. In areas where root pruning is regularly practised, the trees are reported to be shorter-lived than elsewhere.

Root pruning is very commonly practised in Bombay and with oranges in Madhya Pradesh. It is thought to be necessary there because the difference between summer and winter climate is so slight that the trees continue vegetative growth throughout the year and have no well-marked flowering season. The purpose is as much to control the season of fruiting as to increase the amount. If a fruit naturally blossoms at one of two or three seasons, flowering may be induced at the most profitable season. In northern India the seasons are much more distinct, and most fruits bear satisfactorily without root pruning. Even in Madras, where there is very little variation in the temperature Naik (1949) advises strongly against the general practice of root pruning, which has caused much damage to orchards. Perhaps other sections of the country will also abandon the system, except in unusual cases, or where the economic advantage of determining the time of flowering justifies the practice. It should be used only when good general care has failed to give the desired results, and should be only severe enough to accomplish these results.

Ringing and Notching

If fruitfulness can be induced by increasing the concentration of carbohydrates in the top of the trees, without markedly reducing the vegetative activity, this has obvious advantages. Several practices are designed to do this by interfering with the downward flow of the sap. Ringing or girdling is regularly practised with some fruits, and occasionally with others. In its most common form it consists of removing a ring of bark about half an inch wide, or less, around the trunk of the tree or around a branch. The wound may or may not be treated to prevent infection. A milder treatment is to draw a knife around the branch in such a way as to cut through the bark, but not into the wood, either in a circle or in a spiral. Much the same effect can be gained by drawing a wire tightly around the branch, but if this is done it is important to remember to remove the wire later, lest permanent damage be done. In all of these treatments the downward flow of sap is interrupted. It is generally believed that the upward movement is largely in the xylem, which is not cut in careful girdling, and the downward movement in the phloem, which is removed. Girdling may cause the formation of gum in the xylem, and it has been observed that the amount of nitrogen passing into a branch is reduced by girdling. Furr and others (1945) found that ringing with a single knife cut reduced nitrogen absorption somewhat, but that it returned to normal in about two weeks. When ringing was done in such a way as to prevent the repair of the wound, absorption remained low for the rest of the period of observation. They suggest that the reduction in nitrogen absorption may be caused by the reduction of growth and metabolic activities in the root as a consequence of the shortage of elaborated food and growth substances, and by the accumulation of nitrogenous compounds below the ring. Girdling thus increases the amount of carbohydrate above the cut, and decreases the amount of nitrogen, causing a condition favourable to fruiting. It is likely to check the vegetative growth of the top and also the growth of the roots. Ordinarily the wound heals before much harm is done to the roots, but if the ring of bark removed is so wide that new bark does not cover the ring, the parts below are gradually starved to death.

Girdling has long been practised with grapes, and it has recently gained some favour with the citrus growers of California. In the latter case it is practised when the trees are in flower and results in a heavier setting of fruit. The increase in the first year is marked, but according to Shamel and Pomeroy (1934, 1936, 1944), if girdling is not repeated, the next year the decrease in yield is about equal to the first increase, while if it is repeated a smaller increase results. They observed no effect on the quality of the fruit except a slight decrease in size, but by the eighth year a loss in vigour was noticed. The girdling of normal, healthy trees in California is therefore not considered desirable. In the

Mediterranean area, however, it is considered by Auguste (1954) as the best method of securing a good yield from the Clementine, a vigorous variety of mandarin orange. He reports a yield of 16,633 lb. per acre from annually girdled trees, compared to 7,972 from ungirdled trees. With reference to the same variety, Praloran (1954) states that the best results are secured by ringing between full bloom and petal-fall, and again three weeks later, 5 cm. lower on the stem, while keeping the trees in vigorous vegetative condition by irrigation and fertilizing.

Notching is a similar process, but affects only one bud at a time. A notch is cut through the bark, and sometimes into the wood, either just above or just below the bud. Notching below the bud tends to cause a concentration of carbohydrate in the bud, and encourages its development as a fruit bud, while notching above the bud is thought to increase vegetative growth by interfering with the flow past the bud of water and nitrogen. Conflicting theories have been proposed explaining the practice. Gandhi (1924) reports excellent results from notching figs above the bud, and no effect from notching below the bud. In the case of the fig, the desired result is not the production of a flower bud, but of a shoot, along which a number of figs will be borne.

Alternate bearing presents another perplexing problem. It is often observed that a mango tree bears a heavy crop one year, and a very light one the next, and then again a heavy one. Sometimes there will be two or more successive years of failure, and more rarely, two years in which the crop is heavy. Often one branch of a tree will bear one year and another the next. On the other hand, the crop of an entire region tends to follow the same pattern. Records kept at the Saharanpur botanical garden from 1886 to 1912 have been reported by Hartless (1913), who considered that the mango crop had been below the average 15 years, average 3 years and above average 9 years.

A similar condition is found among some other fruits. Certain varieties of the apple are very prone to alternate bearing. The phenomenon has been studied by a number of investigators but is still imperfectly understood. It seems probable that in the year in which a heavy crop is borne, the physiological condition within the branch or the tree is not favourable to the formation of fruit buds. However, attempts to overcome the habit by rigorous thinning in the years in which a heavy crop occurs have not often been successful. It is possible that such thinning might succeed if it were commenced before the tree had ever borne a heavy crop. McCormick (1933) achieved more promising results by thinning the blossoms of two varieties of apples. In the avocado, heavy thinning has proved ineffective, but the complete removal of the young fruits results in a heavy crop the next year. The fact that a large majority of the trees in a region bear at the same time indicates that some climatic factor often determines the "off" and the "on" year. It is probable that conditions which destroy the crop of a whole region one year would start all of the trees alternating with a heavy crop the following year. Local conditions, or factors not at present understood, might change this alternation for some trees or branches, or conditions which affect the fruiting of young trees might not be potent enough to change the habits of older trees. This is fortunate, for if alternate bearing cannot be avoided, it is preferable that not all fail to bear the same year. For in 'off' years the grower has no fruit to sell, and in 'on' years the price may be so low as to bring very little profit.

In addition to thinning, other methods have been used in an attempt to control alternate bearing. In most cases, fairly regular bearing can be obtained by the right combination of variety, rootstock, irrigation, manuring, and pruning. In some cases a combination of the application of nitrogenous fertilizer and a moderate pruning in the 'off' year so increases the vegetative growth that excessive fruit bud formation is prevented. Pruning away part of the bearing branches in the winter before the 'on' year also prevents heavy bearing, and thus favours the formation of fruit buds for the next year. Most of the experiments have been with apples and pears. L. B. Singh (1948) has presented an extensive review of this work. The methods used have not been entirely successful, and there is not sufficient evidence to justify any definite statement as to the control of alternate bearing in most tropical and subtropical fruits. Neither is there much evidence on record as to the relative extent to which different varieties are subject to the habit. Considerable work on the problem of irregular bearing in the mango is discussed in Chapter XIII.

Thinning

Aside from any effect it may have on alternate bearing, the thinning of fruits is sometimes desirable. Some varieties frequently set more fruits than they can mature properly. Especially on young trees is a heavy crop objectionable, as it bends the limbs and damages the shape of the tree, as well as interfering with growth. There is also the danger of broken branches. Thinning also tends to increase the size of the fruit, but it almost invariably reduces the yield per acre. Whether it is justified for the purpose of increasing size is a question of economics. In some markets, very small fruit sells at a distinct discount, while in others the rate per pound for the different sizes varies only slightly. The cost of thinning is only partially off-set by the saving at harvest time.

Much thinning takes place naturally. The number of flowers borne is normally many times the number of fruits which the tree could bring to maturity. Many of the flowers and young fruits fall because of the formation of an abscission layer, which seems to be stimulated by ethylene, according to Murneek (1954). This continues for two or three weeks, and is then stopped by an auxin (plant hormone) formed in the endosperm. This is not naphthalene acetic acid (NAA) according to Luckwill (1953) but, in the case of the apple, is the ethyl ester of indoleacetic acid, according to Murneek (1954). Later the rapidly growing embryo causes a decrease in the amount of endosperm and consequently in the auxin, resulting in the so-called 'June drop.' Then the endosperm increases to its maximum as embryo growth near completion, and there is very little dropping of fruit until the fruit reaches maturity and the auxin again decreases, perhaps with the degeneration and drying out of the endosperm. The application of NAA will sometimes reduce the June drop, but if it is applied during the earlier drop it causes the abortion of many embryos, with a resulting drop, which is delayed because of the action of the NAA on the abscission layer.

Thinning of the flowers is more effective than thinning the fruits as it saves the material used in forming the fruit. But it is a much safer practice to thin after the natural drop is complete. Otherwise the total thinning may be more than is desired. Not infrequently more than half of the fruit is removed in thinning. The young fruits are either pulled or clipped off so as to leave those which remain well spaced on the branches. Because of the high cost of thinning by hand where wages are high, attempts have been made, particularly in the United States, to thin by means of sprays. Very satisfactory results were achieved, at least with heavy-setting varieties of apples, under some conditions, by the use of dinitro ortho cresol and related compounds, referred to as dinitro or DN sprays. One set of experiments is described by Batjer and Thompson (1948) in which they were applied at full bloom. Oil-wax emulsions have also been used effectively at this stage. There is an obvious advantage in thinning after the natural drop of the blossoms, and Flory and Moore (1947) and Kenworthy (1947) report promising results from a very complicated mixture. Luckwill (1953), however, states that the ideal post-blossom thinning agent is yet to be discovered. NAA is effective in thinning the crop when applied 2—4 weeks after petal-fall, but it tends to retard fruit growth and so may fail to accomplish the purpose of thinning. It may also retard the growth of spur foliage, and so does not help to avoid alternate bearing. Hemphill (1954), however, reports good thinning without damage to the foliage from spraying 25-60 ppm of naphthylacetamide at the petal-fall stage. Longley (1954) says that the biennial bearing habit was broken in the McIntosh apple by spraying with 25 ppm NAA three weeks after full bloom. In the Fameuse variety the regularity of bearing was improved, and in both the total yield in the year of treatment and the following year was greater than in unsprayed plots. Edgerton and Hoffman (1955) suggest that N-l-naphthylphthalamic acid (NPA) may prove better than the DN sprays for thinning peaches and, perhaps, other fruits, since its action does not depend on the stage of bloom when it is applied.

Pollination Problems

It is sometimes seen that trees produce abundant bloom, but fail to set fruit. In cold regions this may be due to frost, or the very abundance of bloom may so exhaust the plant that the tiny fruits fall, but it is more commonly due to lack of pollination. Pollination is necessary for the production of seeds, and in most cases for the maturing of fruits. An apparent exception to this statement is the mangosteen, in which pistillate trees without pollination produce fruits with viable "seeds." In this case no true seed is formed, but a primitive adventitious embryo develops from a cell in the epithelium of the inner integument of the ovary. Much more common is the production of seedless fruits, which may result from lack of pollination (vegetative parthenocarpy), lack of fecundation although pollination is necessary (stimulative parthenocarpy), or the abortion of the embryo following fecundation. In the case of stimulative parthenocarpy, it is thought that the fruit develops only with the aid of a hormone from the pollen or growing pollen tube.

Very few fruits are invariably seedless, but this is the normal condition in quite a number, including many varieties of banana and most other triploid fruits. Pollination is not required in the banana and these varieties produce little or no viable pollen. Most of the ovules are also defective, but when the flowers are pollinated with pollen from some fertile species of *Musa*, a few seeds may be formed. In some fruits a few seeds are normally formed, the number depending on the effectiveness of pollination. In other cases the fruit will be completely seedy if pollination has occurred, or completely seedless if it has not. In seedless fruit there may be visible remains of the ovules, as in bananas and citrus fruits, or empty coats which seem like seeds, as in some figs. In some cases the development of the pulp seems to depend on a hormone from the seed, so that the pulp of fruits with few or no seeds may be less than normal. This is markedly true in the case of the papaya, where some seedless fruit will set in the absence of pollination, but is frequently worthless. In the case of the kaki or Japanese persimmon, the amount of pulp is not affected, but its colour and quality may be.

More or less parthenocarpy has been observed in a number of fruits. Lewis (1946) states that parthenocarpic fruits are formed in species with many seeds, but not in those with few or only one. Their occurrence in the date, olive, and jujube, each of which has but a single seed to a fruit, would seem to indicate that this is not always the case. Gustafson (1942), in a review of the literature, mentions parthenocarpy in the following fruits : pineapple, citrus, three species of persimmon, mangosteen, banana, *Spondias mombin* (all vegetative), fig, peach, apple, grape (vegetative and stimulative), pear (mostly stimulative), Chinese jujube (stimulative), three species of *Eugenia*, mulberry, olive, and date. Embryo abortion (stenospermocarpy) is thought to occur in some grapes, the Haden mango, and perhaps in the avocado which produces seedless fruit of an unusual shape but excellent quality either in this way or through parthenocarpy. Certain varieties of guavas produce fruits with few or no seeds.

The possibility of producing seedless fruits, particularly such fruits as the guava and watermelon, where the seeds are a nuisance to the consumer, has aroused considerable interest. This may be done in some cases by preventing pollination and treating the stigma with crushed pollen, pollen incapable of fecundating the plant treated, or certain plant hormones. These are probably effective because they provide the equivalent of the hormone received in the pollen when pollination occurs. The fruits formed are frequently smaller than normal, and in most cases there is little likelihood of commercial application. Venkataratnam (1949) emasculated the flowers of three varieties of mango and sprayed them with 10 ppm (parts per million) of beta naphoxyacetic acid, and secured a set somewhat better than that of these varieties with open pollination. The fruits looked normal, but no embryo development occurred, and they dropped off after reaching the size of a marble, perhaps due to external causes. Raman (1949) has reviewed the literature on induced parthenocarpy. Hormone sprays may also be used to increase the set of fruit in some cases in which pollination is inadequate, as has been done with greenhouse tomatoes. The Bartlett pear is largely self-sterile and DeTar and others (1950) report that when grown in solid blocks in one section of California, more than 90% of the fruits are seedless. They found that branches which were sprayed with 2, 4, 5-trichlorophenoxypropionic acid (2, 4, 5-TP), set more fruit and showed no injury, but in the next year, when entire trees were sprayed, varying amounts of injury to leaves and fruits were noted (Griggs and others, 1951). In that year an increased yield was obtained even where cross-pollination occurred. They recognized that the heavy crop so induced might result in a light bloom in the following year. Batjer and Uota (1951) found no increase from spraying with the same hormone where there was cross-pollination, and in the case of the Anjou pear and two varieties of apples, spraying drastically reduced the set. The use of hormones to replace pollination in the fig is discussed in Chapter XXI.

Several conditions may lead to a failure of pollination. Certain fruits, like some papayas and the date, are dioecious, staminate flowers being borne on one tree and pistillate on another. In such cases it is necessary to have some staminate or male trees present to provide pollen, though they bear no fruit. Some trees produce no viable pollen, and some produce pollen which will not fertilize pistils of the same variety. In such cases cross-pollination is essential. Even this is not always effective, for some varieties are intersterile. With cherries, for instance, it is sometimes necessary to grow some trees the fruit of which is of little value, because the commercial varieties are all intersterile.

Another condition necessitating cross-pollination is that known as dichogamy, in which the pollen is not shed at the time when the pistils are receptive. It may be shed either before or after the pistils are in a proper condition. A very interesting type of dichogamy is found in the avocado. Nirody (1923) noticed that each flower opens twice, the pistils being receptive the first time, and the pollen being shed the second. In part of the trees the first opening is in the morning, and the second in the afternoon of the next day, while the others open first in the afternoon, and the second time in the morning of the third day. The time of opening is a varietal characteristic. It is therefore necessary to have at least two varieties in a plantation. Under certain climatic conditions, however, dichogamy is not sufficiently regular to prevent self-pollination. Oppenheimer states that this is the case in Palestine, but that even so, better yields are secured with cross-pollination.

Pollen may be carried by either the wind or insects, but in the case of most fruits, insect pollination seems to be the rule. In many regions bees are the most important pollen carriers, but flies, beetles, and other insects also take part. The addition of a few hives of bees has often greatly increased the set of fruit in a deciduous orchard. The statement of Rahman and Singh (1943) that all deciduous fruits require the help of insects is not justified, for good crops of some varieties of persimmons and figs are produced without pollination. However, there is much more advantage in providing bees for orchards in temperate climates than on the plains of India, where pollination seldom seems to be a problem. These authors give no evidence for their statement that if the pollination of the banana is helped by bees and other insects, more and better fruit is produced. Certain of the citrus fruits which normally contain few seeds will bear somewhat more heavily when bees increase the amount of cross-pollination, but the fruit will tend to be more seedy. Rahman and Singh state that the most important insects for pollination are the honey bees, bumble bee, solitary bees, and flies of the genus *Eristalis*. The only one suitable for artificial breeding in India is said to be one of the honey bees, *Apis indica*. Even this bee is difficult to keep on the plains of northern India. Weather conditions have an important effect on the activity of insects. In bright warm weather these will travel great distances, whereas in cool rainy weather their activities are greatly decreased.

Insects are especially important where cross-pollination is required, but in some cases the pollination of self-fertile varieties is much better when insects are present than when they are absent. Sirdar Singh (1953) states that individual flies, bumble bees, and honey bees may restrict the area in which they work during one day to one about 30 ft. in diameter, in which case some plans for interplanting self-sterile varieties are unsuitable. Even where there is a row of pollinators after two rows of the main variety, more fruit has been observed on the side of the trees of the main variety toward the pollinators. In some cases it may be desirable to have alternate rows of the two varieties, although this might prove uneconomic unless both were commercial varieties.

Some varieties of the fig require the services of a particular insect in pollination. This insect is a small wasp which carries the pollen from wild varieties to the better kinds, which produce no pollen. The process is called caprification, and will be described in more detail in Chapter XXI.

In hybridization it may be desirable to cross two species of varieties which flower at different times, which involves storing the pollen in such a way that it will remain viable for the required time. S. N. Singh and S. P. Singh (1952) found that most types of pollen deteriorate rapidly at room temperature or with high humidity, but can be stored for longer periods at 30 to 46 °F. and 25% relative humidity. Of the ten species with which they worked, all showed at least some viability at the end of five months, and 8 species remained viable for about two years.

It has generally been assumed that unless plants were to be grown from seeds, any pollen which would fertilize the ovary was satisfactory. This is probably true in most cases. In most fruits any direct effect of the pollen on the endosperm, which is known as xenia, is of no importance. However, after considerable investigation and discussion, it has been established that the pollen may produce a direct effect on the parts of the seed and fruit lying outside the embryo and endosperm. This is called metaxenia, a term suggested by Swingle in 1926. Size, shape, and time of maturity of the seed and the fruit may be affected, but in most fruits the effect seems to be slight. In the date, however, it is sufficient to be of commercial importance. Recent work indicates that metaxenia may be important in the mango.

Chapter IX

HARVESTING AND MARKETING

Commercial fruit growing cannot stop with the production of fruit of high quality, but must extend to the distribution of the produce to the consumer. If distribution is defective, not only does the grower receive an inadequate reward for his effort, but he fails to perform his function in society. That the majority of the people of this country do not receive the amount of fruit they need is partly because the acreage is too small and the yield too low, and partly because of the waste in distribution. Proper distribution involves the preparation of the produce for market, transportation, and wholesale and retail marketing. The part played by the grower in this process varies, but is likely to be rather small. In most cases it would be to his advantage to increase it.

The process of distribution may be taken as beginning with the harvesting of the fruit. The proper time and methods are most important, especially if the fruit is intended for a market at any distance from the orchard. Most fruits have their finest quality if allowed to ripen fully on the tree, and eaten soon after being picked. It is, however, obviously impossible to harvest many kinds of fruit for market after they are fully ripe. In the time required for marketing them, they would become over-ripe and unfit for consumption. Fruit must be harvested while still firm enough to stand handling, and to keep for a number of days. The difficulty of protecting ripening fruit from birds and other pests also encourages the grower to pick his fruit while still green. A few fruits, such as the oranges, are well protected from damage, and may be harvested when fully ripe. Even with such fruits, however, a better price may often be secured by picking them before they have attained their maximum quality, for the early market.

As a result of all these factors, much fruit is picked before it should be. Fruit picked green may attain a fairly attractive appearance, but it never has the quality of tree-ripened fruit. The sale of such fruit may bring an immediate gain to the grower, but the consumer is so disappointed that he does not soon buy more fruit of that kind. The result is a diminished demand and lower prices. In certain instances the sale of immature fruit may be prohibited by law, but for the most part only public opinion, and a sense of responsibility on the part of the grower can prevent this evil.

Fruit should be picked no sooner than is necessary in order to have it reach the consumer in good condition, unless it has already attained high quality. In no case should it be picked so green as to be of little real value. Within these limitations, the time of harvesting may be determined by market conditions. Fruit which can be placed on the market early or late in the season will ordinarily bring better prices than that sold at the height of the season. Under the present unorganized condition of the market, it is difficult to take advantage of the daily fluctuations in supply.

Pre-harvest Drop

When harvest is delayed until comparatively late in the season, part of the fruit is likely to fall to the ground before it is picked. The amount which falls varies, but is frequently enough to cause a serious loss in apples, pears, and citrus fruits. These windfalls are frequently very good for immediate consumption, but are not satisfactory for marketing. A large amount of experimental work has been done in the United States and England on the possibility of reducing the pre-harvest drop by means of plant hormone sprays. Early work, as reported by Batjer (1943) and Vyvyan (1946) on pome fruits indicated that naphthalene acetic acid (NAA) and related compounds frequently were very effective in reducing the drop of some varieties of apples. A little later it was found that some varieties which did not respond to this treatment could be effectively treated with 2, 4-dichlorophenoxyacetic acid (2, 4-D). NAA has been used with good results at the fruit research station at Chaubattia on the Jonathan, a variety which does not respond to 2, 4-D, and 20 ppm seemed somewhat more effective than more dilute sprays. Recent experiments, summed up by Marth (1953), indicate that 2, 4, 5-TP is satisfactory with all varieties on which it has been tried. For different varieties, from 5 to 20 ppm is required. Except at very low dilutions this hormone has the advantage over NAA that exact timing is less important, although the best results are secured by spraying 30-35 days before the harvest. There is less danger of difficulty in harvesting and of a harmful effect on the leaves the following spring than with 2, 4-D. Good results have also been secured with 2, 4, 5-trichlorophenoxyacetic acid (2, 4, 5-T, 2, 4, 5-TA). Under some circumstances, all of these hormones may hasten the ripening (reducing storage life) of early-ripening varieties, and improve the colour of those with red fruits. White (1953) secured the greatest effect on colour by combined treatments; 25 ppm of 2, 4, 5-T with 10 ppm of 2, 4, 5-TP considerably increased the colour of apples borne inside the tree without injury to the foliage or appreciable effect on the firmness of the fruit. With the winter varieties, Batjer and others (1954) found no effect on maturity even when 80 ppm of 2, 4, 5-TP was applied. Where there is danger of causing early ripening, this can be avoided by adding maleic hydrazide (MH) to the spray, without reducing its efficacy in controlling fruit drop, according to Smock and others (1952). They found that the hormones used to prevent pre-harvest drop tended to increase the respiration rate of the fruit both on the tree and in storage, and that 100—600 ppm of MH often checked the respiration rate and always retarded softening.

Much less work has been done on the other deciduous fruits. In general, the stone fruits have not responded as well as have apples, but Rogers and Batjer (1954) report increasing the yield of one variety of apricot 68% by reducing the drop with 2, 4, 5-T. Crane (1955) reduced the drop of one variety of apricot from 52.9% to 6.6% and 6.4% by spraying 25 and 50 ppm respectively of 2, 4, 5-T. In another variety the drop was decreased from 9% to 1.2, 0.8, and 0.6% with 25, 50, and 100 ppm respectively. Serr and Forde (1952) found 10 ppm of 2, 4-D, and 20 ppm of 2, 4, 5-TP effective in delaying the dropping of one variety of almond.

The drop of citrus fruits can generally be checked by spraying with 2, 4-D. Stewart and others (1952) found this effective on the Valencia orange at the rate of 4-48 ppm and applied any time from six months before the drop until after it had begun, although 2, 4-D was found useless with this variety by Reece and Horanic (1952). Davison (1952) reports success with the Washington Navel with 20 ppm of either 2, 4-D or 2, 4, 5-T. Stewart and Parker (1954) found 8 ppm of 2, 4-D more effective in preventing the drop of grapefruit when applied in May than in July. While NAA has not commonly proved effective with citrus fruits, Zanini (1950) reports that 10 ppm applied to mandarin oranges in November or December effectively prevented the drop of the fruit, and Miege (1948) reports success with potassium naphthylacetate on the Clemantine mandarin. While these hormone sprays have ordinarily been applied to prevent pre-harvest drop, it has been found that they sometimes have other benefits. Erickson and others (1952) found that the soluble solids content of Delicious apples was significantly increased by spraying with 2, 4, 5-TP, while the starch content and acidity were not affected. In the apricot, greater changes have been reported by Crane (1953, 1954a, 1955), who found that either 2, 4-D or 2, 4, 5-T increased the average weight of the fruit, in some cases as much as 50%; hastened maturity as much as 18 days; and in at least one case increased the red colour of the fruit; as well as decreasing drop. The sprays sometimes caused some cracking of the fruit, and some damage to foliage. Bradley and Crane (1955) explain the increase in size by the increase in the size of the cells, with even greater difference in the size of the nucleus, and with many more cells highly polyploid. Peaches have been induced to ripen about a week early, according to Blommaert (1953), without other effect, but he reports severe damage to the crop from early spraying.

Important gains from spraying also occur in citrus fruits. Stewart and others (1952) report an increase in size of Valencia oranges as a result of spraying with 2, 4-D, and some increase in size of grapefruit has been reported by Stewart and Parker (1954) provided a sufficiently concentrated spray is applied when the fruit is less than 16 weeks old. The possibility of increasing the size of lemons and securing other desirable effects by spraying with an ester of 2,4,5-T is reported by Erickson and Brannaman (1950). Stewart and Hield (1954) report that a still greater increase in size can be secured by adding about 5 lb. of urea per 100 gal. of the spray.

Fruit from sprayed trees has been observed to have a longer storage life and be less subject to decay, and similar results are secured by treating the fruit after harvest. Stewart and others (1952) found that the addition of from 100 to 1000 ppm of 2, 4-D or preferably 2, 4, 5-T to the wax emulsion or to the wash water increased the storage life of lemons, mainly by decreasing Alternaria rot and the blackening of the calyx ('black button'). It also delayed the development of yellow colour. Stewart (1953) has summed up the work done in California on the effect of hormone sprays on citrus fruits.

Great care must be exercised in the use of hormones, for it is possible to cause much damage to the foliage and new growth. Less dilute solutions of 2, 4-D are very effective in killing many broad-leaved weeds, and even very dilute solutions may cause abnormal growth in some plants. Marsh and Taylor (1947) report that after 2, 4-D had been used to kill weeds and the equipment rinsed until there were no visible traces, it was used for an oil spray on apple trees. The fruit and foliage of some varieties adhered tenaciously to the trees as a result, and the dry leaves hung on all winter. Considerable damage was caused to foliage and fruit the next year. Tukey and Hammer (1949) report that both 2, 4-D and NAA applied in October delayed the opening of buds the following spring and had marked effects on the shape and composition of cherry fruit, mostly undesirable.

Harvesting Methods

Methods of harvesting are also of importance. These will vary with the different fruits, but in all cases care must be taken to avoid damaging the fruit. Methods in common use are often unsatisfactory. Some fruits may be carefully pulled off without damage, but in other cases it is almost impossible to pull the fruit without injuring the skin so that decay organisms may enter. Another common method is that of breaking the stem by which the fruit is attached. This leaves a piece of the stem which is likely to puncture other fruits with which it comes in contact. Those fruits which cannot safely be pulled should be cut loose with shears. Special blunt-pointed clippers with straight or curved blades are made for the purpose.

The picking of fruit borne more than about eight feet from the ground presents a problem. It is commonly pulled off by means of a long hook. It is either allowed to fall into a small bag attached to the hook, or is caught by the picker as it falls. In either case a certain amount of bruising is probable. Much worse are the methods, sometimes seen, of knocking the fruit off with a stick, or with stones, or by shaking the tree. Pickers sometimes climb the tree, but it is seldom possible to reach all of the fruit without danger to the tree and to the picker. The best means of reaching high fruit is by the use of a ladder. This may be either a light ladder which can be leaned against the tree, or a step-ladder. The latter is heavier and more awkward to use, but in some cases may be better for the tree.

In India the picker commonly carries a basket in which he places the fruit as he picks it. This is satisfactory except that it leaves only one hand free for picking. Sometimes an assistant carries the basket. In other countries baskets are sometimes used slung from the shoulders, leaving both hands free. Canvas bags are also commonly used, especially for citrus fruits. These are so made that they hang from the shoulders, are held open at the top, and are closed at the bottom only by folding up the lower portion. They are emptied by unfolding the bottom, so that the fruit can run out gently into a box or basket.

In case of small orchards near the market, the fruit may be carried to the market in the basket into which it is picked, or it may be put into a larger basket, with little attempt at sorting or packing. When larger quantities are handled, sorting and grading are desirable and in the case of fruit shipped to more distant markets, packing is also necessary. At present both grading and packing are commonly done by middlemen, though in some cases the grower or contractor may grade the fruit.

The object of sorting is to remove over-ripe or damaged fruit, which is likely to decay before reaching the consumer, often damaging good fruit in contact with it; and to remove as culls such fruit as is so green or so deformed as to lower the standard of the whole lot. Such culls may sometimes be sold locally at a low price, or used in making by-products. It is obviously to the advantage of all concerned that such fruit be separated from the sound fruit as early as possible.

Sound, marketable fruit may vary in size, quality and appearance. Fruit of superior quality and appearance brings a higher price in the retail market, and in many markets the largest sizes also bring better prices not only per unit but also per pound. Extremely large sizes may sell at a discount, however. In most cases, fruit graded into different sizes and qualities will sell for more than the same fruit ungraded. This is generally recognized by the retailer, who sorts and grades the fruit if this has not been done before. Sometimes this frunction is performed by the wholesale merchant, but seldom by the grower. In some cases the grower may practise a type of grading, but generally in order to put the less attractive fruit at the bottom or in the middle of the basket, out of sight. His naive hope that the buyer will be deceived by this practice is entirely unjustified. This practice leads the trade to assume that there are inferior fruits hidden in every basket and to fix the price accordingly. It would be to the interest of all concerned to have the fruit honestly graded, so that the quality of an entire lot could be seen from the surface, and this is frequently done in other countries, but not commonly in India.

The improvement of marketing was greatly encouraged by the passing of the Agricultural Produce (Grading and Marketing) Act of 1937. Under this Act, standards have been established for a number of fruits and fruit products. In general, the fruit is required to be mature, sound, well picked, and reasonably uniform. Grades are based mainly on size, colour, and freedom from blemishes. Growers or others willing to observe the rules and to submit to inspection, may be granted by the Marketing Adviser to the Government of India the right to use the designation 'Agmark' on their produce, and in advertising. In order to demonstrate the value of this method, the Government set up experimental grading stations for various fruits. At a station in Allahabad district in 1940-41, 179 maunds of guavas were graded and dispatched to market. These sold at a premium of Re. 0-8-8 per maund over ungraded fruit in the same markets, leaving a net gain of about 11% for the grower. The grading of citrus fruits was started in Madhya Pradesh and Bombay in 1937, and by 1939 there were 14 experimental stations and one packer was authorized to grade Santaras, and nine to grade Mosambi oranges, while in 1940 there were nine experimental stations and 37 authorized packers (Anon., 1943 a). During four years fruit valued at Rs. 2,03,272 was graded and sold at premiums of from 5·6 to 37%. A large grower in the Punjab ('Kissan', 1943) also reports good results from the use of careful sorting, grading, and attractive packing. As the public becomes accustomed to the graded produce, ungraded fruits will be at a still greater disadvantage in the market.

Sorting and grading are ordinarily done by hand in India, with little mechanical assistance. This is fairly satisfactory, for the experienced grader can work very rapidly and quite accurately. Machinery is commonly used in some countries, and is justified where the amount of fruit handled is very large, and where labour is comparatively expensive. It is especially efficient with fruit which is roughly round, and not easily damaged. Oranges and apples are better adapted to machine grading than either peaches or mangoes. In a typical orange packing house, the fruit is carried past sorters on a moving belt, and then passes into revolving rollers, close enough together at one end to allow only the smallest fruit to fall through between, and further apart at the other, so that practically all the fruit falls through into bins before reaching the end. Such machinery is not likely to be economical in India under present conditions or with such developments as are now in sight.

Packing

In shipping fruit by rail, packing is a problem of great importance and great difficulty. The most common package now in use in this country is the basket. There are many forms of baskets used, made of several materials, among the most common being bamboo and pigeon pea. Baskets may be large or small, deep or shallow, flat, conical, or cylindrical. Often two baskets are used, one forming the lid for the other. These are sewn together with string or wire, and may be sealed. None of these packages is entirely satisfactory. Frequently, they are not strong enough to stand the rough handling given them by railway crews. They are not sufficiently rigid to make it possible for them to be piled more than two or three layers deep without injury to the fruit in the lower baskets. This means that railway wagons cannot be given a load even approaching their capacity, and as a result freight rates have to be maintained at a higher level than would otherwise be necessary.

A committee on marketing fruit in Bombay (Anon., 1935) came to the conclusion that the use of bamboo baskets was uneconomical and recommended investigations of the possibility of better packages of wood r other material Perhaps as a result, boxes made from the wood of *Bombax malabaricum* have been found more economical for shipping mangoes from Ratnagiri to Bombay than bamboo baskets, according to Cheema and others (1954). The boxes are 15 by 20 in. and made of half-inch boards. They have half-inch holes for ventilation, rope handles, and hinged lids, and are fastened with wire and sealed. They hold 100—115 mangoes of the size of the Alphonso, and may be used at least four times in a season. The loss from damage and pilfering from baskets is put at 16·1%, and from boxes at 3·9%, and the price of 100 fruits is said to be about Rs. 2 to 6 more when shipped in boxes. Boxes were also found more economical in Visakhapatnam district, according to Suryanarayana (1951).

Boxes are used for packing other fruit only to a very limited extent, although they have very definite advantages over baskets. A well-made box is sufficiently rigid to protect the fruit, even if at the bottom of a tall pile. A rectangular box may be shipped or stored more economically of space than a round basket. The reason boxes are not commonly used is, of course, their cost, which is more than that of baskets. Two types of box are used. One is fairly heavy and returnable, that is, it is designed to be returned empty and used a number of times. The other is a lighter box which is used only once. The Howards, (1918, 1920) when at Quetta, experimented with both types, but although they arranged to have the railways return empty boxes free of charge, there was so much difficulty in working out this system that light, non-returnable boxes were preferred. These were first introduced in 1912, and despite the difficulties in obtaining supplies during the war, Rs. 8,000 worth of these boxes were sold in 1919.

Light boxes are used in shipping fruit from the region of Peshawar to distant markets, and for shipping apples and other temperate fruits from the Kumaun and other hill districts. These boxes are made specially for the purpose and are fairly satisfactory, but in some cases are rather expensive. If materials for boxes were prepared in large quantities at saw-mills near the forests in the Himalayas, the cost should be low enough to make their use economical throughout most of northern India. A good box should be light, yet rigid enough to protect the fruit, and should be open enough to allow ventilation. Packing cases are sometimes used, mainly because they can be secured at small cost, but they are not satisfactory, being heavy, too solid to allow sufficient ventilation and not uniform in size and shape. Another possibility is suggested by the increasing use of fibreboard cartons in some countries. Citrus fruits in the United States were formerly wrapped and carefully placed in wooden boxes, but by 1954 almost all the lemons were being shipped in cartons holding half as much as the wooden box, and some packers were using these for oranges also. The fruit is dumped into the cartons unwrapped and mechanically shaken so that the cartons are properly filled. As material suitable for the manufacture of fibreboard is plentiful in India, the expense of such cartons should be much less than that of wooden boxes.

In some cases, it is advisable to wrap fruit in tissue paper before packing it. This is commonly done in other countries, and with apples and peaches in this country. The paper tends to absorb the moisture given out by the fruit, and to delay the ripening process. It also helps to prevent the spread of decay. The Howards (1918) found that in shipping peaches from Quetta to the plains of India, wrapped fruit kept cool longer than unwrapped fruit. The wrapper also improves the appearance of the fruit and offers a convenient form of advertising. Each wrapper can bear the name, address and trade-mark of the producer.

The fruit should be packed firmly in the box or basket, so that no movement is possible. Where the fruit is first graded, it is placed in boxes in a definite arrangement, so many fruits to a row, so many rows and so many tiers to the box. The box is filled so that it has a slight bulge before the top is put on. The full boxes are stacked on their sides to avoid undue pressure on the fruit. The same principles should be followed in packing in baskets. Grass and leaves are frequently used to line the baskets, and are sometimes used between the layers of fruit. Large leaves are sometimes stitched together for this purpose, and such material is sometimes used to form the sides of parcels with baskets on top and bottom. In the case of the more delicate fruits, such as peaches and grapes, small baskets of bamboo or of very thin wood, designed to hold from one fruit to about five pounds, are made to fit into the larger boxes or baskets. *Sann* fibre or other soft packing material is often put around delicate fruits to prevent bruising.

Transportation

The transport of fruit to distant markets is mainly by rail, and presents numerous problems. The railways are often accused of charging high rates for poor service. It is true that the rates are high, and often the service is unsatisfactory, but the railways are by no means entirely responsible. The worst evils are inherent in the present state of the fruit industry and the methods used by the growers and the marketers.

One of the chief factors in the situation is the smallness and lack of concentration of the fruit industry. The economy of shipping a full wagon of fruit from a centre of production to a market is obvious, but very little Indian fruit can be shipped in this way. Most of the fruit is shipped in small consignments, and must be handled along with other parcels. Oranges are shipped from Nagpur in wagon lots during the height of the season, but comparatively few shipping points even approach this quantity. There is nothing in India to compare with centres in England and America from which trainloads of fruit are shipped daily during the season. Nor are there many markets which can handle fruit in wagon lots. In most cities a few baskets at a time is the limit. This condition is bound to remain for a long time.

Another large factor in the problem of transportation is the unsatisfactory packages which are used. It is estimated that it is safe to load a wagon to about one-third of its capacity, when baskets of the common type are used. The cost to the railway is practically as great as it would be if the space were fully utilized. The development and general use of suitable boxes will make lower rates possible.

Charges of rough handling and of pilfering are still too common, though there seems to have been some improvement in the situation in recent years. It will always be necessary for the railways to bring pressure to bear on their employees to avoid damage of this sort, but the shipper can co-operate by using packages which are light enough to be handled easily, strong enough to stand fairly rough treatment, and not easily broken into. If the railways would accept fruit at the railway's risk, at reasonable rates, as is done in some countries, this would encourage more care on the part of railway officials and employees. Obviously only fruit in good condition and well packed could be accepted on these terms.

In recent years transportation by lorry has gained some importance. In some cases, passenger lorries carry small quantities of fruits short distances, a service which is often economical and convenient for the small grower. The use of freight lorries is still restricted, but is of increasing importance, both in carrying fruit to the railways and in competition with the railways. Lorry competition has already considerably reduced the railway traffic in fruit and vegetables from Poona to Bombay, according to Gadgil and Gadgil (1933). The lorries offer not only somewhat lower rates, but better service, taking the fruit directly from the orchard, in some cases, to the market. The same authors give at least one instance in which the railway met such competition by reducing rates. With the improvement of the roads of the country, however, lorry traffic is bound to assume greater importance, as it has in some western countries.

The question of cold storage and refrigerated vans is often raised. These are available in western countries, and contribute greatly to the fruit industry. By making it possible to put fruit in storage when it is plentiful, they lengthen the season when it is available and avoid the extremely low prices resulting from gluts. Cold storage is already available in a number of the larger cities of India. Chand (1943) mentions two cold storage plants in Calcutta, three in Bombay, and one each in Madras, Karachi, Lucknow, and Cawnpore. Chand's calculations showed that storage was very profitable. There is, of course, always some loss in storage. Cold storage plants increased from a bare dozen in 1947 to about 50 in 1949 as a result of assistance given by the Ministry of Agriculture (B., 1949). These were mainly for the storage of seed potatoes, but a number in the large cities were for general purposes. By 1951 there were 113, according to K. K. Singh (1951), with a capacity of 16,40,000 md. About half of the stores are for potatoes only, with the result that much of the space is not utilized for about half of the time. Refrigerated vans have been run on some railways, and are of great value in the shipping of the more perishable crops, but the demand for this service has not been sufficient to encourage its extension.

The conditions of temperature and humidity best suited to different fruits differ widely. Some fruits may be stored at temperatures just above freezing, and remain in good condition for many months. More tropical crops are likely to be damaged by temperatures even far above freezing, and therefore cannot be kept as long. Considerable experimental work has been done at a Cold storage station at Poona and more recently at the Central Food Technological Research Institute in Mysore and the results on a number of crops will be included in the sections dealing with these fruits.

Modification of the atmoshpere in the storage chamber also affects the length of time fruit may be kept in good condition. As Claypool and Allen (1947) point out, the possible benefits of modified atmosphere for fruit preservation were presented by Berard in 1821, and recognized by the French Academy of Sciences. Little attention was paid to the idea until the extensive 'gas storage' experiments by Kidd and West, almost a century later in England. The basis of this method is the reduction of respiration so that the fruit ripens more slowly. This may be accomplished by increasing the proportion of carbon dioxide in the air, or by reducing the proportion of oxygen by adding an inert gas such as nitrogen. Here again, different fruits respond differently, and careful experimentation is necessary. The method is generally used with some degree of refrigeration. Somewhat similar results may sometimes be secured by the use of polyethylene box liners. Schomer and others (1954) report that these lengthened the storage life of four varieties of pears at least eight weeks at about 30° F., the liners being opened when the fruit was taken from cold storage. The quality of the pears and of one variety of apple was improved. On the other hand, polythylene wrappers were found by Boyes (1955) to aggravate internal disorders in stone fruits.

Marketing

The machinery of marketing differs somewhat in different parts of the country, with the distance from the orchard to the market, and with the fruit. Certain features, however, are common to the entire country. Dissatisfaction with the present system is also very common, and is fully justified.

One of the most common, and most objectionable features of the system is the presence of pre-harvest contractors, who take the place of the owner of the orchard in all marketing arrangements. Such contractors handle practically all small gardens, and some large ones. Their functions and the terms on which they buy the crop, vary. They may buy the crop even before blossoming time, or at any time before the fruit is ripe, but ordinarily the bargain is made about the time the trees are in blossom. Most commonly the contractor agrees to pay a fixed sum for the entire crop, in which case he theoretically assumes the risk of damage to the crop by adverse weather conditions. In practice, if conditions turn out so that the contractor loses, he ordinarily fails to pay the contract price. In some cases, the bargain may be to take all of the fruit or a given quantity of fruit, at a fixed price per unit. Occasionally a contract may cover a period of years, but ordinarily, while the contractor may buy the fruit of one garden year after year, the contract is on an annual basis. Gadgil and Gadgil (1933) report that in parts of Bombay one contractor frequently buys more than one orchard and that in Purandhar taluka, each contractor handles about 30,000 orange trees. An extreme illustration of the uneconomic nature of the contract system is provided by Gupta (1955) who states that the mango crop in Malda district is commonly sold five times, beginning when the flowers appear and ending just before harvest.

The work of the contractor always includes the harvesting and marketing of the fruit, and almost always the guarding of the orchard. In most cases, the contractor and his family live in the orchard from the time there is any danger of the crop being stolen or damaged by pests, until the harvest is finished. In some cases the contractor also performs all or part of the cultural treatments, digging, irrigating and manuring the orchard, though the owner ordinarily supplies the water and manure.

Under present conditions, the pre-harvest contractor serves a useful purpose. Most orchards are small, and are owned by comparatively wealthy men whose main interest is elsewhere. The owners are not in a position to handle the orchards themselves, and if they attempt to do so they must hire men to do the work. The expense of hiring reliable watchmen to protect the crop is rather large, whereas the contractor and his family do this for themselves. In the case of smaller growers, the contractor is a means of collecting money in advance of the harvest. The owner is often almost entirely ignorant regarding the proper care of the orchard, and while the contractor may not know much more, he takes the responsibility for this work.

Evils of Contracting System

On the other hand, the weaknesses of the system are obvious. The owner often does not know the real value of his fruit, and in any case he can do nothing but accept the best price offered. The contractors in any one section are not very numerous, and often form rings to hold the prices down. It may even be against caste rules to raise the bid for an orchard. Not knowing how the crop will turn out, or what the market conditions will be, the contractor must be conservative in his offers. The price is ordinarily paid in instalments, and if for any reason the season is a bad one, the contractor seldom completes the payment.

More serious is the tendency of contractors to bend their efforts solely to the production of the one crop of fruit, with no thought for the good of the trees. Cultivation and manuring are often neglected. The presence of a contractor adds greatly to the difficulty of introducing improved methods of cultivation and irrigation, for the contractor is usually an uneducated man who is sure that the traditional ways are the best.

If it is desired to sell a crop to a contractor, the evils may be minimized by care in selecting the man, and in settling terms. The contractor should have a good reputation for honesty and dependability. The duties of the contractor should be clearly stated. Ordinarily there should be a payment when the contract is signed, sufficient to assure its being carried out. At least half of the total price should be collected by the beginning of the harvest, and the rest before more than half of the fruit is harvested. If the contractor is allowed to harvest all of the fruit before payment is completed, he is tempted to leave without paying the balance. In such cases it is very difficult to force payment through a law suit.

The contractor may dispose of the fruit in several ways. Most commonly he takes it to the wholesale market in the nearby city and sells it to dealers. The majority of these are retail merchants who sell the fruit in small shops or stalls, or hawk it in the streets and from house to house. A few may pack and export the fruit to other cities. In many cases the contractor becomes a retail merchant, he or some member of the family peddling the fruit. Occasionally he will sell to what may be termed a country buyer, who goes around to orchards and purchases ripe fruit, which he packs and dispatches to market. In some cases the contractor himself ships fruit to a commission merchant in a distant market. Gadgil and Gadgil (1933) state that in Poona district it is common for contractors to consign produce to a distant market, generally through a forwarding agent, called a *hundekari*. This man receives the fruit at the railway station and sends it to commission merchants, to whom he also sends the receipts, along with his bill which includes about six pies per basket as forwarding charge, a small amount for postage, and whatever he has spent for railway charges and perhaps for cartage. He frequently has an arrangement with the railway staff whereby fruit is delivered immediately to the agent. In small stations this function is sometimes exercised unofficially by the station master.

If the grower does not choose to sell his crop to a contractor, he may dispose of it in any of the ways open to the contractor. In a very few cases the grower advertises his fruit and ships directly to the consumer by parcel post or railway parcel. This method is largely restricted to fruit of a kind or quality not commonly available on the retail market.

City Markets

In the smaller markets, the producer or contractor often conducts his own sales, often with the assistance of a professional salesman who charges a slight commission for his services. In the largest market, and in some not so large, the selling is done by commission merchants. Most of the fruit in such markets arrives by train, and is sold in the absence of the owner. This situation, unless controlled by strict regulations, is apt to encourage dishonesty. The owner is not in a position to discover the actual price his fruit brings, and is dependent on the information sent to him by the commission merchant (*dalal*). The very unsatisfactory situation in the Bombay market has been pointed out by Cheema (1933) and by Gadgil and Gadgil. There the fruit was invariably sold by secret auction, the offer being expressed by means of pressure of the hands under a cloth, a system known *as hatha*. This was made illegal some years ago, but it was recently stated that "The Bombay State is again making an attempt to stop that strange system of 'Hatha' sales of fruits and vegetables" (Anon., 1954 b). G. P. Singh (1954) states that in the wholesale markets of Bihar, mangoes are sold by this system as well as by open auction.

Many of the commission men also conduct retail stalls and sell to themselves, or they may buy fruit and export it to other cities. This combination of functions is very undesirable. Not only is it possible for the commission merchant to sell to himself at a low rate, or report a lower rate than is actually received, but he may report that the consignment arrived in poor condition and had to be wholly or partly thrown away. The situation could be greatly improved by the publication of daily wholesale prices. It should also be made illegal for commission merchants to engage in wholesale or retail trade.

The charges which may be collected during the marketing process are many. In many cities an octroi tax is levied on all fruit as it enters. This is an undesirable form of taxation, not only because it discourages trade in a commodity necessary for the health of the people, but also because, from its very nature, it promotes dishonesty. When fruit is sold in a public market, a small charge is made for the privilege. If the fruit is sold by a *dalal*, he collects his commission; if not, the seller must seek the aid of a salesman who must be paid. If the fruit is taken any distance to the market, cartage or railway freight, or both, are added to the expense, and another middleman may be called in to take his share. In some markets there are additional charges for postage, rental, money changing and charity, the last two, at least, being unjustified. Finally, the retail seller must make his living. He ordinarily operates on a very small margin of profit.

It is frequently said that the producer receives too small a proportion of the retail price, and to a certain extent, the criticism is justified. Certainly something is wrong if, as Gupta (1955) states is the case with Malda mangoes, the wholesale buyer gets 33% of the consumer's rupee, brokerage and storage take 18%, the exporter's men 6%, transport 9%, the wholesaler 10%, and the retailer 12%, leaving only 12% to be divided between the grower and the contractors. On the other hand, it should be remembered that certain middlemen perform a useful function, and that the cost of marketing is just as legitimate an expense as the cost of production. No system of distribution has been discovered which eliminates the middleman except on a very limited scale. Direct sale from the producer to the consumer cannot be expected to provide for any large proportion of the fruit produced in the country.

Much can be done, however, to improve the marketing system, especially if at the same time production and packing are improved. Some of the glaring defects of the large markets can and should be eliminated. The advantages to be gained by the co-operation of producers are almost unlimited, but great care in the organization of growers is necessary.

Co-operative marketing of agricultural produce has been extensively tried in the West, with varying results. Most of the attempts have failed, but a few have been outstanding successes. One of the most successful is Sunkist Growers, organized in its present form in 1905. This organization handles only citrus fruits, and controls about three-fourths of the production of California. It is primarily a marketing organization, but packs practically all of the fruit, harvests much of it, and oversees production of a small amount. It also conducts a purchasing service for its members. Because of the large amount of fruit shipped through the Exchange, it has been able to spend well over a million dollars a year in recent years, for advertising, which has had a large part in expanding the market with increasing production.

Beginnings in co-operation have been made in India. A fruit growers' co-operative has functioned in Kodur, Andhra State, for some years. There was at least one co-operative fruit growers' association in the Punjab before partition and there has been a move to organize the fruit growers of Uttar Pradesh. A Fruit Development Board was started in 1933, and under it a number of district associations have been organized. Most of these are intended in the first place to help the grower to improve his production. Some are already planning to deal with marketing also, and may eventually become true co-operative marketing societies. In the earlier stages, the marketing societies will endeavour to increase the demand for fruit, arrange auctions, both in the market and in member's gardens, and publish market reports. An organization of this kind can do much to improve conditions in the markets, and to free owners from the control of rings of contractors. The time does not seem to be ripe for co-operative packing and sale of fruit in this country, but this may well result after growers gain confidence in their organizations, and in the co-operative principle.

Chapter X

THE HEALTH OF THE ORCHARD

It is a common experience to enter an old garden and find many trees missing or dead, and those which are alive obviously fighting a losing battle against a host of enemies. It is easy to ascribe this condition to neglect and poor care, but the subject cannot be so readily dismissed. Even with the best of care trees are likely to suffer, and the fruit to be injured. The successful grower must be ever alert to protect his trees and keep them in good health.

If one is to combat effectively the causes of injury in the orchard, he must first know what these causes are—the identity and nature of his actual or potential enemies. Against some he can take such precautions that there is little chance of their attack. Others may only be watched for, and fought against whenever they appear. In such cases it is of extreme importance that the attack be quickly and accurately diagnosed. This is one of the most difficult tasks the fruit grower must face, for the causes of poor health are numerous, and the symptoms are often confusing. Even in countries where practically all serious diseases have been studied and described, it is frequently difficult to make a sure diagnosis. Unfortunately, in India comparatively few orchard ills have been carefully studied, and it is frequently impossible to secure accurate information about some disease.

Poor health in the orchard may be caused in a number of ways. Climatic conditions unfavourable to the particular fruit or variety may prevent normal growth and fruitfulness. The soil may be of an undesirable texture, or may lack fertility. If the trees grow well the first few years, and then turn sickly, the cause may be the accumulation of salts, but more likely it is the presence of an impervious layer a few feet below the surface of the soil, or a rising water table. Again, the cause of poor growth may be an inherent weakness of the tree because of a poor rootstock, or improper treatment in the nursery. Some of these causes of failure may be overcome by proper cultivation, irrigation, and manuring, but others yield to no treatment. Many can be avoided by care in selecting the orchard site.

Another type of trouble is that caused by various living organisms, plant and animal, and it is these which are the principal subject of this chapter. These include the fungi, bacteria, viruses, larger parasitic plants, insects, mites, larger animals, and birds. The bacteria are sometimes considered as fungi, but it is more convenient to think of them as a distinct group. For convenience, the term 'disease' will be used for an abnormal condition caused by some fungus, bacterium, or virus, but not for the injury caused directly by insect attack. Abnormalities caused by environmental factors such as poor drainage are referred to as physiological diseases.

In many cases, more than one cause of injury is present in a tree. Unfavourable soil and climatic conditions render plants more susceptible to soem diseases and insect pests, and the presence of one disease may encourage another. Some insects cause direct damage, and are also indirectly harmful in that they spread disease from one plant to another.

Plants have been harmed by diseases and insects since the earliest times in recorded history, but the nature of the troubles was for long unknown. In many cases, the insects damaging crops were recognized, but little was known of their life histories. Fungous diseases were entirely mysterious, and were regarded in some cases as evidence of divine displeasure. Treatment based on such theories was not effective. Pliny, who lived at the beginning of the Christian era, recorded, with apparent faith in their value, such remedies as the burying of a frog in the middle of the field to be protected. Remedies, many of them fantastic, were tried, but, of them all, the only one which has survived into a scientific age is sulphur.

The discovery of the true cause of disease was impossible until the invention of the microscope, and did not actually occur until many years later. Gradually the knowledge of microscopic organisms increased, and methods of combating them in plants as well as in animals, were developed. The science of plant pathology is almost entirely the product of the period since 1880. While insects were studied at an earlier date, modern methods of control have no long history. In both fields, pathology and entomology, there still remains much to be done, but this consists of the application to particular diseases and insects, of the principles which have already been worked out.

Orchard Sanitation

Just as sanitary habits are important in maintaining human health, orchard sanitation is necessary as a basis for fighting orchard ills. Weeds harbour both insects and diseases, and should not be allowed to grow in the orchard, at least for long periods. During the rainy season it may be desirable to allow weeds to grow, along with any cover crop which may be planted, to prevent erosion and provide a green manure. But at the end of the season they should be completely destroyed. Not only are weeds dangerous in the orchard itself, but also in fence-rows, hedges, and neighbouring fields. Cultivation of the soil at some seasons tends to kill certain insects. If diseased branches are allowed to remain in the trees, they may serve as sources of infection. They should, as far as is practicable, be removed. In some cases the infection may be so general that the loss resulting from such severe pruning as would remove all infected branches would be greater than the loss from the disease. This may be true of limes infected with canker. The presence of dead or broken branches, which may readily become infected, is a danger which should be avoided.

Most important of all, in the avoidance of conditions favourable to disease, is the maintenance of vigour by means of proper cultivation, irrigation, and manuring. It is the run-down orchard which is most likely to be attacked by pests.

When trees seem to be lacking in health, the first move is to find out, if possible, the cause. The tree should be examined for the presence of insects, or evidence of insect damage. The leaves may be eaten or deformed. The refuse of borers or bark-eating beetles may be seen clinging to the trunk or branches. If there is no sign of insect damage, there may be evidence of disease. This may consist of the fruiting bodies of fungi, of dead or discoloured leaves or twigs, of gum oozing from the tree, or of dead bark. When either the causal organism or the symptoms are found, it is next desirable to identify the disease or insect. The grower may be able to do this himself, or by consultation with more experienced neighbours. It may be necessary to secure the aid of a trained entomologist or plant pathologist. Such help may ordinarily be secured from the Department of Agriculture. Advice may also be secured as to the best control measures. The more intelligent orchardist will also wish to know the life history of the fungus or insect, so as to be able to attack it when it is most vulnerable.

Biological Control

Measures for controlling insect pests may be divided into the biological, the mechanical, such as hand picking or the destruction of borers by thrusting a wire into their holes; and the chemical, the use of poisons. The latter may again be divided into contact insecticides, stomach poisons, and gases. Repellents are substances which do not actually kill the insects, but protect the plant by making it unattractive to the insects.

Biological control of insects is more important than is generally realized. It consists mainly of the use of other insects which prey upon the pests, or, more rarely, of the encouragement of a disease which attacks the pest. Predators or predaceous insects attack and eat other insects. Parasites lay their eggs within the body of the insect and the young develop at the expense of the host, ultimately killing it. In any area where a particular kind of plant has been growing for a very long time, there are likely to be both insect pests and their parasites or predators which tend to keep them in check. There are present in India certain pests which in other countries have caused great damage, but which here are not serious. This is probably because their natural enemies prevent a large increase in numbers.

When a pest is accidentally carried from one country to another without any parasite, it may cause immense damage, or be controlled only at great expense. In such cases it is now a recognized practice to send to the country of origin for parasites or predators. While the initial expense is comparatively large, this method has often proved an economical control measure. Pruthi (1950) tells how the fluted scale, *Icerya purchasi*, was introduced from Australia about 1900, and temporarily held in check by introducing a ladybird beetle, *Rodolia cardinalis*, from Australia. In 1941 it was found that the scale had become widespread in South India, and a serious threat. By the mass production and distribution of this beetle, and other predators, within three years the danger had been greatly reduced. Subramaniam (1954, 1955) says that it has been well controlled in

Mysore, Travancore, and Madras, although *I. formicarum* was still found on the plains, well parasitized. Five Indian species of *Rodolia*, a predacious caterpillar, *Euzophera cocciphaga*, and a species of the fungus *Caldosporium* were found ineffective in controlling the scale. The situation is complicated by the fact that *Rodolia* grubs are themselves frequently parasitized by *Homolotylus flaminius*. Smith (1948) gives the history of efforts to use biological control on many insect pests of citrus in California, including entomological expeditions to many parts of the world. In several cases the success achieved was outstanding. Ants often protect such insects as scale and aphids which secrete honeydew, from thier enemies, and biological control in such cases requires measures to eliminate the ants. Poison syrup is used for this purpose. As Fawcett (1948) points out, fungous and bacterial diseases of insects are fairly common, but this form of biological control has had comparatively little study. Birds, mammals, and reptiles sometimes feed on insects and help to reduce their numbers.

Biological control is often endangered by chemical treatment of other pests or diseases. This is particularly important in the case of some modern insecticides, the effectiveness of which remains for considerable time after spraying. After mango trees are sprayed with DDT to control the hoppers, mites and scale insects may become serious problems. Ramakrishnan (1954) states that in moist districts, such as Coorg, scale insects are kept under control by entomogenous fungi, and that if it is necessary to use fungicides to control diseases, an insecticide should be added to control the scale. It is clear that chemical means of control should not be used lightly.

In the chemical control of insect pests, contact insecticides and stomach poisons are commonly used. The type to be used depends largely on the feeding habits of the insect concerned. Stomach poisons are effective only against those with biting mouth parts, and a few which lap up moisture from the surface. Even a few of the biting insects cannot be killed with poisons, as they carefully discard the surface tissues. Most of them, however, may be poisoned, and this method has distinct advantages over all others. Once the foliage and fruits are covered with the poison, the tree is protected until new growth takes place, or heavy rains wash the poison off. The material may be applied in advance of the attack, and prevent practically all damage. In general, stomach poisons are less likely to damage the tree than contact insecticides.

Many insects have a long beak or proboscis, which they thrust through the surface, and with which they suck juice from the tissues of the plant. Stomach poisons, on the surface, are obviously of no avail against these. Against such pests, contact insecticides are used. As the name indicates, these kill the insect by coming into contact with it. There are various types of contact sprays and poisons. The most common cause death by suffocation by closing the breathing pores, or by paralyzing the nervous system. It is necessary to bring the insecticide into actual contact with the insect. Thus the treatment must be carried out when the insects are present except in the case of some of the newer insecticides, such as DDT, which retain their effectiveness for some time; it must be very thorough; and it must be repeated when a new batch of insects arrives.

Gases are used in a few cases. They are of great importance in treating stored seed. The most spectacular use of gas in fruit growing is the fumigation of citrus trees with hydrocyanic acid gas to control scale insects. This was first used, according to Woglum (1949), in California in 1886, the gas being generated from potassium cyanide. Later the cheaper sodium cyanide was used, and since 1916 liquid hydrocyanic acid has become popular. In 1922 Quayle found that calcium cyanide dust could be used, and was easier to handle than the other substances. This method has become popular in other countries, and has been used to a limited extent in India. Fumigation is an expensive process, and is used only when other insecticides are ineffective. It involves the use of stout canvas tents to cover the trees during the process, and in order to avoid damage to the trees, must be done at night and when the trees are dry. Certain powders, such as pyrethrum, are generally classed as contact insecticides, but give off gases which kill the insects.

Stomach Poisons

Historically, the first modern stomach poison to come into use is that known as Paris green. It was first used soon after 1860, in the United States. For many years it was very commonly used, but it has now been largely discarded in favour of safer insecticides. It is still used in preparing poison baits, and to a certain extent in spraying field crops. It is not to be recommended for fruit trees, as it is very likely to 'burn' the leaves. Paris green is the aceto-arsenite of copper, and is likely to contain about 4½% of water-soluble arsenic, which is likely to cause damage. It received its name because of its brilliant green colour. If used at all, it should be mixed with lime.

Most of the other stomach poisons are also arsenic compounds. The most commonly used today is lead arsenate, which is marketed as a grayish-white powder or paste. There are two types on the market, the so-called acid or hydrogen lead arsenate ($PbHAsO_4$) and the basic or neutral [$Pb_4PbOH\ (AsO_4)_3$] which is often listed as $PbAsO_4$. The acid form should contain about 32% arsenic acid, as a powder, and 16% when purchased in paste form. Basic lead arsenate contains about 23% and 11% respectively. The acid form is more toxic, but is also more likely to damage the foliage. Under most conditions basic lead arsenate is entirely safe, but about one-third more is required for effective control. Ordinarily from 4 to 8 pounds of paste, or 2 to 6 pounds of powder should be used with 100 gallons of water. Richards and Sharma (1933) advise that 8 pounds of slaked lime be first added to the water.

Lead arsenate is also applied as a dust, in which case it should be mixed with slaked lime or sulphur, the arsenate forming 5% to 15%, or occasionally as high as 50% of the total. With tender foliage it is safer to use at least 20% slaked lime.

Lead arsenate is a dangerous poison, and should be handled with great care. It should be kept out of reach of animals, children, and ignorant persons. In small amounts it has no immediate effect, and it was formerly thought that there was no danger from that which might adhere to fruit sprayed with it. Later it was found that the continued eating of very small amounts might be injurious. Many western countries now make it illegal to sell fruit carrying more than a very small trace of arsenic or of lead, or of certain other spray materials. As a matter of fact, as Talbert (1935) has pointed out, many common foods contain more arsenic, and many samples of drinking water contain more lead, than the legal tolerances of spray residue in the United States. And as Morris (1941) has pointed out, a study of men working with lead arsenate in the orchard, as well as of the consumers of sprayed fruit shows that there is no evidence of harm caused by the spray. Nevertheless, as long as the laws stand or the public is afraid, special efforts must be made in preparing such fruit for the market, to remove all spray residue.

Calcium arsenate is sometimes used as an insecticide, and is both cheaper and stronger than lead arsenate, but it is unstable, and likely to damage the foliage. It cannot be recommended for spraying fruit trees.

There are several plant products used as poison insecticides, the most important being hellebore, made by grinding the roots of the white hellebore plant. It contains alkaloids which are effective both as poison and as contact insecticides. It is harmless to man, and may be used on fruit which is almost ripe. It is comparatively expensive, and therefore not widely used in horticulture. One ounce is used to a gallon of water, or to 5—10 ounces of slaked lime for dusting.

Contact Insecticides

A large number of substances are used as contact insecticides, with varying degrees of success. The most important types are the vegetable products, soaps, mineral oils, sulphur sprays, and organic compounds.

The most important of the plant materials is tobacco, the effective agent being the alkaloid, nicotine. Most insects have the good taste to dislike the smell of tobacco, which is attractive to so many men, and thus it acts as a repellent as well as a contact insecticide. Tobacco decoction is easily prepared, and fairly satisfactory. The coarser and stronger the tobacco is, the better it is for this purpose. One pound of such tobacco can be steeped in a gallon of water for 24 hours, and the process repeated twice with fresh water. The addition of up to one pound of soft soap is recommended. Before use, the decoction can be diluted to make 6 to 10 gallons of spray. It should, of course, be strained and allowed to cool before being used. It can be kept for short periods, but is ordinarily made up only as needed. Hough and Mason (1928) state that boiling should be avoided as the nicotine is volatile, and advocate soaking in cool water. They recommend about half a pound of leaves or one pound of stems for each gallon of water used, with no further dilution. As there is no danger of harming the plant with strong solutions, it is better to use a solution stronger than necessary than one which is too weak. The greatest difficulty in using home-made decoctions is the variation in nicotine content.

Greater accuracy is possible by using commercial nicotine preparations, which are sold under several trade names. The most popular strength is that which contains 40% of nicotine sulphate. These preparations are expensive, but are greatly diluted before use. Recommendations vary from one part of 40% nicotine sulphate to 550 parts of water, to about half that strength. Probably one part to 800 is sufficient under most conditions. For small operations, one teaspoonful in a gallon of water may be used. The dilute mixture, or tobacco decoction, should contain not less than ·05% nicotine, according to Mason (1928).

Tobacco sprays may be mixed with soap, oils, or other spray materials. They are effective only when they actually strike the insect to be killed. They are more effective in hot dry weather than when it is cool. Such soft-bodied sucking insects as aphids are frequently controlled with tobacco sprays.

Dusting is also done. Ground stems of tobacco have long been used, and may be recommended for easily killed pests. Here again the variability is great. Nicotine dusts are prepared by adding nicotine sulphate or free nicotine to a carrier such as lime. These dusts are about as effective as nicotine sprays.

A promising contact insecticide can be made from a plant commonly grown in India, the yellow oleander, *Thevetia nereifolia*. Cherian and Ramchandran (1942), who discovered this fact, found an infusion made by soaking the crushed kernels in cold water for 24 hours, or a decoction made by boiling them for five minutes, the best form. An oil emulsion was also successful. At the rate of one-fourth ounce of kernel to a gallon of water, it was effective for aphids and other soft-bodied insects; twice that amount for most other insects; and one ounce for scale. In order to kill the scale nymphs as they emerge, the treatment must be repeated two or three times at intervals of three or four days. In all cases as much soap should be added as the amount of kernel used. At the rate of one ounce per gallon it was tried on the foliage of plants of a number of species, without damage even to tender foliage.

Pyrethrum powder, sometimes called buhach, is made by grinding the flower-heads and stalks of certain species of *Pyrethrum*. It contains a very volatile oil which is toxic to insects. It must be kept air-tight until used, and loses its toxicity very quickly. It is of value chiefly for use on fruit or vegetables shortly before harvest, as it leaves no harmful residue. Because of its high cost, it is not commonly used. It has long been used for certain purposes, and continues its limited popularity. It is generally used as a dust, but occasionally as spray.

Rotenone is the active drug found in a number of plants, and extracted mainly from cube and derris roots. It is primarily a contact insecticide, but is used to some extent as a stomach poison also. It is not dangerous to man or the larger animals. Its use seems to be increasing, perhaps because of legislation against the more dangerous poisons. Practically all derris is produced in Malaya, where according to Grist (1935), it is a profitable crop. Cube, obtained from two species of the leguminous genus *Lonchocarpus*, is also grown in that region, according to Milsum (1935). A decoction made from chips of quassia wood has also been used, and is about as effective as nicotine sulphate, but as it is as expensive, and more troublesome, it is not much used.

Soap has long been popular as a contact insecticide for very small-scale operations, principally because it is cheap and easy to obtain. It is only moderately effective. It is used to a considerable extent as a spreader with nicotine sprays, and as a flux in making oil emulsions. While ordinary soap may be used, fish-oil soap is to be preferred. Two types are on the market, that being made with caustic potash being soft and that with caustic soda being hard. The latter is easier to handle, but must be sliced and dissolved in hot water. A fish-oil soap containing resin (rosin) is also available, and the resin in it makes it more adhesive. When soap is used alone, about one pound to three gallons of water should be used. A compound made by adding two pounds of powdered resin to one pound of washing soda in one gallon of boiling water, and again boiling, is sometimes used.

Mineral oils are very effective insecticides, but if used undiluted they would severely damage foliage, and even the wood. They are never so used, but in the form of emulsions or as miscible oils. An emulsion is a water-and-soap suspension of oil, while a miscible oil is an oil solution of the soap emulsifier. Even these preparations may be dangerous to most foliage, and are most satisfactory as dormant sprays. They have been largely used to kill scale insects on citrus trees in California, with very little obvious damage to the foliage, but Harding (1953) reports that an oil-emulsion spray significantly reduced the total solids in some varieties of oranges, and also lowered the acid and ascorbic acid content. In making kerosene emulsion one pound of soft soap is dissolved in a gallon of water and boiled, and while it is still hot two gallons of kerosene oil is added, being forced into the soap solution through the jet of a spraying machine. One gallon of the emulsion may be added to from 10 to 30 gallons of water for spraying. Commercial kerosene emulsions may be purchased, and used one gallon to 30 or 40 gallons of water for spraying young foliage and flowers of the mango.

In other countries kerosene emulsions are now little used, distillate, lubricating, and crude oils being more satisfactory. These are prepared in much the same way. Some are heated to the boiling point, and others are prepared cold, with the use of calcium caseinate or other emulsifiers instead of soap.

Sulphur Insecticides

Sulphur insecticides have been used for hundreds of years, and some of them are extremely effective. Sulphur itself is used in several forms, both as a spray and as a dust. It is used against such insects as hoppers and against mites. As it is of more importance as a fungicide, it will be discussed in more detail later.

Undoubtedly the most important sulphur insecticide is that known as lime-sulphur. This also is a powerful fungicide. The form called 'self-boiled' is milder, and is seldom used as an insecticide. Lime-sulphur is a complex mixture of chemicals resulting from the interaction of lime, water, and sulphur. It owes its effectiveness to the presence of polysulphides of calcium, which act as reducing agents, breaking down into calcium thiosulphate and finally calcium sulphate. Lime sulphur, even when diluted for spraying, can damage tender skin. Sprayers often protect their faces with cold cream, and try to avoid getting the spray into their eyes, where it stings badly for a few seconds. The concentrated material must be carefully handled.

Concentrated lime-sulphur may be bought in barrels, and as it is not easy to prepare at home, this is probably the best policy, unless large quantities are needed. In the latter case it may be economical to make it locally, especially if the material must be shipped a long distance. A dry form is also marketed, but the addition of a stabilizer, such as sugar, is necessary. This increases the cost. The effectiveness is also less, so that the cost per acre is much greater.

There are several formulae for making lime-sulphur stock solution. In each, about twice as much sulphur as lime is used. A popular formula is 50 pounds of quicklime, 100 pounds of sulphur and 50 gallons of water. The quicklime should be of high quality and fresh. The sulphur should be finely ground. A large iron kettle is needed. This is put over a fire and the lime is added with enough water for slaking. When this is well started, the sulphur is added, and when slaking is finished, the rest of the water is added. Constant stirring is needed until the solution boils, and occasional stirring, or the adding of cold water may be necessary to prevent it from boiling over. It should be cooked until it has a rich amber colour, showing that the free sulphur has disappeared. This may take from 35 minutes to an hour. The solution should then be drawn off and allowed to stand for a day or two, and then decanted into storage barrels.

The stock solution should be diluted before being used. As the strength of home-made lime-sulphur varies, it can be diluted properly only by testing it with a specific gravity or Baume hydrometer. Scales are available, showing the amount of stock solution to be used. One gallon of stock solution of average specific gravity to 50 gallons of water is a common dilution.

Two more or less similar sprays are the so-called soluble sulphur and barium tetrasulphide, in which sodium and barium, respectively, are substituted for the lime. Neither is as satisfactory as lime-sulphur.

Newer Insecticides

During the second World War, an insecticide known as DDT came into use and proved very effective against a number of insects including flies and mosquitoes. This is dichloro-diphenyl-trichlorethane, and had been discovered many years earlier but never used commonly. It is not only toxic to a large number of species, but keeps its toxicity for a long time after application. This is an advantage, but makes more care necessary in its application. Two related compounds are used to a limited extent, methoxy-DDT, and dichloro-diphenyl-dichloroethane, which is known as DDD. At about the same time that DDT became popular, another organic insecticide was widely introduced, benzene-hexachloride or hexachlorocycolhexane. This is known in India as gammexane, in Britain also as 666, and in the United States as BHC. This is effective against a wide range of insects, as a poison, contact insecticide, and fumigant, but has a musty odour which may be imparted to foods with which it comes in contact.

The popularity of these organic insecticides has led to a large amount of investigation which is still continuing and has already produced several other promising compounds (Hensill, 1950). Lindane is 99 or 100% pure gamma isomer of gammexane and has all the insecticidal properties of it, but has no odour, no accumulation of a poisonous residue in animals, and can be used on plants the sensitive foliage of which is damaged by gammexane. TEPP, tetraethyl-pyrophosphate, is reportedly more than 100 times as toxic as DDT, leaves no poison residue, and is apparently one of the best insecticides for red spider mites and aphids, as well as being effective against some other insects. Parathion, O, O-diethyl O-paranitrophenyl thiophosphate, is another new and highly effective organic insecticide, used against some of the same pests as TEPP, with longer residual activity. As it is very toxic to warm-blooded animals, including man, when swallowed or absorbed through the skin, great caution is required in its use.

Systemic insecticides are those which are absorbed by the foliage, bark, or roots, or are injected into the stem, and are transported to all parts of the plant and kill the sucking insects. Several organic phosphate compounds have been used on annuals, and show much promise in the case of fruit trees, but more information is necessary both as to the best methods of use and the possible harm to the plants or to those who eat fruits from such plants. The method not only protects the plants for several months, in some cases, but has the great advantage of not interfering with biological control. One of the best at present is called Systox and contains about 21% of diethylthiophosphoric acid ester of 2-ethylmeraptoethanol. This is extremely toxic to human beings, but may be applied to plants except within 21 days of harvest without danger of harm from eating the fruit. Metcalf (1954) states that 0.5-1.0 lb. per acre in 400 gal. of water has given excellent protection from red mites on citrus trees for three months. Or 0.5-2.0 oz. per tree painted on the trunks in the spring will protect the tree for about as long. Excessive application may cause the cracking and destruction of the bark. Another material, OMPA or Schradan, is cheaper but more is required so that the cost per acre is about the same. A third chemical, BFPO, is also being tried.

With further development and trial, it seems quite possible that some of these or other organic insecticides may very largely replace insecticides which have been popular for many years. They may make possible more satisfactory control of insect pests than has been possible up to the present.

Fungous Diseases

Plant diseases are controlled mainly by preventing or reducing infection. In most cases, once the organism establishes itself in its host, it can be destroyed only by removing the infected portion. In some cases of mildew, the mycelium, or main body of the fungus, is on or very near the surface, and can be destroyed by spraying. Bacterial diseases, once established, are particularly difficult to eradicate. In recent years, however, it has been found that some of the antibiotics used in treating human disease are effective against some bacterial diseases of plants. Streptomycin and terramycin, separately or combined, have given excellent control of fireblight, a disease of pears, apples, and plums which is estimated to cause an annual loss in the United States of about $ 70 million. Goodman (1954), for instance, states that complete and lasting inhibition of fireblight could be obtained by spraying with 100 ppm of streptomycin, starting early in the flowering period. Good results have been secured with some other bacterial diseases. Unfortunately the method is not yet economic because of the high cost of the antibiotics.

Fungous diseases spread by means of spores which are carried to the host plant by means of wind, water, insects, larger animals, and man himself. If conditions are favourable they germinate and enter the tissues of the plant through wounds or sometimes through the stomata. Insects not only carry the spores, but by biting or piercing the host, provide a convenient entrance. The fungus develops rapidly, spreading to the surrounding tissue, and in a short period is producing spores for further infection. Bacteria spread in much the same way.

Control of diseases therefore lies largely in avoiding sources of infection, and killing the germinating spores, on the surface of the host. By avoiding other hosts, and by removing all parts known to be infected, the supply of spores can be greatly reduced. This is particularly effective if carried out on a large scale. It is of little use for one grower to control the sources of infection on his property, if his neighbours make no similar effort.

Spraying is used mainly to protect the plants from infection. The spores are well protected. When they germinate, however, they are comparatively easily killed by toxic substances on the surface on which they lie. The secret of successful control, therefore, is the coating of the leaves, tender twigs and young fruits with some material which will not injure the host, but will kill the germinating spores. Such a material is called a fungicide.

Bordeaux Mixture

The most popular of all fungicides is that known as Bordeaux mixture. It is also one of the first to be used sucessfully, although sulphur was used as a fungicide somewhat earlier. The history of the discovery of Bordeaux mixture is one of the most famous bits of horticultural lore. It followed upon the introduction into France of the downy mildew of grapes from America. This disease caused much damage. At the same time, growers whose vineyards were along the highways suffered from the theft of their crop. In order to discourage thieves, some of the growers tried to cover the grapes with verdigris, or with a mixture of copper sulphate and lime, so that they would appear to be poisoned. Of those who followed this practice, one, a scientist named Millardet, was observant enough to notice in 1882 that the vines so treated did not lose their leaves from the mildew as did the untreated vines. Thus by accident was it discovered that copper sulphate would prevent the mildew, and that by mixing this with lime, the plants were saved from the damage which made the use of copper sulphate alone impracticable. The mixture soon became known as Bordeaux mixture, from the name of the region where it was first used.

The use of the new fungicide spread to other countries, and it has ever since been the one most commonly used. Many formulae have been developed, and are expressed in terms of the number of pounds of copper sulphate and of quicklime used in 50 gallons of water. Thus a common formula is 4-4-50 indicating four pounds each of copper sulphate and lime. The formula 3-4-50 would indicate three pounds of copper sulphate and four of lime. The strongest solution commonly used is 5-5-50. For very tender foliage it is well to reduce the formula to 2-2-50. Hydrated lime may be substituted for quicklime, using about 6½ pounds instead of 5. Christopher (1941) points out that in some cases a high calcium lime gives better protection than a high magnesium lime. He also advises caution in comparing results by different experimental workers because a small minority use the first figure in the formula for lime.

Bordeaux mixture is easy to make, and should be used fresh to get the best results. It is therefore almost always made where it is to be used. Stock solutions of copper sulphate (bluestone) and lime are made, generally by adding one pound of each material for each gallon of water. If the copper sulphate is merely thrown into the container, it will dissolve very slowly, as the solution remains at the bottom. It should be tied in a cloth, just under the surface. The quicklime should be of good quality, and should be very fresh. It should be slaked, and then the balance of the water should be added. These two stock solutions may be kept indefinitely. When they are used, the lime water is first diluted, and to this the copper sulphate is added while the mixture is stirred vigorously. The mixture can be tested for free copper, which might damage foliage, by putting a polished knife into it for a minute. If copper deposits on it, more lime should be added. Bordeaux mixture reacts with iron or steel. It is therefore necessary that it be stored in vessels of other materials, and that spraying equipment be of brass or bronze.

Burgundy mixture is similar, but contains sodium carbonate (washing soda) instead of lime. It is somewhat more expensive, but does not stain the fruit on which it is used. It may be used where it is difficult to get a good quality of lime. The Department of Agriculture, Bombay (Anon. 1933 a) recommends it for anthracnose of the papaya. It is prepared just as Bordeaux is.

Cuprous oxide is reported by Blackford (1941) to be as effective as Bordeaux mixture in some cases, without adverse after-effects. A solution of 1 pound of bluestone, 1 pint of molasses, and 4 pints of water is mixed slowly and thoroughly with a solution of 5 ounces of caustic soda in 3 pints of water, and allowed to stand for 10 to 15 days, until the colour changes from dirty green to brownish yellow. About 3 gallons are used with 40 gallons of water.

Sulphur Fungicides

Sulphur is a very effective fungicide, and is used in a number of forms. Any finely divided sulphur may be used as a dust. It should be fine enough to pass through a 300-mesh sieve. Ground, sublimed, and precipitated sulphurs are on the market for this purpose. They are commonly used to control powdery mildew of the grape and other crops. Sulphur is exceedingly difficult to wet, and cannot, therefore, be used satisfactorily as a spray, by itself. By adding certain substances, such as glue, flour, calcium caseinate, skim milk, or lime, a sulphur paste can be made which readily becomes suspended in water. This type of spray is known as wettable sulphur. It has become very popular, and is said by Robinson (1935) to be markedly superior to self-boiled lime-sulphur as a spray for trees in foliage. A number of commercial preparations are on the market, and several formulae are recommended. A simple formula is given by Robinson as Oregon cold-mix wettable sulphur. Three quarts of skim milk are diluted with an equal amount of water, and poured into a mixture of 8 pounds of sulphur and one pound of hydrated lime, this being stirred to form a smooth paste. This is then added to 100 gallons of water for spraying. The sulphur should be fine enough to pass through a 300-mesh screen. In warm weather more lime may be necessary to prevent burning. Another form is the New Jersey dry-mix wettable sulphur. In this 8 pounds of sulphur, 4 pounds of hydrated lime and one-half a pound of calcium caseinate are mixed together thoroughly. This is enough for 50 gallons of water.

Other sulphur sprays have long been popular. Lime sulphur, the manufacture of which has already been described, is used as a fungicide as well as an insecticide, especially on dormant plants. A much milder fungicide is made by slaking lime in the presence of sulphur, but without other heating. This is known as self-boiled lime-sulphur, although it is not actually boiled. Some chemical reaction takes place, but for the most part this is a mechanical mixture. Ordinarily 8 to 10 pounds each of quicklime and sulphur are used to make 50 gallons of spray, the water being added only fast enough to keep the lime slaking vigorously. When slaking is finished, the balance is added.

A number of other fungicides have been, and are being used, which are of comparatively little importance. Among the more promising is zinc sulphate, 16 pounds of which, with 8 pounds of hydrated lime, are used with 100 gallons of water.

In recent years, a number of organic fungicides have come into use, particularly for the protection of annual crops from seed decay and damping-off. Some of these are also proving useful in the control of diseases of fruit trees. Fermate, ferric dimethyldithiocarbamate, is one of the more promising, and it and some other nitrogenous fungicides may in some cases improve the nutrition of the trees sprayed. Gases are sometimes used to prevent the decay of fruit in storage. Klotz (1936) reported the successful use, commercially as well as experimentally, of nitrogen trichloride to prevent blue and green molds of oranges, while monomethylchloremine was more effective for grapefruit and lemons. Roistacher and others (1955) report that the same purpose is served by treating the fruit with 0.5% of ammonia gas twice daily for three consecutive days. This prevented decay even when the fruit was inoculated 24-30 hours before the first treatment and held at a temperature favourable to the mold.

Disinfectants, such as creosote, are used to protect wounds, and to treat gummosis of citrus trees. These are painted on the wounds, not sprayed. A paste, similar to Bordeaux mixture, is used in this way.

It is sometimes convenient and economical to combine two or more spray materials, and thus control more than one pest with one operation. This can frequently be done, but not all sprays are compatible. Lime-sulphur is not a stable compound, and must not be added to soaps or oils. If it is combined with lead arsenate one pound of lime should be added to every 10 gallons of spray. Bordeaux mixture, on the other hand, may be combined with lead arsenate, oils, nicotine sulphate, soap, or lime-sulphur. Lead arsenate may also be combined with nicotine sulphate, or tobacco decoction.

Many spray materials do not adhere well to the foliage or fruit, especially when the surface is waxy. They also tend to form large drops, rather than a thin coating over the surface. Materials which help to overcome these tendencies are called spreaders and stickers. Soap is an excellent spreader for nicotine sprays, but cannot be used with all. Casein is also effective, and may be used in several forms, the most common being calcium caseinate. Fresh and dried skim milk are also satisfactory. Blood albumin is now commonly used. Resin is a good sticker. Flour, especially if it has a high gluten content, is very satisfactory, helping both spreading and sticking, and having no chemical reaction with the sprays.

Spraying Equipment

Efficient control of insects and diseases depends not only on the material used, but also on the way in which it is applied. Early in the history of spraying, a whisk broom was the device used, and dusting is still carried on by putting the dust in a cloth and shaking it over the plant. At the other extreme, spraying is sometimes done with pumps capable of throwing a stream of spray 60 feet high, and dusting from aeroplanes is no longer a novelty in some sections. There are numerous devices on the market, suitable for all types of spraying and dusting and all scales of operation. The householder with a few small plants to be protected will not need the same machinery as the grower with many acres of fruit trees.

Small hand sprayers, similar to those sold for killing household pests, may be useful if only a few small plants are to be sprayed, but are of no value in an orchard. Garden syringes are also of little use, as they fail to form a fine mist which is necessary for good spraying.

The essential features of an orchard sprayer are a container, preferably of brass or bronze, a pump, a hose and a nozzle which breaks the liquid up into very small drops. For ease of handling, the nozzle may be at the end of a short or long rod. For spraying small trees, a nozzle attached to the end of a hose may be satisfactory, but for larger trees it is necessary to have the nozzle on the end of a rod, for better control. Bamboo rods, 10 to 15 feet long, enable the operators to bring the nozzles fairly close to the surface to be sprayed. Very short rods, with adjustable nozzles, are known as spray guns. They are lighter to carry, and make rapid work possible, but with them uniform covering of the tree is more difficult. The simplest type of sprayer is the bucket type, in which the pump is set in the bucket containing the spray. The bucket is moved about to enable the operator to reach all parts of the tree. Ordinarily two men are required, one to pump and the other to spray. This type is satisfactory for small trees where spraying is only an occasional feature.

Compressed air sprayers are somewhat more complicated, and more expensive, but they are also more convenient. They can be operated by one man, who first pumps air into the air chamber and then operates the spray until the pressure becomes too low for good spraying. They are ordinarily left on the ground but some models can be slung on the back of the operator, thus increasing his mobility. Other so-called knapsack sprayers have pumps which are worked with one hand while the operator directs the spray with the other. This is hard work. It has the advantage of maintaining an even pressure.

For more extensive operations, or for spraying large trees, more powerful machines are desirable. Strong pumps attached to barrels which are mounted on wheels or on drags provide higher pressure, and make it possible to spray more trees without stopping to refill.

Power spray pumps are commonly used in countries where fruit is grown on a large scale. Some of the common fruits, such as the apple, are subject to attack from many insects and diseases. The market demands fruit which is practically free from blemish. It is therefore necessary to spray the trees several times a year. Excellent spraying outfits are now manufactured. Ordinarily a tank holding 200 to 500 gallons, a sturdy pump, and a petrol or kerosene engine are mounted on four wheels. The outfit may be pulled by animals or by a tractor. Some are mounted on motor lorries. The pump should be capable of maintaining a pressure of at least 200 pounds. Much spraying is done with a pressure of 250 pounds, and some machines will develop several times that much. From one to four hoses may be attached to each pump. Sodhi and Batra (1950) describe the successful spraying of mango trees 50 ft. tall with a bullock-drawn sprayer with a 300-gal. tank and 12-h.p. engine, delivering 20 gallons per minute at 600 to 700 lb. pressure. Many modern power sprayers have a number of nozzles attached to one or two vertical booms, so that as the sprayer proceeds down a row one-half of each tree on one side or both sides is thoroughly sprayed. These allow very rapid spraying with a minimum of human labour.

In very large orchards where much spraying is done, stationary pumps are sometimes installed. Pipe lines lead from these to all parts of the orchard, to which hoses may be attached.

In addition to the use of the right spray material, and satisfactory equipment, there are several factors involved in successful spraying. One of the most important is timeliness. Spraying which one week would give excellent control, may be almost useless the next. Thoroughness is also of great importance. If any part of the tree is missed, the insect or disease is likely to spread rapidly over the whole tree. This is especially true of the use of the older contact insecticides. By well planned, careful work, it is possible to cover the tree thoroughly without an undue waste of material. Careless work may use much more spray without securing satisfactory control.

Just as there are various types of spraying machinery, there are different types of dusters. Hand dusters of two types are commonly used. For dusting small plants at some distance from each other, the bellows type is best, as no material is wasted in going from plant to plant. For most fruit trees, however, it is much better to use a fan-type duster. In this type, by turning a crank slowly with one hand, a continuous current of dust is discharged. The outlet pipe is directed with the other hand.

For larger trees, or for covering large acreages, power dusters are desirable. With one of these, as much as 50 acres can be covered in one day. This makes it possible to time the dusting very accurately.

Larger Parasites

A number of flowering plants are also parasitic, and some of these sometimes attack fruit trees. The most important are the mistletoes and dodder. Both are large groups, attacking many kinds of plant. The mistletoes attacking fruit trees have thick, succulent, light green leaves, pale flowers, and bright berries. The berries are attractive to the birds. The seeds are sticky and those not swallowed may adhere to the beak. In either case they are often carried to other trees. If deposited on a branch, they germinate and send their roots into the tree. They absorb the sap and are thus enabled to grow and spread.

The mistletoes have been placed in the genus *Loranthus*, with about 350 species, most of which are tropical, but the genus has been divided by Danser who puts the Indian species all in other genera. Thus the species listed by Sarma (1952) on citrus trees in Assam as *Loranthus longiflorus*, *L. involucratus*, *L. ampullaceus*, and *L. scurrula* become, according to Danser, *Dendropthoe falcata*, *Tolypanthus involucratus*, *Macrosolen cochinchinensis*, and *Scurrula parasitia*, respectively. According to Kumar (1944), about 55 species have been reported in India, Burma, and Ceylon, causing a very large amount of damage. One species, *L. longiflorus*, is reported (Anon. 1931) to attack 29 plants in Bombay, of which 13 are fruit trees. The mango is frequently seriously damaged.

Several species of dodder attack fruit trees. This plant, of the genus *Cuscuta*, has a long, slender, yellow stem which entwines itself tightly around the host, penetrating the bark at intervals with haustoria which absorb the sap. The seeds of dodder germinate in the ground, and the plants lose their connection with it after attaching themselves to some other plant. They are thus more likely to attach themselves to plants having branches near the soil.

Both types of parasites can be fairly easily prevented from establishing themselves in an orchard, but are difficult to eradicate when established. If not removed, they are likely to kill the branches to which they are attached. As they spread very rapidly, the infection soon becomes general. They can be killed by cutting them out. It is ordinarily best to remove the limb which is attacked, some distance below the point of attachment. Mehta and Gupta

(1951) report that *Cuscuta reflexa* can be killed by a single application of 1% Dicotox (a 2, 4-D ester preparation used as a weed killer) or of 2% Methoxone (sodium MCPA). These were tried on dodder on two hosts : *Ingia dulcis* was little damaged by Dicotox, but *Tecoma stans* showed some injury, especially from Methoxone. Even if the leaves and tender shoots are killed by the treatment, this may injure the plant less than the severe pruning which would otherwise be necessary. If occasional attacks are promptly combated, the damage done is small. It is highly desirable to treat or remove any other hosts in the neighbourhood, as these would otherwise serve as a source of seeds for fresh infestation.

A parasite resembling dodder but with greenish stems, *Cassytha filiformis*, is said by Ramakrishnan (1954) to infest orange trees and to be common in Cuddapah and neighbouring districts in South India.

Birds and animals are often serious pests in orchards. They constitute an especially serious problem in India where a majority of the people believe in the sanctity of all life, and therefore hesitate to kill even the harmful animals. Even when the orchardist is willing to kill these pests, it is often difficult to do so.

Some of the larger animals, such as deer and stray cattle, can be excluded by good fencing. In regions where wild pigs are common, an especially strong fence is required. The numbers may be reduced by hunting and killing them. Monkeys are frequently a serious problem because they can climb over most types of fence, and because in some places there is a strong feeling against shooting them. They waste more fruit than they eat, and break down the trees. Because they are such a serious pest of other crops also and steal and damage other forms of property, the governments of some States have taken steps to have them killed. Fruit growers can well cooperate in this attempt to protect the food resources of the country. Porcupines are sometimes bothersome in nurseries, and they are likely to cut down young papaya trees. They are difficult to exclude from the orchard, but may be shot or sometimes clubbed to death. If their holes can be found, they can be fumigated in the same way that rat holes are treated.

Rats are a common pest of farm crops, and sometimes damage fruit trees by eating the roots. They may be poisoned with strychnine or some other poison. The best method is to impregnate grain with the poison and drop it in the holes. Care must be taken, as the poison is dangerous to other animals and to man. Probably a more satisfactory method is to fumigate the holes. There are pumps on the market by which smoke can be forced into the holes. The exhaust from tractor or motor car may also be used. Most effective of all is the pumping of a cyanide dust into the holes, which when it comes in contact with the moist earth liberates a gas which quickly kills any animal which may be in the hole. Snakes are often killed in this way. Dust and special pumps for the purpose are sold, and while the initial expense is fairly high, the cost per rat is not much.

Squirrels occasionally eat the fruit on the trees, but are seldom serious pests. They are difficult to shoot, but may be poisoned if the damage warrants the trouble. As the poison must be exposed, it is necessary to exclude domesticated animals from the area treated.

Birds, especially parrakeets, do tremendous damage, eating the ripe and half-ripe fruit. Protective measures are limited to devices to scare them away. The most common is the use of watchmen who cry out from time to time, and whenever they see birds alighting. Boards are often suspended in the trees in such a way that by pulling a rope the watchman may cause a clatter in various parts of the orchard. Guns may be fired with the dual purpose of killing a few birds and frightening many. All of these devices are of limited value. In spite of them much of the fruit is damaged. This is one of the main reasons that much fruit is harvested before it is of good quality.

Fruit-eating bats are also common, and are even more difficult to control, as they visit the orchard at night. The common device of stringing a coarse net across the probable course of their flight is of questionable value. The theory is that they become entangled in the net and are thus frightened away. Better methods of protecting fruit from birds and bats are badly needed.

CHAPTER XI

FRUIT PRODUCTS

Most fruits are ripe at certain seasons of the year only. For a short time they are likely to be comparatively cheap and plentiful in the market, but at other times they are expensive if available at all. By means of cold storage, or by importing from other districts, the season may be lengthened, but this is expensive. Cold storage is available in very few Indian markets, and is justified only where there is large population capable of paying somewhat higher prices for out-of-season fruit. This situation is not satisfactory to the consumer, and it is very unsatisfactory to the producer, who has to sell the major part of his crop when it is plentiful and the price is low. In years when the crop is large, the price may fall below the cost of production.

The preservation of fruits partially solves this problem. It takes part of the crop out of the fresh fruit market and thus helps to prevent 'gluts' and very low prices. It also provides a supply of fruit throughout the year. While the preserved fruit differs from the fresh, it is frequently a very palatable product and has many of the dietary values of fresh fruit.

Much the same reasons exist for the preservation of vegetables, although in most parts of India some vegetables are available at all seasons. Many of the same methods of preservation are used, so in this chapter much that is said will be applicable to both fruits and vegetables. It is frequently economical to use the same equipment for both, specially in factories, for it is rarely possible to keep a factory operating throughout the year on fruits, or on vegetables, alone. Other foods, such as fish are preserved in similar ways, but it is seldom feasible to use the same equipment.

While fruit and vegetable preservation has been developed on large scale in some countries, and to a certain extent in India also, more modest operations are also practicable. Certain forms of preservation are suitable as cottage industries, and almost all types may be used by the economical housewife in feeding her own family. Considerable knowledge and skill are required in some forms, but others are very simple. Various types of preservation were studied at Lyallpur, Punjab, before partition, and a fairly detailed report has been published by Lal Singh and others (1951). More recently experimental work has been carried on at the Central Food Technological Research Institute in Mysore. Siddappa (1949) presents a detailed estimate of the equipment desirable for a small fruit preservation unit, with a total cost of Rs. 1,692, but a beginning can be made with less equipment. He also gives the cost of manufacturing a number of products.

India has greatly decreased her imports of fruit products in recent years, partly because of import restrictions and partly because of increased production within the country. The average annual imports for the years 1952-53 to 1954-55 were jam, jelly, and marmalade valued at Rs. 5,46,673; pickles, chutney, sauces, and condiments, Rs. 3,70,440; and canned and bottled fruit, Rs. 2,10,119. This totals Rs. 11,26,232, compared with Rs. 24,60,991 for the same items on the average for the years 1935-36 to 1939-40. Even within the last three years there has been a distinct fall in amounts. But even these smaller figures indicate that there is still room for developing the preserving industry in India. Many of the imported products could be produced at least as well in India and if suitable Indian products were available, the public would doubtless consume less of those products which have to be imported.

The basic difficulty in developing the fruit products industry in India is the lack of large quantities of fruit over a considerable period, at a reasonable price. As long as fruit growing is on a small scale and is scattered, it will be difficult to get enough suitable fruit in one place to keep a plant of a good economic size operating for a long season. If fruits are efficiently grown and the grower makes only a reasonable profit, they can be supplied to the factory at a price which allows it a profit when it sells its produce at a reasonable price. In some countries factories can buy fruit at below the cost of production, because converting part of the crop into products maintains the price of fresh fruit at a profitable level. As long as the price of fruit in India is comparatively high, the factories are likely to succeed only if given the benefit of a protective tariff or some other trade barrier. Other difficulties at present are the high price of containers, the high price of sugar, and the reputation of Indian produce. Because some manufacturers have been willing to use fruit of poor quality, have not used the best methods of preparation, and have not maintained a high standard of sanitation, the reputation of Indian products has suffered in comparison with imported goods.

Another opportunity for advance is in the development of new products. Shunmukhasundaram and Naidu (1941) report promising experimental work on mango 'leather', candied jackfruit, jackfruit syrup, custard-apple jam, butter and chutney, and a powder made from dried wild figs (*Ficus glomerata*) and eaten with milk and sugar, in addition to some of the more usual products. Another satisfactory product of this wild fig has been developed in Mysore. The fruits are collected as they fall, dipped for 3-5 minutes in boiling water containing half an ounce of salt and 1 oz. of lime per gallon, washed in cold water, sulphured, dried first in the sun and then in the shade, and packed in air-tight containers. Work in Kodur, Andhra, indicates that jelly can be made from the same species, or that the juice can be mixed with that of other fruits to improve the physical nature of the jelly. There are doubtless other Indian fruits from which, with a little ingenuity, pleasing products could be made.

If the skin of a fruit remains intact, it will remain edible for some days, but ripening soon proceeds to the stage where the fruit is said to be over-ripe and not fit for consumption. It is by delaying the ripening process that cold storage enables fruit to be kept for some months. But frequently decay enters through some bruise or break in the skin, and the fruit soon spoils. Cooked fruits and vegetables also soon decay or ferment. If the food is to be kept long, this spoiling must be prevented. Intelligent preservation requires an understanding of the causes of spoilage.

Spoilage is caused by the growth of microscopic organisms, including moulds, yeasts, and bacteria. The most common moulds are those belonging to the genera *Penicillium* and *Aspergillus*. *Penicillium expansum* (*glaucum*) is the very common green mould, which often attacks both fresh fruits and fruit products, causing an objectional flavour even in the early stages. About as common is the black mould, *Aspergillus niger*. The bread moulds, *Mucor*, are used to change starch into sugar, but are not important as causes of spoilage. The yeasts are also useful in the manufacture of alcohol and vinegar, but they cause undesired fermentation when present in fruit juices. Alcohol is produced from rice and other grains by a combination of a mould, such as *Mucor* and a yeast, the starch being changed to sugar and then alcohol. Among the bacteria causing spoilage are the lactic acid bacteria and *Claustridium botulinum* (*Bacillus botulinus*) as well as others of less importance. They occur in vegetable products. In most forms of spoilage the product is made unpalatable, but not dangerous, but *Claustridium botulinum* produces a very virulent poison which has been responsible for the death of many persons. The vinegar bacteria are useful, normally developing after alcoholic fermentation has taken place, and converting the alcohol into vinegar.

If infection with any of these organisms could be totally avoided, nothing more would be necessary except the stopping of metabolism and the exclusion of air, to prevent oxidation. But the organisms or their spores are practically universally present, and while their numbers can be, and should be, reduced by cleanliness and sanitation, it is not possible to avoid all infection. Preservation depends on the killing of the organisms present and the exclusion of all others or, the provision of conditions under which the organisms cannot develop. Killing is generally accomplished by heat, though certain antiseptics are sometime used. Other antiseptics, such as sugar, salt, and vinegar, do not ordinarily kill the organisms, but prevent their development. Sugar is not a true antiseptic, but acts by osmosis. No organism can grow in a substance the dissolved solids of which are sufficiently concentrated that osmosis through the cell wall of the organism tends to remove moisture from it. Salt acts both by osmosis and as a poison, while vinegar acts only as a poison. A product must contain about 65% of sugar to be preserved, while 15% of salt or 1% of acetic acid is ordinarily effective. These substances are not harmful to human beings. Benzoic and sulphurous acids are also harmless in small amounts and are effective at about 0.2%. Other chemicals are sometimes used, but are harmful in amounts large enough to be effective. Drying or freezing also prevents the development of the organisms.

Several types of preservation are used. The simplest and cheapest method is drying, and it has the advantage that the product is easily shipped as it is light and can be roughly handled without damage. But the product is generally considered inferior to that which has been preserved in other ways. Quick freezing yields a product practically like the fresh fruit or vegetable, but requires rather expensive equipment, and shipping and storing under refrigeration. Fellers (1936) points out that the type of preservation affects the vitamin content. During ordinary storage there is little loss of vitamins D, F, and G, a slight loss of A and B, and a serious loss of C, especially in vegetables. Sun-drying is destructive to A and C, but dehydration is less so. Fermentation also destroys C. Heat is not injurious to any of the vitamins, but oxidation, which takes place in ordinary cooking, is decidedly injurious to B and C. B, C, and G are dissolved in the cooking water, and may thus be lost. Dhopeshwarkar and Magar (1954) report that in canning mangoes there was more loss of ascorbic acid than of other vitamins, but that 77.8% was retained in canned slices and 50% in pulp. They report little loss in canning pineapple, but more in unblanched papaya than in mango, perhaps because of the action of an enzyme. In the guava about 68% of the ascorbic acid and practically all of the riboflavin were retained.

Canning

The most important form of preservation is that known as canning, using this term to denote preservation either in tin cans or in glass jars or bottles. It depends on the complete sterilization of the product by heat, and the exclusion of other organisms. The temperature neoessary varies with the nature of the substances, particularly with the acidity. Most fruits are sufficiently acid to be sterilized by boiling, even if spore-forming bacteria are present. Fruit juices are generally pasteurized at temperatures of 120 to 150 F., which probably kills all organisms. Tomatoes are also easily sterilized becasuse of their acid content. Most vegetables are slightly alkaline and are therefore much more difficult to sterilize, unless lemon juice or vinegar be added. Even holding vegetables at the boiling point for five hours does not make them safe, and as *C. botulinum* forms spores and is not certain to be killed by this treatment, non-acid vegetables should not be canned in this way. It is much safer to sterilize the vegetables for one hour on each of three successive days, but even this does not eliminate all danger. It is not recommended that vegetables be canned unless there are facilities for cooking them at higher temperatures. At a temperature of 250°F. complete sterilization is rapid. This temperature may be secured in a pressure cooker at about 15 pounds pressure.

The so-called tin can is made of tinplate, which is only about 2% tin, the base being a high quality steel, low in carbon. In the early history of the canning industry, the cans were made with holes in the top through which they were filled. A cover was then soldered in place, with a small vent-hole in the middle which was closed with a drop of solder after the air was removed by heating for a few minutes. This type of can is still sometimes used in this country. As it can be made by hand, it is often available where other types are not. This tin has been largely replaced by the 'sanitary' can, which is almost exclusively used in canning factories, and which is also used in home canning. The lid of the sanitary can is sealed on by a double seaming process, after the can is full, the seal being made perfect by a gasket of thin cardboard or a thin film of rubber.

The sealing must be done by means of a machine. There are small models available for home use, as well as large automatic machines for factories. A special device reflanges the top of a can after on lid has been cut off, making it possible to use the same tin more than once.

Glass containers have long been used, and although the initial cost is comparatively high, the fact that they can be used repeatedly makes them economical for home canning. Several methods of sealing the jars are used. A zinc cap with a porcelain lining which screws on to the jar was formerly popular, but has been largely replaced by a thin metal lid with a sealing compound applied to the lower side near the circumference. This is at first held in place with a ring which screws on, but after the contents have cooled there is enough vacuum inside so that air pressure holds the lid on. A new lid is used each time the jar is filled. Similarly, glass lids may be used which are held on with a clamp until cool. As in the case of the zinc cap, a new rubber washer is used each time the jar is used. Only jars which have been especially made for the purpose should be used. Glass jars are used in factories only for produce of very high quality for a trade willing to pay the higher cost.

Almost all kinds of fruits have been canned, but some are much more suitable than others. Within one species, some varieties are better than others. In some cases a variety may be satisfactory for home canning, but because the sections tend to break up during cooking and so look less attractive, cannot well be canned commercially. Lal and Jain (1947 A) report that trials of 14 varieties of plum, 10 of peaches, 5 of apricots, and 3 of pears showed 9 plums, 2 peaches, 1 apricot and 1 pear to be good canners. It is important that fruits and vegetables for canning be in the proper condition. In the case of most fruits, this means that they should be mature, but still quite firm. No fruit which has begun to decay should be included. The fruit should be carefully handled to avoid bruising and unnecessary infection. It should be carefully washed to remove all dirt and as large a proportion of the organisms as possible. Some fruits should be peeled and in some cases the seeds are also removed. Very large fruits, like the mango, are cut into pieces of convenient size.

In factories the 'cold pack' method is almost exclusively used, and this is preferred by many for home use also, especially where it is desired to preserve the shape of the fruit. In many cases, however, it is satisfactory and simple to use an older method, with glass containers. The jars are sterilized in boiling water while the fruit is cooked in open kettles. When sufficiently cooked, it is poured into the hot jars, which are immediately sealed. They may or may not be further sterilized.

In canning by the cold pack method, the fruit is placed in the can and covered with boiling syrup. If a soldered can is used, the top is next put on. A few fruits, and most vegetables, should be 'blanched', or parboiled to improve the flavour and soften the fruit so that it is more easily packed in the can. The cans should be filled only to about half an inch from the top, to allow for expansion when being sterilized. The cans are next 'exhausted', that is, they are heated for a few minutes in boiling water to expand the air so that much of it is driven out. The cans are then sealed and sterilized, or 'processed'. The length of time required for sterilization depends on the nature of the products, and the size of the container. Mitra (1926) recommends the following periods in boiling water : Mango, orange, carambola, jujube, apple, and pear, 15 minutes; pineapple, guava, jambolan, litchi, rose-apple, and jackfruit, 20 minutes; bael, 25 minutes. A Bombay leaflet (Anon., 1928) indicates somewhat longer periods in the case of the mango (30 minutes), the pineapple and the guava (25 minutes each). Sayed (1924), describing the canning of mango slices and pulp, recommends processing for 13 to 20 minutes in boiling water.

When fruit is canned in glass jars by the cold pack method, the lids are put on lightly before sterilization, and tightened immediately afterward. Some fruits soften in cooking, leaving the jars only partially filled. In such cases it is desirable to cook the fruit at least partially before putting it into the jars.

While fruit can be canned without the addition of sugar, the quality of the product is ordinarily much better if sugar is added. Only in the case of cheap fruit for the restaurant trade is fruit canned commercially without sugar. The sugar is generally added as syrup, the percentage of sugar varying with the different fruits and the different qualities. The more acid fruits require more sugar. The best grades of canned fruits receive syrup of from 40 to 60% sugar, while the cheaper packs may have as low as 10% The syrup may be tested by means of a Balling or Brix hydrometer, or the percentage of sugar may be determined by adding it by weight. To make syrup of 10, 40 or 65%, add to one gallon of water 15 oz., 5 lb. and 10 oz., or 15 lb. and 11 oz., respectively. The syrup should be strained to remove impurities, and added hot.

Preserving with Sugar

Jam, jelly, marmalade, and preserves are all similar in that they contain a large proportion of sugar, and are commonly eaten with bread. They contain enough sugar that they do not spoil quickly when exposed to the air, and some will keep indefinitely, though they are ordinarily sealed in jars or tins, or at least covered with paraffin wax.

Of these, jam is the easiest to make, it being a mixture of the fruit pulp with sugar in which the shape of the fruit is not retained. It may contain skins and seeds. Ripe fruit is ordinarliy used, and this is washed, and generally peeled, except in the case of small fruits and berries. Large fruits may be cut in pieces to allow more rapid cooking. Large seeds are generally removed either before or after cooking. If the fruit is very juicy it is merely crushed and boiled in its own juice; otherwise enough water is added to prevent the fruit from burning. After the pulp is soft, sugar is added, and boiling is continued until the jam has a uniform texture of the desired density. The proportion of sugar to fruit varies, but it is common to use equal weights. Very sweet fruits require less sugar. In the United States, the law requires at least 45 pounds of fruit to 55 pounds of sugar. If boiling is continued until the concentration of sugar reaches 70%, the jam will keep indefinitely, but ordinarily this is not done. Commercially it is the custom to pasteurize the jam at 180° F. for 30 minutes after putting it in the containers.

It is often desirable to mix two or more fruits in order to blend the flavours, especially if one is especially sweet or sour. Cheaper fruits, and occasionally vegetables, are sometimes mixed with the more expensive ones, but this should be permitted in commercial jam only if the percentage of each ingredient is clearly stated on the label. The addition of pectin tends to give jam a jelly-like consistency, and makes it possible to use less fruit without having the jam too thin or syrupy. The quality of such jam is much below that in which sufficient fruit is used so that no pectin is needed.

Fruit butter is similar to jam, but is more highly concentrated and has a finer consistency. It is usually highly spiced, and may be made without the addition of sugar.

Many of the temperate fruits are suitable for jams and butters. The berries make especially good jams. Apples are commonly used for butter, as they do not have enough flavour to make a very good product without the addition of spices. Peaches, plums, and apricots are used in both ways.- Jam can be made from a number of the fruits grown on the plains of India, but none of these except the cape gooseberry is especially suitable. Guavas and jujubes are used for both jam and butter. The manufacture of jam on a small scale is carried on in a number of hill stations, where suitable fruits are available. Unfortunately, little attention is paid to quality or sanitation, with the result that the reputation enjoyed by the product is not good.

The term 'preserves' is often used in a broad sense to include any fruit preserved in sugar, but is also used specifically for fruit cooked in syrup until the concentration reaches 55 to 70%. It is desirable that the fruit keep its shape and be crisp. The fruit is prepared as for canning, and. cut into pieces of convenient size. It may then be boiled with syrup or sugar until the desired density is secured, and then put in cans or jars. If sealed while hot, sterilization is not necessary. A product of better flavour and colour may often be secured by boiling the fruit for a short time on successive days, adding sugar each time, until the syrup is sufficiently dense. Johar and Anand (1952) mention the possibility of spoilage, mainly by yeasts, in *aonla* preserves in which the syrup contains about 65% sugar, and recommend that it be prevented by adding 0·01% of sodium benzoate or sulphur dioxide. Indian "morabba" is essentially a preserve.

Fruit paste is made in much the same way as butter, but is dried in the sun or with artificial heat, until it becomes solid. Less sugar may be used and sometimes nuts are added. It is cut into bars, and used as a confection. "Guava cheese" is a paste of some importance in India.

The process of preparing candied or crystallized fruits is similar to that of making preserves, but is somewhat more complicated. More skill is necessary in order to turn out an attractive product. Whole small fruits, or pieces of larger ones, are slowly impregnated with sugar. Firm fruit should be used, either fresh or canned. Fresh fruit is sometimes placed in a solution of sulphurous acid, which tends to bleach the colour and harden the tissues. The acid also acts as a preservative in case the rest of the process is delayed. The syrup treatment varies greatly. Cruess recommends starting with a syrup of 30° Balling (30% sugar), made with two parts of cane sugar to one of glucose. The use of glucose prevents the product from becoming too hard, and makes it more translucent and attractive in appearance. The fruit is boiled until tender and placed in this syrup, and fruit and syrup are boiled for one or two minutes and set aside for 24 to 48 hours. If the fruit tends to float it should be held under the syrup. The syrup is then drained from the fruit and brought to 40° Balling by adding sugar and glucose in the same proportion. The fruit is brought to the boiling point in this syrup, and again set aside for a day or two. This process is repeated, increasing the concentration 10 degrees each day, until approximately 70°. It is said that a somewhat better product is secured by increasing the concentration only 5 degrees at a time, but this increases the expense considerably. Finally the fruit should be left in the concentrated syrup several days until the sugar has penetrated the fruit completely. The fruit should then be plump and tender. It should be washed in a wet cloth or sponge, or plunged momentarily into boiling water. It is then dried on a screen, at room temperature or at not more than 120° F.

Glaced fruit is prepared by dipping the dried candied fruit into a hot, very concentrated sugar solution for about one minute. This gives it a thin, transparent coating of sugar which improves the appearance and tends to keep the fruit moist. A similar result can be obtained by dipping the fruit in a 1% solution of pectin for one minute and drying it for 2 or 3 hours at 120° F.

Candied jujubes are highly regarded. They may be prepared by following the directions given above, except that either before or after the first boiling they are punctured all over, preferably with a wooden tooth-pick. The rind of citrus fruits, particularly the very thick rind of the citron, is candied, and is an important ingredient of fruit cakes. Lal and Jain (1948) give directions for candying orange and lemon peel, carrots and *petha,* stating the amount of sugar used per pound of the product, and the amount left in the syrup.

Fruit Jelly

When fruit juice is boiled with sugar to a certain concentration and allowed to become cool, it may become a soft solid of a springy consistency. This is known as a fruit jelly. More or less similar jellies may be prepared by adding gelatine or agar agar to fruit juice, but these are not true fruit jellies. Not all fruits are capable of being made into jelly with the addition of only water and sugar. In some the amount of acid present is insufficient, and a jelly can be made when lime juice or some other acid is added. In other cases the failure of the juice to form jelly is due to the lack of a substance called pectin. This is present in most fruits, in varying amounts, but in some is absent. In many cases the amount present is not sufficient for the formation of a good jelly. In the cell walls of green fruits there is a insoluble substance called pectose, which as the fruit ripens turns into soluble, colloidal substances, pectin. According to McCrady and Owens (1954), 'Pectin' (or 'pectins') designate those water-soluble pectinic acids of varying methyl ester content and degree of neutralization which are capable of forming gels with sugar and acid under suitable conditions. They discuss their physical and chemical properties. As the fruit becomes fully ripe, the pectin is converted into pectic acid and methyl alcohol.

The essential constituents of a fruit jelly are thus seen to be water, sugar, acid and pectin. Pectin is extracted from certain fruits, generally apples or citrus fruits, and may be bought as a powder or solution. About 3,000 tons of pectin are made each year from citrus peel in the United States, where it is estimated that 40,000 tons could be produced from the waste materials in citrus processing plants. Johar and Lewis (1955) state that good quality pectin may be recovered from tamarind pulp, which is the only material available in India throughout the year cheaply enough to make the process profitable. With such pectin an artificial jelly can be made, any desired flavour being added. Any acid may be used, but if the product is to be edible, a harmless acid is essential such as those commonly found in fruits. Kalyankar and others (1952) report the amounts of different acids in the sweet orange, lemon, lime, pummelo, carambola, *aonla* and jujube. Citric acid is the most common in these, and also most plentiful in the guava, but malic, oxalic, tartaric, and succinic acids are also reported. A jelly will form only if the ingredients are present in proper proportions, which may vary within narrow limits.

The chemistry of fruit jellies has been studied by a number of investigators, notably Tarr and others at the University of Delaware (1923 to 1929). They found that jellying depends not on the total acidity, but on the hydrogen ion content, which depends on the particular acids present and on the buffer action of the salts which are also present in fruit juice. The minimum concentration necessary was that indicated by pH 3.46, while a good household-jelly was formed at pH 3·3. For a stiffer jelly, such as is desired for commercial purposes, pH 3·2 is necessary. If the pH is much below 3·1, the jelly is subject to syneresis, or 'weeping', a seeping out of the liquid contents. Of the commonly present acids, tartaric is the most efficient, malic next, and citric least.

The best amount of sugar to add is a practical question of great importance, but no easily applied rule is available. Too little sugar results in a very stiff jelly, while too much results in a jelly which is very soft, or in a syrup which will not jelly. The work in Delaware showed that more sugar can be added when the hydrogen ion concentration is greater, and that the difference between the greatest and least amounts which would produce a jelly is also greater. It is thus more important to add exactly the right amount of sugar to a juice of pH 3·4 than to one of pH 3·2. Jellying seems to take place, however, when the sugar solution is approximately saturated, and the jelly ordinarily ranges from 69% to 72% in sugar content. The greater the active acidity of the juice, the more is the sugar which can be added, and the greater is the yield of jelly, when the amount and quality of the pectin are constant.

The jellying power of pectin depends on the viscosity of the pectin solution, which depends on both the quantity and the quality. Commercial pectins, and also those present in fruit juices, vary greatly. No general rule as to the amount of pectin which is necessary, can be given.

In making jelly, the fruit is washed and boiled until soft. Juicy fruits may be boiled without the addition of water, but hard fruits, such as guavas, require fairly large amounts of water. The length of time the fruit should be boiled also varies from two minutes to an hour. In home jelly-making the fruit, when soft, is placed in a cloth bag suspended over a vessel in which the juice is collected. Sometimes more juice is squeezed out after cooling. In factories presses are used in order to extract a large percentage of juice without undue delay. In the case of expensive fruits it may be desirable to add water and extract the juice several times.

In order to make a clear sparkling jelly, it is necessary that the juice be clear. If little pressure is used in extracting the juice, it is likely to be sufficiently clear. In factories it is frequently filtered or otherwise clarified.

The amount of sugar to be added depends on the nature of the juice, and it is highly desirable that the active acidity and pectin content be known before the sugar is added. The housewife usually judges acidity by taste, and with experience can get fairly satisfactory results. In the commercial manufacture of jelly, uniformity is of great importance, and more accurate control is desirable. Apparatus for measuring the hydrogen ion content is too expensive and difficult to operate for the small-scale jelly maker, but may well be used in larger factories.

The approximate amount and quality of the pectin contained in the juice may be determined by a simple test. One spoonful of juice is mixed with one spoonful of methylated spirits. If a jelly-like mass is formed, this indicates that the juice is rich in pectin. If the mixture remains a liquid, or only a small amount of the jelly forms, there is not enough pectin present to make a satisfactory jelly. With a little experience, one can judge sufficiently accurately the amount of pectin present.

If the juice is found to be deficient in acid or pectin, steps should be taken to correct this, before adding the sugar. A common method is to mix the juice with the juice of some fruit rich in the deficient element. Roselle juice, for instance, ordinarily contains both acid and pectin in abundance. A jelly of a very desirable flavour and appearance may frequently be secured by a judicious mixing of juices. If it is not desired to change the flavour, and the deficiency is not very great, the juice may be boiled until a satisfactory concentration is reached. When only acid is deficient, as is frequently the case with guavas, a good jelly can be secured by adding the juice of limes or lemons, although this adds to the flavour also. By using tartaric or citric acid, jelly can be made without the lime or lemon flavour.

If the juice is lacking in pectin, this can be added in liquid or powdered form although these products are not commonly available in the markets of India. The liquid form is easier to use, but more expensive. Pectin may be extracted from fruits rich in it, for home use. To extract pectin from the rind of citrus fruits, cut the albedo (the white portion) into small pieces. This can be done easily by putting it through a food chopper. Add eight tablespoons of lemon juice and eight cups of water per pound of albedo, and allow this to stand two or three hours. Then add as much water again and slowly bring it to a boil and boil it for 10 minutes, with the vessel covered. Then set it aside, and the next day boil it again for 15 minutes. When it is cool, strain it through a cloth. The pectin solution thus prepared may be used at once or sterilized and sealed for future use.

With a juice containing adequate pectin and acid, it is not difficult to make good jelly. The juice is brought to a boil, and if it is thought necessary to concentrate it, this should be done before the sugar is added. If the sugar is heated before it is added, the cooking process is delayed less, but this is not essential. If the juice is rich in pectin and acid, and equal weight of sugar may be added. More often about two parts of sugar to three of juice is all that should be added. The use of too much sugar is a common mistake. It is desirable that the constituents be in the right proportion, so that the juice will need to be boiled only a few minutes after the sugar is added.

Determining the 'end point', when boiling should cease, is one of the most delicate phases of jelly making. A test very commonly used is that of dipping a large spoon into the kettle and allowing the juice to run off the edge. When it has reached the jellying point, it will hang from the spoon in a sheet. The nature of the sheet will vary somewhat with different juices, and some experience is necessary before this test can be used with satisfaction. The use of a thermometer is of great help, especially if more than one batch of the same juice is to be cooked. In most cases jelly will form when the boiling point is about 220 or 221° F. In extreme cases the boiling point may be one or two degrees higher or lower. Once the correct boiling point for a lot of juice is determined, uniform results are secured from boiling all kettles to same end point. Specific gravity determinations are equally accurate, but are much more difficult to make. During boiling, the scum should be removed occasionally.

In the home, jelly is ordinarily put into glasses or wide-mouthed jars. When it has solidified, the top is covered with melted paraffin, which sterilizes the surface and tends to keep out all organisms. Frequently the paraffin cracks away from the glass enough to allow spores to enter, and a certain amount of spoilage takes place. The high concentration of sugar also helps to preserve the jelly. In factories jelly is sealed either in glass jars or in tins, which are pasteurized.

The acids in the fruit tend to react with iron or brass resulting in poor appearance and flavour. It is better to use aluminium vessels, which react very little with the fruit acids. In factories, so-called 'glass-lined' equipment is the best, this being steel onto the inner surface of which a thick layer of enamel is fused.

A number of the fruits grown on the plains of India are excellent for jelly. Guava jelly is world-famous, and may be made from the more sour types without the addition of acid, but with the guavas ordinarily grown in India, additional acid is desirable. B. N. Singh and Dutt (1941) recommend that the fruit be extracted with a 5% solution of tartaric acid, saying that this increases the pectin content to 1·04% as compared with 72% when extracted with water. The karanda makes one of the best jellies, and the roselle is also commonly used. Jellies can be made from the citrus fruits, the cape gooseberry, and, with added acid, the jujube and banana. The woodapple makes a stiff jelly, but the flavour is not very pleasing unless it is mixed with some other fruit. Singh and Dutt state that pectin can be extracted from its rind. They failed to make jelly out of the bael, although it is rich in pectin, because of the presence of a gummy principle.

Marmalade is a clear jelly in which are suspended slices of fruit. It is ordinarily made of oranges, but sometimes other citrus fruits, and occasionally other fruits are used. Some types of jam are often, but mistakenly, called marmalades. The English type of marmalade is made from the sour or bitter orange which is also called the Seville orange from the region in Spain where it is principally grown. In America the preference is for marmalade made from sweet oranges. The *karna* makes a marmalade similar to that made from the sour orange.

In preparing marmalade from citrus fruits, the rinds of some of the fruits are removed, and cut into thin slices. These are boiled in water until they are tender. In the meantime the rest of the fruit is boiled with added water until tender, which usually takes about an hour. It is then strained as for making jelly, and to this juice is added the thinly sliced peel and sugar. The rest of the process is the same as in making jelly, except that the marmalade is allowed to cool partially before it is placed in the glasses or tins. Otherwise the pieces of rind are likely to float to the top.

In an alternative method, the rind and juice are not prepared separately, but the whole fruit is finely shredded or chopped before cooking. This produces a marmalade of excellent flavour, but it is not as clear as that made by the former method.

Other Products

The fresh juice of many kinds of fruit forms a delicious drink, but in few cases is it possible to preserve the juice without sacrificing much of the flavour. Fermentation can be prevented by pasteurizing the juice and sealing it, but heating gives a cooked flavour to many kinds, and others change flavour from standing. Grape and pineapple juices are among those which are very successfully bottled or canned. In the United States the use of canned juices has become very popular, the amount canned increasing from 15 million cases in 1934 to 128 million in 1946. The principal juices canned in that country include grapefruit, orange, pineapple, and tomato. In 1946 the citrus juices made up more than half of the total. According to the rules made under the Agricultural Produce (Grading and Marketing) Act of 1937, the product is defined as 'juice' when unsweetened, as 'cordial' when it contains the prescribed quantity of sugar, and as 'squash' when juice sacks have been included in cordial. Lime and lemon juice, cordial and squash must be free from added substances other than water, sugar, peel oil, harmless colouring matter, and not more than 350 parts per million by weight of sulphur dioxide. Juice must contain nothing else, and cordial and squash must contain at least 30% juice, and 15, 30, and 50% sugar, for the three grades which have been established. Similar rules apply to orange juice and squash, except that the squash must contain at least 35% juice and be free from added substances except water, sugar, citric acid (as a solid or as citrus juice) to bring the total acidity to not more than 2·5%, harmless colouring matter, and not more than 600 parts per million by weight of sodium benzoate.

As the food value of citrus juices depends largely on their content of ascorbic acid, it is highly desirable that as much as possible be retained in the preserved juice. Wahhab and Zamir-ud-din (1954), using up to 400 ppm of sulphur dioxide, found that the retention of ascorbic acid increased with the concentration. Benzoate of soda as a preservative resulted in the best flavour, but the least of the vitamin. Pasteurization resulted in poorer flavour than either of the preservatives. They recommend 400 to 450 ppm of sulphur dioxide (which would be illegal in India) plus a small amount of benzoate of soda. They found no effect on the retention of ascorbic acid from the addition of that acid or of citric acid, but reducing the head space in the bottle increased the retention of ascorbic acid.

Fruit syrups are generally made with sugar, but some of excellent quality are made by concentrating the natural juice. This can ordinarily be accomplished without spoiling the flavour, only by boiling in vacuum pans or by freezing. Both methods require expensive equipment. Fairly satisfactory syrups can be made by extracting the juice much as is done in making jelly, and adding this to a sugar syrup. In order to keep as much as possible of the flavour of the fresh fruit, the initial cooking should be the minimum necessary to soften the fruit. The juice should be allowed to settle, and only the clear juice decanted and used. The settling process can be greatly hastened by adding a small amount of alum or of skim milk. The clear juice is added to the syrup and this is brought to the boiling point and bottled hot; or it may be bottled and pasteurized. There is a considerable demand for fruit syrups, for use in making cool drinks, though most of the so-called fruit drinks which are sold are made with artificial flavours. These are not harmful to the health, but possess none of the special dietetic values of true fruit drinks.

Vinegar is a product in the manufacture of which cull fruits can be used, and it is also of importance in the preparation of pickles and other fruit and vegetable products. While occasionally made in the home, or as a very small-scale industry, high quality vinegar can only be manufactured with fairly elaborate equipment. When vinegar is made from fruit juice, the first step is alcoholic fermentation which is brought about by yeast. Later the alcohol is acted upon by certain bacteria and turned into acetic acid. Vinegar can also be made from starchy vegetables, such as the potato, the starch being first hydrolyzed into sugar. Dutta and Biswas (1942) suggest the use of such fruits as the guava, banana, pineapple, grape, orange, and jambolan, and give directions for making vinegar from these as well as from sugar-cane. The fruits may be over-ripe, and the juice should contain at least 15% sugar, in order to give an acetic acid content of 5 or 6%, which is the minimum for vinegar of good quality. Distilled or spirit vinegar is made from distilled alcohol, and is popular in the manufacture of pickles because of its uniformity and its neutral flavour.

Pickles of the western type are made principally by adding vinegar, with or without sugar and spices, to fruits and vegetables. In some cases, the raw product is allowed to ferment and thus form its own acetic acid. The keeping quality of the pickle depends not only on the vinegar, but also on the salt, sugar, and spices. It will not ordinarily keep indefinitely, and is therefore sealed in jars with additional vinegar, or packed in tins and sterilized.

Indian pickles are of great variety, the preservative being salt, sugar, vinegar, or mustard oil. Frequently two or more of these substances are combined. In making hot pickles, chillies are added, and various other spices are sometimes used. The mustard or other oil prevents decay by excluding oxygen. Lemon or lime juice is frequently added, both for flavour and to help in preservation.

Chutney is a distinctively Indian product, though it is now greatly appreciated in some other countries. The best-known type is mango chutney, but many other fruits and vegetables are used. There are many recipes, most of which contain fairly large quantities of sugar and salt. Chillies are commonly added, as well as many other spices. In many cases vinegar also helps to preserve the product. Crang and Sturdy (1947) state that mould spores develop on chutney only when the acidity is below 1%.

The simplest way of preserving fruits and vegetables is by drying them in the sun, and this is commonly used with, such fruits as grapes, figs, plums, peaches, and apricots in the West. Plums which can be dried without removing the seed, and without fermentation, are known as prunes, and form an important crop in Europe and America. In India, many fruits and vegetables are dried, mostly for home consumption. Ordinarily they are merely cut into suitable sections and placed in the sun until sufficiently dry so that decay does not set in. Unfortunately it is often difficult to protect them from flies and dust. In some countries where the sun is less dependable than in India, specially constructed drying ovens or evaporators are necessary. These make better sanitation possible. Dehydration made rapid progress during the second world war, both in the quantity of foods handled and the quality of the product. Conditions are very accurately controlled. Cruess (1943) points out that for vegetables, the initial temperatures should be high, up to about 300° F. in some cases, while they should be much lower, sometimes below 145°, towards the end of the process. The moisture is reduced to below 5% in most cases. The use of evaporators in India, especially for vegetables, was stimulated by the war. L. Singh and Lal (1941) give a plan for a small evaporator using a charcoal burner, and give instructions for drying vegetables. Khan (1941) describes the drying of peaches, plums, and pears, as done at the Tarnab farm in West Pakistan. In few cases is dried fruit of as high quality as that which is canned, but it is much cheaper.

One of the most common forms of dried fruit in this country is that known by such names as *amsat* and *amras*. It is prepared from the juicy varieties of mangoes. The juicy pulp is squeezed from the stone onto clean plates, mats, or boards in a thin layer, and allowed to dry in the sun. More pulp is added each day for about a week, and when the last layer is dry, the whole sheet is rolled up, cut into smaller rolls, and stored. This product is very popular and it is desirable that a more sanitary method of preparation be worked out. If this is done, the commercial manufacture of *amras* may prove profitable. Another common and very useful household product is made by drying strips of the pulp of green mangoes.

When fruits or vegetables are frozen in nature, or the temperature in cold storage becomes too low, the cell structure is damaged and the material frequently becomes useless. Some foods, however, can be frozen very quickly, kept frozen for long periods, and when thawed have much the appearance and flavour of the fresh product, and may be eaten raw or cooked. This method has become very common in the United States in recent years, but there are still many problems to be solved. Some varieties have been found much more suitable than others. Some have a tendency to turn brown and to develop undesirable flavour on thawing. Fruits are washed, sometimes sliced, and may have sugar added. The addition of about 200 mg. of ascorbic acid per pound of fruit may help prevent browning. The food is placed in a convenient container and frozen in a chamber where the temperature is not above zero, Fahrenheit, and may be as much as 40° below. After freezing, it may be stored at as much as 10° above zero, but better results are secured by storing at about zero. This method is used in three ways in the United States. Large commercial firms freeze fruits and vegetables and ship them under refrigeration to all parts of the country, where they are sold in small refrigerated cases in shops. There are also a large number of co-operative societies, especially in rural areas and small towns which have small freezing units, and refrigerated lockers for each member. The member brings his produce, has it frozen, and puts it in his own locker from which he can take all or part of it at any time. An increasing number of individuals, especially those living far from any town, have their own freezers. Meat, fish, and other food can be frozen and stored in the same units. Many modern refrigerators contain small freezing compartments.

While a number of fruits grown in India, including the mango, guava, papaya, litchi, and jackfruit, have been found suitable for freezing, very little work has been done in this country. The method could probably be used commercially only in the larger cities or institutions where large numbers of people are fed. Rao and others (1952) report that fruits of the mango, cashew, *aonla*, lemon, and orange, frozen and held at—20° F. for 48 hours, yielded 12-20·8% more juice with a corresponding increase in ascorbic acid, than the fresh fruit. Smaller increases were secured by holding oranges at 20° F. and in a household refrigerator.

Frozen citrus juice concentrates became extremely popular in the United States as soon as they were introduced. Any heating of citrus juice damages the flavour, mainly through the loss of volatile substances. It was found that these are present in the fresh juice in greater quantity than is needed, and that by concentrating the juice under vacuum to 60° Balling and then adding one part of fresh juice to two parts of the concentrate, a mixture is secured of desirable flavour. This can be placed in tins and frozen. When diluted to the concentration of fresh juice, the flavour is very similar to that of fresh juice. Other juices may be prepared in a similar manner, and some encouraging results have been secured in partially dehydrating fruit and then freezing it.

CHAPTER XII

THE HISTORY AND LITERATURE OF POMOLOGY

At the dawn of written history, fruit was already being grown, but probably most of the fruit eaten was wild. The story of Adam and Eve living in a garden, where they had only to pluck the fruit, and later being forced to toil for their food, reflects the history of the race. Even men began to plant crops, in order to supplement the wild seeds, roots, and fruits they would naturally choose the annuals, and only at a later stage, with the development of more permanent abodes, would trees find a place in primitive agriculture. But very little is definitely known about the very early history of agriculture.

History begins in the development of the great centres of civilization, around the Mediterranean, in the Tigris-Euphrates valley, India, China, and tropical America. The concentration of population necessary for such advance is possible only where agriculture has been developed. This connection is brought out by Casson (1939) in writing of the region which is now Iraq at about 3500 B.C. 'There is no doubt at all', he says, 'that the city, in the sense in which we know it, was entirely a Sumerian conception. And in that city we find everywhere the remembrances of the great invention of agriculture that gave it birth. The royal graves of Ur reflect this. Ears of grain, of wheat and barley, pomegranates—one of the world's earliest cultivated fruits—and domesticated animals appear represented in the gold jewels and ornaments of the Sumerian kings. . .Bulls and cows rapidly achieved a semi-mystic veneration. For the Sumerians remembered their origins, just as we remember our recent scientific past.' Even older than the pomegranate, and perhaps the oldest of all cultivated fruits, is the date. A religious cult of the date is mentioned in records from this same region from about 7000 B.C., and spread throughout the Mediterranean world. The date achieved importance in Egypt in the third millennium B. C.

Although there is also reference to the peach and almond in an Egyptian manuscript of about 1300 B.C., the first extensive references to fruit in the Mediterranean region are in the writings of the Greeks and Romans. Homer (962-927 B.C.) refers in the Odyssey to the apple, pear, pomegranate, fig and olive. Xenophon and Theophrastus (called the "Father of Botany" by Linnaeus) made important contributions to horticultural literature in Greece in the fourth century before Christ. The Romans were great collectors, both of plants and of information, true and false. They brought in the fig, almond, peach, apricot, and other fruits from the outlying parts of their great empire, and collected many varieties of some of these. Cato (239-149 B.C.) and Varro (116-28 B.C.) wrote works on agriculture, the latter in his *Rerum Rusticarum* mentioning four ways of training grape vines, propagation by seed, cutting, grafting, and inarching (then a new method), the making of wine and olive oil, and the storing of fruit in brine oil, or salt,

Virgil took most of his agriculture from Varro. Collumella, who travelled extensively about 200 years after Cato, and left a very full account of the agriculture of southern Europe, reflects very little improvement in that period. The greatest contribution to our knowledge of Roman agriculture was made by Pliny (A. D. 23-79) whose classic Natural History is a review of more than 1,000 volumes.

Fruit played a prominent part in the life of the ancient Hebrews. References to the grape, the fig, and the olive abound in the Old Testament, including those parts written more than 1,000 years before the birth of Christ. The palm tree is mentioned, but the fruit is not, for it is only in the hottest parts of Palestine that edible dates will mature. Some indication of the importance attached to fruit is the specific prohibition of the destruction of fruit trees by besieging armies, in Deuteronomy, probably written in the seventh century B. C.

The Chinese have been among the world's best gardeners for many centuries and have developed a number of excellent fruits, including the litchi, the persimmon, and several citrus fruits. Horticulture has been a favourite subject for their poets and other writers, some of them writing more than 4,000 years ago. A treatise on the litchi written in A. D. 1056 is said to be the first book in the world dealing only with fruit growing. The attitude of the Chinese is reflected in the remark of the Emperor Kan-hi (1662-1722), quoted by Laufer (1919): I would procure for my subjects a novel kind of fruit or grain, rather than build a hundred porcelain kilns.'

Civilization in tropical America developed much later than in Europe and Asia, and seems to have been based on a less advanced agriculture. However, this region has produced a number of valuable fruits, including the avocado, guava, papaya, and custard-apples. Some of these had reached a stage of development before the arrival of the Europeans which indicates a fairly high type of horticulture. Unfortunately,. these civilizations have left little in the way of legible written records.

It is in India that our interest chiefly lies, and fortunately a great wealth of material is available. But the task of uncovering information about fruit, especially in the Sanskrit writings, is a difficult and complicated one. The very quantity of such literature makes it an immense problem to search out all of the references to fruit and to horticultural practices. It is frequently difficult to ascertain within several centuries the time when a book was written. As in other early writings, legend, superstition, error, and facts are recorded with perfect impartiality. To identify the crops mentioned is generally difficult, and frequently impossible. When it is remembered that the *sitaphal* even today may be either a pumpkin or a custard-apple, and that Watt (1908) says of the sour lime, 'This is the lemon of most popular writers', it is not surprising that many translators have been led astray. At least until much more study has been devoted to this field, many conclusions will have to be tentative.

Early Indian Records

In Sanskrit literature written before the Christian era, there seems to be little mention of fruit The Arthashastra, believed to have been written in the fourth century B. C., refers to land suitable for grapes. It is impossible to date the Brahatsamhita very definitely, but it comes from the period 1200 to 200 B. C. According to Gangopadhyay (1932), it states that the jackfruit, plantain, and other fruits were propagated by cuttings, smeared with cow dung, but that grafting was better, using roots or stems as stock. These methods are obviously wrong as far as the plantain is concerned, and probably for the jackfruit also, but the statement is of importance as an indication that methods of vegetative propagation were used at this early period. Other fruits mentioned are the tamarind, woodapple or elephant-apple, and the *aonla*.

Two early Sanskrit medical works of great importance, the Charaka Samhita and the Sushruta Samhita, mention large numbers of medicinal plants, including some fruits. There is some doubt as to when they were written. Lal (1907, 1911, 1914) claims that the Sushruta Samhita was written at least two centuries before the birth of Buddha, which occurred about 480 B. C., and that the final recension, which is the one now existing, was made by Nagarjuna about the 2nd century B.C. On the other hand, Tolkowsky (1930) seems to be correct in stating that the book was probably written in the 4th century A.D. Chandra considers Charaka earlier than Sushruta, and as Tolkowsky suggests, that he wrote about A. D. 100.

Among the fruits mentioned in these works are the *aonla*, bael, bullock's heart, citron, wild date, wild fig (*Ficus glomerata*), grape, hog plum, jackfruit, jambolan, two species of jujube, karanda, *khirni*, lemon, lime, mango, monkey jack, mulberry, sweet and sour oranges, *paniala*, phalsa, plantain, pomegranate, and woodapple, and the walnut, almond, pistachio, *chiraunji*, and coconut. The difficulty of identifying the plants named is illustrated by the fact that Chandra seems uncertain whether one term means the woodapple, karanda, carambola, or *Citrus medica*. It is therefore, perhaps, not unduly cynical to question the inclusion of the bullock's heart in this list, as it belongs to a genus generally believed to have originated in tropical America, and as the much more common and valuable custard-apple is not included. The identification of some of the citrus fruits is also questionable.

In later Sanskrit books, particularly the Puranas, many fruits are mentioned, but as these were written during this era and some as late as the 14th century, their significance is doubtful. They would, however, probably be limited to fruits indigenous to Asia and Europe. The Matsya Purana, in addition to many of the fruits given above, names the fig, rose-apple, and breadfruit. The inclusion of the last, which is grown only to a slight extent in southern India, and not the much more common jackfruit, suggests a possible error in translation. It is not clear whether the fig is of the cultivated type or one of the wild species. The Krshi Parasara, said to be not earlier than the 6th century, mentions the litchi, in addition to the mango, plantain and coconut. The Sukra Niti, written in the 16th century, mentions, in addition to other fruits, two types of dates, one of which may be the cultivated species.

Varma (1947, 1949) refers to Sanskrit manuscript by an unknown author, entitled Vriksha Ropan Vidhi, and chapter 505 of Variksh Ayurveda, compiled or composed by Barma Sanghita Charya in A. D. 1392. These deal with the importance of fruit culture, propagation, and some aspects of culture. Graftage was known, but was apparently thought to produce hybrids. The difficulties of translation are again illustrated by Varma's use of the word 'lime' for '*jambhir*', although the latter is said to be four times the size of the sour lime.

Before the later of these Sanskrit works, independent testimony had been introduced by Yuan Chwang (Hiuen Tsiang or Huan Tsan) (Beal, 1884 : Walters, 1904), a Chinese Buddhist pilgrim who was in India from A. D. 629 to 645. His interest was primarily religious, and some of his observations untrustworthy, but his list of fruits confirms the presence in India of the mango, tamarind, jujube (but not the species with which he was familiar in China), woodapple, *aonla*, *Ficus glomerata*, plantain, coconut, and jackfruit, and adds a species of *Diospyros*, again not the *D. kaki* of China. He also calls attention to the absence of the loquat. He adds that pomegranates and sweet oranges were grown everywhere. Pears, plums, peaches, apricots, and grapes he found here and there, 'from Kashmir on', but it is not clear whether he meant toward China or toward India. In another place he states that at the time of the Indo-Scythian King, Kaniska (in the first century A.D.), Chinese hostages who resided during the winter in the eastern Punjab planted peach and pear trees, and at the time he wrote the peach was called 'cinani' and the pear, 'cinarajputra'.

The next contribution to the history of pomology in India is that of the Emperor Baber, and no greater contribution has been made. Not only does he give a very inclusive list of fruits in his Memoirs, (Leyden and Erskin, 1826) but the accuracy of his descriptions is remarkable, and he writes with zest which reflects the personality of a great man. His comments on the mango certainly justify quotation at some length : "Such mangoes as are good are excellent. Many are eaten, but few are good of their kind. They pluck most of them unripe and ripen them in the house. While unripe, the mango makes excellent tarts and extremely good marmalade. In short, this is the best fruit of Hindustan. The tree bears a great weight of fruit. Many praise the mango so highly as to give it preference to every kind of fruit, the muskmelon excepted, but it does not appear to me to justify their praise." He mentions two types, those eaten and those sucked, and praises particularly the mangoes of Bengal and Gujarat. It is interesting to notice that Baber, like most adults, remembers as the best of all fruits those he knew in childhood. It does not enter his head that anyone would prefer the mango to the melons of Samarkand. Again, he speaks of the pomegranates in the Baghe-Vafa in Afghanistan as excellent but 'not equal to the fine ones of our country'.

'The plantain has two good qualities,' says Baber, 'the one is that it is easily peeled—the other that it has no stones and is not stringy.' 'They say that the date alone, of all the vegetable kingdom, resembles the animal kingdom in two respects', that it dies when its head is cut off, and that it bears fruit only when male and female palms are both present. The tapping of the trees for juice is described. When the Emperor found a fruit he did not like, he was free to say so. Of the amleh' (*aonla*) he says, 'When made into marmalade it is not bad, and is very wholesome'; while of the *jaman* he is more critical, 'Its fruit resembles the black grape, but has a more acid taste and is not very good'. But of the jackfruit he could say nothing good; he liked neither the flavour nor the appearance which he thought was like 'a sheep's stomach made into a haggis.'

Babar is the first writer to mention a number of the citrus fruits, and about some of these he gives helpful information. Here, however, it is very difficult to know just what fruits are meant. The fruit which he calls 'taranj' 'though the people of India called it 'bajauri', while in Bajaur it was called 'baleng', is probably the citron, especially the type of which he said that it was sickly sweet and the peel was used for marmalade. But when he speaks of another type, with fruit a deeper yellow than the orange, rind extremely thin and knobbed, juice sour and used for sherbet, and leaves smaller than those of the orange, it seems that he must have had some other species in mind. The translators use Seville orange for his 'naranj, narak, or narangi', said to grow in Afghanistan. They also speak of limes the size and shape of hen's eggs, boiled and eaten as an antidote for poison. The 'sengtereh' seems to be the common santara, and is said to make an extremely agreeable and wholesome sherbet. The 'jambiri' with pleasant acid juice is probably the rough lemon, but when this is said to be shaped like an orange, but a deeper yellow, some doubt arises. Other citrus fruits are the 'kilkil' (probably *galgal*), 'sadaphal', a sweet fruit shaped like a pear and the colour of a quince, the 'amratphal', the 'kirneh' (perhaps the *karna or khatta nimbu*), and the 'amilbid' of which he says, 'They say that if a needle be thrust into the heart of it, it melts away.'

The first mention of fruits indigenous to the western hemisphere, seems to occur in the Ain-i-Akbari written about 1590, some seventy years after Babar's Memoirs, and just about 100 years after the discovery of America by Columbus. The only new fruits appearing in this work are the pineapple and the custard-apple, both from tropical America, unless some of the terms which the translator does not venture to put into English also represent new species. A few years later, another Moghal writer (Rogers, 1909, 1914) adds another American fruit, the guava, and includes some temperate fruits not previously mentioned in India proper, sweet and sour cherries, the currant, and the quince.

European Visitors

By this time the first European travellers were visiting India, and beginning the stream of travel books which have added much to our knowledge of the development of fruit-growing in the last 500 years. The great pioneer, Marco Polo, visited southern India late in the 13th century, but seems to have been little interested in the fruits although he had recorded several seen in China. In the fifteenth century, travellers (Bracciolini, 1857) recorded 'vast varieties of fruits, and above all those called *musa* which are more sweet than honey' and coconuts, on the banks of the Ganges, apparently along its lower part. They also mention grapes in Burma but not in India, along with pineapples, oranges, and chestnuts; the durian in the Andamans; and the mango and jackfruit in Malabar. A little later, Eden

(1577) mentions the jackfruit and the 'apolanda' or banana at Calicut. Watt (1908) quotes two other travellers of about this time. Vertomannus, a gentleman of the city of Rome, visited Cananor and Narsinga in South India in 1503, and wrote that 'the soyle beareth neyther wheate nor vynes, or few other fruits, except Oranges and Gourdes'. Varthema was in Cananor in 1510 and also mentions the sweet oranges, but found them less excellent than those of Ceylon, which were, indeed, the finest in the world.

John Huyghrn van Linschoten (Bunell and Tiele, 1885), one of the greatest of the early travellers, began his voyage to the East Indies in 1576, and had much of interest to report about the fruits of India. He speaks of the 'ananas' (pineapple) as having been 'first brought by the Portuguese out of Brasille', and of the 'papaios' (papaya) from the Spanish Indies having been brought from beyond the Philippines to Malacca and thence to India. He found oranges, lemons, and citrons to occur 'throughout all India in great abundance and for goodness and taste surpass those of Spain'. But even better were those of Ceylon of which he writes, 'for oranges, lemons, and citrons it hath not only the best in India but better than any are found either in Spaine or Portingal.' Duly impressed by the banana, for which he uses a term common in early writings, he says, 'Indian Figges there are manie and of divers sorts' and of 'marvellous good taste'. 'They may serve both for bread and butter, and a man may verie well live thereon, without other meate, if need were, as manie in India do live therewith'. After mentioning that they were dried and carried all over India for sale, he concludes that 'it is one of the best and necessaryest fruits in all India, and one of the principallest sustenances of the common people'. Of 'mangas' (mangoes) he has not much to say, except that the green ones were preserved in salt, stuffed with ginger and garlic, or made into *achar*. He reported that the 'Tamarinio groweth in the most parts of India, speciallie in the lands of Gusurate and the north parts beyond Goa.' Other fruits mentioned are the 'Iacas' (jackfruit), 'Iambos' (*jaman*), carambola, 'Brindoijans' (*Garcinia purpurea*), mangosteen and 'Emblicos' (*aonla*), as well as several it is now difficult to identify.

Just twenty-five years later Pyrard (Grey, 1890) began a voyage which brought him also to India, where he found a number of the common fruits, including the 'mirabolans' (*aonla*) which were growing in great numbers in Cochin and Calicut, and were made into conserves and comfits. When he mentions also the durian and 'ramboutan', which are quite tropical, it must be remembered that India to him may have included Malaya, as it did to some other writers. It was also difficult, even at that time, for travellers to find out which fruits were indigenous, and while the general tendency was to assume fruits native unless it was known that they were not, Della Valle (Grey, 1892), in India in 1622-23, included the mango and *jaman* with the papaya, cashew, and pineapple as having been brought from Brazil.

Another keen observer was Edward Terry, Chaplain to Sir Thomas Roe, the first British Ambassador to the Moghul court, who was in India from 1616 to 1619. He also showed rather surprising enthusiasm for the *aonla*, referring to 'those most excellent plums, called Mirabolans', although he found the oranges and lemons inferior to those he had tasted elsewhere. He liked bananas which were 'made like unto tender cucumbers' and tasted 'like unto a Norwich pear, but much better'. The mango was also 'a most excellent fruit' 'which taken and rolled in a man's hand becomes like the pap of a roasted apple, which when sucked out from about a large stone they have within, is delicately pleasing unto every palate that tastes it'—an observation less accurate than Babar's. Best of all he found 'the Ananas, like unto our pineapples, which seems to the taster to be a most pleasing compound made of strawberries, claret-wine, rose-water, and sugar, well tempered together.'

A little later, writers were more apt to refer to specific parts of India. Bruton says in reference to Bengal, 'Good fruits they have in abundance; as coco-nuts, mangoes, pineapples, guavas, limes, lemons and oranges', while the mulberry was grown mainly for silk production. This was soon after 1632, the year in which Mundy (Temple, 1914) reached Agra, where he found apples (although they were scarce), 'orunge', 'mulberrie', mango, coconut, 'figg', and plantain trees. In the bazars he reports 'ananesses', raisins, almonds, pistachios, walnuts, prunes, 'prunellas or dryed Apricocks', 'Musk millions' (*sitaphal*), and 'water millions'. Somewhere in northern India he saw the pear, and also 'A Delicate Fruit resembling a pine, butt when ripe it is soft and of an admirable taste, called Atae', of which a footnote says that this is *Anona squamosa*, and which is referred to again in 1638 at Achin in Sumatra where it was called 'Anona.' At Goa in 1636 he refers to the 'Cajoora', of which the editor says that this is the cashew which had been introduced by the Portuguese in the 16th century.

Pennant (1798) mentions breadfruit in Cochin, and a large number of fruits in the Gangetic valley, including surprisingly, the strawberry, said to grow in the woods around Patna. He shared Babar's low opinion of the jackfruit, saying 'It is wonderful that this and some other Indian fruits should find admittance into a desert. Some compare the smell to garlic mixed with frowsy apples, others to a much more filthy thing.' But in Assam he admired the 'punialeh, a species of *amleh*, which has such an excellent flavour, that every person who tastes it prefers it to the plum.'

Light on the nomenclature of mangoes, and particularly the most famous variety, is shed by Manucci (1907) who was in Goa late in the 17th century, and refers to the abundance of food, principally fruits. 'Among these is the mango, the best flavoured fruit of India...... In Goa the gentlemen are very particular about having good kinds of this fruit. They give them special names taken from the first person to have good mangoes of that kind. Thus they speak of the mangoes of Niculao Afonco, which are the largest and best; Melajassao *mangoes* and Carreynas mangoes.' In another place he spells the name 'Affonso' giving a precedent for the various forms of the name Alphonse now in use. Of the pineapple, he says, 'In no part of India have I seen them in such quantities as in Bengal, where they were large and fine. The reason for this is that it is a low-lying and humid country.' 'There are a quantity of *Jacas* (jack-fruit) like large melons growing on the bark of the tree, with strong sharp thorns on the rind. There are two kinds—the *barca* Jack and the *papa* Jack.' Later he mentions a third kind, *pacheri*, and says that some weigh 80 pounds,

Medical men have contributed much by looking about them with a scientifically trained eye, and among the first to visit India, also toward the close of the 17th century was John Fryer (1909). He was among the first to distinguish between the plantain and the 'bonanoes' which were smaller but better. But he deserves quotation not so much for his facts as for the delightful way in which he gives them. While in 'Canatick', he writes of 'the *Mango* (which they have improved in all its kinds to the utmost perfection) being a Sovereign Medicine; they are the best and largest in *India*.....the Fruit when green scents like Turpentine, and pickled are the best *Achars* to provoke an Appetite; when Ripe, the Apples of *Hisperides* are but fables to them; for Taste, the Nectarine, Peach and Apricot fall short; they make them break out, and cleanse the Blood, and Salivate to the height of Mercurial Arcanaes; and afterwards fatten as much as Antimony, or Acorns do Hogs.' Of the pineapple he writes, 'The Taste inclinable to Tartness, though most excellently qualified by a dulcid Sapor that imposes on the Imagination and Gustative Faculty a Fancy that it relishes of any Fruit a man likes, and some will swear it.'

By 1754 two new names appear on the list of fruits, one probably indigenous, the other imported. That Ives (1793) is the first to mention the 'Pulsa' (phalsa) can be explained by the unimportant position of this fruit, which he found in only one garden in Bengal, although it is probably a native of India. But the 'Chaddock (pumple or pimple-noses)' which he considered 'a fine pleasant fruit', is the pummelo, which is mentioned in earlier writings in China and Java. Ives also speaks of two sorts of custard-apples, which may mean two species; the date, which seems to have been missed by other Europeans, few of whom probably visited the northwest; the guava, and other fruits.

Horticultural and Botanical Works

With a brief reference to another doctor, Buchanan (1807), who found the apples in the gardens of Tippoo much better than those in Calcutta, and the peaches much worse, and who mentions a relative of the mango, *Spondias dulcis*, the reports of travellers may be left in favour of more systematic works. Two events of great importance are connected with the name of that most versatile missionary, William Carey. In 1820 he founded the Agricultural and Horticultural Society of India, and four years later he published the first edition of Roxburgh's (1824) monumental Flora Indica. William Roxburgh, M.D., had come to India in 1776 as medical officer of the Madras Army, but soon became botanist to the East India Company, and from 1793 until 1814 was superintendent of the botanical garden in Calcutta. He also wrote 'Plants of the Coast of Coromandel, and Hortus Bengalenisis.' Roxburgh gives a tremendous list of fruits growing in India at that time, indigenous and introduced, including 23 species of *Zizyphus*, 6 of *Mangifera*, 37 of *Eugenia*, 23 of *Grewia*, and 55 of *Ficus*, not all edible, of course. Strangely enough, he says that the date, *Phoenix dectylifera*, was not known to succeed anywhere in India.

It would be difficult to estimate the effects of the Agri-Horticultural Society and its branches and kindred societies. These grew out of an interest in gardening which perhaps no longer exists to the same extent (the branch in Allahabad in 1841 had 60 members, half of them European), and in turn increased that interest. Between 1837 and 1841, eight volumes of the Transactions of the Society were published. Then Proceedings were published monthly from January 1841 to June 1842, and the Journal from 1842 until 1920, when it had to be discontinued through lack of support. The first volume of the Transactions contains a note written in 1820 by Robert Tyler, M.D., of Allahâbad, describing the agriculture of the district, and stating that he had the following fruits growing in his garden: lemons, limes, the orange, citron, pomegranate, pumplemuss (pummelo), figs, litchis, guavas, peaches, apples, vines, custard-apples, papayas, plantains, *jaman*, jujubes, and mangoes. The chief orchards of the district were said to be mango and *jaman*. The famous guava orchards seem to have been planted later.

Two works of distinct horticultural interest were published in 1839; one by Graham lists only plants growing in Bombay, including several, such as the durian, avocado, and cherimoya, recently introduced by a Mr. Nimmo, which may not have become established. The other, by Royle, covers a wider territory than that indicated by the title, the Himalayas. Other works containing interesting lists of fruit trees are those of Drury (1858) and of Watt (1889, 1908). The latter deals with the history and distribution of a large number of fruits as well as with the industrial, medicinal, and food value of the various parts of many plants.

The interest in gardening shown by both Europeans and educated Indians in the 19th century led to the production of a number of books on the subject, written for Indian conditions, some of which have been revised and are still used. Most of these are intended for the amateur gardener, and devote most of their pages to the flowers and ornamentals, with a shorter section on vegetables, and still less space for fruits.

One of the earliest of these manuals was the Indian Handbook of Gardening, by Speede, first published in 1842, and revised a few years later as the New Indian Gardener. It is typical in that it deals with flowers, vegetables, and fruits, but at least a little is said of each of 57 kinds of fruit. This list is of some interest as showing the fruits which were considered of importance at that time, and the nomenclature used. The fruits are the peach, apricot (rare), almond, *Terminalia cataapa*, plum, native plum (jujube), cherry, Java plum (*jaman*), olive (*Olea dioica*, said to be indigenous in Eastern Bengal), native olive (*Elaeocarpus suratus*), mango, hog-plum, apple, pear, quince, loquat, Malay apple (*Eugenia alba*), leechee, longan, wampee, mangosteen (very rare), custard-apple, bullock's heart, sour sop, avocado, jack, guava, pomegranate, carambola, pierardia (*lutkoo* or *lutka*, *Pierardia sapida*), jasmine flowered carissa (karanda), paneola plum (*Eugenia paniola*), Indian star apple (*Chrysophyllum acuminatum*), papaw, orange (chiefly in the eastern parts of India), citron, lemon, lime, fig, plantain, pineapple, grape, grewia (phalsa), mulberry, raspberry, strawberry, winter cherry (cape gooseberry), the nut (*Corylus avellana*), walnut, musk melon, watermelon, coconut, Borassus (*tar*), elephant or woodapple, Bengal quince (bael), tamarind, and Indian sorrel. It will be noted that some of these have never become of much importance, while certain important fruits such as the date and the pummelo, are omitted.

Probably the most popular book on gardening in India for more than three-fourths of a century has been Firminger's Manual. Thomas A. C. Firminger came to India as chaplain under the East India Company in 1846, and after a few months in Saugor, was stationed in Ferozepore for about seven years. After an extended furlough he spent six years in Bengal, during which he completed the first edition of his book, based on his experience in the Punjab and Bengal, and on extensive travels in northern India and a period at Ootacamund. The first edition bore the title, 'A Manual of Gardening for Bengal and Upper India', and was printed in London in 1864, although, according to his son, Firminger saw the book through the Press before leaving India in 1863. The book has been revised several times, twice by the author, and later by three other men. As Firminger's Manual of Gardening for India, revised and edited by Dr. William Burns, it retains its popularity, and preserves much of Firminger's material.

Other books on gardening followed. Indian Gardening, by Pogson, was publishd in 1872, and deals with much the same list of fruits as did Speede, but in somewhat more detail. G. M. Woodrow, of the Ganeshkhind gardens in Poona, published a modest book in 1876, Hints on Gardening in India, which went through several editions, and later appeared under the title, 'Gardening in the Tropics.' Woodrow's small work on The Mango, published in 1904, is also well known. The first edition of Riddell's Manual of Gardening for Western and Southern India must have been published by this time, as the 5th edition came out in 1884. Later books, revised editions of which are still current, are the Indian Amateur Gardener, by 'Landolicus', which had reached its 3rd edition by 1902 and the Amateur in an Indian Garden, by Lancaster, which appeared about 1929.

Probably the most significant horticultural book written in India is the Cultivated Oranges and Lemons, etc. of India and Ceylon, with Researches into Their Origin and the Derivation of Their Names, and Other Useful Information, by E. Bonavia, M. D., Brigade Surgeon, Indian Medical Service. This work consists of a text of 265 pages and a volume of 259 plates and was published by W. H. Allen and Co. in London, in 1890. It represents a great deal of effort, including keen observation in many parts of India, and the collection of specimens, and of information, from other parts. While stationed in Lucknow about 1870, Dr. Bonavia found time to act as Superintendent of the Government Gardens, and he may have acted in a similar capacity elsewhere. While he did not have much of the information which is available today about the history and classification of the citrus fruits (inadequate as that is !) and while few would now agree with some of his theories, his work is still of value for its contents, as well as historically. It is, perhaps, more highly appreciated in other countries than in India. Unfortunately, it has long been out of print.

Less well known, because of its smaller intrinsic value, and because it deals with a fruit restricted to a smaller area of the earth, is an earlier book by the same author, The Future of the Date Palm in India (*Phoenix dactylifera*). This was published by Thacker, Spink and Co. in Calcutta in 1885, and grew out of enthusiasm engendered when Dr. Bonavia found fresh dates in the market in Lucknow. This led to experiments, and the introduction of a number of good off-shoots into various parts of Oudh. The failure of others to catch his enthusiasm seems to have been due in part to his being ahead of the times, and partly to the unsound nature of some of his proposals. The modern development of the date industry in this country was fathered by Mr. Milne, who began work in 1909, and whose book on The Date Palm and its Cultivation in the Punjab grew out of a circular letter, revised in 1913 and again in 1918. It was published by Thacker, Spink and Co., for the Government of the Punjab.

It will be noted that practically all of these Indian publications have been written for the amateur rather than the commercial grower. This is natural in a country where the production of fruit for the market has been almost entirely in the hands of illiterate cultivators. A good deal of material of value to both the amateur and the professional has been issued from time to time in the bulletins of the various departments of agriculture, and in the agricultural journals of the country. Among these, Indian Farming, a popular magazine, and the Indian Journal of Agricultural Science, more technical, both issued by the Indian Council of Agricultural Research, are of importance. Had horticulture occupied a more prominent place in the research programmes, both the quantity and the quality of these publications would doubtless have been improved. Many of these bulletins have been published in the various Indian languages also, and there have been some books on gardening published in these languages also, but, none of much prominence. An example is Kitabul Asmar (The Book of Fruits) by Nawab Syed Imdad, a *rais* of Patna, published in the last decade of the 19th century by the Paisa Akhbar Press, Lahore. Apparently much in it was taken from the gardening Manuals in English.

Two books of great value to the Indian fruit grower and the student of pomology in this country have appeared recently. South Indian Fruits and their Culture, by K. C. Naik, was published in 1949 and is based largely on research by the author and other workers in South India. Commercial Fruits of India, with Special Reference to Western India was written in 1948-49 by Cheema, Bhat, and Naik, for the Indian Council of Agricultural Research, but unfortunately not published until 1954.

Of special importance to fruit growers in this country is the Indian Journal of Horticulture, published by the Horticultural Society of India which was founded in 1942.

Many journals on fruit growing are published in other English-speaking countries, containing some articles of interest to the Indian horticulturist. The Journal of Pomology is the organ of the horticultural research stations at Long Ashton and East Malling in England. It appears four times a year, and contains articles of scientific interest, but deals almost entirely with temperate crops. Horticultural Abstracts, issued quarterly by the Imperial Bureau of Horticulture and Plantation Crops is extremely valuable as it gives brief abstracts of articles published all over the world, not only in English but in other languages. Many horticultural societies issue publications, among the most valuable to the Indian fruit grower being the Proceedings of the American Society for Horticultural Science, as it deals with subtropical as well as temperate crops.

Sources of Indian Fruits

From the references to different fruits in the writings of various authors, it appears that those now grown may be classified in three groups : those indigenous, those introduced from other parts of Asia and Europe before the great age of exploration which started late in the 15th century, and those introduced later. This does not mean that it is easy to assign each fruit to one of these groups with any confidence. In many cases our present knowledge allows only a tentative classification.

The list of important fruits indigenous to this country is surprisingly small. The mango may belong here, and the jackfruit probably does. Very likely certain of the types of citrus fruits are Indian, but there is much confusion about the genus and it is questionable whether any of the important species is native. It has been thought by many that the lemon is, and the sweet and sour orange, citron, and lime may be. The banana originated in southern Asia, and possibly in India, but probably further east. Some types of figs and grapes seem to have been indigenous, and used in very ancient times, but the commercial varieties appear to be foreign, or possibly in some cases, hybrids of indigenous and foreign types. Fruits of less importance which seem to be Indian include the tamarind, the woodapple, the Indian jujube, the bael, the *aonla*, and the phalsa. The date may be a native of Pakistan as it is believed to have originated along the Persian Gulf but probably not as far south-east as Sind.

All of the fruits mentioned as possible natives of India fall into the second group if not into the first. The relation between India and the countries to the north-west goes back far beyond the dawn of history. Not only were there repeated migrations of people into the country, but there must have been considerable commerce between ancient centres of civilization in Iraq and Sind. Intercourse with China was more difficult, but there were routes across the mountains which were used in very early times, later supplemented by the sea route. Yuan Chwang whose visit to India in the seventh century has been noted, probably came by the long overland route, through Kashmir, and returned by sea. Before the end of the 13th century there seem to have been trading expeditions passing regularly between the ports of southern China and India. Relations with Burma, Malaya, Thailand, and Indo-China also go back to very early times. Thus we find the date entering Pakistan (if it did not originate there) before the dawn of history, and the peach and pear, and perhaps other deciduous fruits, from Europe or western Asia somewhat later. The mango and banana may have come into India from the east in prehistoric days, and some of the citrus fruits either overland or by sea from China long before the 15th century.

With the great impetus to travel and exploration which came with the discovery by Columbus of America, there began an exchange of plants from which India, as well as the rest of the world, has greatly benefited. Not only was the wealth of tropical America available for the first time, but more introductions were made from China and Europe. It has been seen how remarkably soon after the discovery of America the pineapple, custard-apple, and guava were introduced into India. Other fruits which had been established by the middle of the 18th century included the apple, plum, cashew, papaya, and pummelo. Later additions have brought to Indian horticulture such fruits as the apricot, cherry, quince, and strawberry from Europe, the loquat from the Far East, and the sapodilla and avocado from America. The process is not complete. The grapefruit is one of the more recent immigrants to find a place on our orchards, and there are still many tropical and subtropical fruits in other countries which have not yet had an adequate trial here. For instance, Joshi (1946) has suggested the probability that the tropical American palm, *Bactris utilis*, would succeed in India. Nor has the traffic been exclusively in one direction. Choice varieties of the mango have gone from India to enrich other lands, along with the banana and other fruits of southern Asia. That there are yet fruits in India which may profitably be introduced to other lands is probable. The systematic introduction, acclimatization, and testing of new fruits has been carried out in only a few countries, but may yet prove of great value to India.

The history of horticultural practices is much more difficult to trace than that of the fruits. Some evidence has been presented that methods of vegetative reproduction were known in India thousands of years ago, but for the most part this knowledge seems to have lapsed. Whether anything resembling scientific control of pests and disease was developed in ancient time is not known. That good methods of cultivation and manuring were used by gardeners who understood propagation by cuttings and grafting seems probable. By the time of the first European visitors, the practices seem not to have been such as would attract attention. At least, there is little comment on the methods in use. It has been claimed that the Portuguese introduced the practice of grafting mangoes, which would indicate that Indian gardening had fallen to a lower level than it had once occupied. Probably it is fair to credit the Portuguese with starting the revival in horticulture in this country. Much has been accomplished, but much remains to be done to put fruit growing on a scientific basis, even in the most advanced countries. The history of pomology in India is far from being finished.

PART II

CHAPTER XIII

THE MANGO

'The choicest fruit of Hindustan' is still the mango, as it was in the days of the poet Amir Khusrau, who sang its praises in the 14th century. Indeed, the mango has been a favourite fruit in India throughout recorded history, and is frequently mentioned in Sanskrit literature. Foreigners who visited India and left written records of their experience, from the Chinese pilgrims who travelled here in the seventh century A.D., down to modern writers, have all mentioned this fruit. The opinions expressed have differed somewhat, probably because of variations in the fruit tasted, but most writers have recognized in the mango the most important fruit of the country, and one of the most delicious fruits of the world.

Estimates of the acreage of mangoes in the States, taken from various sources, are given in Table III. It will be noted that Uttar Pradesh accounts for more than half of the entire area, but it must be remembered that these figures are misleading because they include many old and unproductive orchards. Many of the figures are estimates and the total is less than the acreage of 2,564,000 in unpublished data with the Agricultural Marketing Adviser of the Government of India.

Table III—Estimated area under mangoes in some parts of India

State	Area in acres	State	Area in acres
1	2	3	4
Ajmer	4	Madhya Pradesh	47,000
Andhra	160,917	Madras	100,459
Assam	5,000	Mysore	27,000
Bhopal	3,128	Orissa	158,963
Bihar	217,517	PEPSU	3,441
Bombay	41,500	Punjab	32,401
Coorg	1,000	Sourashtra	845
Himachal Pradesh	90	Travancore-Cochin	5,402
Hyderabad	19,913	Uttar Pradesh	1,322,656
Kutch	885	West Bengal	183,700
Madhya Bharat	6,000		
		Total	2,337,821

While India would be proud to claim the mango as an indigenous tree, it is not certain that this claim would be justified. Nor could it be definitely denied. De Condole believed that the mango had been cultivated for at least 4,000 years. The mango is found growing wild in many parts of the country, but in most if not all, it has doubtless escaped from cultivation. Early writers mention wild mangoes in Ceylon, and there is a legend that it was brought from that island to India by Hanuman. The importance of the legend may lie in its indication that the mango was regarded as an introduced fruit, but this is by no means convincing. Mukherjee (1950 b, 1951, 1953 a), presents evidence that the genus *Mangifera* originated in the area of Burma, Siam, and Indo-China, or in the Malay Peninsula, but that the mango itself probably came from the region of Assam and Burma. He points out that most of the species closely allied to *M. indica* occur in that region, that truly wild mangoes have not been found in Malaya, but do occur in Assam and the Chittagong Hills, that good cultivated varieties of the mango do not occur in Malaya, and that local names also support this theory. Agharkar and Roy (1951) are in general agreement.

Even though the mango may have come into India from farther east, there can be no doubt that its greatest development has been in this country. It was grown here for many centuries before there is any record of it in other countries. It is generally held that vegetative propagation was introduced by the Portuguese in Goa, though some claim that inarching had been practised for centuries before the coming of Europeans. In either case, superior varieties were first produced in India, and from there they have spread around the world. It has been seen that the famous Alphonso mango was in existence before the end of the 17th century. Cheema and others (1954) state that the huge original tree of the Borsha variety, reputed to be more than 300 years old, is still alive in Kalamsar, East Khandesh. Akbar was so fond of mangoes that he had the Lakh Bagh, supposed to contain 100,000 trees, planted near Darbhanga. English visitors reported some of the original trees still alive three hundred years later.

The mango spread all over India at a very early date. It was found in the Indus valley when the army of Alexander the Great invaded it in 327 B.C. It was not until many centuries later that it was taken to other countries. The historical record is not complete. By the 16th century it seems to have been growing around the head of the Persian Gulf. According to Burns and Prayag (1920) mangoes were growing in Somaliland, on the coast of Africa, in 1931; Yemen in the later 18th century; the Canaries in the 19th century; the Azores in 1865; Hawaii in 1865; the Philippines after 1600; the Moluccas in 1665; southern Italy in 1905; Queensland in about 1870; Florida in 1861 or 1862; and California in the period 1880-85. The same authors state that mangoes were grown in England, under glass as early as 1690, and actually fruited in Kew gardens in 1818. Pope (1929) accepts an earlier date for the introduction of the mango into Hawaii, probably between 1800 and 1820. He believes that they were taken by Spanish traders from the Philippines to Mexico before 1778, and by the Portuguese to Brazil in the 18th century, and thence to the West Indies. Thrum is quoted by Miller and Bazore (1945) as stating that the first mango trees were imported into

Hawaii from Manila in 1824. Mukherjee (1948) states that the mango was taken from Brazil to Barbados, in the West Indies, in about 1742, and that the first introduction into Florida was from Mexico in 1833. Wester (1917), however, states that this attempt failed and that it was not until 1861 or 1862 that seedlings were established in Florida. He says that the first grafts introduced from India in 1885 died, and that of those introduced in 1888 only one, a Mulgoba, survived.

The mango is now an important fruit throughout the tropics and into the milder subtropical regions. From India eastward to southern China, and south through the Malay Archipelago to the warmer parts of Australia, it is commonly grown. It is one of the most important fruits of Java, and the third most important, according to Wester (1925), in the Philippine Islands. It succeeds well in Hawaii and other Pacific Islands. It has long been grown in the West Indies, and to a limited extent in Florida. It has not been very successfully introduced into California or the Mediterranean region. It grows well in Madagascar, and along the coast of tropical Africa. Oppenheimer (1947) states that it is commonly grown in Egypt and will be in Palestine in the not distant future. Some of the better Indian varieties have been introduced into many of these regions, but local varieties of excellent quality have also been developed. Few of these countries have accurate agricultural statistics, so it is impossible to give the acreage of mangoes in the world, or to state how the mango compares in importance with such fruits as the apple in temperate regions, the subtropical grape, olive, and orange, or the tropical banana. If the truth were known, the mango would probably come in the same class as these, as the most widely grown fruits in the world.

India has also given the world the most common names for this fruit. The English name mango, and similar names in other European languages, come from the Tamil, *mankay or mangay*. Like a number of other Indian words, it came into English through the Portuguese. There is some doubt as to whether the name came originally from the Malayan, or travelled east from India, but the Malayan *manga or mangga* is common in Malaya and Java. The Chinese *mang-kwo* seems to have the same derivation. The names used in northern India, such as *am*, come from the Sanskrit.

Botanically, the mango is generally considered as one species, *Mangifera indica* L., but it is likely that other species have contributed to at least some cultivated varieties. While the mango is by far the best of the genus, several of the 41 species are valued for their fruits, especially in Malaya. Charaka mentions a fruit which Chandra identifies as *M. sylvatica*, a species Roxburgh (1824) mentions as growing wild near Sylhet, but which differs only slightly from *M. indica*. Agharkar and Roy (1951) state that it is also found in Nepal, Sikkim, elsewhere in the Himalayas, and in Andaman Islands. Mukherjee (1950 a) describes this species from Assam and the Chittagong Hill Tracts, and mentions another species, *M. khasiana*, supposed to occur in Assam, but not recently found there. Berwick (1940) says that at least eight species are grown in the villages of Malaya in addition to the common mango : *pentandra*, *odorata*, *foetida*, *longipetiolata*, *maingayi*, *quadrifida*, and *caesia*. He describes one variety each of *M. pentandra* and *M. odorata*. Ochse (1931) describes *M. caesia*, *M. foetida* and *M. odorata* as cultivated fruits in Java, and Wester (1925), includes these and the uncultivated *M. altissima* among the food plants of the Philippines. Other species with more or less edible fruits, according to S. K. Mukherjee (1949, 1953c) are *M. cachinchinensis*, *M. oblongifolia*, *M. zeylanica*, *M. logenifera*, *M. kemangra*, and *M. reba*. He points out the possibility of selecting better types of some of these species, especially for growing in areas where the mango does not do well. Hybridization between the species also presents an interesting line of development. In all of the varieties of the mango he studied, all allopolyploids, and in *M. sylvatica*, *M. caloneura*, *M. foetida*, and *M. caesia*, he found the same haploid chromosome number, 20. Most species of *Mangifera* have more or less of the 'turpentine' flavour common to the poorest mangoes.

The family Anacardiaceae, to which the mango belongs, contains a number of plants of horticultural interest, as well as some which are poisonous to the touch. The most important of these is the cashew, *Anacardium occidentale*, which is dealt with later. Several species of *Spondias*, including the hog plum, *amra*, *S. mangifera*, yield edible fruits, some of which are grown occasionally in India. The small nut, *chiraunji*, *Buchanania latifolia*, is another tree of slight importance in Indian horticulture. The pistachio, *Pistacia vera*, is a nut of greater importance, but is not grown in India, except to a very limited extent in Kashmir, being imported from Afghanistan. Of the ornamental trees of this family the most important is the pepper-tree, *Schinus molle*, which is common in Bangalore, and occasionally found in other parts of India.

The mango is too well known to require any complete description, but there are several points which should be kept in mind. One is that the mango is one of the largest of fruit trees, and when planted singly is normally spreading, sometimes with a spread of more than 100 feet, in the case of seedling trees. Such trees are commonly believed to be more than 100 years of age, though accurate records are seldom available. Randhawa (1949) mentions a number of very large trees on unusually fertile soil in a village in Ambala district. One of these, named Chhappar, had a trunk with a circumference of 32 feet and nine branches, close to the ground, of from 5 to 12 feet in circumference, and 70 to 80 feet long. The total area occupied by the branches was 2,700 square yards, equivalent to a circle with a diameter of about 175 feet. The average yield was said to be 450 maunds. Grafted trees are probably somewhat smaller and shorter lived. The growth habit of the mango is also of importance. The tree is evergreen, but grows in several periods during the year, known as flushes. While there is a tendency for flushes to take place at certain seasons of the year, such as early spring, not all trees grow at the same time. In fact, part of a tree may be covered with beautiful red or coppery or pale green new leaves while other branches have only the dark green mature leaves.

The root system of the mango has not been much studied. Roy (1952) reports that a 60-year old Fazli tree in Bihar had anchor roots which descended 3·75 meters and then became horizontal, but the finer roots were confined to the top 50 cm. with the majority in the top 25 cm. on deeper and lighter soils, much deeper penetration probably.

The flowers are small, but borne in immense panicles which are generally terminal, but sometimes axillary. A higher percentage of leaders flower than of lateral shoots, but because of their abundance the laterals are also important in producing the crop. Reece and others (1946) report that if the terminal bud is removed during the flowering period inflorescences are produced from the lateral buds, and that if the decapitated shoot is girdled below some leaves, floral induction takes place in axillary buds within four days. Bijhouwer (1937), working with the Alphonso and seven varieties of Java, found the number of flowers to the inflorescence to vary from 788 to 9,020. In the Alphonso, from 6 to 11% of the flowers were perfect, the rest being staminate. The percentage in the other varieties was higher, up to 55%. Of the perfect flowers, 99% failed to set fruit which stayed on the tree more than a month. Mukherjee (1953 b) reports the number of flowers per panicle on 10 varieties, varying from 978 on the Langra to 5,827 on the Imampasand. The percentage of perfect flowers in these varied from 1.25 in Jahangir to 35.6 in Langra. The number of perfect flowers per panicle varied from 24.5 in Jahangir to 531.4 in Imampasand and 600 in Safdarpasand. In one variety, Kalapahar, the percentage of perfect flowers was found to be 20 on the west side of the tree and 9 on the east. R. N. Singh (1954) reports 1,212 flowers per panicle, 30.6% of which were perfect in the Dasheri and 1,061 and 69.8% in the Langra. Musahib-ud-din and Dinsa (1946) studied two varieties and four seedling trees in the Punjab, and found the number of flowers per inflorescence to be 885 in the Langra, 324 in Aman Dasehri and from 470 to 1,598 in the seedlings. Only about two-thirds of the buds ever opened, and of those that did the percentage of perfect flowers in Aman Dasehri was 77.9; in Langra, 66.8; and in the seedlings from 8.9 to 36.7. There were fewer perfect flowers on the mixed than on the pure inflorescences. There were more flowers, and more perfect flowers on the basal and middle thirds of the inflorescence, although the proportion of perfect flowers was higher in the terminal third, and most of the fruit was borne there, perhaps because there was more viable pollen late in the season when these flowers opened.

It is clear that in all of these varieties there are more perfect flowers than are needed for a bumper crop of fruit. It has been estimated that in some cases half of the perfect flowers are pollinated, but R. N. Singh (1954) found 41% pollinated of the 700 flowers he examined, and Mukherjee (1953 b) reports only from 3 to 35% in the varieties he examined. Nevertheless, he attributed the poor set of fruits not to lack of pollinated flowers, but to a post-fertilization drop, probably caused by deficient nutrition in the many competing developing embryos. Spencer and Kennard (1955), on the other hand, attribute the poor set of mangoes in Puerto Rico to poor pollination, because of the small amount of pollen, its reduced germination because of the dry hot air and bright sun, the fact that anthers and stigma do not mature at the same time, and the lack of insect carriers. Damage by thrips is seen as another factor. If one-fourth of the flowers were pollinated, even in the variety Jahangir, mentioned above as having the least perfect flowers, and half of these developed into mature fruits, a satisfactory crop would be borne. Actually Sen and others (1946) report about half as many mature fruits as panicles. Work at Kodur on the other hand indicates that there is a high positive correlation between the percentage of perfect flowers and the number of fruits per panicle carried to maturity, and that a low ratio of style length to stamen length is favourable to fruit set.

Pollination by means of insects seems to be the most common condition. The pollen is rather heavy and sticky, and R. N. Singh (1954) found very little in the air. However, Burns and Prayag (1920) point out that the flowers are protogynous, but that sometimes the stigma and anther are very close together or touching, and that bagged flowers, from which insects are excluded, often set fruit. Bijhouwer (1937) also found some varieties able to set fruit in spite of bagging. However, he found that the commercially important varieties were all more attractive to bees than some other varieties. While Young (1951) refers to bees and perhaps some flies being the only insects affecting significant transfer of pollen, in India it is the flies which are important. Burns and Prayag (1920) state that the flowers are visited mainly by flies in the genera *Psychonoma* and *Pyrellia*, while R. N. Singh (1954) considers a species of *Melipona* most important, followed by members of the *Syrphidae* and the house fly. Cross-pollination seems necessary in order to get good crops, at least in the case of certain varieties. Ruehle and Lynch (1948) report that the Haden variety, which makes up fully 90% of the plantings of named varieties in Florida, fails to bear well when planted as solitary trees or in solid blocks. The presence of other varieties was helpful, and grafted trees of the Saigon race were more effective pollinizers than those of the Sundersha or Mulgoba groups. They consider that it is probably necessary that a fourth to a half of the trees be of a favourable type in order for the influence to be marked. At the Fruit Research Station at Kodur in Madras State, it was also found that in cross-pollination certain combinations of male and female parents were more effective than others. Thus it was found that with Neelum as the female variety, the percentage of perfect flowers setting fruit with pollen from three males varied from 51.0 to 93.6; with Bangalora and five males, from 65.2 to 79.9; with Chinnasuvernarekha and three males, from 50.0 to 66.9; and with others similar ranges. The possibility of increasing the set with hormone sprays has been suggested by Venkataratnam (1949) whose experiments were mentioned in Chapter VIII.

Not all of the fruits which set remain on the tree until mature, and while much of the drop can be explained by the high winds and other unfavourable climatic conditions which prevail as the fruit is developing, there are probably other factors which are not well understood. Certainly there are varietal differences. R. N. Singh (1954 b) found that the greatest drop at Saharanpur occurred in the first three weeks of April, after which there was very little in the case of the Dasheri, but that fruits of the Langra continued to fall through June, so that only 0.29 fruits matured per panicle. This tendency for the fruit to fall is the only reason this variety is not recommended in some parts of the country The possibility of reducing the drop by means of hormone sprays is suggested by

Gokhale and Kanitkar (1951) who increased the number of fruits of the Alphonso at harvest by from 17 to 23% by spraying with 25 ppm of NAA or 2, 4-D when the fruit was from half an inch to an inch in diameter.

Climatic and Soil Requirements

The mango is tolerant of soil and climatic conditions. It grows from the southernmost part of India to the Punjab and from Assam to the borders of the western desert; from sea level to 5,000 feet above the sea in the Himalayas. It flourishes best where there is enough rain to wet the soil to a considerable depth but where there is also a well-marked dry season and where there is little, if any, frost. Freedom from rain and cloudiness, and from frost, during the flowering season is particularly important. In regions where the humidity is high throughout the year, the mango does not bear well. Popenoe (1920) refers to a beautiful avenue of mango trees in Rio de Janeiro, more than 100 years old, never known to have produced any mature fruit. Berwick (1940) believes that while the bette varieties are uncertain producers in Malaya, where they are grown mostly on the bunds between rice fields, the periodic flooding and draining of the rice fields takes the place of a dry season in checking growth and inducing fruitful-ness. He reports two crops a year, one in May and June and one from the middle of October to the middle of December. In areas of heavy rainfall, such as the Konkan in Bombay, mango trees may be grown without irrigation, bu where the rainfall is less than about 80 inches a year, young trees are generally irrigated. Some varieties in Madras fail to ripen well where there is heavy rainfall at the ripening season.

The susceptibility of mangoes to frost varies with the variety and the age and the condition of the tree. Some varieties will withstand as much as te degrees of frost without damage, while others are severely injured by four o five degrees. Young trees are often protected during the winter because the are easily damaged. At the Government Garden in Saharanpur on one occasio a frost of 8° on February 9th killed a number of two-year-old grafted trees whic had been uncovered as it was thought the danger of frost was past. There wa much variation in susceptibility among seedling plants in the same orchard It was observed that the stronger plants were less damaged than the weaker one If conditions in the autumn favour late growth, frost during the winter is likely t cause more damage. The total amount of heat during the growing season is als of importance and may be the limiting factor at high elevations. Oppenheime (1947) suggests that about 1000 heat units is the minimum requirement for man goes of high quality, a unit being counted for each degree Centigrade abov 17.9 on a day in the warmer half of the year.

The climate influences the time of flowering. There is some variation fro year to year, but greater differences occur in different regions. In northern Indi the mango ordinarily flowers in February, whereas in Bombay it may flower fro late November through January or occasionally in September. In Bombay cit it flowers a month later than along the southern coast or the Province, while a

Poona it is still later. Ripening is correspondingly varied, thus spreading the marketing season over a long period. In Cochin, mangoes ripen as early as February and March, according to Menon (1941). In Madras the main crop ripens from May to July, but some off-season fruits ripen from July to November. There are some varieties which have no definite time of flowering, but bloom more or less throughout the year.

The mango may be found flourishing on a wide range of soils. The deep alluvial soils of the Gangetic plain seem to be well suited. Burns and Prayag (1920) state that the red soils of Dharwar and the red laterite soils of Belgaum, Ratnagiri, and Goa are pre-eminently suited to the mango, and quote Maries in favour of the *Kankar* (nodular limestone) soils of Gwalior. They report a remarkable instance in which trees grew ten feet in two years on a soil in Ahmednagar district, which was underlaid with *murum* and which had been fallow for some time. They recommend that the soil be more than three feet deep, a minimum which is probably much too low for northern India. Sand and clay are considered unsuitable. Deep 'black cotton' soil is also considered poor. The presence of stones may not harm the soil for mangoes. Balakrishnamurti and Jogiraju (1932) state that in Madras the ideal soil is a red loam, fairly deep and with a substratum of loose gravel, but that rich soil and clay are not to be recommended, as they favour vegetative growth with little fruit. Their statement that peroxide of iron in the soil increases the vigour of the trees and sweetens the fruit may be regarded as not proved.

The varieties of mango, even in India alone, are almost beyond number. Mukherjee (1948) says that about one thousand varieties are grown in India. There are millions of seedling trees, some of such excellence that they have gained a local reputation. Many such trees have been propagated as named varieties. Probably the same name has been given to entirely separate varieties in many cases. On the other hand, the same variety may be known in different localities under different names. Five hundred varieties are said to have been collected by an early enthusiast named Maries. Only when fruit growing is a hobby for the rich, a sort of game in which each variety counts in the score, is there any object in growing so many varieties. Burns and Prayag describe 89 varieties which are grown in Bombay Province, but from the descriptions it is obvious that many of these are unworthy of a place in any orchard. Wester (1922) was interested in Indian varieties suitable for planting in the Philippines and compiled descriptions of 285 varieties. He was able to recommened only a few of these. Mukherjee (1948) describes 72 varieties, mostly from Bengal and Bihar, and classifies them according to fruit shape. Naik and Gangooly (1951) classify and describe 325 varieties, including all those of commercial importance grown in South India.

Van Rheede in his Hortus Malibaricus, published in 1638, is quoted by Burns and Prayag as saying, 'Of these other fruits, mangoes, not unlike our apples and pears, are found in several types, which vary greatly according to the nature of the region.' In the three hundred years since he wrote, the number of varieties of apples and pears grown has greatly diminished, and as the mango industry develops, the number of varieties is sure to grow less. Fraser (1924) states that a survey of nursery catalogues in America showed 735 supposedly distinct varieties of apples listed in 1892, while in 1910 a similar study showed only 472. He goes on to express the opinion that no one should plant more than ten varieties, and that three would probably be better than ten. Much the same advice should probably be given to the Indian grower of mangoes.

The number of varieties grown for the market in India will remain considerable, because of regional differences, seasonal variation, and market demands. Different varieties are suited to different sections. Gangooly and Singh (1950) have listed the important varieties grown in each of five climatic regions of India. The Alphonse group is considered by many the best of all, as grown in Bombay, but it has not proved satisfactory in northern India. Even in North Kanara, Holmes-Smith (1911) ranked it fifth in order of merit. In any region, there is room for varieties ripening at different times. Very early or very late varieties of medium quality may bring more on the market than superior varieties ripening in mid-season. While quality is a very important consideration, quantity must also be considered. In order to meet the demand for cheap fruit, varieties bearing regularly and abundantly should be grown, as well as those of superlative quality which may bear less freely.

It does not follow that each grower should produce all of the varieties which are desirable in his region. Each grower should have enough of each variety he grows to provide for economical handling and marketing, even though that limit him to one carefully chosen variety. In larger orchards it is generally desirable to plan to have varieties ripening more or less throughout the season. Allen (1935) suggests two or three varieties of each seasonal group, a total of six to ten varieties in an orchard of moderate size.

In Uttar Pradesh there are about 300 varieties, according to L. B. Singh and Singh (1955), who describe the following table varieties: early, Bombay (green and yellow types otherwise very similar), Gopalbhog, Alphan, Zamurrad, Rataul, and Zardalu; mid-season, Dasheri (Dashahari, Dasehri), Langra, Gulabkhas, Fajari Jafrani (Fazari, Fazli), Khasulkhas, and Krishanbhog; late, Chausa (Samar Bihisht Chausa, Khajari), Taimuria, Benishan, and Fajari White (Safeda No. 1). Of these, Langra is considered by many to be the best, though Rataul, a smaller variety, is increasing in popularity. But the Langra tends strongly to bear irregularly, and the fruit tends to fall before it is mature, so these authors consider the Dasheri the best mango for the State. They also describe four superior sucking mangoes : Mithawa Ghazipur, Raspoonia, Mithawa Sundar Shah, and Hardil Aziz.

Conditions in Bihar are similar to those in Uttar Pradesh, and many of the same varieties are grown. Roy (1952) recommends the following commercial varieties: early, Gulabkhas and Bambai; mid-season, Hemsagar, Langra, Krishanbhog and Bharatbhog; late, Sukul, Sepia, Fazli, and Bathua. Choice varieties, several of which may become commercial, are listed as : Mithua, Zardaloo, Alfanso, Aman Dasheri, Aman Abbasi, Be-Nazir, Ab-e-hayat, Husan Ara, Taimuria, Samar Bahist, Paharpur, Sinduria, and Puttu. In West Bengal the

Langra, Himsagar (Shadwala), and Fazli are also recommended, along with the Bhuto Bombai.

There are a number of excellent varieties grown in Bombay, the best being the Alphonse, of which name Alphonso, Apoos, Afooz, etc. are variations. Probably next in merit is the Pairi. Fernandin and Kavasji Patel are also of importance, the latter for pickling. In Madras, including Andhra, according to Naik (1947 a), about 30% of the production is from seedling trees, 17% of the Bangalora variety, 14% of Neelum, 6% of Swarnarekha, 5% of Banganapalle, and 4% of Peter. This leaves about a fourth of the total production to be provided by the hundreds of other named varieties. Rao (1954 b) mentions Jehangir, Himayuddin, Mulgoa, and Alampur Beneshan as the famous mangoes of Andhra, but unfortunately some of these do not bear well enough to be good commercial varieties. Many of these are described and classified by Naik and Gangooly (1950).

Since names are rather freely used, it is obviously that not all trees with a certain name will be equally satisfactory. Naik (1940 b) kept records for four years on 1,143 trees of the locally important Neelum, Bangalora, Andrews, and Mulgoa varieties. Only one tree flowered heavily each year, and more than 95% of the Mulgoa and Andrews trees gave a poor crop or none in three of the four years. The percentage fruiting heavily in any year was not more than 2·6. Plants were propagated vegetatively from selected Neelum and Bangalora trees, and later Naik (1947 b) reported that all proved efficient producers, with little variation. This illustrates the importance of standardizing varieties and propagating only from trees known to yield good crops of fruit of the type desired.

Although there are already so many varieties being grown, it is still possible to secure improved types through breeding. The task is somewhat tedious and requires patience, as only a small percentage of the pollinated flowers will produce fruit. The efficiency of this work can be considerably increased by pollinating only a few flowers on each panicle and removing all others, according to R. N. Singh (1954 a). He also recommends choosing only healthy panicles and pollen from freshly dehisced anthers, and the spraying of the trees, and later the bagged panicles, with DDT to avoid all damage by hoppers. Sen and others (1946) at Sabur cross-pollinated 3,000 flowers in one year, but because of unfavourable weather secured no mature fruit. In the next three years they pollinated 8,737 flowers and secured 77 fruits which yielded 65 seedlings from which to select. Altogether, according to Roy (1952), 69 hybrids were secured, of which 19 were living and 5 had fruited at the time of his report. Mallik (1953-54 a) has reported on one of these which has been named Provasankar, a cross of the commercial variety Bambai, which has poor keeping qualities, and the Kalapady which has little in its favour except keeping quality. He reports fruit averaging 8 oz. (compared with 6 and 4 in the parents), of very good quality and good keeping quality, ripening a month later than the Bambai. Another tree with the same parents seems promising, and has been named Mahmudbahr. A cross between the Langra and Kalapady is said to have fruit like that of the Langra but ripening a month later.

Similarly, at Kodur 7,308 pollinated flowers yielded 88 seedlings (Naik 1948 a). Here such heavy-bearing varieties as the Neelum were crossed with choice shy-bearing varieties. Rao (1954) report that these have yielded 21 hybrids of promise and describes 8 of the most outstanding ones. He also says that of 36 seedlings from an open-pollinated tree of a good variety, 6 give fruit of exceptionally good quality. If these trees are otherwise satisfactory, this would seem to be a case of better fortune than the plant breeder can expect. Hybridization is also being carried on at Saharanpur, and in Hyderabad, where emphasis is put on crossing good varieties from the North with those from the South. Thus far, hybridization seems to have been limited to varieties in the one species, but the possibilities of inter-specific crossing are recognized.

In both Sabour and Kodur, evidence was found of metaxenia, or a related phenomenon. Sen and his co-workers report the apparent influence of the pollen parent on the size, shape, colour, and odour of the fruit resulting from cross-pollination. At Kodur one seed of Neelum pollinated by a polyembryonic variety gave rise to three seedlings, and Neelum is considered monoembryonic. It has been reported that the Mulgoa (Mulgoba) variety is monoembryonic in India but became polyembryonic when taken to Florida. This might be explained as the result of pollination with pollen of one of the polyembryonic varieties which are common in Florida but not in the parts of India where the Mulgoa is commonly grown.

It is argued by some that in order to secure high yields per acre, India needs good varieties, which are somewhat dwarfed so that more can be planted per acre. This might be one factor to be considered in breeding. Sen (1939, 1941 a, 1942 a) suggests the Kalapadi for this purpose, as trees 20 years old are about 15ft. high and have an excellent fruiting habit. L. B. Singh (1954 a) classifies the varieties Brindabani, Krishanbhog, Totapari Small, and Samarkand as dwarf, with a height of 13-15 ft. and a spread of 14-16 ft. compared to a height of 32-38 ft., and a spread of 30-39 ft. in those classified as vigorous. A still smaller variety found in Vicarabad and called Mahmuda is reported by Chellappa (1954). He says that a full grown tree is about 8 ft. tall, with a spread of 6-8 ft., that it is heavy-bearing, and that the quality is excellent.

In order to deal with the many varieties of mangoes in a more orderly manner, several classifications have been suggested. One type of classification is based on the nature and use of the fruit, such as juicy, table, intermediate, sour or pickle, and a few which are sweet even when green. Most of the superior varieties are table mangoes with firm pulp containing little if any fibre. There is also a considerable demand for juicy mangoes, most of which are more or less fibrous, and which are generally sucked.

Burns and Prayag, on the other hand, have suggested a classification based on the shape of the fruit. Their main classes are round, long, and indefinite. They also suggest that in describing a variety the fruit be placed with the beak to the left, and the following points noted : the nature of the right and left shoulders, the basal cavity, the beak, the apex, and the sinus; the three dimensions; weight, colour; surface; the nature, closeness, and distribution of the glands; the taste, colour, and stringiness of the pulp; the thickness of the skin; and the size, weight, fibre, and markings of the stone. Popenoe (1941), who suggested a similar outline in 1913 uses the mango to illustrate the need for developing the systematic pomology of tropical fruits. He says, 'Next to vegetative propagation itself, it is sincerely believed that there is nothing which would do more to advance the cause of fruit growing in the tropics than detailed attention to this subject' (the description of varieties). Naik and Gangooly (1950) deal with the shape of the tree, the leaves, and the inflorescences, as well as the fruit in their very valuable classification of mangoes in the South. Nand (1955) found that the 17 varieties he studied at Kanpur could be distinguished from each other by the colour of the eaves while still folded and just after unfolding.

Propagation

As with other highly improved fruits, proper propagation is very important in the mango. While some seedlings are of excellent quality, in India the great majority are very poor. This is not true in all other countries. Some races of mangoes are polyembryonic, the extra embryos originating from the nucellus, cotyledons, or hypocotyl, according to Mukherjee (1953 b). This seems to be the case with the famous Carabao variety in the Philippines, seedling trees of which bear uniformly excellent fruit. Some of the varieties grown in Java also seem to be of this nature. Pope (1929) reports that most Hawaiian mangoes are polyembryonic and Grant and Williams (1936) state that this is true of the varieties found in Burma, where they are largely grown from seed. It is also true of all the important varieties in Malaya, according to Berwick (1940). Richards (1952) states that in Ceylon both the most popular variety, the Jaffna, and the type preferred as rootstock, the fibrous *kohuamba*, are highly polyembryonic. Unfortunately, the important varieties in India all seem to be largely monoembryonic. It was reported from Bombay (Anon. 1926) that seedlings of the Alphonse and Pairi exhibited considerable variation in shape, taste, fibre, and colour. According to Sen and Mallik (1940), the Bambai, Langra, and Fazli varieties are monoembryonic, although multiple shoots may occur with a single tap-root, the extra shoots apparently arising from the axils of the cotyledons. Horn (1943) studied 7,880 seedlings of 20 varieties, mostly Indian, in Puerto Rico, and found cases of polyembryony in 17, varying up to 51.41%. The Alphonse was found 13.33% polyembryonic, and the Sufaida 23.07%. On the basis of this report, the growing of seedling trees of these varieties would scarcely be justified.

The possible advantage of using polyembryonic varieties as rootstocks is obvious. Although the greater vigour these are reported to impart to the scion may not be desirable, uniformity is. The Sabre, grown in South Africa, is both polyembryonic and dwarfing, and might prove desirable. There are about ten polyembryonic varieties on the west coast of South India, where they occupy about 50,000 acres, according to Naik (1947). He found that they produced from two to five seedlings per seed, although Sen and Mallik (1940) found some monoembryonic seeds in all of the five varieties of this group which they studied. An observational trial at Kodur is reported by Rangacharlu (1955) who states that during the first ten years of bearing the yield of Baneshan and Neelum was better on Pathutan and Goa than on the other polyembryonic rootstocks tried, the differences between the best and the poorest being very large.

Another method of securing uniform rootstocks is to propagate them by rootage. Early attempts at layering were not encouraging, but the introduction of hormone treatments has changed the picture. Thakurta and Dutt (1941) found that by using branches of trees two or three years old, and applying 1% indoleacetic acid, they could raise plants successfully from 80% of the air-layers attempted. The acid was applied in lanolin to the surface after removing a ring of bark. They also succeeded with cuttings, but in this case 3% indoleacetic acid was necessary. Some success in air-layering is also reported by S. N. Singh and Teotia (1951), who found that varieties varied in their response. Using either 1 or 2% NNA, they induced 100% rooting in the Dasehri. From 1 to 3% IAA, IBA, and phenyl acetic acid gave from 60 to 80% success with this variety, but with the Langra the best result, 70%, was secured with 2% IAA. After the roots appeared, further care was necessary if the layers were to survive. By adding another layer of leaf mould, about 40% survived, but when the layers were pressed into pots filled with leaf mould and left for some time before severing them from the tree, all survived. Results were much better in the rainy season than in the spring. Cuttings failed to grow in spite of hormone treatment. L. B. Singh (1954 a, b) reports success with 1% NAA in lanolin as follows : dwarf varieties : Brindabani, 80%; Krishanbhog, 40%; Samarkand, 22%; Totapari small, 20%; semi-vigorous : Kala, 80%; Anfas, 70%; Rataul, 60%; Dasheri, 60%; vigorous : Machhali, 100%; P. S. Special No. 2, 60%; Banarsi Langra 40%; and Fazri Kalan, 10%. Shoots about two years old responded better than did those twice that age. When sphagnum moss and plastic sheeting were used, all of the layers which rooted were successfully established. Garg (1954) reports excellent results with the Dasheri, but only 40% with the Langra, using moss and plastic wraps, without hormone treatment, at a cost of about four annas per layer. In the case of good varieties with a high percentage of rooting, it may prove satisfactory to grow layered plants. In any case, if grafting is used, a well selected clonal rootstock may be a great advantage to the grower as well as in experimental work.

Stock for graftage is ordinarily grown from seed from seedling trees. Naik (1941) found the difference in the germination and vigour between the progenies of different parent trees to be of commercial importance, as careful selection of parent trees may reduce the time required to produce plants large enough for graftage. Roy (1952), however, reports that although the Fazli and Langra varieties on four different rootstocks showed some differences until they were four years old, no difference in growth or bearing because of rootstock could be noticed when they were 15 years old. Nor was there a significant difference between rootstocks from seed of grafted varieties and those from seed of seedlings. Seedlings from the same variety as the scion seemed neither better nor worse than others. No success was had in finding a dwarfing rootstock, as the rate of growth seemed to depend mainly on the scion, though the slow-growing Fazli delayed the growth of the scion when it was used as rootstock. Nevertheless, Roy reports that in Bihar seeds are being used from 16 strains selected after observation in the nursery from 40 seedling trees selected on the basis of vigour and annual bearing. Of the 16, 5 are considered superior but the basis of this judgment is not given. Balakrishnamurti and Jogiraju (1932) claim that varied stock results in varied quality of the fruit, and a distinct difference in the time of ripening. It is claimed that ordinary grafted plants from Bombay were seriously affected by frost, in a cool part of Madhya Pradesh, but were not damaged when grafted on wild seedlings from the Pachmari hills.

It is generally considered good practice to use plump seeds, but while Naik (1941) found that larger seed gives a slightly higher percentage of germination, neither germination nor the vigour of the seedling depends on the size of the fruit or seed. Pope says that seeds from early ripening fruits do not produce vigorous seedlings, and Barakzai (1918) reports a common belief that seeds from the top branches yield plants which are more vigorous and more nearly like the parent than those from side branches. Seeds from fruit which ripens and falls to the ground are also said to come true to type, but there is no reason to consider these theories true.

The seed should be planted soon after it is removed from the ripe fruit, as it loses its viability in a short time. Burns and Prayag report an experiment in which about 80% of the seed germinated when planted within one month, 48% when planted after 38 days, and only 12% after 71 days. The seed ordinarily germinates within three weeks. If the husk is carefully removed before planting, the seed germinates a little sooner and, according to Naik (1941), the stem and root are straighter, but he does not recommend the procedure because of the expense, and of the poor germination. He found that sowing the seed with the plumule up also helps to avoid the rather common distortion of the seedlings. This is also recommended by Pope. Germination may take place in sand or in garden soil, or the seed may be left uncovered and kept damp. Stephens (1949) recommends planting husked seed on its ventral edge in an eight-inch layer of clean sand on a concrete or iron floor. This prevents the formation of a taproot 18 to 24 inches deep as may occur when the plants are grown in an ordinary seed bed, and favours fibrous root system. The seed should be almost covered with sand, and mulched with straw, grass, or some similar substance. He recommends a light shade three feet high which is removed after the first flush hardens.

A good deal has been said in favour of planting the seed where the tree is to remain in order to avoid transplanting. Balakrishnamurti and Jogiraju felt that this would be an advantage, as the cutting of the tap root was thought to shorten the bearing period of the tree. They recognized, however, that this might be caused by the process of grafting rather than by cutting the root. It is doubtful whether the advantage of planting the seed in its permanent position is sufficient to justify the additional expense involved. If this method is followed, a small grafted tree, growing in a pot, may be placed alongside the young seedling in the orchard, and a branch inarched to the seedling.

In common practice, seeds are planted in beds, and the young seedlings are set out in nursery rows until large enough for grafting, when they are placed in pots. On the basis of an experiment at the Ganeshkhind garden, Burns and Prayag recommended that the seedlings be raised in pots from the beginning. They found that seedlings one year old raised in the field averaged 20 inches in height, while those in pots were only 13 inches. But about a third of the field-grown plants died when transplanted to pots. Even if no better results can be secured in transplanting the seedlings, it may be more economical to grow the seedlings in the field and thus secure more rapid growth while avoiding the larger expense of caring for the seedlings in pots. Naik, (1947 a) on the other hand, found it feasible to transplant seedlings with bare roots, on cool, humid evenings when growth is inactive or under less favourable conditions if they are heavily defoliated seven to nine days before being moved. It is doubtful if the plant can be kept in one pot from germination until it is ready to be planted in the field, without becoming pot-bound. The difficulty is, of course, greater when the seedling is comparatively old when grafted.

The age of the seedling at the time of grafting varies from three weeks to three years. Burns and Prayag quote Wester as saying that in the Philippines seedlings three weeks old are inarched, and are commonly ready to be removed from the parent tree within a month, sometimes in as little as 13 days. They also state that in Hawaii the age at grafting is generally about six months. They were successful in five cases out of 10, with two-month-old seedlings. Sen (1939, 1941a, 1942a) secured the best results by inarching the current year's shoots, about the size of a lead pencil on to seedlings about three months old, using waxed tape. The union was complete in two or three weeks and the plants were ready to set out one year after the sowing of the seed. Naik (1941) succeeded with seedlings four and a half months old. He found no variation in size 18 months after planting trees which had been about 10, 13, and 16 months old when grafted and Rangacharlu (1955) found no significant differences among these trees 14 years later. L. B. Singh (1954a) reports 80% success with seedlings four weeks old with their roots covered with sphagnum moss. They were removed about a month after grafting and within three years were about the same size as ordinary inarched trees planted at the same time.

Most nurserymen graft seedlings when they are a year or two old, and in some places they take advantage of the common prejudice in favour of large grafts, and use seedlings as much as three years old. These are unlikely to have a good root system or to grow into satisfactory trees. Even worse results are inevitable with the practice reported by Patwardhan and Deshmukh (1931) of grafting one large scion onto three or more rootstocks simultaneously. A single rootstock not more than about one year old seems to be desirable.

Inarching is the only method of vegetative propagation of the mango used commercially in India. When well done it yields a satisfactory tree, but careless workmen often produce very poor plants. One mistake is that of grafting the scion upside down, because it is often easier to do this. The seedlings are commonly placed in pots a few weeks before grafting, but Garg (1954a) favours a method which makes it possible to use branches high above the ground and to take many grafts from one tree. He digs one-year-old seedlings with a ball of earth but after a day replaces most of the earth with moss or hay and after dipping the roots in water he stores them upright for 8 days, with further watering if necessary. The rooting material is then wrapped in plastic sheeting, and the seedlings are hung on the tree and grafted. They are left for about six weeks, severed and planted. He quotes figures showing the cost to be about 6½ annas each.

Although Burns and Prayag found that a slightly higher percentage of success could be secured by the method known as tongue grafting by approach, they recommend simple inarching. The former method is a combination of tongue grafting and inarching, and is more difficult. It also requires slightly larger stocks and scions. Inarching by an experienced man ordinarily results in a high percentage of success, but this varies with the variety, and with weather conditions. The rainy season is generally the best time. The grafts may commonly be separated from the parent tree in two or three months, but some varieties benefit by being left longer. During certain seasons, according to Naik (1941), it is possible to plant the grafts in their permanent position immediately without the customary period in the shade, with good results and such plants flush sooner than those nursed in the shade.

Naik (1941, 1948c) also reports success with root grafting, the best method being to lift the seedlings with naked roots, pot them, and later re-pot them with about three inches of the root exposed and extending through a notch cut in the side of the pot. The scion is then inarched onto the root. This may be of value for experimental work, as it eliminates the influence of the seedling stem, which may be as great as that of the roots. In the varieties tested, Neelum and Bangalora, there was no significant difference, however, between root-grafted and inarched trees.

When these two varieties were double worked, each with the other as the intermediate stem piece, trees were significantly dwarfed and the size of the Bangalora fruit was reduced. When three shy-bearing varieties were grafted on Neelum intermediate stems, they were somewhat dwarfed, precocious, and produced more flowers, but not more fruit. Roy (1952), however, reports that in Bihar intermediate stem pieces made no difference after a few years.

Other forms of grafting have been used in this country with very limited success. Most of them seem entirely unsuccessful except in regions of moist climate. Burns and Prayag recommended whip grafting in the hands of an expert under such conditions, and Patvardhan and Deshmukh state that in the Konkan about one crown graft out of four is successful. Gandhi (1942) reports good success in crown grafting using a device which had been used by Woodrow to avoid the extremes of temperature and maintain a moist atmosphere. This is an earthenware pot inverted over the plant, with a large hole in its bottom, which is covered with glass. For top-working, he secured excellent results by making a strawboard case around the graft, filling this with sawdust to cover all but the top bud, and covering it with glass. The sawdust is sprinkled on alternate days. Parsai (1952) also reports success in top-working seedlings on the Pachmarhi plateau by crown grafting during the rainy season, with mature terminal shoots defoliated 10—15 days in advance, as scions.

Side grafting has given encouraging results at Sabour, according to Sen, although there are difficulties to be overcome. The scion wood is not in the best condition at the best time of the year for grafting. In Madras Naik secured better results with scions more than half a centimeter in diameter, from the apical regions of shoots, than with other scions, and had some success with scions cut three to five days before being inserted. Veeraraghavan (1945) reports the success attained as follows : Khader, September to November, 100%; Neelum, October, 90%, November, 100%; Alampur Baneshan, October, 80%, November, 90%; Baneshan, October, 50%, November, 100%. For these varieties, at least, this method is preferred to inarching. Roy (1952) reports 83% success with one form of side grafting. Parsai (1954) was successful only when the humidity was high and the sun not bright. He used seedlings about a year old growing in the ground, either *in situ* or in the nursery. Well matured terminal shoots, thinner than the rootstock, were defoliated and used when the petioles had fallen. The base of the scion was cut to form a wedge with one side 3-4 in. long and the other 1 in. It was inserted with the long cut against the wood after the stock had been prepared as for Forkert budding, and tied with waxed tape. Such grafts, if made in the nursery, were ready for planting in the orchard a year later.

Although early attempts at budding in India were not successful, recent work has been much more promising, and the method is likely to replace inarching as standard nursery practice. About the beginning of this century budding was tried at Saharanpur, but with not more than 5% success. Slightly better results were secured at the Ganeshkhind garden in 1913-14, both shield and patch budding being used. Again in 1925 (Anon., 1926) better results were secured, about 40% being successful with the inverted T method. Ulvi (1940) reported 60% at Mirpurkhas, Sind, in 1940, using buds two inches long inserted while the rootstock was in flush, but the scion was not. The last flush of scion wood was rejected, and the previous flush or two were used. The February-March and August-September flushes were found to be the most suitable seasons for budding. Sen, on the other hand, had better success with buds from the current season's growth which had reached a certain stage of maturity, inserted in July and August. It made little difference whether the wood was retained in the bud or not. He secured an average of 50 to 60% success, with a maximum of 70%. Naik also reported success in budding, especially with the Forkert method. This method has also been very successfully used by Gandhi (1942) who describes and illustrates it. The bud, prepared as for shield budding, is inserted between the wood and a flap of bark which has been cut across the top and down both sides. The bud is loosely covered with the flap, and the whole is bandaged with waxed tape. After three weeks the tape is removed and the flap cut away. Growth begins in about three weeks and the top of the rootstock is then cut off. August and September is the best season for the operation in Poona, as the weather is cool and moist but not very rainy. The budling remains in the nursery for a year, but two months before it is to be removed the tap root is cut. Following this procedure, there has been no casualty in transplanting.

While Roy (1952) reports 76% success with budding, this was somewhat less than he reports with side grafting. In the dry zone of Ceylon also, grafting proved easier and more successful, according to Richards (1952). Cleft grafting on seedlings 3-4 months old was used. A possible improvement in the technique is suggested by Van der Meulen (1954) in South Africa, where the modified Forkert method is used, but the buds are wrapped with tightly stretched plastic tape. Another possibility is suggested by Lynch and Nelson (1950, 1951) who inserted shield buds or scion tips into stocks only three weeks old, like side grafts, and wrapped them in plastic film, permeable to gas but not water vapour. The tops of the rootstocks were removed 7—10 days after budding. Parsai (1952) reports success with shield budding in top working from November to January on the Pachmarhi plateau, using defoliated budwood. He also succeeded in budding nine-month-old seedlings in March to June, using shield buds in a vertical slit.

The age of the rootstock was found to be an important factor by L. Singh and Khan (1943 a). They had slight success with one-year-old plants, 30 to 40% with two-year-old and 70% with three-year-old stock. But when they tried to transplant 102 plants which had been budded at the age of three years, only seven survived. This led them to try planting two seeds at each place in the orchard where a tree was desired, keeping one good seedling, and budding it at the age of three years. They recommend this procedure, inserting buds from one-year-old scions on one-year-old branches, leaving one branch of each seedling unbudded, to be removed after the buds grow. The budwood is prepared by cutting off the immature growth and the blades of about 6 leaves just below it. After 10 to 15 days, when the petioles have fallen and the buds are swollen the budding is done. Without special precautions, the budwood must be used within a few hours after it is cut, but L. Singh and Khan (1943b) suggest a method by which it can be kept up to 48 hours. The wood is cut at least an inch and a half from the last usable buds, and the ends are dipped in melted paraffin, not more than a fourth of an inch deep, and then in cold water. The wood is kept in a thermos jug previoulsy cooled and with about one-fourth of an inch of cold water in it, which is renewed after 24 hours. They prefer shield budding, wrapping the bud with cotton tape dipped in paraffin wax with a melting point of 140 to 145° F. After a fortnight, the shoots are ringed four inches above the buds. Bajwa and Ram (1946) report success in 1943 ranging from 32% in Gurdaspur district to 94% in Multan. In the next two years 5,882 trees were budded *in situ* with about 60% success. April is considered the best time for budding in the Punjab but September gives about as good results except in years of severe frost, although the buds do not start growth until March.

Budding *in situ* may be worth while if no other method is successful, but it has obvious disadvantages. Roy (1952) found that in Bihar the age of the rootstock was immaterial if the shoot is of the same age and in the same condition as that from which the bud is taken. Transplanting of budded or grafted trees may be more successful if done when the trees are not actively growing, and if the tap roots, and perhaps also, a little later, the side roots are cut. This should be completed a month or two before transplanting is done.

Planting and Care

Mangoes are generally planted out in the field early in the rainy season, though where the rainfall is more than 60 inches, it is probably better to delay planting until the rains are nearly finished. While it is generally possible to establish trees at other seasons, special care is then required.

While it is recognized that many groves in this country are planted so that the trees have insufficient space in which to develop, there is much difference of opinion as to the correct spacing. Burns and Prayag recommend planting the trees 30 feet apart, which is an improvement on some of the earlier writers, such as Woodrow, who suggested 20 feet. Balakrishnamurti and Jogiraju recommend putting the trees 40 feet apart in rows 35 feet apart, by the triangular method. This amounts to placing them 40 feet apart by the hexagonal method. Allan (1935) states that while 30 feet may be enough on soil which is not fertile, in the Gangetic valley, they should be placed at least 35 feet apart, while 40 feet would not be excessive. Wagle (1931) states that in the Konkan trees 35 feet apart bear less frequently, and produce fewer fruits when they do bear, than trees 52 feet apart. Foreign authors recommend distances from 30 to 45 feet. Ochse (1931) states that for most varieties the spacing should be 12 to 14 meters (39 to 45 feet). If it is desired that the trees have room to develop normally, under most conditions in northern India, most varieties should be planted 40 or 45 feet apart. Seedling trees, if planted at all, may well occupy as much as 60 feet.

On few horticultural subjects has more been written on less experimental evidence than on the care of the mango. In most orchards, very little attention is paid to cultivation, irrigation, manuring, or pruning and frequently remarkably good results are secured. On the other hand, it is probable that most orchards would be benefited by intelligent care, and that in many cases complete failure could be avoided. Burns and Prayag refer to an experiment indicating considerably better crops each year when the soil is ploughed or dug than when it is not cultivated. In an experiment on 17-year-old Bambai, Langra, and Fazli trees, Sen (1939, 1941a, 1942a) found that uncultivated trees were in poor condition and thought that at least three ploughings a year were necessary for good health. He did not, however, report comparisons of one or two ploughings with three. The cultivated trees tended to bear fairly good crops in alternate years, but without cultivation more than one year seemed to be required for recovery after a good crop. This was specially evident in the Bambai variety, which also suffered most in vegetative growth when not cultivated.

Some work on the nutritional requirements of the mango has been done in Bihar and reported by Sen and Roy (1945), Sen and others (1947), and Patel (1949). One year after grafting on one-year-old rootstocks, Langra plants were transferred to quartz sand in June, 1940, and given a nutrient solution containing nitrogen, potassium and phosphorus until May, 1941, when differential treatments were begun. No attention was paid to the minor elements, and no solution contained copper, zinc, manganese, or boron. The supply of nitrogen seemed to control the uptake of the other elements, and to determine the amount of growth. An increase of nitrogen beyond the optimum amount caused a deficiency in potassium. The trees showed considerable resistance to phosphorus deficiency, but not to potassium deficiency.

The results of this pot-culture experiment have been confirmed by field trials, according to Roy and others (1951) and Malik and De, (1952). They found that the application of nitrogen increases growth, especially when phosphorus and potassium are also added, although these without nitrogen do not. Flowering and fruiting were found to be directly proportional to vegetative growth. They found that providing more nitrogen increased the uptake of potash by the tree and recommend that the two be applied together, and that phosphorus be applied with a slow-acting manure. They also recommend a manurial treatment including for each mature tree 1.6 lb. of nitrogen, 0.4 lb. of phosphate, and 1.5 lb. of potash. This may be supplied by 200 lb. of farmyard manure, 4 lb. of castor cake, 10 lb. of bone-meal, 2 lb. of ammonium sulphate, and 30 lb. of wood ash. In the year of heavy bearing, the amount of ammonium sulphate should be doubled. It is recommended that the ammonium sulphate and half of the potash be applied in June, and the rest in October. Malik and De (1952) give a schedule starting at the time of planting and increasing annually for several years. They refer to four trials in which manuring increased the net income per acre, whether accompanied by irrigation or ploughing and pruning, or by itself.

Sand cultures of two varieties in Florida are reported by Smith and Scudder (1952) in which 11 essential elements were omitted systematically. The omission of Ca, Cu, and B reduced growth, and definite deficiency symptoms are reported for N, P, K, Mg, Mn, and S. No specific symptoms were noted when Zn and Fe were omitted. When the nitrogen was supplied entirely as ammonia, the young leaves showed marginal scorch and the trees died within a few months.

There is general agreement among writers on the subject, that conditions should be such that the young trees will grow rapidly, but that too vigorous growth in older trees interferes with fruitfulness. Manuring the pit in which the trees are to be planted is commonly recommended. Burns and Prayag recommend mixing 100 lb. of well-rotted manure, 5 lb. of bone-meal and 10 lb. of wood ash with the soil of the pit. Allan recommends smaller amounts. He suggests that to the soil which is to fill the lower two feet of the pit, there be added 30 to 40 lb. of manure, 6 lb. of bone-meal, and 6 lb. of wood ash, while to the upper foot there be added 10 lb. of manure, 2 to 3 lb. of bone-meal, and 2 lb. of neem cake. Both recommend increments of these materials each year for several years. Neither seems to base his recommendations on experimental evidence, and in any case, such recommendations can be applied logically only to cases in which it is known that the soil is similar to that of the experience on which the recommendation is based.

In the Konkan, the use of salt is universal and it is regarded as a manure, but the Department of Agriculture (Anon. 1937b) considers it beneficial as a means of stopping vegetative growth. Its use would thus be similar to root pruning.

It is frequently recommended that the manure be applied in shallow trenches which are at first near the trunk and which are gradually moved further away and increased in size. It is seldom suggested that the manure be placed beyond the tips of the branches. These recommendations seem to be based more on the practice of the country than on definite evidence. Some recommend that the manure be given at the beginning of the rains, and others in early winter. It is obvious that many more manurial trials in different parts of the country will have to be conducted before amounts of the different elements and methods and times of application can be confidently recommended.

Young mango trees need to be irrigated frequently in order to keep them growing vigorously. The suggestion made by Burns and Prayag and accepted by Allan, that during the first six months the young trees should be irrigated every third day, and after that about once a week, seems unnecessarily liberal. There seems to be no advantage in irrigating oftener than once in ten days or two weeks, except in the very hot dry weather.

There is less basis for judgment regarding the irrigation of bearing trees. In many orchards no irrigation is given, but it is probable that under most Indian conditions a certain amount is desirable. It is questionable whether the trees should be irrigated at all between the monsoon and the flowering season, though some recommend one or two irrigations. It is thought, that tree irrigation at this time encourages vegetative growth in October and November, which in turn interferes with flowering in February. This cannot be regarded as an established fact, however. It is generally believed that irrigation from the time the fruit sets until the monsoon, tends to prevent the fruit from falling and to produce large fruits. There is considerable evidence that this is true.

Securing Regular Crops

The mango is commonly subject to alternate or irregular bearing. Vegetative and flora growth are closely inter-related. Inflorescences are generally borne on shoots nearly a year old, and the shoots which bear panicles of flowers do not ordinarily produce vegetative growth until after the harvest, although, as Sen has pointed out, if fruit fails to set, or falls early, laterals may be produced early enough to flower the following spring. It is even reported that in Madras shoots produced in October may bear the following year. Sen points out that shoots produced in March and April usually cease growth by July, and flower the next spring and that those ceasing growth by October are much more likely to flower than those growing in October. L. Singh and Khan (1939) agree that shoots growing rapidly and ceasing growth early produce more fruit the next year. It thus appears that the production of many leaders in the early flushes is likely to result in a good crop the following year, and it has also been suggested that an early production of laterals during the spring flush, and vigorous growth in October favour regular bearing.

Evidence that the amount of carbohydrate in the bark, wood, and leaves of one Langra tree was higher in the period of bud differentiation following an 'off' season than after one in which there was normal flowering has been presented by Malik (1953-54 b). He found 8.81% of carbohydrate in November following flowering, which increased to 19.30% in February, fell to 10–13% until July. Following a spring without flowers there was 14.61% in November, 20.45% in February, and then, as a result of flowering and new growth, only 4–8% until July.

There are some varieties, such as the Baramasi, which flower more than once during the year, and in these panicles are sometimes borne on very young vegetative growth. In these varieties, mixed panicles occur frequently, that is, shoots which bear both leaves and flowers, and crops are generally very light. Mixed inflorescences also occur in some varieties which flower only once a year, such as the Fazli. Sen (1939, 1941a, 1942a) observed that the varieties which bear the fewest mixed panicles bear the heaviest crops and are the most markedly alternate bearing.

Efforts have been made to overcome the alternate bearing tendency but with little success. Wagle (1928) found that by ringing and notching he could increase the number of inflorescences and of fruits, on bearing trees, but that he could not secure flowers on trees in a vegetative state. In a later paper (1931) he reports some success with ringing, manuring and pruning off the October-November flush. Sen reports one case in which ringing in August resulted in satisfactory flowering the following spring. Malik (1951) reports a significant increase in the flowering of 20-year-old Bambai, Langra, and Fazli trees following the removal in August of rings of bark one-half inch wide from large branches. The damage which sometimes resulted was avoided by applying farmyard manure and ammonium sulphate at the time of ringing. Manuring without ringing caused a slight increase in flowering. The treatment had to be repeated each year, and the effect of this on the growth of the tree was not reported. L. Singh and Khan (1939) removed part of the panicles from a flowering Langra tree with the result that about 70% of the deflowered shoots fruited the next year. Later these workers (1946) observed three 26-year-old Langra trees during four seasons. One tree and two of the four main branches of another were totally deflowered the first year. The untreated tree and branches continued to bear fairly uniform crops. Strong hot winds cause much shedding of fruits where these trees were growing in the Punjab, and the average crop on the untreated tree was only 166 fruits weighing 6.75 oz. each. Deflowering caused marked alternate bearing on the treated tree and branches, with about the same total production during the four seasons as the untreated tree and branches. Sen, on the other hand, found that removing all of the panicles of the Bambai variety during the 'on' year resulted in a significant increase in the number of panicles borne the next year, but the number in all cases was very small. Similar results were secured with the Fazli. Sen (1939, 1941a, 1942a) states that with the Bambai a very poor flowering follows heavy flowering even if no fruit is set, but that in some other varieties a fair crop may follow. Removing 50% of the panicles of the Bambai had no effect on the crop that year, and removing 75% reduced the crop only 57%, but in both cases there was only a slight increase in flowering the next year. L. B. Singh and Singh (1955) state that the only effective method of controlling alternate bearing is to rub off the flower buds or remove the flowers in the 'on' year, and suggest that 90% be removed.

The importance of cultivation in encouraging fruitfulness is stressed by Sen (1943b). An experiment was started in 1935 with Bambai trees 13 years old, all having been ploughed regularly up to that time. From 1936 to 1942, the average number of panicles per tree in the part of the orchard in which ploughing was continued was 9,283, with satisfactory numbers in three years. In the unploughed part, the average number was 3,233, with satisfactory numbers in only two years. Sen feels that there is little doubt that the fahure of trees to bear heavily for several years is caused by nutritional deficiencies, mainly of nitrogen. In one case, manuring after the harvest of a heavy crop resulted in good flowering the next year.

It thus seems that the problem of bearing has at least two aspects : maintaining the nutrition of the tree, and so managing that there will be some branches ready to bear each year. Sen (1943b) therefore makes the following recommendations: (1) plant varieties which do not have a strong tendency toward alternate bearing; (2) plant the trees well apart and provide a wind-break; (3) plough regularly, ordinarily once in the winter, at the beginning of the monsoon, and in October or November; (4) use up to 10 cartloads of farmyard manure or compost per acre, or even more, depending on the condition of the trees, at the time of the autumn ploughing; (5) if the new growth in the spring is insufficient, apply nitrogen in a quickly available form, such as ammonium sulphate, 5 to 10 lb. per tree about the first of June, and irrigate liberally once or twice; (6) irrigate soon after the fruit has set; (7) where the rainfall is high, or when there are late rains, ring the branches 3 to 5 inches thick at the beginning of August by removing half an inch of the bark and covering the wound with a mixture of one part of fresh cowdung and two parts of soil; and (8) keep the orchard open by pruning or by removing alternate trees. Having secured flowers, it is, of course, necessary to protect them from insect pests and diseases, in order to get a satisfactory crop of fruit.

In the Philippines it has long been the practice to build slow fires in the mango groves some time before flowering, and there seems to be little doubt that this causes the trees to flower earlier than they otherwise would. Borja and Bautista (1932) report that in an experiment on 27-year-old trees, 84% flowered in from 7 to 9 days, and that the effect was apparent up to a distance of 60 metres. The presence of such gases as ethylene in the smoke may explain in part its effect, but Galang and Agati (1936) have shown that a combination of heat and smoke produce a greater response than cool smoke. De Jong (1934a) has reported an interesting experiment in Java, where the mango ordinarily flowers in July. Four fires, producing dense smoke, were lighted under a mango tree on March 3,

A langra mango tree which had been cultivated for several years.

A langra mango tree, 12 years old without cultivation.

Guava tree in an early stage of wilt infection showing a few branches withered.

Completely wilted guava tree.

and the first flowers appeared in 24 days. The fires were continued 8 hours daily until April 10, when the tree was in full bloom. The fruit was ripe in July, and the tree bloomed again in August. The yield in July was 797 fruits, while that in the regular season was 200. Similar trees, unsmudged, yielded about 1,000 to 1,500 fruits. While the total crop was not increased by smudging, the higher price of the fruit out of season might justify the expense. Sen and Mallik (1945, 1947) report no success in inducing flowering by smudging in Bihar, but they sometimes brought about excessive vegetative growth. When they maintained six to eight small heaps of green grass and weeds burning night and day for four weeks in November and December, about 10 feet from the trunk of a tree, and confined the smoke within mat screens around the tree, they caused the shedding of leaves and profuse vegetative growth, part of which was abnormal. But there was no flowering, even on the 'on' years when the control trees flowered heavily. This treatment was more severe than that used in the Philippines. It seems probable that smudging has no effect on bud differentiation, but may hasten the growth of differentiated buds.

Heating the tree after flowering has begun may increase the set in some cases. Robinson (1951) noticed that a Haden tree in Florida was warmed by being near a wash house and never failed to bear. He tried heating with a coke burner a large Banarsi Langra tree which was a shy bearer for five nights and forenoons when the night temperatures ranged from 35° to 58° F. The tree then bore a good crop, better than comparable trees in the same orchard, and after that Robinson used a heater under one of his trees whenever it was cool and foggy, and regularly had good crops. How the heat was effective is uncertain; the warmth may have favoured inset pollinators or prevented some disease, or may have had some direct effect.

Very little pruning is ordinarily given the mango. Young trees should be pruned to form a head about two or three feet from the ground, with a few well-spaced branches. As the tree develops, it may be wise to thin out the top, as it is otherwise likely to be quite dense. Otherwise no pruning is recommended except the removal of dead or injured branches. The best time for pruning seems to be after the close of the monsoon.

Mango Hoppers

A large number of insects have been noticed as pests of the mango in India and in other countries, but fortunately most of these are of comparatively little importance. Undoubtedly the most serious pests in India are the mango hoppers, which are also referred to as jassids. They occur in all of the mango-growing districts of India, and are frequently found in very large numbers during the hot weather, and especially at the flowering season. The three species of the genus *Ideocerus* which are important in India differ from each other in several respects, according to Uppal and Wagle (1944). Both *I. atkinsoni* and *I. niveosparsus* are larger than *I. clypealis*. The adults of *I. atkinsoni* are found mainly on the trunk and branches while the other species are found on the leaves and panicles.

I. clypealis is the most prolific and breeds usually in January and February; *I. niveosparsus* breeds not only during the flowering season but also in June and October; and *I. atkinsoni* also breeds three times a year, mainly on the vegetative shoots, but both latter species produce comparatively few young. *I. atkinsoni* is less common on the flowers, though it may be abundant at other seasons. In the Konkan and Karnatak, *I. clypealis* predominates, and it is reported as a serious pest in most parts of the country. In South India *I. niveosparsus* is said to cause the greatest damage and it occurs along with *I. atkinsoni* in southern Gujarat and the area near Bombay city. In the northern parts of the country *I. atkinsoni* is most commonly found, although *I. clypealis* also occurs.

The minute, translucent eggs are deposited in the tissue of the floral or vegetative shoots or in the unopened flowers. The nymphs, which are yellowish, with red eyes, emerge in about 4 to 6 days in Bombay or 8 to 10 days in the Punjab. They grow rapidly, and moult five times before becoming winged adults in about 10 to 13 days in Bombay or 17 to 19 days in the Punjab. After breeding, the adults of *I. atkinsoni* live on the stems, while the other species prefer the leaves. They spend the winter in crevices in the bark, and become active again just before the trees flower. While some damage results from oviposition, much more is done by the nymphs and adults, which suck the juice from the inflorescence and young fruits. The honey-dew falling on other inflorescences may interfere with pollination, and it sometimes encourages a fungus, sooty mould, which interferes with respiration. The result of an attack by hoppers is that the flowers and young fruits fall, and the crop is reduced, sometimes as much as 60 or even 100%. Hoppers cause damage also in Pakistan and Burma, and Ochse (1931) reports an attack in Java.

Control of the mango hopper with the older insecticides has proved difficult. Among sprays which have been recommended are crude oil emulsion, kerosene emulsion, fish-oil soap, fish-oil-rosin soap, and tobacco decoction. Sen (1946) in addition to other methods, suggests a spray made by boiling 60 soap nuts in about a gallon of water and, after straining, diluting in 12 to 15 gallons of water. Rahman (1946) recommends spraying in the early morning from December 15 to February 7 with rosin compound, made by boiling 6 lb. of third grade rosin, and 1 lb. of washing soda in just enough water to keep it from burning over a slow fire, and adding more warm water until the liquid is a clear deep brown. Dusting with finely powdered sulphur has also proved fairly effective, especially in the areas of Bombay where *I. clypealis* is the common species, according to Uppal and Wagle (1944). The sulphur also helps to prevent or control the powdery mildew which frequently occurs at the same time and is partly responsible for the failure of the crop.

But far more effective than any of the earlier insecticides in controlling the hoppers are some of the modern insecticides, particularly DDT. Excellent results have been reported by Sodhi and Batra (1950) and Latif and Qayyum (1950) in the Punjab, by Roy and Ram (1951) in Bihar, and by Rao (1953) in Madras. Sen and Prasad (1954), also working in Bihar, found DDT better than BHC, Dieldrin, Aldrin, Folidol, or Pyrocolloid, and the only material effective as a preventive and to control an infestation. They say the only advantage of adding Pyrocolloid is its immediate 'knockdown' effect, which impresses the farmers. They report better results from spraying than from dusting, and recommend spraying once in winter and once in the spring before the flowers begin to open, as spraying the open flowers may reduce the set of fruit. About 1 lb. of 50% DDT in a wettable form, such as Guesarol 550, in 300 lb. of water seems satisfactory. The main difficulty lies in getting the spray applied at the proper time. Spraying mature trees with hand equipment is slow and difficult, and few growers have power sprayers. In Bihar and Madras the Government has undertaken to spray large numbers of trees for the growers, in some cases charging only four annas per tree although the actual cost was figured at Rs. 1-12.

In using such an insecticide as DDT, there is always the danger of killing the parasites or predators of other pests, with the result that there is a severe attack of a pest which had been held in biological control. This is pointed out by Patel and Hadli (1953) who state that 'DDT, when used by itself has led, in many cases, to disastrous epidemics of mites'. They, therefore, advocate mixing an equal amount or twice as much sulphur with 5% DDT, or an equal amount with 5% toxaphene, either of which they found to kill 95–98% of the nymphs, compared with up to 80.8% with sulphur alone. They worked in a part of Bombay where *I. atkinsoni* is the principal species. The sulphur not only helps to control the hoppers and mildew, but helps to control the mites, as well as reducing the cost of the treatment. The use of DDT may also enable scale insects to increase in numbers so as to require treatment, which, unfortunately is much more difficult and expensive than the treatment of mites.

Other Insect Pests

Another pest which sometimes does great damage, is the stem borer, the grub of a large, long-horned beetle, *Batocera rufomaculata* (*rubus*, *rubra*, *rubiginosa*, *cruentata*). The eggs are laid in chinks in the bark, and the young borer makes straight, zigzag, or spiral tunnels in the bark and later bores into the wood. If neglected, the pest may not only destroy many branches, but actually kill the tree. Rahman (1946) recommends, as measures to prevent attack, the destruction of severely infested trees, wrapping 1/6 in. mesh wire gauze loosely around the trunk of the tree in July and August, when the eggs are laid, and the collection and destruction of the adult beetle. Control, especially in the early stages, is not difficult. The tunnels may be found by noticing the hard dry pellets of excreta which are pushed out of the opening, or by tapping the trunk and branches. At first the grubs can be scooped out with a knife, or destroyed with a stiff wire. Later, when it is difficult to force a wire to the end of the tunnel, the grubs can be killed by putting kerosene, carbon bisulfide, tar, turpentine, or a mixture of creosote and chloroform into the hole and closing it. Rahman also recommends placing one or two grains of potassium cyanide in the tunnel. Chowdhury and Majid (1954) also recommend the collection of the beetles by hand and by attracting them to light.

Fruit flies are not as serious pests in India as in some countries, but some damage is caused, especially in the South. Unfortunately, the better varieties are more subject to attack than the poor ones. The flies are slightly larger than the common house flies, and of a reddish brown colour, marked with black and yellow. The eggs are laid just under the skin of the ripening fruit, and the larvae burrow around in the pulp, making it unusable. They emerge, drop to the ground and pupate in the soil. Ayyar (1940) says that about half a dozen species, chiefly of the genus *Chaetodacus*, have been noted attacking mangoes in Madras. The nomenclature is somewhat confused. One species frequently attacks many kinds of fruits, and so may be given several common names. The term mango fruit fly has been applied to *Dacus dorsalis* and to *Chaetodacus* (*Dacus*, *Strumeta*) *ferrugineus*, which may be the same fly as is called *Chaetodacus ferrugineus var. dorsalis*. This species is said to be severe in Western India and is probably widespread in the country. Also severe in Bombay is the peach fly, *Dacus zonatus*, which Rahman (1946) says is most destructive to mangoes and guavas, as well as the peach, in the Punjab. Chowdhury and Majid (1954) refer to a peach fly which also attacks mangoes in Assam as *Dacus persicae*. In other countries mangoes are damaged by the Mediterranean fruit fly, *Ceratitis capitata;* the Queensland fruit fly, *Strumeta* (*Chaetodacus*) *tryoni;* the Mexican fruit fly, *Anastrepha ludens;* and the melon, cucurbit or cucumber fruit fly, *Chaetodacus* (*Dacus*) *cucurbitae*. The last is reported by Rahman (1944) as being common in the Punjab, and may attack mangoes there.

There is no practicable method of controlling the adult fly, but the numbers can be greatly reduced by collecting the attacked fruit, before or as it falls from the tree, and destroying the larvae by boiling the fruit or burying them deeply. As there are five or six broods in a season it is obvious that the destruction of the first brood is of greater importance. If green mangoes which fall from the trees a fortnight before harvest are punctured and left under the trees, some of the flies will be attracted and will lay eggs in them. They can later be collected and destroyed. Rahman (1946) also recommends stirring the soil to destroy the pupae and spraying 1 lb. of lead arsenate, 2 lb. of molasses, and about 6 gallons of water on a small patch of foliage or on a board hung horizontally in the tree, once a week or oftener from June to August. Rivnay (1954) reports that spraying at short intervals with 0.5—1% methoxychlor, DDT, and BHC as wettable powders gave adequate control, in that order of efficiency, of the Mediterranean fruit fly. Shaw (1955) reports on tests of a number of modern insecticides in poison-lure sprays against the Mexican fruit fly, in which parathion and malathion formulations proved fairly effective. In limited experiments, 4 lb. of tartar emetic with 20 lb. of sugar gave as good results. This would seem to be worth trying in India where considerable risk is run in using such highly toxic materials as parathion.

The giant mealy bug, or mango white bug, *Drosicha* (*Monophlebus*) *stebbingi*, occasionally causes damage in northern India, but as it produces only one generation in a year, it is ordinarily not of much importance. Sen (1955), however, states that it has been increasing in recent years and is second in importance only to the hoppers in Bihar. It feeds on as many as 62 different plants, of which the mango, citrus fruits, jujube, and guava suffer most, according to Rahman and Latif (1944). The soft, white, slow-moving insect is to be found on the tender shoots, from February to May or June, sucking the juice. The adult female, about half an inch in length and covered with white wax, crawls down the trunk at the end of the season and lays her eggs in the ground. The winged male adult is also seen at this time. The eggs remain in the ground until the following January or February, when they hatch and the young, which are brown, crawl up the trunk of the tree. They have many enemies. Rahman and Latif (1944) report that in Lyallpur an unidentified Dipterous parasite is common in March and May, 10% of the nymphs collected on March 25 being parasitized. In April and May a species of *Phygadeuon* oviposits in the nymphs. They mention eight insect predators, and state that the common babbler also feeds on the females and nymphs in March and April.

A fair degree of control may be secured by hand picking of the bugs in the case of small trees, and the capture of the adult females by means of a trench with a steep outer wall, around the trunk of the tree. Greased bands around the trunk in the early spring prevent the young from reaching the branches. The reports of the United Provinces Department of Agriculture for 1935-36 and 1939-40 mention experiments in which the crop was doubled by banding the trees. Many eggs can be destroyed by cultivating the soil under the trees after the monsoon. Rahman and Latif (1941) report finding 1,526 nymphs on weeds near a garden in which the trees had not been banded, and only 430 near banded trees. Later, however, Rahman and Latif (1944) report that most types of banding are either ineffective or temporary, especially the sticky ones. Fluffy cotton bands were effective until the birds and squirrels stole the cotton. Black oilcloth bands two inches wide largely prevented the nymphs from climbing the tree, but did not prevent the descent of the adult females. They recommend a material called 'namhar' when applied twice a season at a cost of less than an anna a season per tree. Some caution is necesary in using this mixture, however, for when it was applied to the trunk of citrus trees at Allahabad, serious damage was caused. Still later, Rahman (1946) recommends the use of 9-inch bands of cotton wool, or rope, soaked in a mixture of coal tar and crude oil emulsion, or in three parts of rosin dissolved in one part of rapeseed oil. When large numbers of nymphs collect below the band or adults above it, they can be removed and destroyed. He also suggests the burning of the rubbish from under the tree and the use of the top 4 to 6 inches of soil as litter for animals, and spraying the females with fish-oil rosin soap solution. Sen (1955) found 'namhar' effective for 2-3 weeks, and other banding materials for not more than 6 days, except the proprietary 'Ostico' bands which he recommends as giving protection for 83—99 days at a cost of 6 annas per tree, and which he says are best applied in the third week of December. Chowdhury and Majid (1954), in addition to some of the treatments already mentioned, suggest treating the soil within three yards of the trunk with equal parts of 5% BHC and road dust. Experiments in Uttar Pradesh have shown more than 90% of the mealy bugs killed with 0.1% parathion sprays, the nymphs being more easily killed than the adults. A carbon and sulphur insecticide, 'Rhodiatox' is reported very effective in Orissa.

Related to the mealy bug are the scale insects, of which several species attack the mango. Burns and Prayag list five species, of which *Aspidiotus destructor* is the most serious, as it sometimes covers the tender parts of the tree. Ansari (1947) refers to this species as the transparent bourbon scale, common on many plants in India and sometimes severe on grafted mangoes and guavas. He states that it is generally kept under control by its natural enemies, but that if necessary to use other methods it may be sprayed with 4-4-50 Bordeaux mixture to which 2 to 3 pounds of fuel oil has been added, or with a rosin wash. He indicates the importance of the inspection of nursery stock to prevent the spread of this scale. Berger (1935) recommends spraying with an oil-emulsion or miscible oil, preferably with about 1% of white oil. He found spraying with 1 lb. of fish-oil soap to 6 or 8 gallons of water less effective. A species of *Coccus* (*Lecanium*), perhaps *C. hesperidum*, has been found on mangoes at Allahabad. *Leucaspis indica* may do considerable damage by encircling young branches under a black mould. *Chionaspis dilatata*, *Pulvinaria psidii*, and *Icerya seychellarum* are given as less serious pests. *Chionaspis vitis* has also been recorded. Lal (1950) mentions *Pulvinaria polygonata*, *P. pergandei*, and *Lepidosaphes gloverii* as pests in Uttar Pradesh, but states that as far as is known, they attack only young plants. Rahman and Ansari (1941) report *Aonidiella aurantii*, *A. orientalis*, *Parlatoria oleae*, and *P. pseudopyri* as also occurring on the mango. The remedy suggested for these is a rosin wash.

A bug, *Spilostethus pandurus*, attacks a number of fruits in South Africa, and is reported by Ahmad (1945) as a fairly serious pest of the peach in Jhelum district, and as a pest of mangoes in Agra. It sucks juice from the fruit, causing it to fall. Little is known of its life histroy or control.

The mango weevil lays its eggs on the young fruit, and the grubs enter the pulp and seed and develop and pupate in it, the weevils then eating their way out through the pulp. They belong to two species of *Cryptorhynchus* (*Sternochetus*), *C. gravis* being found in eastern Bengal and Assam and also in Java, and *C. mangiferae* in South India and in most other mango-producing countries. Control is possible by destroying the infested fruit, removing all litter from under the trees, cultivation and if necessary spraying the trunk with kerosene emulsion after harvest, to kill the weevils hiding in the bark.

Among other weevils of minor importance to Indian mangoes are two which eat the leaves in Bombay, *Myllocerous maculosus* and *Astycus lateralis*. L. B. Singh and Singh (1955) report species of *Myllocerus* attacking the tender leaves, shoots, and inflorescences except in winter, in Uttar Pradesh. They also refer to *Deporus* (*Eugnamptus*) *marginatus*, a weevil which lays eggs along the midrib of the leaf and then cuts the leaf so that it falls to the ground, toward the close of the rainy season. Destroying the cut leaves, raking the soil beneath the trees, and dusting the leaves with lead arsenate or 5% BHC when the weevils are about to attack are possible control methods. Apparently more serious is the flea weevil, *Rhynchaenus mangiferae*, which S. M. Singh (1954a) says has been known in South India and Ceylon, but has now become serious in Uttar Pradesh, especially in the western districts. The adult is active from February to May and lays eggs in the flowers and young leaves. The infested flowers and buds dry, and in severe cases leaves are eaten. It is stated to be one of the main reasons for the poor setting of fruit in the western districts. Anantanaryanan and Subramanian (1955) report that it had been considered a minor pest, but that a severe attack occurred in Coimbatore in February-March, 1955. It can be fairly well controlled by spraying with DDT.

The caterpillars of many moths are found on the mango, but in most cases the damage done is not great. The mango shoot-webbers, the caterpillars of *Orthaga exvinacea*, are reported by Cherian and Ananthanarayanan (1943) to cause considerable damage to the leaves of the mango trees throughout Madras State. They can be controlled by hand picking the infested clusters or by spraying with calcium arsenate. The bark-eating caterpillars, *Indarbela quadrinotata* and *I. tetraonis*, are much less serious pests of the mango than of some other fruits. A shoot borer, *Chlümetia transversa*, sometimes kills small twigs. Cheema and others (1954) state that this is a major pest during the rainy season in Bombay and recommend spraying with 0.5% lead arsenate and cutting off and burning the affected twigs. L. B. Singh and Singh (1955) state that in Uttar Pradesh there are three overlapping generations from September to the middle of November. The larva of the Pyralid moth, *Noorda albisonalis*, has recently been found widespread in Puri district, boring the green and ripening fruit. A species previously known as a pest of forest trees, *Lymantria mathura*, is reported by S. M. Singh (1954b) to have appeared in unusual numbers in Dehra Dun in 1953 and in the next year to have caused severe damage to mango and litchi trees. More than 80% were killed by two dipterous parasites, and the young caterpillars in the trunk could be killed with a 2% tar oil wash. Among caterpillars which eat the leaves are *Circula trifenestrata*, which defoliates trees in lower Bengal and Burma and which is dangerous to handle because of its poisonous spines; *Natada velutina*, which also has irritating spines; *Parasa lipida*; and *Euproctis scintillans*. These can be controlled by use of a stomach poison, if necessary. Aiyar (1943) calls attention to three caterpillars attacking mango inflorescences in Travancore, of which a species of *Chlorocylstis* is considered a serious pest. The others, which are potentially serious in that State are *Eublemna angulifera* and *Argyroploce aprobola*, which more commonly attacks the jambolan.

Another insect eating the flowers of the mango has been reported by Banerji and Chatterji (1951). This is a shiny blue flea-beetle, *Alitca* (*Haltica*) *coerulea*. It seems to be limited to an area within 10 miles of Gosaba in the 24-Parganas of Bengal, but there swarms of the beetles appear just before flowering and are very destructive. They are said to infest about 45% of the trees. This discourages the planting of mangoes in that area, and presents a threat to other areas.

Galls are formed on the leaves and, more rarely, on the shoots of the mango by a number of insects. Lal (1949, 1950, 1953) and Chaturvedi (1954) in Uttar Pradesh have reported on 11 types of galls on the leaves, two on the stems, and one on the inflorescences. The most common type is caused by a Cecid fly, *Procontarinia matterana.* They also mention *Rhabdophagi mangiferae, Amrodiplosis viridigallicola,* and *Dasyneura mangiferae,* a heavy infestation of which at Dharwar is reported by Kulkarni (1955). Kulkarni and Patel (1953 a, b) report on a Cecidomyid fly, *Allasomyia tenuispatha* and a wasp of the genus *Platygaster.* Severe damage is reported by Gupta (1953) and S. M. Singh (1954 c) in the hill valleys and within 40 miles of the Himalayas by *Apsylla cistellata,* which modifies vegetative buds into green conical galls. The relationship of the insect to the formation of the galls, however, has been questioned. A tar-oil wash in September before the eggs hatch or from February to May greatly reduces the infestation. Control methods for some of the other gall-makers have been worked out but may not ordinarily be required.

Termites are frequently blamed for damage to mango trees as well as to other plants and Lal (1950) states that trees up to three years of age are often damaged or killed. Patel and Patel (1952, 1953) state that termites, notably *Trinervitermes biformis* damage mango and other trees in Bombay. For large trees they recommend 5% DDT in light oil or 5% BHC in crude oil, and for small trees, 2% DDT in water. In northern India the termites frequently eat the dead outer bark, but do no harm to old trees, and it may be questioned whether even young plants are damaged unless weakened by some other agent. For young trees, cultivation, irrigation, and such deterrents as kerosene emulsion and oil-cakes are recommended.

The red ant, *Oecophylla smaragdina,* is listed by Lal (1950) as a pest of mango and other fruit trees with large or medium leaves. It makes nests by sewing many leaves together, and as it bites viciously when disturbed, it interferes with harvesting and other orchard operations. To control this ant, Lal suggests the persistent destruction of the nests. Trehan and others (1949) advocate piercing the nests, dusting the nests and then dusting the entire tree with 5% Hexyclan (0.65% BHC) or Gammexane, or DDT, with added sulphur which keeps the tree free from ants for more than 12 weeks. Other ants are harmful mainly in protecting aphids, scale insects, and other insects from their natural enemies.

Many other insects have been found on the mango. Most of them do little or no damage. Some which are pests in other countries are not found in India, or if found, seem to be held in control by nature.

A condition called malformation of the inflorescence or abnormal or bunchy inflorescence was reported by Watt in 1891. In it the flowers are crowded on short thick stems and open very late if at all. They very seldom set fruit but sometimes the inflorescence persists and becomes vegetative. All or part of the panicles may be affected. Sattar (1946) reports that it is increasing rapidly in the Punjab, and this seems to be true of northern India in general. Sharma (1953) reported that near Lucknow 30—60% of the panicles of Dasheri, Khajri, and Husnara were affected, while other varieties fared better. A somewhat similar condition of the vegetative shoots, with clusters of short thick shoots arising from a leaf axil, has been called bunchy top by Garg (1951) and Nirvan (1953 b). Later Tripathi (1954) presented evidence that the two were closely related, and that Bombay Yellow and Fajri Jafrani were more susceptible than some other varieties. For a long time no cause could be established, but Narasimhan (1954) reported that the malformation of the inflorescence was caused by a mite, a species of *Eriophyes*. S. M. Singh (1955) found mites in all of the malformed panicles and shoots, but reports that they are the copra itch mite, *Tyrophagus castellanii* and species of *Typhlodromus*, probably *T. asiaticus*. The mites are active in February—April, take refuge in the dried panicles and bunchy shoots, and are plentiful from July to October. Although removing and burning the malformed panicles seems a logical measure to reduce infestation, Singh reports that this, the application of sulphur dust, and spraying with a 2% tar-oil wash all proved ineffective. However, now that the nature of the trouble is established, it may be hoped that an effective means of control will be found.

Diseases

While it is clear that considerable damage is done to mangoes by diseases, there is much confusion about the nature of the diseases and the best means of control.

In different parts of India, and in other countries, one of the most serious diseases is caused by a fungus, or a group of fungi, variously named. The term anthracnose has been widely used for a disease caused by a fungus which has been known as *Colletotrichum gloeosporioides*. It attacks leaves, stems, inflorescences, flowers, and fruits. A related fungus, *C. mangifera*, is said to be the cause of mango die-back, attacking only twigs and branches, in Uttar Pradesh. In Bombay a similar disease, called blight and attacking flowers also, is attributed to *Gloeosporium mangifera*. This fungus is considered the most serious in Java where it attacks seedlings and fruit, as well as other parts of the plant. That these may be synonyms for one disease and one fungus is suggested by Sattar and Malik (1939), who use anthracnose as the name of the disease, and *Glomerella cingulata* for the organism, giving *Colletotrichum gloeosporioides* as a synonym. They think that *Gloeosporium mangiferae* may be identical. In the Punjab the disease was first reported in 1934, and has become very serious in several districts. The optimum temperature for the germination of the spores was found to be about 25° C. (77° F.), and the spores were viable after two years on twigs on the ground, after at least 19 months on twigs on the trees, and after 14 months on leaves on the ground. This emphasizes the value of removing all dead and diseased leaves. They also found spraying with 3-3-50 Bordeaux mixture effective in nurseries. Sattar (1946) states that the young plants, which are very susceptible, should be kept away from infected trees, including citrus trees suffering from withertip, a disease which may be caused by the same organism. He recommends spraying all mango trees in infected areas with Bordeaux mixture in February, April and September, as do Chowdhury and Majid (1954) in Assam. Baker (1938) and McKee (1940) found that freshly prepared 1% Burgundy mixture, sprayed throughout the season, gave good control of the disease. Conover and Ruehle (1949) found bioquin-1 (copper-8-quinolinolate) as effective as Bordeaux without leaving a visible residue on the fruit at harvest time. Workers at Jeolikote have reported die-back and the destruction of the graft union of mango trees in the *tarai* region of Uttar Pradesh, caused by a species of *Gloeosporium*.

Powdery mildew often appears during the flowering season and may reduce the crop, especially on certain varieties. It is caused by *Erysiphe cichoracearum* or, where the perfect stage is not found, *Oidium mangiferae*. The disease is prevalent in Bombay. U. B. Singh and Garg (1949) report an outbreak in Lucknow, said to be the first recorded in Uttar Pradesh. Bose (1953 a), however, states that on the plains of that State it attacks inflorescences and young plants but that in Kumaun it is also severe on the leaves of grown trees, especially between 2,000 and 4,000 ft. above sea-level, where it is found at all times, especially in the spring, causing the premature fall of the leaves and fruit. He says that Sandolin (dinitro cresol) gave the best control of the fungicides tried. Sulphur is a fairly effective treatment, and may well be used as dust or as wettable sulphur along with treatment for the hoppers which are often present at the same time. Rains during the flowering season encourage mildew and Raisinghani (1945) states that by shaking the branches after each rain the loss in the yield may be reduced by 50—75%.

Black stem, caused by *Rhinocladium corticolum*, is of little importance except as it is associated with a scale insect. Sooty mould, caused by *Capnodium mangiferum*, lives on the secretions of the hoppers, or sometimes of aphids, and is controlled by killing these insects. It does some damage by interfering with respiration, whereas red rust, caused by an alga, *Cephaleuros mycoidea* (*virescens*) is considered practically harmless.

Die-back, caused by a species of *Fusarium*, is reported in Hyderabad by Vaheeduddin (1954) who states that the small branches dry out from the tip downward and that there is a white growth, turning pink or red, on the bark and sometimes in the wood. He recommends applying Bordeaux paste after removing the infected parts, and spraying with Bordeaux mixture.

Slight to severe damage to leaves, especially of young trees has been observed, caused by *Pestalotia* (*Pestalotiopsis*) *mangiferae*. Tandon and others (1955) were able to cause symptoms on the leaves, and also rotting of the fruits, by inoculation with this weakly parasitic species, and to control it on the leaves with zinc sulphate dust.

Fruit rots are of some importance and Verma and Kamal (1951) report one caused by *Aspergillus niger* which affects about a fourth of the fruit on seven varieties around Lucknow, especally Gola and Safeda. This may be the same disease which is stated to spoil 25—30% of the crop in some districts around Bombay and in the Konkan. Another disease of the ripe fruit is black rot, caused by a species of *Lasiodiplodia* and may be prevented by spraying with Bordeaux mixture, or soaking the fruit in one ounce of formalin in two gallons of water, before storage.

Bacteria cause a number of diseases and fruit rots of the mango. Patel and others (1948 a, b) report small necrotic spots on the leaves, fruits, and tender stems of the mango and also affecting the cashew. It seems similar to a very serious disease which is apparently confined to South Africa, but as the pathogen differs, they call it *Pseudomonas mangiferae-indica*. L. B. Singh and Singh (1955) say that it has apparently existed in India for long and that in 1953 it caused severe loss in western Uttar Pradesh. Vaheeduddin (1954) reports a disease caused by *Erwinia mangifera* which is found mainly on the fruit, which becomes spotted and falls, but also on the leaves and stems. He recommends collecting and burning the infected parts and spraying with Bordeaux. Patel and Pandhye (1948) report a soft rot of the fruit caused by *Bacterium carotovorus*.

It has long been noticed that mangoes grown in the vicinity of brick kilns are frequently damaged. Pal, Chatterjee, and Ranjan (1937) described the effects as the formation at the distal end of the fruit of black spots which gradually harden, the retardation of the growth of the fruit, and its falling before maturity. The fruit was found to be physiologically riper than the undamaged ones. The tree is apparently unharmed. The disease is referred to as black-tip. Sen (1941 a, b, 1942 a, b, 1943 a) produced the disease by burning coal in an orchard, with no brick kiln within three miles. In a survey, he found that black-tip occurs near kilns in Bengal, Bihar, Uttar Pradesh, and the Punjab, mostly in the lee of the kilns, and in inverse ratio to the distance from the kiln. Although different varieties were damaged to varying degrees, all were affected when growing within 500 feet of a kiln. The maximum distance at which damage was observed was 700 yards, but cases of damage up to a mile away were reported. In Madras, and other sections where the modern type of brick kiln is not in vogue, the disease was not reported. He found that it could be produced only during the period of active development, April 24 to May 3, those treated later showing only a tendency toward early ripening. He recommends that where there are kilns near orchards, the chimneys rise at least 50 feet, or the kilns be not operated from the first of March through the mango season. Gupta and others (1950) were able to produce the disease in only a very small number of fruits by burning coal in orchards, and they could attribute the necrosis to none of the commonly known harmful constituents in brick kiln fumes, such as sulphur dioxide, carbon monoxide, and ethylene. They could cause symptoms by introducing into young mangoes the sterile juice of mangoes which had been subjected to brick kiln fumes, or of necrotic fruits. One fraction of the ether-soluble constituents of the fumes, as yet unidentified, when dissolved in mango juice and injected into fruit, caused necrosis. This work seems more likely to lead to a solution of the question than that of Ranjan and Jha (1940) who found that ethylene, at the comparatively strong concentration of 1 : 1000, produced characteristic symptoms while more dilute gas caused more rapid respiration, increased sugar content, and softening. Sulphur dioxide, with or without ethylene, had a similar effect, but caused the general condition of the fruit to deteriorate.

Somewhat similar symptoms are described by Verma (1950) on four varieties growing in Uttar Pradesh. As the fruits approach maturity the tips become prematurely pulpy and turn dark brown, but the fruits never ripen properly. It is said that a fourth of the total crop is lost in this way. No evidence could be found of any fungal or bacterial cause.

The grafted mango begins to bear commercially in 4 or 5 years. Frequently younger trees will blossom, but the infloresences should be removed. By the time a tree is 10 years old it should bear 300 to 500 fruits in the years of heavy bearing. Frequently mature trees bear 1,000 to 1,500 fruits, but the average over a period of years would seldom approach that figure. Balakrishnamurti and Jogiraju are probably closer to the average when they estimate this at about 100 fruits. L. B. Singh and Singh (1955) state that the Dasheri should produce about 100 fruits per annum between the ages of 6 and 10 years, and that from the 15th year on it should average 400—500 fruits. This many fruits of the size indicated, weighing about 6 oz., would mean a yield of about 2·5 tons per acre if the trees are 36 ft. apart by the square system. This is the same yield per acre indicated by figures collected by the Agricultural Marketing Adviser for the whole of India, but much less than the average of 3·42 tons (93·4 md.) given by Naik (1947 b) for the old Madras State, which he said produced about 855,000 tons on 250,000 acres. However, there are no satisfactory statistics on yield, and the average over a period of years may not be more than 1·5 tons per acre. L. B. Singh and Singh (1955) state that a mature orchard near Saharanpur may yield a net profit of Rs. 1,000 per acre, but while this may be possible elsewhere also, it is obvious that most orchards produce far less. In South Africa grafted trees start bearing at the age of about three years, according to Marloth (1947 a), and at 10 years average 60 to 300 fruits, while at 20 years the average is 160 to 600 fruits, with some orchards yielding three to five times this number.

Harvesting and Marketing

For home consumption, the mango may be allowed to become soft on the tree, but it is ordinarily harvested while still firm, and this is necessary for the market. Harkness (1951) and Harkness and Cobin (1951) studied the ripening of fruit on and off the tree in an attempt to find the best time of harvesting. They found that the reducing sugar remained constant at about 3-4% from a very immature stage until ripeness and that while sucrose starts low and increases, it may be more than 1% at harvest, and is not a suitable test. Acid was also unsatisfactory, as it does not change much until the final stages of ripening. Fruit with a specific gravity of 1·02 was found to ripen well, and it is suggested that a combination of colour change, length of time after full bloom, and specific gravity may furnish a satisfactory basis on which to determine the time of harvest. They state that the quality of fruit requiring more than 10 days at room temperature to ripen is likely to be poor.

The firm fruit stands shipping well, although even so, much of it is ruined by the rough handling it sometimes receives. Much of it is shipped fairly long distances. Naik (1947 a) states that normally about 21,000 tons are exported from Madras. Formerly some of this fruit went as far as the North-West Frontier Province and Burma. Bombay (Anon. 1938) reports fairly successful shipments by sea to England. R. S. Singh and Gupta (1950-51) report on the experimental shipment of two varieties from Uttar Pradesh to the United Kingdom in 1950 by air. This proved highly profitable in the latter part of June, before the abundance of local fruit on the market brought down the price. There seemed to be only a limited market for mangoes at a profitable price. The variety Dasehri proved superior to the Khajri which ripens late in the season.

The fruit may be kept in straw until mellow, when it is ready to be used. Burns and Prayag recommend that the fruit be first exposed for two days on a layer of mango leaves at least four inches thick, and then transferred to straw, preferably in a single layer. If they remain exposed, ripening is delayed. They state that after ripening, the fruit can be kept at room temperatures for 12 to 25 days, without decay. The fruit is ordinarily separated from the stem when harvested. They found no advantage in keeping part of the stem attached, or in waxing the stem end. Pope in recommending similar practices, emphasizes the importance of good ventilation and a fairly uniform temperature. He says that wrapping the fruit in tissue paper before ripening improves the keeping quality, and is essential if one is to place mangoes of the highest quality on the market. Wardlaw and Leonard (1936) also recommend wrapping the fruit in moisture-retaining paper and packing it in two layers in wooden boxes padded with wood-wool. Berwick (1940) states that in Malaya the fruit is frequently ripened by placing it in baskets or boxes lined with banana leaves and containing calcium carbide. This results in a uniform colour in two or three days, but is thought to make the fruit rather insipid. Marloth (1947 a) states that in South Africa mangoes are frequently kept in piles in a warm place for a day or two to hasten ripening for the early market, but that such fruit is always heavily infected with the "black spot" disease before it reaches the consumer, although this disease can be controlled by spraying the trees with Bordeaux mixture within two weeks of harvesting, or dipping the fruit in a 4-4-50 Bordeaux mixture. He reports some success in ripening mangoes picked 7 to 10 days earlier than usual with careful handling and treatment in one part of ethylene to 5,000 parts of air, with a temperature of 70 to 80 degrees and 85 to 90% humidity. He also says that the exudation of juice from the stem, which tends to mar the appearance of the fruit, can be largely avoided by picking the fruit with at least four inches of the stem attached, which is removed at the time of packing. K. K. Singh and Mathur (1952) demonstrated the value of ripening mangoes at temperatures lower than those ordinarily used. Badami (Alphonso) and Totapuri (Bangalore) ripened at 67-70° F. suffered less wastage, were of a better colour, and had a higher content of soluble solids and of acids, including ascorbic acid, than those ripened at room temperature, 75—80° F. At both temperatures the percentage of ascorbic acid increased in the Badami and decreased in the Totapuri.

Most of the mangoes shipped in this country are packed in baskets, but these containers are not entirely satisfactory. Boxes are now recommended in some States, as was noted in Chapter IX. On the other hand, Cheema and others (1954) state that large quantities of the Bangalora, a hardy variety, are shipped from Madras to Calcutta, Hyderabad, and Bombay without packing, in railway wagons. But in Madras and Bombay the common package is a bamboo basket, and the mangoes are packed between layers of rice straw. Such baskets generally hold from 50 to 100 fruits. Little or no sorting or grading is done, although this would be well worth while. The Bombay Mango Marketing Committee, in 1925, estimated that about 20% of the mangoes entering the city had been picked so green as to be worthless, and another 20% were rotten. This large loss could be very largely avoided by care in plucking and packing the fruit. As has been pointed out earlier, there is also much room for improving the marketing of the mango.

Experiments reported by Cheema and Gandhi (1926), Banerjee and Rao (1933), Wardlaw and Leonard (1945), Karmarkar and Joshi (1940 a), Cheema and others (1939, 1950), and Cheema and Karmarkar (1939) showed that many varieties picked when fully mature but firm could be stored for about a month or even seven weeks at temperatures ranging from 39° to 48° F. Much of this work was done at Poona, where the Alphonso was found to behave better than other varieties in cold storage as it did in ordinary storage. More recent work at Mysore has shown that most varieties are best stored at 42°—45° F., with 85—90% relative humidity. Details are given by K. K. Singh and others (1953, 1954), and Mathur and others (1953 a, b). After such storage, the fruits ripen well at room temperature or, preferably, at 67—70° F. At temperatures above 40° F. most of the loss is caused by the fungus causing anthracnose; lower temperatures reduced this, but increased physiological damage. Gas storage was tried in Bombay (Anon., 1944 b) but from 5 to 15% of carbon dioxide in the atmosphere was found harmful. Bose and Basu (1953) report that mature firm fruit coated with paraffin and stored at 55° F. was kept for 42 days, while unwaxed fruit spoiled within 15 days. They dipped the fruit for 10 seconds in paraffin with a melting point of 70—75° F. held at 80° F.

Food Value

The mango is useful from the time the fruits are small and green until they are fully ripe. This is an advantage, in that it makes it possible to use or sell the fruits which fall, but on the other hand the crop must be guarded from thieves during a long season. The green fruits are used in many ways. Roy and Singh (1952) describe slices (amchur), powder, candied pulp, jam, paste, jelly, 'cheese', juice (used in souring food), squash, chutney, preserves, cider, ketchup, and pickles. Only the last use was considered not very successful. They consider that the best use of fallen mangoes after the fifth week is in jelly, which is made in much the same way as guava jelly except that no acid is added. The best yield of jelly was with fruit eight weeks old. Green mangoes are also used with milk and sugar to make a sauce or drink known as 'mangofool.'

The principal use of the ripe fruit is as a dessert fruit, but it is also used in cooking. The juice, particularly of the fibrous varieties, is squeezed out and dried on plates.

Mandlekar and others (1951) report that as much as 40% of the fruit of a cheap variety, the Raival, grown in Bombay and elsewhere, is wasted, and that the product made in the villages by warming and sun-drying the juice and pulp with sugar, in shallow pans has poor keeping quality. In an experiment on a semi-commercial scale, hand-pressed juice of fully ripe mangoes, with a moisture content of 80 to 90%, was spread to a depth of ⅛th inch and dried for from 4 to 6 hours at temperatures no higher than 50° C. (122° F.). It was further dried for one hour under vacuum at 50° C. and became crisp. The addition of 10% sugar improved the taste. Sulphuring improved the colour but harmed the flavour. When stored in air-tight containers the product remained in good condition for more than two years.

Bose and Dutt (1952) report that a good product was made by drying the ripe pulp in a vaccum double-drum drier with little loss of nutrient value. The product had to be stored in moisture-proof containers. Basu (1954) reports on a similar experiment with the Fazli mango in Bengal, in which the pulp was dried on hot rolls. The water content was reduced from 82·6% to 3·145 % in eight seconds, and the product was light yellow with the flavour and nutritive value of the fresh mango. These qualities were well preserved for eight months. According to a newspaper report a pilot scheme has been started to help solve the problems of the growers in Malda district where there are said to be 50,000 acres of mangoes without easy access to a market.

The mango can be canned very successfully, as far as the quality of the product is concerned. Lal and others (1952) found the Badami (Alphonso) better for this purpose than the four other varieties tested. Commercially, the industry has made very little progress, although it seems probable that under efficient management a very good trade could be developed, both internal and export. Several canneries have been started in the better mango districts of India. The Bombay Mango Marketing Committee reported in 1925 that there were three factories in that province canning mangoes, one with an output of 50,000 12-ounce cans. The committee gave the cost of canning 5,000 cans as Rs. 2,650, excluding interest and depreciation, while the receipts were Rs. 3,440. These cans retailed at Rs. 9 to Rs. 11 a dozen. The equipment was admittedly poor, and conditions insanitary. This may explain the fact that ten years later only one cannery was operating in the province. By 1942 there were again three factories, one of them large, according to Sayed (1942) who considered that there was a large scope for the industry, but that government subsidies and trade protection were necessary. He described the process of canning slices and pulp in some detail. Lye peeling for canning or other purposes is recommended by Bose and Basu (1955) as being quicker and less wasteful than other methods of peeling. They recommend dipping the fruit for 8 minutes in three parts of sodium oxide to one of sodium carbonate, and washing in a spray or in running water.

The cost of canning mangoes on a small scale has been estimated by Siddappa (1952) at about 15 annas per A2½ tin. Such tins could retail at Rs. 1-12 each, which is considered a reasonable and competitive price. He found that about half of the fruit, by weight, could be made into slices suitable for canning, while 12—14% was trimmings and scrapings, useful for jam. He calculated on costs of Rs. 1,150 a year as interest and depreciation, and Rs. 2,400 for overhead, and assumed a production of 100 units a day, 25 days a month, 6 months a year. These costs thus amounted to four annas a unit.

Mango squash is another excellent product being used as a drink and as flavouring for ice-cream. L. Singh and others (1943 a) have reported that the best results are secured by extracting fully ripe fruits with a pulping machine, and mixing equal parts of pulp, water, and sugar with enough citric acid to bring the acidity of the finished product to about 1%. Potassium metabisulphite, added at the rate of 0·05% (0·8 oz. per 100 lb. of the finished product) gave better results than pasteurization or the use of sodium benzoate as a preservative. Seedling mangoes were used, those from some districts proving superior to those from others. The cost per 24-ounce bottle, exclusive of overhead charges, worked out at 7 annas 9 pies, with the fruit costing Rs. 4-3-6 a maund.

Preservation by freezing of the sliced and diced firm pulp is very satisfactory, although whole mangoes do not freeze well, according to Mustard (1951). Riper fruit can be made into puree and frozen. Green mango puree, with up to the same amount of sugar as pulp and a spiced compote are also recommended.

The composition of different varieties of mango varies considerably, particularly in the percentage of sugar, which may be as low as 11% or higher than 20%. Pope gives the following analysis of 8 varieties : edible, 63·77%; total solids, more than 20%; carbohydrates, 15 to 25%; acids, ·122 to ·279%; ash, ·277 to ·469%; protein, ·438 to 1·075%; fat, ·032 to ·530%. In the ripe fruit there is considerable tannin, but no starch. Lal and others (1952) state that there is much variation in the analysis of different fruits of the same variety but that a typical Badami fruit contains 7·13% reducing sugar, 11·42% non-reducing sugar, 0·38% acid, 1·02% protein, and 0·39% ash. Leley and others (1943), who studied the ripening of this or a closely related variety, found that the fully ripe fruit contained 2·19% glucose, 0·41% fructose, and 13·98% non-reducing sugars, which increase during ripening. Of the varieties tested by Cheema and others (1950), the Hemsagar and Langra contained more than 16% total sugar, while Kawasji Patel contained the least, 11·2%. Reducing sugars varied from 1·4 to 4·83% and non-reducing from 8·19 to 13·81%. Acid, taken as malic, varied from 0·18% in Kawasji Patel and the Alphonso of Ratnagiri to 0·56% in Fazri Zafrani. The unripe fruit contains fairly large amounts of malic and tartaric acid, and also some substance in the rind which protects the fruits from insect attack. In some varieties this is strong enough to prevent the hatching of fruit fly eggs. It is thought that it is the persistence of this substance in the ripe fruit of some varieties which causes what is called 'mango poisoning' in some persons.

Various parts of the mango tree and fruit are considered to have medicinal properties, and some varieties, at least, are excellent sources of vitamins A and C. Ripe mango contains more carotene than any of the other fruits and compares well with many of the leafy vegetables according to Aykroyd (1951). Banerjee and Ramasarma (1938) and Ramasarma and Banerjee (1941) tested 30 varieties at Bangalore and found a great deal of variation between varieties, and even within the same varieties. Small mangoes were found to contain a higher percentage of vitamin C than large fruit from the same tree. The formation of carotene and of sugars was greater and quicker and the fall in vitamin C during ripening was less in mangoes plucked when mature than when immature. Bajwa and Musa-hib-ud-din (1946) reported finding 200 to 600 mg. of ascorbic acid per 100 ml. whereas Bhutiani (1946) also working in the Punjab, found only 13·2 to 80·3 mg. per 100 g. in seedlings and seven named varieties. He found 121·9 to 363·8 mg. of carotene per 100 g. With relation to both, the varieties Dr. King and Langra stood high, while the seedlings were lowest. Mustard and Lynch (1945) in Florida found that ascorbic acid in 32 varieties ranged from 8·8 to 107·4 mg. per 100 g., the amount being greater nearer the skin. Munsell (1946) who examined two fruits of each of 26 varieties in the West Indies found ascorbic acid varying from 9·13 to 130·81 mg. per 100 g. Differences within a variety, even with fruits grown in different places, were found not greater than 9 mg. per 100 g. He found the mango relatively rich in carotene, riboflavin, and thiamine. Marloth (1947 a) reports similar findings, with ascrobic acid running from 17 to 178 mg. Miller and Bazore (1945) in Hawaii found the ascorbic acid content to vary greatly up to 150 mg. per 100 g. in the half-ripe fruit and 119 in the ripe fruit. The Pirie was the only variety tested for carotene, of which it was a good source, and thiamine, of which it was only fair. This variety was never found to contain more than 16 mg. of ascorbic acid per 100 g. They consider a sauce made from half-ripe mangoes a good source of this vitamin. Lal and others (1952) found 52·7 mg. of ascorbie acid in 100 g. of pulp of the Badami, and 4907 international units of carotene.

The ascorbic acid content of tender green mangoes of the variety Raspuri (Peter) was studied by Siddappa and Bhatia (1954 a), and was found to vary from 329·0 and 348·5 mg. per 100 g. in fruit weighing 0·55 and 1·46 g. respectively down to 39·1 mg. in those weighing 158 g. This was true ascorbic acid which varies from 46 to 70% of the total. Storage at room temperature for six days caused a loss of 10% in ascorbic acid. Sun-drying also destroyed the ascorbic acid but dehydration after steeping in potassium metabisulphite solution was better and the product retained 38% after a year. Mathur and others (1953 a) found 28·53 mg. per 100 g. in the mature green Raspuri and 39·96 mg. in the Badami.

The people of the Kond hills and in certain other parts of the country eat a flour made from the kernels, according to Wilkins (1942). The kernels are crushed, washed for hours in running water, or by moving them through still water, and dried. The washing removes the astringency which is caused by tannin. The food value compares with that of rice, without taking into consideration an oily substance which may not be utilizable, and no toxic substance seems to be present. Although it is relished by all in the sections where it is made, it is a staple food in the months of scarcity before the rice harvest, and may be of value as a famine food elsewhere. As it is manufactured, it does not keep long. Ochse says that in Java flour is made from the seeds, which is used as a sort of porridge with cocoanut milk, and that the seeds are also used in a side-dish. Kehar and Chanda (1946) report on work done at the Veterinary Research Institute, Izatnagar, on the value of the kernels as cattle feed. They contain 8·50% crude protein, 8·85% ether abstract, and 74·49% soluble carbohydrate, on a dry matter basis. Animals took two or three weeks to acquire a taste for the kernels but later relished enough to provide half of their digestible protein. They estimate that every year 70 million pounds of digestible protein and 780 million pounds of starch are available in this form, and are now largely wasted. Biological tests with rats indicated that the kernels could well replace 60% of the wheat or maize in the ration.

The use of starch from mango kernels as sizing for textiles is advocated by Das and Banerjee (1952). They estimate that a million tons of seeds, containing 7000,000 tons of kernels are available each year, and that from these 140,000 tons of starch can be prepared, with tannin and fat as by-products. They describe a suitable method of preparation.

CHAPTER XIV

THE CITRUS FRUITS

Although authorities may disagree violently as to the history, classification, nomenclature, and best cultural methods of the citrus fruits, none can dispute their importance, both from the point of view of the size of the industry, and as delicious and wholesome fruits. In acreage, the citrus fruits probably rank third among the subtropical fruits of the world, with more than 2,000,000 acres, as compared with about 26,500,000 acres of vinifera grapes and 13,500,000 acres of olives. Statistics about subtropical fruits are admittedly inaccurate. In Italy, one of the most important producing countries, several crops are frequently grown mixed in the same orchard, and the total area is included under the heading of each fruit. Complete statistics are not available for much of the worlds, including India.

While the citrus fruits are grown in tropical and subtropical regions throughout the world, the leading producer is the United States, with nearly 40% of the total recorded acreage. The following estimated acreages are based largely on a statement by Webber (1943 c) relating to the situation before the Second World War : the U. S. A., 650,000; India, 254,641; Spain, 209,000; Italy, 180,000; Mexico, 137,000; Japan, 103,350; South Africa, 60,000; Brazil, 55,000; and Australia, 50,000. The figure for Mexico relates to 1951, and is more than four times that of 1939. The acreage in Japan, largely of mandarins, is for the year 1952 and is based on Camp's (1954) report. The figure for South Africa is based on an estimated six million trees in 1955. Before the virus disease, tristeza, practically wiped out the citrus industry of Brazil, there were about 200,000 acres in that country. When Chapman (1954) reported 50 to 60 thousand acres there, the orchards were mostly less than 10 years old and it may be supposed that the area will continue to increase for some time. A concentrated industry in Israel, where there are now about 35,000 acres, may also be expected to increase, for before the war there was more than twice that acreage. World production in 1951 for the countries for which statistics are available amounted to nearly 380 million boxes (of about 70 lb.), of which the United States produced 46%. Sweet oranges are by far the most important species, but in most cases figures are given for these and mandarins combined. Next in order come grapefruit, lemons, and limes. The U. S. A. and the Mediterranean countries lead in orange production; the single State of Florida produces three-fourths of the world's grapefruit; Italy leads in lemons, followed by California; and Mexico and India are the leading producers of limes.

The industry has been growing rapidly. The area in Andhra and Madras increased from 4,960 acres in 1921-22 to 31,270 in 1939-40 to 55,293 in 1955.

In Madhya Pradesh, which has the largest acreage of citrus fruits of any State, Bombay, Assam, and Coorg large increases have also occurred. The total acreage according to Table IV is nearly twice that given in the Report, 130,000, although most of the citrus fruits in the Punjab were in the part now in Pakistan.

TABLE IV

Estimated area under Citrus fruits in some parts of India

State	Area in acres	State	Area in arces
Ajmer ..	207	Madhya Pradesh .	40,000
Andhra ..	28,263	Madras ..	27,030
Assam ..	28,000	Mysore ..	6,000
Bhopal ..	216	Orissa ..	31,000
Bihar ..	12,764	PEPSU ..	4,929
Bombay ..	27,900	Punjab ..	4,262
Coorg ..	21,108	Sikkim ..	2,500
Himachal Pradesh ..	100	Saurashtra ..	120
Hyderabad ..	10,392	Travancore-Cochin	1,802
Kutch ..	500	Uttar Pradesh ..	1,692
Madhya Bharat ..	3,500	West Bengal ..	2,356
		Total ..	254,641

The estimated acreage of citrus fruits in the different parts of India, according to the Report on the Marketing of Citrus Fruits in India, was in 1943 : Madras, 31,270; Madhya Pradesh, 22,947; the Punjab, 17,150; Bombay, 16,100; Assam, 14,025; Coorg, 10,071; other provinces and States, 18,148.

The origin and history of the citrus fruits are not fully known, the most that can be said with confidence being that they are natives of southern Asia. Some are from China and probably some from India, while others may have originated in the region between these two great countries and in the Malaya Archipelago. Bhattacharya and Dutta (1951) suggest that two species in Eucitrus, (the sub-genus containing the edible forms), *Citrus indica* and *C. assamensis*, and three species of Papeda, *C. ichangensis*, *C. latipes*, and *C. macroptera*, are definitely indigenous to Assam. They think that *C. aurantium*, *C. magaloxycarpa*, and one variety of *C. reticulata* are probably indigenous also. The spread of the citrus fruits to Europe and other parts of the world occurred comparatively recently, and even in modern times western botanists and pomologists have shown slight appreciation of the wealth of species and varieties which occur in India and other Oriental countries. Many of the problems involved in the history of the citrus fruits are discussed by Tolkowsky (1938) in his large volume on the subject. He goes into great detail, especially in dealing with these fruits in Europe, but is less complete in the sections dealing with Asia, and accepts too uncritically some statements regarding the occurrence of certain species in India.

While De Condolle does not include the citrus fruits in his list of those which have been in cultivation for 4,000 years, there seems to be evidence that some of them have been cultivated at least that long in China. Hu (1934) states that Chinese literature written as early as 2200 B.C. refers to the cultivation of some species of citrus. There was intercourse between India and China in very early times and citrus fruits may have been carried from one country to the other or from other points to both, before the earliest records.

The citron seems to have had the most western origin of any of the citrus fruits, and has commonly been considered a native of India. This was the first of these fruits to reach Europe. The Creeks found citrons growing in Media and Persia, hence the name *Citrus medica*. They were probably growing in Persia by the time of Cyrus the Great, in the sixth centruy B.C., although the first clear mention of the citron seems to be by the Greek botanist Theophrastes, who wrote about 310 B.C. At that time it apparently did not grow as far west as Babylon. Theophrastes's report that there were some flowers without pistils which developed no fruit, is perhaps the earliest record of this phenomenon in the history of botany. No other citrus fruit was known to the Europeans at that time. Some authors have accepted the Jewish tradition that the 'fruit of a goodly tree', mentioned in the book of Leviticus, was the citron, and have placed its introduction into Palestine in the sixth century B.C. This view is refuted by Tolkowsky (1930, 1918) who thinks that it was introduced between 250 and 200 B.C. By the beginning of the Christian era the citron was used in Jewish ritual, and must have been produced in large numbers. It seems to have spread to Greece and Italy by the end of the third century.

The suggestion that the citron may have been in Egypt at a very early date is made by Hodgson (1954), who writes, 'What clearly appears to be a citron occurs on a relief in a temple at Karnak, said to date back to the 15th century B.C. And there exists in the Louvre Museum in Paris a model of a citron fruit taken from a tomb of one of the Pharaonic dynasties dating back to the 12th centruy B. C. The present surmise is that this fruit was brought from the Middle East by Thotmos III during one of his wars of conquest there. Another evidence of antiquity is cited by reference to the ancient Coptic word *gitri* (meaning sour fruit) which is believed to have given rise to the much later Latin word *citrium* (of the same meaning), from which the word *Citrus* was derived.'

It is frequently stated that the citron occurs wild in India, on the basis of reports by Wight, Roxburgh, Royle, and others that it was found in the Nilgiris, Assam, and the lower Himalayas. It is clear that fruits classified in the old species *C. medica* occur wild in India, but this species included the lime, lemon, citron, and probably other types. Watt (1908) suggested that the 'lemons' reported growing wild were probably limes, but in his sub-species *C. medica* var. *acida*, he included the *jambiri*, *kaghzi*, *khatta* and other types. Even if botanists of the 19th century found the citron growing wild, it does not follow that it is indigenous to this country, although this has frequently been assumed. As it seems probable that other species, of more value than the citron, were indigenous, it is difficult to believe that these were left behind, and the citron taken to Media, Persia, and the West. And Bonavia (1890) points out that the common Indian names for the citron, *turanj* (from the Persian) and *bajoura* (from Bajour in Afghanistan) indicate that some varieties, if not the whole species, entered India from the west. The earliest Chinese description of the citron is said by Tolkowsky to date from the 4th century A.D. On the whole, it seems most probable that the citron originated in the area northwest of India.

The lemon is commonly said to be indigenous to India, although Bonavia reached the conclusion that it originated in Malaya. He quotes Rumphius as saying that all citrus fruits were called by the Malays *lemoen*. Bonavia thought that this was the origin of the English word and that the species probably came from the same region. As already pointed out, there has been much confusion about the identity of the citrus fruits reported growing wild in this country. The rough lemon, *jamburi*, seems to occur wild in the lower Himalayas, and is an important rootstock in parts of the country. The ordinary lemon of the West, on the other hand, is still comparatively rare in this country. The so-called hill lemon is more likely indigenous, especially if this is the '*puhari kaguzee*' or '*bihari nimboo*' of Royle (1839). If one or both of these fruits is placed in the species of the lemon, then it may be considered probable that some forms, at least, of the species are indigenous to India.

The introduction of the lemon into Europe has generally been placed in the 10th century, as suggested by Gallesio in his classic work on the citrus fruits published in 1811. Tolkowsky, however, has found evidence in art and literature which convinces him that both the orange and lemon, as well as the citron, reached Europe by the middle of the first century A.D.

The lime is frequently confused with the lemon, which makes it very difficult to trace its early history. It is very commonly grown all over India, but does not seem to occur wild. Perhaps the most probable theory is that of Bonavia, that it also originated in the Malayan region. He points out the possibility that both the English word 'lime' and the Indian '*nimbu*' or '*limbu*' may have come from the Malayan '*lemoen*'.

The Oranges

Again in the case of the oranges, there is much confusion, as at least three species are commonly called by this name, and it is frequently difficult, if not impossible, to tell which one is meant. The sour orange was probably the first to reach the Mediterranean, although Tolkowsky believes that both sour and sweet oranges reached Europe at about the same time, in the first centruy A.D. He thinks that the fruits mentioned by Mas'udi as having been introduced from India into Oman and thence into Syria, Palestine, and Egypt, early in the 10th century, were merely new varieties. This reference has generally been taken as the first record of the orange in the West, and it is thought to refer to the sour orange, which was well established in Europe before the end of the 15th century. It was one of the first immigrants to America, where it landed in the 15th century, and soon escaped from cultivation. It thrived so well that many have supposed it to be native to Florida. Hodgson (1954) refers to the belief in Egypt that both the sour and sweet orange were known in that country before the 10th century.

As to the Indian origin of the sour oranges there is some doubt. Words such as '*narangi*' and '*naranj*' have no very specific meaning. Hooker seems to have been the only early botanist to report sour oranges growing wild in India, from Garhwal to the Khasia Hills, and he said that they were botanically nearer the sweet than the sour orange, so it is difficult to know what fruit was meant. Bonavia thought there was evidence of the sour orange having been in South India from prehistoric times, and that it may have originated there, but that more likely it was indigenous to China or Cochin China. It is not commonly grown in China, and unless Tolkowsky is right probably originated further south or west than the sweet orange, for it is obvious that the latter would have spread westward at least as rapidly as the comparatively useless sour orange.

It is generally agreed that the sweet orange originated in southern China or in Cochin China, although it is rarely cultivated in China. Bhattacharya (1950) considers the Soh Niangriang, which occurs in several places in Assam, a sweet orange and the only one of the species indigenous in Assam. That it has been grown there for a considerable time is indicated by the fact that it is taboo to one Khasi clan, but it is quite possible that it entered Assam from further east, in contrast with other and better varieties which entered later from the west. It seems strange that this most important of the citrus fruits, with about two-thirds of the commercial acreage of the world, is comparatively little grown in any place in eastern Asia where it must have originated.

When Vasco da Gama returned from his historic trip around the Cape of Good Hope in 1498, he took sweet oranges with him to Portugal from the Far East. Many have regarded this as the first introduction of the sweet orange into Europe, a theory to which weight is given by the fact that this type of orange gets its common names in most European languages from the name Portugal. Others have held that the sweet orange was early introduced from China into South India, and thence to Europe, perhaps two centuries before the time of Vasco da Gama. Webber (1939) has pointed out that there was considerable trade between the ports of China and India as early as the 13th century, so that it seems easily possible that the orange had been introduced and become well established in India in time to be taken to Europe much earlier than 1498. Tolkowsky, of course, places the introduction of the sweet orange into Europe in the first century.

If the sweet orange reached South India before it reached Europe, it seems not to have spread very rapidly in this country. The names used in other parts of India such as Malta and Mosambi (from Mozambique) indicate an introduction from the West. Even in Madras, as Ali (1941) points out, there is the tradition that the Nagari variety was introduced by Dutch settlers. Other names used in the South, such as Chini (probably referring to sweetness rather than to China) and Sathgudi, give no indication as to the history of the fruit. The name Batavian suggests that at least one variety was introduced from Java, perhaps at a comparatively recent time.

The place of greatest importance, both in China and India is taken by the loose-skinned oranges commonly known as mandarin oranges or mandarins, of which there are many types. Some, at least, of these are of Chinese origin. While mandarins are now commonly grown in various places in India, their spread over the country seems to have taken place since the time of Baber, when they were not found west of Bengal. Their importance in the hills of Assam points to their introduction from further east. Bonavia makes a good case for this view, suggesting that they may have been brought by the Shan people who migrated westward from Yunnan, China, and reached south-east Assam by the beginning of the Christian era. The orange gardens which are said to have flourished in Coorg by 1815 (Vardarajan and Subramanian 1953) were probably of mandarins. Oranges of this type were very late in reaching Europe, arriving about 1828. They soon spread across the Atlantic, but in neither region have they become of great importance, perhaps because they do not stand transportation and storage nearly as well as the sweet orange.

An interesting illustration of the danger of basing history on nomenclature is afforded by the pummelo. The English name, with its variations, is derived by some from the Latin '*pomum melo*' and it seems quite reasonable that such a large yellow fruit might be called the 'melon fruit'. But Bonavia is apparently right in deriving the name from the Dutch 'pomelmoes', the origin of which is uncertain, or from the same source. Such forms as 'pumpelmuss', 'pompelmose', and 'pimple nose' occur in the early English literature. Some vernacular names such as 'papanas' in Bombay and 'bambalinas' in Madras, may have the same derivation. In North India the most common names are '*mahtabi*' and '*chakotra*', and for these, again certain pundits have very plausible explanations. The former is supposed to compare the fruit to the moon, '*mahtab*', while '*chakotra*, is said to come from '*chak*,' a wheel. Bonavia, on the other hand, derives '*mahtabi*' from '*batabi*' from Batavia, and '*chakotra*' from Jakatra, the ancient and now revived name for Batavia. If he is right, as seems likely, this is an indication that the pummelo came to India from Java where many varieties are now cultivated, although it may have been imported from other regions also. De Candolle thought that the spec es originated in the islands east of the Malaya Archipelago, including Fiji and the Friendly Islands. Siam produces a great variety of pummelos, including some very good ones. This indicates that they have been grown there for a very long time, and it is possible that they originated on the mainland of south-eastern Asia, rather than in the island region. Bretschneider (1898) on the other hand, states definitely that they are indigenous to China, and Tolkowsky points out that they were mentioned in a collection of Chinese documents written between the 24th and 8th centuries B.C. The pummelo seems to have followed the sweet orange to Europe, where it has never become important except as the grapefruit, which is thought to have originated as a variation of the pummelo. The name shaddock, sometimes used for this fruit, is said to have come from Captain Shaddock, whose ship was one of the first to take the fruit to the West Indies, in the 16th century.

Of the citrus fruits of less importance, several species are indigenous to China, and others probably originated in the general region south and west, as far as India. The trifoliate orange and the kumquart are among those native to China.

The great development of the citrus industry has come in modern times. In Europe there has been much interest in citrus fruits since they were first introduced, and greenhouses were first built to make it possible to grow oranges in northern Europe where it was impossible to grow them in the open. But commercial plantings were small until transportation facilities developed. The Spanish and Portuguese settlers in the new world apparently took citrus fruits with them, and from these developed the orchards of Florida, where St. Augustine was established in 1655 and California, where the first mission was started at San Diego in 1769. In both States, commercial production assumed importance only in the second half of the 19th century. These two sections still produce the bulk of the crop, although there has recently been a large expansion in Texas and some citrus fruits are grown in other southern States. In South America, Brazil is the most important producer. Fruit is also exported from the West Indies.

South Africa has a rapidly growing citrus industry. The first European settlers planted a few trees. According to Powell (1930), the first introduction of orange trees was in 1654, but the large-scale plantings are of recent date. Australia has a smaller citrus industry, which is also developing steadily.

In India also, citrus fruits have been grown commercially only in modern times, although some types have been found in gardens for ages. Even now, most orchards are small, and seldom devoted exclusively to any one type. The mandarins or loose-skinned oranges are the most important, with an area of more than 90,000 acres, of which about 36,000 is in Madhya Pradesh, the home of the famous Nagpur Santara. Assam and Coorg each claims about 20,000 acres, while the other States have much smaller acreages : Madras and Andhra, 8,000; Sikkim, 2,500; Bengal, 2,000; Bihar, 1,487; Hyderabad, 1,350; and Mysore, 1,000.

The sweet orange stood second in area when the Report on the Marketing of Citrus Fruits in India (Anon., 1943 a) was published. Out of 27,321 acres, the Report credits 10,996 to Bombay, 8,230 to Madras, and 6,683 to the Punjab. By 1948 Bombay reported 20,402 acres. Naik (1949) estimated 15,000 acres in Madras, which would bring the total, without the Punjab, to 36,814 acres. Rangacharlu and Venkatarao (1954) state that at least 500 acres of Sathgudi oranges are planted each year in Andhra.

Limes are grown in all parts of the country, with a total in 1943 of 20,881 acres, including 11,760 in Madras, 2,786 in Bombay, 1,560 in Bengal, and 1,546 in Punjab. Naik (1949) estimates 16,600 acres in Madras and 300 in Mysore, while Bombay in 1948 had 2,569, and Bihar in 1953 estimated 5,960. So, in spite of the loss of some acreage in Bengal and the Punjab, the total has risen to 25,429, counting only that in four States.

There were 4,100 acres of what the Report calls sour oranges, in Madras, only 42% being in full bearing. By 1959, this area had increased to 5,000 acres, according to Naik. This is not the true sour orange, but is the *kichili* or *vadlapudi* which Tanaka called *Citrus maderaspatana*. Sweet lemons or limes, mainly in the Punjab and Madars, occupy 2,200 acres. There were said to be 1,475 acres of pummelos in Madras, Bengal, and Uttar Pradesh. L. Singh and others (1940) report more than 10,000 grapefruit plants which would mean about 100 acres, in the Punjab, now largely in Pakistan. The grapefruit trees planted by Mitchell in the Punjab in 1925 seem to have been among the first in India.

Classification

No more complicated problem exists for the systematic pomologists than the classification of the citrus fruits. Early attempts by Europeans resulted in very simple classifications, limiting the entire group to about half a dozen species in one genus. Such classifications not only group in one species such diverse forms as the lime and citron, but leave out entirely a large number of fruits which occur in Asia, but are either unknown or of rare occurrence in Europe and America. Modern authorities recognize a larger number of species, but do not agree as to how far the process should go.

Certain reasons for the chaotic condition are apparent. Very few scholars have had a personal acquaintance with the whole region in which the species have originated; many have seen only those which are grown in the West. The tendency to group together types thought to have a common origin has made the problem more difficult. Nature has failed to co-operate, for wherever the boundary line is drawn between species, intermediate forms are likely to be found. Many of the characteristics on which classifications are commonly based are not constant within the species. New forms seem to occur more frequently than in most genera. Shamel and Pomeroy (1937) have reported 1,341 striking bud mutations of economic significance in two varieties of the sweet orange, 202 in lemons, 32 in grapefruit, and 68 in other citrus fruits, as compared with 394 in apples, 154 in peaches, 95 in grapes, and 26 in plums. At the Fruit Research station, at Kodur in Andhra, 13 bud mutations had been located which were considered desirable, including a pink-fleshed *vadlapudi*. Of these, seven had been propagated. Many hybrids have been produced by artifical cross-pollination, and it as probable that natural hybrids account for some of the forms which seem to combine characteristics of different species. The *khatta nimbu*, for instance, has some characteristics of the sour orange, and tinted flowers such as occur in the lemon, citron, and Rangpur lime, but not in any orange.

Variation in popular names is fully as great as in the botanical names which have been applied, and makes it difficult to know what fruit is meant unless it is fully described. This is true both in English and in the vernaculars. The terms 'lime' and 'lemon' are frequently used interchangeably, and 'lime' is used for a number of fruits. '*Jamburi*' and its variations, '*narangi*' and '*khatta*' are also indefinite terms.

There is no classification which has found general acceptance, and it is likely to be some time before pomologists and botanists agree on a solution to this complex problem. Botanists are not agreed on any accurate definition of the terms 'genus' and 'species'. The general rule that a species must be described from a truly wild specimen would, perhaps, eliminate the entire genus, for even the generally accepted species are found only in cultivation or as escapes from cultivation. No one suggests denying specific status to well established species because of a suspicion that they are of hybrid origin, and few would give specific names to man-made hybrids. To what extent specific recognition should be given to types which give some indication of hybrid origin and the specific names of which have not been commonly accepted, is debatable. Important modern contributions have been made by Swingle and Tanaka. The late Walter T. Swingle, long with the United States Department of Agriculture, studied citrus fruits and their relatives in most of the countries where they are grown, although, unfortunately, not in India. He bred a large number of hybrids, including some closely resembling forms he found in remote sections of Asia. He wrote on the subject from 1893 until the appearance of his 346-page chapter on the botany of citrus fruits in the first volume of the book, The Citrus Industry, edited by Webber and Batchelor and published in 1943. He recognizes only 16 species and is not sure that all of these deserve such classification. Tyozaburo Tanaka, the leading Japanese authority, once worked with Swingle, but has done much independent work in many parts of the world, including India, and has come to take the opposite attitude regarding species, of which he recognizes 145 (Tanaka, 1945).

All the citrus fruits were formerly considered members of the genus *Citrus*, but modern classifications recognize two other genera of the family Rutaceae. The trifoliate orange was formerly called *Citrus trifoliata*, but is now known as *Poncirus trifoliata*. As the name indicates, it has a compound leaf, with three leaflets. It is a small, spiny tree with an inedible fruit, and is used only as rootstock. As it is the only one of the citrus fruits which is deciduous, it is the most hardy and is therefore used as a stock in regions where the frost hazard is great. It is almost unknown in India, but in China is a preferred rootstock for a fruit very similar to, if not identical with, the Nagpur *santara*. The trifoliate orange seems to be indigenous to central or northern China.

The kumquats comprise the other new genus, *Fortunella*, and were formerly classified as *Citrus japonica*. They are small trees with small orange coloured fruits which are juicy and acid, but with a sweet and edible rind. There are several species, native in China, the more important being *F. margarita*, the oval kumquat, and *F. japonica*, the round kumquat. They are of very little commercial value, but are grown occasionally for ornament. Khan and Mazhar (1954) give recipes for candied fruit, preserves, marmalade, and jelly. They state that kumquats grow fairly well in the Punjab, probably better than in the warmer parts of India. The so-called kumquat of northern India, the *hazara*, is similar to the true kumquat, but is the calamondin, which has been thought to be a native of the Philippines. It has been classified as *Citrus microcarpa* (*mitis*). Swingle (1943) considers it reasonably certain that the calamondin is a hybrid between the genera *Citrus* and *Fortunella*, probably between a sour mandarin orange and a true kumquat, and thinks that it probably arose in China. Tanak, however, calls it *C. madurensis*.

The genus *Citrus* contains all of the citrus of commercial importance (except some that are used as rootstocks, and perhaps some inter-generic hybrids) and a number of minor fruits. There is a great wealth of forms growing over large parts of southern Asia. Swingle assumes that most of these are chance hybrids or mutations. Some of the hybrids produced under carefully controlled conditions are so different from their parents or from any other types, that on the basis of appearance alone it would be necessary to classify them as new species, or even genera. Because of polyembryony, these hybrids come true from seed very largely. Cross-pollination by insects is not difficult, so it is reasonable to suppose that the forms similar to known hybrids are likewise hybrids, the result of insect pollination. Others, different from any artificial hybrids, may have arisen in the same way.

Even some of the well-known species may possibly have arisen as hybrids. Swingle uses the term 'satellite species' for a species of doubtful validity, which may be a natural species of comparatively recent origin, or may be a chance hybrid or sport. Further investigation may lead to a change in the classification of such fruits.

The genus is divided by Swingle into two subgenera, *Eucitrus*, containing the important edible species, and *Papeda*, the pulp-vesicles of which contain droplets of acrid oil, so that the fruits are not very pleasant. There are also distinguishing characteristics of the leaves and flowers.

Of all the citrus fruits, the citron is probably the least subject to dispute. All authorities accept the Linnaean name *C. medica*, from Media, the ancient country corresponding to part of modern Iran, where the Greeks first saw the citron. This is a small tree with an indistinct trunk and straggling branches. It is thorny, with large, glabrous leaves which are tinged with purple when young. Typically, they are not articulated, but this character seems not constant. The flowers are large and before opening they are frequently curved. The outside of the petals is generally purplish. Frequently the flowers are staminate. The fruit is large, yellow, and frequently very rough, with a very thick rind and scant juice which may be acid, or in varieties with white flowers, somewhat sweet. The fruit is used mainly in the preparation of candied peel.

Linnaeus and other early writers included with the citron in the species *medica*, the lemon and lime, but most modern authorities give these separate specific standing. The lemons, especially, have much in common with the citron, having a similar style of growth, similar leaves, except that they are ordinarily articulated, and rather similar purplish flowers. The fruit is quite different, however, being smaller and having a thin rind and plentiful acid juice. The fruit is three to five inches long, oblong or ovoid, with a terminal nipple. The lemon was first called *C. medica*, var. *limonum*, but later classifications called it *C. limonia*. However, Tanaka pointed out in 1924 that the fruit which Osbeck described, and to which he gave this name, was not the ordinary lemon, but the Canton lemon or Rangpur lime, a very different fruit. Swingle agrees that Osbeck was not describing the true lemon, although he says that the plant described was the white, not the red, lemon of the Cantonese, both of which he considers hybrids. Both Tanaka and Swingle accept *C. limon* for the lemon, but the latter considers this species a satellite of the citron, and thinks it may possibly have arisen as hybrid, perhaps of the citron and lime. The relationship of the true lemon and the *jamburi* or rough lemon, is not clear. One may be a hybrid or sport of the other. They differ in the vigour and form of the tree, in their resistance to certain diseases, and in the form of the fruit. The rough lemon is not readily marketable, because of its appearance, but is serviceable for home consumption. Because of its vigour and disease resistance, it is widely used as a rootstock, both in India and in other countries. It has been placed by Lushington (1910) in a separate species, *C. jamburi*, but this is not recognized by Swingle, although it is by Tanaka.

There seems to be less justification for classifying the lime as *C. medica*. var. *acida*, as has been done. It is now recognized as *C. aurantifolia*. While there are intermediate forms between the lime and the lemon, the typical lime is a more bushy tree with smaller leaves not more than slightly tinged purple when young, and with winged petioles. The flowers are small and pure white, and the fruits round or oval, sometimes mammillate, and not more than two inches in diameter. The rind is thin, and the pulp greenish, as compared with the yellow pulp of the lemon. The flavour is also slightly different. The Tahiti lime differs markedly from the common one, having a larger fruit which remains green in colour, growing on a tree with larger leaves and much of the appearance of the sweet lime. Webber (1943) thought it might be a hybrid or even a distinct species, a suggestion supported by Hodgson (1955). It is a triploid, and produces no pollen. Even when cross-pollinated, it produces very few seeds, according to Krug and Bacchi (1943). It is believed to have arisen from a seed of an ordinary lime imported into the United States from Tahiti. It is grown mainly as the variety Bearss, which probably originated as a nucellar seedling. There is no other known natural triploid citrus fruit, but triploid plants have been produced by crossing the tetraploid *Fortunella hindsi* which belongs to the subgenus *Protocitrus*, with the diploid limequat which is a hybrid between the round kumquat and the ime. These are called procimequats because of this origin, Pro-(to) c (itrus x 1) imequat. The lime and lemon are used for much the same purposes, for making refreshing drinks, for pickles, and in cooking. In Europe and America the lemon is much more important, but in India the lime is more popular probably because the lemon suffers from sunburn. Both are more tender to frost than most species of citrus fruits.

There are a number of more-or-less lemonlike fruits which are occasionally grown in India but which have not been thoroughly studied. The hill lemon, or *galgal*, has leaves, flowers, and fruits which are considerably larger than those of the common lemon. It also differs in bearing only one crop a year, whereas the common lemon flowers throughout the year. The common lemon is rather sensitive to extreme temperatures, while the hill lemon is more hardy to both heat and cold. The hill lemon bears large crops of fruit of excellent quality, and seems to deserve more extensive planting. It is doubtful if it should be kept in the same species as the common lemon.

The *gajanimma* of South India is grown more as a rootstock than for its fruits which contain much pleasantly acid juice. Tanaka (1954), who calls this *C. pennivesiculata,* considers it the same as the *attarra* which Bonavia reported in Madhya Pradesh. It is also very similar to the *ada jamir* or *soh sying* of Assam, although it seems to lack the aroma of the crushed leaves and rind of the latter, which is said to resemble eucalyptus or ginger (*ada, sying*). Dutta and Bhattacharya (1951) describe the *ada jamir* as a new species, *C. assamensis* and state that it is distinct from the *gajanimma* and cannot be suspected of being a hybrid, but do not defend this statement.

Juice resembling that of the lemon is found in types with large round fruits and with foliage which does not always resemble that of the lemon. Some are of good quality. The *amilbed,* which Bonavia included with the pummelo, is of less value. The fruit is very sour, and Baber records the saying that a needle thrust into the heart of one melts away. Lushington (1910) suggested the name *C. megaloxycarpa* for this fruit. Swingle would, probably, consider all of these forms natural hybrids.

The sweet lime is rather commonly grown in different parts of India, perhaps because of its hardy nature and its fruitfulness, and the fact that it ripens late in the rains when other sweet citrus fruits are not available. The quality of the fruit would not seem to justify extensive planting, for while it is thin-skinned and juicy, the juice is decidedly insipid. It is mildly sweet with practically no acidity. The tree is large and spreading, with leaves about the size of those of the sweet orange, but of a lighter green colour. The flowers are large and pure white. In habit of growth, foliage, and fruit it more nearly resembles the Tahiti type of sour lime than the limes commonly grown in India. The classification of the sweet lime is thus questionable. It is sometimes included with the true limes. A similar fruit growing in Europe has been called *C. limetta,* but Tanaka considers the Indian sweet lime different and calls it *C. limettioides.* The sweet lime of Palestine seems to be the same as the one grown in India. The sweet lime is ignored by Swingle. Sweet lemons, which may be acidless mutants of the ordinary lemon, occur in some countries.

The sour, bitter, bigarade, or Seville orange, in spite of its many names, is of minor importance. It is grown in Spain and exported to Great Britain and other countries for the manufacture of marmalade. In many parts of the world it is used as a stock on which to grow other citrus fruits. It is a fairly large tree, thorny, with dark green leaves the petioles of which are broadly winged. The flowers are large, white, and very fragrant. The fruit is round, orange in colour, about three inches in diameter, and acid, with bitter membranes. When ripe, the centre is hollow. The commonly accepted name is *C. aurantium*, but *C. vulgaris* and *C. bigaradia* are synonyms. The bergamot orange of Europe, from the rind of which bergamot oil, used in perfumes, is extracted, is considered by many as a form of the sour orange or as a hybrid, but by others has been classified separately as *C. bergamia*.

A fruit of considerable commercial importance in Madras is the *kichili*, sometimes called the *vadlapudi*, or Guntur sour orange. Naik (1949) distinguishes between the *vadlapudi* and the *kichili* which he says is rarely sweet at any season and is grown only as stray trees. Siddappa (1952) says that the *vadlapudi* contains from 9·7 to 12·2% soluble solids and from 1·34 to 2·13% acid, while these figures for the *kichili* are 11·6 and 2·345. This has been included with the true sour orange, and Bonavia put it with the mandarins. While the foliage somewhat resembles that of the sour orange, the fruit differs in having a looser and rougher rind and pulp which turns sweet when fully ripe. Tanaka (1937 b) placed it in a separate species, *C. maderaspatana*.

The term sweet orange, applied to the tight-skinned oranges such as the 'Malta' and 'Mosambi', is not entirely satisfactory. It serves well to distinguish this group from the sour orange, but it seems to ignore the loose-skinned oranges, which have as much right to the adjective 'sweet'. However, the term is established, and no other designation seems satisfactory, so it will probably continue to be used. The sweet orange is readily distinguished from the sour by its leaves, which are not as dark a green and which ordinarily have only small wings on the petioles. The flowers are slightly smaller. The fruits differ mainly in that those of the sweet orange are sweet or sub-acid. While some early writers considered the two types to be varieties of the same species, the separate standing of the sweet orange as *C. sinensis* is now generally recognized.

The Pummelo and Grapefruit

The pummelos present a more difficult problem. They have generally been treated as a distinct group, although Bonavia questioned this. Because pubescence is not a constant, nor an exclusive characteristic of the group, although it is a common feature of it, he felt that no case was made for putting them in a separate species. He may have been unduly influenced by his theory that in most or all cases, small citrus fruits have their large or 'elephant' counterparts, developed by living for generations under conditions of luxuriant growth. He suggested that the pummelo was the elephant form of the sweet orange. Even if both originated from a common ancestor, there seems to be as much justification for separating them as there is for the other species. In few of the species is there one constant factor which distinguishes it from all other species. Classifications are based on a group of features, and even then it is not always easy to place a tree in its proper species.

The leaves of the pummelo are dark green, leathery, and with large wings on the petioles. The amount of pubescence varies, but in some cases it is considerable, and may remain on the young branches for a year or more. The flowers are large, white, and heavy, with conspicuous oil glands. The fruit is larger than that of any other important species, weighing several pounds in some cases. It may be globose, oval, flattened or pyriform, and the rind varies from moderately thin to very thick. The pulp is frequently rather dry and sour, but in the better varieties is of excellent quality. The membrane surrounding the segments is tough, but in some cases the segments are open in the centre. A number of names have been used for the species. Swingle and Tanaka agree on *C. grandis*, but Chatterjee (1948) maintains that *C. maxima* is correct. Another fairly common synonym is *C. decumana*.

The grapefruit is very similar to the pummelo and is considered by some as *C. grandis* var. *uvacar pa*. The modern tendency, however, is to recognize it as a separate species, *C. paradisi*. Swingle accepts this as a satellite species, although recognizing that it may be a hybrid between the pummelo and sweet orange. There is some evidence that at least one variety, the Triumph, is a hybrid between the grapefruit and orange. The grapefruit has never been found in Asia except where it had been imported, and is therefore thought to have originated as a seedling or bud mutation from the pummelo, in the West Indies. The first mention of it, according to Morton and Morton (1946), is in 1750 in the published writings of Griffith Hughes who referred to the 'forbidden fruit' of Barbados. Six years later another writer refers to the 'forbidden fruit' or 'smaller shaddock' cultivated in Jamaica. It was not until 1814 that the word 'grapefruit' first appeared, in Lunan's Hortus Jamaicensis, and not until about 1885 that commercial production began. While it is ordinarily not difficult to distinguish a grapefruit tree from a pummelo, this is done by means of a group of characteristics, rather than any one distinctive feature. The leaves tend to be somewhat smaller, slightly lighter in colour, and less leathery. The wings on the petioles are smaller. The leaves and young shoots have little, if any, pubescence. The fruit is generally smaller, has a thinner rind, is more juicy, and has a somewhat different flavour. Both pummelos and grapefruit have varieties with pink or red pulp as well as pale yellow or grayish. Some grapefruits also have a pink blush on the outside.

American horticulturists have contributed to the confusion of names, by adopting the term 'pomelo' for the grapefruit, pronouncing the word in the same way as 'pummelo'. Thus they distinguished the pomelo (grapefruit) from the pummelo (shaddock). Even in the United States, however, the fruit is known popularly and in trade as the grapefruit and the attempt to introduce the other term has been largely abandoned. In India, where the term 'pummelo' is well known and 'shaddock' is not used, it would certainly be unwise to call the grapefruit a pomelo.

There are other citrus fruits occurring in India which have been largely neglected by western writers. These include the *karna* and the *attani*.

The *karna, khatta nimbu, id nimbu, or kharna khatta* is a fruit having no English name, although it is frequently referred to in this country as a citron, which it in no way resembles. The tree is very vigorous, and is commonly and successfully used as stock. In some ways the fruit resembles that of the sour orange, but Bonavia recognized that it was distinc , and proposed calling it *C. aurantium* var. *khatta.* Its flowers are tinged with red, like those of the lemon, but the leaves are very distinct from those of either species, having neither the large wings of the sour orange nor the distinct scent of the lemon. The fruit is large and round, but generally mammillate, and sometimes very rough. Both the rind and the pulp are orange in colour. The juice is plentiful and very sour. It has been suggested that this fruit represents a natural hybrid between the sour orange and the lemon. It has been called *C. karna.*

The position of the *attani* (or *atanni*) is not so clear. The name is supposed to be derived from *ath anne,* meaning eight annas. Bonavia was told that this was because the fruit was half as large a pummelo. Another explanation is that it is thought to be a hybrid, half orange and half lemon. The leaves are similar to those of the mandarin, except that they are pubescent when young, and Bonavia suggested that this might be the 'elephant' form of the Santara. The fruit is large with a thick rind, with pulp which is juicy and sub-acid. It is very pleasant when eaten like grapefruit, with sugar. Lushington follows Bonavia in putting it in the same species as the Santara, making it the botanical variety *decumana.* Tanaka (1937 b) calls in *C. rugulosa.*

The Loose-skinned Oranges

The loose-skinned oranges have never received adequate treatment by any European or American authority. The term 'mandarin' is used for the entire group as well as for one section of it. These fruits were introduced into the West at a comparatively late date, and do not play an important part there, as they do in Asia. At first they were grouped in a single species, *C. nobilis.* Swingle formerly recognized three botanical varieties : *C. nobilis* proper, the King orange; the variety *delicioso,* the mandarin and tangerine oranges; and the variety *unshiu,* the Satsuma orange. Hume (1926) and Tanaka felt that these should be recognized as separate species. Later Swingle became convinced that the King orange, which was the type of Lourerio's species *C. nobilis,* is a hybrid between a mandarin and some other fruit, possibly a sweet orange, pummelo, or a hybrid of the two. This would invalidate the name for the species, and Swingle accepts the name Blanco applied in 1837, *C. reticulata.* He now recognizes only one botanical variety, *austera,* the sour mandarin. He suggests that the Rangpur lime may be a form of this sour mandarin, or a hybrid of it. This is a decorative tree bearing large numbers of fruits similar in appearance to mandarins, but sour, and used for the same purposes as lemons and limes. It bears only one crop a year, but as this is usable from August until March, it makes a good addition to the home garden. Tanaka maintains *C. nobilis* for the King orange and *C. unshiu* for the Satsuma, while he restricts *C. reticulata* to the type commonly grown in India.

Undoubtedly the most important mandarin in India is the Santara or Nagpur orange, which Lushington (1910) called *C. chrysocarpa,* and which Swingle and Tanaka both call *C. reticulata.* The very similar mandarin grown in the Kashi hills of Assam would have to be included in this group. Tanaka assigned specific names to five other mandarins in India, mentioned other species, still unnamed, and suggested the probable existence of others. Swingle tentatively accepts two other species of more or less similar fruits, *C. tachibana*, an inedible fruit of Japan and *C. indica*, which Tanaka described as growing wild in the Khasi hills, although Swingle thinks it possible that it may prove to be a hybrid with *C. latipes*, a member of the subgenus *Pepeda*, native to that area.

It is not clear whether the name Santara (Santra, Sangtra) should be considered the name of one variety, the Nagpur orange, or should be used for the group containing this and similar varieties, such as the Coorg orange. It may even be used for the entire species, in which case it should not be capitalized. Bhattacharya and Dutta (1949 a) recognize two varieties of the Khasi mandarin, the common one which ripens from the end of October until February, and one grown in a limited area of the Khasi hills ripening from March to May. They consider that the late ripening is due mainly to environmental factors, however.

The mandarins are ordinarily recognized without much difficulty. The leaves are ordinarily rather small and slender, and have a characteristic scent. The flowers are solitary, white, and small. The fruit is oblate, generally smaller than the sweet orange, and frequently reddish orange in colour. The rind and segments are loosely attached, and the seeds, when cut open, are generally green.

To a much greater extent than the mango, the citrus fruits tend to be polyembryonic. This probably explains the comparative uniformity of the fruit of seedling trees, such as those of the Khasi hills, where vegetative propagation is rare. Except for those rather recently introduced, there are few clonal varieties. Nurseries offer named varieties, but these are seldom well established, and frequently merely refer to the place from which the parent plant was obtained.

None of the Indian varieties of the sweet orange has the reputation of such foreign varieties as the Washington Naval, the Valenica and the Shamouti, the last being the most important variety in Palestine, and reputedly one of the best oranges in the world. The most largely grown sweet orange in India is the Mosambi, produced mainly in Bombay, and the Sathgudi or Chini which is the most important in Madras The Batavian, also grown there, is very similar, and may prove merely a synonym. In northern India, the sweet orange is called the Malta, and this term is sometimes used for a particular variety. The Blood-red Malta of the Punjab is highly regarded. None of these terms, however, always refers to a clonal variety, as some orchards are of seedling trees. The true Mosambi is probably a clonal variety, but other similar types are given that name, which is, indeed, sometimes used for all the sweet oranges. Foreign varieties grown in the Punjab include the Pineapple, said to be the best, Excellencis, Vaneille, Seville, and Valencia. Although the Valenica in the Punjab is rather sour and lacking in juice, it brings a good price because it ripens in March whereas the other varieties are on the market in January and February. Randhawa and Dinsa (1947 a) point out that this variety produces fruit of high quality in regions having a hot climate, and should find a prominent place in plantings there. Choudhury and others (1947 a) report that it is a promising variety in Assam, where it, the Washington Navel, and Duncan and Marsh grapefruit were introduced about 1925. The original trees grew well, but as propagation was entirely on the pummelo, which is not congenial, these fruits were neglected. It does well on the rough lemon, which is recommended, and on certain other lemons.

Most of the mandarin oranges are grown under regional names. Ahmed and Ullah (1950) report that the Kinnow from the United States and Feutrell's Early from Australia are more promising in the canal colonies of West Punjab than the local mandarins which suffer from sunburn, and they may be valuable in India also. Feutrell's Early ripens in November, and has a very low acid content. The Kinnow ripens in January and February there and contains more sugar and more acid. This variety has also done very well in Allahabad, where it ripens by December. The pulp resembles that of the Santara but the rind is not separated from the pulp. This means that there is less danger of damage to the fruit in marketing.

In the case of the limes, vernacular names are used, but it is not clear to what extent these represent varieties rather than being local names for the species. This is largely true of the lemon also, except for recently introduced varieties. There are many 'indigenous' varieties in Assam, according to Choudhury and others (1947 b). These are varieties with vernacular names and have been grown in Assam for generations, although there may be doubt as to their being truly indigenous. A variety called by such names as China Kagzi, Chinapati, and Sarbati, and which appears to be a true lemon, but immune to scab which affects the imported Eureka and Genoa, has been selected as suitable for cultivation, and is referred to as the Assam lemon. The trees are apparently rather small, as it is suggested that they be planted 12 to 18 feet apart. As it bears throughout the year and so does not stand drought well, it is said to do better on the plains, where irrigation is practised, than on the hills. Although lemons are not grown commercially in Assam, they seem to be more important there than in most other parts of the country, for it is said that there are not more than 1,000 acres in the State. In Andhra the lemon is considered a promising crop by Rao and Sundararao (1954) who state that the trees start bearing at the age of 18 months and produce about the same weight of fruit as the lime. They bear throughout the year, but most heavily from August to November. They recommend a variety called Nepali Oblong as producing the heaviest crops of seedless fruit and being resistant to canker.

There are undoubtedly a number of distinct varieties of pummelo, but varietal names are not well established. The grapefruits grown in India are almost entirely imported varieties, including the Marsh, Duncan, Excelsior, Walters, and the pink-fleshed form of the last, Foster. As polyembryony is very common in the species, seedling trees are frequently very satisfactory, and perhaps should be considered as nucellar trees of the varieties from which they came.

Considerable work has been done, particularly by Swingle in America, on the hybridization of citrus fruits, and this has resulted in a number of promising hybrids. A very large number of cross-pollinations is required in order to get a reasonable number of hybrids from which to select. Only a small percentage of the cross-pollinated flowers develop into fruits, and not all of the fruits have viable seed. Many of the seedlings are apogamic, only a few being true hybrids. Nevertheless, much has been accomplished. In an effort to secure varieties which can be grown in regions subject to frost, the sweet orange has been crossed with the trifoliate orange. The result, called the citrange, is generally rather sour, and with more or less of the bitterness of the trifoliate orange. This hybrid has been further crossed with the kumquat to produce the citrangequat. The limequat, produced by crossing the lime and kumquat, bears fruit similar to that of the lime, and in some cases equally good, and is more hardy than the lime. Most promising of all is the tangelo, a hybrid of the tangerine (mandarin) and the 'pomelo' (grapefruit). The fruit commonly resembles that of the sweet orange, but with a distinctive and pleasant flavour. The tangors, hybrids between the mandarin and sweet orange, include one known as the Umatilla which resembles the tangelos, as well as some which are commonly considered mandarins. Miss Janki Amal (1953) has reported a plant which she considers a natural hybrid between a lemon and citron found in a garden in south Malabar and which she named the Sukumari citrolemon. Its fruit is said to resemble the citron, but to be borne in bunches like the lemon, thus being more abundant. In making hybrids it is sometimes desirable to cross species which do not flower at the same time. Soost and Cameron (1954) report success with trifoliate orange pollen stored 36 days at 4°C. over calcium chloride. Great possibilities lie before the plant breeder who will develop hybrids between the various citrus fruits grown in India.

Although most of the citrus fruits probably originated in regions of tropical climate, most of them thrive in a subtropical climate, and produce fruit of better quality than that grown in the tropics. Nevertheless, none of them except the trifoliate orange can stand much frost. There is a difference in the hardiness of the different species, but all are seriously damaged if the temperature falls to 16° F. A temperature of 28°, especially if maintained for several hours, is likely to damage fruits and young shoots. Hodgson and others (1950) report on the comparative resistance of many varieties shown during the freezes of 1948 and 1949 in California. Almost all of the important regions of citrus production are subject to occasional frost damage, and in some of them the growers go to great expense to protect the trees from injury, mainly by means of orchard heaters and wind machines.

Other climatic factors than frost rarely prevent the growth of citrus fruits, but they may influence greatly the quality of the fruit and the choice of varieties, and they affect the cost of production. Thus the Shamouti orange is grown on the coastal plain of Israel but does not do well in the hot interior valleys where grapefruit of good quality is grown. Cheema and others (1954) state that neither the Santara nor the Mosambi does well in heavy rainfall tracts except where drainage is very good, as in Coorg. They say that in Bombay the Santara requires a drier climate than the Mosambi, but that both are sweeter where there is less rainfall. On the other hand, the pummelo is said to stand heavy rain and to fail to bear good fruits in the drier Deccan area, while the sour lime does well with either heavy or light rain. In California, according to Caprio and others

(1954), warmer than average autumns and winters are associated with larger sizes of both Washington Navel and Valencia oranges, but warmer springs and summers are associated with larger Navels but smaller Valencias. This difference between varieties may be connected with the fact that the Valencias are carrying two crops during these months. Harding and others (1954), however, were unable to correlate the decrease in fruit size in most areas of California from 1945 to 1949 with any single feature of the climate, although they consider that rainfall, temperature, wind, light, and air pollutants all affect the size of the fruit, as do many other factors. Climatic factors are considered by Barnard (1949) and by Bain (1949) who contrasts the production of citrus fruits in Trinidad, near the equator and near sea-level, with that in California which is well within the temperate zone and relatively dry. Rainfall seems to be unimportant if irrigation is provided, but atmospheric humidity makes a great difference. In general, low humidity results in good colour and external appearance, whereas high humidity favours thin skin and plentiful juice. Exposure to strong wind, whether hot or cool is also important, and in windy districts windbreaks are commonly used.

Maximum temperatures are not very important, except in desert regions where exposure to very hot sun may be harmful, but the total heat during the growing season is extremely important. Little growth takes place when the mean temperature is below 55°F. or above 97°F. A unit of heat is taken as a degree above 55° daily mean temperature, and heat indices of the growing season have been calculated for some important areas as follows : grapefruit, 5,617 to 6,781; Washington Navel oranges, 2,706 to 3,462; Valenica oranges, 2,672; lemons 1,854. In Trinidad, the heat units during the growing season are calculated at 6,560, and as dormancy is brought about by drought rather than coolness, there is likely to be some growth outside the growing season. In California, on the other hand, some of the heat units may not be utilized because of too high temperatures. Bain therefore estimates that the effective units at Riverside, California, in an important citrus area, are only about 2,800 and thinks that this explains why an average 10-year-old tree in California is no bigger than one 5 to 8 years old in Trinidad. Although Riverside has considerably less heat than the places where grapefruit is at its best, fruit of fair quality is produced there. But while pummelo trees of excellent varieties thrive at Riverside, the fruit is sour, indicating that the heat requirement of the pummelo is considerably greater than that of the grapefruit. Allahabad probably has about 5,700 units in the warmest six months, and considerably more in the growing season, which lasts most of the year.

Washington Navel oranges ripen in about 7 months from flowering in Riverside, and in half that time in Trinidad. Likewise, grapefruit and Valencias require about 15 months in California and from May to December in Trinidad. Colour seems to develop at the end of the growing period and the beginning of the dormant season. Washington Navels ripen in winter in California, where they develop good colour, but in Trinidad, as in India, they ripen during warm weather and remain green. Grapefruit and Valencias ripen in winter in Trinidad and India, and develop good colour. Granulation is a problem with the Valenica in

California and the Navel in Trinidad, and Bain considers that it is a normal stage of maturity that is reached when the required number of heat units for the variety have been utilized in growth. He states, 'It has been shown that when during the normal process of fruit maturity the acid content reaches a certain low point, starches are formed instead of sugar, thus giving the juice sacs the appearance associated with granulation.' When fruit ripens in hot weather, it soon passes from maturity to granulation.

Bain states that citrus trees in California need about twice as much nitrogen as those in Trinidad, and explains this partly by the fact that in Trinidad the trees never carry two crops at the same time (nor do Navels in California), but mainly by the greater amount of sunshine in California as trees with more light use more nitrogen.

Some of the loose-skinned oranges as well as some lemons will ripen well in regions of comparatively cool summers. The King orange and the Santara, like most of the sweet oranges require more heat. High temperatures at the time of flowering result in a poor set of fruit in the case of some varieties. Hot summers cause sunburn in some cases, including sweet oranges and mandarins in the Punjab, according to Bajwa and Ram (1943). Sunburn on the fruit is said to be very common, and the bark is sometimes affected. In one case trees with a spread of 12 to 14 feet were growing 20 feet apart. Part of the trees were protected by having a row of *Sesbania egyptica* planted on the south-west side, parallel to the tree row, and about a foot from the periphery of the tree. The protection reduced the damage from 10·6% to 6·1% in the case of the sweet orange, and from 12·3% to 4·2% in the case of the mandarin. The Sesbania may be planted by March 1, and by July will protect the fruit. No damage is done after October 1.

L. Singh and Khan (1942) found that fruit of the Blood-red Malta developed better colour when protected from the sun by the tree or by Sesbania, although the fruit borne in the interior of the tree had no red colour. It is probable that the development of red-colour depends on low temperatures. K. K. Singh and Singh (1948) report that on rough lemon rootstock, less than 20% of the oranges developed the red colour in 1943-44, a mild winter, compared with 56% in the following more severe winter. The rootstock was also shown to exert an important influence. The most colour was developed on the *kharna khatta* which is incompatible and caused almost complete defoliation in the winter, allowing the fruits to lose heat by radiation. This produced colour in 35·7% of the fruits in 1943-44, whereas *Jullunduri khatti* produced it in 4·7%, and the sweet lime not at all. Cold storage after harvesting also increases both the amount and the intensity of the red colour. Temperatures of 36 to 39° F° increased the colour distinctly in 1943-44. The next year the temperatures used were 32 to 39°F. and the amount of colour increased rather rapidly for six weeks and more slowly until, at the end of 14 weeks, 96% of the fruit showed colour. When this variety is grown in areas having no frosty weather, it develops no colour, and cold storage then has no effect.

In spite of all these limitations, the citrus fruits are grown under a wide variety of climatic conditions. Particularly for commercial production, care should be taken to choose the varieties best suited to local conditions, but if this is done good citrus fruits can be produced ractically throughout the tropics and subtropics. More experience is needed to show which species and varieties are best suited to different parts of India.

Citrus fruits are grown successfully on a wide range of soils. Near Nagpur, most of the orchards are on rather heavy black soil, underlaid with *murrum* which provides good drainage. Oranges of similar type and quality are grown on sandy or gravelly soils in the Khasi hills. In the Punjab also, the soils are mostly light. The depth of the soil and the nature of the subsoil are of more importance than the texture of the surface soil. The citrus fruits are sensitive to poor drainage, and should not be planted where there is danger of the soil around the roots becoming water-logged. Rock or hardpan within five feet of the surface should be avoided. In some cases soils which are naturally poorly drained may be made suitable for citrus fruits by artificial drainage. Heavy soils, if well drained, may produce good crops, but increase the difficulty of cultivation. Very light soils are likely to lack in fertility and to dry out quickly. The ideal soil would seem to be a medium or light loam with a slightly heavier subsoil. The soils of most important citrus districts are well supplied with lime, and it is thought that this contributes to the success of the orchards. On the other hand, Haas (1939, 1940) claims that citrus trees grow better in an acid than in an alkaline medium, and that the idea that they grow well in soil with a pH value as high as 8·5 is based on faulty technique. The harmful effects of a high pH value seem to be indirect, probably mainly relating to the availability of minerals, for Guest and Chapman (1944) found that when the indirect effects were eliminated as far as possible, there was no harmful effect on sweet orange seedlings growing in cultures when the pH ranged from 4 to 9. Death was caused in a few days at 2 or 11. Bhattacharya and Dutta (1949 a) state that in Assam citrus fruits do best on soil with a pH value of 5·5 to 6·5.

Propagation

In some areas, such as Madras State and the Khasi hills, propagation is largely by seed, and in the case of species in which polyembryony is the rule, this results in less variation in the fruit than is the case with most fruits of good quality. Even so, Naik (1940) reports that in the Sathgudi orchard reputed to be the best around Kodur, only 17·40% of the trees bore heavily in the main crop, whereas 12·62% bore few or no fruits. In another orchard 19·8% bore heavily, but 30·21% bore lightly. Obviously, neither orchard was satisfactory in this respect. Experimental trees budded from a single mother tree showed less variation than these orchard trees, while carefully rogued seedlings, presumably apogamic, were still more uniform. However, seedling trees are slow in coming into bearing, tend to be thorny, and grow tall and slender. Vegetative propagation is, therefore, desirable in most cases.

Sometimes varieties which have been propagated vegetatively for many generations become somewhat lacking in vigour. Hodgson and Cameron (1938) and Frost (1938) have pointed out that such varieties may have their vigour restored by being grown once from apogamic seedlings. For this process of rejuvenation, Swingle in 1932 coined the term 'neophyosis', from the Greek meaning 'causing to grow anew'. The loss of vigour in old clones may be caused by unknown virus infection, which would explain the greater vigour of the seedlings. Swingle, (1948) states that nucellar seedlings of citrus are completely free from virus apparently because the embryo sac and immediately adjoining tissues are at flowering time impregnated with some powerful substance which kills all the virus. It is thought that this substance may be desoxyribose nucleic acid. He also points out that nucellar seedlings are more resistant to frost, and that in the case of Washington and Thompson Navel oranges, the nucellar seedlings had no true navel but only a round hole 1/8 to 1/16 of an inch in diameter in the slightly depressed tip of the fruit. The Bahianinha variety, which is thought to be a nucellar seedling of the Washington Navel, has a smaller, firmer fruit without a navel, and so has better shipping quality and has become of great importance in Brazil. On the other hand, as Frost (1938) points out, there may be certain undesirable fruit characteristics, including more ragginess in the pulp and earlier over-ripeness. Batchelor and Cameron (1950) mention the undesirable features, but also the fact that in some cases the fruit is larger and in some it has a higher total solids content. Some nucellar clones seem to produce less fruit, at least when young, but this is not true of all. Cameron and Soost (1952) report on an orchard planted mainly in 1933 in which nucellar seedling line plants were grown along with their parental line. The average cross section of the trunk of the young line (nucellar) trees was from 6 to 108% greater than that of the old line trees, and the volume of the tops was similarly greater. Except in the case of the Lisbon lemon, the yields were 33 to 102% greater. The size, shape, and percentage of juice of the fruits were generally similar. The percentage of soluble solids was similar or slightly higher and of acid similar or slightly lower, in the young line trees. Some tendency toward a thicker rind and coarser pulp, and in two navel-orange varieties, the smaller size of the navel, persisted. The tendency for the young line trees to have fewer seeds was decreasing. It would seem that this method of renewing the vigour of an old clone offers considerable promise, but must be used with care. Such nucellar seedlings will tend to be thorny, but it has been observed that branches arising after about three years are less thorny, and if buds are taken from these branches for propagation, excessive thorniness may be avoided.

Budding is, by far, the most common method of vegetative propagation, and is very successful. Shield budding is probably the best form, and may be practised in mid-winter, or during the early part of the rainy season at Allahabad. L. B. Singh (1954 a) reports 80 to 85% success in budding sweet oranges on *karna* rootstock in June, and lower percentages in March and September. Naik (1940 a) reports a significantly higher percentage of 'takes' when the wood is left in the bud than when it is removed, in the case of the sweet orange and lime on two rootstocks. Khan (1942) agrees that the wood is necessary in the case of the lime, and is better when the budwood is immature, but in other cases, removing the wood increased the 'take' by about 25%. It decreased the number of plants a man could bud in a day in the same proportion. K. Singh and Singh (1947), also working in the Punjab, found that in budding the mandarin on the rough lemon, the removal of the wood delayed the growth of the buds but gave a better percentage of success,

83·3% in spring and 51·7% in summer, compared with 74·1% and 42·3% with the wood left attached to the bud. The skill of the budder may be questioned, for in the United States, where the wood is ordinarily left in the bud, a professional budder would expect better results. One such budder reports in correspondence placing about 34,000 buds in one nursery with the loss of about 0·5%, although he experimented with several different types of budwood. K. Singh and Singh report that a microscopic examination of cross sections through the bud union showed better results when the wood was removed. Nandi and others (1945) in Assam tend to favour leaving the wood in the bud of the Khasi mandarin, budded on *katajamir*, a lemon. In one case one man achieved 88% and 72% success with the wood and 56% and 60% without it, using T and inverted T budding respectively. Stevenson (1947a), working with Santara on rough lemon, reports 93% success in T budding and 87% in inverted T budding after removing the wood from the bud, as compared with 77·5% and 80·5% when the wood was left. Both methods proved superior to the one commonly used in Madhya Pradesh, in which the bark is cut and lifted from the budwood without taking any wood with it, and which gave 54% and 53% success. Stevenson (1948) also emphasizes the importance of having rootstocks of the proper size. Budding the Santara on rough lemon, the percentage of success varied with the girth of the rootstock as follows : 3·6 cm., 66%; 3·7 cm., 78%; 3·8 cm., 87%; 3·9 cm., 90%; 4 cm., 81·67%. Also working in Madhya Pradesh, M. P. Singh (1948) found that sweet and sour limes were seldom budded because of the thorny nature of the budwood, which made it impracticable to remove the wood from the bud. Allowing the wood to remain gave poor results with mature budwood, but was very successful with immature budwood. Probably this question may well be left to the preference of the individual.

Lopping the top immediately after budding was found by K. Singh and Singh (1947) better than delaying this action with the sweet orange and sour lime, and with the mandarin in summer but not always in the spring. The vigour of the rootstocks did not affect the percentage of 'takes', but the larger stocks gave the larger budlings a year later. Naik (1940 a) found no advantage in lopping the rootstock at the time of budding, although this caused the bud to start growing somewhat sooner, and as it reduced the 'take' in the case of the lime, he recommends that lopping be delayed until the bud has grown at least two inches. Similar results were secured in Assam. If it is necessary to use buds which are not swollen, however, it may be desirable to lop off the top after the bud has united with the rootstock, to force it into growth. Orillos (1954), working in the Philippines, secured better growth by bending the rootstock about 10 cm. from the ground immediately before budding than by bending or cutting it 3 or 8 weeks after budding.

Grafting is sometimes done and Nandi and others (1945) found bark grafting the Khasi mandarin on the rough lemon successful in very wet weather when budding was not satisfactory. Inarching is fairly common in India, but as it is cumbersome and does not give as good plants as budding, it should not be used. The pummelo, lime, and sweet lime are commonly propagated by layering or air-layering, and Nandi and others (1945) report 100% success with the citron, lemon, sweet lime, Mosambi orange, and *C. macroptera* in from 20 to 44 days, while in from 40 to 55 days they secured 90% success with the Khasi mandarin, 80% with the sour orange and grapefruit, and 70% with the Valencia orange. They failed to grow the mandarin from stem cuttings even when using a plant hormone which improved the growth of the species which could be grown in this way. They succeeded in growing plants from root cuttings only in the cases of the citron, rough lemon, and sweet lime, cuttings 4 to 6 cm. in diameter proving better than those half that size. S. N. Singh (1955 b) increased the percentage of success with air layering from 60 to 100% in the case of the sweet lime by treating the cut surface with 1% a-NAA plus 1% b-IAA, which also increased the number and length of the roots. Similar improvement in the roots was secured on the sour lime and grapefruit by hormone treatment, although 100% success was secured without treatment. For the grapefruit, b-IAA was best but for the sour lime a mixture of this and b-IBA, all of these at 1%. As Halma (1931) has shown, many species of *Citrus* can be grown from small leafy cuttings by using a special technique. While this may be of advantage for certain experimental purposes, it is not likely to prove of value for commercial propagation. Halma (1947) compares the growth of Washington Navel and Valencia oranges and Eureka lemons grown from stem cuttings with those budded on sweet orange and grapefruit rootstocks, up to from 11 to 16 years of age. The lemon cuttings were consistently less productive, and except for the first four years, less vigorous than the budlings, while no consistent differences occurred in the oranges. Neither rootstock maintained a taproot system for more than five years, and the cuttings developed good root systems, so there must be some other reason for the failure of the lemon cuttings.

The question of rootstocks on which to grow the different species of citrus fruits is a complicated one. Not only do the different species require different stocks, but a combination of stock and scion which is satisfactory under one set of conditions may fail entirely under other conditions. Wallace and others (1953) show how the reaction of the soil may affect the choice of rootstock. They grew Eureka lemons on five rootstocks at 5·0, 6·4, and 7·5 pH. The greatest growth in 15 months occurred at 7·5 in the case of the sweet orange, rough lemon, and grapefruit, but there was little difference attributable to pH in the case of sour and trifoliate oranges. The concentration of iron in the leaves was highest at 5·0 in the sour orange and rough lemon, at 6·4 in the trifoliate, and at 7·5 in the sweet orange and grapefruit. Both the pH and the rootstock affected the amount of nitrogen in the leaves. This means that local experimentation is necessary to discover the best stocks for each species in each region where citrus fruits are grown.

The most commonly used stocks in the world are the sour, sweet, and trifoliate oranges, and the rough lemon. Hume (1926) estimated that 75% of the citrus fruits of the world were produced on sour orange stock, which has been very popular in Europe and America. It is more hardy than the others except the trifoliate orange, is resistant to gummosis, and has a good root system. In

Florida it proved unsuitable for the Satsuma orange, the lime, or the kumquat. It is very susceptible to a virus disease or group of diseases, and thousands of acres of sweet oranges on this rootstock have died. It is, therefore, likely to be much less used in the future. The sweet orange is less hardy, and is susceptible to gummosis, but is otherwise a good stock, and is used to a limited extent in most countries. The rough lemon is probably second in importance to the sour orange, being used on light soils in Florida, and almost entirely in South Africa. It seems to be compatible with all of the important species, at least under some circumstances. It is a vigorous grower, and is resistant to gummosis. The main objection to it is that particularly while the trees are young, the fruit is frequently of poor quality. The trifoliate orange is the most hardy stock, and is used in regions subject to severe frosts, such as Japan and Central China, and for the Satsuma in the United States. It generally, but not always, tends to dwarf the trees of which it is the stock. Benton and others (1953) state that it is the most resistant of all rootstocks to *Phytophtora citrophthora* root rot which makes the rough lemon unsatisfactory in New South Wales, and that some of the stunting may be avoided by selecting budwood from trees free from the scaly butt virus. It is used there for the sweet orange and mandarin with some satisfaction. Martin and others (1955) point out that it is more sensitive to high soil sodium or potassium or a combination of these, than are some other species. It thrives in soil too moist for other rootstocks, and results in early bearing, better quality, and increased yield, especially during drought.

Hybrids, particularly those with the trifoliate orange as one parent, may furnish good rootstocks. The Troyer citrange, a hybrid with the Washington Navel, seems particularly promising, at least in California. Batchelor and Bitters (1952) state that it is highly polyembryonic, and in limited trials has given higher yields of the Valencia orange and Lisbon lemon than other rootstocks with Valencia fruits slightly larger and of at least as good quality as those on sour orange roots. It seems to be tolerant to tristeza. Bitters and Batchelor (1953) report that it is extremely resistant to gummosis. However, as Weathers and others (1955) have reported, it is a failure with the Eureka lemon, resulting in death in the third year with damage to the tissues below the bud union. The cause may be a virus, but as nucellar Eurekas are affected, any virus would have to be seed-borne in the Eureka or, less probably in the Troyer, or very readily transmissible.

Most mandarin oranges are unsuitable rootstocks, but one, the Cleopatra, gives good crops of sweet oranges of excellent quality, is fairly resistant to gummosis, and seems tolerant to tristeza. According to Batchelor and Bitters (1952), it is likely to be widely used in California. The Empress mandarin is said by Marloth (1954) to be a promising rootstock for the Tomango orange.

A number of other species of *Citrus* have been used to a greater or less extent, including the pummelo, grapefruit, lime, sweet lime, citron, mandarin, and hybrids. The Imperial Bureau of Fruit Production (Anon. 1932) in a very complete review of propagation methods, gives information regarding some 14 species of *Citrus*, and 33 species of other genera of the family Rutaceae, which have been tried as stock, or seem promising for this purpose. Among the genera which seem most promising are *Feronia* and *Aegle.* Wester (1913) reported citrus fruits growing successfully on *A. glutinosa.* De Jong (1934) found that only a small percentage of buds on *A. marmelo* (the bael) grew at all, and that these died within a year, but after initial failures he obtained 65% success in budding grapefruit, mandarins and sweet oranges on *Feronia limonia* (*elephantum*) and *F. lucida.* Cheema and Bhat (1928) reported inarching Santara and Mosambi oranges on stocks of *Feronia limonia* and *Aegle marmelos,* in an attempt to secure plants which would succeed under soil conditions unsuitable for trees on citrus roots. Some of the grafts bore fruit, but did not live long. Badami (1941) reports similar experiments, and states that both Santara and Mosambi oranges can easily be inarched on the bael. In Madras• (Anon. 1944 a) it was found that the Sathgudi bore mainly in clusters of 5 or 6 fruits each when budded on *Feronia limonia.* The plants are precocious but severely dwarfed. The same variety budded on *Atalantia monophylla* had not fruited in four years.

The virus disease or diseases attacking the sour orange rootstock are of considerable interest because of the importance of this rootstock, the peculiar nature of the disease, and the way in which the problem has been attacked. The trouble was first noted in South Africa about 1899, when it was found that sweet oranges budded on sour orange rootstock remained sickly and stunted. This was dismissed as incompatibility under local conditions. The failure of this combination in Java was even more marked. The scions would grow well for two or three months and then within a year the plant would die. Toxopeus (1936) concluded at the end of some interesting experiments that in Java the sweet orange produced some substance toxic to the sour orange. In these countries the only effect of the disease was to prevent the use of the sour orange as rootstock. But in 1932 it was discovered that sweet orange trees on 'sour stock' in Argentina were mysteriously sickening and dying, and in 1937 it was observed that this condition had been developing in Brazil for several years. In 1939 a similar condition was noticed in California and by the beginning of 1945 it was estimated that 9,500 trees were affected. In these three countries there were large acreages of sweet orange trees, of all ages, growing on sour stock, and the situation was recognized as alarming. Scientists started investigating, and in California the problem was divided among a group of scientists, one or two men investigating one phase of the problem. When Fawcett and others (1946) issued a preliminary report, they were able to give the external and internal symptoms and to eliminate fairly well all possible causes except a virus, a cause Webber (1943 a) had earlier considered most probable. In affected trees the leaves turn yellowish green or ashen and there is frequently a large crop of fruit which may turn orange prematurely. The leaves curl and fall, and twigs die, but in most cases some new leaves are developed, and the tree remains for some years in an 'equilibrium stage', staying alive, but useless. Some trees die quickly. It was found that the sieve tubes degenerate at and below the bud union and become blocked, so that the roots starve for carbohydrate and begin to rot. Bitancourt (1944) had showed that there was frequently an accumulation of starch above the bud union which could be demonstrated by applying iodine to the scraped bark. A little later Fawcett and Wallace (1946) offered proof that the disease was caused by a virus.

It is now known that the same virus or group of viruses cause different symptoms on different scion-rootstock combinations and seedlings. In the form commonly called stem pitting, the wood above or below the bud union, or both, is pitted or grooved. It is severe on grapefruit trees, and Oberholzer (1953) estimates that it has rendered almost 40% of the grapefruit orchards of South Africa valueless. Hughes and Lister (1953) describe a die back of limes caused by the virus in West Africa. Seedling trees are more severely damaged than those on rough lemon rootstock, but even the latter are said to yield economic crops only for about 10 years. There seems to be evidence that some forms of the virus are more virulent than others and Costa and others (1955) indicate that different stionic combinations react differently to these forms. Grant and others (1951) report some evidence that the presence of a mild form of the virus protects the tree from severe forms. McClean and Van der Plank (1955) suggest that the virus has two components, one of which causes stem pitting and the other the symptoms known as seedling yellows, a severe yellowing of the leaves and stunting of the tree (Fraser, 1952).

Because of the various symptoms, the disease is known by different names. In South America it is called tristeza (meaning melancholy) and in California, quick decline. Other names which have been used include bud-union decline and rootlet rot.

The disease has been reported in Queensland by Oxenham and Sturgess (1953), and, in a mild form, in Florida by Grant and Schneider (1953) and in Texas by Olsen and Sleeth (1954). That it is also present in India is suggested by the behaviour of sweet oranges on sour orange rootstock brought from the North-West Frontier Province (now Pakistan) to Allahabad in 1934. Only two of these trees ever grew well, and there was much die-back; eventually all proved failures, although sweet oranges on their own roots and on *karna* rootstock, growing near them have grown and fruited fairly well. Its presence in Bombay also is suggested by Nagpal (1954), who cites symptoms including sudden collapse of trees, stem pitting, and vein clearing on the lime. He suggests that this may be an important factor in the so-called 'die-back' of citrus in that State. He found severe pitting on *galgal* and *karna* rootstocks, some on the sweet lime and rough lemon, but none on the Rangpur lime or when the Mosambi was budded on the rough lemon. The clearing of the veins of the sour lime after it is budded with buds from an infected tree is commonly used as a means of testing for the presence of the virus in trees which show no distinct symptoms.

The vector which seems to be responsible in South America (Meneghini, 1946, 1948; Bennet and Costa, (1949) and Africa is the black orange aphid, *Aphis citricidus* (*A. tavaresi*, *A. citricola*, *Dorsalis tavaresi*, *Paratoxoptera argentinensis*). This aphid does not occur in the United States, where the melon aphid, *A. gossypii*, is the culprit in California (Dickson and others, 1950) and, with the green citrus aphid, *A. spiraecola* in Florida.

While tristeza was discovered in connection with the sour orange rootstock, and it is of great importance mainly where that rootstock is used, it has now been found that other species may also be affected. Grant and others (1950) report the results of extensive trials in Brazil. The virus may be present in any species, but symptoms develop only when the sweet orange, mandarin, grapefruit, or one of certain limes or lemons is budded on a non-tolerant rootstock. All of the 19 sour and bittersweet oranges, 10 grapefruits, and 19 pummelos, shaddocks, and their hybrids which were tested were non-tolerant. The 12 sweet oranges and 26 mandarins tested seemed tolerant. Also non-tolerant were 10 tangelos, 18 lemons, 3 limes, a citremon, the Nippon kumquat, *Citrus macroptera* and 2 forms of *Severinia*. Tolerant varieties included 16 tangelos, a trifoliate orange, 6 citranges, 6 citrumelos, and 2 sweet lemons. The situation regarding the rough lemon as a rootstock was not yet clear, but it seemed that some types might be tolerant and some non-tolerant. Grant and others (1951) report that while sweet oranges and mandarins may be safely grown on tolerant rootstocks, grapefruit and some limes may gradually decline on tolerant roots.

Even with non-tolerant combinations, there will be no symptoms, of course, unless the virus is present. If buds are taken from an area in which the disease is not found, and placed on seedlings, the resultant trees are likely to be healthy until infected by means of aphids or perhaps other insects. Oberholzer (1947) has shown that healthy trees can be grown when buds are taken from nucellar trees in infected areas. However, wherever sour orange or other non-tolerant rootstocks are used, there is always the danger of the virus being introduced. Care should be taken not to bring into such areas trees from any affected area, for even a completely tolearnt tree may carry the virus. For instance, the Meyer lemon has shown no symptoms in California, but Wallace and Drake (1955) report tests which show that most of the trees of this variety carry the virus, which was probably present on the trees originally introduced from northern China in 1908. In fact, this may have been the only introduction of the virus into that State, although it seldom seems to spread from the Meyer to other species. It would thus seem that the only safe way to introduce a citrus type from an area where the virus occurs is by means of seed, with the subsequent selection of apomictic seedlings.

Once tristeza appears in an orchard, there seems to be very little which can be done to protect non-tolerant trees. DuCharme and Knorr (1953) state that in South America the destruction of visibly affected trees, the sterilization of the soil, and the control of aphids proved of little or no value, and the inarching of tolerant roots or inducing scion rooting were successful only under certain conditions. They recommend replacing the affected trees with those on tolerant rootstocks.

In new plantings, whether in India or in other countries, it would seem wise to use a tolerant rootstock if a suitable one is available.

A disease of lemons, somewhat resembling quick decline, with a characteristic pattern of sieve-tube necrosis, has been increasingly common in California for 25 years, according to Calavan and others (1951). It is more common on lemon trees on grapefruit or sweet orange rootstocks than on others. While it is transmitted by budding, its virus nature has not been proved.

The only way to find out the most suitable stock to be used for each species under given soil and climatic conditions is to conduct comparative stock trials. These may produce certain valuable information within a year or two, but as deficiencies sometimes appear after as long as twenty years, trials should not be considered conclusive in a shorter period. One of the earliest trials of citrus stocks in India is that conducted by Brown (1920) at Peshawar. Although this experiment dealt with only two varieties and four rootstocks, it is especially interesting in that it showed that there was a remarkable difference in compatibility and a decided influence of the stock on the fruit, and that a stock suitable to one species might be entirely unsatisfactory for another. In fact, because of uncertainty as to the identification of some of the rootstocks used, this is almost the only value of the experiment.

In Bombay and Madhya Pradesh, the most common stock is the rough lemon, called '*jamburi*' or '*jamberi*'. Srivastava (1931) states that the best stock is the sweet lime, but that the *jamburi* is generally used. Allan (1934) recommends the *jamberi* (which he calls rough citron) for the Mosambi and the grapefruit but states that the sweet lime produces the best quality of Santara fruit, although the branches of the tree tend to break on this stock. He considers the *karna* best for the Malta. This is a very vigorous stock which is very commonly used in Uttar Pradesh, and which seems to be compatible with a number of species. In Bombay a rootstock trial has been conducted since about 1943 which indicates that of the species tried, only the Rangpur lime and rough lemon are even reasonably satisfactory (Nagpal, 1954). The rough lemon has shown the greatest growth and yield and the largest size of fruit but the best quality fruit is found on the trees on Rangpur lime roots. The *karna*, *galgal* and sweet lime were also tried.

Further experiments on rootstocks are needed in the different parts of the country, and several are being conducted. At Kodur, in Andhra, the more important varieties of sweet orange and sour lime grown there have been budded on the following stocks : rough lemon, *kichili*, *gajanimma* (*C. pennivesiculata*), *billi-kichili* (a tangerine), pummelo, sour lime, and sour orange. Naik (1940a) reported that at the end of the first year in the orchard the rough lemon was making the best growth. Later Naik (1949) sums up the results in the nursery stage, but states that the performance of the trees in the orchard remains to be seen. In general, the rough lemon appeared to be the most suitable rootstock. The *gajanimma* was the most vigorous, but its low germination, high variability, and susceptibility to gummosis were against it. The pummelo, being entirely monoembryonic, was variable. On *billi-kichili* the 'take' varied, and this stock lacks vigour in the first year and does not transplant well. The *kichili* was more satisfactory, except with the lime, but the germination is not very satisfactory, and the trees are not very uniform. The lime failed to transplant well, and is less vigorous than the rough lemon. A trial started in 1938 suggests that for the important Sathgudi orange, rootstocks of the same variety or of the *kichili* are likely to prove suitable.

More evidence of the value of the different rootstocks for the lime is available than for the other rootstocks in Andhra. Naik (1944, 1948b) reports that the budded trees were significantly larger and more fruitful than seedling limes after 89 months in the orchard, although the seedlings were doing better than in the first years of bearing. During the first 63 months, trees on *gajanimma* stock had produced more than ten times as much as the seedlings. Of the budded trees, those on rough lemon and *gajanimma* were slightly larger than those on lime, and those on *gajanimma* and lime had yielded more than those on rough lemon. As the *gajanimma* rootstock had overgrown the lime scion in nearly three-fourths of the trees, it seemed that this rootstock might not be permanently satisfactory. Because of better root systems, it was thought that this and the rough lemon might be preferred in regions where high winds sometimes uproot the trees. Rao and others (1954) report later, when the trees were about 16 years old. For the first 12 years the budded plants were more vigorous than the seedlings, but later there was no difference. During the first 11 years the trees on *gajanimma* roots bore the heaviest crops, and the seedlings the least, but again there was no significant difference after that period. At the time of the report the plants on *gajanimma* seemed to be the best, but it was recognized that in the end the seedlings might prove to be about as satisfactory.

An experiment was started in 1937 in Montgomery in the Punjab and a report up to 1940 was published by L. Singh and Singh (1942a). The Malta orange, Santara, and grapefruit were budded on apogamic seedlings and cuttings of the sweet lime, rough lemon, citron, and *kharna khatta* (*karna*), and, on seedlings of shaddock and a type received from Ceylon under the name *nasnaran*, said to be *C. japonica*. This last in Ceylon has been identified by Tanaka as the calamondin, according to Richards (1955). There is some doubt as to the type grown under this name in the Punjab, for S. Singh (1951) says that it has winged petioles and pinkish flowers, and Khan and Haq (1954) identify it as *Citrus aurantifolia*. Bijwa and Singh (1945), report that in all cases in which rootstocks were grown from cuttings, the scions budded on these were more vigorous and more fruitful than those on seedlings. S. Singh and Nagpal (1954) make exceptions in the cases of the local Malta on citron and Bloodred Malta on *karna* after 1943, and add that they were also more precocious and higher yielding. With all scions except the Bloodred Malta, *karna* was most vigorous until bearing started, and it continued so with the Sangtara. Because of heavier cropping with the Malta (local) and grapefruit, the trees of these dropped behind those on rough lemon in size. Citron and sweet lime dwarfed all the scions, and were considered unsuitable, except possibly for the Sangtara. *Nasnaran* produced nearly as much fruit of the Malta (local) as did *karna* and there was some evidence that the fruit was of better quality.

The Bloodred Malta on *karna* started well, but according to L. Singh and Singh (1944), and S. Singh and Nagpal (1954), showed delayed compatibility. There was much splitting of the bark beginning when the trees were about two years old, and the trees which did not die were largely defoliated each winter. For this scion the rough lemon was outstandingly the best rootstock. In this connection, it is interesting that Provan (1933) reports that in Victoria, Australia, most varieties of the sweet orange do well on the rough lemon, but that the Maltese Blood variety was a failure on this stock. The local Malta, during the first four years of bearing was best on *karna* followed closely by *nasnaran* and rough lemon. Khan (1949) reports that up to the age of five years, the Valencia orange was most vigorous on 'Jamberi' which is said to differ from the rough lemon slightly in the shape and colour of the fruit, but should probably be considered a form of it. Other fairly vigorous rootstock for this variety were the *karna*, rough lemon, sour orange, and three types more or less similar to the rough lemon.

The effect of the rootstock on the quality is obviously important, but in most Indian trials has not been measured. K. K. Singh (1954) reports on the composition of fruit produced at Montgomery in 1943-45, on the common and Bloodred Malta. Strangely enough, the rough lemon which ordinarily results in very poor quality is said to have given the best results. The sweet lime and citron rootstocks resulted in fruit of poor quality. In the case of the common Malta, *nasnaran* and *karna* were almost as good as the rough lemon.

S. Singh and Nagpal (1947) report that through the first four years of bearing, Marsh grapefruit had proven vigorous and most productive on *karna* rootstock, although after bearing began the trees on rough lemon had grown a little more rapidly. Rough lemon and shaddock were fairly satisfactory. A high negative correlation was found between growth increment and cropping. The grapefruit on rootstock grown from cuttings were all larger than those on seedlings, and in 15 out of 16 comparisons, out-yielded them.

Although most of the oranges in Assam are seedlings, and under favourable conditions these have a long, profitable life, under some conditions, especially on the plains, they lack vigour, bear poorly, and do not live long. To find a satisfactory rootstock under such conditions, an experiment has been started at Burnihat, with the Khasi mandarin and other scions budded on a number of rootstocks. When Nandi and others (1943) reported on the trees 28 months after budding, the most vigorous plants were on *Pani jamir* which is said to be a lemon, but as the fruits are somewhat sweet, it cannot be considered the true lemon. Later, however, Woodford (1948) reported signs of incompatibility on this rootstock, while the rough lemon (*soh myndong*) has proved the best of five rootstocks for the Khasi mandarin, and apparently suitable for most species. Das (1948) considers it best for the sweet orange as well as the mandarin. Grape fruit did well on the pummelo (*rabab tenga*) but this rootstock and the sour orange (*karun jamir*) were not suitable for the mandarin. Later reports, however, indicate that the sour orange was second only to the rough lemon in growth and fruitfulness. The *satkora* (*Citrus macroptera*, of the subgenus *Papeda*) was definitely dwarfing, and the citron (*bira jora*) was also unsuitable. The *Kata jamir* of the Surma valley, or *Tulia tenga* of the Assam valley was found generally compatible with the various scions tested, and may be useful in some circumstances. This and the *soh myndong* are both placed in the species *C. jambhiri* by Bhattacharya and Dutta (1949a), although the former has smooth round fruits.

Along with this statistically designed experiment, an observational trial with the same rootstocks and five others and six scion varieties was conducted. Bhattacharya and Dutta (1952) report that the rough lemon was good for the mandarin, Valencia, and Mosambi, but slightly dwarfed the Duncan grapefruit and Washington Navel orange, and induced granulation in the latter. The sour orange was of doubtful value for the mandarin and Valencia, and the pummelo was suitable only for the grapefruit. The Khasi mandarin was of doubtful value for the Mosambi, and the *ada-jamir* (*C. assamensis*) for the mandarin. Failures were the citron, the *pati-lebu* described as a citron-lemon type, the *pani jamir* and another lemon-like fruit, *soh-synteng*, and the *karna*.

At Peradeniya, Ceylon, four varieties of grapefruit were budded on sour orange, rough lemon, pummelo, and a hybrid. Richards (1938, 1945) reports vigorous healthy growth on the rough lemon, but variable growth on the sour orange and the hybrid, with most of the plants stunted and chlorotic. (Richards, 1954, reports symptoms of tristeza on most varieties growing on the sour orange.) The pummelo was a failure in all cases. Similar results were observed at Hingurakgoda and Nalanda. At Nalanda the Nagpur Santara grew well on the sour orange, although other mandarins, Beauty of Glen Retreat and Emperor, failed. Where conditions are more favourable, symptoms on the sour orange rootstocks are less severe, according to Richards (1948). The failure of sweet orange, mandarin, and Tahiti lime on the European lemon (which flourishes) at semi-dry Malpotha, at an elevation of 3,500 feet, is attributed to a virus disease. All citrus fruits do well on the rough lemon at this station. Richards (1954) reports that the *heen naran*, said to be Lushington's *C. crenatifolia* var. *lycospersiformis*, shows great promise for one sweet orange and the Santara. It is highly polyembryonic and vigorous, and gives more than 95% bud-take.

Frequently the quality of the fruit seems to be poorer on the more vigorous stock. Richards (1940), working in California, found that of five rootstocks, the rough lemon produced the most vigorous trees of six different scions, but fruit with the lowest content both of acid and total solids. Trifoliate orange was the most dwarfing, but produced fruit of the highest acid and total solids content. Such fruit is generally preferred. He also found that the invigorating stocks tended to hasten granulation. The undesirable effects of too great vigour are likely to become less marked as the trees grow older. That lack of vigour does not always result in fruit of superior quality is evident from an experiment reported by Halma (1943), in which the Eureka lemon as rootstock not only dwarfed the Valencia orange, in comparison with sweet orange stock, but produced fruit with a thicker rind and a lower content of both acid and total solids. The tendency of the juice of the Washington Navel orange to turn bitter was found by Marsh and Cameron (1950) to be related to the rootstock. Fruit grown on grapefruit rootstock contained very little of the precursor of bitterness and this disappeared early in the season. Slightly more occurred in that grown on trifoliate and ordinary sweet orange stock, and considerably more in that on sour orange stock or from trees grown as cuttings, while the rough lemon had the worst effect. The general quality of the juice followed much the same pattern, being best in fruit grown on trifoliate stock and poorest in that on rough lemon.

Although seeds for propagation may be taken from a ripe fruit with fair results, it is frequently better to use seeds from immature fruit. B. Singh (1945) reports that in the Punjab, seeds of *karna*, rough lemon, and lemon taken from green fruits as early as August 25 were viable, and that after September 7 the percentage of germination decreased. Similar results have been noticed at Allahabad, in the case of *karna* seeds. Nandi and others (1945) found that seeds of the Khasi mandarin increased in percentage of germination from 47·5 in September to 93 or 95 in the period from the middle of November to the middle of December, and then decreased to 81 by the first of January. The time taken for germination increased from 42 days early in the season to 76 at the end.

Citrus seeds lose their viability if stored for very long, especially if they are allowed to become dry. It has been reported (Anon., 1942) that at Montgomery seeds lost nearly 50% of their viability within 15 days, and that practically none grew after three months in storage. Nandi and others (1945) found that all citrus seeds deteriorated in storage, but that the larger kinds tended to retain their viability longer than the smaller ones. Exposure of the seeds to sunshine for even four hours reduced germination, and after 36 hours in the sun none of the seed grew. It is ordinarily preferable to plant the seed soon after they are removed from the mature fruit, although Bhat (1929) reports that *jamburi* seed could be kept up to 131 days without a decrease in the percentage of germination. He found that germination began in about 20 days when fresh, but required twice as long in the case of older seed. With more precautions, viability may be prolonged somewhat. Childs and Hrnciar (1949) report that seeds of 29 out of 34 varieties dipped in a disinfectant such as 8-hydroxyquinoline sulphate and stored in moist sawdust or moss at 35°F. in unsealed containers gave over 90% germination after 6 months and in most cases more than 80% after 8 months.

The seedlings are subject to damping off if conditions are favourable to this disease. Srivastava and Singh (1954) report that severe damping off of grapefruit seedlings at Kanpur was caused by *Pythium de Baryanum* and *Rhizoctonia solani*. The application of formaldehyde dust at the rate of 30-40 g. per square foot of the seedbed gave excellent control, better than with 20 g. or with 0·1% to 1·0% mercuric chloride. The seedlings should be transplanted when two or three inches high, and may be moved again before budding. Stevenson (1947b) in Madhya Pradesh found it desirable to shelter the seedlings so that no sunshine struck them between 10 a.m. and 3 p.m. About 12% of the leaves of unshaded seedlings were scorched in the hot weather, while a third of them died and others failed to grow well in the rainy season, supposedly because of too much water around the roots.

The importance of discarding the weak seedlings at the time of the first transplanting, and again just before budding, has been pointed out by Webber (1932). As polyembryony is common, the majority of the seedlings in most species arise from unfertilized embryos, and resemble the parent plant very closely. The sexually produced seedlings vary a great deal, and are likely to be lacking in vigour. By discarding these small seedlings, stock can be secured which is uniform and strong. It has been found by careful observation and recording that trees grown on these small variants never become as large and fruitful as those grown on the apogamic stock. As a result of work by himself and other investigators, Webber gives the percentage of apogamic seedlings in different species as follows : sweet orange, 40 to 45; sour orange, 75 to 85; grapefruit, 60 to 95; mandarin orange, 10 to 100; lemon, 10 to 95; citron, 40 to 50; and trifoliate orange, 72. Some of the hybrids which are promising stocks seem to be practically 100 percent apogamic. Nandi and others (1945) report on the percentage of seeds in several species producing more than one seedling (part of those producing only one were doubtless also polyembryonic, with only one embryo developing). The highest percentage, 36·84, was in the sweet lime, followed by two lemons, 33·5 and 32·93; the Khasi mandarin, 27·08; rough lemon, 24·64; *Ada jamir* 15; sour orange, 13·41; and the citron and pummelo, 0. Out of 380 seeds, 138 produced two seedlings each, and only two produced as many as four each. L. B. Singh and Singh (1955), working on 10 types, found no correlation between the percentage of seeds producing more than one seedling and the percentage of nucellar seedlings. For instance, they report only 4% of the trifoliate orange seeds producing more than one seedling, but of all the seedlings produced, 71% were nucellar, whereas the percentages in the Florida rough lemon were 40 and 57. The highest percentage of nucellar seedlings was found in the *jamberi*, 91% The high percentage of seeds they report giving rise to multiple gametic seedlings suggests that they may have counted as gametic some seedlings which were apogamic but weak. They report the sour orange having 25% multiple apogamic seedlings and 60% multiple gametic seedlings, with only 55% of all the seedlings apogamic, whereas Webber reported 75-85%. Agrawal (1947) counted the number of embryos in the sweet lime, and found that while nearly half of the seeds produced only 1 seedling, and none produced more than 4, 92% were polyembryonic, and some contained as many as 7 embryos.

In growing the young budded trees in the nursery, care is necessary in order to produce a straight clean stem. Bhat (1929) has pointed out that there is a tendency for several shoots to arise from one Santara bud, and this is true of other types also. All but one should be removed, and later, when branching is allowed, the branches should be well spaced. In a tree with many branches arising close together near the ground, the treatment of gummosis and the stem borer is unnecessarily difficult. In order to develop a good straight stem, the young plant should be staked, a light bamboo stake being quite satisfactory. Side branches tend to take the lead over those arising from the terminal bud and may be allowed to take their place. In most citrus areas of the world except Israil, the preference is for a rather low-headed tree, with the lowest branch perhaps a foot and a half from the ground.

The age at which rootstocks are ready for budding depends on the species and on soil and climatic conditions, varying from less than a year to several years. In areas such as Allahabad where the growing season is long, vigorous rootstocks are ready in about a year, but in the Punjab growth is much slower. In order to lessen the time in the nursery, Bajwa and Chhabra (1946) suggest sowing the seeds in August or September, ¼ to ½ inch deep, 1 to 2 inches apart, in rows 9 to 10 inches apart. Good care is given to encourage rapid growth, including covering the seedlings at night with a thatch in mid-winter. The larger seedlings may be transplanted in February, and the rest in the next monsoon season. All the plants in every third line are transplanted, and the others are thinned to 6 to 9 inches apart. The plants removed are replanted at that distance in pairs of rows 10 inches apart, with 20 inches between pairs. The seedlings which have not been transplanted are said to be ready for budding when 1 or 1½ years old, and the others a year after transplanting. The budlings are saleable one year, in the case of those not transplanted, or 1½ years after budding.

Culture

The citrus trees, being evergreen are best transplanted during the monsoon season. Unless they are to be moved long distances, no special precautions need to be taken.

Considerable difference of opinion exists as to the correct distance at which to plant the various citrus fruits. This will vary with the variety, the stock, the soil, and the cultural methods used. If the orchard is crowded, cultivation will have to be done by hand. However, there is a tendency in California at present to favour close spacing, at least in one direction. The trees may be kept from crowding by pruning, and later part may be removed, but good yields are being secured in some orchards in which the trees form hedges. In such orchards 'non-tillage' is commonly practised, the weeds being controlled by spraying. Many Indian citrus orchards, like those of other fruits, are so closely planted that oxen cannot work between the trees, and the yield of mature trees is less than it would have been with sufficient spacing. The Report on the Marketing of Citrus Fruits states that in all parts of the country the older orchards are irregular and crowded, with such extremes as 300 limes per acre in Madras and 500 oranges in Assam. In Bombay the older orchards both of Mosambi and Santara are said to have the trees about 10 to 12 feet apart, while in the newer plantings 15 to 21 feet is allowed between plants. Similar distances are given for other provinces. The tendency is toward more space, and in the newer orchards in Madras about 27 feet is a common spacing for sweet oranges and up to this distance is allowed for the lime. Still greater distances, 30 to 36 feet, are used in the *kichili* orchards. Naik (1949) says that Sathgudi seedlings are planted 27 to 30 ft. apart, but that 20 to 25 ft. seems sufficient for budded plants of this variety and of the lemon and pummelo. Rangacharlu and Venkatarao (1954), however, recommend 28 ft. Naik suggests 25 to 30 ft. for seedling limes, and at least 20 for budded plants; 18 ft. for grapefruit at Coonoor and at least 20 ft. on the plains; and 22 to 25 ft. for seedling mandarins.

The common practice seems to have influenced most writers on the subject, who tend to recommend rather close planting. Allan (1934) recommends not less than 16 feet for the sweet orange, 18 to 20 feet for the Santara and grapefruit, and 22 feet for the pummelo. Paranjpye (1937) suggests 18 feet for the sweet orange, but only 15 feet for the Santara in Poona and 18 feet in Khandesh. Conditions in Assam apparently do not encourage growth, for Bhattacharya and Dutta (1949 a) urge that trees be planted so that the branches will never touch, but suggest as a general rule, the following distances : Khasi mandarin, 15-20 ft.; sweet oranges, 20-25 ft.; limes, 12-15 ft.; lemons, 12-18 ft.; pummeloes and grapefruit, 22-25 ft. In most of the important citrus-growing countries, wider spacing is parctised, 20 to 25 ft. being common for oranges, lemons and grapefruit. Palestine is an exception, some of the older orchards having trees 10 or even 6 ft. apart. The present tendency there is to increase the distance to about 20 ft. Some kinds of loose-skinned oranges form rather small bushy trees, but this is not true of the Santara. The latter is at first a rather slender tree, but after it begins to bear, it spreads out. Under most conditions, even the smaller types of citrus fruit grown commercially in India should probably be planted at least 20 ft. apart. In some cases it may be wise to plant the trees at about 15 by 20 ft. and later to remove alternate trees so as to leave them 20 by 30 ft.

The citrus trees produce many fibrous roots in the surface soil, so that it is ordinarily impossible to cultivate the soil at all without breaking some of the roots. Some cultivation, however, is ordinarily necessary in order to control the weeds and incorporate organic matter in the soil. The increasing use of spraying to control weeds, with no cultivation, in citrus orchards in California has been mentioned in Chapter V. It was formerly considered good practice to cultivate thoroughly after every irrigation, so that no weeds might grow. This is unnecessary and may be harmful. It is probably sufficient to plough or dig the orchard once a year, deep enough to cover a green manure crop, and cultivate frequently enough to prevent weeds from going to seed. Mulching with organic matter may take the place of cultivation, but has some dangers. It increases fire hazard and gives shelter to rodents. Its possible effect on the termite population would need to be watched. With the spread of sprinkler irrigation in the United States there is much less danger of fire in mulch, and more interest is being showed in this method. De-Wolfe and others (1954) found that in some cases mulching increases the yield, and that it increases certain soil fungi which parasitize *Phytophthora* and others which capture and kill the citrus nematode.

Cultivation in Assam presents special difficulties as much of the fruit is grown on steep hillsides. Most growers do not cultivate at all, but cut the undergrowth before harvesting. Woodford (1948) reports that a higher yield was secured by a light hoeing three times a year, and Bhattacharya and Dutta(1949 a) consider the effects of failure to cultivate so serious that they recommend terracing, or at least levelling a circular bed 5 or 6 feet in diameter for each tree. Even on the plains tillage is often neglected, and these authors (1949 b) report on an experiment in a private orchard on typical old alluvium of the Brahmaputra valley with seedling trees 25 years old and in a state of decline. Part of the trees were hoed and sprayed with Bordeaux mixture, and bore significantly more fruit than those which had no care except the cutting of weeds before the harvest.

Irrigation is necessary in order to keep citrus trees in a healthy condition under most Indian conditions, and in most other citrus-growing regions of the world. Mandarins are grown in Coorg without irrigation on well-drained black and red loam soils 2,500 to 4,000 feet above sea-level, with 25 to 200 inches of rain a year. However, lack of water is considered an important factor in the deterioration of many orchards there (Anon., 1954 b), and mulching is said to be an advantage. Other factors are erosion, lack of nutrients, and diseases. The citrus orchards of Assam are also unirrigated except for some on the plains, but irrigation would be beneficial. Mitra and Khongwir (1928) suggest that the appearance of mottle-leaf and die-back in the dry season is caused by a lack of moisture. The situation may be aggravated by the killing of roots when the soil is water-logged in the rainy season. Any lack of moisture when growing fruits are on the tree is likely to reduce the rate of growth and result in smaller fruit, or even to cause the fruit to fall. Huberty and Richards (1954) report on an experiment at Riverside, California, where water is used rapidly, which has been carried on since 1934. A highly significant increase in yield was found from trees irrigated with furrows every three weeks in the season, compared with those irrigated less frequently, but only a slight increase in trunk growth. Applications intended to wet 80% of the root zone did not increase the yield in comparison with those wetting only 40%. On the other hand, Marloth (1955) reports that in a long-term experiment in South Africa, trees irrigated by basins yielded more than those by furrows, and that there was a significant decrease in yield where irrigation was given on only one side of the tree.

Too much irrigation is harmful, even on fairly well-drained soil, and any water-logging is to be strictly avoided. Water-logging frequently reduces the area in which the roots are effective, and may make more frequent irrigation necessary. Phatak (1934) states that the Santara garden at the Nagpur Agricultural College showed great improvement as a result of drainage, and that it was then necessary to irrigate only once a month, as compared with weekly irrigation given in the neighbouring orchards.

In heavy soils, the great majority of the roots are to be found in the top two and a half feet of the soil, and even in light soil, most of the roots are in the top four feet. It is obviously undesirable to irrigate below the root zone, except occasionally to wash undesirable salts from the surface soil under conditions in which these are likely to accumulate. Irrigation should be so planned as to wet the root zone frequently enough to keep it from drying out. Rangacharlu and Venkatarao (1954) advise irrigation when the top 9-12 in. of the soil become dry, which, in Andhra, means from 15 to 20 times a year. As most of the roots are fairly close to the surface, the upper soil is likely to dry out more quickly, in which case one or more light irrigations may be given between the more thorough irrigations. While a soil augur is the best means of determining the time of irrigation, much can be told by the appearance of the leaves, which begin to curl when the water supply is inadequate. If the tree is not getting enough water, some may be withdrawn from the fruit during the day, and by careful measurement of the fruit in the morning and evening this can be detected. In very hot weather it may be well to reduce the temperature of the soil by giving light irrigations more frequently than would be necessary to supply the needs of the tree.

The exact method of irrigation is not important, provided no water is allowed to touch the trunk of the tree. Furrow irrigation is commonly practised, but flooding is also satisfactory where water is abundant and cheap. Naik (1949) feels that the furrow system has not been adequately tried in India, and is not satisfactory on light soils, and that the extended basin system is the only one which can be recommended at present.

Maintaining the fertility of orchard soils is a complex problem, as has been seen in Chapter V. More experimental work has been done with citrus fruits than with any other fruit commonly grown in India, but there is still much to be discovered and more to be understood. Differences in requirements between the different kinds of citrus fruits seem not to be great, but there is a great deal of difference between desirable treatments on different soils and under different climatic conditions. Nutrients are likely to be leached from the soil if the pH is below about 5·5, and to be unavailable if it is more than about 7. It is comparatively easy to maintain fertility in a soil with a pH of about 6.

Nitrogen is required in fairly large amounts in all cases, more apparently being needed in parts of California, where as much as three pounds per tree per annum is recommended, and in Arizona, where Finch and McGeorge (1940, 1945) stress its importance, than in Florida, although the soils there are poor and sandy. As has been seen, Bain (1949) explains the greater need in California mainly on the basis of the greater amount of sunshine there, but Chapman (1951) believes that there are other reasons. He states that while many growers add from 200 to 400 lb. of nitrogen per acre each year, the trees remove only from 40 to 60 lb. Much is lost by leaching, especially as in many California orchards the root development is poor in the areas where the fertilizer and water are applied, and because the nitrogen increases in the surface soil during the summer and is carried down by rains in the winter when the trees need it least. Nitrogen is also lost by volitization under fully aerobic conditions, especially when decomposable organic matter is present. This may be one reason why less nitrogen is required under non-tillage, as organic matter is not added. In neutral or alkaline soils, such as are common in California, as much as a fourth of the nitrogen added may be lost by the volitization of ammonia. The comparative abundance of phosphorus in the soils there seems to produce symptoms of nitrogen starvation, perhaps by increasing the activity of the organisms causing volitization. The larger amounts of potassium in the soils of Florida and Texas tend to increase nitrogen absorption by the trees there.

Under the mild conditions of the coastal zone of southern California, where light rainfall and light irrigation result in little loss by leaching or run-off, less nitrogen is needed than elsewhere in that State. Wallace and others (1952) report an experiment in an orchard in that area, with non-tillage, in which for 11 years all of the trees had received about 3 lb. of nitrogen each, per annum. Then for 9 years half the trees were given no nitrogen and the rest 4 lb. each, per annum. They report no significant depression in the yield of the trees receiving no nitrogen, and an adequate amount in the soil and in the leaves at the end of the 9 years. Apparently sufficient had been stored in the soil for this period, at at least. That less than 3 lb. per tree is needed in other parts of the State also is indicated by a survey made by Aldrich and Taylor (1954). They interviewed growers in all citrus areas of the State, and found that while two-thirds were using 2-3 lb. of nitrogen per tree, the others were getting excellent production on less than 1·75 lb., applied, generally, in several doses. They particularly commend the growers who were applying nitrogen on the basis of soil analysis, so as to maintain 5 or 10 ppm of nitrate in solution. These were among the most economical users of nitrogen in their areas, and had average or better production.

In South Africa the importance of nitrogen has been emphasized by Powell (1930) and Morris (1937), but the quantity required may be less than in California, for Anderssen (1937) reports an experiment in which the application of nitrogen induced a marked increase in the crop, but with no significant difference between trees given 2, 4 and 6 pounds of ammonium sulphate. It is possible to decrease the yield by adding too much nitrogen, but in India the danger of this happening seems very small. If too much nitrogen, particularly in soluble form, is added at one time there may be considerable loss through leaching. Rohrbaugh (1946) also warns that if too much is added along with organic matter where the aeration is poor, some of it may be changed to nitrite which is highly toxic to the trees. It is commonly recommended that at least half of the nitrogen be applied in the form of bulky organic matter, partly for the beneficial effect of this on the structure and flora of the soil, and partly because the organic matter contains other elements, some of which may be needed. However, only 40% of the successful growers in the survey made by Aldrich and Taylor (1954) used any manure.

That the time of application may be of great importance is pointed out by Martin (1940) who found that in Arizona the application of nitrogen and the practice of clean cultivation, both in winter, advanced the spring growth by as much as 10 days, increased the nitrogen content of the trees prior to bloom and tended to maintain a satisfactory yield. On the other hand, the same practices in summer resulted in coarse fruit. This is explained by Jones and others (1944) who found that the application of nitrogen in winter markedly increased the amount in the leaves, but not in the maturing fruit. Van der Mere (1952-53) also stresses the need for plenty of nitrogen at flowering time, and a low level when the fruit is ripening, in the case of the Washington Navel orange. He reports the highest yields when nitrogen is applied as nitrate, and states that trees receiving ammonium produced coarser fruit with a higher acid content. It is possible that the results would have been better had the ammonium been applied earlier in the season so that more would have been converted to nitrate by flowering time. As Wallace and others (1952) point out, the use of ammonia tends to decrease the pH of the soil, which is desirable under some conditions. In their experiment the pH was reduced from about neutral to 4·1 in the surface soil and to 4·2 in the second 6 in. under heavy applications of ammonium sulphate, while the surface soil under the trees receiving no nitrogen increased to 7·4, partly because the leaves which fell contained about 7% calcium.

Phosphorus is rarely a factor limiting the growth or yield of citrus trees, although symptoms of deficiency can be readily produced in water or sand cultures. Haas (1936) describes the symptoms in trees grown in sand culture, the leaves of which contained only 0·05 to 0·07% phosphorus, whereas those of orchard trees contained several times as much. Chapman and Rayner (1951) tentatively suggest that orange leaves of the spring flush, when 5-8 months old should contain 0·12 to 0·13% of phosphorus. Aldrich and Coony (1951) and Haas (1951) report that lemons need more phosphorus than do oranges. Where the deficiency in the soil is extreme, the addition of phosphorus has sometimes given good results. It is often difficult to apply it so that it is available to the trees, and Bathurst (1945) found that in South Africa, where the soils are notoriously low in phosphorus, in only one orchard did an application increase the yield. More phosphorus than is needed should not be applied, for an excess causes damage. It had long been a standard practice to use superphosphate in Florida when Reuther and others (1949) reported that it did not increase the yield and in some cases interfered with growth. The amount in the soil also tends to increase when large amounts of farmyard manure are used and Chapman and Fullmer (1951) found that while about 10% of the orchards in California would respond favourably to applications of phosphorus, as many were suffering from too much.

The situation regarding potassium is similar. Where there are deficiencies, trees may not grow well, there may be leaf symptoms, or, more commonly, the fruit tends to be small. As Chapman and Harding (1955) point out, citrus trees may use from 150 to 235 lb. of potassium per acre each year, so a deficiency may develop. On the other hand, if manure is applied potassium as well as phosphorus tends to increase in the soil and they say that reductions in growth have occurred where potassium has become more than 15% of the exchangeable base complex. Haas (1948 b) states that 1% of potassiun in the dry matter of leaves is ample, and that 0·2% indicates a deficiency, but that the interpretation of values between these two is doubtful. Apparently most orchard soils are adequately supplied.

Deficiencies in phosphorus and potassium are more likely to affect the composition and quality of the fruit than the yield or the growth of the tree. Jones and Parker (1949 a) report that the application of nitrogen, phosphorus, and potassium each increased the percentage of that element in the juice, while winter cover-crops reduced nitrogen and potassium, and slightly increased calcium. They found significant correlations between potassium in the juice and acidity; and between phosphorus in the juice and the percentage of juice (probably because of the thinner rind) and low acidity and the low ascorbic acid content. Van der Plank and Turner (1936) refer to the common occurrence of sourness in oranges and grapefruit in South Africa, and state that the addition of phosphorus to the soil increased the amount of juice in the fruit and decreased its acidity, while adding potassium increased the acid. This was confirmed by Morris (1937) and Anderssen (1937). The latter found a high nitrogen content of the juice associated with high sugar and acid content and good keeping quality, while a high phosphorus content seemed to induce a thin rind and low acid content. Anderssen and Bathurst (1938) found that in Navel oranges, the more the nitrogen in the juice, the less was the phosphorus and that the yield increased with the nitrogen in the juice to about 1,000 ppm, after which it fell. During three years the maximum yield came when the ratio of nitrogen to phosphorus was between 8·7 and 9·9 to 1.

In sand and water cultures, out of doors, Chapman and others (1943) found that a low nitrogen content in a complete nutrient solution resulted in slower growing trees and in fruit with smooth thin skins and a high juice content, probably because phosphorus accumulates under such conditions. Plentiful nitrogen and low phosphorus gave the opposite results. Their findings agree with those of others that an excess of potash increases acidity, and if this is carried to extremes the fruit becomes very rough and coarse, while an extreme deficiency results in small fruit. In similar experiments Chapman and Brown (1942), found that in a solution with a high potassium and low calcium content, Valenica oranges seemed more susceptible to gummosis, and Navels were subject to the attack of other fungi under this condition, or when the phosphate content was high. Chapman and Rayner (1951) found that trees with an abundant phosphorus supply were more susceptible to a root-infecting fungus, *Thielavia basicola,* and to red scale. Innes (1946) found that on deficient soils, adding potassium increased seediness and the thickness of rind and core, while phosphorus reduced the thickness of the rind and the total solids and acid in the juice. In soils deficient in potassium, its addition improved the quality of the juice, but where nitrogen and phosphorus were deficient, potassium increased the acidity more than the other solids. He considered a N: K_2O ration of 1·7 about optimum.

Smith and others (1949) found no effect of added superphosphate on Pineapple oranges in Florida, but a decreased percentage of solids, including acid and ascorbic acid, in the Valencia. They considered the changes accompanying phosphorus fertilization there not to benefit fruit quality, but to harm it in the case of the Valenica. Finch and McGeorge (1945) found no effect on the quality of grapefruit in Arizona from any fertilizer treatment. In the same area, Jones and others (1945) found that grapefruit matured under a declining level on nitrogen in the soil had a relatively high ratio of total solids to acid, a high ascorbic acid content, earlier colouring with no re-greening of the fruit, and relatively thin, fine-textured fruit, compared with fruit matured under a continuing high nitrogen supply. Jones and Parker (1947) found that at Riverside the amount of nitrogen in the juice varied with that applied in the fertilizer, and that there was an inverse correlation between nitrogen in the juice and ascorbic acid in Navel oranges. When part of the nitrogen was added in the form of organic matter there was a highly significant decrease of nitrogen in the juice, but no more ascorbic acid.

The lack of a number of other elements, in addition to nitrogen, phosphorus, and potassium sometimes causes serious trouble. This has been particularly marked in Florida where citrus trees are grown on very light acid soils, subject to leaching by heavy rains. Camp and others (1949) discuss deficiencies in zinc, copper, manganese, boron, iron, magnesium, and some which have not been found in the field. A deficiency of molybdenum in Florida has been reported by Stewart and Leonard (1952 b, 1953) which is more serious where the rootstock is grapefruit and where the pH of the soil is below 5·6. Leaves with the deficiency contained 0·02 to 0·08 ppm of molybdenum. Spraying with 0·1 to 0·4 oz. of sodium molybdate in 10 gal. of water per tree resulted in satisfactory recovery. Deficiencies in a number of these elements particularly zinc occur in California and have been discussed by Chapman and others (1945), Rohrbaugh (1946), and Batchelor (1948 a). These authors do not consider magnesium commonly lacking in that State, but Haas (1948 a) states that symptoms of its deficiency are increasing there. The effect of even 1 ppm of zinc in the nutrient solution of lemon cuttings has been noted by Brusca and Haas (1955), who could see some benefit from as little as 0·4 ppm, while up to 15 ppm caused no harm. A deficiency of iron has been found in almost every major fruit-growing area of the world, and is the most difficult of all to correct, according to Stewart and Leonard (1952 a). As has been seen in Chapter V the use of chelated iron is promising, especially on acid soils. Manganese deficiency has been observed in Australia, where it is more severe in plants on sweet orange rootstocks than in those on rough lemon, according to Connor (1954). She reports an improvement where the pH of the soil was decreased by the use of ammonium sulphate. Boron deficiency seems to have been found only in India and in South Africa, where Morris (1938) cured the 'hard fruit' disease by adding small amounts of borax to the soil. The possibility that aluminium may play a part in the nutrition of citrus trees is suggested by Haas (1947), although he does not claim that it is essential. He found considerable improvement in the plants when it was added in solution and soil cultures. One of the most striking effects of a deficiency of these minor elements has been seen in Florida, where trees which were deficient suffered much more severely from frost than neighbouring trees which had been properly fertilized.

As in the case of phosphorus and potassium, there is also a possibility of toxic accumulations of these minor elements. Great care must be taken in adding boron as damage may be caused by as little as 16 ppm in the soil (Penman, 1949). Reuther and Smith (1953) refer to damage from copper accumulating in the soil as a result of the use of copper fungicides, and, to a less extent, from zinc and manganese. They state that when the soil pH is less than about 5 and copper exceeds 150 ppm, chlorosis develops. Both deficiencies and excesses of a large number of elements and salts are dealt with by Chapman (1953) who states the percentage present in normal leaves and discusses the interactions of one element on another.

While many deficiencies may be recognized by their symptoms, this is not possible in all cases, and a deficiency of more than one element often complicates the problem. Proper leaf analysis, which requires expensive equipment and experienced technicians, may be required for diagnosis. While many elements can be supplied by applying them to the soil, this method is not satisfactory in all cases. Van der Plank and Turner (1936) did not consider the addition of phosphorus commercially practicable because it soon formed insoluble compounds and very little was available to the trees. Anderssen (1940) reports that it was possible to reduce the acidity of the fruit strikingly by phosphate sprays. Chelated or, possibly, acidified, iron sprays offer some promise. Even partial improvement in the colour of the leaves may be accompanied by increased intake of water and minerals and production of carbohydrates. Considerable improvement is sometimes seen in as short a period as 11 days. Zinc can easily be supplied by spraying with zinc sulphate and lime, and copper by spraying with Bordeaux mixture.

Little can be said with confidence regarding the manuring of citrus fruits in India. There is general agreement that nitrogen is needed, and that farmyard manure is ordinarily the best form in which to add it. Mitter and Khongwir (1928) state that farmyard manure is not uncommonly used in Assam, and they recommend it and lime, as the soils there are mostly acid. Bhattacharya and Dutt (1945) report on a trial of nitrogen, phosphorus, and potassium, with and without lime in an orchard on good soil, but previously unmanured and declining. They report that 4 lb. of ammonium sulphate per tree increased the yield, while the other elements apparently did not. Nevertheless, these authors (1949 a) recommend the application of nitrogen, phosphorus, and potassium, and even suggest the exact amount of each from the first to the 14th year of the tree. They do state that these amounts are only indicative. To correct the acidity of the soil they recommend applying 15 to 30 md. of lime per acre every six or eight years.

It is said that only such manures as are rich in nitrogen have proved beneficial in the Punjab. L. Singh and others (1941), assuming that potassium and phosphorus were not limiting factors because the Punjab soils are richer in these elements than the average American soil, experimented with 4, 8, and 12 pounds of ammonium sulphate per tree of Malta orange. This significantly increased the yield, compared with controls, but there was no significant difference between the different amounts. Unfortunately, because of the appearance of mottle-leaf, 60 pounds of farmyard manure was given to each tree, including the controls, in spite of which the yield of all dropped markedly in the last two years of the experiment. This was thought to be because of the depletion of the organic matter in the soil, but the occurrence of mottle-leaf suggests the deficiency of zinc or some other element or elements. If this deficiency had been corrected, the results from the application of nitrogen might have been different. By applying 1·3 lb. of nitrogen per tree of sweet orange Bajwa and Kaura (1952) were able to increase the number of fruits borne, in comparison to the control trees without added nitrogen, 21% when only farmyard manure was used, 51% when ammonium sulphate was used, and 60% when half of the nitrogen was added in each form. The treatments proved profitable in almost the same proportions.

Srivastava (1931) states that farmyard manure serves the requirements of the trees in Madhya Pradesh but also says that potassium and phosphorus may be used with advantage. A. A. Khan (1945) writing of the same State emphasizes the need for nitrogen, stating that under-nourished trees have shorter productive lives and bear only a few hundred fruits a year, compared with 1,500 to 2,000 on trees in properly maintained orchards. He recommends using 20 lb. of farmyard manure (containing 0·5% nitrogen) per tree in the first year, rising to 240 lb. in the 12th year, or half these amounts plus one-fourth pound ammonium sulphate rising to 3 lb. He suggests applying the manure about a month before flowering and the ammonium sulphate just before and after flowering. He states that soils in Madhya Pradesh contain sufficient potassium and calcium, and probably sufficient phosphorus. Allan (1934), while recommending nitrogenous manures for young trees in Uttar Pradesh states that the use of phosphorus, and on some soils, potassium is required, as these elements influence both the quantity and the quality of the fruit. He refers to no experimental evidence in this country. In Bombay, Cheema and others (1954) recommend placing in the pit, preferably some time before planting, 5 lb. of bonemeal (or 10-20 lb. of bones), 100 lb. of cattle manure, and 10 lb. of wood ash. A year after planting they would apply 20 lb. of manure, 3 lb. of ash, 1 lb. of bonemeal, and 2 lb. of oil cake; these amounts they would increase until the 5th year when each tree would receive 100 lb. of manure, 15 lb. of ash, and 10 lb. of oil cake. These amounts would be continued, except that after the 5th year there would be only 5 lb. of cake. They recommend manuring young trees at the beginning of the monsoon and giving bearing trees ash at the time of the treatment to induce flowering and nitrogen when the fruits have set. They state that nitrogen before flowering hinders it, but seem more correct at another place when oil cake before flowering is said to stimulate it. Probably both oil cake and manure would be more effective if applied several months before flowering, so that by that time the nitrogen would be available.

Somewhat heavier manuring is recommended in Andhra by Rangacharlu and Venkatarao (1954) who suggest 1-2 lb. of nitrogen for each mature plant. They state that at Kodur good results have been secured by suing 150-200 lb. of manure or compost, 7-8 lb. of groundnut cake, and 7-8 lb. of ammonium sulphate, so as to supply about 3 lb. of nitrogen per tree. This is usually applied half in May or June and half in December or January.

The lack of adequate experimental evidence regarding the manuring of citrus trees in India is obvious. Excellent crops are grown with the addition of farmyard manure alone, but it is not clear to what extent this could be replaced with nitrogenous fertilizers, such as ammonium sulphate. Except where there is definite evidence of the need for other than nitrogenous fertilizers, it would seem wise to spend no money on them. Green manuring gives good results under most conditions.

There is already evidence that minor elements are lacking in many citrus orchards, although the subject has not been sufficiently studied. Deficiencies of iron and zinc seem to be very common, having been reported from Assam (Chowdhury, 1954 a), the Punjab (Choudhury, 1936), Baroda (Bhat, 1945), Madhya Pradesh (Anon., 1940 b; M. P. Singh, 1953), Bombay (Cheema and others, 1954), and Madras (Ramakrishnan, 1954). Zinc deficiency is also reported from Coorg by Varadarajan and Subramanian (1953). J. N. Mukherjee (1949) reports evidence of a lack of manganese in the Punjab, Madras, and Coorg, and others have mentioned it in these States and in Bombay, while Sulaiman (1954) includes it among the elements deficient in Hyderabad.

As has been seen, India is one of the two countries in which boron deficiency is known to exist. Chowdhury and Dutta (1950) reported symptoms of it on pummelo and sour orange leaves in Assam, and Chowdhury (1954) reports it on the fruits also. Ramakrishnan (1954) states that it has been observed affecting leaves and fruit of the sweet orange in Cuddapah and Tirunelveli districts in South India. These areas also report a lack of magnesium, Ramamoothy and Desai (1946) reporting it in Assam and Ramakrishnan (1954) in Cuddapah on the sweet orange and in Kotagiri and Wynaad on the mandarin. Copper deficiency is reported at Saharanpur by M. P. Singh and Singh (1953) and in Hyderabad, Madras, and Coorg. Only in the hills of Madras is deficiency of calcium known.

The fact remains that excellent citrus fruits are grown in India with the addition of only farmyard manure, and until there is evidence that other fertilizers are required, it would seem wise to spend no money on them. Green manuring gives favourable results under almost all conditions.

Cropping

While some citrus fruits blossom more or less throughout the year, most of them have one or two distinct seasons. The most common period of flowering in northern India is in the early spring, generally in February. Practically all varieties of citrus are in bloom at that period, if there is sufficient moisture in the soil. Some frequently blossom also early in the rainy season. S. N. Singh and Tomar (1949) report a heavy flowering of limes at Kanpur in the early spring, and a lighter flowering in June and July. The fruit ripens six to twelve months after flowering but in some cases may be left on the tree even after the next year's flowers appear. This is necessary for satisfactory quality in grapefruit and the Valencia orange in California and is desirable for at least part of the crop of these fruits in India. That leaving the fruit on after the next crop has set may reduce the yield is suggested by Jones and Cree (1954) who found that at Riverside over 15 years harvesting on June 4 resulted in higher yields of Valencias than on July 24, which in turn was better than on September 21. The July harvest resulted in the largest fruits. Marloth (1955), in South Africa also reports higher yields when Valencias are harvest not later than at flowering time. If grapefruit is allowed to remain on the trees until the end of the season, some of the seeds may germinate and impart an undesirable flavour to the fruit.

In South India the flowering seasons are longer and less distinct. Naik (1949) says that the main crop of Sathgudi oranges ripens from November to March from blossoms which opened from December to April, but there is a considerable off-season crop ripe from June to November from flowers opening from September until the beginning of December, and occasionally a third crop which ripens from March to June from flowers appearing from June to September. This crop is of poor quality, but sells well because of the small number of fruits on the market. There may thus be flowers on the trees in every month but May, and ripe fruit throughout the year. The mandarins also generally produce two crops in each district, and are on the market throughout the year except in May and

June. Limes are harvested throughout the year, with the main crop varying in different sections.

In the northern part of the country, where there is a distinct winter, no special measures are ordinarily necessary in order to induce flowering. In Madhya Pradesh and Bombay, the means used to determine the time of flowering form an important part of the orchard management. If the spring flowering, known as the *ambe bahar* because it occurs at about the time of the mango blossoming, is desired, water should be withheld about two months before the normal flowering season. After about a month it is customary to remove four or five inches of soil, exposing many of the roots and removing the small ones. After a few days the soil is returned, mixed with manure, and a light irrigation is given. Three or four days later and at normal intervals thereafter, heavier irrigations are given. Cheema and others (1954) state that only on deep, heavy soils is root pruning necessary in Bombay. The tree sends out new shoots and on these the flowers appear. If the July flowering, or *mrig bahar*, is desired, the treatment is delayed until shortly before the rainy season. Because of the rains, it is not possible to treat the orchard so as to induce flowering in the third season, the *hasta or hatti bahar*, in September-October. But if there is no set in the earlier seasons this one may give a poor crop. It is considered desirable that the same crop be taken, each year in any one orchard. This treatment is said to be necessary for the Santara, and in a less severe form for most other citrus fruits except the lime.

In an experiment in the Punjab, L. Singh (1934) practised root pruning, followed by manuring, and irrigation, for three years. The earth was removed in a circle three feet wide, starting one foot from the trunk, to a depth of 9, 12, or 15 inches. The treatment increased the yield during this brief period, the largest crops being secured by an annual exposure of the roots to a depth of nine inches. The vigour of the trees was decreased in proportion to the severity of the treatment, and in consideration of this Singh recommended that the practice be used only in cases of excessive vegetative growth and shy bearing, and then only in alternate years.

In other places also root pruning has been found harmful to the trees. Ali (1941) says that annual root pruning of the Nagari orange was widely adopted in Madras, as it increased the crop at first. Later the yield was reduced to practically nothing, disease increased, and many of the farmers were ruined. Rao (1941) also reports damage from the practice, and urges that efforts be made to find some other method of regulating bearing, and that in any case root pruning be not done oftener than once in two or three years. Naik (1949) points out that the method was not ordinarily practised in South India to control the time of flowering, but only to increase fruitfulness. He considers it undesirable, except in the case of extremely vigorous and unfruitful trees. In such cases the soil may be removed to a depth of about 9 inches beginning 3 feet from the trunk, in December or January. The biggest roots should not be disturbed, and where there are heavy winds, propping may be necessary. The soil should be returned within a week, followed by immediate irrigation. He says that if this treatment does not produce blossoms within a month, it is idle to repeat it in subsequent years.

Ringing or girdling is not commonly practised in India and is probably not desirable unless it should prove a satisfactory substitute for root pruning. As has been stated in a previous chapter, experience in other countries shows that the yield of oranges can be temporarily increased in this way, but that the effect is not permanent, and the process, if repeated, tends to dwarf the tree. L. Singh and others (1940), in order to avoid the adverse effects of root pruning on the Sangtara, tried ringing, which invariably increased the yield of shy-bearing trees about 10 years old. They found it necessary to treat the wounds in order to get proper healing, and drew no conclusions about the effect of the process on the vigour of the trees. S. Singh (1940) reports that in the case of 16-year-old Sangtara trees which had never borne an economic crop, root pruning failed, and ringing increased the crop markedly, but the highest yield secured was only 180 fruits.

Ordinarily a considerable proportion of the flowers fail to set fruit, sometimes a very heavy bloom results in a crop failure. This may be because the nitrogen supply is exhausted by the flowering. Haas (1948 c) states that there is also an excessive loss of potassium, the flowers in one collection containing 1·163 to 1·806%. Some varieties such as the Washington Navel produce no pollen and have almost no seeds, and others have little viable pollen and contain few seeds. Pomeroy and Aldrich (1943) were able to increase the set of Navel oranges and Marsh grapefruit by hand pollination with pollen from seedy varieties of grapefruit, although the application of naphthalene acetic acid failed. El-tomi (1954) reports that pollen from 12 varieties was tried on the Navel, but only that from a pummelo increased the set. Aala (1953) reports that a popular Siamese variety of pummelo in the Philippines is a shy-bearer, and that while hand pollination with its own pollen increased the set, pollen from other varieties was still more effective. Nautiyal (1952) reports that the Chakaiya pummelo at Saharanpur proved entirely self-sterile. The Italian, Lucknow Seedless, and Nepali Oblong lemons are seedless when self-pollinated or when pollination is prevented, according to Naidu (1955 a, b) but pollen from the Lisbon variety, which is seedy, increased the set by about 33%. Lack of the stimulatory effect of pollination may be one reason why seedless varieties sometimes fail to get good crops.

Sometimes thinning is recommended to secure large fruits. Parker (1934) reports experiments with oranges in California, indicating no economic advantage from thinning. He found that in the year of thinning the fruits were larger, but the total volume was less than on corresponding unthinned trees; while in the next year the yield was heavier, but the fruit smaller. There is no reason to think that thinning of citrus fruits would be desirable in India, except to avoid the breaking of limbs in the case of very heavy setting.

Pruning

There is a good deal of difference of opinion regarding the pruning of citrus trees. It is generally agreed, however, that less pruning is needed than in the case of most fruits. The lemon is a possible exception to this rule, but the very severe pruning formerly given the lemon has largely disappeared.

The young tree should be so pruned as to form a strong framework, with the lowest branch about one and a half or two feet from the ground. If the young tree is gone over frequently, unwanted branches can be rubbed off or cut off with a knife and those which tend to become too long may be pinched back. There is a tendency for several branches to arise from the same point and this should be discouraged.

Some growers do no pruning after the tree is two or three years old, and the results are frequently satisfactory. Most varieties of the sweet orange and the grapefruit naturally produced desirable heads. Small branches inside the tree ordinarily die in a few years, and it is generally considered wise to remove this dead wood, though comparatively little damage seems to be done if it is allowed to remain until it falls naturally.

In many species there is a strong tendency for suckers and water-sprouts to grow. If they are allowed to remain, they grow out to the surface, branch and eventually bear fruit. The fruit is likely to be coarse for a few years, but later is indistinguishable from that on other branches. It is desirable to remove some of the water-sprouts as soon as they appear, but some may be usefully kept, especially when they can be trained to fill an empty place in the tree. If one is kept, it may be necessary to head it back once or twice to prevent such long slender growth that the branch would bend badly or break with its first load of fruit. It is, of course, very important that all suckers arising from the rootstock be removed.

Some authorities advocate further pruning, particularly the thinning of the top to allow more light to enter. Prest (1935, 1947) recommends a light thinning for sweet oranges and a somewhat heavier pruning of mandarins and lemons, in Queensland. The Sundays River Research Station (1944) reports that in that section of South Africa, a light annual or heavy biennial pruning of grapefruit increased the size and yield of fruit, and improved the health and the vigour of the trees. The consensus in most citrus-growing countries, however, is against this practice.

The lemon requires somewhat different treatment from the other citrus fruits. It tends to produce long rambling branches which bear at the end, and thus bend very badly. In order to produce strong trees it seems necessary to prune them rather severely when young, and to shorten or remove very long branches even in mature trees.

Insect Pests

Insects seem to be as fond of the genus *Citrus* as are human beings, but prefer the foliage to the fruits in most cases. Insect control is a problem in every important centre of production, and its cost is sometimes a major item. A great variety of insects attack the leaves, branches, flowers, and fruits. Clausen (1933) lists 200 species which attack citrus trees in tropical Asia including 96 found in India. Fortunately, many of these are of little importance. The largest group is that of the scale insects which are probably the most serious pests from a world point of view. They are of less importance in tropical Asia, probably because they are kept in check by natural enemies. Quayle (1938) gives detailed descriptions of many of the pests, with their predators, parasites, and diseases, and suggests methods of control. Boyce (1948) also describes many pests and gives the recommended insecticidal treatment, while Smith (1948) deals with insect parasites and predators, and Fawcett (1948) with parasitic fungi and bacteria. Pruthi and Mani (1945) deal with more than 160 pests of citrus trees in India, including 49 species of Coccidae, 39 of Lepidoptera, 12 of Aleurodidae, and 12 of Coleoptera.

Fortunately, India does not suffer as much from these insects as some other countries. There are, however, a number of pests which do cause damage, and which must be guarded against. Among those which cause the most obvious damage are those which eat the foliage, sometimes denuding young trees in the nursery or even in the orchard. Mature trees are seldom seriously injured by them.

The most important of these is the caterpillar of the lemon butterfly, *Papilio demoleus*, and other species of *Papilio*. *P. polytes* occurs all over India while *P. polymnestor* occurs in South India and *P. helenus* is said to be very destructive in the hills of South India and to be a minor pest in Shillong. They are serious pests in the nursery, and on young trees in the orchard. Sontakay (1943), moreover, reports serious outbreaks in Madhya Pradesh in July, 1940, and again a year later, in which some orchards were completely defoliated. As many as 1,000 caterpillars were collected from one tree of medium size.

The lemon butterfly is easily recognized, being about three inches across and bluish green, with yellow markings and two eye-like spots on the hind wings. The female lays her eggs, which are about the size of the head of a pin and pale yellow in colour, on the young foliage. According to Paranjpye (1937), there are broods in April, June, November, and sometimes December in Bombay, but these broods seem to be so spread out that some caterpillars may be found almost throughout the year. The eggs hatch in from three days to a week, depending on the temperature, and the tiny caterpillar eats voraciously and is full grown in two to four weeks. Its protective colouration is interesting. At first it is dark with an irregular white streak, so that it resembles a bird dropping. Later it turns a dark green, blending with the foliage. It also protects itself when disturbed by thrusting out a forked flesh-coloured structure at the back of its head, and emitting an unpleasant, sweetish odour. It pupates on the tree, suspending itself by silky threads. Pupation lasts a week in summer and as much as twelve weeks in winter.

Hand picking of the caterpillars, and of the eggs when noticed, is ordinarily sufficient to control this pest. If further measures are necessary, the butterflies may be caught in hand nets, or the plants may be sprayed with lead arsenate or some other poison insecticide. One ounce of lead arsenate to four gallons of water, with a little fish oil rosin soap or *gur* as a sticker was found effective by Sontakay (1943). He also found it possible to collect the caterpillars which had turned green by shaking the branches of the larger trees. As the young caterpillars did not fall off, the process had to be repeated several times at intervals of a few days.

Other leaf-eating caterpillars are of less importance. The orange leaf caterpillar, *Psorosticha* (*Tonica*) *zizyphi*, is a small, active larva which folds the young leaves over its slender light green body with a dark brown head. In spite of its name, it probably does not attack plants in the genus *Ziziphus*. It is plentiful in Madhya Pradesh from July to September, according to Gupta (1954), who gives its life history and recommends fish-oil rosin soap spray for its control. It is also considered serious enough in the South to justify spraying. The orange hairstreak, *Tarucus theophrastus*, is bright green, short and squat, and very slow-moving. Both of these caterpillars attack very young shoots, and may cause their death. They are serious only in the nursery and on very young orchard trees but occur widely in India. Pruthi and Mani (1945) state that *Euproctis fraterna* is common throughout India and is a sporadic major pest in several parts, sometimes completely defoliating plants. It can be controlled by dusting ashes on the plant or brushing the caterpillars off with brooms. They also mention *Heliothrips haemorroidalis* which is commonly found feeding on the leaves of plants, including citrus, and sometimes feeds on the surface of fruits. Several other species of thrips are said to be quite common on citrus, but the extent of the damage caused is not known. Ramachandran (1954) mentions *Thrips florum*, *T. subnudula*, and *T. nilgiriensis* as occasionally being found on the flowers and says they can be controlled with a 0·025% BHC wash.

The orange leaf miner, *Phyllocnistis citrella*, occurs widely in India and, according to Clausen (1931), in the other countries of southern Asia, as far as Japan. The miner is the larva of a tiny moth, which lays almost invisible eggs on the leaves and shoots. On hatching the larva bores under the epidermis, and makes a serpentine tunnel feeding on the sap. It never leaves this tunnel until after pupation. There are nine overlapping generations a year in Uttar Pradesh, where the maximum activity is in July and August, and the minimum in May and June, according to Lal (1949). In the Punjab, where the life cycle lasts from about 12 to 65 days, Rahman and Yunus (1945) found peaks of population in March to May and September to November. Sontakay and Gupta (1945) found that in Madhya Pradesh from 34 to 46% of the leaves of young trees were attacked from the end of July through October, with the incidence falling to 2% in January, and 1·2% in March. In May and June none were found. The direct damage done is not very great, even when the miners are present in great numbers, as frequently happens. It has been supposed that the disease, canker, enters the leaves more readily through the injured leaves, but Latif and Yunus (1950) were unable to establish any connection between the miner and canker. Control is very difficult, as the caterpillar is protected from insecticides, and hand picking is impracticable. The removal of the infested leaves and spraying with nicotine sulphate have not proved very effective. Spraying with 1% DDT was better, according to Lal (1949) killing up to 70% of the miners, and in 1953 he reports 85·7% killed by a suspension of DDT in nicotine sulphate, and 100% killed by 0·1% parathion As it is difficult to protect the leaves in this way during the rainy season when the miners are most harmful, there is some promise in the report of Lal (1949) that injecting 0·4 g. of potassium cyanide into the stems of small trees killed 82·9% of the larvae and pupae within 10 days and was effective for about 4 months, with no harmful effect on the trees.

The citron is the species most susceptible to miner attack, and the sour lime the least, according to Latif and Yunus (1951) who recommend that the citron be excluded from gardens and hedges. However, the miners feed on all types of citrus plants, and on the bael, *Aegle marmelos*.

The caterpillars of the citrus flower moth, *Prays citri*, feed on the flowers and cause much damage. They have been reported from several places in India and are probably widespread. When necessary, they may be controlled by spraying or dusting the trees with barium fluosilicate, according to Pruthi and Mani (1945).

Although the sucking insects are not as serious in India as in many countries, there are a number which attack citrus. Several types of scale have been reported. Pruthi and Mani (1945) mention about two dozen species, most of which are minor or sporadic pests of citrus trees. The California red scale, *Aonidiella aurantii*, and the Florida red scale, *Chrysomphalis ficus* (*aonidum*), occur widely in India and are sometimes very serious pests. Rahman and Ansari (1941) mention several species causing damage in the Punjab. The cottony cushion or fluted scale, *Icerya purchasi* has been widespread and rather threatening in South India, as has been seen in Chapter X, but now seems under fairly effective biological control. Ramachandran (1954) says that the purple scale, *Lepidosaphes becki* is often a pest in Wynaad, though kept in check to a considerable extent by the entomophagus fungus, *Spherostelbe auranticola*, unless this is killed by a fungicide. The soft (soft brown) scale, *Coccus* (*Lecanium*) *hesperidum* has attacked citrus at Allahabad, but is kept under control by its enemies unless protected by ants. Oil emulsions have been used with considerable success against different scale insects, in India and elsewhere, but tend to cause leaf-drop and reduce the soluble solids in the fruit. This can be counteracted by adding 4-8 ppm of 2, 4-D to the spray. Parathion, by itself or with oil, is increasingly used, and Ramachandran (1954) recommends spraying with 0·025% parathion or 0·2% HETP. Fumigation with hydrocyanic acid or powdered calcium cyanide is very commonly and effectively used in other countries, and has been tried with success in India. It is comparatively expensive, and is not recommendod to the farmers. Biological control is especially important, and in India is generally sufficient.

Closely related to the scale insects are the mealy bugs, one of which, the citrus or common mealy bug, *Pseudococcus citri*, is a serious pest in many parts of the world. It occurs practically throughout India, often as an important pest. Spraying with tobacco decoction and dusting with lime sulphur are mentioned by Pruthi and Mani as control measures, while Mitra and Khongwir (1928) recommended spraying with kerosene oil emulsion. This and other species were formerly serious pests in California, but have been very satisfactorily controlled biologically. Chowdhury and Majid (1954) state that in Assam the lady beetle, *Cryptolaemus montronzieri*, and the fungus, *Entomophthora fumosa*, help in the control of the mealy bug. Two other species are listed by Pruthi and Mani (1945), *P. corymbatus*, said to be widespread in India and an important pest of citrus trees in Godavari district; and *P. lilacinus*, said to be occasionally serious in South India.

A number of species of white flies attack citrus plants. The name mealy wing is also applied, both names being descriptive of the adult, although in one species both the larva and the adult are smoky. The larvae are attached to the leaves from which they suck the sap, sometimes causing considerable damage. There seems to be some confusion in the identification of the species. Among those causing serious trouble seem to be *Dialeurodes citri*, *Aleurocanthus husaini*, *A. spiniferus*, and *A. woglumi*. They seem to occur in all parts of the country and to be preyed upon by a number of parasites and fungi. One of the fungi occurring in Kumaun has been identified by Bose (1953 b) as *Aschersoni papillata.*

Control of the white flies is difficult. Pruthi and Mani (1945) emphasize biological control, including the spraying of the trees with suspensions of entomophagus fungi as well as encouraging parasites and predators. Woglum and others (1949) report that parathion was effective, but too dangerous to be recommended and that DDT in kerosene was effective but harmed the trees.

Several species of aphids are sometimes found on the young citrus leaves, but are ordinarily kept in check by lady-bird beetles or other natural agencies. The black citrus aphid, *Aphis citricidus*, which has been mentioned in connection with tristeza, is one of the more common. Nicotine sprays and dusts have been the standard fungicides, but Boyce (1948) reports good results with rotonone, while some of the newer materials such as TEPP and hexethyl tetraphosphate are promising.

The citrus psylla, *Diaphorina citri*, is widely distributed, but seems to be serious only in the Punjab. Pruthi and Mani (1945) report that there and in the North-West Frontier Province of Pakistan it is the most destructive of all citrus pests, and may ruin the industry. The damage is done by the nymphs which move about actively, sucking the sap from the tender parts of the buds, leaves, and branches, and injecting into them a toxic substance. The leaves are badly curled and fall prematurely, resulting in some cases of complete defoliation. Any fruits which mature are small and of poor quality. The branches and sometimes the entire tree may die. The nymphs secrete honeydew in such enormous amounts that the tree may appear white, and on this a black sooty mould grows. The life cycle lasts from 15 to 47 days, and the adult may live 190 days. There are 8 or 9 generations a year. Tandon (1941) reports satisfactory control by spraying with rosin compound in January or February and again in July or August, at a cost of only one anna a tree. As the preparation of the rosin compound is laborious and needs some skill, Rahman (1941) reports trials of dusts, nicotine sulphate in sulphur proving most effective, but costing about eight times as much. Pruthi and Mani (1945) also suggest a crude oil emulsion as fairly effective, but stress the importance of cultural methods to increase the vigour of the trees. Several predators and parasites are found, but they seem unable to keep the numbers of psylla down in the Punjab.

A green bug, or citrus stinkbug, *Rhinchocoris humeralis*, is reported as a serious pest all over Assam and also occurs in Kumaun and the eastern Himalayas. Entomologists at Jeolikote report that it is becoming a serious pest in the valleys of Kumaun. Chowdhury and Majid (1954) state that in Assam the eggs are laid from May to September, and hatch in about a week. The nymphs mature in about a week and some adults live over winter. The nymphs and adults puncture the fruits, mainly mandarin and orange, and preferably partly ripe, and suck the juice. Brushing the bugs off into pans of water with a layer of kerosene on top, spraying with tobacco decoction, and dusting with 5% BHC have been suggested, but no very satisfactory method of control is known. The pumpkin bug, *Nezara viridula*, is common throughout India and is a sporadic major pest when other hosts are grown near citrus trees. It also may be brushed off into oil, or nursery trees may be sprayed with nicotine sulphate. Other bugs which are minor pests are *Cappoea taprebanica*, widely distributed and *Leptoglossus membranaceus*, in South India and Assam.

Borers are serious pests in some parts of the country, especially in old or neglected orchards. Two closely related caterpillars, *Indarbela tetraonis* and *I. quadrinotata*, bore into the wood of citrus and many other trees, and damage them mainly by eating the bark. They are widely distributed throughout the country, often occurring side by side. Sontakay (1945 a, b) describes the life history of *I. quadrinotata* in Madhya Pradesh, where it is said to be one of the most important pests of citrus trees. The eggs are laid in May and June, glued to the bark, and hatch in from 8 to 11 days. The caterpillars live under the bark until September, when they tunnel into the wood. They pupate in the spring. Limbs may be ringed, the vitality of the tree is lowered, and in some cases of severe infestation, death may result. Asthana and Nayak (1947) report a survey in Madhya Pradesh, in which 9·45% of the 14,362 trees examined in 10 districts were found to be infested. The highest incidence was found on trees growing on black soil in an area of very heavy rainfall, 42·33%. Of 6,746 mandarin trees, 17·24% were infested. by both this borer and another, *Stromatium barbatum*. The latter occurs all over India, mainly in dry wood, but sometimes boring into living branches. The most common control measures for the *Indarbela* caterpillars consist of inserting a small amount of petrol, carbon bisulphide, chlorasol, or two parts of chloroform to one of creosote into the hole and plugging it with clay. Shah (1946) found these methods expensive, and advocated the introduction of hot water into the hole by means of a cheap syringe, but the inconvenience of this method is obvious. Another method, said to be very successful, is painting the galleries and surrounding bark with Paris green.

One of the most serious pests of citrus trees in Assam is the trunk borer, *Monohammus versteegi*, which is also one of the borers causing much damage in Sikkim (Hayes, 1945). Chowdhury (1954 b) states that 15-60% of the Khasi mandarin trees in different orchards are attacked, while the rough lemon and, more rarely, other species are also infested. He recommends the use of fumigants such as petrol or the placing of small crystals of paradichlorobenzene in the holes before plugging them with mud. For prevention, he recommends painting the trunks every month or two with water-dispersible DDT or BHC at the rate of 1 lb. in 10 gal. of water. At the citrus research station at Burnihat, Assam, no new attack took place on 10 trees the trunks of which had been treated with DDT (½ lb. Guesarol 550 per gallon of water) compared with 7 attacks in 10 untreated trees.

The lime-tree borer, *Chelidonium cinctum*, is common in South India, particularly in Mysore, and attacks other citrus trees as well as the lime. Kannan (1928) reports it as serious in Madras, but Cherian (1942) considers it only a minor pest. This and a very similar species, *C. argentatum*, have become very serious in Wynaad, according to Ramachandran (1954). The eggs are laid in June-July on young branches and hatch in 10-12 days. The grubs enter the branch with a spiral cut which weakens it and first bore toward the end of the branch. After 2-6 weeks they turn and make their way into the trunk. If the wilted branches are broken off while the grubs are still in them, the grubs are unable to get into the trunk and die. If they get into the trunk they live there the rest of the year, unless killed by petrol fumigation. Kannan says that a single borer can kill a young tree, and that the damage in Coorg was probably at least four lakhs of rupees annually. Another sporadic pest, especially in Coorg and Assam, *Chloridolum alcmene*, can be controlled in the same way.

Moths which fly at night and suck the juice from the fruits occur all over India, and in other citrus districts of Asia, and in some cases cause very serious loss. Sweet oranges, mandarins, and sweet limes are commonly attacked. The moths pierce the rinds of the ripening fruits, thus making possible the entrance of decay organisms. Ordinarily the fruit falls within a few days, and is worthless. Bajpai (1955) states that 20% of the mandarins and a higher percentage of Mosambi fruits in Madhya Pradesh are ruined. Pruthi and Mani (1945) mention moths belonging to eight genera, one of which, *Ophideres*, is credited with 12 species attacking citrus fruits in India. One of these species should probably be placed in the genus *Othreis*, and some of the others sometimes are so placed. The most important pests of citrus in this group seem to be *Othreis fullonica*, *Ophideres materna*, *Achaea janata*, *Calpe ophideroides*, *C. emarginata*, and *Anua coronata*. Ayyar (1943) deals with those which are important in South India, and Lal (1949) and Chaturvedi (1950-51) those causing damage in Uttar Pradesh. The larvae of *Anua coronata* feed on the ornamental creeper, *Quisqualis indica*, and those of *Achaea janata* on a variety of wild and cultivated plants. Most of the other species breed on wild Menispermaceous plants, including *Tinospora cordifolia*, and species of *Cocculus*.

The elimination of the larval host plants is a method of protecting the orchards which naturally suggests itself, and Susainathan (1924) reports excellent results from this procedure in the northern part of Madras. In other places, however, this has not been found feasible, as the hosts are widespread and the moths are capable of flying long distances. Lal (1949) found that the elimination of all host plants within half a mile of an orchard was not effective. Chaturvedi (1950-51) on the other hand considers this the most promising method and mentions a case in which it saved 75% of the crop at a cost of six annas per tree. The cost might be less in subsequent years. Baptista (1944) describes *Othreis fullonica* and summarizes the methods which have been tried. These include the capture of the moths by hand or with nets, light traps, baited traps with or without poison, smudging, and the prompt disposal of fallen or decaying fruit, the last being the most important, along with early harvesting. Lal (1949) tried several of these methods and also deterrent sprays. Some of these decrease the attack somewhat, but none is even fairly satisfactory. Bajpai (1955), on the other hand, claims that both eliminating the host plants and poisoned bait are effective, and recommends dissolving ½lb. of molasses in 10 lb. of water and adding a few drops of vinegar and ¼oz. of lead arsenate. A small amount of the solution is placed in wide-mouthed bottles which are hung in the trees and covered to keep out the rain but to allow the moths to enter. The bagging of the individual fruits is effective, but is expensive and laborious. Rakshpal (1945) concluded that the only feasible method is to avoid the presence of ripening fruit in the autumn when the moths are present. He found it very satisfactory in the case of the sweet orange in Gwalior to allow only the June or September flowering, and found that the fruit was not only safe from attack, but sold at a higher price than that from the January and February flowering. If a large number of growers adopted this practice, however, the price might be less favourable.

Fruit flies seem to be serious pests of citrus fruits only in limited areas, perhaps only in the cooler subtropical regions. They cause a very large annual loss in Sikkim, where the ground under the trees may be covered with the fallen infested fruit (Hayes, 1945). There is some confusion regarding identification and nomenclature. Pruthi and Mani (1945) consider *Chaetodacus diversus* the most widespread, and a sporadic major pest in several parts of the country. They also mention *C. caudatus* and *C. ferrugineus dorsalis*. The last is the Formosan fruit fly which is important throughout tropical Asia and was introduced into Hawaii during the second World War, where it has caused great damage and worries the fruit growers in California. The difficult problem of controlling fruit flies has been discussed with reference to the mango.

Mites often pass unnoticed unless the infestation is severe, but probably occur throughout the country. Cheema and others (1954) refer to a deep brown coating on Mosambi fruits, caused by mites when the soil remains moist all year or is over-irrigated. Chowdhury and Majid (1954) mention partial or even complete defoliation caused by mites which attack the fruit and bark as well as the leaves, with a resultant reduction in the size of the fruits. Among the species in Assam are *Tetranychus sexmaculatus* and *T. telarius*, while *T. hindustanicus* is reported from Andhra. Lime sulphur and other sulphur sprays are used to control mites where biological control is not sufficient.

The red ant which was mentioned on mango trees also makes it difficult to work in some citrus groves, and other ants need to be controlled where they interfere with biological control of pests.

Citrus Diseases

Citrus trees are subject to many diseases. Fawcett (1936) in his excellent book on the subject, deals with more than two hundered diseases, mostly parasitic.

Many of these are capable of causing severe damage, but fortunately, in most regions only a few are of much importance. A briefer and somewhat more up-to-date treatment is given by Fawcett and Klotz (1948). Fawcett mentions about 18 diseases which have been reported in India, and it is possible that others also occur. Only those of commercial importance are discussed here.

Citrus canker is one of the most prevalent diseases in India, although it has frequently been confused with scab. It may have originated in this country, as herbarium specimens sent from Dehra Dun to Kew prior to 1831 show the disease. It may, however, have originated in some other part of Asia. It has spread to many of the citrus areas of the world. It became established in Florida and neighbouring States, and was eradicated only by destroying more than a million orchard trees and twice that many nursery trees. The seriousness of the disease is indicated by the fact that it was considered worthwhile to eliminate it at a cost of $2,500,000. In South Africa all infected trees were destroyed in 1918, but the disease was discovered again in 1924. No sign of the disease has been seen there since 1926, according to Doidge (1938) and a period of ten years without evident infection is considered proof of eradication. It has also been eliminated from Australia. Such a method does not seem practicable in a country like India where the disease is widespread and long established.

Canker affects the leaves, twigs, thorns, and fruits. The lesions first appear as small yellowish spots which enlarge to a diameter of 3 or 4 mm., and become raised and rough or spongy, and tan or brown. They are surrounded by characteristic yellow areas or halos. In severe cases the lesions become irregular and may coalesce. The halos commonly are missing on the fruit. The lesions vary somewhat under different conditions and on different species. The causal organism is a bacterium, first called *Pseudomonas citri* and then *Phytomonas citri*, but now *Xanthomonas citri*.

There is a great deal of difference in the susceptibility of different species. The lime is very susceptible, which together with the fact that the lime is widely grown, accounts for the widespread occurrence of the disease. Fortunately, under Indian conditions at least, the damage is not very severe. The appearance of the fruit is marred, but this does not prevent its sale, and the trees seem to flourish in spite of heavy infestations. The grapefruit is also very susceptible, and the damage is sometimes more severe. Not only is the appearance of the fruit affected, and in rare cases the quality also damaged, but there is frequently a considerable loss of leaves and young shoots. The *ada jamir* and Washington Navel and Mosambi oranges are also severely attacked in Assam, according to Chowdhury (1951 c, 1952) although the Valencia and some other sweet oranges are highly resistant, as are the Khasi mandarin, the Santara, and the lemon. The rough lemon and sour orange seem to be immune.

Climate has a great effect on the spread of the disease. Optimum conditions are found when the temperature is around 86° F. and the leaves and fruits are wet. Such conditions prevail during the rainy season. Young leaves are frequently present at that time, and are very likely to be infected. Fortunately, most of the fruit, in the case of grapefruit and sweet oranges, is set in the spring and is fairly well grown before the rains begin, and so is not so badly infected as would be the case with fruit set during the rains.

As has been indicated, control of the disease, short of the destruction of all infected tress, is probably impossible under conditions favourable to its development. A good deal can be done to lessen the damage, however. Foremost comes the growing of resistant species and varieties. The use of lemons or Rangpur limes which are resistant, in place of the common lime might be desirable, although the preference of the consumer is a factor difficult to overcome. Good resistant oranges are available, but there seems to be no satisfactory substitute for the grapefruit.

Infection can be largely prevented by keeping the leaves and fruits covered with some fungicide, such as Bordeaux mixture, but this is scarcely practicable during the rainy season when infection is most common. The sources of infection are old lesions on the branches and infected leaves on the ground. By collecting the leaves as they fall, and pruning out the infected twigs, before the rainy season, the amount of new infection can be reduced. With this treatment, damage to grapefruit at Allahabad has been negligible except on young trees. In the Punjab, Luthra and Sattar (1942) reduced the incidence of infected fruit from about 25% to 6% by spraying sweet oranges with 4-4-50 Bordeaux mixture. This, combined with the removal of the infected leaves before spraying, reduced the incidence to less than 1% and after two years' treatment, only a trace of the disease remained. They had no success, however, with the more susceptible lime. Chowdhury (1951 c) recommends spraying with cuprous oxide or 2-2-50 Bordeaux plus 8 oz. of white oil per 100 gal. Naik (1949) says that canker is not very serious in South India, and that the only treatment necessary is removing the diseased parts and spraying with Bordeaux mixture. Varma (1949 b) on the other hand says that the use of this spray for five years was an utter failure but that by the use of a contact insecticide against aphids and the leaf miner on each of the first three flushes on more than 6,000 grapefruit and sweet orange plants, canker was entirely eliminated. On the fourth flush, unsprayed, there was about 10% infection, so he advises spraying this also.

Scab, which has frequently been reported in different parts of India, often mistakenly for canker, seems to be of much less importance, although Chowdhury (1955 a) states that usually from 25 to 55% of the fruits of susceptible varieties in Assam are ruined. The lesions occur on the same portions, and are somewhat similar in appearance. Identification is made more difficult by the fact that several different organisms are frequently found in old lesions. Scab lesions project on only one side of the leaf, whereas those of canker are raised on both sides, and scab lacks the characteristic yellow halo. On both leaves and fruits the lesions are generally accompanied by some distortion.

In order to distinguish it from Australian citrus scab, which occurs only in Australia, and sweet-orange fruit scab, found only in South America, this more general disease is called sour orange scab or verrusosis. It is caused by a fungus which was called *Sphaceloma fawcetti* until the discovery of the perfect stage in 1936 led to its being reclassified as *Elsinoe fawcetti*.

Here again there is a great difference in susceptibility among the species. Chowdhury (1955 a) says that in Assam, where scab is one of the most serious diseases, the rough lemon, *ada jamir*, lime, *karna*, citron, and one mandarin are highly susceptible, while the pummelo and *kata jamir* are less susceptible and the Khasi mandarin, most fortunately, is immune. In other countries the sweet orange is reported immune and the lemon susceptible.

As in the case of canker, scab spreads most rapidly when weather conditions are favourable and there are young leaves or fruits present. Like canker it can infect tissues only when the surface is wet, but it prefers a lower temperature, the maximum, according to Fawcett (1936) being about 81·5 °F. This probably explains why the disease is not very severe in the warmer parts of India. It is reported to be severe in Kumaun, especially above an elevation of 4,000 ft., as well as in Assam.

If control measures are necessary, infection can be greatly reduced by keeping the young growth covered with a copper fungicide. Fawcett recommends a 3-3-50 Bordeaux spray, and this has been found effective in Assam. But satisfactory results from this, or cuprous oxide, or white oil emulsion, are secured only when spraying is repeated whenever a new flush appears and whenever there is heavy rain immediately after plants have been sprayed.

Withertip or anthracnose is a disease which occurs throughout India and other citrus regions, but is generally of minor importance. In most places it appears only on trees weakened by some other disease or by the lack of proper care. All types of citrus grown are affected, but the sweet orange and Santara suffer most. Several species of the fungus *Colletotrichum* are commonly present as saprophytes and are able to produce the disease. The one most commonly occurring in India is *C. gloeosporioides* (*Glomerella cingulata*), of which there seem to be a number of strains, varying in virulence. According to Chaudhuri (1936) it is only in the Punjab that withertip is a serious disease in India, and there the most badly damaged orchards are found in the low hills and within a hundred miles of the mountains. Bhattacharya and Dutta (1949 a) state that in Assam the disease is serious, attacking limes, lemons, and citrons. Naik (1949) says that withertip caused by a species of *Gloeosporium* is serious on the lime, and that the more common form also occurs. Rather sharp but brief outbreaks of similar symptoms occurred on some trees in Allahabad in the winters of 1941-42 and 1942-43. *C. gloeosporioides* was isolated from dead twigs, but some other organism may have been responsible for the attack. This species is also blamed by R. S. Singh and Sinha (1954) for three types of fruit drop of the grapefruit at Kanpur. In Kumaun it is said to be severe on mandarins and sweet oranges and, along with a species of *Alternaria*, to cause a rot of grapefruit.

The most commonly observed symptom of withertip is that which gives it its name. The leaves fall off the small twigs, and the latter gradually die and turn a greyish colour. Frequently small black dots, the acervuli of the fungus, appear on the dead twigs. Sometimes the leaves are spotted before they drop, the spots appearing light green at first and soon turning brown. The fungus also attacks the stem end of the immature fruits, causing them to fall. In severe cases, the branches may die back to such an extent that in a few years the tree dies.

Under most conditions in India, no treatment is required except proper culture and orchard hygiene. In the Punjab, however, it frequently seems desirable to take specific measures in addition. Chaudhuri (1936) secured good results by spraying with Bordeaux mixture, 5-5-50, and recommends that this be used in February or March and again late in September, in addition to good orchard practice and the pruning off and burning of all diseased twigs each winter. He emphasizes the necessity of control of the disease in the nurseries, as much nursery stock is affected. The removal of infected branches and spraying with Bordeaux are recommended in Assam, followed by the use of manure and good cultivation to restore vigour. Sattar (1945) emphasizes the importance of soil and other environmental conditions, and says that root infection by fungi is connected with the disease.

Gummosis

Gummosis or gum disease is of frequent occurrence throughout the citrus areas of the world. The production of gum on the lower part of the trunk, and sometimes on the main roots, may be caused by a number of different fungi. The most common forms are caused by members of the genus *Phytophthora* and are called brown-rot gummosis, becasuse the same fungi cause a rot of the fruit characterized by a pale brown colour and a distinctive smell. When the attack is at or below the surface of the soil, it is frequently called foot rot. Not all cases of gummosis in India have been studied, but it is probable that the brown-rot gummosis is the one which most commonly occurs. At least three species cause the disease, *P. citrophthora*, *P. parasitica*, and *P. palmivora*. Naik (1949) and Chowdhury (1951 a) report *P. parasitica* causing gummosis in Madras and in Assam where it is frequently accompanied by *Fusarium lateritum*. Member of this common genus of soil fungi are unable to cause the disease, but in India and elsewhere often complicate the disease.

Symptoms vary somewhat in the different species, but in general the first indication of the disease is the exudation of gum from the bark of the trunk. The bark cracks more or less extensively, and in the later stages dries up and falls off, exposing the wood. If the bark is scraped in the early stages, it is seen to have become brown through the cambium layer, but only for a short distance into the wood. Secondary infection by other organisms is frequent, and may cause a decay of the wood itself. If conditions are favourable, the infection spreads rapidly vertically, and slowly horizontally. Even mild attacks interfere markedly with the vigour and productivity of the tree, and severe attacks frequently cause death, or at least make the plant worthless.

Infection takes place through the bark, frequently at the point of the bud union. Any injury to the bark aids infection, but this is not necessary. It is necessary for the bark to be wet, either by rain or irrigation. Temperature is also important. Uppal and Kamat (1936) found that *Phytophthora palmivora*, the species occurring in Bombay, grows most rapidly at temperatures around 80 or 85° F.

Susceptibility varies greatly. Uppal and Kamat (1936) found the Mosambi and pummelo very susceptible, the Santara only mildly so, and the lime practically immune. The grapefruit and tangelo have seemed particularly susceptible at Allahabad. Chowdhury (1951a) reports the pummelo, sweet orange, *karna* lime, lemon, and *ada jamir* most susceptible to *Phytophthora parasitica* in Assam, while the rough lemon is less susceptible and the mandarin and sour orange are immune. The rough lemon which is commonly used as a stock in Bombay, is highly resistant there, but is quite susceptible in America.

Much can be done to prevent gummosis in new plantations. One obvious method is the use of resistant or immune stock, together with budding at least six inches above the ground. The fungus lives in the soil, and there is every likelihood of infection if the susceptible scion touches the soil or is low enough that rain water splashes upon it. For the same reason, deep planting and the heaping of soil around the trunk are to be avoided. It is important that irrigation water should not touch the trunk.

Under certain conditions, however, no immune stock is satisfactory for other reasons. In such cases, in addition to practices which keep the trunk free from standing water or wet soil, much can be done by the application to the trunk of Bordeaux paste or a powder of copper sulphate and lime, or a mixture of 12 parts of zinc sulphate, 1 part of copper sulphate, and 6 parts of hydrated lime. These may be dusted on the trunk, or applied in a cylinder of heavy tarred paper fastened around the trunk loosely, using 1 part of the former to 10 parts of sand, or equal parts of the latter and sand. Such treatments are specially important in the first few years of the life of the orchard.

Where infection has taken place, treatment is possible if undertaken in time. The bark should be scraped to find out how much is diseased. The fungus extends somewhat beyond the brown area. The bark should be removed to the wood over an area extending about half an inch beyond the limits of discoloration on the sides, and two inches above and below. The wound is covered with a fungicide to prevent reinfection. Fawcett (1936) recommends a paste or wash made of 1 pound of zinc sulphate, 1 pound of copper sulphate, and 2 pounds of lime to 2 gallons of water. Uppal and Kamat (1936) secured very good results by using crude carbolic acid diluted with an equal amount of water, but prefer a 25 to 30% creosote oil. Klotz (1943) found the copper fungicides, with 'stickers' satisfactory, but considered tetrachlora-p-benzoquinone very promising in case it becomes available at a reduced price.

In addition to attacking the bark of the trunk and large roots, *P. citrophthora* has been reported by Fraser (1942 a, b) as causing lesions on the smaller roots and the premature decay of the fibrous roots, in Australia. Brown rot is a very serious disease of mandarins in Coorg, according to Rajen and Aiyappa (1944), although they refer to it only as a leaf-fall and fruit-rot disease. They say that at least half of the area there is infected, and that the annual loss is estimated at two lakhs of rupees Ramakrishnan (1954) refers to it in Wynaad and some areas in the Pulneys also. The cause is *P. palmivora*. At the onset of the monsoon there is a shedding of the lower leaves which proceeds upwards and may result in completely denuding the trees. The infected fruits develop a pale brown rot and emit a peculiar and offensive odour. To control the disease they recommend the collection and destruction of fallen leaves and fruit and a single spray of 1% Bordeaux mixture late in May, sometimes repeated in August or September. In four trials, the net profit from spraying varied from Rs. 30 to Rs. 208 per acre.

Another type of gummosis is reported in South India by Ramakrishnan (1954), caused by *Diplodia natalensis* and another species. These are weak parasites so trouble may generally be avoided by keeping the orchard in good condition and avoiding wounds. Gumming and the death of the bark and of whole branches, often in the upper part of the tree, are symptoms and where they appear the affected tissues should be removed and the wounds disinfected.

Pink disease, caused by the fungus *Pellicularia* (*Corticium*) *samonicolor*, has been reported from Assam, Madhya Pradesh, and South India. This is a disease which attacks a great variety of crops in the tropics, causing severe damage and frequently death. Its name comes from the pink mycelium on the surface of the branches at one stage. Dastur (1941) reports that it is epidemic in Balaghat district of Madhya Pradesh, where the rainfall between June 1 and October 31 averages more than 60 inches. He found cutting out the diseased branches and spraying, the measures which are ordinarily sufficient, not entirely satisfactory, as it was difficult to prune the large trees completely enough, and to keep the spray on the trees in the rainy season. He recommends searching for cankers in the dry season and scraping them and the bark at the crotches where dormant mycelium has been observed and treating the wounds with Bordeaux paste or creosote. Frequent examination and the removal of diseased portions in the wet season is also necessary. *P. alba* has also been noted on citrus stems by Dastur (1946).

Powdery mildew causes considerable damage in South India, particularly to mandarins in comparatively cool, moist regions. Devarajan (1946) states that it was long considered a minor disease in Coorg, but became very serious in 1943 when scarcely a tree escaped damage. Greenish white patches of the mildew appear on the leaves, mainly on young ones, causing them to curl, dry, and fall. The trees lose vitality and, in severe cases, the twigs die. Damage in nurseries is more severe than in orchards. The cause is *Oidium tingitaninum* according to Ramakrishnan (1954), although the fungus in Coorg has been thought to differ from this species. Dusting with 200-mesh sulphur when the trees are wet with dew or from spraying with water, at cost of Rs. 1-4 (plus labour) for 10 mature trees, was found entirely satisfactory, and better than spraying with Bordeaux.

Sooty mould which develops on the secretions of insects, reduces yields in South India, according to Naik (1949). It is caused by *Capnodium citri* which is also the most common cause in Assam, where Chowdhury (1955 b) also mentions *Meliola butleri*, *Cladosporium herbarium*, and *Acrothecium lunatum* as causes. In Kumaun much damage is said to be caused to sweet oranges by sooty mould caused by several species of *Chaetothyrium*, fairly well controlled by spraying dinitro cresol.

The felt disease is so called because of a felt-like covering of the twigs caused by *Septobasisdium Pseudo pedicellatum* and other species. It is reported by Chowdhury (1951 a, b) to be common in all the citrus areas of Assam and by Ramakrishnan (1954) to occur on mandarins, sweet oranges, and limes in several parts of South India. It seems to cause no direct damage, but frequently protects scale insects. Control is achieved by giving the trees favourable growing conditions, and the spraying of the scale insects if necessary.

Ganoderma root rot is reported by Ramakrishnan (1954) on the sweet orange and lime in Cuddapah district and on the mandarin in Wynaad. It is caused by *Ganoderma lucidum* and other species which have a wide range of host plants. The fungus generally starts on dead wood in the soil and spreads to lateral roots and up these to the trunk. Bracket-like fruiting bodies appear on the trunk. In early stages the diseased wood may be removed, the wound protected, and 1-2 lb. of sulphur mixed with the soil around the tree. If not treated in the early stages the tree should be removed, including the roots. Infected trees should be isolated with a trench a foot wide and 2-3 ft. deep.

A rust of grapefruit caused by *Uredo citri*, resulting in defoliation, has been reported by Vaheeduddin (1955) in a humid section of Hyderabad.

Melinose is reported by Chowdhury (1955 c) to be common in all of the citrus-growing areas of Assam, particularly in the older orchards. It is caused by *Phomopsis citri*. Sweet oranges, mandarins, pummeloes, sour oranges, and lemons seem about equally susceptible, and more so than other species. The fungus infects leaves, twigs, and fruits, causing minute spots which on the fruits sometimes take a 'tear-streak' pattern. In severe cases, the fruit may crack, but the main damage is a lowering of the market value of the fruit. The fungus lives on dead wood, and infection takes place mainly in the wet months of May to August. Control is by pruning out and destroying the dead wood and keeping the young fruits covered with a fungicide until about six weeks after they have set. Of seven fungicides tried, Bordeaux oil emulsion was best, but any copper fungicide was effective if applied a week after setting and again two weeks later.

A bacterial rot of fibrous roots, occasionally affecting roots up to two inches in diameter, has been reported by Asthana (1947) on mandarins and oranges in Madhya Pradesh. In advanced cases the bark also cracks, and the tree shows symptoms of die-back. A bacterium, probably a new species of *Bacillus*, was isolated and was able to cause the disease, but poor soil conditions and neglect were considered very important predisposing causes. In advanced cases, *Fusarium* was also always present.

Khasi mandarin trees more than five years old have recently been found infected with 'foam' or 'weeping' disease, according to Bhattacharya and Dutt (1949 a) and Chowdhury (1950 b, 1953). White foam or froth exudes from longitudinal cracks in the bark of the trunk and branches from ground level to a little more than one foot above. The bark rots and the wood emits disagreeable odour and turns slightly brown. The symptoms start at the beginning of the monsoon season, and continue until September. The bark then peels, and eventually the trunk may be girdled. The wounds give entrance to borers. Extensive experiments indicate that the trouble is physiological. Although only the mandarin is known to be affected, growing it on other rootstocks has not affected the disease.

The term 'die-back' has been used for the condition resulting from a deficiency of copper, but is commonly used in India for any condition in which the shoots and sometimes large branches die slowly, beginning at the end. There may or may not be gumming. In some cases, the cause may be tristeza and in some malnutrition, including copper deficiency. Malnutrition may be brought on by a naturally poor soil and lack of manuring, or by poor drainage which restricts the root zone. In the hills of Assam, where many trees have died, the most important factor may be the long period of drouth each year. It has been suggested that there new plantations should be on terraced land in order to make better culture possible.

A premature dropping of citrus fruits in Bihar has been studied by Sinha and Malik (1950). In the case of the Nagpur Santara they found that the amount of the drop varied from place to place and from year to year, but was greater in the 'off' years, and when the rain was heavy. It begins in August and stops by the end of October, with the maximum drop in the third week of September. There was very little drop from trees treated for the second crop. The sweet orange was observed to be more badly affected than the mandarin, and the sweet and sour limes were also commonly affected. Premature dropping has also been investigated by Nauriyal (1955) at Saharanpur, who found that about half was of fruit which had split. Disease was another cause, but some of the fruits which fell seemed quite perfect. Dropping was more in the case of the pummelo and mandarin because of a greater tendency for some varieties of these fruits to crack.

Harvesting and Marketing

Granulation is likely to be a problem especially in the latter part of the season, and affects both sweet oranges and grapefruit in northern India. While this may be a normal stage in the ripening process, as Bain (1949) claims, there are distinct differences between trees in the same variety in the same orchard. Bartholomew and Sinclair (1947) made a thorough study of the subject in California without being able to explain the differences. They found that certain root-stocks tend to increase the amount of granulation in one locality and to decrease it in other places. The tendency toward granulation may be associated with the root, for top-working trees failed to change the tendency to produce much or little, and budlings did not consistently follow the pattern of the parent trees. Granulation is more prevalent in fruit from the inside or north side of the tree, but shading did not increase it. Conditions favouring vigorous growth and large fruit favour granulation. Decreasing the amount and frequency of irrigation generally reduced granulation without affecting the quantity or quality of the fruit otherwise. The granulated juice sacs contain more water and inorganic matter, less acid, less sugar, and less carotin. In the intermediate stage they contain twice the normal amount of pectin. The only feasible method of avoiding damage was found to be to pick the large fruit early before granulation set in.

The citrus fruits are very well designed for marketing. The harvesting season is comparatively long, but in some cases all the fruit on a tree can be picked at one time. In South India, however, where the flowering season is prolonged, and ripening is uneven, the common practice of harvesting all the fruit at one time is said by Naik (1949) to lead to disastrous results. After fruit reaches maturity it can be allowed to remain on the tree for several weeks without deteriorating. In some cases, however, there is danger of granulation, or the fruit may become dry. In such cases it is desirable to harvest the fruits as early as possible. The sweet species should not be harvested until reasonably mature, and in some countries laws forbid their sale until they have attained a certain ratio of total solids to acid. Total solids are considered because they are mostly sugar, and are much more easily determined than sugar. In the United States a ratio of 8 parts total solids to one part acid is considered satisfactory for the sweet orange, although good fruit is likely to have about 10 to 12% total solids, and ·872 to 1·125% acid, giving a ratio between 10 and 13. The sugar orange or Bortugan of Egypt, Tunisia, and Algeria, known in Spain as the Imperiale, has such a low acid content that the ripe fruit has a ratio of 90 or 100 to 1 (Hodgson, 1954). It can be marketed when immature and is popular where grown, as it might prove to be in India.

Naik and Sugurappa (1943) state that Sathgudi oranges in Kodur have 8·2 to 9% solids (degrees Brix) and ·441 to ·482% acid during the main season, in November and December, with a ratio of 18·05 to 19·83. In the second season, July and August the amount of acid was almost twice as great and the total solids only slightly larger, with a ratio of 12·14 to 12·68. They state that South Indians prefer a fruit with a low acid content, and this probably holds for other parts of the country as well. They and Siddappa (1952) have suggested standards, but Narayanrao (1955) says that these are unacceptable to the trade, even for the main crop, partly because of the variability of the seedling trees.

In Madhya Pradesh also, there is a great difference in the composition of mature fruits of the two crops of Santaras. M. P. Singh and Kunte (1949) found that ripe fruit on December 3, 1948, averaged 8·48% total solids in the stylar half and 8·84% in the stem half, with ·566 and ·514% acid respectively. On March 9, when the second crop was equally ripe, the figures were 13·03 and 12·42% total solids and ·808 and ·688% acidity. In both cases the ratio is high, 15·30 and 15·51 in December and 16·28 and 18·44 in March, but the quality of the second crop was unquestionably superior. The fruit of the early crop in October, when marketing had begun, had a ratio of less than 7 to 1. Siddappa and Bhatia (1954 b) compared mandarins from different sections and report ratios of 20·9 (Gauhati), 36·4 (Khasi hills), 23·2 (Coorg), 21·6 (Nagpur), and 7·8 (Wynaad). The fruit from the Khasi hills was reported to be flat, while the Wynaad fruit with 6·14% sugar and 1·44% acid, was obviously unsatisfactory. It may be doubted if the samples were really comparable.

In some cases it may be desirable to increase the ratio of soluble solids to acid, either to meet the preference for a sweet fruit or to hasten maturity. This can be done, at least in some cases, by spraying the trees with lead arsenate. Harding (1945) reports that 1 lb. of lead arsenate in 100 gal. of water increased the ratio in Florida grapefruit and produced a more palatable fruit, though slightly smaller. Crous (1940, 1947) produced similar effects on Valencia oranges in South Africa, and says that an application of 2 lb. in 100 gal. was effective for three years. Deszyck (1953) says that the arsenate slightly increases the soluble solids as well as decreasing the acid. The percentage of juice is reduced, but the ascorbic acid content is increased. He recommends using 1¼ lb. of lead arsenate soon after fruit-set. Deszyck and others (1954) say that basic copper arsenate is a satisfactory substitute. On the other hand both copper and borax sprays tend to increase acidity.

Lemons are frequently picked by size, without reference to maturity, as they are of as good quality when green as when fully ripe. They are coloured before marketing by storage or by the use of ethylene gas.

The yield per acre varies greatly in different sections, but it is estimated (Anon. 1943 a) that the average yield of oranges in India is about 98 md. placing it fourth in a list of nine leading producing countries, with Japan producing 42 mds. and the United States 132. The yield of sweet oranges is estimated at about 100 md. per acre in Madras, the Punjab and Uttar Pradesh, 140 in Bombay and 180 in Hyderabad. The mandarin group varies from 50 to 364 md. In the important area in Madhya Pradesh the yield is put at 85 to 250 md. (but Karmarkar and Joshi (1942) estimate only 107 md. per acre for this region). Varadarajan and Subramanian (1953) state that the average production of bearing orchards in Coorg is only about 22 md. per acre. Limes are estimated at from 79 to 300 md., pummelos at from 83 to 400, and sweet lemons at 100 to 152. As it is stated that from 30 to 50% of the trees have not yet reached full bearing, it is to be expected that the yield will increase rapidly in the next decade. Rao (1946) gives estimates falling within these ranges, with an average of about 3·8 tons or nearly 104 md. per acre for all citrus fruits. Naik (1949) gives much lower figures for Madras, about 38 md. of oranges, 33 md. of mandarins, 65·5 md. of limes, and 82 md. of *vadlapudi*. The higher estimates are probably higher than are justified by the facts.

Citrus trees live for a long time, and with proper care continue to bear well. Harding (1951) reports that in a survey of 43 sweet orange orchards in California, selected for high yields, it was found that 35 were at least 30 years old, 14 were at least 50 years old, and one was actually 70 years of age. It is said that some trees in Coorg may be expected to give an economic yield until about 50 years old and that some trees there and in Sikkim are still producing when about 100 years of age.

The figures given in the Report on Marketing for the prices received by the growers indicate that the industry is very profitable. Prices paid by contractors for the fruit on the trees are given for periods of several years in different places. Sweet oranges sold for Rs. 157 to Rs. 750 per acre in Cuddapah, for Rs. 225 to Rs. 323 in Bombay and for Rs. 344 to Rs. 688 in U. P. Loose-skinned oranges sold for as little as Rs. 52 to Rs. 165 in Salem, but in most places brought better prices. The highest prices recorded are for the Santara in Katol tahsil, the leading producing area in Madhya Pradesh, where for the seasons 1931-32 to 1939-40, the price per acre varied from Rs. 650 to Rs. 3,900, averaging Rs. 2,358. (Here again Karmarkar and Joshi give a more conservative estimate of Rs. 321 as the average price per acre in M. P.) Limes sold for from Rs. 200 to Rs. 600 per acre in West Godavari district, and the *kichili* for Rs. 233 to Rs. 384 in Guntur.

Naik (1949) gives the actual production costs, without capital or management charges, of 4·4 acres of Sathgudi budded oranges and 1 acre of limes, mostly budded, from 1938, when they were planted, until the spring of 1946. The costs per acre were manual labour, Rs. 288 and 417; bullock labour, Rs. 105 and 74; irrigation, Rs. 197 and 333; manure Rs. 146 and 281; other expenses, Rs. 79 and 198; plants Rs. 32 and 75; total, Rs. 849 and Rs. 1,381 for oranges and limes respectively. He does not explain the differences in expenses between the two. He also gives some instances of high returns, including a Sathgudi orchard which averaged Rs. 166 per tree in one year. One grower in Coorg reported an average yield in 1946 of 1,000 fruits per tree and a gross income of Rs. 800 per acre. In one case the net income of Batavian oranges in their eighth years was Rs. 1,500 per acre. Rao and others (1954) say that in Andhra the lime had for several years been the most profitable fruit and that in 1954 the fruit of 180 trees was sold for Rs. 12,000.

Although the citrus fruits have fairly thick rinds, they should be carefully handled during picking and marketing. In this matter, there is room for much improvement in India. In most cases, they should probably be cut from the tree, rather than pulled. Special shears, with blunt, curved blades are manufactured to enable the picker to cut the stem very close to the fruit without damaging the rind. The fruits may well be dropped gently into canvas bags, and then transferred to boxes or baskets. The practice of hauling oranges to the Nagpur market piled loose in ox-carts, like that of dumping them into boats in Assam, results in much damage. Later they are frequently packed in light bamboo baskets which do not provide adequate protection. In both cases the fruit is the comparatively delicate loose-skinned orange, and a large proportion of the fruits spoil before reaching the retail market. Sikkim is ahead of the rest of the country in that practically all of the mandarins exported are packed in strong wooden boxes. Unfortunately, Agmark grading was not continued after a trial period, as the packers felt that the market preferred fruits of different sizes in the same box.

In other countries citrus fruits are frequently washed, dried, sorted, graded, wrapped in tissue paper, and packed in light wooden boxes, with the result that there is comparatively little loss. In the United States, as has been seen in Chapter IX, there is a tendency to place unwrapped fruit in fibreboard cartons. Naik and Sugurappa (1943) report that the Kodur Fruit Growers' Co-operative Society, Ltd., has done much to improve the marketing of oranges, and has introduced a simple, cheap, and satisfactory hand-grading machine. The first grading centre under the Agmark scheme was established in 1937, and a number were established in the following years. The fruit so packed is said to bring a premium of from 5·6 to 37%. Standards have been established for Santara and Mosambi oranges, based on size, stage of ripeness (in indefinite terms), and external appearance. It was felt that more exacting standards would have to wait until vegetative methods of propagation are generally adopted, and here is more uniformity in the fruit grown.

Most of the citrus fruits may be kept for some time at ordinary temperatures and for several months in cold storage. Some, such as the grapefruit, may be kept in a cool cellar for about six months. As L. Singh and Hamid (1942) point out, temperatures ranging from 32 to 50° F. have been recommended. Rose and others (1941) recommend 32-34° for sweet oranges and grapefruit, 45-48° for limes and 55-58° for lemons, the relative humidity in each case being kept at 85-90%. Miller (1946) recommends similar temperatures and mentions several factors leading to physiological disorders in storage. These are a high percentage of potassium in the fertilizer, high moisture and organic matter in the soil, the susceptibility of the variety, harvesting after relatively high mean temperatures, storing of fruit from the outside branches, storing fruit that is physiologically immature, processing in the packing house, and a low relative humidity in storage. He had success using an atmosphere containing 10 to 15% of carbon dioxide, but found that with a high carbon dioxide content, prolonged storage resulted in injury to the rind or harm to the flavour of the fruit. Biale (1953) increased the storage life of lemons markedly by reducing the oxygen to 5 or 10%.

Cheema, Karmarkar and Joshi (1937), Cheema and Karmarkar (1939), and Karmarkar and Joshi (1940 a, 1942) found that the Santara suffered from chilling at 35°, but kept well for 3 months at 40°, or for 6 weeks at 52°, or for one month at 52° plus 3 months at 40°. The Assam orange is said to have brown specks on the rind normally, which spread and cause decay in storage, reducing storage life to about 6 weeks. They report that the Mosambi kept well for 4 months at 52° or for 5 months at 40°. The colour changed very slowly at the lower temperature. The Malta kept only 4 months at 40°. L. Singh and Hamid tested the Malta and Santara at 29-32°, 36-39°, and 40-43°, and found that both did better at 36-39° than at either of the other temperatures. The Mosambi did not keep quite as well as other varieties of sweet orange, for about 3 or 4 months, while the Santara kept only 4 or 5 weeks. Wrapping the fruit in butter paper increased the storage life. Srivastava and Mathur (1954) recommend that Coorg mandarins be stored at 42-45°, at which temperature the green fruits may be kept 62-85 days in boxes treated with lysol, while yellow fruits could be kept only about 50 days. Mathur and Singh (1954) say that the rainy season crop could be stored only about half as long as the main crop, at this temperature. They recommend the same temperature for the Sathgudi, but 47-50° for the lime.

Orange marmalade has long been an important product, and is one of the main uses of the sour orange. Sweet oranges, grapefruit, and other types are also used in this way. Orange, lemon, lime, and grapefruit juices are bottled and canned to a considerable extent, although it is difficult to secure a product with a satisfactory flavour. The flavour is less damaged when preservation is by means of chemicals rather than by heating. Lal (1944) found that preservation with sulphur dioxide was more effective in conserving the vitamin C in orange and lemon squashes than sodium benzoate or pasteurization. The orange squash lost more of the vitamin than the lemon. Preheating decreased the loss in orange squash and increased it in lemon. There was less destruction at 45° Brix than at 65°. The ascorbic acid content of different varieties of sweet orange varied from 45·43 mg. in Dulcis to 84·42 mg. in Pineapple, per 100 ml. The Eureka lemon had 38·1 mg. and Sangtra mandarins about 25 mg. Lal and Jain (1947 b) report that Coorg mandarins made a good squash, but as they did not contain enough pectin, made satisfactory marmalade only when mixed with '*khatta, C. aurantium*'. Lemon barley water has been prepared from the common lemon and the *galgal*, with satisfactory results, by L. Singh and others (1943). There is also difficulty in preserving a good flavour in canning the pulp. In recent years, however, large quantities of grapefruit, oranges, and mandarins have been canned. Lal and Jain (1951) report success in canning both sweet oranges and mandarins, peeling the segments by immersion in 2% boiling lye for 25-30 seconds, followed by washing. The peeled segments were packed in 55° Brix syrup in plain cans, exhausted at 175-185° F. for 20 minutes, and sterilized at 180-185° F. for 30 minutes. The addition of an ounce of an orange essence per 4·5 gallons of syrup resulted in a flavour which remained satisfactory for two years. As has been seen in Chapter XI, the production of canned juice and pulp, and particularly of frozen concentrated juice, has been increasing very rapidly in the U. S. A.

In parts of Europe, the manufacture of essential oils and perfumes from citrus flowers, leaves, and fruits is of considerable importance. Other commercial products are citric acid and pectin, made primarily from cull fruits and from fruits kept off the market in order to maintain a satisfactory price for fresh fruit. The Sunkist Growers, a great co-operative organization in California maintains its own factories for the manufacture of these products, and returns to the growers several million dollars a year for such fruit which would otherwise be wasted. Patel and Kale (1938) produced lime oil and calcium citrate both experimentally and on a commercial basis in Bombay. The oil is much more important than the citrate, and on the basis of the prices prevailing for the oil in the three seasons before 1938, the value of the limes used was about Re. 1-14 a maund. This does not compare very unfavourably with the prices realized for limes by the growers in Madras which, during the same period, varied from 14 annas to Rs. 4 per 1,000 fruits (somewhat less than a maund) (Anon. 1943 a). Patel and Kale state that during the peak seasons, tons of limes are sometimes thrown away because marketing is not profitable when the roads are in bad condition. Chopra (1941) considers that the oils, pectin, citric acid, juices, preserves, essences, and cattle feed are among the produces which might be economically made from poor grades of citrus fruits in the Punjab. Bhat (1943) claims that it has been proved that every part of the sour lime can be preserved and sold with profit. The fruit is said to yield 65% raw juice or 25% clarified juice, while the average yield of lime oil is 7·1 lb per ton. The peel is used in powder and pickles, and the residue as a metal polish.

Chapter XV

THE BANANA

The banana is one of the most ancient of food plants, having been used, and perhaps cultivated, at the dawn of recorded history. It is one of the most common of plants in a large part of the world, yet its production is more highly industrialized than that of any other fruit. When it was first introduced into Europe, it was regarded as a rare luxury, and is still considered a fruit of excellent quality. Disraeli wrote that "the most delicious thing in the world is a banana." On the other hand, it is a staple food for thousands of poor people, and is sold thousands of miles from where it is grown at prices frequently lower than those of local fruits.

In India, the banana is one of the most important fruits, occupying more land than any other fruit, except the mango. As plantations are easily established, and ordinarily changed after a few years, the area varies more than with most fruit plants. The acreage seems to be increasing less rapidly than that under many fruits. Of the total of 400, 550 acres reported in the Report on the Marketing of Bananas in India (Anon., 1945 a), about 100,000 acres were in the part of Bengal which is now in Pakistan. According to Table V, this loss has not yet been made up by increased production in India.

Table V

Estimated Area under Bananas in some parts of India

State	Area in acres	State	Area in acres
Andhra	21,674	Madhya Bharat	500
Andaman Islands	181	Madras	123,562
Assam	40,000	Mysore	17,000
Bhopal	11	Orissa	8,666
Bihar	20,000	Saurashtra	200
Bombay	46,500	Travancore-Cochin	40,246
Coorg	2,000	Uttar Pradesh	1,860
Himachal Pradesh	45	West Bengal	26,000
Hyderabad	7,332		
Kutch	700	Total	346,477

As the banana was commonly grown in southern Asia from India to China, and in the islands to the south and east, before the earliest written history, it is impossible to say with assurance just where it originated. It is generally agreed, however, that all of the edible bananas and plantains are indigenous to the warm, moist regions of tropical Asia, probably in the mountainous region where Assam, Burma, Thailand, and Indo-China meet. Very ancient Egyptian and Assyrian bas-reliefs have been taken as evidence of the culture of the banana in that region prior to 1,000 B.C., but it seems more probable that the plant represented is the African species, *Musa ensete*, which is inedible. Had the western world so early known the banana, the Greeks under Alexander would scarcely have been so impressed when they found the plant growing in the Indus valley in 327 B.C. The Arabs seem to have introduced the banana from India into Palestine and Egypt perhaps in the seventh century A. D. It soon gained great popularity. It seems to have been carried across from Asia to the eastern coast of Africa at a very early date, and may have spread across the country, for it was found on the west coast when Europeans first visited that section. It was spread throughout the islands of the Pacific before they were known to Westerners, and there were several varieties growing in Hawaii when those islands were discovered by Captain Cook in 1778. The arrival of the banana in tropical America, where it was to spread so rapidly that many persons a little later thought it to be native, and where it was to have its greatest commercial development, seems to have occurred in 1516 A.D. It was taken by a pioneer missionary, Friar Tomas de Berlanga, from the Canary Islands to the island of Santo Domingo, and soon reached the other islands of the West Indies, and the mainland.

While bananas are grown throughout the tropical world, the greatest production is in the countries of tropical America. The industry there has been developed to supply the markets of the United States, Canada, and Europe. The trade was started slowly in the last half of the 19th century, and in 1899 several concerns were united to form the United Fruit Company, which now controls about half of the bananas exported from tropical America. The United Fruit Company claims to be the biggest farmer in the world. It has many large plantations of its own, although it buys from other planters also. It operates a fleet of about a hundred ships, all built to carry bananas, and has done a great deal to improve the sanitation of the areas in which it operates, as well as to care for the health of its own employees. The plantations are laid out on a large scale and are often established after cutting down virgin forests. Railways, with branches running through the plantations at convenient distances, carry the fruit to the ports.

No estimates are available of the acreage of bananas in many of the countries where it is largely grown. Statistics of the number of bunches entering international trade, prepared by the office of Foreign Agricultural Relations in Washington, are quoted by Von Loesecke (1949). The average number of bunches exported each year in the period 1934-38 was : North America, 72,251,000; South America, 18,044,000; Africa, 11,959,000 (including 5,730,000 from the Canary Islands); Asia, 6,398,000; Oceania, 653,000; total, 109,312,000. Later the number diminished somewhat, because of the war and the spread of disease in tropical America. Jamaica and Mexico were, about 1940, the largest producers, but the industry there and in Cuba was nearly wiped out, while Ecuador increased her production ten-fold to become the leading exporter, with about 20,000,000 bunches a year by 1954. Brazil and West Africa have also increased, and the total of all countries has remained about the same. Simmonds (1946) estimates 125 to 159 bunches per acre per annum in Central America, and 500 to 750 in the Canary Islands. At a very rough estimate, 666,000 acres produce bananas entering international trade. As most of the bananas grown in India and many other countries are consumed within the country, the total area under bananas in the world is probably between 1 and 1·5 million acres. According to Eastwood (1946), the area in New South Wales during ten years fluctuated between 15,000 and 22,000 acres. In South Africa the acreage is reported to have increased from about 12,000 acres in 1950, to 17,000 in 1955. Hawaii has a small industry, but cannot very well compete with Central America.

The banana is an herbaceous plant reaching a height of more than 30 feet in some cases, although its only true stem is the underground rhizome. The pseudostem is formed of the bases of the leaves, and from its centre emerges the inflorescence, which is an elongated spike. In most varieties the spike bends over, so that the bunch of fruit hangs down. One set of roots extends horizontally in the top two feet of the soil, while another grows vertically to a depth of about six feet. The main roots are nearly uniform in thickness, and possess numerous small rootlets. The flowers are arranged in clusters of two spiral rows each and are of three types. Those at the base of the spike open first and are pistillate. Towards the end of the spike are the neutral flowers, with neither pistils nor stamens well developed, and the staminate flowers. In most cultivated bananas the fruits are seedless, and pollination is not required.

Classification

The bananas belong to the genus *Musa* of the family Musaceae. These names are said by some to have been given by Linnaeus in honour of Antonio Musa, physician to the Emperor Augustus, and by others to come from Arabic term, *Muz*, applied to the banana and plantain. The latter is probably the correct explanation. There has been much confusion about the classification of the genus and in recent years cytogenetical studies, particularly by Cheesman at the Imperial College of Tropical Agriculture in Trinidad have thrown much new light on the subject. The most important species, *M. paradisiaca*, containing most of the varieties which are eaten raw, is thought to have developed from the wild seedy species, *M. acuminata*. Some may have come from another wild species, *M. balbisiana*, while the other important commercial species, *M. sapientum* is thought to have arisen by hybridization between the two wild species. Most varieties in it are edible only after being cooked. Gandhi (1956), following Cheesman's classification, places seven of the commercial varieties of Bombay, including the Rajeli, which is always cooked, in the species *M. paradisiaca*, and the remaining three in *M. sapientum*. Another type, not much cultivated, and differing considerably from the common bananas, seems to be a parthenocarpic form of *M. fehi*. Many of the seedless varieties are triploids, thought to have arisen by the union of reduced and unreduced gametes in diploid species. Parthenocarpy and female sterility may have arisen earlier as gene mutations. The origin of these species is discussed by Chakravorti (1951). Unfortunately, for many years the Linnean name *sapientum* was commonly applied to the varieties edible raw, and *paradisiaca* to the others. These names are said to refer to the legend that the banana was the tree of the knowledge of good and evil in the Biblical story of the garden of Eden. Another explanation given is that the wise men of ancient India used to sit in the shade of the plant and eat its fruit.

In addition to the varieties with edible fruits, there are several species of *Musa* of some economic importance. The most valuable of these is *M. textilis*, the Manila hemp, the basis of a great industry in the Philippine Islands. *M. basjoo* is used in Japan for the manufacture of coarse fabrics, and other species, including the banana itself, yield fibres of less importance. Both the rhizome and the pseudo-stem of the African species *M. ensete*, which may now be placed in the genus *Ensete*, are said to be used as food.

The English name, banana, seems to have come from terms used in the languages of the Guinea coast of West Africa, and was probably made current by the Portuguese navigators and explorers. In American usage the term 'plantain' is reserved for the kinds used only when cooked, but in India this rather useful distinction is not commonly made, and the two names are regarded as synonyms. Cavendish, Chinese, Canary, and dwarf banana are some of the names applied to the varieties which are usually not more than about six feet high.

In the confusion of the hundreds of named varieties of the banana, one variety is of outstanding importance. This is the Gros Michel (pronounced 'Gro Mishel') also known as the Jamaica or the Bluefields. It was introduced into Jamaica from Martinique by a French botanist and planter, Pouyat, in 1836 and soon became very popular and spread to other sections. Heavy production, superior shipping and marketing qualities, and excellent quality combined to make this almost the sole variety in the great industry which developed in tropical America. It is also grown in other parts of the world including Siam, Burma, and Ceylon, and is said to be identical with a popular variety in Malaya and the Dutch East Indies. Jacob (1940) states that it has been introduced into Coimbatore and thrives under a wide range of conditions. It is a tall tree with long, comparatively slender, yellow fruit. The crop of this one variety has been estimated to have a value of about $40,000,000 a year.

The Cavendish bananas are also of great importance, being the principal type grown in the Canary and Hawaiian Islands, and in a number of other countries, including India. It has a distinct advantage over the taller type in areas where damage by wind is an important factor.

A large number of varieties are grown in India under a tremendously larger number of varietal names. Jacob (1952) states that in the old Madras State not less than 500 names were used for bananas, which, when grown at Coimbatore could be classified into 53 varieties, 15 sub-varieties, 5 ecotypes, and one unstable type. All of these he placed in 9 groups. The situation is complicated by the frequent occurrence of mutants and ecotypes (ecological types). These latter vary so much in size, disposition of the inflorescence, arrangement of fruits on the rachis, and the colour, taste, flavour, odour, and consistency of the pulp of the ripe fruits that they have separate names and sell at different rates. Yet when grown at one place for a few years, these ecotypes become indistinguishable.

The most important variety in India is undoubtedly that known as Poovan, Chakrakeli, Lal Velchi, Champa, and Chinichampa. According to the Report on the Marketing of Bananas (Anon., 1945), it accounts for more than half of the acreage in the old Madras, about half of that in Assam, and important acreages in Travancore-Cochin, Bombay and elsewhere. Probably second in importance is the dwarf banana, with a still longer list of synonyms : Basrai, Mauritius, Vamanakeli, Kabuli, Jehaji, Bhusawal, Pacha Vazhai, Hirvi, and Bengali. The Harichhal of Bombay, Pedda Pacha Arati of Andhra, Malbhog of Bihar, or Sapri of Assam is considered by Nayar and Bakthavathsalu (1955) to be a semi-tall mutant of the Basrai. This dwarf banana is by far the most common in Bombay, but is also popular in other sections of the country.

Other commercial varieties in South India, according to Nayar (1954) are the Rasthali (Sonkel, Martaman), Chakkarakeli or Raja Bale (which Jacob, 1942 a, says is the best banana in the world, but with poor keeping quality), and Mala Vazhai (hill banana, Vannan, Sirumalai), all for eating raw; the Nendran or Rajeli, a dual-purpose variety; and for cooking, the Monthan.

Gandhi (1952, 1956 a) describes the ten varieties which he says are the only ones grown commercially in Bombay: Basrai, Harichhal, Lal Velchi, Safed Velchi, Mutheli, Rajeli, Rajapuri, Lalkel, Bankel, and Bhurkel. In Travancore-Cochin the Palankodan seems to be the most important, followed by the Yethen and the Nendran. In Assam the Champa, as India's most common variety is called there, occupies about half of the acreage. This and other cultivated varieties have been described by Dutta (1952). The Alpan is prominent in Bihar, where other promising varieties are discussed by Roy (1952). Jacob (1942 a, b) lists varieties grown in Mysore and Travancore, and Nauriyal (1954) has suggested 11 varieties for trial in Uttar Pradesh. Most areas report local favourities, and until more study has been devoted to the subject, it is difficult to know which of these are distinct varieties and which are better known varieties listed under a local name.

Although there are already so many excellent varieties, attempts to breed new ones are going on in different places, notably at the Imperial College of Tropical Agriculture, the work at which from 1922 to 1946 has been reviewed by Cheesman (1949). In the section of the genus, *Eumusa*, to which the edible bananas belong, the basic chromosome number is 11. The fertile species are diploids, but most of the edible bananas are triploids, a few being diploids. The most promising crosses are tetraploids resulting from the union of normal pollen of a wild diploid with an unreduced triploid gamete. In tropical America the Gros Michel is considered almost ideal except for its susceptibility to wilt (Panama disease) and leafspot, so it is being used as one parent. A search is being made for a suitable diploid parent, but as the most likely place for the search is the area where the genus arose, little progress has been made since this area became inaccessible during the Second World War. In India, breeding work is being done under the Indian Council of Agricultural Research. Venkataramani (1949) has pointed out that one of the species probably involved in the ancestry of the cultivated bananas, *M. balbisiana*, occurs in South India, while the other, *M. acuminata*, has been reported from Assam. Roy and Sharma (1951) and Nauriyal (1954) state that if commercial varieties are neglected for a few years, they begin to produce fertile pollen and viable seeds so that it is possible to use these varieties in breeding.

The banana is grown from the southern tip of India to an elevation of several thousand feet in the Himalayas, and is thus subject to a wide range of climatic conditions. Some of the varieties will stand several degrees of frost without serious damage. The most suitable climate, however, is one with warm, moist weather throughout the year, without strong winds. Such ideal conditions are hard to find. Hurricanes are one of the major risks in banana growing in Central America, severe storms sometimes breaking down every tree in a plantation. In India the most satisfactory conditions are found along the coast in Bengal, Madras and Bombay. Three factors operate against the extension of the industry in northern India: a long dry season, making much irrigation necessary; cool winters, causing damage to some varieties; and hot winds in the summer which shred and dry out the leaves.

The physical condition of the soil does not seem to be very important, provided it is deep and well drained. Naik (1949) says that three feet of rich, uniform soil is sufficient, and that even wet rice land is suitable if drainage is provided. Fertility is important, as the banana is a gross feeder. In tropical America, plantations are generally made on virgin forest soil, with its accumulation of humus, and under such conditions banana can be grown for many years without manuring.

Culture

As most commercial varieties do not produce viable seeds, propagation is invariably by vegetative means, except in experimental breeding. Selection of outstanding stools for propagation has been advocated (Anon. 1941 b) and it has been suggested that in the case of the Cavendish banana, selection should be for the more open bunches. The most common form of vegetative propagation in this country is by the use of suckers. These arise in large numbers from the parent rhizome, and are of two types. 'Sword suckers', with long narrow leaves are considered superior to the broad-leaved 'water suckers'. Nair and Sundararaj (1950) found that water suckers are produced only when the rhizome is diseased or injured or other conditions are unfavourable. On the other hand, Oppenheimer and Gottreich (1954) state that the suckers arising from the rhizome after the pseudostem has been removed are mostly water suckers, while young plants produce sword suckers and that both are satisfactory planting material. For the ratoon crop, however, they found that sword suckers flowered somewhat later but produced larger bunches.

From experiments in West Bengal, it appears that for planting in May or June, it makes little difference whether the suckers have just emerged (when they are called 'peepers') or are several months old, but that for planting in September or October, suckers 3 months old give a higher yield of fruit than those either younger or older. Larger suckers, and those lightly pruned, are likely to produce somewhat earlier than others. It is, however, commonly considered desirable to remove all of the expanded leaves, at least. Some authorities recommend that the suckers be kept for several days before planting to allow the cut surface of the rhizome to dry out.

In Central America and the West Indies, the more common form of propagation is by the planting of 'bits' or sections of rhizome. This method is more convenient in large-scale operations, particularly where the forest has been only partially cleared, and some of the felled trees are still lying on the ground, as is frequently the case in that section. The bits must contain at least one bud and better results are obtained by using bits of at least eight pounds weight. 'Heads' or 'heart suckers' are obtained by cutting back a sucker, or an old stem, within a few inches of the ground, removing enough of the central bud to prevent it from growing, and removing all but two or three of the other buds on the rhizome, which is then planted whole. This gives good results, but is an expensive method and is not commonly used.

The United Fruit Company conducted experiments comparing the different methods of propagation, and came to the conclusion that while heads bore fruit sooner, and sword suckers bore somewhat larger bunches, satisfactory results could be secured by any method. Small bits, however, resulted in poor germination and weak growth and should not be used.

The time of planting varies in different places. In South India it may be at any season, though most varieties are not planted in mid-winter. In Bengal it was found that plants set out in May-June produced more than those planted in September-October. In Madhya Pradesh and most of northern India early in the rainy season seems to be the best season, though planting may continue up to December. Sometimes large pits are dug and then filled with a mixture of manure and soil before planting. In other cases the pits are only large enough to receive the base of the sucker, and sometimes the suckers are placed in position on the level field, and enough earth is heaped around them to hold them upright.

Many different systems are used in growing bananas in different parts of the world, depending on the variety, the climate, the soil, and other conditions. Several of these are commonly found in India. Commonly with the Basrai, and sometimes with other varieties, only one crop is taken and the land is then used for some other crop before bananas are again planted in it. This is the case in East Khandesh, where by far the largest area of Basrai bananas in India is grown. According to Nayar and Bakthavathsalu (1955), they are grown on black cotton soil, and before planting about 50 tons of manure per acre is incorporated with the soil. In July the suckers are planted in deep plough furrows, about 4½ or 5 ft. apart. Four plants form a bed and there are channels between the beds which are filled with water about 70 times between November and May. In addition to the first application of manure, the State Government recommends 0·4 lb. of nitrogen per plant, and this is frequently given as two applications of groundnut cake at the rate of 2 tons per acre, but some growers replace this at least partially with ammonium sulphate. Rather similar methods are used with this variety in South Arcot.

The same variety is extensively grown in the 24-Parganas of Bengal, but here two ratoon crops are generally taken. This requires somewhat more liberal spacing, but probably not the 9 ft. commonly allowed. In fact, in experiments, greater yields per acre have been secured with plants 6 ft. apart than 9 ft. At the time of planting and about four months later, each plant may be given about 30 lb. of silt, 2 lb. of mustard cake, and 8 oz. of ammonium sulphate. Although the water table is within 5 ft. of the surface, the plantations are irrigated in summer. Somewhat similar methods are used in many places with different varieties, and the plantations are maintained for about five years.

The term, 'perennial plantation', however, is generally limited to those kept for a much longer period. Both Jacob (1952) and Nayar (1954) describe two types of perennial plantations in the South. In Coorg and on the lower slopes of the Palni hills, where there is heavy rainfall covering much of the year, they are grown without irrigation. The plantations are on well-drained fertile soil from about 3,200 to 5,200 feet above sea-level. The Mala Vazhai variety constitutes about 90% of the plantings, and a spacing of about 11 ft. is maintained. The soil is dug 6-8 times a year. In October or November this digging may be as much as 9 in. deep, and all plant waste is then incorporated in the soil. Most plantations receive no other manuring, but some are given farmyard manure. Such plantations are maintained up to 60 years. In some cases the banana plants are grown partly to provide shade for coffee or citrus trees which may be planted 24 to 30 ft. apart. They are also used for shade on the lower slopes of the Ghats, but in this case they are kept only about five years.

On the deep, rich clay loams at high levels in the Cauvery delta of Tanjore district, plantations are frequently kept 50 years, and those 100 years old are reported. Here the variety is mainly the Poovan, but some Monthans are also grown. The spacing and general culture are similar to those in the hills, except that here irrigation has to be provided. Trenches are dug about 2 ft. wide and 1½ ft. deep with two rows of plants between two trenches. Earth, when the trenches are dug, and the silt which accumulates, once a year, are thrown around the plants. From about the end of June until January the trenches are flooded often enough to keep the soil moist; in the rainy season they provide drainage.

It will be seen from the above that the banana requires much water, which would be expected because of the very large leaves. Shmueli (1953) states that under conditions in the hot, dry Jordon valley, the moisture content of the soil should not be allowed to become less than two-thirds of the total available water, as less than this is not readily available to banana roots. There is probably no justification for the extreme practice of irrigating every alternate day from

February to June, reported in Cochin by Venkitasubban (1948). But Naik (1949) recommends water every 5-10 days in dry weather, and Gandhi (1952) recommends irrigation at intervals of 10-15 days from October to February, and of 6-8 days from March to May or a total of 40-45 irrigations in the 18 months a plantation is maintained. Roy (1950 c) thinks three times a month from December to June sufficient in Bihar.

Except on very rich soil, manuring is also important. The plant is reported by Baillon and others (1933) to use exceptionally large amounts of potash, but the application of this element in India has not ordinarily given good results. Nayar (1953) reports an extensive experiment at the central banana research station at Aduthurai in Tanjore, where an analysis before treatment showed the soil to be fairly well supplied with lime, nitrogen, total and available phosphorus, and total potassium. Each plant received 25 lb. of farmyard manure and, except for the control plants, all received 0·5 lb. of nitrogen in various forms; some also received potassium or phosphorus or both. Half of the amount of each treatment was applied three months after planting, and the rest two months later. The best treatments hastened growth and fruiting, and gave the largest crop. The application of nitrogen alone, half as cattle manure and half as ammonium sulphate proved significantly better than the next treatments in which the nitrogen came from groundnut cake and ammonium sulphate and from groundnut cake and manure. There was no response from the separate applications of potash or phosphorus. In experiments at the Ganeshkhind garden, Poona, from 1933 to 1947, the application of potash was not helpful, according to Gandhi (1952). On the other hand, Dhareshwar (1952) reports an experiment at Poona in which there is some indication that with the application of 0·8 lb. of nitrogen per plant, potash increased the yield and improved the quality, but 0·4 lb. of nitrogen in farmyard manure was the most profitable treatment.

In Bengal, it was found that 8 oz. of nitrogen per plant hastened fruiting and resulted in a larger yield than 4 oz. In Bihar, 1 lb. of nitrogen is said to be desirable, along with 0·27 lb. of phosphorus and 2 lb. of potassium.

The importance of adequate nutrition early in the life of the plant is emphasized by Nayar (1954), who points out that flower bud initiation occurs very early and determines the number of hands and fingers. In one experiment at Aduthurai, plants receiving ammonium sulphate were producing the first ratoon flowering at the same time that the first inflorescences were appearing on plants which had been given no quick-acting nitrogen.

The possibility of forcing the growth and increasing the yield by providing conditions which may not normally be economic is mentioned by Jacob (1952). He says that this is done by growers on the Malabar coast in order to have ripe Nendran fruits for the Onan festival, 9-10 months after planting. He also mentions having forced the Basrai, which ordinarily matures in about 14 months, to produce a bunch weighing 58 lb. in about 10½ months, whereas the largest bunch in a commercial planting weighed 38 lb. On the other hand, he claims that perennial plantations with little care give fruit of better quality than results from intensive cultivation.

Numerous suckers are produced in most varieties, the large majority of which must be discarded. Where only one crop is taken, it is obviously desirable to keep only enough suckers for purposes of planting, which would normally be one per plant. Results at Aduthurai suggest that the best procedure is to allow one good sucker to start when the inflorescence emerges and to remove it for planting just after harvest. Where ratoon crops are taken it may be desirable to allow more than one sucker to grow, and some growers like to have one sucker half grown and another starting when the inflorescence appears. Jacob (1952) suggests allowing only the third sucker to grow and cutting it back if necessary, in order to secure four bunches in three years. He also suggests allowing more suckers to grow in the borders, to make a more efficient windbreak as well as to provide more leaves for sale. Similarly, in the last year all plants may be allowed three or four suckers.

In removing the unwanted suckers, care should be taken to cut them off from the parent rhizome completely, so that they will not resume growth, but with a minimum of damage to the roots of the clump. J. H. Mitchell (1950) states that in Queensland the approved method of desuckering is to cut off the sucker a few inches above the ground, gouge out a small part of the central section and pour in about 1/3 of a teaspoonful of kerosene. Suckers are produced throughout the year, so it is necessary to repeat the operation at frequent intervals, in order to remove the suckers before they have used up much food material.

In South India bananas are often interplanted with areca or coconut palms or mango, jackfruit, coffee, mandarin, or other trees. This also tends to protect them from the wind, as well as giving them some shade.

In regions subject to strong winds it is desirable to have windbreaks, and for most tall varieties to prop the plants. This is sometimes done with crossed bamboos, but Nayar (1954) recommends placing a single bamboo on the side of the plant away from which the plant leans, and tying it in two or more places with wet banana leaf midribs. This should be done when the inflorescence emerges. He estimates the cost of bamboos, which should last five years, at about Rs. 300 per acre. *Sesbania grandiflora* is said to be suitable for use as a windbreak.

As soon as the pistillate flowers have set fruit, the remainder of the inflorescence, known as the heart, should be removed. The removal of the dead parts of the flower about 10 days after flowering is said to improve the appearance of the fruit and, in some cases, to reduce disease.

In Australia it has been found that the weight of the bunch and the quality of the fruit can be improved by covering the developing bunch with a plastic cover. (Anon., 1953 a.) Maturity is also hastened. Material of different colours is used. In one experiment, blue plastic gave a bunch weighing 64 lb., compared with an uncovered bunch of 48 lb., but yellow was considered most satisfactory. In another test, red caused the greatest increase in weight and blue the greatest acceleration of maturity. This method seems not to have been used in India.

Pests and Diseases

The most serious pest in India is the rootstock borer, a weevil, *Cosmopolites sordidus*. It has been reported in South India, Bombay, Assam, Bihar, and Delhi, as well as in other countries, and may occur wherever bananas are grown in India. As the name indicates, the grubs bore in the rhizome and weaken the plant. Sen and Prasad (1953) state that in Bihar the attack is greatest from April to October, and that the Malbhog is by far the most susceptible variety. They report that spraying with DDT three times at intervals of a fortnight reduced the infestation from 17·5% in an unsprayed section of the plantation to 2·5%. Another treatment is to place small heaps of thin sections of the pseudostem and rhizome, dusted with Paris green or some other poison, in the plantation. But Simmonds and Simmonds (1953) consider it cheaper and more effective to apply a mixture of aldrin and dieldrin to the soil around the plants. Cuille (1953) recommends placing 50 g. of 25% BHC in a ring around each plant. Obviously it is desirable that all planting material be free from the pest.

Another weevil attacking the pseudostem is *Odoiporus longicollis*, which has been reported in Uttar Pradesh by Lal (1950) and in Assam, while Batra (1952 a) found it in Delhi and says it is an important pest in South India. Control seems to depend on the destruction of the plants which have been attacked.

Probably more important is the leaf and fruit beetle, *Nodostoma subcostatum* (*viridipennis*), which spoils the appearance of the fruit and is thought to impair the flavour. It has been reported in Assam, Bihar, Uttar Pradesh, and Delhi. Sen and Prasad (1953) report that this species, along with the rootstock borer, has caused a great set-back to the banana industry of Bihar. The beetle appears in May, causes the greatest destruction in August and September, and disappears by March. It hides until about the middle of the morning, and prefers to feed on the leaf which is about to emerge. The Alpan, Malbhog, and Champa are said to be most attractive. As the grubs are found near the roots of grasses, clean cultivation is desirable. Spraying with DDT or BHC is also fairly effective.

A number of minor pests occur. Brahmachari (1938) reports appreciable damage in Madras from a bagworm which eats holes in the leaves, and Jacob (1952) mentions *Heliothrips kadaliphila*, while Roy and Sharma (1952) report another thrips, *Scirtoithrips signipennis*. Several species of scale insects are mentioned by Rahman and Ansari (1941) and by Jacob (1952). Roy and Sharma (1952) say that the rootknot nematode is increasingly serious in Bihar, while Naik (1949) mentions only 'very casual' nematode damage in Madras.

The banana is subject to a number of diseases, but fortunately these are not as serious in India as in some other countries. The dread 'Panama disease' or banana wilt, which occurs widely in Central America and the West Indies, has been largely responsible for abandoning banana cultivation on thousands of acres. This disease was first noticed in Puerto Rico in 1903, and the causal organism, *Fusarium oxysporum cubense*, was described in 1910. It is said by Jacob (1934) to be prevalent on the Rasthali variety in parts of Trichinopoly district, and Cheema and others (1954) state that this variety is the most susceptible in Bombay, where it is called Sonkel. Bhat (1940) reports it in Baroda, and Chowdhury and Majid (1954) in Assam. Roy (1950 c) states that the acreage of two important varieties in north Bihar, Alpan and Malbhog is decreasing because of this disease and root rot. Fortunately the Poovan is highly resistant and the Basrai immune. The same, or a closely related, fungus is reported to attack the fruits in storage. With good drainage and the selection of healthy suckers for planting, it should be possible to avoid serious damage in India. A similar disease occurring in Bengal was reported by Basu (1911). Another *Fusarium* rot of the leaves, pseudostem, and sometimes the fruit bunch, but differing from Panama disease in being slow and not always fatal, has been described by Dastur (1915).

Perhaps no less important in the world is the Cercospora leaf spot, sometimes called the Sigatoka disease. It is caused by *Cercospora musae*, the ascigerous stage of which is *Mycosphaerella musicola*. Fortunately, it is much less severe in India than in tropical America, where treatment is so expensive that the only hope seems to lie in finding or breeding resistant varieties. Chowdhury and Majid (1954) report that the leaves of banana plants in Assam are sometimes largely destroyed, but that burning the diseased leaves and cultural practices to provide vigorous growth are ordinarily sufficient for the control of the disease. Nayar (1954) says it is not serious in Madras, and may be controlled completely by spraying with 4-4-50 Bordeaux. It seems to be one of the diseases reported but not identified by Chona (1933) in the Punjab.

A number of fungous diseases attack both the plants and the fruit. Anthracnose, caused by *Gloeosporium musarum* is primarily a rot of the ripe fruit from infection when the fruit is young and green. It seems to occur wherever bananas are grown, and was reported from Madhya Pradesh by Dastur as early as 1916. Jain (1950) says that it also causes a rot of the immature fruits. In Bengal the bunches are wrapped in dry banana leaves long before they are mature as a protection from it, and Bordeaux is sometimes sprayed. The Gros Michel is said to be very resistant. Chona (1933) reports that a species of *Gloeosporium* and one of *Botryodiplodia* cause a pseudostem rot of newly planted suckers, a rot of the main stem of the bunch, perhaps only following sunburn, and storage rots. Black-tip or finger-tip, a rot of immature fruits, especially severe in the rainy season, is also caused by a species of *Botryodiplodia*. Venkatakrishnia (1947) reports a pseudostem rot in Mysore caused by *Sclerotium rolfsii*. Species of *Diplodia* are reported to cause fruit rots in Madras, where *Macrophoma musae* causes specks on leaves and fruits (Jacob, 1952). Roy and Sharma (1952) say that the Moko disease, caused by *Bacillus musae* is serious in Bihar.

Much more of a threat to the industry is carried by a virus disease which has commonly been identified as bunchy top. This disease occurs in other countries, and Cann (1952) reports that in Australia control measures have reduced the incidence at a cost of about $28,000 a year. If the disease in India is not identical, it is very similar. It seems to have been reported first in 1939 in Puri district, but not to have spread extensively there. It was also reported early from Assam, but this may have been a mistake. It seems to have appeared in Travancore about 1941, according to Verghese (1945). It is spread by an aphid, *Pentalonia nigronervosa*, and control measures involve spraying with kerosene to kill the aphids and then destroying the plant. It is said that in Travancore from 1943 to 1947 about 600,000 plants were destroyed in a vain attempt to prevent the spread of the disease. Kamat and Patel (1951) report that a survey showed an incidence of 25 to 70% in Khandesh, 10-15% in Poona, and 25-30% in Surat. It is also found in Madras and Hyderabad.

In badly infected plants the leaves are stunted, with short stalks, and are bunched together to form rosettes. The yield is greatly reduced. As no resistant variety is known, the importance of preventing the spread of the disease and, if possible, eliminating it, is obvious.

Harvesting and Marketing

Bananas are harvested while still green, but after they have reached almost their full size and become plump. If they are to be shipped for a long distance they are cut somewhat sooner than if intended for the local market. The bunch should be cut with at least ten inches of the stem above the first fingers, and should be handled gently in order to avoid bruising. As soon as a bunch is cut, the pseudostem on which it was borne should be removed. Nayar (1954) says this should be done in three stages, a month apart.

The first crop of fruit is ordinarily borne in somewhat more than a year after planting. Successive crops are secured at intervals of from 5 to 10 months, depending on the climate and the management. The yield varies greatly in different varieties, and under different conditions. Simmonds (1946) gives the average yield of the Gros Michel in Central America as 125 to 159 bunches per acre per year, with a mean weight of 60 lb. making 3·8 tons per acre, with the maximum about 21 tons. In the Canary Islands, he says the average yield is 500 to 750 bunches, weighing 55 to 86 lb., giving an average yield of 16 to 19 tons. In India, according to the Report on the Marketing of Bananas, it varies from less than 2 tons per acre in Mysore to about 18 tons in Bengal, with nearly 10 tons for the whole country. In Madras the yield of the hill plantain is given as only about 2·5 tons per acre, while the other varieties vary from about 6 tons to over 10 tons in the case of the Poovan. Nayar (1954), however, estimates more than 16 tons per acre for that State, although the yields he quotes for different varieties would indicate a lower average. Menon (1941) estimates about 8 tons per acre in Cochin. Gandhi (1952) estimates the annual yield of the Basrai variety in Bombay as 20 tons per acre, and of other varieties as 10 tons. He reports a yield of 59,000 lb. per acre of Basrai bananas at the Ganeshkhind garden in Poona. He gives the total production of the State as 723,000 tons, and states that 341,754 tons of Basrai bananas were shipped to northern India in one year.

The banana is ordinarily a profitable crop in sections of India where it does well. Dani (1928) gives figures for five years which show expenses of Rs. 1,824, including water at the rate of Rs. 40 per annum per acre, and an income of Rs. 4,593, leaving a net profit of Rs. 554 per acre each year in Bombay. Dhareshwar (1942) states that there are 80 to 150 fruits per bunch, worth Rs. 6 to Rs. 8 per thousand. If the plants were 4½ feet apart, as he recommends, and each bore one bunch a year, the income per acre would be more than Rs. 1,000 at the lower figures for yield and price. Perhaps not all bear, for he gives the income at Rs. 600 to Rs. 800 per acre, with expenses amounting to half as much. Naik (1949) says that net profits of Rs. 537 to Rs. 1,000 per acre have been reported in Madras. Jacob (1952) gives figures showing net profits in different districts of the same State varying from Rs. 200 to 500 at pre-war prices, which would amount to much more in purchasing power than Nayar's (1954) estimate of Rs. 300 from perennial plantations to Rs. 759 per acre. Roy (1950 c) gives figures showing the expenses for the first and second years as Rs. 505 and Rs. 367 respectively, with incomes of Rs. 711 and Rs. 1,658 per acre. It is doubtful if many growers actually make nearly as much profit, however, as these figures indicate.

The economic value of the leaves is stressed by Sundararaj (1952) who says that about 2,000 acres of bananas are grown in Tanjore district largely for the leaves. He says the plants are desuckered the first year, but that in the second about 50 leaves are harvested per clump and sold in bunches of 100, half large and half small for an average price of Rs. 3 per bunch. He gives the cost of cultivation as Rs. 500 the first year and Rs. 400 the second, and the income from fruit the first year as Rs. 1,000 and from leaves the second year, as Rs. 1,500.

Most bananas, both in India and in other countries, are shipped without protection, each bunch forming a unit. The dwarf varieties need more protection than the tall ones and in the Canary Islands and Israel they are crated, and in Australia they are cut into hands and packed like other fruit. In the Canary Islands they are crated, and in some places they are wrapped in burlap. If they are to be shipped long distances, refrigeration is necessary. By controlling the temperature, the time required for ripening can be determined very accurately. In storage and during transportation, the temperature should be kept between 53° and 55° F., according to Wardlaw and McGuire. For ripening, it should be about 70°. Rose and others (1941), however, state that in storage the temperature should not be below 56°, and for ripening, 62° to 70°. They say the humidity should be 90-95% when the fruit is green, and somewhat lower, but not below 85%, when ripe. Von Loesecke (1949) states that while the temperatures used for ripening in Great Britain and in the U. S. A. differ somewhat, satisfactory rapid ripening can be secured by storing the fruit at 70° F. for 24 hours, then at 68° until coloured, and then at 66°. For medium ripening, the temperature should be 64°, and for slow ripening 60° to 62°, with the air being changed 3 or 4 times an hour. Ethylene is evolved by the ripening fruit, and additional ethylene is used for uniformity and to hasten slow ripening fruit, it having little effect on fruit already ripening rapidly. Gas storage experiments have given conflicting reports, but there are indications that about 5% carbon dioxide and 5 to 7% oxygen in the atmosphere in cold storage will prolong the life of the fruit. Gane (1952) states that there is some ripening of Gros Michel bananas during transport from the West Indies to Europe at 53° F., and that on a large scale the control of the atmosphere is feasible only by restricted ventilation, and that this allows some of the more mature fruit to ripen. Limited experimentation had suggested that this difficulty might be overcome by adding ozone to the atmosphere. The use of 2, 4-D and 2, 4, 5-T accelerates softening, but not colouring. In Queensland, the normal loss of weight during ripening of about 4·5% has been reduced one-third by dipping the fruit in paraffin-base emulsions.

Karmarkar and Joshi (1940 a) found that the Sonkel ripened satisfactorily at 68, 60, and 56°, in 2, 3, and 4 weeks, respectively, while the Basrai chilled at 56°. K. K. Singh and Mathur (1953 a) found that for Mysore dwarf bananas the optimum temperature was 52-55° F., at 85-90% relative humidity. Fruits turning yellow could be kept 12 days, those which were still green and difficult to peel, 22 days. Chilling, according to Von Loesecke (1949) produces many effects including more or less complete closure of all or part of the stomata and more or less breakdown of the tissues. Slight chilling may produce only a duller colour of the skin, but severe chilling makes the fruit useless. The optimum temperatures give a better quality than can be obtained if the fruit is ripened at higher temperatures, as is generally the case in India. The Report on the Marketing of Bananas in India, however, expresses the opinion that refrigeration is too expensive to be used on such a cheap fruit as the banana. Smearing the cut end of the stem with vaseline, or applying melted paraffin, as recommended on the basis of experiments in Bombay (Anon., 1933 b), not only protects the bunch from disease but causes the fruit to remain fresh longer, and to ripen with a more attractive colour.

While lower temperatures would frequently result in bananas of better flavour, in India it is customary to hasten ripening. The most common method, according to the Report on the Marketing of Bananas, is smoking the fruit by burning various fuels in store rooms or in heaps or pits plastered with mud to hold the smoke in. In some places they are stored in paddy straw, covered with green banana leaves, or exposed to the sun. Naik (1949) states that the smoking lasts 24 to 48 hours, and that in some trials, but not all, applying vaseline to the cut end of the bunch, or inserting garlic into it, also hastened ripening.

One reason for the great importance of the banana is the amount of food produced per acre. Extravagant claims are sometimes made, placing it far ahead of any other crop in this respect, but as Simmonds (1946) has shown, these claims do not bear critical analysis. He compares two varieties for which accurate records of yield are available, with the potato, one of the other high yielding crops. He calculates that about 59% of the weight of a bunch of bananas, and 95% of the weight of potatoes is edible, and that in both cases about 25% of the edible portion is dry matter, mainly carbohydrate. On this basis the yield of edible matter per acre for an average crop would be 3·2 tons for the Gros Michel, 12·6 tons for the dwarf banana in the Canary Islands, 2·9 tons for the potato in the United States and 5·7 tons in Britain, while the maximum yield for bananas would be about 28·2 tons and for potatoes about 29·5 tons. He recognizes that the figures for bananas are on the basis of the bunches exported, and that if they had been left on the tree until fully mature, for local use, the weight would have been about a third more, and that there are other inaccuracies in the estimate. He concludes that the banana and potato fall into the same general class as producers of food per acre, and on the basis of figures for papaya in Trinidad, puts that fruit in the same class. The yield of bananas in India is about half way between that in Central America and that in the Canary Islands.

The food value of the banana does not depend solely on its carbohydrate content. Von Loesecke (1949) gives the following percentage composition of the fresh ripe pulp of four varieties: moisture, 70·6 to 75·9; reducing sugars, 4·10 to 10·73; non-reducing sugars, 6·12 to 16·08; starch, 2·93 to 6·54; total carbohydrate, 19·78 to 24·70; protein, 0·48 to 1·49; crude fat, 0·24 to 0·47; pectin, 0·34 to 0·62; protopectin, 0·29 to 0·43; ash, 0·70 to 0·84; normal sodium hydroxide to neutralize 100 g. of pulp, 4·05 to 4·46 c.c. A culinary variety showed only 63·8% moisture, or no non-reducing sugar, but 18·89% reducing sugars and 11·69% starch. It was about twice as acid, and the other constiouents fell within the limits for bananas, Jacob (1952) also reports a lower moisture content for the dual-purpose Nendran, 64·2%, than for four other varieties which ran from 73·75 to 78·16%. Reducing sugars ran from 10·02 to 19·76%, with 23% in the Nendran, and non-reducing sugars from 0·20 to 5·02%, with 2·52% in the Nendran. It is interesting that the Nendran contained by far the greatest amount of sugar, 26·42%, while the popular Basrai was lowest, with 15·04%. The Nendran contained only 0·41% acid, while the others varied from 1·00 to 1·22%. Several of the less important varieties contained 25% or more of sugar, the Ney Poovan having 27·7%, and several were high in protein, the Rasthali containing 1·69%. Cheema and others (1954) also place the Basrai toward the bottom of the seven varieties on which they report, with 16·03% total sugars, while the others ranged from 15·07 to 22·44%. Lulla and Johar (1954, 1955) found only citric and malic acids, but state that all ripe bananas contain maltose, sucrose, glucose, fructose, and three or four unidentified sugars, while the culinary Monthan contained only glucose.

Von Loesecke (1949) states that 20 reports on the vitamin C content vary from 2·1 to 24 mg. per 100 g. One report on carotene showed from 71 to 95 international units and another showed larger amounts, especially in a culinary variety. Other vitamins are present in varying amounts. Miller and Bazore (1945) report that the Gros Michel and Cavendish bananas are a fair source of vitamin A, a poor source of C and contain negligible amounts of thiamine. They also report a culinary variety with more vitamin A, 1,200 international units. Von Loesecke says that bananas are quite rich in potassium, magnesium, sodium, and phosphorus, and a fair source of calcium and iron. Barnell (1940) makes the statement that, 'The banana is on every count a more valuable food than the apple.'

Since the banana is also highly digestible and palatable, its value is obvious. Some people have considered the banana difficult to digest, but this is true only before it is fully ripe. As Von Loesecke suggests, ripe bananas may well be the first solid food given to infants. He states that they are useful in treating celiac disease of children and in diseases of the alimentary tract. They are slightly laxative. Green bananas and the culinary varieties contain considerable starch and become easily digestible only when cooked. The possibilities of increasing the consumption of bananas in India are indicated by the figures given in the Report on the Marketing of Bananas, showing the amount used per person in Uttar Pradesh as half a pound annually, whereas the average for India is about 23 lb. and in Bengal 87 lb.

While a very large proportion of all bananas are eaten as fresh fruit, and most plantains are cooked as vegetables, both types are also made into a variety of products. The Report on the Marketing of Bananas states that 26,833 tons of bananas are used each year in this way. The ripe fruit has long been dried for domestic consumption, and this product, called banana figs, is also on the market. In India, the drying of bananas on a large scale has been limited to a few centres. The village of Agashi in Bombay Province has long carried on the industry, and when Kulkarni (1911 b) wrote, the annual output was said to be 160 tons, worth Rs. 27,000.The ripe bananas were merely peeled, spread in the sun, and turned daily until dry. Burns and Joshi (1920) noted that bananas dried in the open developed maggots in a few months, and that covering them with muslin or wire gauze failed to keep out the dust. They made a successful drier with a hinged glass top, holes for ventilation in the sides and bottom, and a false bottom of lattice-work. The legs are stood in water to prevent the entry of ants. The ripe, but not over-ripe, fruit is peeled and scraped and put in the drier in the sun. The ventilating holes are closed when the sun temperature falls below 95°, and the drier is covered with cloth at night. The fruit is turned daily until dry, the process taking four to six days. By covering the bananas with cardboard the last two days, a light saffron colour is secured which changes to an attractive red in storage. The dried fruit should be packed in tightly closed jars or tins, and examined after two months for maggots or mould. The fruits thus dried are said to make a delicious sweetmeat or they may be made into jam. Cheema and others (1954) agree that glass driers give a better product, but state that they have proved uneconomical. Jacob (1952) says that the dehydrator is not only more expensive, but that sometimes its product is inferior. Sulphuring after peeling the fruit is necessary in order to secure a bright product. He considered drying economical only in the case of cheap varieties, small bunches, or fruit which is not within easy reach of the market.

Green bananas or plantains are also dried and ground, forming what is variously called banana flour, plantain meal, pisang starch, and banana meal. It is very nutritious, and easily digested, and thus makes an acceptable invalid's food. Stanley and other early explorers in Africa used it very largely, especially when ill. The preparation of banana meal by sun drying has long been a cottage industry on the wes coast of Madras and in the districts of Tanjore and Trichinopoly, according to Naik (1943). He reports experiments with dehydration. Satisfactory results were secured with two comparatively simple dehydrators. In a small home drier, the temperature was kept at 145 to 150°F., while in a dehydration room it was about 10° cooler. Ripe or slightly unripe bananas were dipped in boiling water for 2 or 3 minutes to facilitate peeling, peeled, and halved or quartered lengthwise before drying, which took from 9 to 22 hours, depending on the temperature and the variety. Sulphuring the fruit for 20 minutes improved the colour. When dry, the slices were either powdered to make flour or cut into small pieces to make figs. It is suggested that a tunnel dehydrator might give even better results. Fully ripe fruits were not found well suited for making figs, as the product became dark in storage, but flour from the ripe bananas was definitely better in taste and sweetness, though more difficult to prepare. It was found very suitable for making beverages. Varieties of banana differ in the quality of the product as well as the time required and the percentage of recovery. The figs were found to contain about 50% reducing sugars, and the flour more than 80% carbohydrates and 3·4 to 5·0% protein. The vitamin C content was low.

A modern method of manufacturing banana flour is described by Von Loesecke (1949) in which the green bananas are peeled, exposed to the fumes of sulphur at the rate of 200 mg. to 100 g. of fruit, and dehydrated at 140 to 167°F., with a relative humidity of 20 to 25%. Instead of sulphuring, the fruit may be dipped in 1% citric acid. The yield is 20 to 30% of the weight of the unpeeled fruit. He uses the term banana powder for the product made by passing ripe fruit through a food chopper and drying it on steam-heated drums, much of the vitamin C being lost in the process.

Various other minor products are used. Jam is sometimes made, but is not very popular. Jacob (1952) recommends adding to 100 ripe fruits of a suitable variety, 6 lb. of sugar, the juice of 6 limes, and 3 pieces of cinnamon bark which is removed before bottling. The same ingredients are used for jelly, except that 3 limes are considered sufficient, and slightly green fruit is preferred. Dias and others (1955) report that slices have been successfully canned at Mysore, with the addition of 0·2% citric acid. Vinegar can also be made successfully. The Report on the Marketing of Bananas says that largely in connection with one temple, about 2,000 md. of a product called *panchamrutham* is made annually. To the sliced pulp of bananas is added such substances as treacle, honey, sugar candy, *ghi* and raisins. In Travancore and Cochin the figs are fried in oil and coated with sugar. Bananas are also baked or fried, the Nendran variety grown in South India always being cooked, as it is rather hard when raw, although ripe and fairly sweet.

Other parts of the plant are also used for food. The neutral and staminate part of the inflorescence or heart, before it opens, is used as a vegetable, and is especially popular in Bengal. The tender centre portion of the pseudostem and the lower part of the peduncle are also cooked and eaten. The ash of the plant is used in food in Assam, and also for washing clothes. The leaves are used as plates, and the stems are used as fodder for cattle. It has been shown in Bombay (Anon., 1919) that banana stems, cut into short pieces, can furnish as much as half of the ration of roughage for work oxen without harm.

While not as valuable as Manila hemp, banana fibre is also useful. During the second world war, when the supply of Manila hemp was cut off, an attempt was made to secure a substitute in Madras. Naik (1946) reports that *Musa-*

textilus grown in Madras is far inferior to that produced in the Philippines, but that the yield is much more per acre than that of banana fibre. Some varieties of banana yield an excellent fibre, and as it is at least as good after the fruit is harvested as before, it seemed possible to develop a profitable side industry. But the cost of extraction, either by hand or with the machine which was devised, was so great that profitable operation seems possible only when the work is done by men who would otherwise be unemployed. The fibre is extracted in that way for home use. Kelkar (1953), however, is more optimistic, although admitting that the small amount of fibre extracted in Bombay becomes brittle on drying. He states that about 0·1 lb. of raw fibre per pseudostem can be extracted with a Raspadore type machine, and that by retting the fibre for two weeks with a curd solution, or by treating the dry fibre with 1% sodium carbonate, 0·1% nitric acid, 1% soap solution, or 0·1% white oil, a superior fibre may be produced, weighing 60% of the weight of the untreated fibre. According to his calculations, about 2,000 tons of fibre of excellent quality could be produced in Bombay State each year from material now largely wasted.

Thus in some primitive cultures the banana furnishes food in a variety of forms, fodder for the cattle, thatching for the house, and fibre for a number of purposes. Few other plants are so useful.

CHAPTER XVI

THE GUAVA AND ITS RELATIVES

The guava is one of the most common fruits in India, and because of the large amounts sold at moderate prices, is of great importance. The tree is very hardy, growing with little attention, or even wild. This has led many to think it indigenous to this country, but such is not the case. It originated, along with a number of other important fruits, in tropical America, and seems to have been growing from Mexico to Peru when European explorers first visited that region. It has now spread throughout the tropics and subtropics, and in several sections has become a pest. It has become the most common of the newly introduced subtropical fruits in Israel, but is not common in the Mediterranean region or in the United States, but has become widely grown in southern Asia. In the Hawaiian Islands it is said to be the most common wild fruit, but the quality is so poor that the fruit practically never reaches the market. In Cuba, however, the wild guavas are used largely in the manufacture of various products, and the crop in 1944 was estimated at about 89,285 tons, all from wild trees, according to Ruehle (1948).

It is not known just when or how the guava reached India, but it must have been at a very early date, as it is mentioned by Bruton who was in India early in the 17th century. It is grown in Ceylon from sea-level to an elevation of 5,000 feet, and throughout Burma. The great importance of Uttar Pradesh with more than half of the entire acreage of guavas in India, is apparent from Table VI.

TABLE VI

Estimated Area under Guavas in some Parts of India

State	Area in acres	State	Area in acres
1	2	3	4
Andhra and Madras ..	2,550	Madhya Bharat ..	2,700
Assam	1,200	Madhya Pradesh ..	11,209
Baroda	915	Mysore	1,000
Bhopal	206	Orissa	600
Bihar	19,982	Saurashtra	15
Bombay	8,100	Uttar Pradesh	70,000
Coorg	50	West Bengal	2,000
Hyderabad	4,800		
		Total ..	125,327

Allahabad has the reputation of growing the best guavas in the country, and perhaps in the world, but other sections also produce very good fruit.

The Myrtle family, to which the guava belongs, is a large one containing many members of horticultural interest. In addition to the common guava there are other, less important guavas and a number of minor fruits, such as the jambolan (*jaman*). Several spices, such as cloves, nutmeg, cinnamon, and allspice are found here, as is the famous and useful Australian genus of trees, the eucalyptus. Many prominent stamens are a feature of this interesting family. The guavas belong to the genus *Psidium*, the common guava being *P. guajava*. This name, which is sometimes, but incorrectly, written *P. guava* or *P. guayaba*, like the English name, comes from the common name for the fruit in Spanish-speaking tropical America, *guayaba*.

The common guava was formerly considered by some to be of two species, the pear-guava *P. pyriferum*, and the apple-guava *P. pomiferum*. This was ordinarily based on the shape of the fruit, though Firminger called the red-fleshed type apple-guava. As there are many variations in shape, there seems little point in making any such distinction.

Although a number of varietal names are used, varieties are not well established. The most popular in U. P. is the Safeda, a round, smooth-skinned, white-fleshed, sweet guava. The Chittidar is similar, but with red spots on the skin and perhaps somewhat sweeter pulp. The Hafsi has a round smooth fruit with red flesh, not as sweet as the white ones, but with a flavour preferred by some. Naithani and Chandra (1954) describe these and a seedless variety which they call Beybugee, as well as three un-named types, the 'apple colored', with a tree somewhat smaller than the ordinary types and fruit which, on standing a few days, has a solidly red skin; the pear shaped; and the spotted pear shaped. The Karela is a pear-shaped guava with a rough skin and sweet, white pulp.

Seedless varieties are reported in several parts of the country and one of these at Poona was studied by Kumar and Ranade (1952) and found to be a triploid, with 33 chromosomes instead of the normal number of 22. This seems to be the first report of triploidy in the guava. This would explain the absence of seeds in this variety, and possibly in other seedless or nearly seedless varieties. The advantage of a fruit containing few or no seeds is obvious, but the seedless varieties seem to be vigorous trees bearing poor crops of rather small, irregular fruit, so are of little commercial importance.

In other sections, different names are used, many of them being names of places where the variety or type is supposed to have originated. Thus in Bombay, the following names are given by Cheema and Deshmukh (1927): Sind, with fruits round or elliptic, with soft white or reddish pulp; Lucknow, with bushy trees and fruits round and somewhat acid; Dholka, with vigorous trees and large fruits; and in the southern part of the State, varieties which are of poorer quality, but which keep well, such as Nasik, which is bottle-shaped and rough; and Dharwar, which is elliptical. Cheema and others (1954) state that out of 600 seedling trees at the Ganeshkhind gardens in Poona, eight were selected as promising and are being propagated. Of these, the Lucknow 49, which seems to be similar to the Safeda, has already become popular within the State and elsewhere. Ramasomayazulu (1953) says that this variety was introduced into the Araku valley, at about 3,000 ft. elevation in Andhra, with a temperature range of from about 36 to 90° F., in 1947, and that it produces better crops there than on the plains where the winters are warmer. This variety is also among the promising ones tested at Kodur, according to Rangacharlu (1954). Ibrahim (1943) describes six types grown in Madras, the only red-fleshed one, and one of the white, being distinctly inferior. Roy and Ahmad (1951) have described the varieties Harijha, Safeda, Habshi, and Seedless as grown in Bihar. These, except Habshi, are being used in breeding.

It should be remembered that few of these are clonal varieties, and in many cases the terms are merely descriptive. The selection of unusually good trees, and their propagation by vegetative means, as named varieties, offers a means of great improvement. Dutta (1953) describes seven types and recommends two with white flesh and two with red. The breeding of new varieties also offers good prospects, and has been begun on a limited scale. Naithani and Chandra (1954) share a rather common belief that the Safeda of Allahabad is not as choice a fruit as it once was, and so feel the need for breeding better varieties. None of the very large-fruited types seems to be of good quality, but it may be possible to combine size with quality, and possibly with seedlessness. In the meantime, propagation from the many poor strains should be discontinued. Cheema and Deshmukh (1927) report that bud mutations are not rare, so care should be exercised in selecting material for propagation.

The guava is grown widely in tropical and subtropical regions, and succeeds under a wide variety of climatic conditions. It seems to produce more abundant crops of better quality in areas having a distinct winter than in more tropical areas. On the other hand, the tree cannot stand more than a few degrees of frost, although there may be considerable variation among different types in this respect. Young trees have been severely damaged and even killed on low ground at Allahabad. Older trees are more hardy, and even if killed to the ground, generally send up new shoots which grow rapidly and may be bearing in two years. The guava is more resistant to drought than most fruits, and may be grown without irrigation in regions like Uttar Pradesh.

Few plants are so tolerant of varying soil conditions as is the guava. It is grown on heavy clay soils and very light sandy soils, as well as on those more commonly considered suitable for fruit production. Ruehle (1948) states that in Florida the guava thrives on light soils with a pH value as low as 4·5, and on limestone and marl soils with a value up to 8·2. It will grow and produce some fruit on soil too poor for most fruits. But as the flowers are borne on the new growth, and there seems to be no antagonism between vegetative growth and productiveness, apparently no soil is too rich for it.

Propagation

Most of the guavas grown in India, and in some other countries, are grown from seed. Seeds ordinarily germinate readily in two or three weeks, but may take much longer under unfavourable conditions. Seeds planted the middle of May, in the open at Allahabad have failed to germinate until the middle of July. Boiling the seeds up to five minutes has reduced the time required for germination somewhat without lessening the percentage of germination. Soaking the seed for two weeks before planting also decreases the time required, as does brief treatment with strong sulphuric acid.

Guava seeds retain their vitality for many months, but it is considered desirable to sow them fairly promptly. Seeds taken from the winter crop should be planted no later than the following monsoon. They should be removed from the ripe fruit, washed, dried thoroughly, and carefully stored. They are frequently mixed with ashes before drying, and it is said that in Gujarat they are repeatedly washed in the belief that this makes the fruit on the resulting trees whiter. This custom is about as useful as the one in Satara, where the seeds are rolled in sugar to make the fruit sweeter. The seeds may be broadcast or sowed in lines. When the seedlings are two or three inches high, they should be transplanted, and the weaker ones discarded. If conditions are favourable, the seedlings are ready for planting in the field, or for grafting, one year after planting, but in some cases they are allowed to remain for two years. Occasional transplanting is desirable to keep the roots in check, as long as they are in the nursery.

While seedlings are most commonly grown, it is certainly wiser to use vegetative propagation. A great deal of variation may be observed in seedling trees, both in the growth of the tree and in the fruit. Most commonly the trees grow rapidly, putting out long straight shoots, but trees making a slow, twiggy growth are also observed. Seedlings from a specially selected, uniform lot of fruit showed great variation in size, shape, quality, and season of ripening, in an experiment at the Agricultural Institute, Allahabad. DuPreez (1943) states that seedlings raised from a single fruit may bear fruit varying in colour from white to pink. There is also considerable variation in the yield of seedlings. Williams and Choong (1944) studied the yield for five years of 16 trees each of the progeny of 6 trees, and found considerable variation within the groups, while some groups yielded more than twice as much as others.

In one experiment, Dasarathy (1951) found no fruit setting when the flowers of three varieties were self-pollinated. On the other hand, at Saharanpur it was found that self-pollination was the rule, although there was more setting from flowers open to the numerous bees which visit them.

A very common method of vegetative propagation in India is inarching in the same way as is done with the mango, and with about equally satisfactory results. Seedling guavas are always used as stock, any vigorous seedling being regarded as suitable. It is probable, however, that careful testing would show that some strains were more desirable than others, and it may prove possible to regulate the size of the trees somewhat by the choice of rootstocks. At least one of the choice types selected at Allahabad is showing a marked tendency to overgrow the stock when grafted on unselected seedlings, and might make a vigorous rootstock. As has been noted, the red-skinned type tends to make a small tree. Other forms of graftage are somewhat difficult. Shield budding is most successful if buds 1-1·5 in. long are inserted in the winter or early spring into young rootstocks with the bark just thick enough to receive them, according to Ruehle (1948). Smith (1934) in Uttar Pradesh also reports some success with budding. In Java Forkert and modified Forkert budding have given excellent results. Wrapping with plastic tape may be an advantage. Nelson (1955 a) recommends veneer grafting with scions 1·5-2 in. long from terminal flushes, still green and quadrangular but with well developed axillary buds, only the best of which is kept. The grafts are wrapped in vinyl plastic film, with a small opening at the top through which the bud can emerge.

Where there is danger of trees being frozen to the ground, there is a distinct advantage in growing guavas on their own roots. Layering and air-layering are fairly common in India. Rangacharlu (1954) says that layering is the method used in South India, but that it is too expensive and should be replaced by grafting. The prejudice against this method because of the alleged shallowness of the root system and danger of the trees blowing over, is probably unjustified. Ruehle (1948) reports excellent results from air-layering with plastic wraps. He recommends removing a strip of bark one and a half times as wide as the diameter of the branch, which should be at least half an inch. The girdled area is bound with moist sphagnum moss and wrapped with a sheet of heavy plastic, tied at each end with rubber bands. Nothing more is done until sufficient roots are visible through the plastic, when the layer is removed and planted. This takes three or four months. A piece of paper tied loosely around the wrap protects it from damage by birds and prevents the moss from overheating. This method has been used successfully at Saharanpur. The application of NAA is beneficial, according to S. N. Singh (1950), who also had fair success in rooting cuttings of one variety, but not of another. Kuperberg (1954) reports 18% success in rooting cuttings by keeping them in mist for three months.

Another method which is easy, and satisfactory unless the parent tree has been produced by graftage, is the use of root suckers. If lateral roots are severed from the tree, or wounded, two or three feet from the trunk, they will, in most cases, send up shoots, which may then be transplanted to the nursery. Or the roots, may be dug up, cut into lengths of five to eight inches, laid flat and covered with two to four inches of soil. Occasionally the suckers which are produced abundantly around the trunk may be removed with a few small roots, and grown.

The use of stool-beds is recommended by Du Preez (1954). A tree on its own roots, 3-5 years old is sawed off just below the surface of the soil in the spring. The shoots which appear are allowed to grow about three months, when they are thinned and copper wire is twisted several times around the bases of those which are left. Soil is banked round and between them, and after nine months the shoots are removed and those with good roots are planted in the nursery.

Grafted plants are ordinarily ready to set out in the field one year after grafting. The rainy season is the best time for this. The correct distance from plant to plant is subject to dispute, although it is generally agreed that most orchards are too closely planted. The most common distances are 12 to 18 feet, but such extreme crowding as results from planting two trees in each pit, with the pits 10 feet apart, is not unknown. Naik (1949) states that in Madras seedling trees are planted about 15 ft. apart on river banks, and receive no irrigation after the first year, while layered or grafted trees are planted 20 ft. to 25 ft. apart on good orchard soil and are given better care. Rangacharlu (1954) favours at least 25 ft. This is about the maximum distance ordinarily recommended but at this distance the field will be completely occupied under favourable conditions in Uttar Pradesh; seedling trees on good soil and with good care should be allowed at least 30 ft.

Culture

Ordinarily the guava is given very little care, and it does remarkably well in spite of this neglect. But in order to get satisfactory crops, some cultivation, irrigation, and manuring are necessary, and some pruning is desirable, at least in the early stages. In the absence of more definite recommendations, it may be assumed that ploughing and cultivation suitable for other fruits will meet the needs of the guava. Trees receiving such care will bear a small commercial crop in the third year, and at five years will be about the same size as neglected trees twice their age.

Cultural operations depend to a considerable extent on the crop which is desired. In tropical regions including Madras, if irrigation is given, the guava may bear more or less throughout the year, but in India there are generally two or three rather distinct crops. In northern India the main crop comes from flowers in the rainy season, and ripens in mid-winter. A second crop is ripe during the rainy season, from flowers which appear in the early spring. In Bombay and Madras there is a third crop, with flowers appearing in October. The common practice is to treat each orchard for only one of these crops, and this is probably wise. In Uttar Pradesh the winter crop is the one ordinarily desired, as it is not only larger, but of much better quality. The fruits borne in the rains are rather insipid and watery, and do not keep well. In many cases, the trees will bear some fruit in the rains and then so much in the winter that branches are broken. However, Smith (1934) states that the total quantity of fruit borne in a year is greater if only the winter crop is taken. Ordinarily, all that is necessary to avoid the rainy season crop is to withhold irrigation after December or January or even February. In that case any young fruit which sets in the spring is likely to fall off. The trees lose many of their leaves. This is the common custom, whether from the conviction that it is the best treatment for the trees, or in order to save the expense of irrigation.

Root pruning has been advocated, even in Uttar Pradesh where it is definitely undesirable. There is more reason for it in Bombay where the fruiting seasons are less definite and the crops tend to be smaller. Even so, Cheema and others (1954) say that it is needed only on deep heavy soils. For the winter crop they recommend withholding water and removing the earth from around the upper roots and then, about June 10, returning the soil, mixed with manure.

Two light irrigations are to be given before a normally heavy one, if the rains have not started.

Whether the roots are pruned or not, manuring is desirable. It helps young trees to become large enough in a few years to bear large crops. As the fruit is borne on the new growth, manurial treatment which brings about vigorous growth also encourages fruiting. Rangacharlu (1954) says that good results have been obtained at Kodur by applying 200 lb. of leaf compost and 7 lb. each of groundnut cake and ammonium sulphate per tree each year, thus supplying about 3 lb. of nitrogen. He refers to no experiment in which this was compared with other treatments, and it is possible that somewhat less nitrogen would prove adequate. Farmyard manure may well be applied after the rainy season and readily available nitrogen just before the time flowers are desired.

Severe symptoms of zinc deficiency have been reported from the Pushkar valley, near Ajmer. Interveinal chlorosis was observed, with a reduction in leaf size, poor growth, die-back, scant flowering, and the drying and cracking of any fruit which set. A virus disease was suspected, but spraying with 1 lb. of zinc sulphate, 0·7 lb. of hydrated lime, and 16 gal. of water, twice, restored the trees to health (Vasudeva and Raychaudhuri, 1954).

In order to secure good growth, young trees may well be irrigated so as to keep the soil in the root zone moist. Mature trees are ordinarily irrigated only from the end of the rainy season until the fruit is harvested. In Uttar Pradesh two or three irrigations are sufficient, and it may be doubted if the programme reported at the Ganeshkhind gardens is justified. There eight or nine irrigations of two acre inches each are given between June and December. If the rainy season crop is desired, irrigation must be continued until the rains start.

Pruning

While very severe pruning has been advocated by some, and very light pruning by others, little or no pruning is commonly practised in northern India. A certain amount is undoubtedly desirable, at least to the extent of forming a strong framework, and of removing the suckers which appear at the base of the tree. Where other culture is largely neglected, this may be all the pruning which is necessary. Under such conditions growth is relatively slow, and crops are light. But if good culture results in rapid growth and heavy cropping, great care is needed in order to avoid excessive breaking of the trees. Proper spacing of the branches and the avoidance of weak crotches will generally prevent splitting, but the wood is rather brittle and under the weight of fruit which is borne toward the end of the branches, the branches are likely to break. In some cases the entire top of the tree is ruined. To prevent this, rather severe pruning is justified, especially in the case of young trees. Frequent nipping back of young shoots may avoid the necessity of much heavy pruning. This is likely to result in the growth of at least one bud in each leaf axil within several nodes of the cut, and not more than one of four of these should be retained. It may also be desirable to develop low branches which, when weighted with fruit, will rest on the ground and give some support to the branches above them.

In trees which have been bearing for some years, a light annual pruning may be desirable to stimulate growth and flowering. There is also a tendency for the branches to lie on each other and shade the lower ones too much, so moderate thinning is also needed. In spite of efforts to build a strong tree, some branches are likely to break, and these should be removed.

As the fruit must be harvested frequently, this becomes a problem, especially where labour is expensive. Oppenheimer (1947) recommends pruning which will keep the tree low enough so that the fruit may be harvested by hand from the ground, even if this means rather heavy pruning in alternate years. It is possible that dwarfing rootstocks would be highly desirable under such circumstances. Bearing trees should be pruned after harvest. Dasarathy (1951) states that in Madras the bearing shoots ordinarily die after the fruit matures (which is not the case at Allahabad) and recommends pruning off such wood and also removing about half of each vegetative shoot.

In connection with pruning, a peculiar system of training of the trees, practised in Bombay, should be considered. After the young trees begin to bear, the branches of adjoining trees are bent down and tied to each other. This is called "bending". By holding the branches in a more nearly horizontal position than they naturally assume, this forces dormant buds into growth, and as the fruit is borne on the growth of the current season, the crop is thereby increased. Frequently the branches are broken in the process, which may also stimulate fruiting, but if it is done frequently, is likely to damage the tree seriously. Gadgil and Gadgil (1933) state that in Poona the trees are treated in this way in alternate years, and bear about 300 fruits per tree in the years they are treated, and only about 25 in the other years. Three hundred fruits per tree is a very low yield as compared with that of untreated trees in Uttar Pradesh. It is obvious that "bending" would interfere with other cultural operations in the orchard, and that the amount of labour required for the operation would be considerable. Nevertheless, it is practically a universal custom in some districts.

In an attempt to secure good crops of superior fruit without the disadvantages inherent in "bending", pruning investigations were carried on at the Ganeshkhind gardens, which have given interesting results, as reported by Cheema and Deshmukh (1927). In May the growth of the last season is removed, leaving only one or two buds at the base. From these, new shoots come out, on which the fruit is borne. In one experiment with 600 trees, the average yield for the unpruned trees was 464 fruits weighing 1·58 ounces per fruit, as compared with a yield of 234 fruits weighing 2·27 ounces from the pruned trees. While the yield per tree was thus less from the pruned trees, the latter were planted 15 feet apart and the unpruned ones 20 feet so that the yield per acre was 6,641 pounds for the pruned trees and 4,998 for the unpruned. Of greater importance than the difference in yield is the larger size of the fruit from the pruned trees. Other advantages claimed are that the pruned trees flower three to four weeks earlier, with the fruit ripening earlier and in a shorter period, and that the fruit is better protected from birds and bats. However, the method was not definitely recommended to the growers, and has not been widely adopted.

A very similar method is recommended by Smith (1934) in the Uttar Pradesh, but without reference to any trial of the method. Although the rainy season begins later there than in Bombay, he states that the pruning should be done in April or May. In an experiment at the Allahabad Agricultural Institute, trees were planted in 1932, half 15 feet apart and half 25. As soon as the trees in the 15-foot block began to crowd, this system of heavy pruning was introduced. Each year, part of the trees were pruned May 1, part June 1, part and part July 1. A few rows in this block, and all in the 25 foot block were given only ordinary pruning. The results up to the 1942-43 season have been reported (Hayes, 1943). While the fruit from the heavily pruned trees was larger, and the number of trees per acre much greater, the number of fruits per tree was so much smaller that the yield per acre was less than half of that in the 25-foot block. Up to 1942-43, the lightly pruned trees 15 feet apart yielded slightly more than those 25 feet apart, but soon after severe crowding began to reduce the yield. There was little difference between the trees pruned on different dates, except that those pruned on May 1 were badly sunburned the first year, and never recovered.

The so-called trellis system has also been used in Bombay. The trees are planted 15 feet apart in rows 8 feet apart. The branches along the row only are allowed to grow, and three branches in each direction are encouraged, at heights of 2½, 4, and 5½ feet from the ground. The branches of adjacent trees meet and all along them fruiting spurs are encouraged. Cheema and Deshmukh (1927) state that this method is easily employed for ornamental purposes. As the yield is reduced, it is not suitable for commercial orcharding. Naik (1949) states that at Kodur trees trained as cordons have proved attractive and yield good crops, about 200 fruits a year. Ordinarily, however, no pruning or 'bending' is done in Madras.

Pests and Diseases

Insect pests play a comparatively unimportant part in guava cultivation. The worst, in Uttar Pradesh, is the bark-eating caterpillar, *Indarbela tetraonis*, which has been mentioned as a pest of the mango and citrus fruits. It seems to prefer the guava to all other hosts, and is frequently found in large numbers in neglected orchards. It probably contributes to their deterioration, although the exact extent of the damage is difficult to assess.

The leaves are frequently eaten at Allahabad and in some cases are reduced to lace. It is difficult to find an insect doing this damage, but a small gray weevil, *Myllocerus maculosus*, is thought to be the culprit. This weevil and two others, *M. discolor* and *M. sabulosis* were reported on the guava at Pusa in 1917, but were thought to be unimportant. Again it is difficult to know how much damage is caused, for trees bear well in spite of a heavy attack.

Tender leaves and buds are eaten by a caterpillar which closely resembles the orange leaf caterpillar, *Psorosticha zizyphi*, except that it is gray instead of green. It has become common at Allahabad, and also been observed at Delhi. The damage is not serious except as it interferes in the training of young trees by destroying buds which have been selected.

The guava scale, *Pulvinaria psidii*, is said to be the only serious pest in Bombay (Cheema and Deshmukh, 1927) where the method of control recommended is spraying twice with fish-oil rosin soap, one pound to 8 gallons of water, or with crude oil emulsion, 15 pounds to 100 gallons of water. On the only occasion this scale has been noticed in Allahabad, it was parasitized by chalcids, which may explain the fact that it is not a serious pest there. Other scale insects reported on the guava by Rahman and Ansari (1941) are *Aonidiella aurantii*, *A. orientalis*, and *Aspidiotus destructor*. Ansari (1947) says that the last is generally under natural control in the Punjab, but sometimes causes severe damage. To control it he recommends the inspection of nursery stock, and where necessary spraying with 2 or 3 lb. of fuel oil in 4-4-50 Bordeaux mixture, or with rosin wash.

The mealy bug is reported to be a prominent pest in Mysore, but kept under control by its predator, *Cryptolemus montrouzierie*. Ibrahim (1943) reports the fruit-sucking moths and scale insects as pests in Madras. Fruit flies cause damage to the rainy season crop in Uttar Pradesh and in some other places. Cheema and others (1954) say that the fruits in Bombay are frequently infested with *Dacus ferrugineus*, *D. ferrugineus dorsalis*, and *D. zonatus*. Oppenheimer (1947) says that the Mediterranean fruit fly is the most important pest in Palestine, but that the damage may be kept low by harvesting the crop frequently and before the fruit is fully ripe. In Assam the larvae of the stem borer, *Microcolona leucosticta*, feed on the pith of tender twigs, generally near the tip according to Chowdhury and Majid (1954). They pupate in the stem, and may be controlled by fumigation with carbon bisulphide or petrol. Larvae of two moths are potential pests. Mitra (1945) reports *Taragama siva*, a pest of acacias, eating the leaves of guava in Calcutta, while Ansari (1945) noted a pest of castor, *Dichocrocis punctiferalis* boring in guava fruits in Ferozepore, Punjab. Other minor pests include aphids and the pomegranate butterfly but none of these is commonly serious.

A combination of insect and fungus attack results in what is called scab, canker, or blister disease which was reported by Patel and others (1950) in Bombay and which is said by Puttarudraiah (1952) and Venkatakrishnia (1952, 1954) to be common in Mysore. It causes some young fruits to drop, and some which remain on the tree until mature have brown or black spots and are malformed. Some dry up on the tree. Occasionally there are small rusty brown angular spots on the leaves. These symptoms are caused by two fungi, *Pestalotiopsis (Pestalotia) psidii* and *Glomerella cingulatum* or *G. Psidii*. These are weak parasites which affect the fruits and leaves only after injury. This is most commonly the puncture of a capsid bug, *Helopeltus antonii*. Control measures may therefore be directed against either the bug or the fungi. Both BHC and DDT are reported effective, as are Bordeaux and lime sulphur. In Kumaun scab is reported to be caused by another species of *Pestolotiopsis* and to be better controlled, although imperfectly, by cuprous oxide than by lime sulphur.

By far the most serious disease of the guava, and one of the most serious disease of any fruit tree in India, is the Fusarium wilt. This seems to have attracted attention first near Allahabad about 1935, but to be widespread in the eastern districts of Uttar Pradesh. It is estimated that 5-10% of the trees are killed each year in the badly infected districts of Allahabad, Farrukhabad, Lucknow, Faizabad, and Unnao. Mehta (1951) states that the disease seems to occur on soils with a pH above 7·5 and to be more severe on the more alkaline soils, up to a pH of about 9. Symptoms are likely to appear during the rainy season, apparently after the fungus has been present in the tree for months. Branches wither and die, one after another, and in a few weeks or months a tree which had seemed entirely healthy will be dead, often with a good crop of half-grown fruit on it. As soon as wilting starts, a discoloration of the cambium region can be discovered.

Early reports on the disease referred to species of *Fusarium* and *Cephalosporium*, but Prasad and others (1952) point out that there is no consistent difference between these genera, and propose to call the cause of this disease *Fusarium oxysporum* f. *psidii*. It is not yet known how the disease spreads, except that it is likely to proceed most commonly to adjacent trees. Nor is any control measure known, though it seems wise to remove a tree as soon as symptoms are noticed. Jain (1956) reports somewhat promising results from the injection of 8-quinolinol sulphate which delayed the development of symptoms in diseased plants. A symptomless plant which was injected still showed no symptoms 15 months later, while eight other healthy plants in close proximity to it developed the disease and died. Investigations are continuing, and it is hoped that a resistant rootstock may be found. Trees planted where others have died have grown and fruited for a number of years without symptoms.

Another wilt disease is serious in the Jhargram area of Midnapur district of West Bengal. Sen and Verma (1954) report a survey of 15,029 trees within 2·25 miles of Jhargram, which showed 88% of the trees had been attacked and 78% were dead. The first visible symptom, according to Chattopadhyay and Sen Gupta (1954, 1955), is partial or complete failure of new growth on some branches. Then the leaves wither and fall, leaving bare twigs which gradually die. In three or four years the tree becomes defoliated and eventually dies. New trees planted where the disease is established are stunted and generally die before bearing. The soil is reported to be of about pH 6·5. Both *Fusarium solani* and *Rhizoctonia bataticola* have been found, together or separately, in the diseased tissue, and the addition of either to sterilized soil has caused the disease in young trees planted in it. The disease is thus quite distinct from the wilt in Uttar Pradesh, and a different name would be desirable for it, but 'die-back', which has also been used, is no improvement.

One tree with symptoms similar to Fusarium wilt in Allahabad was found to be affected by *Macrophomina phaseoli* (*Sclerotium bataticola*) which commonly affects non-woody plants.

In the western districts and in the *tarai* region of Uttar Pradesh anthracnose of the guava is reported to be a serious problem. Mehta (1951) reports that this is caused by *Colletotrichum psidii* and that the fungus may be carried from season to season on mummified fruits. The symptoms vary and are serious only on the crop ripening in the rainy season. Bose and Mehta (1951) refer to this and other minor diseases. This is probably the same as the anthracnose attributed by Cheema and others (1954) to *Gloeosporium psidii*, in which the fruits shrivel, turn brown, and have round decayed s ots. They recommend spraying with Bordeaux mixture to control the disease. This organism is the cause of what Tandon and Agarwala (1954) call die-back, which is said to cause the death of many new shoots in the rainy season near Allahabad. It also attacks buds and flowers, resulting in mummified fruits, but fruit which they inoculated rotted only as it ripened. Their report that trees wilted may indicate confusion with the Fusarium wilt which is common in the area and may infect the same trees. They report that spraying with 3-3-50 Bordeaux reduced the loss.

Uppal (1936) reports a canker caused by *Physalospora psidii*, not known to occur anywhere else in the world, than in Bombay. It may kill branches and eventually the entire tree. Rai (1956) reports a rare stylar-end rot of fruit in the orchard or in storage caused by an undescribed species of *Phomopsis*. Both die-back and fruit rot are reported in lower Kumaun caused by *P. psidii*.

Serious damage is done by birds and bats, the so-called 'flying-foxes'. Control is difficult, and in most cases no attempt is made to do more than scare these marauders away. Watchmen are employed, and various noisemaking instruments are used. Cheema and Deshmukh (1927) recommend the use of nets of 9 to 10 inch mesh, over the trees, but even though these may be used for several years, this is a fairly expensive measure of doubtful utility. The practice of 'bending' is said to give partial protection from birds and bats.

Few other tree fruits begin bearing so early in life as does the guava. Seedling plants flower in the nursery, and will produce fruits if they are allowed to do so. Young trees will frequently bear such heavy crops the first year or two after being planted in the orchard that many limbs are broken or badly bent. They should be protected by removing the flowers, or young fruits. Well grown trees in the third year may be allowed to bear some fruit on branches which will not be broken or badly bent by their weight. Even in older trees, damage from heavy crops is not infrequent. Under favourable conditions in Uttar Pradesh, a commercial crop may be secured in the third or fourth year. Thereafter the trees ordinarily bear regularly and heavily. Thinning may sometimes be done with advantage, resulting in larger fruits as well as fewer broken branches.

The bearing life of the trees depends on the treatment they receive, but there seems to be no reason why they should not continue to produce satisfactory crops for 30 or 40 years, provided they are not seriously affected by disease. Kulkarni (1911) states that plantations generally last about 40 years, but that they deteriorate after about 15 years. Cheema and Deshmukh (1927) report that the orchards are ordinarily kept about 20 years, but that after such a period they may be rejuvenated by severe pruning. The way orchards are commonly planted there is not room for trees to mature normally. Lack of proper care also contributes to a comparatively early death.

Production

Accurate production figures are not available. Oppenheimer (1947) suggests an average of 110 lb. per tree, and as he states the trees in Palestine are planted only about 16 ft. apart, this would mean about 165 trees per acre, yielding about 18,000 lb. Rao (1946) estimates only about 2·2 tons per acre in India. Chhattopadhyay and Sen Gupta (1955) estimate that healthy orchards in West Bengal produce about 10,000 lb., or nearly 4·5 tons per acre. One report from Bombay states that the variety Lucknow 49 will produce 24,000 lb., or about 10·7 tons per acre. Prasad (1936) estimates the average crop in Allahabad District at 450 fruits weighing six ounces each, per tree. This amounts to 172 pounds per tree or, if it is assumed the trees are 15 ft. apart on the average, nearly 15 tons per acre. This figure is probably somewhat high. As he indicates a wholesale price in 1934-35 of more than 12 annas per basket of 120 fruits, the value of the fruit would be about Rs. 3 per tree, or between Rs. 500 and Rs. 600 per acre. Roy and Ahmed (1951) report that at Sabour, Bihar, three varieties yielded from about 264 to 328 lb. per tree, while the seedless yielded only 164 lb. As the trees were small they could probably be planted 20 ft. apart, which would mean up to 16 tons per acre, in two crops each year. Barakzai (1920) estimated average yields at only 30 or 40 lb. per tree. Ten trees planted 25 ft. apart at Allahabad in 1954-55 produced from 30 to 168 lb., with an average of about 120 lb. per tree or more than four tons per acre. Ibrahim (1943) in Madras, estimates a yield of 100 to 300 fruits in the rainy season, when the price is high because of scarcity, although the quality is poor, and of 300 to 500 fruits in the winter, when the price is low. He estimate an income of only Rs. 20 to Rs. 30 per acre for the poor varieties, but Rs. 100 to Rs. 150 for the better types. Naik (1949) states that at Kodur a red-fleshed variety yields more than 700 fruits a year, Allahabad varieties about 500, and a seedless variety about 125.

While the guava is not a fruit of the highest quality, it is very popular as a fresh fruit, as well as for the manufacture of jelly and other products. It is a valuable food, but the actual composition varies greatly. Thompson (1914) reports the following analysis of two varieties, in percentages : edible portion, 84, 87; total solids, 17·78, 18·75 ash, 0·531, 0·676; acids as sulphuric, 0·363, 0·451; protein, 1·125, 1·525; reducing sugar, 6·61, 5·73; sucrose, 0·77, 2·53; total sugar, 7·33, 8·26; fat, 0·524, 0·412; and fibre, 4·445, 5·105. This may be contrasted with a analysis in California, reported by Popenoe (1920) showing no sucrose, and only 5·45% total sugar. Oppenheimer (1947) reports only 4·8% sugar. Riaz-ur-rahman and others (1954) report that 11 unnamed varieties in the Punjab contained from 5 to 7·7% sugar. K. K. Singh and Mathur (1954a) report that Safeda guavas grown in Mysore had 10% total solids in the small fruits and 10·7% in the larger ones.

The growth period of the fruit in South Africa varies from 115 to 280 days, according to Le Riche (1951). He found that in the ripe fruit the sugar is practically all fructose. The ascorbic acid increases very slowly for about 100 days after setting and then rapidly until full maturity. The weight of the fruit of different varieties and in different places varied from 76·3 to 116·9g. (about 2 to 4 ounces).

The outstanding value of the guava as a source of vitamin C has been recognized by workers in India and other countries. Aykroyd (1951) reports 299 milligrams per 100 grams, as compared with from 31 to 68 mg. in citrus fruits.

K. K. Singh and Mathur (1954 a) found slightly more than 100 mg., while Riaz-ur-rahman and others (1954) report 91·8 to 266·8 mg. Golberg and Levy (1941) found 300 to 450 mg. in ripe, firm fruit, while green fruit had somewhat less, and over-ripe, soft fruit only 50 to 100. Le Riche (1946), however, found only insignificant changes, with a tendency for ascorbic acid to increase during ripening in early varieties, but to decrease in late varieties. Even over-ripe fruit which had dropped to the ground without injury to the surface, has as much as at earlier stages. Golberg and Levy (1941) report the proportion of ascorbic acid in the skin, outer pulp, and inner pulp to be 12 : 5 : 1, but Webber (1944) quotes Boyes and de Villiers as placing this ratio at about 3 : 2 : 1. Golberg and Levy (1941) found that the pink-fleshed varieties in South Africa were usually slightly less rich in vitamin C than the white-fleshed, but Webber (1942, 1944) reports that in tests of 6 varieties in 1941 and 19 in 1942, at Riverside, California, the Rolfs, a pink-fleshed variety stood highest both years. In 1941 this variety was reported to contain 971 mg. per 100 c. c. of peel and pericarp, while in 1942 another man made the analysis and found only 319 mg. per 100 g. The other varieties also seemed to contain much less in 1942. It is not known whether the differences were due to the analytical methods used or to environmental or seasonal differences. There were large differences between varieties, even between 8 which were seedlings of one open-pollinated fruit. No correlation was found between ascorbic acid and colour of flesh, acidity judged by taste, or season of ripening. The late ripening fruits within a variety seemed to have somewhat more than those ripening earlier. The highest concentration seemed to be just before the fruits begin to mellow. Cruess and others (1945) surveyed 25 varieties at the same station and found the vitamin C to vary from 55 to 529 mg. per 100 g. Hayward (1942) reports a greater range found by workers in Florida, where several types varied from 37 to about 1,000 mg. per 100 g. of fruit, averaging 564. Van der Merwe (1944) found that vegetatively propagated varieties, selected for their quality, contained more ascorbic acid than seedlings. Similarly, Le Riche (1946) found that of 7 varieties studied in South Africa, the Frank Malherbe, a late variety with deep red flesh was the largest, had the highest percentage of outer flesh ($63 \pm 4{\cdot}568$, compared with minimum of $43{\cdot}5 \pm 2{\cdot}39$) and the highest ascorbic acid content (960 ± 213 mg. per 100 g., compared with minimum of $118{\cdot}4 \pm 24{\cdot}02$). But it had the least fructose at maturity (4·4%, while the highest was 6·24%). In Australia, the Division of Food Preservation (1945) reports a range of from 100 to 500 mg. per 100 g., with the pink-fleshed varieties tending to contain more than the white.

The content of other vitamins is much less. Miller and Bazore (1945) state that the guava in Hawaii is a fair source of vitamin A, but poor source of thiamine. Campos (1943), however, claims that in Brazil it is a good source of both thiamine and riboflavin. Miller and Bazore say it contains much iron, but that 80% of this is in the seeds and not utilizable. It is a fair source of calcium and phosphorus.

The vitamin C in the guava is largely retained in various products. Golberg and Levy (1941) found 200 to 300 mg. per 100 g. in canned selected firm fruits. By quartering the fruits, blanching them for two minutes and drying at 128 to 136° F. for 10 to 12 hours, they produced a powder with a pleasant odour and practically no taste, containing up to 4,500 mg. per 100 g. Webber also prepared an attractive dehydrated product in preliminary experiments, varying from 170 to 1,890 mg. per 100 g., the variation illustrating the importance of using the proper technique. Unsatisfactory methods may account for the fact that Naik (1943) reports only from 280 to 580 mg. per 100 g. in guava flour made from six varieties. Webber also kept a frozen puree for two and a half years, after which it still had a flavour like the fresh fruit and contained 288 mg. of vitamin C per 100 g. Miller and Bazore (1945) found that guava juice kept well and could be used as a satisfactory substitute for orange or tomato juice in feeding babies. Cruess and others (1945) describe guava paste, pie, jam, jelly, ice-cream, mild-shake, and nectar, and canned, frozen, and dehydrated guavas. They found that there was a slight loss in ascorbic acid in canning and in freezing.

Guavas which are just beginning to turn yellow may be kept at 47-56° F. for about four weeks, according to K. K. Singh and Mathur (1954 a). There was less loss in weight at lower temperatures, but the fruit did not develop an attractive appearance.

Guava jelly is an important product in India, and in some other countries is the form in which the fruit is most commonly used. The better Indian varieties do not contain enough acid to make a good jelly without the addition of acid and are likely to have only a fair amount of pectin. The sour types, less desirable as fresh fruit, are better for jelly, and Abbott (1931) states that in some the acid and pectin are so concentrated that three times the weight of sugar may be added to the juice, yielding 350 lb. of jelly from 100 lb. of fruit. A rather large industry has grown up in Cuba, based on the wild guavas growing there. According to Coit (1945), one factory shipped 250,000 lb. of concentrated jelly base and 3,000,000 lb. of other guava products in 1944, including jam, syrup, jelly, dried powder, juice, and paste. Other factories processed from 8 to 10 million pounds. Ruehle (1948) states that guavas freeze exceptionally well, and that the frozen product is practically indistinguishable from the fresh fruit.

Relatives of the Guava

The genus *Psidium* contains about 150 species, but only a few of them are of any horticultural interest, and no other species compares with the common guava. The Brazilian or Guinea guava, *P. guineense*, is a small fruit of poor quality, resembling the common guava, but with branchlets round rather than 4-angled. Considerable confusion has existed about this species, and the specific name has been given to varieties of the common guava and to other species.

Next to the common guava, the most important species is the strawberry, or Cattley guava, *P. cattleianum*. This is a smaller tree, or shrub, capable of withstanding more cold than the common guava, but otherwise much the same in its requirements. It may be planted at a distance of 10 to 15 feet. The leaves are glossy green, making the plant of value as an ornamental. The fruit is little more than an inch in diameter, and is a handsome purplish red, except in the yellow-fruited type, *P. cattleianum var. lucidum.* The latter is a larger tree, sometimes reaching a height of 40 ft. in Hawaii. It seems to come fairly true from seed, and vegetative propagation is seldom used. The fruit is most commonly used for jelly, but is also eaten fresh. While it has been grown in India for some time, it has never become at all common. Naik states that it thrives at elevations of 2,500 to 5,500 feet above sea-level, and also on the plains.

Several minor fruits of the myrtle family are now placed in the genus *Syzygium* instead of *Eugenia,* which is now limited to species of American origin. One of these, the pitanga, Surinam cherry, or Brazil cherry, *E. uniflora,* is grown to a slight extent in India. This is a shrub or tree attaining a height up to 20 ft. The beautiful bright red angular fruits average a little less than an inch in diameter, but some trees produce fruit of about twice that diameter, according to Chandler (1950). He states that the aromatic oil flavour is rather pleasant in those fruits which have the least of it, but often the flavour is distinctly unpleasant. Yields of 6-8 lb. per plant are reported from the hills of South India where it thrives from an elevation of about 1,500 ft. to that of Coonoor. It also grows on the plains of northern India and may be of some importance if varieties of good quality are established. Miller and Bazore (1945) report as much as 22% carbohydrate in the fruit, mostly sugar, and also a large amount of acid, giving a pH value of 2·7 and in two samples. In volume 3 of the series, the Wealth of India, it is credited with only 6·06% sugar, however. It is said to be a fair source of vitamin A.

Except for the guava, the most important of the fruits in this family in India is the jambolan (*jaman*), *Syzygium* (*Eugenia*) *cuminii* (*jambolana*). This common tree is a native of India or the East Indies, and occurs wild as well as along roads and occasionally in gardens, all over the country. The small, purplish red fruit is extensively eaten, but not very highly valued. It is grown entirely from seed, and exhibits a large amount of variation. There are some types with superior fruit, and selection and vegetative propagation would undoubtedly be useful. Miller and Bazore (1945) mention one type with purple flesh and another with larger fruits, whitish flesh, less astringency, and much pectin, which makes a good mild jelly. It is questionable, however, if commercial production would be profitable, even with the best sorts.

The possibility of using *jaman* seeds as cattle-feed has been investigated at Izatnagar (Anon., 1954 c). The seed was found to be fairly rich in protein and carbohydrate and rich in calcium, but poor in phosphorus. Seeds were collected, washed and dried at a cost of Re. 1 per md. They were gradually added to the concentrate mixture until they constituted 20% of it. They were readily eaten. It was pointed out that the villagers could collect the seed in their spare time at very little cost.

A number of insect pests of the *jaman,* the worst being the leaf-eating caterpillar, *Carea subtilis,* which in South India may defoliate trees, are reported by Anantanaraynan and Venugopal (1952, 1954, 1955).

A whitefly, *Dialeurodes eugeniae,* is said by K. Singh (1949) to infest the trees in practically all parts of India.

The rose apple, *Syzygium* (*Eugenia*) *jambos*, is an ornamental tree with beautiful fruit of comparatively little value. In India it is often called *gulab jaman*. Like the jambolan, it is indigenous to southern Asia, and it prefers a mild climate to the extremes of northern India. Naik (1949) states that it is a popular tree in home gardens up to an elevation of about 4,000 ft., and that while layering is possible, it is commonly propagated from seed, being polyembryonic. Roy (1953) states that the apogamic embryos are nucellar, and that usually only these develop. This may be explained in part by the fact that it is a tetraploid with two extra chromosomes and irregular pairing of chromosomes. The yield is given as about 5 lb. a year. It is eaten fresh and according to Morton and Morton (1946), stewed candied, or made into preserves, jam, syrup, or, with lemon juice, jelly. Another species, *S. javanica*, is grown under similar conditions, according to Naik (1949), and is very prolific. It has 45 chromosomes, one less than *S. jambos* and is even more irregular. The *jaman*, a hexaploid, has 66. Only stray trees of a similar species, *E. malaccensis*, are found in South India. Naik (1949) also mentions *S. zeylanica*, a small tree with edible fruits found in the Western Ghats. Other species with edible fruits are *S. acuminatissima* in the Andamans, *S. formosa* in the eastern Himalayas and Assam, and *S. kurzii* in all of these areas.

A number of other members of the family are fruits of more or less importance. The downy myrtle, *Rhodomyrtus tomentosa*, occurs in the mountains of southern India and is eaten fresh and as jam. The feijoa, *Feijoa sellowiana*, a wild fruit of South America, has recently gained considerable importance in California and the Mediterranean region and Naik (1949) states that it is adapted to the same regions as the pitanga. The variety popularly grown in the hills of Madras has red fruit with bronze markings, although more commonly the fruit is of a dull green colour. Schroeder (1947a) in California found that the feijoa was pollinated by insects, mainly bees, and that most varieties set markedly larger crops when cross-pollinated. One variety showed complete self-fertility.

Chapter XVII

THE PAPAYA

From the botanical, as well as the horticultural point of view, the papaya is an unusually interesting plant. Its importance among the fruits of India is great, and seems to be increasing. It is, perhaps, the easiest fruit to introduce among pepole who have not been in the habit of growing or eating fruit. It is easily propagated and grown, and produces fruits, under tropical conditions, in less than a year and in northern India in about a year and a half. Although the plant may live as long as 15 or 20 years, according to Pope (1930), and reach a height of more than 30 feet, its useful life is generally less than the period required by some fruits to come into bearing.

The papaya comes from tropical America, and may have originated as a cross between some species of *Carica* in Mexico. After the discovery of the western hemisphere by Europeans, it spread rapidly throughout the areas of the world with suitable climatic conditions. It may have spread to the islands of the Pacific at an earlier time, as is indicated by the presence of two Hawaiian names, which were not ordinarily given to plants introduced by Europeans. On the other hand, it is included in a list made in 1831 of plants introduced by one Don Marin. As has been seen, it reached India before van Linschoten, who began his voyage in 1576. Kumar and Abraham (1943) refer to the belief that it was introduced into India from Malacca in the 16th century. It must have become naturalized quickly, for Fairchild (1913) records that it was introduced into China as an Indian plant, as early as 1656. The papaya is one of the most important fruits in Hawaii and is important also in Malaya, Burma, Ceylon, and India. It has not been very successful in California, but does well in southern Florida, Queensland, South Africa, Tanganika, Kenya, and other tropical and subtropical regions.

Statistics regarding papaya production in India are even less satisfactory than those for some of the other fruits, partly because of the very short life of the plantations, so that the acreage varies greatly from year to year. One estimate in 1949 was that there were about 31,000 acres of papayas in the country. This included some States not represented in Table VII. As extension workers have been encouraging the planting of papayas, the present acreage may be considerably more than that in 1949.

Table VII

Estimated Area under Papayas in some parts of India

State	Area in acres	State	Area in acres
Andhra and Madras	1,000	Madhya Bharat	600
Assam	5,500	Madhya Pradesh	434
Bhopal	9	Mysore	100
Bihar	9,700	Saurashtra	1,000
Bombay	2,700	Travancore-Cochin	980
Coorg	50	Uttar Pradesh	672
Hyderabad	419		
		Total	23,173

The name papaya is supposed to be a corruption of the Carib name for the fruit, *ababai*, which has given rise to similar names in other languages. It probably accounts also for the English name papaw, but the latter should not be used, as it is also applied to a minor fruit of the southern United States, *Asimina triloba*. The term tree-melon is also sometimes used and is not entirely unjustified, as the papaya has a certain resemblance to the melon, to which it is distantly related, and is used in much the same way.

The genus *Carica*, to which the papaya belongs, has been included in the family Passifloreae, or even in Cucurbitaceae, but is best considered a member of the small family, Caricaceae, sometimes called Papayaceae. The genus contains about 40 species, but only three are of horticultural importance. Only one of these, *Carica papaya*, is grown in India to any extent. The mountain papaya, *C. candamarcensis*, will stand more frost, and thrives at elevations of from 5,000 to 7,000 ft. in the Nilgiris and Palnis. The trees reach a height of only about eight feet. The fruit is three or four inches long and sub-acid, ripening mainly from May to August. It is grown from seeds. It is also grown in the mountains of Ceylon. Swingle (1947) describes another species, *C. monoica*, which may prove of value in India, although it is at home in the upper Amazon basin where the rainfall is about 150 inches a year, the thermometer never falls below 50°F. and there is no very hot or dry weather. It ripens fruit in 3 or 4 months from planting, and is short-lived. Each flower cluster contains female and male flowers. The cooked leaves, or entire young plants are used as greens, and the fruit when cooked with lemon and sugar is said to resemble stewed peaches or apricots.

Although the papaya is most at home in the tropics, where it produces ripe fruit throughout the year, it also produces large crops of fruit of excellent quality in the milder subtropical areas. In northern India frost is a distinct hazard to young trees, but only occasionally seriously damages trees more than a year old. This is more because the tender growing point of the older trees is above the coldest layers of the air, than because of any increased hardiness. Even on the plains of the Punjab the papaya can be successfully grown, according to Bajwa and Jawanda (1952), though sheltered locations are desirable and protection from frost is essential. For this they recommend grass shelters opening toward the east. Interplanting among tall trees which will provide some protection from frost is also recommended.

In order to grow papayas successfully, it is necessary to have some knowledge of the botany of the plant. Most strains are dioecious, but some have perfect flowers, and there are many variations and graduations. The normal pistillate flower is heavy, yellow, about an inch long, with five large, twisted petals. It is borne singly or in groups of about three, on short stalks arising from the axils of the leaves. The staminate flowers are much smaller, and are borne in long racemes. The rudimentary pistils function in some cases, leading to the development of small fruits, which are of very little value. Thus 'male' trees are sometimes seen bearing a few, or even many, small fruits. Kumar (1946) mentions two trees which were observed to bear only pistillate flowers on long branched inflorescences.

The plants which are regarded as hermaphrodite have short racemes containing usually not more than 15 flowers which vary in size. In some plants they are little larger than staminate flowers, and in some almost as large as pistillate. Most of them are bisexual, but part of the year, or throughout the first year, may be female-sterile. Kumar and others (1945) are referring to plants of this general type when they state that 'Some papaya plants which at the commencement of flowering produce female or bi-sexual flowers, later produce only male flowers.' The fruit tends to be large, but is not infrequently irregular in shape. Storey (1937) describes three distinct types of perfect flowers. These are frequently called pentandra, intermediate, and elongata. The flowers of pentandra resemble pistillate flowers, but have five large stamens, and produce squat fruit with deep grooves and well-defined petal scars. The flowers of elongata have smaller elongate pistils with the petals united part way, forming a collar around the ovary, and produce long narrow fruit which tends to bulge at the apex. The intermediate forms, as the name indicates, cover the transition from pentandra to elongata, with various degrees of sexual development and often malformation of flower and fruit. Agnew (1948) points out that all types may occur on the same tree, but that commonly either pentandra or elongata predominates, or the two may predominate alternately.

All varieties studied by Kumar (1952) contained some hermaphrodite plants. Plants of the pistillate type produced 0·91% pentandra flowers. Fertile hermaphrodite plants had some pistillate flowers, and tended to swing toward maleness in summer and femaleness in winter.

Much has been written about the sex behaviour of the papaya, and particularly about the change of the sex. Kulkarni (1915) reports the change from a purely staminate to a purely pistillate plant, in eight stages, and others have made similar statements. It is frequently not clear, however, whether the change is from a typical staminate plant, or from one of the hermaphrodite type, in which, as has been said, the flowers do not always function. It seems to be very rarely that a plant with the typical long, branched inflorescence of the staminate type changes to a typical pistillate plant.

More important than occasional changes in sex, is the claim, frequently made, that it is possible to bring about such a change at will. The most common method advocated is the cutting off of the top of the plant, but injury to the root is also suggested. Mallik and Singh (1952) report that the decapitation of male plants produced some females, but this happened so seldom as to be of no practical value. If such a method proved uniformly effective, it would be of great value, but unfortunately, it is probably never successful. The tops of a large number of typical staminate plants were removed over a period of several years, at the Allahabad Agricultural Institute, without a single one changing sex. Kulkarni (1915) and Pope (1930) report similar experience. The basis of the common claim may be the fact that a hermaphrodite plant which has been barren the first season, begins to bear after an injury. Whether the injury causes the change, or merely happens to precede, it is not certain.

If sex cannot be changed, at least with any regularity, it would be highly desirable to find some method of selecting the seeds which will produce female plants, or failing that, of determining the sex of the plants before they are set in the orchard. Claims of such methods are made from time to time. It is believed by some that seed from one part of the fruit is more likely to produce female plants than that from another, but careful experiments do not indicate any difference. Kumar (1951) reports that in the Washington strain there is some evidence that seeds of a deeper brown produce a somewhat higher proportion of pistillate and hermaphrodite plants than do those of lighter colour. Much more common is the idea that the more vigorous seedlings are largely male. Thus Head (1932) states that in his own experiments he found that a large proportion of the vigorous plants were male, while if the less vigorous plants were set out, there might be no more males than were desirable for pollination, one in twenty or more. Cheema and Dani (1930) also state that the vigorously growing plants are generally males. On the other hand, Pope (1930) states, 'The writer has not learned of a single substantiated instance of anyone's being able to determine the sex of young seedling papayas previous to the appearance of the inflorescence.' Mallik and Singh (1952) also found no connection between the vigour of the seedling and their sex. A claim once made that the sex of a young plant could be determined by observing the way a piece of iron suspended over it swings has also been found unjustified. At the Agricultural Institute, Allahabad, 1,824 seedlings were planted in 1935, of which 909 proved to be males and 915 females. Of 153 which were noticeably vigorous when planted, 80 turned out to be males and 73 females. At the same time, 312 plants which seemed lacking in vigour yielded 165 males and 147 females. This lends no support to the popular theory, which may be explained by the fact, observed at the Institute, that the staminate flowers tend to appear earlier than the pistillate. Also it is observed that staminate plants tend to grow somewhat taller than pistillate ones, probably because they do not have fruits to compete with vegetative growth for the available food material.

There have been chemical tests used to distinguish male and female plants in some species, but with only partial success, and these tests seem not to have been applied to the papaya. This latter is a promising field of research.

It has been seen that in the experiment at Allahabad, approximately half of the plants were of each sex. This seems to be true of most strains, but some, including the Honey Dew variety, are said to produce more females. This may account for the observation of Pope (1930) that in eight years' work with the dioecious type, considerably more pistillate than staminate plants were found. Naik (1949) states that at Kallar about 70% of the plants of the Burliar Long variety are pistillate. It is possible that in these cases some of the 'females' are hermaphrodite, for Storey (1953) states that with controlled pollination of male and female types, there are equal numbers of both in the offspring. When a female is pollinated with pollen from a hermaphrodite, the offspring are again equally divided. When a hermaphrodite is self-pollinated or crossed with another hermaphrodite, the offspring are in the proportion of one female to two hermaphrodite. Selfing or crossing 'males' results in one female to two males. The cross between male and hermaphrodite results in equal numbers of male, hermaphrodite, and female plants. The males and hermaphrodite are enforced sex heterozygotes and the combination of dominants is lethal, so 25% of the seed is not viable.

There is considerable literature on the various aspects of sex in the papaya, and much of this has been reviewed by Narasimham (1949). Storey (1953) deals thoroughly with the genetics of the papaya.

Pollination and Breeding

Cross-pollination is required in the dioecious type, and is common in the hermaphrodite type also, although in the latter case, good fruit may be produced by self-pollination. Perfectly formed fruit sometimes occurs without seed, but even in such cases the stimulation of pollination seems to be required. Agnew (1948) observed occasional trees with well-developed fruit containing not more than two seeds and found evidence that this was due to embryo abortion. He thought this might be heritable. Strains with few or no seeds are also reported in India. When flowers are bagged to prevent pollination, the fruit may fail to set, or it may be very small, and of poor quality. It is also frequently noticed that in parts of the fruit where the seeds are plentiful the pulp is likely to be thicker than where they are missing. Prest (1955b) states that within the limits of the strain, the more seeds, the larger will be the fruit.

It is possible to induce parthenocarpy, and Ordonyo (1951) reports success with an ether-extract of maize pollen, 10 and 50 ppm of indole-butyric acid, or 50-90 ppm of naphthaleneacetic acid. The resulting fruit was inferior to the normal except in the case of 80 ppm of NAA, which produced slightly larger fruit.

There seems to be no clear evidence as to how far the pollen can be carried. Pollination seems to be effected by insects, and in Florida it is believed that the hawk moth is probably the principal agent. Prest (1955b), on the other hand, states that pollination is accomplished by air currents. Pope (1930) mentions cross-pollination in trees one-eighth of a mile apart. Hofmeyr (1936) states that a pistillate tree growing 15 miles from the nearest staminate tree flowered profusely, but did not bear any fruit. Where the dividing line between these two distances is, remains to be discovered, and it will probably vary under different conditions. The question of the proportion of male trees necessary to insure good pollination is of more practical importance, but here again no definite answer can be given. Hofmeyr (1936) says "At least 10% of trees in a grove must be male trees to ensure adequate pollination." Head has been quoted as indicating that half this precentage would be sufficient, and there are indications that two or three trees per acre may be enough. Wolfe and Lynch (1940) recommend planting about 4% of males, but the number required may vary with local conditions and most growers prefer to have a higher percentage in order to assure the best quality, which results from full pollination. Defective pollination is said to be one of the chief cultural problems in central and southern Queensland (Agnew, 1948). It was observed that the staminate trees produced large amounts of pollen except for occasional periods of 2 to 3 weeks, when pollen was absent. There were two such periods in 1940-41. Prest (1955b) says that these periods may be in the winter, when it is too cold for the production of pollen or when there is a wide difference between day and night temperatures.

The papayas commonly found on the market vary greatly in size, shape, colour of skin, colour of pulp, thickness of pulp, texture and flavour. Much can be done by selection and breeding to improve the quality of the fruit. If seed is saved only from fruit with desirable characteristics, the average quality gradually improves. But this is like trying to improve a dairy herd by selecting calves of the better cows, without reference to the bull used. Controlled pollination is necessary for the best results. Some breeders prefer to work with hermaphrodite types, and some with the dioecious. There are obvious advantage in the hermaphrodites, if a satisfactory strain can be developed. One can then be sure that practically all trees will bear fruit, and the need for male trees vanishes. The fruit tends to be cylindrical with thick flesh, and is preferred for shipping long distances. Storey (1953) states that the leading variety in Hawaii, the Solo, was originally highly variable, producing unisexual and hermaphrodite flowers, and that by self-pollination or crossing of hermaphrodites, it has become fairly uniform, producing pistillate and hermaphrodite flowers. He says that since genetical studies were started in 1936, the yield of marketable papayas per acre in Hawaii has increased 114 per cent. He adds that it now seems fairly simple to convert any dioecious variety to such gynodioecism by pollinating pistillate flowers with pollen from a good hermaphrodite, followed by backcrossing until the desired varietal characteristics have been restored.

More uniformity of size and shape seems to be possible in the dioecious types. Here the most promising method seems to be pure line breeding, using pollen from full brothers, and selecting for the desired characteristics. This decreases the vigour of the strain, and for commercial orchards seed should be used resulting from the crossing of two pure lines. This is similar to the method used very successfully with maize, and as in that case, there is also evidence of hybrid vigour in the papayas. Marloth (1954) states that hybrid plantings in South Africa already show considerable improvement in yield and quality, but that further inbreeding is necessary.

In either case, controlled breeding involves the necessity of bagging the flowers before they open, and with the dioecious ones, pollinating them by hand. This requires a good deal of time, but only an extremely small percentage of the flowers need to be so treated. The bulk of the orchard may be left to open pollination, but seeds should be saved only from fruits which have been artificially pollinated. After some generations of controlled breeding, it may be found that fairly satisfactory results may be secured from open pollination. The commercial grower may, however, prefer to leave the production of seed to professional breeders.

Another possible method of securing improved strains of the papaya is the use of colchicine or similar substances which cause changes by increasing the number of chromosomes. Hofmeyr (1941) applied 0·06 to 0·1% colchicine solution to the terminal buds of seedling papayas, causing swelling and a temporary retarding of growth. Out of 64 seedlings treated, 14 showed signs of having the number of chromosomes doubled, and this proved true in the case of two plants studied. The trees were more vigorous, and the fruit was of an unusual shape, being wider than long and the flesh was half an inch thicker than usual. The commercial value of the new type was considered questionable. Even less promising results were secured by R. N. Singh (1955) at Saharanpur. Of 150 seedlings treated, three males and three females became tetraploids. They were dwarfed, with leathery dark green leaves and few small, round, thick-fleshed fruits. They were almost completely male—and female—sterile, and of the few seeds formed, only 28·5% contained normal embryos. Of six seeds sown, three germinated but only one plant survived.

Propagation

Vegetative propagation would seem to offer a means of avoiding the difficulty arising from the dioecious nature of the common types, and of standardizing the quality. Both grafting and the growth of cuttings are possible. Yet these methods are almost universally condemned as yielding unsatisfactory plants. Pope (1930) found that vegetatively propagated plants failed to reproduce the varietal characteristics, and in some cases were as variable as seedlings. Cuttings ordinarily develop more slowly than seedlings, and both cuttings and grafted plants seem to lack in vigour and to bear poorer fruits than their parents. It has been generally noted that the size and quality of the fruits deteriorate as the plants become old. It would seem that senility is passed on to the vegetatively propagated plants. The third or fourth generation is commonly of practically no value.

More promising results have been reported by Traub and Marshall (1936), using a solar propagating frame or a greenhouse. They secured a high percentage of success within a month whereas Pope had reported that cuttings rooted in from 2 to 5 months. The temperature of the soil was kept about 85 or 90° F., with the air somewhat cooler. Best results were secured with entire branch cuttings with the basal swelling attached. In one experiment, treatment with indole-acetic acid increased the percentage of cuttings which formed roots. At the time of the report, many of the plants had fruited, having behaved like seedlings in every way except that they came into bearing sooner. Sen Gupta and Chattopadhaya (1954) report that lateral branches all produced roots in about a month when treated with 3 or 5% indolebutyric acid. No roots were formed in the control, or with treatment with NAA.

Grafting may be done with the young seedlings, or after they have flowered. In the former, either cleft or whip grafting may be used, the seedling being a fourth to a half inch in diameter. Scions should be branches of about the same size, from good plants. In larger plants, cleft or saddle grafting may be used. It should be remembered, however, that grafting is not recommended.

For the present, at least, seedling plants should undoubtedly be used. This involves no difficulty, but some care is necessary to secure strong stocky plants. Although Grant and Williams (1936) recommend sowing the seeds in the permanent positions, four or five seeds at a place, planting in seed-beds is generally preferred. Well-prepared beds, providing good drainage and plenty of plant food, should be used. The time of sowing is of importance. The seed may be planted as soon as it is taken from the mature fruit, or it may be dried and used later with very little loss of viability. Mehta and Kulkarni (1912) mention one case in which seed sown in August germinated when conditions became favourable the following June. Koyamu (1951), however, reports that in Madras it is customary to sow the seeds immediately, as it is believed that they lose their viability on storage. But in one case seeds of the Washington variety germinated poorly when sowed immediately. Seeds dried in the shade and stored for three months gave a germination of 28% compared with 6% when sown fresh. Rubbing the seeds with ashes before drying increased the germination to 55%, and soaking them in cow's urine brought this up to 67%, and the urine of pregnant cows to 76%. Under favourable conditions, the seedlings are ready to transplant to the field in a month or six weeks. The seeds should be planted at such a time that they will be ready for transplanting when desired.

While Head (1932) recommenus planting in February in order to have plants ready to plant out early in the monsoon, this is entirely too early under most conditions. Seed planted early in June in Uttar Pradesh will ordinarily be ready by the time the rains are well established. R. S. Singh and Singh (1952) recommend sowing the seed in February or March and planting in the field in April where there are good facilities for irrigation and for protecting the plants from the hot wind. Otherwise, they suggest sowing in June and setting out in July. Bajwa and Jawanda (1952) recommend sowing from February to April and transplanting after two or three months. Sowing in the spring has the advantage that the plants are comparatively tall when the first frost occurs, and is satisfactory if the plants grow rapidly and produce a crop in the first year. If seed is sown at the beginning of the monsoon, the seedlings may ordinarily be set out by the middle of the season, and become of good size for the first crop, the winter of the following year. Seeds planted before the rains begin require more attention than those planted later, and if the rains are late, the seedlings become larger than is desirable before they can be set out. If planting is delayed until the end of the rains, the seedlings will still be very small when the weather in north India becomes cool, and very little growth takes place until the following spring. In Bombay, Cheema and Dani (1930) state that seed can be safely planted until October or November.

The time of planting is important as it influences both the time of bearing and the height of the plant when it begins to bear, and thus the height throughout the bearing life. As it is more difficult and expensive to harvest the fruit when they can no longer be reached from the ground, it is desirable to have the first fruit borne as close to the ground as possible. There are some varieties which are reputed to be dwarf and to bear low on the stem, but Gandhi (1947) believes that dwarfness is caused by external factors rather than heredity. Close planting undoubtedly results in comparatively tall, slender plants, and the time of planting is also a factor, especially under conditions under which fruiting is restricted to part of the year. Even in the Poona district, where the first crop is matured within 12 months of planting, irrespective of the season, he found that the Washington variety planted in August fruited at a height of 4 ft. on the trunk; planted in December, at 2 ft. 4 in.; and planted in March, at 3 ft. 3 in. Seedlings raised in their permanent positions, or transplanted to them in the early spring in northern India should be ready to flower in the rainy season and mature their first crop in the following winter. They would probably bear lower on the stem than those transplanted during the rains, but they would also require much more attention during the hot dry weather.

The seed should be planted about half an inch deep, and the soil should be kept moist. The bed should be protected from the hot sun and from heavy rain, until germination is complete. Either the seed should be placed about six inches apart, or the small seedlings should be transplanted to this distance before crowding begins. If crowding is allowed, the plants become tall and slender, and are then much more likely to suffer when set out in the orchard. Some prefer to transplant the small seedlings into post, but this is cumbersome if large numbers are involved.

Culture

The papaya is normally a rapidly growing plant, bearing large amounts of fruit, and requiring plenty of nutrients. It can be grown on comparatively poor soil, provided an abundance of manure is used. Oppenheimer (1947) says that in Palestine the papaya does well on soils of very high lime content, and when irrigated with alkaline water. Good drainage is very important, and for this reason heavy soils are to be avoided. Even an inch of water standing around the trees for a few hours is likely to kill them. If the drainage is good, depth of soil is not so important as with most fruits, but Naik (1949) says it does best on rich loams which are uniform to a depth of 6 ft.

The distance from plant to plant varies from about 3 to 12 ft. The problem is simpler if hermaphrodite types are grown, as only one plant is put at a place. With the dioecious type it is possible to plant three or four seedlings 6—12 in. apart and leave only one after they have flowered, but it may be more economical to leave two plants if there are two good females. This would justify a somewhat greater distance between places. Extremely close planting is recommended by Thorold (1949) under conditions where diseases make it unprofitable to keep a plantation for more than 10 months of bearing. He favours setting the plants only 3 ft. apart in each direction although he found that with fairly heavy manuring, twice that distance gave a better yield. He favours close planting because it saves cultivation, as no weeds grow after the first months, and because the loss of some of the plants from disease is not so serious.

It is probably not advisable to keep trees 3 ft. apart for more than one crop, but it might be economical to plant at that distance, remove most of the males, and after the first crop thin to a minimum spacing of 6 ft. Or three plants may be set at a place, 5 ft. apart and thinned to a single plant. This will undoubtedly result in less fruit per tree than 10-ft. spacing, but might be economical because of the larger number of plants per acre. With close planting more manure and water will be necessary. It is unlikely to be economical to leave more than 10 ft. between plants unless they are encouraged to branch, and there is no evidence that this is a wise procedure. Another possibility is to have rows 10 ft. apart, which will allow bullock cultivation, with single trees placed about 3 ft. apart in the row, or several at 5 ft.

As with other fruits, the digging of large holes is commonly advocated, Head (1934) recommending holes four feet in diameter, dug two months before the plants are set out. These are to be filled to within six inches of the top with a mixture of one part manure to three of soil, just before planting. It has been seen, however that excellent growth results from planting in holes just large enough to receive the ball of earth around the roots, in good soil. The use of farmyard manure and other fertilizers in the pit is also commonly suggested, and may be desirable on poor soil.

The young plants may be transplanted at any size up to a height of four or five feet, but the best height is not more than one foot. Gandhi (1947) emphasizes the desirability of transplanting with the least possible damage to the fibrous roots, and so favours transplanting at a height of 6 to 9 inches. If conditions are not favourable for setting out in the field when this height is reached he says the plants should be transplanted to another place in the nursery, and that in no case should they be more than a foot tall when set in the field. Transplanting more than once tends to produce stocky plants and is said to be common practice in spring planting in Bombay. If the plants are stocky, a reasonably large ball of earth is taken with them, and they are carefully handled, little wilting should occur. It is well to remove a few of the lower leaves, however, and if conditions are not satisfactory, it may be desirable to remove all of the large leaves. Cloudy weather is best for the operation. The plants should be placed no lower in the soil than they have been in the nursery. If a few inches of the stem is buried, it is very likely to decay.

In order to secure a stand with a large percentage of female trees, it is well to plant several seedlings at one place if these are of the dioecious type. If only one plant is put at a place, about half of the plants, being males, will have to be removed, and their places filled by others, which, in half the cases will also be males, and so on. If three plants are set together, about 87% of the places should contain at least one female. If the plants are set about six inches apart, and the others are cut out as soon as one produces pistillate flowers, little damage is done to the plant which remains. The staminate plants should be removed as soon as they flower, except where all in one place prove to be staminate, when one may be left. It is also possible to grow some plants in large pots or keep them well spaced in a nursery, and use these to fill up vacancies where all the plants in a hole turn out to be males. A few male plants should, of course, be retained, to provide for pollination.

Cultivation is much the same as for other fruits, but as the papaya has many shallow roots, ploughing, if done at all, should not be deep, and should not come very close to the plants. Especially with close planting, cultivation may be restricted to hoeing to control weeds. Intercropping is normally limited to the first months of a plantation, though Cheema and others (1954) state that when the trees are at least a year old beans may be trained up the stem, but stopped below the fruit, with profit.

Irrigation is necessary, and Cheema and others (1954) recommend watering once in 8—10 days in winter and in 6 days in summer, in the Deccan, with more frequent irrigation on the alluvial soils of Gujerat. This seems excessive, and is certainly more than is needed in northern India. Awada and Ikeda (1953) report that the increase in yield from heavy irrigation of hermaphrodite papayas in Hawaii was not statistically significant and resulted from an increase in carpellodic but not of marketable fruit. Cheema and Dani (1930) report healthier trees, flowering a month earlier, and bearing larger fruits, when irrigated by the ring system, as compared with the basin system. Unless the soil is unusually rich, rather heavy manuring is necessary. Cheema and others (1954) recommend 40 lb. of farmyard manure in the pit at planting, 80—100 lb. 4 or 5 months later, and as much when a year old. Roy (1952) says that in a trial at Sabour, ammonium sulphate gave better results than manure or oilcake, but an earlier application of manure or cake might have been as good, or perhaps better, for he says that applying phosphate and potash along with nitrogen significantly improved the yield, though not the growth of the trees. This is probably sound advice.

In tropical climates, the papaya bears throughout the year, but in northern India the first fruit ripens about December, and the crop is practically finished in five months. There is one variety or strain which is said to ripen as early as September, but it is not common. The fruit should be left on the tree until fully mature, but unless picked before it begins to get soft, it is difficult to protect it from birds, and to market it without spoilage. In many varieties, the fruit shows some yellow colour when mature, but some remain green in colour even when fully ready for eating. When the latex ceases to be milky and becomes watery, the fruit may be considered ready for harvest. Even when picked while the latex is still milky, good quality is said to be secured by using ethylene to ripen the fruit. Overnight treatment with one part of ethylene in 5,000 is sufficient, but as the gas enters the cavity of the fruit, aeration for 24 hours is necessary. The fruit should then be consumed within two or three days. After harvesting, fruit to be consumed locally should be stored in a single layer in straw until mellow. If intended for a distant market, it should be packed in soft material and shipped while still firm. Wrapping each fruit in paper, and placing each in an individual compartment in the basket or box will afford further protection. A suitable case and packing methods used in Queensland have been described (Anon., 1944). From Hawaii, papayas have been successfully shipped to continental America in cold storage. In Trinidad, however, cold storage was not very successful. It proved possible to store fully coloured firm fruit at 45° F. for two weeks in some cases but not in others, while less mature fruit was not stored successfully at any temperature. In the cold storage experiments in Poona, the papaya was found to chill at 68° F.

Papayas of the dioecious type frequently set such a heavy crop that the fruits are crowded and poorly shaped. Thinning when the fruits are small results in larger, well-formed fruit, but in a decrease in the total yield. Market conditions will determine whether this is an advantage or not. There is perhaps more need of thinning in the older trees, where growth is less vigorous, the internodes are shorter, and the fruits closer together. But the cost of thinning is greater on these taller trees.

Most strains of papaya tend to grow as a single stem, until the plant is several years old, when some branching may occur. It is possible to force branching of young plants by removing the terminal bud, and some persons prefer to do so. They thus secure several branches along which the fruit is borne, and perhaps a larger number of fruits. But unless the plants are set farther apart, the branches interfere with cultivation and the practice is not to be recommended. On the other hand, in the strains which tend to branch naturally, it is probably desirable to prune off the branches, at least high enough to allow free cultivation.

As the crop is grown almost entirely from seed, varieties are not very well defined. In northern India no named varieties are of much importance. Varieties with medium-sized fruit are generally preferred to those with very large fruit, the flavour of which is regarded as inferior. In Bombay the Washington variety, with dark red petioles and yellow flowers, is the most popular. It has medium-sized fruits of excellent sweetness and flavour. A local type, known as Gujarat, with large round fruits, also does well. Other varieties, known by such place names as Singapore, Hawaii, and Ceylon, are also mentioned. Naik (1949) says that the Washington and Honey Dew varieties are popular in South India, and that they breed fairly true to type. A famous variety in Hawaii, called Solo is said to require a uniformly warm moist climate, so is not likely to be successful in most parts of India.

Because the quality of the fruit decreases as the plants become old, harvesting becomes more difficult as the plants grow very tall, and some of the plants are likely to be lost by accident and disease, it is well to keep the plants only a few years. Grant and Williams recommend keeping the plants five or six years, and planting seed between the trees in the fifth year. More commonly, about three crops are taken from the plants before they are removed. Cheema and Dani mention the possibility of renewing the plants for another year by cutting back the main stem and allowing several branches to grow, but do not recommend this procedure. In Florida, some growers cut off the trees 1½ or 2 feet from the ground, allow the shoots to grow until 2 or 3 feet tall, and then remove all but one which should be staked. This process is repeated three times, allowing a total of four crops before the trees are removed. It is claimed that this results in larger fruits, as well as avoiding the expense of harvesting from tall trees. It is probably unwise to replant in the shade of the old plants, but better to move the plantation and grow some other crop in the field for a year or more before putting in papayas again. Some growers prefer to divide the plantation into several sections, replanting one each year.

Pests

The absence of any serious pest or disease is given by Cheema and Dani (1930) as one reason why the cultivation of the papaya was increasing in Bombay. Unfortunately diseases are now a serious problem, but it remains true that insects are not. None of the Indian fruit flies has an ovipositor long enough to thrust its eggs inside the fruit. In Bombay the caterpillar of *Dasyses rugosellus* sometimes bores in the stem, and should be cut out, and wound should be treated with tar. The red spider mite is more serious, according to Cheema and others (1954), causing the leaves to turn yellow and the fruit to become roughened and brownish. Dusting with sulphur or spraying with lime-sulphur is said to control the mites. Much more difficult is the control of root-knot nematodes, which Mallik and Choudhury (1955) report at Sabour. Yellowing and curling of the leaves and ultimately death result from a severe attack. Soil fumigation, which will kill nematodes, is now too expensive to be recommended, so soil which is badly infested should not be used for papaya or any other highly susceptible plant.

Several diseases cause damage to papaya plantations in India and elsewhere. One of the most common is called stem rot, foot rot, or collar rot, and may cause such severe losses as to lead to the abandoning of papaya growing.

The stem is affected near the ground, occasionally as high as five feet. The first symptoms, a water-soaked appearance and softness, often escape notice. Later the bark cracks, frequently a foul-smelling liquid oozes out, and the tissue breaks down rapidly. The lesion ordinarily extends rapidly up and down the stem, but may also girdle the plant and cause it to fall. The disease proceeds rapidly during the rainy season, and is generally checked by the return of dry weather. It is caused by *Pythium aphanidermatum*, a soil-dwelling fungus. Good drainage may help to avoid infection. That infection may also be avoided by treatment with Bordeaux mixture is indicated by Nirvan (1953 a). He reports an experiment at Saharanpur in which 120 trees selected at random were sprayed with 6-6-50 Bordeaux; two inches of soil were removed from around the base of the plant and the stem and exposed soil were drenched before the soil was returned. In the first year there were three treatments at 20-day intervals, beginning with the first rain in July. In the second year a sticker was added to the spray and there were only two applications. In the first year the incidence of the disease was 6% in the treated and 20% in the untreated, and in the second year, 2·5% and 22·5%. Other fungi, bacteria, and insects may cause secondary infections. If the early symptoms are noted, Mittra, in Head's bulletin (1932) recommends that the infected area be cut out, the surface painted with an antiseptic solution, such as a 4 or 5% solution of lysol, or a 50% solution of crude carbolic acid, and then protected with coal tar. In more advanced cases, the plant should be removed and destroyed, and its place allowed to remain vacant for some time.

Root rots have caused great damage to papaya plantations in Allahabad in some years. They have sometimes killed so many trees as to make it impracticable to secure more than one or two crops from a planting. Vestal (1947) found *Pythium aphanidermatum*, *Rhizoctonia solani*, and a species of *Fusarium* almost constantly associated with this disease. Although the incidence varies from year to year, he could find no connection between it and the weather. Root rots also occur in other countries, and probably elsewhere in India. No method of control has been discovered, although in similar diseases very heavy manuring has some-times proved effective in increasing the population of other fungi in the soil and decreasing that of the pathogens. Avoiding damage to the roots in cultivation, and perhaps the sowing of the seed direct in the field are other measures which may help.

The same species of *Pythium* and *Rhizoctonia* cause the death of seeds and of seedlings before or after they emerge from the soil, according to B. Singh and Paharia (1952), who found from 10 to 65% damage near Kanpur. Treatment of the seed with such organic fungicides as Ceresan and Agrosan GN was fairly effective, but better control was achieved by treating the soil with 2·5% formaldehyde solution or dust, which involves covering it for 48 hours and an interval of at least 15 days before sowing.

Anthracnose, caused by species of *Gloeosporium* or *Colletotrichum* has been reported by Gammie and Patwardhan (1929) and Cheema and Dani (1930) in Bombay, by Naik (1949) and others in Madras, and by Chowdhury and Majid (1954) in Assam.

It has occasionally occurred in Allahabad, and is probably found in other sections also. It may affect the fruit while it is green on the tree, or when ripe. A light yellow patch appears on the side exposed to the sun, which softens, turns brown and extends to half the fruit. Later black acervuli in concentric rings, and pinkish pustules appear. Control may be secured by spraying with Burgundy mixture, and the destruction of the affected fruits and leaf stalks. Akemine and Arisumi (1953) report that if the fruit is not sprayed on the tree, the incidence of decay in storage may be materially reduced by putting the fruit in water held at 110-120° F. for 20 minutes. This improved the appearance without much effect on the rate of ripening, aroma, or taste.

A disease of considerable local importance in the North Cachar Hills of Assam, but not known to occur elsewhere is a leaf-spot reported by Chowdhury (1944). It is prevalent from September to January and produces spots which are almost white in the centre and yellowish or brownish at the margins. Later the tissue falls out, leaving shot-holes. The organism causing the disease is a new species for which the author, who publishes a technical description proposes the name *Phyllosticta sulata*. It seems to live from one season to the next on plant debris in the soil. The spores are disseminated by the wind. It may be prevented by spraying the plants with 2-2-50 Bordeaux mixture or 4 lb. of cuprous oxide in 100 gal. of water late in August and in mid-September and mid-October, repeating immediately if a heavy shower falls soon after spraying

Chowdhury (1950 a) also reports a fruit rot appearing on half-grown fruits and affecting from 10 to 15% of the papaya fruits in Assam. It has also been reported from other countries, but not from other parts of India. It is caused by the fungus *Ascochyta caricae*, which, under controlled conditions was found to spread most rapidly at 30° C. (86° F.) and 100% humidity. It was controlled by spraying with 2-2-50 Bordeaux mixture at intervals of 21 to 30 days, so as to keep the fruits thoroughly covered from the time of setting.

Severe damage to papaya seedlings at Poona by a powdery mildew is reported by Chiddarwar (1955). It is caused by a species which seems to be new, and for which the name *oidium indicum* is proposed.

Several virus diseases of the papaya have been reported, at least two of them in India. One, commonly known as leaf curl, is often seen in northern India. The young leaves remain small and are curdled and crinkled, the plant is dwarfed, and the fruit does not develop properly. The trees do not die quickly, but they are not known to recover. Sen and others (1945) established the virus nature of the disease by inoculating healthy seedlings with the juice of diseased plants. It has been observed that the disease is more common where drainage is poor, and they found that many plants growing in pots resting on the ground in such a way as to interfere with drainage developed the disease without inoculation, while similar plants in pots set on broken crocks did not. Seedlings grown from seed from diseased fruit were healthy, as is generally true in the case of virus diseases. They did not identify the vector, but Martorell and Adsuar (1952) state that in the Antilles and Florida the virus is carried by the leaf-hopper, *Empoasca papayae*, and perhaps by *E. dilitara*.

Capoor and Varma (1948) discuss a very different virus disease discovered on papaya plants in Bombay and Poona in 1947, the vector of which seems to be an aphid. In this case the symptoms are first dot-like necrotic spots all over the lamina. Later, blister-like patches of green tissue are found distributed indiscriminately over the yellowish green lamina, the petiole is greatly reduced, the lamina is reduced and occasionally malformed, water-soaked areas appear on the stem and petioles, the top leaves assume an upright position, and the fruits are few and small. As the disease was spreading rapidly, vigorous eradication by destroying all diseased plants was called for. Chowdhury and Majid (1954) report this or a very similar mosaic disease in Assam, and state that several species of aphids are vectors. A disease with some similar symptoms appeared in Allahabad about 1953 and has spread very rapidly. If a plant is attacked before it starts flowering, it is likely to be useless, but in older trees the damage seems rather slight. This may be the same as the mosaic disease reported by Mishra and Jha (1955) to be increasingly destructive in Bihar.

Papaya fruits may be somewhat disfigured by an alga, *Cephaleuros mycoidea* which is common in Uttar Pradesh, according to Garg (1951). As no other damage is done, control is probably not necessary.

Larger pests are frequently more troublesome than the insects and diseases. Birds and bats are attracted by the fruit as it ripens, and have to be scared away, or the fruits may be protected by netting or sackcloth. As crows frequently perch on dead or dying petioles emerging from the lower part of the bearing portion of the stem, or just below it, their attack can be decreased by removing these petioles. Civet cats sometimes climb up and eat fruit, but may be kept away by tying a bundle of thorns around the stem. The stems of young plants are sometimes cut off by porcupines.

The yield of papayas varies tremendously, depending largely on the fertility of the soil and other cultural conditions, but also on the variety. Naik (1949) says that in Madras the yield commonly ranges from 30 to 150 fruits per tree, each weighing from 1 to 16 lb. He thinks the average yield per acre may be between 30,000 and 60,000 lb. He mentions one acre at Hessarghatta which produced in a year 13,000 fruits weighing 43,500 lb. Assuming 400 bearing trees per acre, this would be an average of only 32 fruits per tree. The Washington variety averaged 4·1 and the Honey Dew 3·3 lb per fruit. Cheema and Dani (1930) report an average of 27 fruits per plant, weighing 2·2 lb. each. Bajwa and Jawanda (1952) consider a crop of 15 to 25 fruits, weighing about 1·5 lb. each satisfactory in the Punjab. Experience at Allahabad suggests that a yield of less than 80 lb. per tree should be considered unsatisfactory, but that heavy manuring is needed to secure such crops. Agnew (1951) reports an average yield in Queensland of 30 fruits weighing 90 lb. per tree, and as the trees are 8 ft. apart, if 90% bear, this would mean about 24 tons per acre. Wolfe and Lynch (1940) state that in Florida trees ordinarily bear about 75 to 150 lb. each in from 12 to 18 months, while some trees bear as much as 300 lb. Simmonds (1946) refers to a report of up to 48 tons per acre produced in Trinidad.

Even without the exceedingly high yields reported by some of these authors, papaya cultivation is quite profitable. In growing the crop referred to above, Cheema and Dani (1930) state that an intercrop of vegetables paid all costs during the first year, and that in the second and third there was a net profit of Rs. 1,078 per acre. Sankaram (1942) reports that at the very low price of Rs. 2 per 100 fruits, the crop was worth Rs. 480 an acre in the first year and Rs. 400 in the second, with the cost of cultivation about Rs. 150 and Rs. 110 respectively. No records of yield at the Agricultural Institute, Allahabad, are available, but at the prices which prevailed until about 1953, a good crop brought about Rs. 4,000 per acre on the trees, or Rs. 6,000 at wholesale prices. This meant prices higher than could be justified, and if the fall in price since that time represents increased production rather than a decrease in purchasing power, it is to be welcomed. However, because of the hazard of loss by frost or disease, it is to be expected that a good crop should bring more than one of a safer fruit.

Kumar (1952) gives figures based on one acre at the Fruit Research Station, Saharanpur and four acres privately owned. Costs per acre for four years were: raising papayas, Rs. 2,612·5; papain production, Rs. 6,355·5; '*petha*' production, Rs. 48,370; growing an intercrop, Rs. 221. The yield is given as 1,150 md. (42·1 tons) of fruit and 390 lb. of papain. The sale value is given as Rs. 426 for the intercrop, and Rs. 13,250 for the fruit; or, if papain is made, Rs. 13,650 for it and Rs. 7,430 for the scarred fruit; or, if '*petha*' is made instead of selling the fruit, Rs. 69,000 for it. The '*petha*' is the candied immature fruit, and it is assumed that it would sell at 12 annas a pound, half of the price for ordinary *petha*. On this basis, the aggregate profit for four years would be Rs. 25,517·8 per acre if papain and '*petha*' are produced; Rs. 12,317·8 if papain is made and the scarred fruit sold, and Rs. 10,843·3 if the unscarred fruit is sold. The yield of '*petha*' is given as 350 md. per acre, and it is very questionable if the produce of many acres could be sold in this way at a profitable price.

The papaya is pre-eminently a dessert fruit, being eaten when fully ripe, just as it is, or with salt, pepper, sugar, or lime juice. The seeds are also eaten by some for their sprightly flavour, or for their reputed medicinal value. The unripe fruit is used as a vegetable. It can also be made into pickles similar to those made from melons. Preserves of various kinds and marmalade can be made from the ripe fruit, but are rather lacking in character. The fruit is also candied. In the United States considerable quantities are used in making soft drinks either still or carbonated, generally with the addition of citric acid and sugar. Ochse (1931) reports that even the young leaves are eaten in Java, as well as the unripe fruits. The papaya is a very wholesome fruit, and Aykroyd (1951) ranks it second only to the mango as source of the precursor of vitamin A. While this vitamin is generally associated with carotene, the yellow pigment in the papaya is not this but caricaxanthin. Miller and Bazore (1945) report 2,500 international units of this vitamin, as compared with 5,500 in the mango and 1,200 in a culinary banana. They found 84 mg. of ascorbic acid per 100 g., this increasing as the fruit ripens. It proved a poor source of thiamine, but a good source of calcium and other minerals. Analyses of the fruit vary considerably. Thompson (1914) reported total solids varying from 10·59 to 14·41% and sugars from 8·02 to 11·12, in Hawaii. Stahl (1935) in Florida found total solids from 8·4 to 10·1% and sugars from 5·20 to 6·28. Malan (1953) in South Africa reports 12·5% total solids and 10% sugars.

Mature fruit can be stored three or four weeks at 40-50° F., according to Cheema and others (1954), and has been shipped from India to England in good condition.

King and others (1951) report the manufacture of a powder rich in minerals, protein, fat, pectin, and carbohydrate which is used in a number of foods. The seeds are removed and the whole ripe fruit is sliced and dried at temperatures not above 150° F. to a moisture content of 6%. It is then ground so as to pass through a 20-mesh screen. The loss of ascorbic acid is minimized by drying under a vacuum, but is not great with air drying.

Papain

When the skin of an unripe papaya is broken, a white latex comes out, which contains a large amount of an enzyme, papain, which is able to digest protein. It is very similar to the animal enzyme, pepsin. Use is made of this faculty in a number of ways. Tough meat may be rubbed with a slice of green papaya, or cooked with it, and is said to be made more tender in this way. Skin blemishes are also said to vanish when treated with the enzyme. M. B. R. Singh (1949) refers to a number of alleged medicinal uses, including the treatment of cancer, but it would be obviously very unwise for the victim of any such serious disease to attempt treatment except under the direction of a skilled physician. Large amounts of commercial papain are used as digestive, and according to Lewis and Woodward (1950) in the treatment of ulcers and peritoneal adhesions after operations, and in dissolving the membranes in diptheria. It has certain industrial uses as in the fellmongering of sheep skins (separating the wool from the skin), pre-shrinking wool, tanning, the manufacture of chewing gum, and the clarification of brewed beverages, 80% of the beer made in America being so treated. They state that there are five or more enzymes in the latex, the proteolytic one predominating. The principal market is the United States, imports into which country increased from 54,344 lb. in 1925 to 315,021 lb. in 1945, to 476, 247 lb. in 1949, and to 505,368 lb. in 1953.

The production of papain has long been an important industry in Ceylon, which led the world in this industry until 1945, when it was surpassed by Tanganyika, which started production only in 1937. Ceylon took advantage of unsettled conditions in East Africa to regain the lead by 1953 when it produced three times as much as in 1949. The Belgian Congo has also become an important producer, with an export to the United States of 11,625 lb. in 1953, compared with 968 lb. from India. In that year the price varied from about Rs. 19 to Rs. 28 per pound. In Ceylon the papain is secured from a large number of small farms, whereas in Tanganyika it is grown on large estates. Before the war the Japanese exported some from one of the Caroline islands. It has been produced on a small scale in India, with considerable success, and it may be put on a commercial basis. An extensive study of the subject was undertaken at the Harcourt Butler Technological Institute, Kanpur, the results of which have been reported by Sen (1931) and the Principal (1932).

The process of collecting and drying the papain is simple, and requires no elaborate equipment. Fruits grown for this purpose should be thinned so that each one hangs separately. The unripe fruits are lanced with a non-metallic knife, or one of stainless steel, and the latex is collected in glass or porcelain vessels. Full grown fruits yield more latex of higher quality than smaller fruits. It was found that four cuts on a fruit gave better results than a larger number. Lancing may be repeated on successive days, but the amount and the quality of the latex decrease, so that more than five tappings are not worth while. The latex hardens in about 15 minutes and should then be put in alcohol. Sodium bisulphide added at the time of collection acts as a preservative and improves the quality of the product. Commonly the latex has been dried at temperatures not above 130° F., either in the sun or over fire.

A new method has been worked out at the Fruit Research Station, Saharanpur, which is said to give a product of distinctly superior quality. The papain is prepared by precipitating the latex with alcohol and the precipitate is then washed with acetone and dried under vacuum over sulphuric acid at room temperature. During storage, the activity of the enzyme actually increased for seven months, and after 10 months was still above the original. This is measured by noting its hydrolysing effect on egg albumin. Agnew (1946) refers to extensive technical examination of the product. Tainter and others (1951) give detailed technical discussions of the entire subject.

The yield per plant or per acre varies greatly. In Tanganyika it is reported by Lewis and Woodward (1950) to be from 3 to 8 oz. per tree or 80 to 175 lb. per acre, while Haigh (1946) reports that the best variety tested averaged 11½ oz. per tree, with the best tree giving more than a pound. He reports a positive correlation between the yield and the rainfall at the time of tapping of 0·50, apparently because of increased root pressure. Agnew (1946) also reports that in Queensland the best yield is during the wet summer months, some collectors claiming to get a pound per tree. He also found that potassium starvation had disastrous results on the yield, while a relative lack of phosphorus did not.

In the experiment at Kanpur the yield per plant was found to vary from one-fourth to one pound, within the same variety, and some varieties produced more than others. The yield, however, seemed to be proportional to the yield of fruit. R. S. Singh and Singh (1952) estimate that a tree with 60 fruits will produce half a pound of dried papain in a season, and that an acre should yield 175 to 200 lb. in the first year of bearing, falling to 150 lb. in the third year. Cheema and Dani (1930) report that the Gujarat variety averaged 4 oz. and the Singapore twice as much, per tree.

As has been seen, the industry may well prove profitable, although competition from other countries is likely to increase. Much may depend on the profitable use of the scarred fruit. The quality of this seems not to be affected, but the appearance is less attractive. It is reported that when unscarred fruit was selling in Saharanpur for eight annas a seer, the scarred fruit sold at half an anna to an anna less. Dass and others (1954) suggest that as the green fruits, whether scarred or not, contain about 10% of pectin on a dry-weight basis, it might be possible to use them profitably for the production of pectin.

Chapter XVIII

THE LITCHI

One of China's best gifts to India and other subtropical regions is the litchi. This is a fruit of excellent quality and appeals immediately to practically everyone who tastes it. Unfortunately, the climatic conditions under which it is commercially successful are rather limited, both in India and in the world. It is indigenous to southern China, and the most important centre of production, by far, is that region, particularly the provinces of Kwangtung and Fukien, where it is the most important fruit. India probably ranks second, with important centres in north Bihar, where there are 23,616 acres, according to Roy (1950), about a third of the acreage being in Muzaffarpur district; the submontane districts of Uttar Pradesh, where there are 348 acres according to Chand (1943); and near Hooghly in Bengal. Although it may have reached India through Assam, it is only recently that it has been grown to any extent in that State, which now reports about 500 acres. Naik (1949) says there are probably not more than 100 litchi trees in South India, although they thrive all over the plains and up to a height of 3,500 ft., doing best on the humid hill slopes. It was introduced into the Araku valley of Andhra in 1947, where its success seems to justify extensive planting. In South Africa some 16,000 trees were reported in 1934, and about 38,600 in 1946, with prospects of another 30,000 by 1956, according to Marloth (1947 b). There are very small, but increasing acreages in Florida, with 15,000 trees in 1955, and in Hawaii.

The litchi has had a long and honourable history in China, where it has been carefully cultivated and greatly appreciated for many centuries. The first reference to this fruit in literature may be as early as 1766 B.C., but this is questionable. There can be no doubts as to a reference in the literature of the Han dynasty (140 to 86 B. C.). A monograph on the litchi written by Ts'ai Hsiang in 1059 A. D. is considered the first publication in the world devoted to fruit. Groff (1921), whose book is the most complete work on the litchi in English, lists eight other monographs published by 1826. These, and the numerous poems and works of art featuring the litchi give some indication of the place this fruit has played in the life of South China.

Apparently the litchi reached Burma and eastern India by the end of the 17th century or shortly thereafter. Roxburgh reported receiving specimens from old trees in the Garo hills, while the trees in Bengal were still small. The litchi had reached the West Indies by 1775, the Hawaiian Islands about a century later, and Florida by 1883. It reached Europe early in the 19th century, but has never succeeded there. It was introduced into Natal about 1869, according to Marloth (1947 b), but only in 1903 into the Lowveld of eastern Transvaal, where its greatest development in South Africa has taken place. Stevens (1955) says that it was introduced into Queensland in 1854, but has not become a commercial crop largely because of the difficulty of vegetative propagation.

The Sapindaceae or Soapberry family, to which the litchi belongs, is a large family, mostly tropical and subtropical, with only a few members of much horticultural interest. Four of these are in the subfamily Nephelieae, the litchi and longan being subtropical with arils free, and the rambutan and pulasan being tropical with arils adhering to the seed. All four were formerly classified in one genus, *Nephelium*, and this is still done by some, but the modern tendency is to reserve thie genus for the rambutan, *N. lappaceum* and the pulasan, *N. mutabile*. The litchi then becomes *Litchi chinensis* instead of *Nephelium litchi*, and the longan becomes *Euphoria lorgana*. *Dimocarpus litchi* and *D. longan* are also synonyms. A more tropical species, *Litchi philippinensis*, is of comparatively little value, except possibly as a rootstock for *L. chinensis*. Other fruits in the family are the akee, *Blighia sapida*, of Africa, and an American species, *Melicocca bijuga*. The akee is not unknown in India, and Kamal (1953) of Lucknow refers to a leaf blight of it. Here also is classified the lutqua, *Pierardia sapida*, a small tree considered indigenous to Assam and Burma. The fruit has a yellow skin, and is said to resemble the loquat. Opinions differ as to its value, some considering it equal to the litchi, and others as of very poor quality. The botanist Hooker listed 12 species of the old genus *Nephelium* growing in India.

The genetics of the litchi have been studied by Liu (1954), who suggests that the species may have been derived from more than one wild progenitor. Haploid chromosome numbers of 14, 15, 16 and rarely 17 were found. He considers the so-called 'mountain litchi' clearly distinct from the varieties commonly cultivated. This is a type with poor fruit which is more resistant to frost than the better varieties.

The longan or lungan is commonly grown along with the litchi in China and while it is a smaller fruit, and generally considered distinctly inferior to it, it has the advantage of ripening after the litchi is off the market. DeCandolle considered it a native of India and reported that it grew wild from Ceylon and the Konkan to the mountains to the east of Bengal and in Pegu, Burma. The Chinese are said to have introduced it into the Malaya Archipelago and China. Naik (1949) states that there are only a dozen trees of rambutan in South India, but that they thrive on the lower slopes of the Nilgiris, and as the fruits are of good quality, preferred by some to the litchi, their cultivation should be extended. He states that the female trees seem to set fruit by self-pollination, although Ochse (1931) states that the anthers on the staminodes of the female flowers are sterile.

The English name, 'litchi', comes from the Chinese, and has been pronounced in two ways and spelled in many. The Chinese name is written in the same way throughout the country, but in South China the first syllable is pronounced like the word 'lye' while in Mandarin both syllables rhyme with 'me'. Arguing that the pronunciation should be that used in the great litchi-growing region, Groff spells the name 'lychee', but this has been widely adopted in the United States.

The other pronunciation is exclusively used in India. The phonetic spelling, 'lichi' is sometimes used, but 'litchi' has the advantage of being identical with the name of the genus, which cannot be changed, and is well established. Other forms which have been used include 'lici', 'licy', 'li-chi', 'lichea', 'lichee', and 'leechee'.

The litchi region of China has a moist subtropical climate, and this appears to be very satisfactory. The limiting factors appear to be frost in winter and dry heat in the summer. The exact amount of frost which the tree will stand depends on several factors, such as the variety, age, and condition of the plant. Young trees need protection for several years where there is danger of any frost. Trees which have been kept dormant by continued cool weather are less subject to damage than those in flush. Groff (1921) reports that at Saharanpur little damage was said to have been done by a temperature of 21° F., but temperatures this low, or a few degrees higher have killed trees to the ground in other places. The intensity of sunlight is also a factor. Groff (1943) states that young trees especially are harmed by intense light, and recommends that seedlings and layers should not be exposed to strong sunshine for a year or two.

In India, the limiting factor is more likely to be dry heat while the fruit is ripening, especially when accompanied by wind. The *lu* which blows at just this period over much of Uttar Pradesh is likely to prevent the successful culture of the litchi in a region which might otherwise be well suited. It has been suggested that with wind-breaks this difficulty might be overcome, but this is doubtful. Under these desiccating conditions, the fruit is likely to crack before it is fully ripe, and then rapidly to spoil. Even at Saharanpur this is considered by L. B. Singh and Singh (1954) the most serious defect of the litchi. Its causes and possible control are being investigated. While the rainfall in the China litchi region is about 60 inches a year, and high humidity is the rule (between 69 and 84% at Canton), these conditions do not seem to be necessary. In northern India rainfall and humidity are much less, and where irrigation is possible, are probably not limiting factors.

The litchi grows well under a variety of soil conditions, but seems to prefer a fairly deep loam. In Florida and India it has done well on sandy loam, but a considerable proportion of clay may be an advantage. Vyas (1938) notes that the lime content of the best litchi regions of Bihar is high, about 30%, and suggests that in regions where lime is deficient, it may be desirable to add it to the soil. Roy (1952) also recommends the use of lime and says that where its deficiency is marked, the trees respond clearly to its application. That this may be desirable only where very little calcium is present is suggested by the fact that the litchi has failed on the alkali soils of Israel. It has also failed on the limestone land of southern Florida, but this may be because there only a very thin layer of soil, or none, is found above the soft limestone. Preference for an acid soil is suggested by an experiment reported by Coville (1921). In greenhouses, seedling litchis were potted in ordinary potting soil, and in a soil consisting of two parts peat and one part clean sand. The seedlings in the acid soil not only made a much better growth of stem and root, but the roots were covered with tubercles filled with mycorhizal fungi. Groff does not give the reaction of the litchi soils in China, and was not aware of the presence of tubercles on the roots of the trees there. Marloth (1947b) states that in South Africa litchi trees make much more vigorous growth on acid than on neutral or slightly alkaline soil. He advocates the use of soil from under old trees for propagating new ones, to assure the presence of the mycorhizal fungi. It would seem, however, that the litchi is probably capable of growing well on either acid or basic soils. The Chinese are said to believe that the nature of the soil has a marked influence on the quality of the fruit.

Propagation and Culture

Layering and air-layering are the most common methods of propagating the litchi, and are fairly satisfactory, although they do not seem to produce as strong a root system as that of the seedling trees. They are easily used in the moist climate of South China and are very common there as well as in other countries. Li and Li (1949) state that in China a ring of bark an inch wide is removed from a branch one-third of an inch to two inches in diameter. A mud ball containing rotted plant material is applied, and the branch is kept on the tree for about 100 days. They had good success in 40 days by using damp sphagnum moss wrapped in heavy paper treated with tung oil, without watering. This oiled paper is less expensive than the plastic wraps used by Grove (1946) in Florida. L. B. Singh (1951 a) used terminal branches 18-24 in. long, preferably with a fork near the top. He removed a ring of bark an inch wide, and scraped the wood to remove all the cambium layer. The branch was treated with a hormone preparation, Rootone, and the base above the wound was covered with damp sphagnum moss and wrapped with plastic material. After two months the layers were removed and grew well. The use of plant hormones in preparing litchi layers is also recommended by Marloth (1947 b). In Bihar Roy (1952) recommends ringing in July, applying a mud plaster a week or two later covering with straw and another coat of mud in August, and separation in September. The mud is prepared by mixing 1 md. of pond earth, 10 sr. of sand, 5 sr. of rotten castor cake, 1 lb. of ammonium sulphate, and 5 sr. of rotten gunny, and should be kept a week before using. Vyas (1938) prefers starting the process in the hot weather, separating the layers in August, and planting them in the field early in October. Alternatively, he would start in August, separate the layers in October, and plant them in the following monsoon season. Nelson (1954) recommends potting the severed layers and placing them under partial shade, with constant mist for two weeks which is gradually reduced in the third. At the end of the fourth week they may be set out in the field. Layered trees come into bearing in from three to six years. If seedlings are grown, the seed must not be allowed to become dry as it loses its viability if exposed to the air for four or five days. By leaving it in the fruit, or keeping it in moist packing material, it may be kept for about two months. The seedlings grow slowly, and do not bear until from 8 to 12 years of age, or even older. There is great variation among seedlings, so that their use is not to be recommended.

Other methods of propagation are possible, but are not commonly used. Softwood cuttings may be grown with bottom heat and carefully controlled conditions. Sen (1941 c) reports xcellent results in inducing rooting by treating two-year-old cuttings for about 24 hours with from 50 to 100 mg. of indole-butyric acid per litre of water. Stronger solutions or longer treatment had a retarding effect, and younger wood was less suitable. Roy (1952), however, says that while such cuttings rooted very well, the buds died so the cuttings did not grow. Ochse (1953), using 'fog' propagators to maintain very high atmoshperic humidity, had excellent results with cuttings taken when the trees were in flush in April and May, in Florida, but no rooting of cuttings taken from November to March. Inarching is comparatively easy, and is used to a slight extent by the Chinese. Grafting is also used in China, especially for top-working old trees, and has been extensively tried in Hawaii, with fair success. Budding was unknown to the Chinese, but has been used with some success in Hawaii and the Philippines. Nelson (1955 b) reports success in chip and shield budding and veneer grafting in Florida. He used scion wood from vigorous flushes of terminal growth which still retained some green colour and had prominent axillary buds. The grafts were wrapped in plastic film. Litchi seedlings may be used as stock. The longan at first gave promise of being a suitable stock, but trees budded or grafted on it have either died soon, or failed to produce much fruit. There is room for further experimentation with other relatives as stock.

In China the litchi is most commonly grown on low land with dykes to hold the rivers back, and may be planted on the dykes. Such trees may have their roots submerged for periods of 10 days or two weeks during the flood season, without serious injury. But such trees never reach the size of those on higher, better drained soil and may be planted at a distance of 20 to 25 feet apart. Or they may be planted on raised beds, with deep ditches about 30 to 40 feet apart for drainage. A row of trees is planted on either side of the bed, resulting in considerable crowding. On upland land, the trees are planted in orchard form, at least 30 feet apart. This should be the minimum distance wherever the litchi grows well. Marloth (1947 b) recommends a spacing of at least 40 feet, and under the best growing conditions, of 50 feet. In drier regions, where it may be desirable to crowd the trees somewhat for greater protection from the desiccating wind, it may be well to reduce the distance to 25 feet.

As the litchi is grown in China, cultivation is reduced to the minimum. When the trees are planted on dykes or raised beds, little can be done beyond removing weeds, and even when they are set in regular orchards, little cultivation is given after they are mature. Under Indian conditions, cultivation similar to that given the mango is probably desirable, remembering that the litchi is rather shallow rooted, so that deep tillage is dangerous. Because of this factor, Marloth is opposed to ploughing in a litchi orchard. For the same reason, Stephens (1955) suggests the use of a mulch.

Irrigation, on the other hand, is important under Indian conditions, except where the rainfall is heavy. In Bihar, where the climate is favourable and the soil fairly retentive, mature orchards are not ordinarily irrigated but it is recognized that rain late in May is helpful and irrigation at that time would probably be an advantage. In Uttar Pradesh it is ordinarily necessary to irrigate from January until the rainy season, as that is the time the fruit is being formed and ripening, and as rain is not ordinarily expected during these months. Judging from the conditions under which litchis are grown in China, there is no danger of giving them too much water.

Manuring is considered very important by the Chinese, who use night-soil very largely for this as for other crops. Groff (1921) reports that they give each tree at least 500 lb. of this rich fertilizer every year. In order to overcome the tendency for the young plant to grow slowly, Marloth recommends liberal manuring in the hole in which the tree is to be planted, and continued manuring during the life of the tree. He says that while the exact requirements are not known, krall (farmyard) manure is good and may be applied at the rate of 50 lb. per young tree up to 500 lb. per tree of 20 years or more. In India the litchi is grown for the most part on naturally fertile soil, and little or no manure is given. M. P. Singh (1952) analysed the fruit of one variety and found that it contained much potash, which suggested that this might be important in manuring. Roy (1952) reports a trial of nitrogen, calcium, phosphorus, and potassium at different levels in Bihar. Nitrogen induced a significant response, but without any significant difference between the different amounts applied. Calcium was also thought to improve the health of the trees, and where there were symptoms of a deficiency of it or potash, the trees revived after the application of the deficient element. Marloth says that on soils where citrus trees show signs of zinc deficiency, there is a bronzing of the foliage of litchis and that a foliage spray of 8 lb. of zinc sulphate, 4 lb. of hydrated lime, in 100 gal. of water is beneficial.

Pruning seems to be relatively unimportant in the litchi, most writers agreeing that after the young tree has been given a good framework, little is needed. It is customary in harvesting to break off several inches of the branch along with the cluster of fruit. This is thought to cause the growth of new twigs which bear the crop the next year, and by some is considered necessary. Groff states that the Chinese do some pruning early in the winter, but does not indicate the nature of this. Grant and Williams (1936) recommend the removal of branches when crowding occurs, and state that in Burma both branch and root pruning are necessary when the growth becomes too vigorous, the latter being practised every second or third year. Vyas states that heavy pruning is done only when the trees become old and the fruits tend to be small. This rejuvenation is said to produce large fruits for a couple of years, but to be impracticable commercially because of the small yield obtained.

Serious diseases and insect pests seem to be rare. The warm moist climate of South China provides the conditions favourable to many fungi, but even there no disease of importance has been reported. India also seems to be free of fungous diseases. The most important pest is the mite which produces a condition called leaf curl or erinose. Vigorously growing young trees are most likely to be attacked and seriously damaged. Nursery stock may be destroyed. The mites, which are whitish and so small they cannot be seen with the naked eye, are species of *Eriophyes*. They live at the base of the hairs on the underside of the leaf, and cause a brown velvety growth, which, with the curling of the leaves, is a characteristic sign of the infestation. At first pits are formed, which may develop into galls. The leaves become thickened, and curl up, sometimes forming tight rolls. The mites suck sap from the leaves, causing them to dry up. The mites then move to new leaves. The female, according to Misra (1912), lays her eggs among the hairs. The nymphs resemble the adults, and the life cycle probably takes only a couple of weeks. Activity starts about the middle of March and lasts until November. The adults pass the winter on the leaves.

Control of the mites involves the removal and burning of infested leaves, including those which have fallen, the banding of the trees in order to prevent the mites climbing up from the ground, and spraying with a contact insecticide. Misra (1912) recommends spraying in May and November with crude oil emulsion and flowers of sulphur, but found kerosene emulsion or even soft soap a satisfactory substitute for crude oil emulsion. Groff (1921) reports that in Hawaii a solution of nicotine sulphate and whale-oil soap gave very good control, better than either sulphur dust or self-boiled lime-sulphur spray. Roy and De (1950) report that at Sabour the mites were first observed in 1949, and then on only the Bedana and Dehra Rose varieties, out of ten varieties in the collection. They secured good control by spraying with 0·5% DDT in water, at a cost of 10 annas a tree, including labour.

Several other insects have been reported doing slight damage to the litchi in India, including the bark-eating caterpillar, *Indardela spp.* Chaturvedi (1954) reports that the incidence of these caterpillars on the litchi is high, and that he reduced the population by 96·79% by spraying with 0·1% parathion; DDT and BHC were less effective. S. M. Singh (1954 d) states that the caterpillars of *Lymantria mathura* which caused severe damage to mango trees at Dehra Dun in 1954, also attacked litchi trees. Rehman and Ansari (1941) report the scale, *Parlatoria pseudopyri*, on the litchi. Birds and bats often cause much damage, both in India and in other countries. Sometimes trees are protected by means of netting, but more often the only defence is an attempt to scare the marauders away.

Yield and Marketing

Numerous small inconspicuous flowers, without petals, are borne in terminal panicles, mainly on new shoots. The flowers are both staminate and hermaphrodite, some functioning as female, and some with anthers which function and pistils which generally do not. Flowering takes place at about the same time as in the mango. The first flowers to open are males, according to L. B. Singh and Singh (1954) followed by hermaphrodites functioning as female, and then those functioning as males and more which are staminate. They say that pollination is mainly by insects, of which they observed 10 species, including the honey bee, flies, an ant, and a wasp. Presumably the 'seedless' fruis , in which the seed is shrivelled, result from a lack of fertilization, and such varieties must be self-sterile, and perhaps cross-sterile also, while those with normal seeds are probably self- and cross-fertile. It is thought that pollination is necessary even for the 'seedless' type, this being a case of stimulative parthenocarpy. Only a small percentage of the flowers develop into fruits, twenty fruits to a panicle making a good crop. Failure in setting, and the drop of many of the fruits during the first month may be caused by lack of fertilization or embryo abortion, resulting from the chromosome irregularities which have been mentioned.

After the trees come into bearing, the yield should increase for at least twenty years. Under favourable conditions, the litchi bears heavily and regularly, although Stephens (1935) states that in Queensland a crop is borne only once in two or three years. He indicates that an average crop is about 200 or 300 lb. per tree, the same figures that are given by Popenoe (1920) for Hawaii, with an occasional yield as high as 1,000 lb. Similarly, Marloth indicates that trees 30 years old should yield at least 250 lb. a year. Groff states that in China, yield up to 1,500 lb. are sometimes obtained. Vyas states yields in terms of the number of fruits as well as by weight, his average of 4,000 to 5,000 being equivalent to his estimate of 2 to 4 md. (164 to 328 lb.). His statement that an individual tree in an open area may give 15,000 fruits suggests that the orchards are commonly too crowded for the best results. That the litchi is highly profitable is indicated by the statement of L. B. Singh and Singh (1954) that the price varies from Re. 1 to Rs. 2-8 per seer. The litchi is a long-lived tree, and although references in Chinese literature to trees 800 years old need not be accepted as accurate, it seems probable that trees may remain in profitable bearing for more than a century. Under the unusual conditions prevailing at Bangalore, in South India, the litchi is said to bear two crops a year, in May and December.

Yields have been increased by two methods in Hawaii. Bonner and Liverman (1953) refer to a statement in the report of the Experiment Station for 1948 that spraying the trees in the autumn with NAA increased flowering the following spring. It is suggested that spraying caused faster maturation of the growing points by either killing new growth or temporarily slowing growth. Nakata (1953) reports a significant increase in yield in the Brewster variety by girdling branches and trunks by running a pruning saw around them in September or November.

As has been indicated, in harvesting the whole cluster is removed, together with a bit of the stem and some leaves. This is said to delay the wilting of the fruit. For the local market, the fruit can be allowed to remain on the tree until fully ripe and of a beautiful red colour. For shipping, it is better to pick it when just beginning to turn red. The bright red colour soon becomes a less attractive brown. The fruit must be handled carefully to avoid breaking the skin. It is generally packed in small baskets, which should be not more than 10 inches deep, to avoid crushing the bottom fruit. Moss or the leaves of trees, used as packing material, helps the fruit to reach the market in good condition. In South Africa the fruit is dried for a few days, removed from the cluster and packed in excelsior.

In spite of the perishable nature of the fruit, the Chinese have been very successful in transporting it all over their country. Even in the days before modern transportation, 'tribute litchis' were regularly sent to the Emperor and other officials in the north. With refrigeration, the litchi can be kept for some time or shipped to more distant markets. Cheema and Karmarkar (1939) and Karmarkar and Joshi (1940 a) were able to keep the fruit in good condition for three months at 30 to 45° F. In India, up to the present, the supply is not large enough to create a serious marketing problem. The advantage of the grower marketing his crop without the aid of a contractor is indicated by Vyas who says that while individual trees have been known to produce a crop sold for more than Rs. 100 and an average crop should bring from Rs. 10 to Rs. 20 per tree, the crop is sold to a contractor for Rs. 2 or 3 per tree. The contractor, of course, runs the risk of the loss of part or all of the crop from unfavourable weather conditions, and has to guard and harvest it.

In India, the litchi is eaten almost entirely as a fresh fruit, but in China large quantities are dried. They are spread out in bright sun, at first attached to the cluster, but for the final stages they are removed. The aril shrinks as it dries, separating from the thin, brittle skin, so that when shaken it rattles. About two-thirds of the weight is lost. The flavour changes completely, but is still pleasant, and highly regarded by the Chinese. If weather does not permit sun drying, the process is carried on in special ovens. The product is not only used when the fresh fruit is not available, but is shipped all over the world where there are Chinese. There is only a very limited market among other prople. To establish the possibility of drying in India, Pal (1951) successfully dried two baskets of fruit by spreading them on a stringed bed with its legs in water (to prevent ants and other insects from climbing to the fruit), covered with a fine muslin sheet.

The litchi makes an excellent canned fruit, and in modern times a considerable industry has been developed in China. This product has a much wider appeal than the dried 'nuts'. Some canning has been done in India, with excellent results. If production is expanded, this seems to offer a means of profitably marketing those not demanded by the fresh fruit trade. In China various other products are made, including pickles, preserves, and wine. The fruit is said to be very well adapted to quick freezing.

Many named and carefully described varieties of the litchi are grown in China. Groff (1921) lists 49 varieties of Kwangtung, and states that about fifteen of these are grown commercially. In India the situation is far different. Varieties are not well established, and the names used are largely descriptive. Successful varieties in Bihar include the China, Purbi, Deshi, Bedana, and Delhi Rose. L. B. Singh and Singh (1954) recommend the Rose-scented, Early Large Red, Kalkattia, Gulabi, and Late Seedless out of the 12 varieties they describe. It is not difficult to understand their failure to recommend the Pyazi, which tastes like boiled onions. Out of eight varieties tried in West Bengal, the China and Muzaffarpur are regarded as suitable in regard to both quality and yield.

The food value of the litchi lies largely in the sugar content which varies largely between varieties and in different climates. The varieties described by L. B. Singh and Singh (1954) range from 6·74 to 13·86% sugar and from 0·201 to 0·644% acid, and the five recommended average 11·835% sugar and 0·405%

acid. The sugar content in Florida is said to vary from 12 to 15%, while Miller and Bazore (1945) in Hawaii report one variety with 11·8% and one with 20·6%. Popenoe (1923) quotes another analysis in Hawaii, showing 15·3% sugars, 0·54% ash, 1·16% acids, and 1.15% protein. Miller and Bazore found the two varieties studied good sources of phosphorus and poor of calcium, while the sweeter one was also a fair source of iron. They report the litchi a good source of ascorbic acid but a poor source of thiamine. The value of the fruit is also affected by the percentage of the total weight which is pulp. In the varieties described by L. B. Singh and Singh (1954), this varied from 64·42 to 83·19%.

The longan is considered native to the Western Ghats from the Konkan to the Tinnevelly hills, where it grows up to an elevation of about 5,000 ft. It is also fairly common in Assam up to 3,500 ft. It is cultivated to a slight extent for fruit, shade, and ornament in Bengal, where it is known as the *ashphal.* In China it is a fruit of some importance. It is generally recognized as less delicious than the litchi as a fresh fruit, but some esteem the canned longan more highly. The tree is propagated by the same methods as the litchi, but is more commonly inarched. It is a more vigorous tree and attains a height of 40 ft. Cultural practices in China are similar to those used with the litchi, including generous manuring. The fruit is smaller, with a relatively large seed, and with a smooth skin. On ripening it turns yellow or russet. The clusters are tighter. The Chinese practise severe thinning, sometimes removing three-fourths of the inflorescences, and later part of the fruit on those which remain. The sugar content is much less than that of the better varieties of litchi.

The longan is less tender to frost than the litchi, and can therefore be grown in cooler regions. If some of the better varieties from China, where Groff (1921) lists twelve good ones, were tried out in this country, it might be found profitable to grow the longan in areas unsuited to the litchi, as well as in the same region. As the longan ripens later, it would not come into competition with the litchi on the market.

Chapter XIX

THE GRAPE

Grapes are grown on far more land than is used for any other subtropical fruit. There are probably more than 26 million acres of grapes in the world. Of these, by far the larger part is grown in the Mediterranean region, particularly in France, Italy, and Spain. Unfortunately, about 82% of the grapes produced are used in making wine. Of the remainder, about half are dried and marketed as raisins, and about half are eaten fresh.

This subtropical grape, *Vitis vinifera*, is the most important member of the genus, and of the family Vitaceae (Ampelidaceae), but there are a number of other species, several of which are cultivated. The vinifera grape is indigenous to the region stretching from the Caucasus to Pakistan, and has been grown in Europe for thousands of years. It is not clear whether early references to the grape in Sanskrit literature refer to this or to some other species. There are about 25 species found in India and Burma, mostly in the sub-Himalayan tract, where they are found mainly at elevations between 3,000 and 6,000 feet. Four of these wild species produce edible fruit: *Vitis barbata* in Bengal, Assam and Burma, *V. parviflora* in Kashmir and Kumaon, *V. rugosa* in Kumaon and Burma, and *V. rumcisperma* in Sikkim and Assam. North America is also rich in species of grapes, the most important being *V. labrusca* and *V. rotundifolia*, which are cultivated to a considerable extent in the temperate sections. These differ from the vinifera grape in that the skin separates easily from the pulp.

A species formerly included in the genus grows wild in the Colegaon forest on the border of the districts of Bhagalpur and Santhal parganas of Bihar, according to Syamal and Patel (1953). It is now classified as *Ampelocissus latifolia*. It has large underground tubers by which it lives over the winter and hot weather and from which new shoots emerge after the first rains. The berries ripen from the end of July to the middle of October, and are of poor quality. As it grows luxuriantly and is highly resistant to disease and insect pests, it may have value in breeding.

Vinifera grapes are classified according to their use, into wine, raisin, and table varieties. Some varieties are excellent either for raisins or for eating fresh, but those used for wine are generally restricted to that purpose. The raisins made from two varieties of small seedless grapes grown mainly in Greece, are known as currants, but are not to be confused with the small fruit of the same name, of the genus *Ribes*, grown in the cooler temperate regions and never dried. Table grapes are further classified according to colour as white, red, and black varieties, the last being a very dark blue or purple.

In India, grapes are grown only for eating fresh, except for about 35 acres in the Simla Hills which are used for wine. A successful raisin industry can probably be established if production ever exceeds the demand for the fresh fruit. An attempt is now being made to establish a small rasin industry in a remote and very dry valley in Himachal Pradesh. There is now no reason for making raisins from grapes which can be marketed fresh, as the country does not produce enough to meet the demand for fresh grapes. When the Report on the Marketing of Grapes (Anon., 1940 b) was published, it estimated 1,419 acres producing 172,126 md. of grapes in what is now India and nearly twice that acreage in what is Pakistan. Now Bombay probably has more than 1,000 acres, about 90% in Nasik district, and Mysore is credited with that acreage. Madras has between 300 and 400 acres, mainly in Madurai district, and Andhra about 50 acres. Hyderabad reports 322 acres, and Himachal Pradesh 38 acres. So there may be nearly 3,000 acres in India. The consumption of fresh grapes could undoubtedly be greatly increased if grapes of good quality were grown in those parts of the country which now depend on imports from distant places.

In most parts of the world where grapes are grown they are dormant in the winter, and produce fruit in summer. The dormant vines can stand considerable frost. It is important that the weather while the fruit is ripening be dry, as rain at that time is likely to cause the berries to crack and spoil. Dry weather at the time of flowering is also desirable. Some varieties do well with summer temperatures up to about 115° F. while others prefer a moderate climate. These requirements can be met in northern India for varieties which mature before the rainy season begins, and if varieties are found or developed which will do so and which have other desirable characters, an important industry may develop.

Conditions in the important grape-growing areas in India are quite different and have forced the use of different methods. Relative freedom from frost makes it possible to have the main crop develop in the winter or early spring. In Bombay this involves the danger of frost damage, and according to Cheema and others, frequent losses have discouraged the growth of the industry there. No fruit is ripening during the rainy season, but the second crop, which ripens after the monsoon, is of poor quality. In the other regions there is no frost hazard, and Naik (1949) says, 'Experience in viticulture in South India has proved that the yields and quality of grapes produced in certain situations under the tropical conditions of South India are in no way less than those reported from what are usually considered as the ideal home for the fruit.' He believes that the grape can become one of the most profitable fruits in that area.

Fairly light soils are ordinarily preferred for grapes, and good drainage is essential. In Nasik the soil used is a medium black soil with a lime content of from 3 to 5 per cent. Naik (1949) states that while a deep, well-drained loam is considered best in South India, some of the best vineyards in Madurai are on gravelly soil, and produce more than the same varieties do in Baluchistan. In other parts of the South, other soils, including clays, are used. Because of the poor quality of the soil in Madurai, much care is considered necessary in preparing the pits or trenches in which the vines are to be planted. These are dug about three feet deep and wide about six months before planting in December, and are filled with successive layers composed of two feet of green leaves covered with soil, sometimes after adding one or more of the following : bone meal, tank silt, well rotted sheep or cattle manure, loose red earth or ant-hill earth. Water is given repeatedly, and the mixture is turned over occasionally. When it sinks, another layer is added. At the time of planting, a small hole for the roots is made in this compost.

Cuttings are almost universally used in India and in other countries where the phylloxera is not a pest. Ripened wood is cut into pieces about 9 to 18 inches long, the lower cut being just below a node. They are planted with one or two internodes exposed. In most varieties these grow readily, but if not, layering can be used. In Europe and the eastern part of the United States vinifera grapes are grafted on the American species. This presents no difficulties, the ordinary cleft graft being commonly used. Seedlings may easily be grown, but as vegetative propagation is so easy, and the seedlings vary greatly, seeds are used only in breeding new varieties. In Bombay the cuttings are started in a nursery in October, and set out in January. In Madras it is considered better to plant the cuttings in nurseries, but some are planted directly in the vineyard. Rangacharlu (1952) says that four or five cuttings are planted in one pit, of which two are allowed to grow, and that they are protected from termites by a mixture of neem cake and sand. Gandhi (1956 b) states that direct planting results in bearing one year earlier than in the case of transplanting, and that sometimes a maximum yield is secured in the second year. However, he considers this method impracticable because of the expense of caring for the young vines in the field.

Methods of Training

The training and pruning of the vine are matters of great importance, and influence very largely all other operations, from planting to harvesting. In the long history of grape growing, many different methods of training have been developed, varying all the way from practically no care to extremely heavy pruning twice a year. Unpruned vines, growing on pergolas or over buildings, often become very large, and a single plant may produce a tremendous amount of fruit. In commercial production, however, heavy pruning is generally practised.

The system used in Bombay State is called the single-stake method. In this, live stakes of *pangara* (*Erythrina indica*) are used to support the vines. Two rooted cuttings are transplanted at each place, according to Gandhi (1928), so that if one dies, one will still remain. The distance between permanent vines is generally 7 or 8 feet. All side buds are removed from the growing stem until April, when the topmost four are left. The vines are then about five feet tall. Cuttings of *pangara* about six feet long are planted nine inches to the leeward of the vines, and in May the lower half is whitewashed and the upper part painted with coal tar. These supports take root and grow, but as they are shallow-rooted, it is thought that they do not compete seriously with the vines. The four buds which are left in April of the first year become the basis of all future pruning. In October the canes coming from these four buds are pruned back to a length containing three or four buds which shoot out and in April are in turn pruned back to single buds. Thereafter, each year the shoots are pruned back to three or four buds in October. Those nearest the end grow and bear fruit, but at least one bud ordinarily remains dormant. In April the cane is pruned back to a single dormant bud, which then grows and bears. Gole (1943) complains that the growers tend to leave too many buds which results in a large crop of poor quality. The fruit is borne in a few clusters near the base of the shoot. At about five years of age, four strong canes are sometimes tied to those from adjacent vines.

A modification of the single-stake system is that which originated in Junnar and is used to some extent in Bombay. In it four vines are planted and kept in one pit, with resulting crowding. Cheema and others (1954) state that in a trial at Poona, this system resulted in a considerably higher yield, but made bullock-cultivation, irrigation, and spraying difficult. Greater increases in yield are possible by training the vines on wire trellises, one report stating that the yield is three times as great as by the single-stake system. Kamath (1955) reports that the record crop for Poona district was on vines so trained, planted three feet apart in rows eight feet apart.

In Hyderabad, the system used is similar to that in Bombay, according to Venkataratnam and others (1952), except that when the vines reach a height of about six feet, two branches are allowed to grow in opposite directions to a combined length of 8-10 ft. The shoots arising from these are trained along bamboos 1·5 ft. apart and are pruned in April and October-November. The first week of November is preferred, as earlier pruning seems to increase scab.

In Madurai the vines are trained on temporary supports and side branches are removed, for 4-6 months, by which time they are 5-6 ft. high. Then a *pandal* or arbor is constructed, about 8 ft. square, with live supports of *pangara* or of *Erythrina indica* or with supports of wood, stone, or metal. Side shoots are then allowed to grow in various directions and are tied down to the *pandal*. When bearing starts, about 18-22 months after planting, regular pruning begins. Following the harvests in March-April and October-November, water is withheld for a fortnight so that new growth stops, and the vines are pruned in May-June and December-January. The method is not standardized, but commonly the main leaders and laterals are left and side shoots are cut back to from 1 to 5 buds, depending on their vigour. Some growers prune more lightly in winter.

The head system is somewhat similar to the single-stake, but in it the vine is kept much shorter, from one and a half to four feet high. It is necessary to stake the vines only for four to six years, after which the stem is strong enough to stand by itself. This is the method most commonly used with vinifera grapes in America, and is reported by L. Singh and others (1940) to be successful in the Punjab with some varieties making poor vegetative growth. Pruning is done only once a year.

Several systems using wire trellises are popular in various parts of the world, and have been used in India. They are not common here because of the relatively great expense. In the Kniffen or Espalier system, one or two wires are strung from posts, and a single stem is trained as far as the top wire. There permanent arms are trained along the wire in both directions until they meet the arms of the adjoining plants. If there were two wires, another pair of arms follow the lower wire. The bearing canes hang down from the arms, and are pruned back each year. A number of modifications of this system are in use. Cordon training is somewhat similar, but in it the main stem is taken up to the wire and then along it, each vine growing in one direction only. This system was found best for some of the vigorous varieties on good soil in the Punjab. At Saharanpur, where trellises are used, L. B. Singh and Dikshit (1952) tried pruning on November 10, instead of the usual time in the last week of December, in an attempt to hasten growth and the maturity of the crop. The only effect noticed was a decrease in growth and yield.

In addition to the heavy annual or semi-annual pruning, some pruning of the growing vines is frequently desirable. Patwardhan (1919) recommends that each shoot be pinched off at about the fourth leaf beyond the bunch of fruit. All secondary branches arising along the shoots may well be removed. The earlier in the season this work is done, the more profitable it is. In case the 'head' becomes too dense, it may be necessary to thin out some of the branches at the time of the semi-annual pruning, along with any dead wood.

Girdling has long been practised on certain varieties of grapes, and seems to be necessary in order to get a satisfactory crop in the varieties which yield currants. It has not been used to any extent in India. Dhillon and Singh (1949 b) found that ringing the canes of the Black Prince, a vinifera grape, at Lyallpur, increased the yield and the size of the berries. It also hastened the achievement of the colour at which they were harvested, but apparently not true maturity. In another experiment (1949 a) they seemed to find that this colouring was hastened more by a combination of cane and trunk ringing than by either alone, but there are so many unexplained variations in the data that the results are questionable, and as trunk ringing in experiments elsewhere has seemed to decrease the vitality of the vines, they do not recommend it.

Another possible method of increasing the size of the berries is treatment with 4-chlorophenoxyacetic acid. Weaver (1952, 1953) reports that spraying or dipping clusters of the Black Corinth variety in 10-15 ppm resulted in large berries and compact clusters; at 50 ppm the berries were so large that girdling had no additional effect. Only those clusters actually treated showed the effect. Ordinarily treatment at 10 ppm 4-10 days after full bloom resulted in acceptable clusters. The berries contained few, if any, hard seeds. Satisfactory results were also secured with the Thompson Seedless, a combination of hormone treatment and girdling giving the largest berries. Blommaert and Meynhardt (1955) report promising results from treating the Zante currant with 20 ppm of PCPA as a substitute for girdling.

Root pruning is commonly used in some parts of South India, according to Naik (1949), water being withheld for a fortnight, after which a trench is dug around the vine, 4 or 5 feet deep and the roots are exposed for a few hours before the soil, mixed with manure, is returned. The expense involved must be very large, and as Naik says that it is not certain that the treatment is desirable, there seems little justification for the practice.

Cultivation, irrigation, and manuring are needed. Naik (1949) stresses the importance of frequent shallow cultivation to remove the weeds. As warm, dry weather is essential during the growing season, irrigation is important. Gandhi (1928) recommends that at Nasik not more than ten irrigations be given, starting a month and a half or two months after the monsoon, until March, and thereafter three until the next rainy season. Cheema and others (1954) say that in the Deccan irrigation is necessary throughout the year except when there are adequate rains and for a few weeks at the time of each pruning. They recommend that the first two or three irrigations after pruning be light, and that during the fruiting season the vines be watered once every week. Rangacharlu (1952) reports even more extreme treatment, with four irrigations a week in summer and two a week in winter, unless there is rain. A visitor from Israel has noted that in that country mangoes are irrigated every two weeks, but grapes are grown without irrigation, or with four irrigations, at most, during the long dry summer. Possibly the growers in both countries tend to pamper the crops which are new to the region.

India also tends to use more manure than some other countries. With the very intensive culture practised in Madurai, heavy manuring is considered necessary. Rangacharlu (1952) states that just before pruning, 25 tons of green leaves are dug into the soil, and that during the year the same amount of farmyard manure is given per acre. Sultan (1935) recommends the addition of 2-3 lb. each of bonemeal, fish, and castor cake to the soil around each vine in Hyderabad. Cheema and others (1954) say that after the April pruning in Bombay 60-100 lb. of farmyard manure per plant is generally given. Without giving the experimental basis, they recommend in addition, 100 lb. each of bonemeal, potassium sulphate, and ammonium sulphate, or 100 lb. of bonemeal and 200 lb. blood manure, per acre. In the Punjab, however, the application of phosphorous, alone or with nitrogen and potash gave the poorest results except no manuring, according to L. Singh and others (1940). The best results at first were from the use of ammonium sulphate and later from farmyard or other organic manure. On this basic soil nitrate of soda was good for a year or so, and then harmful.

Windbreaks are valuable, as strong winds cause the flowers to shed, and injure the young shoots. Cheema and others (1954) state that under some circumstances windbreaks raise the temperature on cold nights two or three degrees. They found that flooding the vineyard or building wood fires raised the temperature only a degree or two, while oil-heaters raised it about six degrees, but at a cost of Rs. 75 a night. They consider no method of frost protection satisfactory.

Pests and Diseases

The grape suffers from a large number of pests and diseases. Only one of a large number of harmful insects in Europe and America is the aphid, *Phylloxera vastatrix*, reference to which has been made in this and in a former chapter. The most important insect pest in India is the flee beetle, *Scelodonta strigicollis*. This small beetle eats the buds and causes substantial damage in Bombay and South India. The biology and control of this pest have been described by Trehan and others (1947). The eggs are laid from March to October beneath the bark and in crevices in it and hatch in from 4 to 7 days. The larvae feed on the cortical portion of the roots but are not considered pests. They pupate after 6 or 7 weeks, and the adults emerge in 7 to 11 days. The adults live 9 to 12 months, hibernating in mid-winter, under the bark or in dried leaves. They sometimes kill canes as well as damaging the buds. Even in well-managed vineyards they may cause 11 to 31% damage. The tassel method of catching them in dried banana leaves was found to be unsatisfactory, and these authors recommend shaking the beetles into inverted umbrellas early in the morning in September. Removing the loose bark after the April pruning is also important, reducing the population about 42% in two experiments. Adding a pound of Paris green to 100 gallons of Bordeaux mixture for spraying killed 87·8% of the beetles in one experiment, at somewhat less cost than that of shaking them into umbrellas. Lead arsenate was less effective. Appanna and Maheswaruah (1954) report good control in Mysore by spraying after pruning with one part of 5% DDT and four parts of 0·65% gamma isomer BHC. An ingenious method of catching this pest is used. Bundles of dry banana leaves are tied around the stems of the vines and the beetles take shelter in the leaves, which are then removed and burned, or the beetles are shaken out of them and killed. Dead bark which may harbour the beetles should be removed. Another method is to pass burning bundles of sann-hemp over the vines just after sunset, 6, 8 and 10 days after pruning.

Termites are reported by 'Kissan' (1942) to be the most serious pest in the Punjab. Intensive hand cultivation was the only method found which would protect the plants, and this was not economic, although it was found possible to produce many varieties. Parakeets and other birds, and ants which attacked the fruit on the drying trays, were also pests.

A number of other pests are mentioned by Naik (1949). The leaf roller, *Sylepta lunalis* is a caterpillar sometimes found in large numbers but generally checked by parasites. When control is needed, hand-picking or spraying with lead arsenate may be used. The cockchafer beetle, of which Ayyar (1940) names two species, *Adoretus lasiopygus* and *A. versutus*, sometimes defoliates vines after the first heavy rain. In Bombay *A. ovalis* is mentioned. The beetles hide in the soil during the day, when they can be handpicked, or a poison spray may be applied. The grapevine sphinx, *Hippotion celerio* is a large caterpillar and can easily be controlled by hand-picking. A minor pest is the leaf-miner, *Phyllocnistis toparcha* which can be controlled by destroying the infested leaves. The vine-girdling beetle, *Sthenias grisator*, can be controlled by burning the canes it kills. A scale of the genus *Aspidiotus* sometimes interferes with the growth of buds, and even kills vines. Infested portions should be removed in pruning, and if necessary, the vines may be sprayed with crude oil emulsion or fish oil rosin soap. A mite, *Paratetranychus punicae*, appears in such large numbers on the tender leaves in some seasons as to reduce the yield. It can be very effectively controlled by dusting with sulphur. Ayyar (1940) also mentions the grape thrips *Rhipiphorothrips cruentatus*, which lacerates the leaves and sucks up the juice, causing the leaves to fall. It is reported to be a minor pest in Bombay, but occasionally to cause severe damage. It can be controlled by spraying or dusting with nicotine. Increasing damage to young fruits by the bug *Helopeltis antonii*, is reported by Puttarudria and Appanna (1956) in Mysore.

The most destructive disease of the grape in Bombay is the powdery mildew, caused by the fungus *Uncinula necator*. It causes much damage in some years in Madras, particularly in warm sultry weather. All green parts of the plant are attacked. White patches appear on both sides of the leaves and on the shoots, and in severe cases the vine appears wilted. Flowers are frequently attacked, and may fail to set fruit. Berries attacked when young fall off; when half grown, they may be irregular in shape, covered with mildew, and may even crack. Some that ripen have disfiguring spots. The ripe berries are not attacked.

The fungus can grow at temperatures between 50 and 100° F., the optimum being 85 to 95°. It is favoured by high humidity and cloudiness, but actual rain seems to interfere with its growth, perhaps washing the spores on to the ground. Weather conditions in Bombay during the winter, especially October and November, are nearly ideal, and it is at this time that the disease causes the most damage. Formerly spraying with Bordeaux mixture was commonly practised. Control is imperfect, however, and the berries are stained. Uppal and others (1930) report that dusting with sulphur gives better control without any staining, and recommend three applications in the winter. The first is given when the shoots are 6 to 8 in. long, the second during or just before blossoming, and the third 40 to 50 days later. Rarely a fourth application 15 to 20 days later is required. The sulphur can be adulterated with some inert powder up to 20% and this reduces the injury which may be caused by high grade sulphur in hot weather. The cost of three applications on vines of average size is given as Rs. 8-8 an acre.

Anthracnose is of much less importance than powdery mildew, but at times causes considerable damage in Bombay and Madras. It is caused by the fungus *Elsinoe ampelina*, the imperfect stage of which is *Sphaceloma ampelinum* or *Gloeosporium ampelophagum*, which flourishes in wet weather, and at lower temperatures. The disease is therefore of importance only when the rainy season extends into October and November. Ramakrishna and Sundaram (1955) say it is prevalent in Madurai and Salem districts. It causes cankers on the leaves and shoots, may prevent the setting of fruit, and produces red spots with gray centres, called bird's-eye spots, on the fruit. By spraying with Bordeaux in May and again about the end of July, it can be largely prevented. Diseased shoots may be removed, and the wounds painted with a mixture of 5 lb. of ferrous sulphate and ½ pint of sulphuric acid in a gallon of water. Early pruning of the vines, in an attempt to secure an early crop, increases the danger of a serious outbreak, and is therefore discouraged. Irrigation may also be restricted if the disease has appeared during the monsoon.

Downy mildew is another fungous disease which flourishes in wet weather, and occasionally causes severe loss. It is caused by *Plasmopara viticola.* In Madras it is said to be more harmful, though less common, than powdery mildew. Measures taken against powdery mildew and anthracnose are usually sufficient to control it. In Madras it is recommended that all the vines be pruned at the same time, and that the prunings be destroyed. A programme suggested for all three diseases includes spraying three times with Bordeaux, followed by three or four dustings with sulphur.

Root rot, a very destructive disease in Europe, was found in 1926 near Nasik. It is caused by *Dematophora necatrix.* Should it appear again, the affected plants should be dug out and destroyed, and the area should be isolated by means of a trench to avoid the spread of the fungus through the soil. Ramakrishna and Sundaram (1955) mention three other diseases. Black rot, caused by *Guignardia bidwellii*, which is prevalent in most grape-growing countries, has recently been found in Madurai, probably newly introduced. It is severe on certain varieties, causing the berries to rot. It is controlled by one or more sprays of Bordeaux, which may stain the berries, or other copper sprays. Rust, caused by *Phakopsora vitis,* is found in some places, mainly on Black Prince in the winter. It is controlled by dusting with sulphur. Brown leaf spot, caused by *Gercospora viticola,* is a minor disease controlled by good cultural methods and the spraying necessary for other diseases.

In the southern part of the country there are two fruiting seasons a year, but the fruit which ripens from August to October is sour and of such poor quality that in most places it is disregarded. This amounts to about a third of the annual production at Madurai, however, and 45% of that at Krishnagiri. The main crop lasts from December to May or even June, and is at its height in March. There is thus little competition with grapes from Pakistan which are on the Indian market from July to November.

The size and shape of the bunch varies greatly with different varieties. The preference is for a fairly compact bunch but loose enough that the berries are not crowded out of shape, and the bunch may be fitted in with others in the basket or box. Some varieties are benefited by the removal of some of the berries while small, slender scissors or knives being used. Farrag (1955) reports that one variety in Egypt was effectively thinned by spraying at full bloom with 0·05% NAA. This increased the average weight of the berries without much effect on the weight of the bunch. In the case of very loose bunches there is not much which can be done.

A very large number of varieties of grapes are grown in different parts of the world, but comparatively few are grown commercially in India. By far the most important variety is the Bhokri, which is said to constitute 99% of the crop in Bombay. This is a round green variety which produces good bunches and the highest yield. The quality is good, although the skin is thick and tough. A selection from this, number 94, is said to be as prolific and to be of better quality and to produce bunches of better size and shape. Fakdi (Fakri) has a vigorous vine, but is a shy bearer with loose bunches of smaller, oval, green berries with thin skin. The quality is superior, but it does not ship well, and this, coupled with the poor yield, prevents it from being largely grown commercially. However, it is reported that one grower increased the yield 12% and improved the flavour, by grafting Fakdi on Bhokri, and this practice may lead to the larger use of this variety. The best of the varieties grown in Bombay is the Pandhri Sahebi, with long green berries as large as those of Bhokri, a firm pulp and a skin which is thick enough to make this a good keeper, but not tough. The vine is slow-growing and a shy bearer. Being partly self-sterile, it produces a good many small seedless berries when planted by itself, but when planted near Bhokri vines it bears good bunches. Next in quality comes the Kali Sahebi, also a shy bearer, but vigorous, with compact bunches which are sometimes very large, but unfortunately ripen irregularly. It ripens about 15 days later than Bhokri, and as the name indicates, is a dark purple when ripe. Other varieties reported promising in Bombay are the Karachi, Black Prince, Black Hamburg, and Bangalore Purple.

In Madras the common varieties are Pachai-drakshai, meaning green grape, Speen Kishmish imported from Baluchistan, and Bedana probably imported from Peshawar. The Speen Kishmish is the Sultana, a small greenish-yellow, seedless grape largely grown for raisins in some countries, and the Bedana may belong to the same group. The Haitha from Baluchistan and other foreign varieties are under trial. The most important variety in Mysore is called Aurangabad, Blue, or Bangalore Blue, and belongs to the species *V. labrusca* or is a hybrid.

In Hyderabad the Bhokri, Sahebi, and Habshi are commonly grown, according to Venkataratnam and others (1952), who state that the Anab-e-shahi is superior to these and growing in popularity. This, according to Vankataratnam (1953), is a bud sport of the Fakri.

Extensive trials of grape varieties have been carried on at Poona and Lyallpur, including those from other countries as well as from all parts of India. Out of 116 varieties, L. Singh and others (1940) found eight they considered promising for Punjab conditions; these averaged from 6 to 25 lb. of fruit per vine. Of these, the quality of Foster s Seedling, Black Prince, Kandhari, and Seedless was better than of Pandhri Sahebi, Dakh, Waltham Cross, and Black Hamburg. L. Singh and Singh (1940) have described 66 of these varieties after studying the characters of the vines and the grapes useful in classification. The features used in identification, in order of importance, are (*a*) leaf shape and pubescence, (*b*) colour of berries, (*c*) shape of berries, (*d*) colour and pubescence of growing shoots, (*e*) cane characters, and (*f*) some characters of the peduncle, pedicel and skin. Short, popular descriptions of 112 varieties have been given by the same authors (1942 b). An editorial note in the Punjab Fruit Journal for April, 1947, states that of the foreign varieties which grew well at Lyallpur, all were of poor quality and that breeding work, started in 1937, had produced eight promising seedlings. Varma (1947 a) reports on a trial of seven labrusca, or hybrid varieties planted from 4,000 to 5,000 feet above sea level in Patiala. The most productive variety, the famous American variety Concord, yielded at the rate of 5,836 lb. per acre when about four years old. Because the fruit is subacid and seedy, the market price was only about half that of vinifera grapes, but even so, the crop seemed an economic success. In Uttar Pradesh (Anon., 1941 a) more than 40 varieties are reported under trial at Saharanpur and elsewhere, some of which are regarded as promising.

Breeding work of a different nature which may prove of value in India has been done by Fennell (1945) in Florida and the West Indies. He used as female parents some of the 14 or more species growing in the humid tropical climate of that region, and as pollen parents some of the temperate zone grapes of high quality. From some 10,000 seedlings he has selected some with satisfactory size, quality, yield, vigour, and disease resistance, and says they do well both on water-logged soils in Puerto Rico and on poor dry soils in southern Florida. Some of them might prove successful in India. The quality of these hybrids is not as good as that of vinifera grapes, according to Popenoe (1953), who considers *Vitis labrusca* and its hybrids most promising for the tropics.

The possible use of induced polyploidy is stressed by Dermen (1954) who states that within two years, by treatment with colchicine, polyploidy has been induced in 10 varieties of American bunch grapes (largely *Vitis labrusca*), one variety of *V. vinifera*, and 16 of *V. rotundifolia*.

Yield and Marketing

The yield varies greatly with varieties and conditions. The vines start bearing in about the fourth year, and should bear regularly from the 6th, starting with about five pounds per vine, according to the Report on Marketing. Naik (1949) says that in Madras the vines begin to bear in the second or third year. The vines are ordinarily considered to live about as long as men, but some live much longer. A vine planted in 1769 in Hampton Court in England was recently reported to be bearing 1,700 bunches of grapes a year, and vines planted about 1761 in Kandahar are said to be still bearing.

The average yield in India was estimated in the Report on Marketing Grapes as 7,380 lb. per acre. This compares well with yields reported in other countries : California, 7,678 lb. ; Australia, 4,220 ; France, 4,054 ; and Spain, 2,405. But the Report included large areas in Baluchistan, where the yield is relatively low. The average in India is much higher. The Report estimates 11,160 lb. of Bhokri per acre, and 11,610 of Bangalore Blue. One grower in Poona has now produced 40,388 lb. of Bhokri grapes (Kamath, 1955) but this is still less than yields reported in Madurai. There yields up to 70,000 lb. an acre are reported, 50,000 in March and April and the rest in the autumn. This is the green grape, which Rangacharlu (1952) says ordinarily produces 12,000 to 15,000 lb. in the first crop and 7,000 to 8,000 in the second. The seedless varieties yield less, but, according to Naik (1949) may produce 24,000 lb. a year. Venkataratnam (1953) estimates a yield of about 35,000 lb. per acre in the case of the Anab-e-shahi variety in Hyderabad.

Establishing and maintaining a vineyard in South India requires a large investment and brings a large return. Rangacharlu (1952) estimates costs per acre at Rs. 1,475 the first year, Rs. 850 the second, and Rs. 1,450 thereafter. He puts the income at Rs. 1,400 in the second year and Rs. 5,040 in the third, so that by the end of the third year there is a net profit of Rs. 2,665. After that the income is about Rs. 5,200, leaving a net profit of Rs. 3,750 per acre each year. In well-cared for vineyards, where the yield is 25,000 lb. or more per acre, the net profit may be as much as Rs. 5,000 It is obvious that the acreage should be expanded until such profits are impossible. At the time of the Report on Marketing, the highest return per acre was given as Rs. 1,350 at Bangalore. Iyengar and others (1954) describe a new plantation near that city on which an expenditure of Rs. 5,000 per acre had been made in the first two years, in addition to the cost of the land, but in the second year the crop was worth about half this amount. Cheema and others (1954) say that before the second world war, costs in the Deccan were about Rs. 1,000 per acre and receipts up to Rs. 1,500 except when frost spoiled the crop, and that after the war both income and expenditure were three or four times as great.

The fresh grape is highly perishable, unless kept in cold storage, but with careful handling grapes are successfully shipped over northern India, and to Burma, from Baluchistan, while Bombay and Madurai ship as far as Calcutta. The grapes should be picked when fully ripe, as they do not ripen off the vines. The practice of picking them before they are ripe, for the early market, or in order to complete harvesting in one operation after the major part of the crop has been shipped, is condemned by the Marketing Report. The sale of immature, sour fruit injures the market. The bunches should be carefully cut with shears in the morning or evening, but not when the berries are wet with rain or dew. The bunches should be placed on shallow trays. In the packing shed they should be carefully scrutinized, any defective berries removed with fine scissors, and only the good bunches packed. Grading of the fruit is profitable. Cold storage is used in other countries, Rose and others (1941) recommending a temperature of 30 to 31° F., with a humidity of 85 to 90%.

Many types of containers are used, most of which are not very suitable. Bamboo baskets are common in Bombay, where large earthenware pots are also used. The latter have the advantage that everyone handling them realizes that they must be treated gently, lest they break. But they are heavy, and the grapes must be removed from them for inspection. The need for stronger containers is stressed in the Marketing Report, and the use of wooden crates, where these are not too expensive, is recommended. Soft, dry packing material, such as straw, chaff, wood-wool, and plain white paper, should be used. It is common to use green grape leaves, which decay and generate heat, and so damage the grapes. At present, it is generally necessary for exporters in the local wholesale markets to re-pack the grapes, which is bad for the grapes and increases the cost.

Co-operative societies for selling grapes have been organized in Madras, with encouraging results. The Government has set up rules for grading a number of varieties of grapes and the use of the 'Agmark' label.

The grape enjoys a very good reputation, not only as a delicious fruit, but as a suitable food for invalids. Its value is probably due largely to the high content of sugar in an easily digestible form. Gandhi reports analyses of Bombay varieties which show from 13·55 to 22·94% sugar, and 0·37 to 1·28% acid. The Marketing Report states that the sugar content varies from 11 to 22%, and that the Bhokri at Poona tested 18 60%. Siddappa (1942) states that at the best stage for eating, the Kishmish variety contains 23 to 24% solids and Haitha 18 to 20%, the total solids : acid ratio in both cases being about 40 to 1. Venkataratnam (1954) states that the reducing sugars in 35 varieties grown in Hyderabad varied from 9·83 to 20·63% and acid from 0·298 to 4·4552%, although only one variety had more than 2·612% acid. Grapes contain practically no sucrose. The ratio of sugar to acid varied from 3·596 : 1 to 56·96 : 1 (in Barbarosa). The Bhokri, which had the highest yield, contained only 12·63% sugar and had a ratio of only 7·46 : 1. Siddappa and Bhatia (1954 c) found 12·67% sugar in the local purple grape and 14·54% in the white. These figures are typical of labrusca grapes, while most vinifera varieties contain more sugar. In the United States, a sugar content of at least 17% is often required for harvesting vinifera grapes, and raisin grapes are not considered suitable for picking until they show 24%, and 26% is preferred. The iron content of grapes, and particularly of raisins, has been emphasized by some, but actually the grape seems to be only a fair source of iron and other minerals, and a poor source of vitamins.

Grapes of the Kishmish variety were canned in 40° Brix syrup with excellent results by Siddappa and Ishaq (1950). The Haitha berries tended to split open when canned, but also gave a good product.

Most raisins are dried in the sun, often by spreading them in thin layers on trays in the vineyards. Occasionally evaporators with artificial heat are used when there is danger of rain. Choice varieties are sometimes marketed on the cluster, but more commonly they are removed from the bunch. The small seedless varieties are largely used for raisin, and sometimes the seeds are removed from the seedy types.

CHAPTER XX

THE FIG

Although wild figs have grown in India for thousands of years, and dried figs are imported in large quantities, the common fig is not much grown. This is in spite of the fact that soil and climatic conditions which seem to be suitable are commonly found in this country. There are apparently opportunities for growing figs in the neighbourhood of cities for the fresh fruit market, and possibly for extending their cultivation in the most favourable districts for drying. Much remains to be done, however, in order to find the best varieties and the most suitable cultural methods. Bombay formerly had by far the biggest fig industry in India, mainly in Purandhar taluka, where Gandhi (1924) reported 1,230 acres. The area in the State has been rather steadily shrinking, however, and in 1948 was only 287 acres. Cheema and others (1954) state that many orchards have been removed because of the damage caused by the disease, rust. Naik (1949) reports an estimated 250 acres in South India, although he says, 'It seems clear that good crops of fig can be raised under all the diverse conditions of South India, provided the suitable varieties are chosen for each tract.' There are small industries around Mysore and in Hyderabad, and some figs are grown in various parts of the country.

The fig occupies a much more important place in the horticulture of some other countries, particularly around the Mediterranean. The leading producers are Italy, Spain, Turkey, the United States, Greece, Algeria, and Portugal. These countries account for a large part of the estimated 1,625,000 acres of figs in the world, with a production of perhaps 350,000 tons, on a dry basis.

The original home of the fig may have been southern Arabia, but it soon spread westward. An indication of its prominence in the Mediterranean countries is given by the frequent mention of it in the Bible. Not only are Adam and Eve said to have made the first clothing by sewing fig leaves together, but when Micah thinks of the time when 'nation shall not lift up sword against nation, neither shall they learn war any more', he says that 'they shall sit every man under his vine and under his fig-tree'. The fig also appears in Egyptian hieroglyphics, and in the writings of Homer and other early Greek authors. The advanced state of its culture is indicated by the fact that Homer received from his father trees of 20 named varieties (Condit, 1955). Some authorities maintain that certain figs now grown in Italy are clones listed by Pliny. The fig tree was considered sacred in all of the countries of southwestern Asia and in Egypt, Greece, and Italy, according to Condit (1947), who cites many references to figs in the mythology and literature of that region.

The genus *Ficus* is a very large one, containing more than 1,000 species. It belongs to the family Moraceae, which includes the mulberry and jackfruit, and which is considered by some botanists as part of the family Urticaceae. The common fig is *Ficus carica*, although some varieties are probably hybrids between this and other species. Several species bear edible fruits, but are not ordinarily cultivated. Among these is *F. glomerata*, of which Shunmukhasundaram and Naidu (1941) state that the dried fruits may be ground into a powder which is eaten with great relish with milk and sugar, as a base for porridge, or in home-made sweets. Naik (1949) states that *F. roxburghii* on the west coast of South India produces fairly large crops of brick-coloured fruits of poor quality. Many species are grown as ornamentals, including the very common banyan, peepul, and a species which clings to walls. *F. elastica*, the rubber tree, is grown as an ornamental and is used to a small extent for making rubber, although the much more important Para rubber tree is a member of an entirely different family.

The fig grows under a wide variety of climatic conditions. It is a deciduous tree, and can stand winter temperatures as low as 18° F. or even 15° in the case of dormant mature trees, according to Condit (1933). Young trees are much less hardy. On the other hand, there is little need for chilling to break the rest period, and in regions of warm winters growth may be almost continuous. Warm weather while the fruit is ripening is necessary for good quality, but satisfactory figs are produced under glass in England. Summer temperatures up to about 115° seem to do no harm except that fruit ripening at the time may be sunburnt. Condit (1947) however, points out that when the temperature is much above 100° F., the fruit tends to ripen prematurely, to have a tough skin, and to be deficient in pulp. Rainy weather while the fruit is ripening is undesirable, as the fruit may be insipid under such conditions, and is likely to spoil even before it is fully ripe. The climate has a greater effect on the characteristics of the fruit than is the case with most species. Condit (1950) states that the size, shape, bloom, colour of the skin and of the pulp, quality, and tendency toward parthenocarpy may all be markedly influenced. The differences in the colour of the skin and pulp are frequently such as would indicate a difference in variety. In some cases, fruit of better quality is secured in the comparatively cool and moist coastal belt of California than in the dry, hot interior valleys, although the latter may encourage a higher sugar content, and be better for drying. Fewer parthenocarpic fruits mature in regions of hot climate. Cheema and others (1954) report that in Poona half of the fruits are sunburned, and that the stems of young trees should be protected by foliage, straw, or paper. As the fruiting season is long, and in India tends to last throughout the year, it should be possible to arrange for a fair part of the crop to mature at a time when weather conditions are favourable.

The fig is grown commercially on a wide variety of soils, and is known to do well on heavy clays, rich loams, and light sandy soils. Sandy soils are more subject to nematode infection which, in some countries, is a limiting factor and which may explain the failure of European varieties in some places in India. Such soils also require more frequent irrigation, and may need more manuring in order to produce vigorous growth and heavy bearing. But excellent crops of figs of high quality are possible on most soils. It is frequently stated that a large amount of lime is required, and it is true that the soils of the most important fig-producing areas are well supplied.

Propagation and Culture

Propagation is very largely by cuttings, which root very easily and grow rapidly, so that it is possible to have a small tree bearing fruit within a year of the time the cutting is made. Any mature wood up to an age of two or three years may be used, but that about ½ to ¾ of an inch in diameter, with short internodes, is preferred. It is well to cut each piece just above one node and just below another. Cuttings 8 to 12 inches in length give good results. These are ordinarily planted in the nursery in much the same way as those of other plants, with from one bud to half the cutting exposed. Condit (1933, 1947), however, states that in California the practice is to tie bundles of the cuttings together, bury them upside down in sandy soil in January or February at the time of pruning and plant them upright in furrows about the middle of March. They are then ready for planting out the next winter. In Bombay (Anon. 1929) cuttings are made at the beginning of the rains and planted out a year or 15 months later. Smith (1940) states that in Uttar Pradesh cuttings made in December are ready to plant during the following monsoon season. Actually, under favourable conditions, they may be rather large for transplanting by that time. In Europe, according to Condit (1947), the practice of planting cuttings directly in the ground where the tree is desired is probably more common than that of planting them in nurseries.

Other methods of propagation are feasible, and Smith (1940) prefers air-layering. Top-working to change the variety of established trees, is sometimes practised, and may be done by means of shield or patch budding or cleft or bark grafting. Naik (1949) reports success in the sidegrafting of figs on *Ficus glomerata* and *F. hispida*. As *F. glomerata* seems to be resistant to nematodes, it may be desirable to use it as a root-stock where these pests are a problem. *Ficus palmata* is also reported to be resistant to nematode attack. Dorasami (1951) states that Poona and other varieties were budded on five plants tentatively identified as *F. palmata*, and that all had a greater girth and had produced more fruit than any of the 65 varieties of fig received with them from Bezwada and grown as cuttings. One European variety grafted on *F. palmata* at Allahabad lived for about two years, after which the scion died, although the root-stock continued to grow. De la Cruz and Gonzalez (1953) report that *F. hauili*, *F. odorata*, and *F. ampelos* were found compatible with *F. carica* in the Philippines, and in view of their vigour at early stages and probable resistance to the fig borer, were considered promising rootstocks. They found nine other species incompatible.

The distance apart at which the trees should be planted depends on the size of the tree, and this in turn depends on the variety, the soil, and especially on the type of pruning to be followed. Great extremes are found in this matter. Some fig trees live for a very long time. Condit (1941) refers to one said to have lived for 800 years in England before being killed by lightning. It was apparently slow growing, for the circumference of the trunk was only five feet at the base, while Condit mentions trees of the Mission variety in California less than 100 years old with circumferences, four feet above the ground, of from 11 to 14 feet. The largest had a spread of more than 60 feet, but Condit (1933) mentions another tree with a spread of 310 feet. Such size is impossible in orchards, for even in California, figs are rarely planted as much as 40 feet apart. Whatever the distance, crowding may be prevented by pruning. One variety in California does well when planted as close as 6 by 8 feet and pruned practically to the ground every year. Spacing as great as 50 feet is reported by Cheema (1926) in Turkey.

Not only the size, but the natural shape of the tree varies in the different varieties, some being spreading and others more erect. The shape is ordinarily controlled by pruning. Figs for drying are frequently allowed to drop from the tree, in which case the tree may be allowed to grow tall. Hand picking is necessary in the case of figs marketed fresh, and this is much more economical in case the trees are kept comparatively low. The type of pruning thus depends on the variety, the purpose for which grown, and the ideas of the grower.

To produce a 'standard' tree, the young plant is headed back a few feet from the ground, as is done with most fruits, but in some places a 'bush' type is produced by cutting the trunk off a few inches from the ground level, and selecting six or seven main branches, some of which rise below the surface. This method is particularly well adapted to regions where there is danger of frost. Cheema and others (1954) state that in Bombay most fig trees are planted 15 ft. apart, but that this allows only hand cultivation and that a spacing of 18-20 ft. facilitates interculture. In Mysore, according to Naik (1949), the figs are planted 6 to 9 feet apart, and are trained to a bush form by annual pruning which leaves only about two buds on each shoot of the previous season's growth. In Madras, although the spacing allowed is only about 12 feet, little or no pruning is done, with disastrous results. Smith (1940) recommends heading at a foot or 18 inches, whereas Gandhi (1924) advises heads about four feet from the ground. A framework is then developed to suit the type of the tree the grower wishes.

The amount of annual pruning is related to the habits of growth and bearing of the variety. The figs are borne singly or in pairs in the axils of the leaves. They develop as the branch elongates, and in some varieties, and especially in regions with well-marked winters, there are two or three distinct crops. Sometimes young figs remain on the dormant trees and mature early in the spring. This first crop is called the breba and the second, the main crop. Petrucci and Crane (1950) report that in the Mission fig in California, fruit bud differentiation occurs in the terminal buds of young shoots throughout the growing season, April 1 to July 15. Breba figs are produced from buds which differentiated the previous year ; the second crop from either the previous or the current year. One of the main objects of pruning is to produce plenty of shoot growth to bear a large number of fruits during the season. The amount of pruning necessary to produce vigorous growth, and the amount which can be done without inhibiting fruitfulness, vary with the varieties and the environment. Ordinarily rather heavy pruning is possible.

For centuries a special type of pruning has been common in Europe, in which the terminal bud of each shoot is removed just before growth starts in the spring. This is said to cause earlier development and maturity of the fruit, and a larger yield. Condit (1947) refers to experiments with such disbudding in southern California, with good results in one variety, but negative results with 24 other varieties.

In Bombay, the main crop of figs ripens during the dry spring and summer months, and the trees are more or less dormant and lose most of their leaves in August and September. Under these conditions, Gandhi (1924) recommends pruning early in July, just after the crop has been harvested. Only a light heading back of the shoots which have just borne the crop is given. Several new shoots come out near the ends of the pruned branches, at the end of October. Fruits which form on this new growth by November or December have time to mature before the next rainy season. In northern India, on the other hand, the trees are more or less dormant in the winter, and Smith reports satisfactory fruit only from April through June. He lays great emphasis on pruning, saying that without it no edible fruit will be formed. He recommends rather severe annual pruning in December, leaving only three or four buds of the previous year's growth. He deals with only one variety, however, and it is possible that other varieties may be found which will respond to somewhat different treatment, and perhaps produce crops at other seasons. It may prove practicable to produce figs during the rainy season, as is done in some parts of the United States, and if this is done, the season may well be extended into the winter.

The method of pruning used in Bombay is likely to result in rather long stems with a cluster of branches near the end. In a short time the trees become straggly, and much of the fruit is borne far from the trunk. To reduce this tendency, notching has proved effective, and is best done in July. Notches are made within a quarter of an inch above the bud, sloping slightly so that the latex which comes out may not cover the bud. Just enough bark is removed to delay healing until after the bud has started growth, which occurs in about eight days. Plump buds in the middle portion of the branch are most suitable, and not more than two should be notched on one branch. The number of notches on one tree should depend on the state of the tree, straggly trees requiring more than those which naturally produce many branches. Gandhi reports that in one experiment 82 shoots from notched buds on 11 trees produced a total of 588 fruits. This amounts to about five pounds per tree. It is assumed that the notching had no adverse effect on the other branches and that this is a net gain. Not all growers in that area, however, are convinced of the desirability of notching.

Comparatively little has been written regarding the cultivation, manuring, and irrigation of fig trees in this country. Where figs are grown for drying, and are allowed to fall from the tree, it is desirable that the soil be clean of weeds and smooth. This requires careful cultivation. Otherwise similar cultivation to that given to other fruits is sufficient. Naik (1949) states that in South India heavy manuring, frequent irrigation, and weeding at least twice a year are necessary for the production of good crops. Cheema and others (1954) state that in Bombay about 20 lb. of rotten manure per tree is given in the first year, increasing to 100-160 lb. in the eighth. In the first and second years this is applied at the start of the monsoon, and thereafter at the end of September. In California growers feared that the application of nitrogen would increase the splitting of the fruit, but Proebsting and Warner (1954) found that it increased both growth and yield without increasing splitting, even when 12 lb. of nitrogen per tree was applied.

The fig is fairly drouth-resistant, and in Europe, Israel, and Turkey is seldom irrigated after the trees are established, but in many seasons they undoubtedly suffer from a deficiency of water. In California it has been observed that unirrigated trees grow very slowly and fail to produce economic crops. In India, also, irrigation is the practice, at least during the dry season when the fruits are growing and maturing. Figs are irrigated from October to May in the Deccan, where it is reported that the fruits are larger and sweeter when irrigated once a fortnight than when more frequent irrigation is given. In South India also, too much water is said to make the fruit insipid, but irrigation twice a week is considered suitable. Smith (1940) recommends heavy irrigations twice a month from the time the figs are the size of a marble until harvesting is finished. Excessive irrigation while the fruits are ripening may increase the amount of cracking and souring.

Pests and Diseases

The stem borer, *Batocera rufomaculata*, is widely distributed, and in some localities makes fig growing impossible, according to Husain and Khan (1940) who report that of 53 trees planted at Lyallpur in 1925, only 3 survived until 1932. It has also been reported causing some loss in Bombay, where it is said commonly to attack the stems close to the ground, thus escaping attention for some time. It causes serious damage in Uttar Pradesh according to Lal (1950). At the fruit research station at Hessaghatta, Bangalore, practically all fig trees are attacked, but *Ficus palmata* appeared to be unattractive to the borer. This borer has been mentioned as a pest of the mango and occurs on trees of 11 families, including various species of *Ficus*. The adult beetle feeds on the bark, leaves, and fruits, but is not serious. Little harm is done by the grub when it bores in the wood, but by eating the inner bark and xylem tissue it may girdle and kill limbs or the entire tree. Its presence is indicated by debris collected below the entrance hole. Where there is much danger of attack, it is recommended that the trunk of the tree be protected with paper painted with coal tar, or with 1/16 inch mesh wire gauze. The grubs may be killed with a knife, or by injecting kerosene of a chloroform-creosote mixture into the hole.

A leaf-eating caterpillar, *Ocinara varians* is often a serious pest in the Deccan, according to Cheema and others (1954) who recommend hand picking or spraying with lead arsenate or DDT. Another caterpillar, *Phycodes minor*, is recorded by Lal (1950) as causing a severe webbing of the leaves in Uttar Pradesh. Mites also attack the leaves, and may be controlled by sulphur dusting if the damage justifies this. Batra (1952 b) reports one fig tree at New Delhi severely infested with the midge, *Anjeerodiplosis peshawarensis*, which is a pest in West Pakistan. The infested fruit is abnormally long and contains hundreds of maggots. The Oriental yellow scale, *Aonidiella orientalis*, has been reported on the fig by Rahman and Ansari (1941).

The only common disease is the fig rust caused by the fungus, *Cerotelium* (*Physopella, Uredo*) *fici*. This is very common, but ordinarily the damage is not great. It is characterized by small, rusty, raised spots on the underside of the leaf. As has been noted, it causes severe damage in Bombay, especially in cool wet winters. It causes the premature fall of the leaf, but ordinarily this does not occur until late in the season, after the figs are mature. The last part of the crop may be somewhat affected and in cool wet winters in Bombay the damage may be appreciable. Spraying with Bordeaux mixture is advocated in other countries, but has not proved very effective in India. Naik (1949) states that in South India dusting with sulphur has been recommended.

A shot-hole disease of the fig has been reported from Kanpur by Mehta and Bose (1947). It is caused by *Cylindrocladium scoparium*, and may involve the greater part of the leaf. Mehta (1951) also refers to a zonate spot of the fig, caused by *Cephalosporium fici*.

Numerous other pests and diseases are found in other countries, including organisms which cause the sugar in the ripening fruit to ferment, and the ordinary black mould, *Aspergillus niger*, which makes the fruit repulsive and worthless.

Birds are attracted to the ripening fruits, and are likely to cause considerable damage.

Types of Figs

The fruit of the fig is called a syconium, hollow receptacle on the inner surface of which the flowers are borne. At the apex there is a small opening which has been called the eye, ostiole, or mouth. Condit (1941, 1947) distinguishes between the eye, the external opening and the ostiole, the complete passage to the interior of the syconium. The eye is more or less closed by a ring of bracts, more so in the earlier stages than later, and more in some varieties than in others. Many of the best varieties of figs without pollination develop fruits with empty 'seed' coats, and this type is known as the common fig. Some varieties, on the other hand, fail to set fruit unless they are pollinated, and the syconia soon fall from the tree. As the principal varieties grown for drying in Turkey are of this sort, it is called the Smyrna type. A third type, known as the San Pedro type, is of much less importance. In it the breba crop develops without pollination, whereas the second crop may also develop parthenocarpically under some conditions but require pollination under others, or may set a better crop if pollinated. In all of these types, if the ovaries are fertilized they develop into viable seed. The size, shape, colour, and flavour of the fruit which develops after pollination in the common fig are different from those in that which develops without pollination. On the whole, the unpollinated fruit is likely to be better.

Pollen is produced in Europe and America only by a more primitive type of fig, known as the caprifig, 'goat fig'. In it there are staminate flowers borne near the ostiole. Pollination is accomplished solely by means of a very small wasp, *Blastophaga psenes* (*grossorum*). The wasp lays its eggs in the short-styled flowers of the caprifig, and most of the life history is passed within the ovary. After impregnation, the adult female emerges from the flower and finds her way out by the eye. She then looks for other flowers in which to lay her eggs. If she enters another caprifig, she lays her eggs and the species is carried on. If she enters a fig of the other type, however, she is prevented from ovapositing by the long style which characterizes this type of flower. She may leave the syconium, or she may die in it. In leaving the caprifig, she collects pollen which she automatically distributes in the syconium she enters. She thus performs an essential function in the Smyrna type of fig. This is known as caprification.

If figs of the Smyrna type are to be grown, it is therefore necessary to have some trees of the caprifig, both to supply pollen and to maintain the supply of blastophagas. The caprifig also produces three or more crops, the spring crop, corresponding to the brebas being known as the *profiche*, the summer crop as *mammoni*, and the winter crop, in which the wasps are carried over from one year to another, as the *mamme*. The fruits of the *profiche* are gathered just before the blastophagas emerge, and are distributed in the trees to be pollinated, preferably in wire baskets. From about 36 to 100 fruits are necessary for each tree, and these may be produced on from three to five caprifig trees per hundred trees to be pollinated.

Most of the caprifigs are of the species *F. carica*, but *F. pseudocarica* and *F. palmata* are sometimes used for the purpose. Even when caprifigs are not infested with blastophagas, they are ordinarily useless, though edible varieties are known.

The situation regarding the varieties of fig commonly grown in India is still rather obscure. Many of them frequently produce a large number of syconia, all or most of which fall from the tree without maturing. Rao (1944) reported that of 10 varieties being grown at Kodur, only three produced mature fruits normally, but that a crop could be secured from the others by artificial pollination. This was accomplished by inserting a bamboo needle into an immature syconium of the wild fig, *Ficus glomerata* and then into an immature syconium of the variety to be pollinated, and revolving the needle. A little later, work at Allahabad indicated that in some years, at least, mature figs could be secured by bringing in and scattering among the trees, immature syconia of this wild fig. The wild figs are frequently inhabited by *Blastophaga psenes*. Some of the cultivated figs may also be infested and at Allahabad in 1950 a considerable number of figs matured on trees where these insects were found, without bringing in any wild fig syconia. There was no wild fig tree within several hundred yards of these trees. Naik (1949) reports that at Kodur the Poona, Black Ischia, and Brown Turkey were parthenocarpic, whereas in Allahabad trees of the Poona variety, and one secured under the name of Black Ischia failed to set fruit. The Black Ischia tree was received from Lucknow, where this variety is said to set fruit without known pollination. If pollination were brought about naturally by insects, it is quite possible that the growers would be unaware of this. If any of the varieties grown at Allahabad produces some pollen (the cultivated varieties of Europe and America do not), and wasps are present, the production of seedy fruit, as at Allahabad, would be easily explained.

Caprification in California is an expensive process, and encourages the spread of disease, so an alternative method of securing good crops of the Smyrna type fig would be valuable. Work in recent years indicates that this is possible by the use of plant hormones. Crane and Blondeau (1949 a) experimented with a number of hormones, and secured good results with indolebutyric acid, but at a cost which prevented its commercial use. Later Crane found it possible to secure a satisfactory crop with 60 ppm of para-chlorophenoxyacetic acid (PCPA) at the rate of 5 gallons a tree, at a cost of less than a rupee an acre for the material. No damage was done to the foliage. Crane and Blondeau (1951) found 80 ppm still more effective, producing 17% more fruits than the caprified controls, but higher concentrations than this were less effective. The hormone was more effective when applied to the leaves than when applied to the young syconia. The same authors (1949 b) secured astounding results with 2, 4, 5-trichlorophenoxyacetic acid, which not only induced parthenocarpy, but caused the fruit to ripen in 60 days instead of 120. Rather severe damage was caused when this was used at more than 10 ppm, which caused only 56% of the syconia to set. Similar acceleration was caused by some other substances. Acceleration was also produced by injecting 1,500 ppm of indolebutyric acid, or certain other hormones, into the syconia. All of the substances which were effective produced mature syconia similar to those resulting from pollination except for the lack of seed. The sugar content may be slightly higher. The effect on the developing fruitlets, which have commonly been called achenes, but which Crane and Baker (1953) decided were more properly to be called drupelets, differs markedly. In all cases there is no embryo, but as Crane (1952 a, b), points out, in some cases they lack an endocarp, in others it is present but non-sclerified, and in still others it is sclerified as in the case of pollinated drupelets.

Harris (1950) in Australia, induced rapid growth with the same hormones used in California, but the quality of the fruits was unsatisfactory. Attempts to induce parthenocarpy with the varieties grown at Allahabad with PCPA failed. More experimentation, with different hormones, would be desirable.

Another method of hastening the maturity of figs has been practised at least since the third century B.C. and Condit (1947) refers to its use in different places from that time down to the present. This method is the anointing of the eye of the immature fruit with olive oil, or occasionally with other oils or acids, and is known as oleification. The practice has been opposed by some as reducing the quality of the fruit. Clements and Pentzer (1950) in California found that the application of olive oil to the eye hastened maturity and colour and increased the size of the Mission fig considerably when applied within a narrow range of dates, and of the Lob markedly over a wide range of dates starting as much as three weeks before harvest. The flavour and appearance were normal, and the treated fruits were equal to or better than the controls in sugar content. A saturated solution of tartaric acid also caused rapid growth and ripening. Experiments with a local variety at Coonoor are reported by Rangacharlu and Rao (1952). A single application of linseed oil in the syconium caused the fruit to ripen in 43·3 days on the average, compared with 59 in untreated fruits, to ripen more uniformly and be sweeter and of better colour. Weekly applications of sesame oil caused ripening in 14·9 days compared with 37·1 in the control, and in this case there was not only improvement in the colour and sweetness, but the treated fruit weighed an average of 2·3 oz. and the untreated 1·6 oz.

As is to be expected in a fruit which has been cultivated for thousands of years, there are many named varieties. Condit (1955) describes 711 varieties and gives 946 synonyms in addition to 98 which he mentions as having been listed by other authors. Condit (1941) has dealt exhaustively with the characteristics on which the varieties may be classified, including the colour, which varies from green or pale yellow to very dark purple, and the form of the fruit; its neck, stalk, ostiole and eye, eye scales, and skin; the pulp which is the developed floral parts; the meat, which is the wall of the syconium, between the skin and the pulp; the seeds; the flavour; the form, size, and texture of the leaf; and the size, habit of growth, and fruitfulness of the tree.

The leaf of the fig is typically lobed, but much variation occurs. There are commonly three, five, or even seven lobes, and these are often separated by deep sinuses. Several types of leaf may be found on the same tree. Indian varieties are characterized by leaves only slightly lobed or entire. *F. palmata*, *F. glomerata*, and some of the other species have entire leaves, and it is possible that the Indian figs represent hybrids between *F. carica* and some other species.

The main variety grown in Bombay is called the Poona fig, the fruit of which is bell-shaped, light purple with rosy flesh, weighing about an ounce and a half. Cheema and others (1954) say that a common fig called Coimbatore was becoming popular in Baroda and other parts of Western India, and that the Bezwada grafted on *Ficus palmata* has given good yields. Other varieties grown in Bombay are the Ganjam, Bangalore, and Mycerum, the last being a popular variety in Hyderabad. Smith lists the following varieties as growing successfully at Saharanpur : Black Ischia, Cabul, Bangalore, Lucknow, and Brown Turkey. Of these only the first is recommended as doing very well in Lucknow. The Brown Turkey for which Condit (1955) prefers the name San Piero, is fairly extensively grown in other countries. Naik (1949) states that in Madras varieties are not standardized, but that the Poona is the most prolific on the plains while the Marseilles crops well at elevations above 5,000 feet. It will be noticed that a number of names of varieties grown in India are taken from the names of the places where they have been grown, and where they may have originated as seedlings. Even in the case of those having the names of European varieties, there may be question as to identification. The leaf of the Black Ischia grown in Lucknow is very different from that of that variety at Riverside, California. Western varieties introduced into India have generally not grown very well, whereas the Indian varieties flourish. One possible explanation would be that the nematodes injure the western varieties, whereas the Indian types have inherited resistance from *F. glomerata* or some other resistant species. One of the most famous western varieties is the Lob, which is the most important of the figs grown near Smyrna. It is also called the Smyrna fig and in California, the Calimyrna.

Very little information is available on the yield of figs in this country. One reason for practising notching in Bombay is said to be the unsatisfactory yield without it. Cheema and others (1954) say that there should be a good crop from the fourth year, and that at Sawad in Poona district, each tree bears 40-50 lb., or that the yield is about 10,000 lb. per acre. The crop there ripens from March through May. In South India the heavier, more valuable crop is borne in the spring from February to May, and a second crop is ripe from July to October. In Mysore, where the trees are planted closely and heavily pruned, the yield, according to Naik (1949) is about 180 fruits per tree. In other places, it may be about 300 fruits on unpruned trees, giving about the same yield per acre, but the unpruned trees decline in yield after about 10 years. In California yields of dried fruit vary from 1½ to 2½ tons per acre.

The fig is a very wholesome and nutritious food, with an especially high sugar content. Gandhi reports the total sugar content of one lot of Poona figs as 17·2% and some analyses in other countries run as high as 28% although the average is much lower. The acid content is unusually low. Miller and Bazore (1945) state that figs are a good source of calcium and that fresh figs in California have been reported to be a fair source of vitamin A. But they found the Brown Turkey in Hawaii a poor source of vitamin A, thiamine, and ascorbic acid. Figs are also valued for their definite laxative effect, and because of the alkalinity of their ash. In the dried state the sugar content varies from about 45% to 65%.

Figs do not increase in sugar content after harvest, so should be allowed to ripen fully on the tree. At ordinary temperatures they then spoil in a few days, which makes marketing difficult. It was found in Bombay (Anon., 1947) that they could be held in good condition for a month at 32-35° F. Other experiments have favoured higher temperatures, but Claypool and Osbeck (1952) favour 40° F. or below for the Mission fig in California. They found no advantage in controlling the percentage of carbon dioxide in the storage atmosphere, but say that an initial exposure to pure carbon dioxide at 41-50° F. for 36 hours seemed to reduce the subsequent respiration rate and delay the growth of microorganisms.

While the fresh ripe fig is a very delicious fruit, because it is highly persihable the great bulk of the world production is dried. The common practice in most countries is to allow the figs to stay on the tree until they drop, at which time they are already about three-fourths dry. They may be allowed to lie on the ground until drying is completed, or they may be gathered and placed on trays. Some varieties are subjected to sulphur fumes in order to bleach them, to avoid fermentation, and to facilitate drying. Too much sulphuring is likely to damage the flavour of the fruit. In Europe some figs are split open before drying. Gandhi (1924) gives directions for drying figs in Bombay, where the best results are said to be secured by sulphuring the freshly picked figs and then drying them in the sun on bamboo matting supported three or four feet above the ground. They are turned daily for five to seven days. The quality of the dried Poona fig is fair, but not as good as that of the Smyrna fig. That a ready market awaits any dried figs of good quality which can be produced economically in India is shown by the fact that Bombay State alone imported 500,000 lb. annually before the second world war.

Figs may be preserved in several ways, and preservation is practised to a considerable extent in some places, especially where there is danger of rain interfering with drying. Fig preserves, in a rich syrup, are generally considered the choicest product, but the market is limited. As they are very sweet, not much is consumed at a time, and they are comparatively expensive. Larger amounts are canned. In either case they must be allowed to ripen on the tree and be very carefully handled, with very little delay between harvesting and processing. The outer waxy part of the skin is removed by blanching or by dipping in a boiling 2% lye solution. Fig jam is easily made, and is highly regarded by some, but has never become commercially important. Jelly has also been made in Bombay. Some varieties are much better for canning or preserving than others.

CHAPTER XXI

THE CUSTARD APPLES

The term 'custard apple' is ordinarily applied in India to the *sharifa* or *sita phal*, *Anonna squamosa.* In other parts of the world, this term is applied to at least three other species, including the pond apple, *A glabra* (*palustris*), which is scarcely edible, though the smooth, glossy, yellow fruit is decorative. The best usage is, perhaps, to make it cover the entire genus, or at least the edible members of it. Other names for *A. squamosa* are sugar apple and sweetsop, both names sometimes being hyphenated.

Fortunately, there is very little confusion in botanical nomenclature, although the family, *Annonaceae* and the genus *Annona* are sometimes spelled *Anonaceae* and *Anona.* The family contains more than forty genera, of which two besides *Annona* produce edible fruits. The biriba, *Rollinia deliciosa*, is highly regarded in northern Brazil, and may be of value in sections of India which are free from frost. The papaw or pawpaw, *Asimina triloba*, is a wild fruit of temperate United States with some possibilities of development.

The genus *Annona* contains more than fifty species, of which five produce edible fruits of some importance. A number of others may be of value in breeding or as rootstocks. Most of the members of the genus, including all the major fruits, are indigenous to America. A few species are believed to be native of Africa; probably none of Asia. Several species were commonly grown in America before the discovery of those continents by Europeans, and terra cotta vases were made in the shape of the cherimoya in pre-historic Peru. It was formerly thought that the custard apple at least was indigenous to India and there is considerable evidence in favour of such a theory. The existence of Sanskrit names, and paintings and carvings which seem to represent the fruit at Ajanta and elsewhere strengthened the supposition based on the fact that the tree grows wild in many parts of the country. De Candolle studied the question, however, and came to the conclusion that the fruit was of American origin, and other scholars have agreed with him. Watt (1889) quotes one General Cunningham who did not dispute the theory that the Portuguese brought the custard apple into India, but thought that it was already in this country also. He wrote, 'My identification of this fruit amongst the Mathura sculptures has been contested on the ground that the tree was introduced into India by the Portuguese.....I can now appeal to one of the Bharhut sculptures for a very exact representation of the fruit and leaves of the custard apple.' To this, Watt replies, 'The representation referred to by General Cunningham might be associated with a large number of plants; they may prove to be conventional representations of the jack-fruit tree or some other allied plant : they are not unlike the flower-heads of the sacred *kadamba* or *Anthocephalus*.' He also says that there is not the slightest indication of either *A. squamosa* or *A. reticulata* being indigenous in any Indian forest, and concludes that there seems to be hardly any doubt as to *A. squamosa* being an introduced plant, although the date of the introduction was very obscure. However, there is increasing evidence that plants were taken across the South Pacific in one or both directions hundreds of years before the time of Columbus, and it is possible that the custard apple has been in India for thousands of years. Because of the presence of many close relatives, it still seems probable that the genus originated in tropical America.

There can be no doubt that the custard apple has been growing in this country for several centuries. It must have spread very rapidly after the discovery of America, for it is mentioned in the Ain-i-Akbari, written about one hundred years later. Within about another century it had travelled on through Arabia to Egypt. It is now very widely distributed throughout the tropics and warmer subtropics, although it has not succeeded in most Mediterranean countries or in California, where the winters seem to be too cool for it. Oppenheimer (1947), however, states that it is of commercial importance in Egypt and Central Africa, as well as southern Asia, and that it is very successfully grown in Israel.

Aside from the question of frost, or too much cool weather, the custard apple is not particular as to climate, and Oppenheimer (1947) states that it is only slightly damaged by temperatures several degrees below freezing. It is said to prefer a dry climate, at least during the flowering season, and is not damaged by the hot, dry 'khamsin' winds in Israel. On the other hand it ordinarily sets no fruits in northern India until the beginning of the rainy season, although flowers are produced during the hot, dry weather; and low humidity apparently interferes with pollination in parts of Egypt. Oppenheimer also notes that almost no fruits are set during the first weeks of the flowering season, and thinks that this is probably because of the lack of humidity. Possibly the ideal conditions during the flowering season would be high humidity but freedom from rain. In any case, it is known to flourish under very dry conditions, and to withstand drought well. Parsons (1932) states that in Ceylon it thrives in both the wet and the dry zones from sea level to an elevation of 3,000 feet.

As regards soil conditions also the custard apple is very tolerant. The fact that it grows well on rocky soils has been commonly marked, both in India and in other countries. The Aztec name in Mexico meant 'zapote which grows on stony ground', and Sturrock (1940) reports that it is at home in potholes in the coral lime rock of the Florida Keys. This does not mean, as some have thought, that the tree requires such stony ground for its best growth. It probably does better on sandy soil, and Parsons (1932) states that it grows well in quite heavy soil as well as in almost pure sand. Oppenheimer (1947) thinks light soils best, but that heavy soils with good drainage are also suitable. He says that the custard apple will tolerate as much as 50% lime in the soil, and that irrigation water containing about 300 ppm of chlorine has caused no harm. The tree is rather shallow-rooted, so does not require a deep soil, but drainage must be good, as it suffers from water-logging.

Although the custard apple occurs widely in different parts of India, and wild trees bearing satisfactory fruit are abundant in various areas, its commercial cultivation is limited. It is said that custard apples grow wild on more than 100,000 acres in Hyderabad, and Naik (1949) states that while it is not cultivated on a large scale in Madras it is produced in such enormous quantities in the forests as to vie in annual production with most cultivated fruits except the mango, banana, jackfruit and citrus fruits. The Department of Agriculture in Assam has estimated that there are more than 6,000 acres in that State. There are a few hundred acres in Uttar Pradesh.

In India custard apples are almost entirely grown from seed, and fairly good results are secured in this way. The value of vegetative propagation is recognized by most authors, as there is great variation among seedling trees, in quality as well as in yield. Khan and Rao (1953) report that the mean weight of fruit produced on seedling trees at Kodur was 6·2 oz., and that these fruits contained 38 seeds each, whereas fruit from selected trees averaged 12 oz. in weight and contained only 20 seeds. Ahmed (1936 a) holds that such differences are due to environment rather than inheritance and that selection is of no value. While the conditions under which the fruit is grown undoubtedly have a great influence on it, there seems to be no evidence that seedlings do not vary genetically. There seems to be a great opportunity to select seedlings for propagation, giving consideration to yield, size, number of seeds, and the quality of the pulp. Rodriguez (1954) reports the finding of an annona tree with seedless fruit in Cuba, but it is not clear to which species it belongs. If a good seedless custard apple suited to Indian conditions can be found, there could be no doubt of the value of vegetative propagation. Selection and propagation have been started in Hyderabad.

Inarching seems to be the most successful form of vegetative propagation, with 100% success in some cases. Layering is less successful. Venkataratnam (1955) reports 75% success in budding in June, and almost as much in January and March, in Hyderabad. Side-grafting was also used, but with less satisfaction.

In graftage, the rootstock is most commonly the seedling custard apple, but other species may prove better, especially the bullock's heart, *Annona reticulata*. Khan and Rao (1953) report that while all grafts on *A. squamosa*, *A. reticulata*, and *A. muricata*, and most on *A. palustris* grew for a time, those of the latter two species were dead within eight months. The grafts on *A. reticulata* grew somewhat more rapidly than those on *A. squamosa*, but both set fruit eight months after planting, while seedlings took 22 months. All were set out in 1948, and by 1953 the average production per tree had been 41·1 fruits on *A. reticulata*, 29 on *A. squamosa*, and 24·2 from the seedlings. Buell (1955) also reports lives of only a few months on *A. muricata* and *A. palustris*, and better results on *A. reticulata* than on *A. squamosa* both in the growth of the trees and the size and quality of the fruit. But doubt is cast on the success of grafting, for within 11 years all of the trees on *A. squamosa* were dead, and a third of those on *A. reticulata* showed signs of decline. Venkataratnam (1955) reports that trees grafted on *A. cherimola*, as well as those on *A. squamosa* and *A. reticulata*, were making good progress.

In growing seedlings for rootstock or as trees, it is recommended that fresh seed be used although Ahmed (1936 b) says that the seed remains good for three or four years, and that germination is better after exposure for a week than when absolutely fresh. The seed has a hard coat, and may take a month or more to germinate, but this time can be reduced by scarification or soaking for three days in water. In Hyderabad, however, it is said that planting the seed without soaking gives a higher percentage of germination, and planting the seeds in flat beds in the rainy season is recommended. The seedlings should be ready to bud or graft in about a year.

Two types of breeding work have been started. Venkataratnam (1954) reports crossing *A. squamosa*, *A. reticulata*, and *A. cherimola*. In one year 1,939 cross pollinations yielded fruit of 12 different combinations, containing a total of 3,389 seeds. Islam (1953) working at Dacca, East Bengal, produced tetraploids by colchicine treatment, which had larger, thicker darker green leaves and which flowered earlier than the controls.

Culture

The custard apple has rarely been grown in commercial orchards, or where any serious attempt has been made to provide scientific care. Very little is known, therefore, as to the best cultural methods. The trees never attain very great size, and if planted 20 feet apart, are not likely to be crowded. Closer planting is recommended in some countries, and Ahmed (1936 b) points out that in the desert regions of Egypt thick planting may improve pollination by raising the humidity of the atmosphere. Oppenheimer (1947) believes that the spacing used in Egypt, about three metres, is insufficient, but that the spacing of five metres used in Israel is too great.

The need for manuring custard apples in order to get good crops is generally recognized. Naturally, it is more important where the trees are grown on poor, sandy soil than where the soil contains a good supply of nutrients. Firminger's Manual recommends the use of old lime or mortar and cow dung during the winter. Ahmed (1936 b) recommends the application of nitrogen, phosphorus, and potassium to the sandy soils of Egypt, while Sturrock (1940) states that the custard apple responds well to organic fertilizers, the size and quality of the fruit depending chiefly on the vigour of the tree. On very light soils, Oppenheimer (1947) recommends 132 to 176 lb. of manure per tree each year, supplemented by commercial fertilizer, especially nitrogen. Further experimentation was needed before this general recommendation could be made more specific. As the fruit is borne on new as well as old wood, there is probably little danger of providing too much nitrogen. This fact also indicates the desirability of good cultivation, although very little has been written about this.

The custard apple is frequently grown without irrigation, and in established orchards in India is able to produce fair crops. This is explained in part by the fact that the fruit is set during the rainy season and ripens before the soil has become very dry. Trees grow more rapidly, however, and probably bear better crops if irrigated during the summer. One irrigation while the fruit is ripening may be of value also. Very heavy irrigation is needed in Egypt, according to Ahmed (1936 b) who recommends watering the plants at least twice a month on the heavier soils and 80 times a year on sandy soils.

If left unpruned, the custard apple forms a bush with a large number of stems of various sizes and ages. In India it is customary to allow the plants to assume this shape. In order to make room for some of the shoots which keep appearing, to develop, and to avoid very old branches, which may not bear well, it is probably advisable to cut out the older stems from time to time. Sometimes only dead wood is removed. By pruning off all shoots as they appear except one, it is possible to train the plant into a standard tree with one trunk and several well-spaced branches. Such treatment retards the growth of the tree, but avoids the crowding and the crossing of branches which are inevitable in the bush form. Whether it results in the production of more or fewer fruits is questionable. Budded or grafted plants would naturally be trained to a single stem, and all shoots arising below the union would be promptly removed. Stephens (1936) stresses the importance of pruning in order to maintain vigorous trees which can produce fruits of good quality. After heading back to form a strong framework he recommends thinning and heading back to prevent crowding and to maintain healthy annual growth. He warns against pruning until the buds are ready to start growth in the spring lest earlier pruning cause the tree to die.

One of the worst faults of the annonas as a group is their tendency to bear few fruits. The custard apple is better than some of the other species in this respect, but frequently fails to produce a very satisfactory crop. This seems to be due to the failure of many of the flowers to form fruits, which in turn is sometimes caused by lack of pollination. In northern India the custard apple blossoms over a long period, beginning in the hot weather and lasting well into the rains. Unfortunately, little or no fruit sets before the beginning of the rains. As fruit which is still immature late in the season never becomes edible, no matter how long it is left on the tree or kept in storage, the setting of fruit early in the season is important.

In Egypt a similar problem exists, as under dry conditions very little fruit sets. Ahmed (1936 a) reports that the yield can be greatly increased by hand pollination. Flowers on the extremities of branches or weak flowers in clusters are unlikely to set fruit, so these are collected and used for pollen. This is applied with a camel's hair brush before the stigmas have a chance to dry out. Only as many flowers are pollinated as the tree can carry to maturity. This has proved a very satisfactory solution in Egypt, but in India, at least under certain conditions, this method is not entirely successful because the early flowers produce no pollen. It is possible to increase the set of fruit during the rainy season. In one experiment at Allahabad, hand pollinated flowers gave an 85% set, as compared with 30% in the controls.

Anothet factor which may affect the set of fruits is dichogamy. Some custard apple trees shed pollen in the morning and others in the afternoon. The stigmas are not receptive when the pollen is shed.

Both seedling and budded or grafted plants ordinarily come into bearing in from one to four years. All trees begin bearing within two years after planting in Israel according to Oppenheimer (1947) who says that good trees five years old yield about 50 fruits each, while older trees bear up to twice that number. He says that as the trees get old, the size of the fruit decreases, and that it is doubtful whether an orchard is profitable for more than 10 or 12 years. Ahmed (1936b) says that at five years of age a tree produces about 120 fruits, and should increase for at least 20 years to a maximum of about 500 fruits. This is probably somewhat higher than the ordinary yield in India. Seedlings 8 years old at Allahabad have produced from 31 to 288 fruits, averaging 149. Naik (1949) says that good trees in South India average 60 to 70 lb. a year, and that in some cases low yields may be because of lack of pollination. Individual performance records in Hyderabad indicate yields ranging from about 5 to 20 lb. per tree. Even if all of the trees were like the best in these tests, and were planted 15 ft. apart, this would mean less than 2,000 lb. per acre.

If left on the tree, the fruits split open and decay rather than becoming soft and ready to eat. They are therefore harvested while still firm, but after the skin between the segments has turned a creamy yellow and may have begun to crack. This requires going over each tree every day or two. The fruits are generally kept in straw for a few days until soft. After they are ready to eat they are very delicate and must be handled with the utmost care. This means that the fruit should reach the consumer within a few days of picking, and makes transport to distant markets very difficult. If picked prematurely, the skin holds together better even after the pulp is soft, but the quality is damaged. In India, custard apples are usually sold locally, and are marketed without any packing, but in other countries they may be packed and shipped short distances.

Cold storage is not promising in the case of the custard apple. It was found in Bombay (Anon., 1947) that hard, immature fruit was chilled at a temperature of 60° F., or below, and that while ripe fruit could be held for six weeks at 40° F., with the pulp in good condition, the skin became brown and unattractive.

The custard apple is almost entirely eaten as a dessert fruit, although the pulp may be mixed with milk to form a drink, or made into ice-cream. The pulp has a pleasant texture and flavour, sweet with a slight acidity. It does not have a flavour distinctive enough to antagonize those who taste it for the first time, but for the same reason it often fails to engender great enthusiasm. It is considered the best of the tropical annonas, with the possible exception of the ilama. The food value lies mainly in the sugar content, which compares well with that of other sweet fruits, such as the fig. The variation in the custard apple is illustrated by different analyses. Stahl (1935) reports five analyses in Florida, showing the edible portion varying from 28·6 to 36·9%, sugar from 12·4 to 16·6%, and acid from 0·26 to 0·65%. Wester (1925) shows the edible portion varying from 52 to 55·73% and sugar from 15·99 to 18·15%. Oppenheimer (1947) reports 16 to 20% sugar, and 1·2% protein. Much better quality is indicated by Sturrock who states that analysis in Cuba shows 72% edible portion and 21·5% sugar. These differences may be due in part to the conditions under which the fruit was grown, in part to inherent differences, and perhaps in part to sampling.

A possible economic use for the seeds is reported by Naidu and Saletore (1954), who report that an oil suitable for soap making can be extracted, leaving a cake for use as manure. On the basis of the collection of the seed at Hyderabad and Secunderabad, it was estimated that the oil would cost about a third as much as groundnut oil. They calculated that from the seed available in Hyderabad State each year about 4,000 tons of oil and 9,000 tons of cake could be made.

The custard apple is virtually free from insect pests and diseases in India, and the entire genus in all parts of the world seems to have no major troubles.

Other Annonas

Next to the custard apple, the most commonly grown annona in India is the bullock's heart, bull's heart or *ramphal*, *A. reticulata*. It is also known in some places as the custard apple or sweetsop. Morton and Morton (1946) say that according to the publication Standard Plant Names, the approved name for the fruit is custard apple and for the tree, bullock's heart custard apple, but one can hope that such a confusing standardization will never become established. The fruit is slightly larger than that of *A. squamosa*, and the carpels are fused to form a rind marked with hexagonal areoles. It has the advantage of containing fewer seeds, but the pulp is less delicately flavoured. There is much variation in quality, but even the best are not as good as the average custard apple. The sugar content is slightly less.

The climatic and soil requirements of the bullock's heart are such that it can be grown in much the same area as the custard apple. It is somewhat less resistant to cold than the custard apple, and prefers a somewhat heavier soil. The tree is quite similar, and cultural operations are much the same, although it must be admitted that here again the best methods are not known with any certainty. The fruit takes longer to mature, and in tropical regions some fruit may be ripening throughout the year, although the bulk of the crop comes in a period of a few months. In India it ripens during the hot weather, and thus is not in competition with the custard apple. It is rarely grown commercially, but if some of the superior strains were to be propagated vegetatively they might be economically grown. Naik (1949) states that it thrives all over the plains of South India, and to an elevation of 4,000 feet on humid hills, and that individual trees at the Burliar station yield from 75 to 100 lb. a year.

A dry rot of the bullock's heart fruit is reported by Chowdhury (1947 b) as common in Sylhet district, where it sometimes spoils from 15 to 20% of the crop in an orchard. It is caused by *Glomerella cingulata*, and may be controlled by spraying with 2-2-50 Bordeaux mixture when it appears or is about to appear in the middle or latter part of December. This saves all of the fruit not infected at the time of spraying.

Much less commonly grown in India is the soursop, *A. muricata*, commonly known in Spanish-speaking countries as the guanabana. This is the most tropical of the genus, and is not suited to most of northern India. It is grown to a certain extent in Assam, and in lower Burma. Naik (1949) states that in Madras it does better on the plains than in the hills, but that it is liked by few persons. This may be because of the absence of the best varieties. It is a favourite fruit in Cuba, and is grown to a certain extent in other parts of the tropics, including Ceylon. The fruit is larger than that of any of the other annonas, weighing from three to six or even eight pounds. As the name indicates, the fruit is comparatively sour, containing two or three times as much acid as the custard apple, and somewhat less sugar. The sugar content, however, compares well with that of a good many fruits, running from about 11 to 14%. In Burma the soursop is eaten as a dessert fruit, but is not as well liked as the custard apple. In Cuba and other parts of America it is used in ices and icecream, or mixed with milk to form a famous drink. Ochse (1931) states that the soursop is one of the best fruits of Java. The pulp is pressed through a sieve and eaten, preferably with syrup and ice, or by some, mixed with wine or brandy. The young fruits are used in a kind of soup. One of the main drawbacks to the cultivation of the soursop is the small number of fruits borne on a tree. This varies a good deal, but even the most prolific will rarely exceed two dozen.

The cherimoya is generally considered to be the best of the genus, and indeed, one of the best fruits in the world. It is not as sweet as the custard apple, but has a more distinct flavour. Another form of the name is cherimoyer and the scientific name is *Aanona cherimola* (*cherimolia*). This is the least tropical of the genus. It originated in the highlands of tropical America, probably in Ecuador and Peru, and grows well only under similar conditions. It can stand only slightly more frost than the custard apple, and does not do well where the humidity is either very high or very low. The summers of the plains of northern India are probably too severe for it. Venakataratnam (1953) reports that, surprisingly, the cherimoya has been found to do well on the coarse red sandy loam soils of Telingana, where it is more resistant to drought and produces larger crops of larger fruits than *A. squamosa*. An average crop is said to be 109 fruits weighing an average of 6·58 oz., compared to 26·64 custard apple fruits weighing 5·36 oz., and 15 bullock's hearts weighing 7·4 oz. These trees came from seedlings purchased from a nursery in Calcutta as cherimoya, but it is doubtful if they really are. They are known locally as *lakshmanphal*, whereas at Poona trees which are also suspected of being hybrids are called *hanumanphal*. The cherimoya is grown to a slight extent in the hills of South India and Ceylon, and its cultivation might be extended if varieties of superior quality and productiveness were secured. It thrives at elevations from 1,500 to 7,000 feet above sea level in South India, according to Naik (1949), and while production is limited it has some promise as being one of the few fruits available in the hills in December and January. No named variety is grown, and the trees are mostly seedlings producing fruit resembling the custard apple, but with a smoother skin which is dark when ripe.

The cherimoya can be inarched on the bullock's heart, and at Burliar such grafted trees came into bearing in about the 6th year while seedlings started bearing in the 11th. Oppenheimer (1947) says that in Palestine patch budding and cleft grafting are successful, and that budding is easy on the cherimoya rootstock, but that the custard apple is apparently incompatible. In other parts of the world there are a number of named varieties of excellent quality. Some bear better than others, though none is very prolific. Schroeder (1943) reports that in California hand pollination may cause 60% or more of the flowers to set fruit, compared with about 2% in the controls. This was not effective, however, when the temperature was above 90° F., and the humidity below 30%. It was not found possible to store the pollen more than one day. When the flowers first open the pistils are receptive; later the pollen is shed and the pistils function to a much smaller degree. Oppenheimer (1947) found that although the trees flourish in Israel, practically no fruit is borne without hand pollination and that in one experiment, only 16% of the pollinated flowers set fruit, and these produced lop-sided fruits, indicating imperfect pollination. Naik (1949) also suggests that lack of adequate pollination may be responsible for yields which generally do not exceed 100 fruits in a year.

One of the best of the annonas, and one which should succeed in some sections, at least, of India is the ilama, *A. diversifolia*. Although it is an important fruit in Mexico and Central America, it was not tried in other sections as early as were other species, and still seems to be entirely unknown in India. Trees from seed planted in 1925 were growing in Ceylon, but had not fruited when Parsons reported in 1932. The climatic requirements are said to be similar to those of the custard apple though it probably will not stand quite as much frost. The fruit of some varieties is said to be similar to that of the custard apple, while that of others more closely resembles the cherimoya.

As has been noted, the 'cherimoyas' in Bombay and Hyderabad are suspected of being hybrids, probably with the custard apple. This cross is called the atemoya (from the Philippine names of the custard apple and cherimoya) and is important in some countries. Most atemoyas resemble the custard apple in climatic requirements, but are somewhat more resistant to frost. Some prefer a heavy soil, as does the cherimoya, but some do well in light soil and can stand much alkalinity. The better ones have fruit which resembles that of the cherimoya and yield at least as well as the custard apple. Oppenheimer (1947) thinks that some of the heavy-yielding 'cherimoyas' of Egypt are atemoyas, and states that chance hybrids seem common in Israel. Prest (1955 a) suggests that the 'custard apples' of Queensland are actually atemoyas. These are vigorous trees requiring a spacing of 30-40 ft. and bearing up to five bushels (perhaps 225 lb.) of fruits, each of which weighs 1-2 lb. The fruit of the largest and most popular variety is about six inches in diameter. It would seem desirable to give the atemoya or the 'cherimoya' of Hyderabad, a trial in all parts of the country where custard apples are grown. As the fruit ripens late in January in Hyderabad, it is not in competition with the custard apple.

Another fruit which is promising for India is the atemoya, a cross between the custard apple and the cherimoya. Its climatic requirements are similar to those of the custard apple, but the fruit more closely resembles the cherimoya. Like both parents, it is inclined to be a shy bearer, but Sturrock reports that in southern Florida it bears good crops of fruits of excellent quality. Oppenheimer also reports that chance hybrids seem common in a Israel, and that some of them approach the cherimoya in quality and the custard apple in yield. He suggests that some of the heavy-yielding 'cherimoyas' of Egypt and Queensland may actually be hybrids. Hybrids have also been produced at the Ganeshkhind garden at Poona, and a few selections have been made and propagated by inarching. As the atemoya is a hybrid, seedlings cannot be expected to come true to type, so budding or grafting should be employed. Custard apple seedlings are said to make a satisfactory root-stock. This is a fruit which should certainly be tried extensively in India.

CHAPTER XXII

THE PINEAPPLE

Many fruits are unfortunate in their names. The English term 'pineapple', with its reference to the inedible cone of a tree of temperate climates, is an unhappy selection for one of the most delicious of tropical fruits. Surely those languages did better which based their word for this fruit on the name used in its native country where, in the Guarani language, *a* means 'fruit' and *nana* means 'excelling'.

The excellent fruit is probably indigenous to Brazil, although it had spread to the other parts of tropical America by the time of Columbus, who took it to Europe. There it immediately became popular and efforts were made to grow it, with some success even in cold countries where by the 17th century it was grown under glass. With the traffic then springing up to all parts of the world, its spread was very rapid. It seems to have reached India by 1548 and probably Malaya at about the same time, or soon afterwards. In the Philippines, pina cloth was being made from the fibre extracted from the leaves in the sixteenth century. The history of the pineapple in South Africa dates from about 1655. It is not known definitely when the first pineapples were introduced into the Hawaiian Islands, where the industry was to reach its highest development, but some were planted in 1809. A start was made in Queensland in about 1854. The canning industry was started on a small scale in Hawaii in 1892 and in Singapore at about the same time. These two centres have become the most important. Hawaii has about 90,000 acres available, but as the land is left fallow or planted to other crops in rotation, not all of this is producing pineapples at any one time. Malan (1954) quotes figures showing about 82,000 acres in Hawaii, 60,000 in Malaya, 36,000 in South Africa where not more than 10,000 tons were produced in 1938-39, but about 75,000 tons in 1953-54, and 6,800 acres in Queensland. The West Indies also have an industry of some importance, and the fruit is grown on a smaller scale in Formosa, the Philippines, and several other countries.

Although the pineapple is not canned to any extent in India, and the industry has not been intensively developed, it is of considerable importance. A bulletin on the marketing of various fruita (Anon., 1950) estimates the acreage in 1941-42 as 11,178, of which perhaps about 8,000 is now in India. This is now obviously much too low a figure, for Travancore-Cochin alone reports 9,745. Somewhat less accurate are the estimates of 6,500 acres in Assam and 3,600 in Bihar. There are said to be about 3,000 acres in the northern part of West Bengal, and about 1,400 in Madras and Andhra. Smaller plantings in the Uttar Pradesh *tarai*, Bombay, and elsewhere bring the total to more than 24,500 acres.

The pineapple is the only member of the family Bromeliaceae of any great importance, although a few of the 900 species are cultivated as ornamentals and fibre is extracted from some. The genus of the pineapple is *Ananas* and the species is *comosus*, with *sativus* as a very common synonym, and *sativa* and *ananas* more rarely used. Certain other species produce small fruits more or less like the pineapple, but these are of no use horticulturally except possibly as parents which might contribute resistance to pests or unfavourable conditions to hybrids.

The pineapple differs greatly from other fruits, being one of the very few which are monocotyledonous. It consists of a very short stem practically hidden by a rosette of stiff leaves, and a poorly developed root system. The leaves are stiff and waxy on the upper surface, with stomata in furrows on the under surface, protected by a thick growth of hairs. Transpiration is thus held to a minimum. The leaves are so arranged that very little rain gets past them to the ground, and they are slightly concave, so that the water is conducted to the base. Heavy dew is collected in the same way. A slight amount of water will be held in the pocket where the leaf clasps the stem, and only when these pockets overflow will water reach the ground. The roots grow from buds in the axils of the leaves. The lower ones enter directly into the soil, but those higher on the stem grow in these pockets and may circle the stem. Some of them eventually reach the soil. The roots probably derive most of their nourishment from the soil within a radius of one foot. The plants are poorly anchored and have a tendency to fall over. Both of these facts encourage close planting so that the plants may support each other.

The flower stalk is an extension of the main stem. It bears a head of flowers, each borne in the axil of a bract, and above the flowers are other bracts which form the 'crown' of the fruit. The flowers develop into berries which fuse to form the multiple fruit. The receptacle and bracts are included in the fruit. Some varieties are self-sterile, and in most of the better types, viable seeds are rare.

A mild tropical climate seems best suited to the pineapple, such as is found in the tropics near the sea or at some elevation above it. Johnson (1935), in his excellent and comprehensive book on the pineapple, suggests that temperatures varying from 60 to 90°F. are best. Injury is caused when the temperature falls below freezing, at least if by more than a few degrees. On the other hand, some cool weather in the winter seems to improve the quality. Very strong sunshine is undesirable, but complete shade is also harmful. In India, pineapples are frequently grown under mango trees, but the decline of such plantations may be caused by the shade becoming too dense. Naik (1949) says that partial shade from cocoanuts or young mango trees on the west coast does no harm, and that on the plains some shade may be necessary. Lighter shade is used in Malaya, where there is more moisture in the air and the sunshine is less bright, while in such mild climates as that of Hawaii, no shade is provided.

It is frequently stated that heavy rainfall is necessary, especially if water for irrigation is not plentiful. Actually, the pineapple is grown undeu a wide range of moisture conditions, and Johnson (1935) states that where a paper mulch is used in Hawaii, the crop can be grown with an annual rainfall of as little as 20 inches, without irrigation. Wind is much less of a factor than in the case of many crops, but Johnson reports that wind may bruise the ends of the leaves and the bruised portions then become decayed.

The pineapple is grown on many different types of soil, ranging from the very poor, white silica sands of Florida to the clay loam and clay soils of the Philippines. In the West Indies the soils are generally light and rather poor. The soils of Hawaii are of as fine a texture as clay, but are laterite soils which do not remain sticky and can be more easily worked. In South Africa about 80% of the pineapples are grown on loam or heavy loam soils. In Queensland there is great variation, but sandy loam is considered best. Near Singapore they are grown on both wet soil with a high humus content and a coarse gravelly soil. The fruit is larger on the heavier soil, but it is said that the flavour of the fruit grown on the lighter soil is richer. Laterite hill slopes and the sandy and loamy soils of the west coast are said to be the most suitable in South India. Good drainage is regarded as very important, but the soil does not need to be deep, and in the case of the wet soil of Singapore, the water level is only three feet from the surface, although Ochse (1931) warns of the danger of too high a water table.

A peculiar condition exists in the soils of Hawaii, which for a time threatened to restrict the development of the industry drastically. Most of the soils there are very rich in iron, aluminium, and, especially, manganese, with a pH value of from 5·5 to 7. In the presence of such a high percentage of manganese, the iron is unavailable, and the addition of iron to the soil is of no value. It was discovered fortunately, that the deficiency in the plants could be rectified by spraying them with iron sulphate several times a year, and this is now standard practice in Hawaii. Barnes (1944) advocates spraying the plants with a weak solution of ferric sulphate where the presence of manganese prevents the absorption of iron from the soil in Queensland, but he emphasizes the desirability of keeping the pH of the soil down to 4·5 or 5, adding sulphur if necessary to attain this object. An excess of lime in the soil may also inhibit the absorption of iron and cause chlorosis. In Puerto Rico this is successfully treated by applying sulphur to the soil, and Pennock (1949) prefers a pH of 5 or slightly below. He and Schappelle (1942) recommend spraying 'diligently and regularly' with iron sulphate, as even slight chlorosis during the growing or early fruiting period reduces the yield.

Propagation

Except for breeding purposes, vegetative propagation is universally practised. Several parts of the plant may be used. Shoots which grow in the axils of the leaves are called suckers; those which come out below the surface of the soil are called ground suckers or ratoons. Shoots borne on the fruiting stem, below the fruits, are known as slips. Suckers and slips are the most commonly used planting materials. In most countries, suckers are preferred, as they mature the first crop of fruit several months sooner. In Hawaii suckers produce fruit in from 15 to 18 months, while slips require from 20 to 22. Under less favourable circumstances, both may take longer. Slips produce larger fruits in the first or 'plant' crop. In Hawaii slips are preferred because when they are planted in the autumn, after the crop is harvested, they produce the first crop in the summer of the second year, when the fruit is sweeter than that which matures in the winter or spring. On the other hand, if the crop is to be sold on the fresh fruit market it brings a better price in the winter or spring, when there is less fruit ripening. In Ceylon large slips or suckers are planted in May or June in order to produce fruit the next year, or smaller ones are planted from October to December and produce fruit in from 18 to 20 months. Naik (1949) says that suckers are preferred in South India because they give a crop in 18 months, as compared with two years when other material is used. Chowdhury (1947 a) prefers suckers which will flower in 6 or 7 months, as very large ones flower too soon and give weak plants and small fruits.

The crown or top of the fruit is sometimes planted, and under favourable conditions will grow well, although it ordinarily takes at least two years to produce ripe fruit. Crowns are extensively used with the Smooth Cayenne variety in South Africa. They are available at canning factories, but not where the fruit is shipped fresh. Shoots sometimes grow on the crown, and are called crown slips, but are very small and of no value.

In some places, stumps are used, these being the stalks after the fruit has been harvested. They are planted in furrows in much the same manner as is sugarcane. The shoots which develop along the stump are later removed and planted, but as they are slow and irregular in growth, the method is not very popular.

The type of planting material to be used will depend on local conditions and the desires of the grower, and also on the variety of pineapple. Some varieties produce very few suckers or slips, and the grower may be forced to use any material he can get, especially where pineapple cultivation is expanding. The health and vigour of the plant from which the material is taken are of great importance. Even if poor growth is due to lack of fertility, suckers or slips from weak plants seem incapable of producing strong plants, even when given the best of care.

In the development of new varieties, one difficulty is the time taken to produce planting material for the industry in case an improved variety is secured. Only a limited number of slips, suckers, crowns, and stumps are produced, and many years would be required to produce the hundreds of thousands necessary for commercial production. To help solve this problem a method was reported by Walters (1932). A stem which has not yet fruited is stripped and cut into slices not more than one-fifth of an inch thick. The slices are soaked in potassium permanganate solution and planted. When rooting has occurred, each slice can be cut into three triangular portions and replanted. In this way from 80 to 100 plants can be secured from one foot of stem, and will be ready to plant out in the nursery in about six months. A similar method is sometimes used in Malaya, where each slice is thick enough to contain two or three buds, and is not further divided. Evans, (1952), however, prefers splitting the crown into eight vertical sections before planting, as this gave him maximum shoot production in 93 days, compared with 342 days when discs were used.

While the first crop of fruit is developing, slips and suckers are also growing. If left on the plant, some of these will in turn produce fruits. They sometimes send their own roots into the soil. From them develop still more slips and suckers, but these are likely to be rather weak, and the second ratoon crop comes mostly from suckers of the plant crop which did not fruit during the first ratoon season. The process can be carried on indefinitely, and in some cases plantations on very fertile soil have continued to produce satisfactorily for more than 30 years. Ordinarily, however, it is better to discontinue the plantation in a much shorter time. In Malaya by the time the plantation has ceased to yield good crops, the young rubber trees among which the pineapples are planted have reached a size such that they shade the ground too much for pineapples. Grant and Williams (1936) state that in Burma the life of a plantation is about 10 or 12 years, after which the soil is given very thorough cultivation and heavy manuring before being replanted. In many parts of the world it is considered better practice to plant some other crop for a few years, or at least to allow the land to lie fallow for a year. In Hawaii, the practice is to take only from one to three ratoon crops.

The length of time a plantation is expected to remain determines very largely the system to be used in planting. If only a few ratoon crops are contemplated, cultivation is of less importance, and the plants can be set closer together. For more permanent plantations, more room must be left for cultivation and for the larger numbers of leaves and stalks in the ratoon crops. The plants are placed in beds of from one to six or seven rows, and formerly even wider beds were used. In single rows the plants are placed from 1 to 2 feet apart, and the rows about 2½ feet apart. This allows the use of animal-drawn cultivators, but the plants do not support each other and in some cases fall over and then suffer from sunburn on the side of the fruit. In the double row system, the plants are frequently placed about 12 to 14 inches apart both ways, with the beds 5 or 6 feet from centre to centre. This provides for some mutual support and still leaves a chance for considerable cultivation. Single or double rows 9 feet apart proved unsatisfactory in Queensland, and for a time 4 ft. was left between double rows which were 2 ft. apart, with 1 ft. between plants in the row. But Mitchell and Cannon (1953) favour 5½ or 6 ft. between double rows, allowing 15,800 or 14,500 plants per acre. When there are three rows, the middle row gets less cultivation and sunlight, and is likely to give smaller fruits than the outer rows. If the spacing is 18 to 24 inches, good results may be had, but in Hawaii it is preferred to have the same number of plants per acre by closer spacing in two rows. The four-row system is popular in Hawaii, using mulching paper 54 or 58 inches wide, with plants 14 to 19 inches apart in rows 15 or 16 inches apart, and beds 7 or 8 feet from centre to centre. This method gives the largest number of rows that can be reached from the passageways. More than four rows in a bed are used only on very sandy soil, where cultivation is not so important.

Double rows, with 2 ft. between and 5 ft. between pairs, with 18 to 20 inches between plants in the row, are strongly recommended by Sane (1935) for Uttar Pradesh, while Firminger's Manual favours planting at distances of 2 by at least 3 feet. Chowdhury (1947 a) in Assam recommends rather wide spacing, 3 feet by 4 ft. or planting in beds 5 ft. apart with 2, 3, or 4 rows 2 feet apart, with plants 2 ft. apart in the row. He says that in the hills they should be planted along contours, either terraced or in trenches, with 12 to 15 ft. between rows on an average hill. Naik (1949) reports that in South India the plants are set from 2 to 6 ft. apart, either with wider spacing between rows than between plants in the row, or with a path 4 to 6 ft. wide after 3 or 4 rows. The system advocated by Sane allows 6,223 plants per acre, while Chowdhury would allow from 3,630 to 6,700. Gandhi (1949) reports that in Bombay a spacing of 3 ft. each way is used, allowing 4,850 plants per acre. On the other hand 10,000 plants per acre is not unusual in other countries, and in Hawaii it is customary to plant from 11,000 to 18,000. Briant and Tidbury (1942) found that in Zanzibar close planting largely increased the yield, although it reduced the average size of the fruit.

Planting

The need for thorough cultivation before planting is recognized in most countries, although it is said that little or no cultivation is given in Singapore. In Hawaii, according to Johnson (1935), a cover crop is ordinarily ploughed in about a year before the pineapples are to be set, followed by five to seven ploughings and harrowings. Subsoiling is also practised, especially where there is any danger of poor drainage. Sane (1935) recommends three ploughings during the hot weather, each followed by harrowing or discing.

Before planting suckers or slips, a few of the lower leaves are stripped off, and they are generally allowed to dry. In Hawaii they are stood upside down for a week, or less if they have partially dried before stripping. Barnes (1944) says that planting material can be stored for several months in single layers, butts up, either in the shade or in the open. If fresh material is planted in moist soil, it is likely to rot, and if the leaves are allowed to remain the roots may have difficulty in getting into the soil, especially under rather dry conditions.

The suckers or slips are planted from two to five inches deep, depending on their size, so as to leave the bud or 'heart' about an inch above the surface. Care must be taken to prevent soil from getting into the heart. The soil should be made firm around the plant. In Hawaii a 'planting iron' is used, this being a blade about an eighth of an inch thick, two inches wide and about eight inches long, with a curved handle. This is very similar to the *khurpi* which may well be used for the same purpose. In some countries it is customary to plant in furrows instead of making individual holes.

In India it is considered best to plant pineapples during the rainy season, when they start growth quickly and no irrigation is needed for several months, but if planted in dry soil they can withstand considerable drought and then grow when water is provided by rain or irrigation. Chowdhury (1947 a) says that in Assam it is desirable to avoid either heavy rains or drouth in the first months, and that therefore August is a suitable month for planting. Firminger's Manual recommends planting on ridges, which may be an advantage where heavy rains are frequent. Gandhi (1949) recommends planting in September-November in Bombay.

After planting, the main purpose of cultivation is to control the weeds. As the root system of the pineapple is not extensive, the plant is not able to compete well with weeds, and the removal of the latter is important. Hand work is generally necessary in addition to that done by machines where the system of planting allows their use. Care should be taken to avoid damaging the roots, especially those of plants maturing fruit. Naik (1949) says that a few growers in South India mulch with dry leaves or straw, with obvious benefit.

Reference has been made to the use of mulching paper in Hawaii, a practice which was begun about 1920, and has become almost universal in the Islands. Heavy paper impregnated with asphalt is furnished in rolls 36 to 58 in. wide and 300 to 600 ft. long. This is rolled out onto the beds, leaving a passage between strips. Holes are made through the paper in planting, and some weeds are likely to grow through these which have to be removed by hand. No other weeding or cultivation is needed, and this saving of expense was the greatest benefit which was expected. It was discovered, however, that the paper mulch increases the crop 15 to 25%, and improves the quality of the slips produced. Whether the increased crop comes from the increased temperature of the soil, better moisture conditions, or some other factor, is not clear. The use of a paper mulch has not spread to other countries, at least to a large extent, and is probably undesirable where there is heavy rainfall. Mitchell and Cannon (1953) and Malan(1954)recognize its advantages, but state that it is not much used in Queensland or South Africa, low labour costs in the latter country making it uneconomical.

Rather heavy manuring is practised in most countries where the pineapple is grown, although there are comparatively few experiments to show just what is needed. In the case of the very sandy soils of Florida and the West Indies, nitrogen, phosphorous, and potassium are all added in fairly large amounts, and as the soil contains very little plant food, their use is probably justified. The virgin soils of Hawaii are rich, and no manuring is needed for several crops. After that nitrogen must be applied in large amounts. The pineapple seems able to absorb nitrogen in the form of ammonia, and perhaps prefers this to the nitrate. Ammonium sulphate is considered the best fertilizer in Hawaii. Pennock (1949) also found this better than ammonium nitrate in Puerto Rico. Depending on soil conditions, it may be desirable to add potassium also, and possibly phosphorous, and minor elements. As noted in a previous chapter, it has been found possible to apply nitrogen, phosphorus, and potassium as foliage sprays in Malaya. It has been noticed that iron is unavailable in some soils; deficiencies of zinc and copper have also been reported.

Recommendations in India thus far are based on entirely inadequate experimental evidence. Sane (1935) recommends 1 md. of ammonium sulphate, 2 md. of potassium sulphate, and 3 md. of superphosphate per acre, apparently on the basis of an experiment in Singapore.

Naik (1949) recommends planting on well manured soil and adding 25 to 50 cartloads per acre of well-rotted manure in one or two applications within 6 to 12 months after planting. Chowdhury (1947 a) says that in Assam manuring is generally neglected, but that it is necessary in order to get good crops. He recommends 5 to 10 tons of rotted cowdung or oil-cake before, or at the time of, planting, and an application of 30 to 40 lb. per 1,000 plants of a 10-6-10 mixture soon after planting, with two or three more applications of 50 lb. each during the year. This may be worked into the soil around the plants, but it is best to apply a soluble mixture in the leaf bases. Ammonium sulphate is preferred to nitrate. Superphosphate, finely ground bone meal, basic slag, and potassium sulphate are said to have given good results. A top dressing of 3,500 lb. of fish manure is recommended in two doses, three and five months after planting, in Bombay (Gandhi 1949).

Irrigation is not a prominent feature of the pineapple industry because of fairly well-distributed rain in most countries where the fruit is grown. In parts of India, however, irrigation is necessary, and Firminger's Manual states that it should be given from February until the beginning of the rainy season. In northern India it is desirable to commence irrigation earlier in the season, especially in years of scanty rainfall. Because of the very limited nature of the roots of the pineapple, light and comparatively frequent irrigation is more efficient than heavy applications.

In parts of Bombay, the industry has been limited by lack of irrigation water, according to Dhareswar (1950) who suggests a method of overcoming this difficulty. In a 20-year-old cocoanut plantation, trenches 18 in. wide and deep, and 30 ft. long were dug in one acre in September and October, and left until the beginning of the following monsoon, when pineapples were planted 3 ft. apart in them, and they were filled with organic waste. More was added at 6-week intervals, for two more years. No manure or water was given. The cost in the first two years was Rs. 500, and the income Rs. 1,175. During the second season only the 500 plants which had previously failed to flower produced fruit worth Rs. 161. The third season the suckers from the first crop fruited and brought in an income of Rs. 655 with an expense of Rs. 70. The fruits the first and second seasons weighed 3 to 5 lb. each, but those from the ratoon crop only 2 to 4 lb. For the four years, the expenditure was Rs. 620 and the income Rs. 1,993, while the yield of the cocoanuts increased from 100 to 200%. As there are many cocoanut plantations in the area, this method seems to offer a good way to increase production.

About two suckers may well be left on each plant for the ratoon crop. Other suckers and slips not needed for planting should be removed from time to time, as the development of these may weaken the plant. It is also considered good practice to earth up the plants after the harvesting of the first crop, in order to encourage the rooting of the suckers.

As it is customary in India to plant suckers in the rainy season, and the first crop matures in from 15 to 20 months, the first fruit is likely to ripen during the winter or spring. Thereafter the main season is July and August from flowers appearing in February and March. The greatest growth ordinarily takes place just after the harvest, but sometimes another flowering occurs at this time, resulting in a winter crop. This is undesirable, as the fruits ripening in winter are likely to be sour. In most other countries the pineapple ripens mainly in the summer months, but in Malaya there are two crops, one in May and June and another in November and December, and a similar condition exists in South Africa.

Various methods have been used to control the time of flowering of the pineapple, including smudging, and more commonly the placing of a small amount of calcium carbide in the axils of the upper leaves, where it gradually reacts with moisture to produce acetylene. This treatment in an experiment in Bombay induced 65% of the plants to flower within two months, compared with 28% of the untreated plants. More recently plant hormones have given very promising results. Van Overbeek (1946) and Van Overbeek and others (1946) report that in Puerto Rico flowering can be induced in any month, and that as the size of the fruit depends on the number of leaves, it is possible to control both the time of harvest and the size of the fruit. Some flowers were induced by as little as 0·05 mg. of NAA, and 0·25 or 0·50 mg. caused practically all plants to flower. This treatment increased the number of slips up to 70%, whereas treating with the cheaper 2,4-D was equally effective in inducing flowering but inhibited the formation of slips and reduced the average weight of the fruit, perhaps by its adverse effect on the development of young leaves. In Costa Rico, Perez (1949) found it possible to secure ripe fruit in six months by treating plants with a 0·0015% solution of 2,4-D. Of several hormones tried in Queensland, Groszmann (1950) found alpha NAA most suitable for use in the spring and early summer, when at 5 ppm it induced flowering and increased the weight of the fruit from 7 to 14%. On the other hand, a concentrated spray several weeks before the normal time of harvesting delayed maturity, but also increased the size. The results of applying NAA in the autumn were even more variable than when acetylene was used. Mitchell and Cannon (1953) report that 2 fluid ounces of 10 ppm alpha NAA is commonly used in Queensland. Kraus (1954) states that the tonnage can be substantially increased without the loss of quality or sugar content by applying B-naphthoxyacetic acid, whereas certain other growth regulators decrease the quality in increasing the yield.

The action of these substances is partly explained by Bonner and Liverman (1953) who state that the native auxin in the pineapple seems to be IAA, which is low at the time of flowering. Acetylene and ethylene decrease the amount of IAA in the plant and thus induce flowering. NAA and 2,4-D appear to act as antiauxins, and so favour flowering.

Pests and Diseases

Sane (1935) is able to dismiss the subject of pests and diseases of the pineapple in India with one sentence, to the effect that there is none which is serious. Although this is not entirely true, the country is comparatively fortunate. It is not surprising that under the intense cultivation of Hawaii, the enemies of the pineapple are legion. Nematodes of the species *Heterodera radicola* (*marioni*) cause very serious loss, and can be partially controlled by treating the soil before planting, with chloropicrin gas. This is an expensive treatment, but seems to have other beneficial results, producing improved growth and yield. Alvarez-Garcie and Lopez-Matos (1954) found soil fumigation with Dowfume W-85 most effective against nematodes in Puerto Rico, where it increased the yield of fruit from 6·2 to from 10·8 to 15·9 tons per acre and at least doubled the number of suckers and slips. Several species of mealy bugs, particularly *Pseudococcus brevipes*, cause the plants to lose chlorophyl and turn a reddish yellow. Abraham (1953) reports that this has become a serious pest in the Wynaad area of Madras. He recommends planting suckers that are free from infestation or treating planting material with parathion, cyanogas, or methyl bromide. If treatment in the field is desired, the plants may be sprayed with parathion of HETP. The latter can be used in the last month before harvesting, as it is hydrolised in a few hours. Other pests include the pineapple scale, *Diaspis bromeliae;* and the pineapple mite, *Stigmaeus floridanus*, and other mites.

Pineapple diseases in Assam have been described by Chowdhury (1945 a, b, 1946). Leaf-rot, base-rot, and fruit-rot occur throughout the growing area, and are caused by *Ceratostomella (Thielaviopsis) paradoxa.* They are reported to be very serious in Java, and to occur in Gorakhpur district of Uttar Pradesh, and in other countries. In Assam the leaf-spot is negligible, but the base-rot destroys 4 to 10% of the plants, and the fruit-rot 3 to 15% of the fruits, more of them in transport and storage than in the field. Suckers affected with the disease fail to grow. The fungus is a facultative parasite, lives over on trash in the soil, and is disseminated by insects, wind, men, and planting material. Heart- or stem- rot, caused by *Phytophthora parasitica* is highly sporadic, some fields being free and some with 7 to 25% of the plants affected. Although not reported from other parts of India, it is common in other countries. It causes a slight wilting and twisting of the leaves, discoloration, and sometimes the disintegration of the stem. Control measures include good drainage, careful handling to avoid wounding the planting material, and dipping this material in 1-1-3 Bordeaux mixture. A strain of the same fungus causes wilt, which is invariably associated with rotting of the roots. It occurs in certain parts of Assam only, though a similar disease caused by *P. cinnomoni* occurs in Queensland. The disease is prevalent in the rainy season, especially if the rains are excessive. Plants a year or two old are most susceptible, and while they may take months to die, any fruit present fails to develop properly.

Harvesting and Canning

The immature pineapple fruit contains very little sugar, and no starch, so there is no chance of increasing sweetness after harvesting. Fraser (1924) states that during the last two weeks of the development of the fruit, the sugar content increases from 4% to the maximum which may be as high as 15%. It is thus obvious that harvesting even a few days early may seriously reduce the sugar content. Fruit picked immaturely also suffers in flavour and appearance. If to be consumed or canned immediately, the fruit may be allowed to become fully ripe before harvesting. But for shipping it must be picked somewhat earlier. This explains in part the superiority of some canned pineapple compared with much that is marketed fresh. Spraying with parachlorophenoxyacetic acid (PCPA) 10 days before harvest was found by Miller and Marsteller (1953) to reduce physiological breakdown during transport and storage. When there was no sound fruit left in the control, the lot sprayed with 400 ppm of PCPA had 35%, and that sprayed with 800 ppm, 63% sound. The sprayed fruit also contained significantly more ascorbic acid. Spraying a month before harvest proved undesirable.

There are several indications of approaching maturity, the most important, perhaps, being the colour. The dark green of the unripe fruit gradually changes to light green, then yellow, and then, in some cases, a deep orange. A greenish yellow colour may be taken to indicate a stage of maturity which will yield a fruit of satisfactory quality. At the same time the fruit becomes less angular about the eyes, and the ends of the bracts which project at the eyes dry up. Johnson (1935) also recommends snapping the fruit with the finger and judging maturity by the sound.

Yields vary to a large extent with the soil and climatic conditions, culture, number of plants per acre, and the variety. Ordinarily the first or plant crop gives the highest yield in Hawaii, but where the first crop ripens in winter, and where the method of planting allows for a greatly increased number of fruits in the ratoon crops, the first crop is likely to be small. The highest yields in the world are obtained in Hawaii, where formerly 10 tons per acre was considered satisfactory but where, with improved practices, 25 to 30 tons are expected, and the maximum may be as high as 40 tons in the plant crop. The first ratoon may give 20 to 25 tons, and the second much less. Ordinarily the yield in one cycle, before replanting, will be 50 to 60 tons, with 75 tons as about the limit. In other countries an average yield is about 10 tons of Smooth Cayenne, or 6 to 7 tons of Queen or other smaller varieties. On account of the wide spacing used in South Africa, yields of 5 tons of Smooth Cayenne, and about 2 tons of other varieties are recorded. Sane (1935) quotes experimental yields in one field in Ceylon for four years, ranging from about 4 tons to 10, with an average of less than 7 tons per acre. Figures are not available for the different parts of India, but as has been seen, Rao (1946) estimates only 2·4 tons per acre for the entire country. Naik (1949) estimates 5·5 tons in South India, with as much as 10 tons of the Kew variety. Chowdhury (1947 a) estimates a yield of 4,000 fruits per acre in Assam, which may mean nearly 9 tons. Valuing the fruits at two annas each, he calculates an income of Rs. 500 per acre, and he estimates the cost of production at Rs. 310 per acre. As has been seen, Dhareswar (1950) reports an average profit of Rs. 343 per acre from growing pineapples as an intercrop in cocoanuts.

The fruit of the Smooth Cayenne variety may be rather easily snapped off, without damage to the plant or fruit, and this is done in Hawaii. In some other countries, and with other varieties, it is preferable to cut the stem with a sharp heavy knife. Sane recommends cutting the stalk below the slips and then cutting it again just below the fruit. Whether the fruit is to be canned or sold fresh, great care should be taken to avoid bruising it. It should be graded and carefully packed in boxes or baskets and taken to the market or factory as quickly as practicable. In some countries each fruit is wrapped in glazed paper. If the fruit has been carefully handled, ripe fruit may be stored for about a month at 40 to 45° F., while mature green fruit should be held at 50 to 60° with a humidity of 85 to 90%, according to Rose and others (1941). Ginsburg (1953) in South Africa found a temperature of 46·5° F. most suitable for shipping the two varieties tested, the Queen and Cayenne. In the cold storage experiments at Poona it was found that the ripe fruit could be stored for a month at 32 to 52° F. but that immature fruit chilled at temperatures below 45° F.

The quality of the pineapple depends largely on the amounts of sugar and acid present. As has been seen, the amount of sugar depends largely on the ripeness of the fruit, but it also depends on the variety and the conditions under which grown. Johnson (1935) quotes analyses of a number of varieties in different countries, showing the sugar content to vary from about 8 to 15%, and the acid from 0·3 to 0·85%. The average may be taken at about 12% sugar and 0·6% acid. Johnson also quotes reports that canned pineapple is an unusually good source of vitamins A, B, and C, as well as minerals and acids which add to its value in the diet. This does not agree with the report of Miller and Bazore (1945) that the Smooth Cayenne is a poor source of vitamin A, fair to poor of ascorbic acid, and fair of thiamine; and that fresh pineapple is low in phosphorus and iron, and only a fair source of calcium. In Australia also, the pineapple is reported less rich in carotene and ascorbic acid than are most tropical fruits. Lal and Pruthi (1955), refer to reports of from 2·9 to 165·2 mg. of ascorbic acid per 100 g. of pulp or juice of different varieties. They found 6·1 to 10·2 mg. in the juice of the Giant Kew, 14·0 to 16·6 in the Kew, and 19·3 to 24·8 in a local Mauritius type. The retention of ascorbic acid in canned juice and slices was good at temperatures up to 86° F. but poor at 99°. There is also present in the fresh fruits, but not in the canned products, an enzyme, bromelin, which digests protein. Miller and Bazore suggest that the soreness of the mouth and esophagus which results from eating some varieties, is caused by this enzyme along with the acid and crystals of calcium oxalate.

While the fresh fruit is very highly esteemed, most of the crop is canned, and the canned pineapple is also of very high quality. The great centres of the canning industry are in Hawaii and Singapore, and in neither would it be possible to grow pineapples except on a small scale were they sold only as fresh fruit. Crawford (1937) gives figures showing a 10-year average of nearly nine million cases, each containing 25 cans of about two pounds each, as the output of Hawaiian factories. In one year the production was 12,726,291 cases. The industry in Malaya developed rapidly from about 1920 to 1935, based largely on pineapples grown without much care in young rubber plantations. In 1937 the industry turned out two and a half million cases, constituting 27% of the world's production and 80% of the export trade, according to Courtnay (1947). Later hilly land in South Johore was used, but poor methods continued, and the canned pineapple was of poor quality, and was the cheapest canned fruit in international trade. Conditions were improving until the second world war almost entirely stopped both growing and canning. After the war the industry has been revived.

The canning of pineapples presents no special problems other than peeling and coring. This operation is performed at a rate of more than 50 pineapples a minute by a very ingenious machine, known as the Ginaca machine in honour of its inventor. This is standard equipment in Hawaii, but in Singapore practically all operations are still performed by hand.

A number of by-products are produced in the canneries. In the canning operation, more juice is obtained than it is desirable to include in the cans, and for years this was a waste product of very little value. More recently, however, a demand for canned juice has developed to the extent that some fruit has to be crushed to meet it. Hawaii produces about four million cases of juice. The dried waste, known as pineapple bran, is a valuable stock feed. Other products are alcohol, calcium citrate, citric acid, and vinegar. A very fine fibre can be extracted from the leaves by a laborious and rather expensive process, and this is used in the Philippines for making a very light, rather stiff cloth.

Many varieties have been grown at some time and place, and have been given names. Johnson (1935) lists about 125 names, representing probably 80 or 90 distinct varieties. These were divided by Hume and Miller (1904) into three groups : the Queen, the Cayenne, and the Spanish. The last is a group of vigorous varieties, not of the highest quality, but largely grown in the West Indies and Florida. Of all the varieties, the Smooth Cayenne is by far the most important, being grown almost exclusively in Hawaii, and to a considerable extent in Queensland, Malaya, Ceylon, and India. It is also called the Kew and the Giant Kew. The Queen is very important in South Africa and Malaya, and along with a very similar variety, the Ripley Queen, in Java and India. The Red and Green Ripley are other members of the Queen group grown in India. The Red and Yellow Mauritius, grown in Ceylon and elsewhere, are members of the Spanish group.

In India, as in many countries, types of distinctly inferior value were early introduced, and are still grown to a considerable extent. Dhareswar (1950) says that in Bombay 80 or 90 varieties are grown but that the Kew and Queen are preferred. Chowdhury (1947 a) says that in Assam the Giant Kew is the most popular, being a large fruit averaging 6 lb., with fruits weighing 10 to 15 lb. commonly, and occasionally up to 22 lb. Second in importance is the Queen with fruits of excellent quality weighing 3 to 5 lb. Naik says that in the South the leading variety is called Kew or Giant Kew, but is different from the variety grown under that name in Assam. It produces fruits weighing from 8 to 16 lb. Second in importance is the Mauritius, weighing 3 to 5 lb., while the Queen, considered to have the best taste, is smaller, the crop at one station in Mysore averaging just more than a pound each. In West Bengal the Queen is preferred.

a The confusion concerning the Kew in Assam and South India may be explained by the statement of Collins (1951) that, 'the present Cayenne is a miscellaneous collection of clones.' He also says that this group is highly heterozygous and exhibits hybrid vigour.

Some hybrids have been produced in an effort to secure even better varieties, and some of these show considerable promise. Mendiola and others (1951) report not only inter-varietal crosses, but intergeneric crossing with *Cryptanthus zonatus*, in the Philippines, where colchicine treatment has also been used. Matations occur fairly commonly, and may present an opportunity for selection, but for the most part they merely present a problem, for if they are not carefully excluded in selecting planting material, undesirable types may be multiplied.

CHAPTER XXIII

OTHER TROPICAL FRUITS

As was mentioned in Chapter II, there is no clear distinction between tropical and subtropical plants. There are some, like the mangosteen, which will not grow in India except in the most tropical sections, and which are clearly tropical. Others, like the tree tomato, do not grow on the plains, and can readily be classified as subtropical. Others have a wide range and their inclusion in this chapter or the next is somewhat arbitrary. Some of the fruits, such as the cashew and jackfruit are of such economic importance as to justify separate chapters, were there sufficient information available concerning their culture. In other cases extensive literature tempts one to devote more space to a fruit than is justified by its importance in this country. Some of the fruits dealt with will continue to be grown only on a very small scale, either in a strictly limited area or as scattered trees in gardens; others are likely to be grown on a much larger scale in the future than at present.

The Cashew

A Brazilian relative of the mango, the cashew is a very interesting plant of considerable commercial importance. It seems to have spread to the entire tropical American seacoast and to the West Indies before the first voyage of Columbus to the New World. It soon spread, and is said to have been introduced into India in the latter half of the 16th century, where it was first used primarily to check erosion. It has become abundant on both coasts of Africa, in Tahiti, and to a more limited extent in Malaya.

There are various estimates of the acreage of cashews in India, and these vary widely. The Report on the Marketing of Cashewnut in India, issued by the Government in 1944, says that there are about 45,500 acres in Madras (including Andhra), 40,000 in Travancore, 8,300 in Cochin, and 500 in Mysore, a total of 94,300 acres, but the Report considered these estimates unreliable. One may also question the accuracy of the figures given by Kaikini (1955): Madras, 135,000 acres; Travancore-Cochin, 83,000; Bombay, 4,500; Mysore, 500; Coorg, 150; total 2,23,150. Rao (1954 c) states that there are 5,969 acres in Andhra and the Director of Agriculture reports that there were 95,583 acres in Madras in 1953-54. There are also limited acreages in Orissa and Bengal. Sayed (1939, 1951) has surveyed the possibilities of developing the industry in India, and urges that the area in Bombay, where 42,000 acres are suitable, be greatly expanded.

Temperature is the limiting factor in determining where the cashew can be grown, a mild tropical climate being most suitable. When seeds were planted at

Allahabad, they germinated well in the rainy season and flourished until winter, when most of them died. The few which survived the cold season succumbed to the heat of the following summer. Even mature trees are likely to be injured if the temperature falls below the freezing point. In South India they may be grown at elevations as great as 3,000 feet, but do best below 1,500. As regards soil, they are very tolerant, and are grown on the sand hills of the west coast which would perhaps produce no other economic crop. Nevertheless, they do best, according to Naik (1949) on deep loam. They are given no irrigation, manuring, or other care and seem to thrive as well with 35 inches of rain on the east coast as with 120 to 150 on the west.

The cashew is ordinarily a rather small, spreading tree although it may reach a height of 40 ft. The botanical name is *Anacardim occidentale*. The most important product is the nut, which is the kernel of the hard, dry fruit which is borne outside the 'fruit'' or cashew apple, which is the swollen peduncle and disc. Economically, the oil from the shell is also more important at present than the apple.

In India the cashew has been propagated almost entirely from seed but there is evidence to suggest that vegetative propagation would be well worth while. In one study of 97 seedlings, the yield varied from nothing at all to 2,247 nuts, and there is a similar variation in quality of both fruit and nut. Layering and inarching seem the best forms of propagation, but side-grafting and patch and shield budding are also possible.

There is much variation in the spacing of cashews, partly because much of the acreage is on rough hilly land in which regular planting is not practicable. Moosad (1953) says that in Madras the seed is planted direct except where there is much danger of its destruction by rats or crows, in April-May. Two seeds are put in a pit, with about 10 ft. between pits. They germinate in about 15 days, and one seedling is kept in each pit. During the first five years about three-fourths of the trees are removed, leaving about 100 per acre. This is probably satisfactory on poor soil, but on good soil the plants should be 30-40 ft. apart. Actually, plantations may have from 50 to 250 trees per acre (Anon., 1955 b).

Because the export of cashew products brings India desirable dollar exchange, much interest has been shown in recent years in improving the crop. The selection of planting material is promising, but attempts to improve cultural operations are faced with great difficulties. Most of the plantations are given almost no care, but because of the terrain, irrigation would be possible only by the expensive sprinkler system, cultivation would encourage erosion, and manures would be rapidly washed away. Even where these operations are possible, there is yet little evidence of their usefulness. Little pruning is done, and little is known of its value.

The trees may begin to flower when about two years old, and may produce an economic crop in the fifth year and be in full bearing by the 10th. They continue to bear well for 25-30 years. There are a number of pests : thrips, stem-borers, caterpillars which damage the leaves and flowers, birds, rats, squirrels, die-back, and mildew. Thus far little attempt seems to have been made to study and control these.

Accurate figures on yield are not available, and this obviously varies greatly under different conditions. The Report on the Marketing of Cashewnuts in India estimated that about 45,210 tons were grown. As it adds that the production had increased about ten-fold in 15 years, it is not surprising that Moosad (1953) estimates 50,000 tons and Rao and Rao (1953) 60,000 tons. If Kaikini's (1955) estimate of acreage is approximately correct, this would mean only about 600 lb. per acre, whereas Rao and Rao (1953) say the average on the west coast is 20 lb. per tree; on the east coast, 30 lb.; and in Orissa, 40 lb. Some trees are said to produce 100 lb. each. A survey of 10 fairly well maintained plantations in Madras showed an average production of 14·6 lb. per tree or 1,820 lb. per acre. Part of the acreage is, of course, of non-bearing trees.

The shell of the fresh nuts contains about 25-30% oil which contains cardol and anarcadic acid, substances which blister the skin and which must therefore be removed. This was formerly done by roasting in open pans or later, when the value of the oil was recognized, in rotary cylinders or in oil baths. The shells could then be removed by hand. Now, according to Moosad (1953), the approved method is to remove the kernels from the shells by a pedal-operated machine, the hands of the operators being protected with castor or linseed oil. This gives a better quality of kernel and the oil which is then expressed from the shells with an hydraulic expeller is also of better quality. The kernels are about 20-22% by weight of the raw nuts.

The world's production for export is largely in India, and British and Portuguese East Africa, with smaller amounts in Egypt, Brazil, and the West Indies. Until about 1953 the nuts from East Africa were sent to India for processing, and amounted to about the same quantity as were grown in India. This gave India a dominating position in the world market. Now processing plants have been established in Portuguese East Africa and Tanganyika, where production has been increasing rapidly. Mehta (1954) states that in 1951-52, India exported 21,000 tons, including African nuts processed here, two-thirds going to the United States. The value of the exports is given as Rs. 8,89,00,000. This is a somewhat greater value for a smaller amount than the figures quoted by Iyengar and Kale (1951) for 1950. The latter say that shell oil worth more than Rs. 60,00,000 was exported in 1950.

The kernels are not only delicious, but of great nutritional value. According to Iyengar and Kale (1951) they contain up to 47% fat, 21·2% protein, and 22·3% carbohydrate, as well as useful amounts of calcium, phosphorus, and iron, much vitamin B_1, and some niacin and riboflavin. The shell oil was formerly used as a preservative for boats and nets and to protect wood from termites. It is now largely exported and used in the manufacture of plastics, indelible inks, waterproofing compositions, and other industrial products.

The fresh cashew apples contain about 11% sugar, a pleasant amount of acid, and according to K. K. Singh and Mathur (1953 b), about 185 mg. of ascorbic acid per 100 g. Small quantities are consumed, but the tannin content makes them unpleasantly astringent. They can be stored for about five weeks at 32-35° F., but unfortunately the ascorbic acid is rapidly lost.

There seems to be more hope of using the apples in bottled juice or other products. A pleasant drink was made at Kodur by precipitating the tannin either by boiling or adding citric acid or lime juice.

The manufacture of a number of products of the fruit has been described by Jain and others (1951). They estimate that 55,00,000 md. (201,339 tons) of fruit are available annually of which only about 15% is used fresh and for making of liquor and vinegar. They found the juice yield 50 to 60%, of 13·5° Brix, containing 12·28% sugar (all reducing) and 0·33% tannin. The acid, as malic, was 0·27% Most of the astringency which makes the raw juice unpleasant could be removed by cooking for 3 or 4 minutes in a 2% salt solution or steaming at 5 lb. pressure for 5 minutes. The slight degree of astringency remaining could be removed by adding 3·6 oz. of gelatin to 10 gal. of juice, or by adding 26 parts lime juice to 74 parts of cashew juice. The further addition of 5 or 6% of sugar is said to make a delicious product. A syrup was made by concentrating the juice to 36° Brix, and this could be diluted three times to make a drink. Jam was made by immersing the fruit in 2% salt solution for three days, washing, steaming at 15 lb. pressure for 15 minutes, adding an equal amount of sugar, and cooking to a temperature of 217° F. The fruit was also candied. More details are given by Jain and others (1952).

The Jackfruit

Probably indigenous to India, perhaps to the Western Ghats, the jackfruit is widely grown and highly esteemed in most parts of the country. Assam claims the largest area, about 20,000 acres, and Bihar estimates nearly half as much. Travancore-Cochin reports 5,130 acres. Naik (1949) says that it is rarely planted in orchards in South India, but estimates more than 100,000 trees, which would occupy nearly 3,000 acres. It has been reported that there are 660 acres in Uttar Pradesh. The tree grows from sea-level to about 5,000 ft. elevation in the South, and into the foothills of the Himalayas. It is said to produce more food per acre than any other fruit in South India, and Naik (1949) considers that the total production there is as great as that of any fruit except the mango and banana. It is commonly grown in Burma and Malaya, and to a considerable extent in Brazil. It has not become popular in some other tropical countries, as the flavour and texture do not appeal to some people.

The English name, which is derived from the Malayalam term, is variously spelled. 'Jack', 'jaka', or 'jakfruit' are used, and may be better forms, but 'jackfruit' is now well established. Along with the fig and the mulberry, the jackfruit belongs to the family Moraceae or Urticaceae. The genus is *Artocarpus*, from the Greek for breadfruit, and the species has been considered *integrifolia* or *integra*. Sturrock (1940), however, states that this is because of a consistent misinterpretation of the original description, and that *A. integra* properly refers to another species, while the proper name for the jackfruit is *A. heterophylla*. Chatterjee and Randhawa (1952) call it *A. heterophyllus*.

Several other members of the genus are of some importance. The breadfruit, *A. altilis* (*communis, incisa*) is more tropical in its requirements, and is not much grown in India, but is of greater importance in the world, being one of the staple foods in Polynesia. It is connected with one of the great epics of the sea, for Captain Bligh had loaded a thousand breadfruit plants on his ship, the 'Bounty', in Tahiti and was taking them to the West Indies when the majority of the crew mutinied and put him and the few loyal sailors into an open boat. After an almost impossible trip they reached the East Indies, and later Captain Bligh succeeded in introducing both the breadfruit and jackfruit into the West Indies, where they proved of very little value. It flourishes on the west coast of South India and on the islands off that coast, according to Naik (1949), who says it also grows on humid hill slopes up to about 3,500 feet above the sea, and even in the drier parts when planted in a sheltered spot in the midst of thick vegetation and well supplied with water. The seedless type is preferred and is commonly propagated from root suckers. K. F. Khan (1945) reports 90% success with root cuttings about 1 in. in diameter and 9 in. long, planted horizontally, while those planted vertically gave only 40% success, and stem cuttings failed at the Burliar Fruit Station. Bearing starts in about 6 years and the average yield in South India is given as about 50 lb. per tree, with some trees giving more than 200 lb. The starchy fruits are much smaller than those of the jackfruit, and are eaten cooked.

The monkey jack, *A. lakoocha*, is a handsome tree, said to be a native of Bengal, bearing an irregular fruit, three or four inches in diameter. Both the pulp and the seeds are edible, but are not highly esteemed. The tree occurs wild in different parts of India and Burma, but is very seldom cultivated. Naik reports that this and another species, *A. hirsuta* are both semi-wild and bear edible fruits. The Johore jackfruit, *A. champedon* is a small fruit which is eaten but has a strong odour resembling that of the durion.

The jackfruit is of interest because of the queer way the large fruits, sometimes weighing 100 lb., are borne. Spikes of flowers are borne on footstalks which are short deciduous branches arising on the trunk and the primary and secondary branches. Smaller spikes are formed at the ends of small branches. All are staminate except some of those on the thicker footstalks which contain pistillate and sterile flowers and develop into the fruits. Pollination, according to Sambamurty and Ramalingam (1954 a), seems to be entirely by means of the wind. They found that hand pollination increased the number of flowers fecundated and the weight of the fruit. The common belief that fruits are also borne on the roots may be based on their appearance at the base of the trunk, below the surface of the soil.

In India the jackfruit has been universally grown from seed, and this method is largely used in other countries also. Sonwalkar (1951) found that four fruits of a culinary type in Madhya Pradesh contained from 378 to 491 seeds each, compared with about 100 in table varieties. Most of the seed weighed from 3 to 6 grammes each, and those smaller than this were unsatisfactory for propagation. Germination required from three to eight weeks, and was only slightly lessened and retarded by storing the seeds for a month at room temperature. Germination was poorer when the seed was placed with the embryo up, and soaking the seed in water for 24 hours increased and hastened germination. The larger seeds gave better germination and seedlings which at three months were more vigorous. Transplanting when the seedlings had more than four leaves resulted in 20% mortality. It is better to transplant the seedlings before the food reserves in the cotyledons are exhausted. and some growers prefer to plant the seed where the plant is to be grown.

Khan (1946 b) reports successful inarching in South India. Inarching on *A. hirsuta* and on jackfruit seedlings in July gave 67% success, and on an inferior variety of jackfruit, called Rudrakshi, in December, 70%. S. N. Singh and others (1949) had no success at Kanpur with any vegetative method except air layering. Their best results, about 60% success, were achieved when shoots 2 or 3 years old were prepared in the last week of August or the first week of September by removing a ring of bark 2 or 2½ inches wide. This section of the stem was covered with clean sand and kept moist for about 2½ months. As the roots emerged from the sand they were covered with successive layers of leaf mould, and when they emerged from the third layer a notch was made half through the branch and a week later the gootee was removed. Those planted in pots became dormant and later died, but those planted in a shaded nursery grew. S. N. Singh (1955 a) tried several hormones singly and in combination and had outstanding success only with 1% beta indolebutyric acid, which gave 100%, compared with 50% in the control. Shoots 1-1·5 cm. in diameter responded well.

L. B. Singh (1951) at Saharanpur reports only 12% success without the use of hormones, but with 0·025% Seradix A, 72% and with 0·025% alpha naphthalene acetic acid, 56%. In Java it is successfully budded by the modified Forkert method, and Ochse (1931) recommends the use of non-petioled budwood on rootstocks of *Artocarpus champeden*, although *A. rigida* or the jackfruit itself may be used.

Very little has been written about the culture of the jackfruit. While for the best production it needs plenty of water, poor drainage is very injurious. In the flood of 1948 in Allahabad, jackfruit trees were severely injured or killed when mangoes and other trees under the same conditions were uninjured. Naik (1949) considers rich, deep soil of medium or open texture best, but states that on deep gravelly or laterite soils trees sometimes become large and bear well. The tree grows to a large size, and under favourable conditions would be crowded at the distance of 30 ft. which is sometimes recommended. Naik believes that from 30 to 40 ft. is satisfactory. Ochse (1931) is probably not too generous in allowing 39 to 46 feet. As the fruit is borne on the trunk and main branches, there is no objection to the tree growing tall, and little pruning is desirable except to secure a strong framework. As there is a tendency towards narrow crotches which may split, care should be taken to avoid these. Except where there is plentiful rainfall throughout the year, irrigation is necessary. Manure is sometimes given.

Insect pests and diseases are of comparatively minor importance. Chowdhury and Majid (1954) say that in Assam substantial damage is caused by the stem borer, *Margaronia caesalis*. The larvae of this moth attack both tender stems and developing fruits and may be controlled by hand picking or spraying with BHC or DDT. This pest has also been reported from Andhra and Uttar Pradesh. The small, whitish grubs of the Brown weevil, *Ochyromera artocarpi*, are also said to bore into the tender buds and fruits in Assam and may be controlled by destroying the fallen fruits and buds, and by collecting grubs and adults. The borer, *Batocera ruformaculata*, and the larvae of the moth *Perina nuda*, have also been reported damaging the jackfruit.

Chowdhury (1949) reports that in the principal jackfruit areas in Sylhet and Cachar districts of Assam, 15 to 32% of the fruits were found suffering from a soft rot which causes them to fall. This is caused by *Rhizopus artocarpi*, which grows best at 26 to 28° C. (78·8 to 82·4° F) while the fruiting bodies form better at temperatures about 1° C. lower. The male, but not the female, inflorescence is also attacked. The fungus survives as a saprophyte on organic matter in the soil. Spraying with Bordeaux mixture at 3-week intervals from January to March gave partial control. A brown leafspot, caused by *Phomopsis artocarpina*, has been observed in northern India which does not seem to do much damage.

Seedling jackfruit trees come into bearing in from four to eight years in the warmer parts of the country, but in northern India these figures have to be doubled. Richards (1950) states that the Singapore variety comes into bearing in about 18 months under favourable conditions in the low wet zone of Ceylon, but takes two years or more at higher elevations. Rangacharlu and Rao (1951) state that of 12 trees of this type planted at Kallar, four bloomed when three years old and one set fruits which were mature 42 months after the trees were planted. By that time they were 16 ft. high on the average, with a spread of 7 ft. and a girth of 13½ in. The fruit is of a good dessert type and much of it ripens when trees of the ordinary type produce little, so this seems a promising type.

In northern India, the blossoms appear in winter and the fruits mature in the summer, but in more tropical regions cropping continues throughout the year.

Heavy crops of fruit are produced, and where the price is good, as it is in northern India, the trees are quite profitable. A single large tree may produce a crop worth Rs. 50 to 75 a year. Naik (1949) indicates a tendency toward alternate bearing, saying that a fair average yield in a poor year is 75 lb. while in a good year it is 350 lb., with a maximum of twice this amount. If an average of 212 lb. per tree is taken, and it is assumed that there are 35·5 trees per acre (at 35 feet) the production would be 7,526 lb. per acre, about like that of the mango, but much less than the banana. Richards (1950) says that after harvest, the stalks should be cut off flush with the stem, to encourage flowering shoots the next season.

Two types of jackfruit are commonly recognized, one with firm, sweet pulp and the other with softer, more acid pulp. Naik (1949) recognizes that there is much variation, but divides the jackfruit into three types, one with tender, mushy pulp, one with crisp pulp, and the Rudrakshi, with fruit only the size of an ordinary pummelo, smoother and less spiny than the other kinds, and pulp of slightly inferior character. The quality deteriorates at high elevations, and he says that fruit borne above 4,000 feet is fit only for cooking. As vegetative propagation is only beginning to be used, there are no established varieties.

While the ripe fruit is sweet and is enjoyed by many, the bulk of the crop is used, before it is ripe, for cooking. The seeds are also cooked and eaten. In Java the inflorescences and young fruits are also eaten. Sturrock quotes an analysis made in the Philippines, showing 23·53% carbohydrates and 1·87% sugar, while Patwardhan (1928) reports 27·56% digestible carbohydrate in the ripe pulp. Bhattia and others (1955) report that the 'bulbs' form 29% of the ripe fruit, the seeds 12%, and the rind 59%. The bulbs contain about 75% sugar on a dry-weight basis, a fair amount of carotene, and very little ascorbic acid.

Mature jackfruit may be stored for 3-6 weeks at 52-55° F., according to K. K. Singh and P. B. Mathur (1954 b). They also report that slices of the fruit in 50% sugar syrup with 0·5% citric acid, frozen at —20° F. and stored at 0° F. were in excellent condition at the end of a year.

While the jackfruit has not been preserved to any extent, several products are possible. Siddappa (1951) reports that the 'bulbs' have been successfully canned in syrup. Siddappa and Bhatia (1952) report that the edible bulbs form only 25-30% of the whole fruit, and that the rind, which contains about 8% sugar, and the undeveloped bulbs, but not the gummy core, can be used in the preparation of a jelly of good consistency, taste, and aroma. A little citric acid is added to the water in which the rind is boiled, and more may be added later. A palatable beverage concentrate may be made from 10 lb. of pulp, 22½ lb. of sugar, 7½ lb. of citric acid, and 15 lb. of water (Anon., 1954 e). After cooking, the mixture is mashed and strained, and may be preserved by adding an ounce of potassium metabisulphite per 100 lb.

The Sapota or Sapodilla

In tropical America, where the sapodilla is indigenous, it is one of the best fruits, and is largely cultivated as well as growing wild. Several of its too numerous names, sapodilla, sapota, zapote, and chiku (chikku, chikoo, chico) are obviously derived from the native term *tzicozapotl*. 'Sapota' is commonly used in India, but has the disadvantage of similarity with the name 'sapote' which is applied to a number of fruits. 'Naseberry' or 'Neesberry', derived from the Spanish name of another fruit, is also used, as are 'dilly' and 'bully tree' which are applied to several species of the family, the Sapotaceae. The botanical nomenclature is also confused. The sapodilla is called *Achras zapota*, *A. sapota*, *Sapota achras*, *S. zapotilla*, and *Manilkara zapotilla*. *Achras zapota* is also used for another fruit, the sapote or marmalade plum which enjoys the distinction of having been placed in four genera.

The sapodilla is at its best in a strictly tropical climate, and is grown all around the world where conditions are suitable. In India the largest acreage seems to be in Bombay, especially in the tract from Bombay city to Surat, where, according to Cheema and others (1954) there are about 2,000 acres. The area there is said to be fast increasing. Andhra is said to have 1,100 acres, Madras and Mysore each 100, and Saurashtra about 150. There are also considerable plantings in Bengal, the western districts of Uttar Pradesh, and the Punjab. Where the fruit has not been grown it is not immediately popular but a market can be developed, and it seems probable that the industry will expand in various parts of the country. The tree is ornamental and may well find a place in gardens even where conditions are not suitable for commercial production.

The tree has been known to withstand temperature as low as 28° F. and according to Naik (1949) it thrives up to an elevation of 4,000 ft. in South India, but seems to bear better below 1,500 ft. The Cricket Ball variety with large fruits of good quality appears to produce fruits which are more tasty when grown below 1,000 ft. Even in Ceylon and Java, it is said to do best in moist areas near the sea. Temperature may be more important than humidity, however, for Oppenheimer (1947) says that in Israel it seems more adaptable to the interior valleys, where it is not damaged by hot, dry winds than on the cool coastal plains, where it develops slowly.

A deep sandy loam, rich or well manured, is said to be most satisfactory, but sapotas are grown on a wide range of soils. A high lime content in Israel seems not to harm the trees in Israel, even when combined with rather alkaline irrigation water. In the Gholwad area in Bombay, also, the trees seem undamaged even when salts encrust the surface as a result of a high water table, often only a foot from the surface in the rainy season, and brackish water.

In tropical America the tree sometimes reaches a height of 75 ft., but in India it is ordinarily much smaller. It is slow-growing, and this may encourage too close planting. In India spacing as close as 15 ft. is sometimes advocated and used, but Sultan (1935) is safer in recommending 25-30 ft. In Bombay the trees are planted from 20 to 40 ft. apart with a tendency toward wider spacing in the new plantations. Naik recommends from 20-35 ft., depending on the variety and on the soil and irrigation facilities. In Java, where the sapodilla seems to do very well, Ochse (1931) recommends 39 to 46 ft.

Seedling trees are commonly grown, but vary greatly in productivity as well as in the quality of the fruit, and are slow in coming into bearing. Vegetative propagation is therefore very desirable. Layering, air-layering, budding, and grafting are all used. Budding is said to be possible by the shield method with the same precautions as are necessary with the mango, or by the Forkert method. Air-layering is preferred by growers in Bombay, according to Cheema and others (1954) as grafted trees are thought to bear fruit with more granular pulp. In that State the layers are prepared in May or June and if watered regularly from October to January may then be removed; otherwise they are not detached until after the next monsoon. This is also the practice in parts of South India. Even with this long period, some varieties do not root well. The use of hormones to aid rooting seems not to have been tried. Naik (1949) says that layering is also most popular in Madras, but that inarching is gaining in favour. This is the most common form of grafting, but side-grafting has given some indications of success in the South. Fahmy (1952) found a positive correlation between the amount of carbohydrate in the tissues and graft union in Florida, and ays that good success was obtained by grafting in early spring.

A number of rootstocks are possible, in addition to seedling sapotas. These include the *mohwa*, *Madhuca* (*Bassia*) *latifolia*; *M. longifolia*; and *Sideroxylon dulcificum*. But the most promising is the *khirni* or *rayan; Manilkara* (*Mimusops*) *hexandra*. In the Philippines a high degree of compatibility was shown between the sapota and three species of *Palaquium* (Gonzalez and Fabella, 1952). In Poona and Gandevi in Bombay State, trials have been conducted comparing layered plants and those grafted on the sapota and on *Manilkara hexandra*. In both places the last proved best in vigour and bearing; at Gandevi the yield is reported to be 50% larger than from layered trees and double that of trees grafted on sapota seedlings. Goswami (1954) reports an experiment, presumably at Anand, with six replications of nine trees each, and three treatments, started in 1942. The cumulative production from 1947-48 to 1953-54 was 962 lb. from the layered plants, 1,091 lb. from those inarched on the sapota, and 3,159 lb. from those on *M. hexandra*. Nambiar (1954) reports that two years after planting at Taliparamba in South India, trees on *M. hexandra* were much larger than those on sapota, while nearly half of those on *Madhuca latifolia* had died.

The sapota is said by Cheema and others (1954) to do best with rather heavy irrigation, and they recommend giving water every eight days. They say that when water is scarce in the hot weather the interval is increased to 10 days but that this results in the falling of many flowers. This may be because of the very limited root zone in many of the orchards. In other parts of the country irrigation is limited to the hot dry months, and to orchards on light soils. In Navsari, irrigation with brackish water is considered beneficial to this fruit. Probably more irrigation in these parts would be an advantage. Cultivation is also largely neglected, though it is said that in Bombay the soil is dug nine inches deep in September. Fairly heavy manuring is also reported in that area.

Little experimental work has been done on pruning, but as the tree grows rather slowly and tends to shed any branches which die, pruning is probably not important.

Frequently the sapotas are classified only as those bearing oval fruits and those bearing round, although Cheema and others (1954) state that the two types may be found on the same tree at the same time or at different seasons. There are a number of named varieties in Bombay, of which the Kali, Dhola Diwani, and Large Calcutta are important. Near Vizianagram there are about a dozen named varieties, but the nomenclature is not yet standardized. The size of the fruit varies greatly, some being as much as four inches in diameter, but varieties with smaller fruit are likely to bear more of it. Texido and Alvarez (1954) in Cuba report a seedless variety of promise.

Very few pests and diseases have been reported. A caterpillar, *Nephopteryx eugraphella*, feeds on the leaf and flower buds, and the tender fruits and leaves, and causes considerable loss, according to Cherian and Anantanarayanan (1942). It forms tunnels of webs and grass, and also fastens the leaves together with silken threads, and feeds inside. The larvae are found on the tree throughout the year at Nagpur, according to R. L. Gupta (1955), but are most active in June and July and least from November through February. It has also been reported from the Punjab, Bengal, Bihar, and Madras, and also attacks *Manilkara elengi.* Two natural enemies have been noted, but they seem not to control the pest. Spraying with calcium arsenate is recommended. The scale insect, *Pulvinaria psidii*, and a borer of the fruit and stem are reported from Hyderabad. Cheema and others (1954) report damage by mealy bugs, *Phenacoccus iceryoides*, which attack the tender shoots, a fruit borer, and the bark-eating caterpillars which are only a minor pest. They consider the galls on the stems a hereditary physiological trouble. Diseases are not important, but Bose and Mehta (1951) frequently isolated *Pestalotia* (*Pestalotiopsis*) *sapotae* from fasciated branches and mummified fruits.

Flowers appear more or less throughout the year, but there are generally two or three seasons when more fruit ripens than at other times. Little is known about pollination in this country, but the failure of an isolated tree at Allahabad to set more than half a dozen fruits at a time from thousands of flowers suggests a large degree of self-sterility, at least in that variety. Gonzalez and Feliciano (1954) report that in the case of a variety with large fruits of fine quality in the Philippines, crops were often unsatisfactory, but hand pollination with pollen from common varieties resulted in fruit setting from 30·67% of the flowers pollinated. Examination indicated that this variety produced no viable pollen. The common type set about 10% with natural self-pollination, and 39·60% with hand self-pollination. They report several insects acting as pollinators. Sambamurty and Ramalingam (1954 b) also report insect visitors, and say that bagged unemasculated flowers failed to set, but they consider the wind the main agent of pollination.

The fruits are ripe about six months after the flowers appear. Bearing begins in the third year in the orchard, according to Cheema and others (1954) and a fair income may be expected from the fourth or fifth year, but bearing increases for about 30 years. They suggest that an average 10-year-old tree should produce about 2,000 fruits. Naik (1949) estimates only half this number, on the average. Sambamurty and Ramalingam (1954 b) report a tree of this age of the Oval variety bearing 1,158 fruits weighing 184 lb., while a tree of the Cricket Ball variety about the same age bore only 353 fruits, weighing 112 lb. Venkataratnam (1954) gives as the maximum yield of one tree in Hyderabad 8,151 fruits, weighing 461 lb. In Bombay and northern India, March-April and August-September are the main seasons, while in the South more fruit is ripe in February-June and September-October.

With fruits purchased in the Nagpur market, presumably of one variety, M. P. Singh (1951 a) found a uniformly high correlation between fruit weight, seed weight, ratio of length to transverse diameter, and sugar content. Fruits weighing not more than two ounces frequently did not contain enough sugar to be satisfactory, possibly because they had been picked when too green, and the percentage of edible flesh was only 27·33 as compared with 69·19 in fruits weighing eight ounces. In another study, M. P. Singh (1951 b) measured length and diameter of the developing fruits from September 16 until April 10, and found somewhat more rapid growth in the first and last months. The fruits which were largest at the first measurement, presumably because they set first, continued to be the largest. No evidence of the cyclic growth which has been observed in some other fruits was found. The number of seeds varies from nine to twelve.

The fruit is ordinarily picked while still firm, in which condition it can be shipped successfully. It is entirely inedible until fully ripe. Cheema and Karmarkar (1939) and Karmarkar and Joshi (1940 a) report that it ripens satisfactorily at 52 and 56° F. but not at 45, and remains good for 5 weeks, while ripe fruit can be kept for about 6 weeks at 32 or 35° F.

K. K. Singh and Mathur (1954 c) found they could keep full grown hard fruits eight weeks at 35-38° F., after which they could be kept not more than five days. During storage the ascorbic acid content, which was not high at the beginning, decreased rapidly.

The fruit is used almost entirely as a dessert fruit, but is reported (Anon., 1954 f) that it can be canned by heating for 20-25 minutes in boiling water. The product is said to be delicious and retain the characteristic flavour.

Products in the West Indies mentioned by Morton and Morton (1946) include a fine syrup made by boiling down the juice, vinegar, jam, and combined with citrus fruits, delicious marmalades. The mashed fruit is also added to bread and pancakes. Stahl (1935) gives analyses showing only about 8% sugar, while Sturrock (1940) quotes analyses showing 11·20% sugar in the round type and 12·70 in the oval. In tropical America the trees are tapped for the milky latex, chicle, which is the basis of chewing gum.

Reference has been made to the *khirni*, *Manilkara hexandra*, as a rootstock for the sapodilla. This is a large tree found in many parts of India, producing a small, sweet fruit in the summer. It is occasionally included in gardens. *Sideroxylon tomentosum* grows wild in the Western Ghats and Circars, according to Naik (1949), and its fruits are used. A number of other sapotaceous fruits are grown in the American tropics, but do not seem to have been introduced into India. The white sapote, *Casimiroa edulis*, which is occasionally grown, is not a member of this family, but of the Rutaceae. It may deserve more attention than it has had. Everett (1947) recommends extending its growth in New Zealand where it gives fair crops of fruit of high quality. It can be propagated by shield budding using fairly mature budwood and rootstocks in active growth.

The Mangosteen

One of the most delicious of tropical fruits is the mangosteen, *Garcinia mangostana*, of the family Guttiferae, and it is to be hoped that its culture in this country will spread beyond the 25 acres or so reported by Naik (1949) on the lower slopes of the Nilgiris and near Courtallam in Tinnevelly district. It is indigenous to the East Indies, and according to Hume (1947), is also grown in the southern islands of the Philippines, Burma, Malaya, Cochin China, Siam, Ceylon, and in a few orchards in the West Indies and continental tropical America. Attempts to grow it in slightly cooler climates such as the northern Philippines and Florida have failed. In the tropics it is grown at altitudes up to 1,500 feet, but is at its best near sea-level. It needs either heavy and well distributed rainfall or plenty of irrigation, and a water table within 6 feet of the surface is considered desirable. But drainage is also necessary. Soil with a high organic matter content is important, as is protection from the wind.

Although 'seedling' trees are commonly grown, the mangosteen has no true seed. The fruits generally contain one or two 'seeds', but fecundation does not take place and growth is from primitive adventitious embryos or hypocotyl-tubercles. According to Hume and Cobin (1946), swellings occur on opposite ends of the 'seed' and the shoot comes from one and the root from the other. The original root usually dies, and is replaced by a root system from the base of the stem. There are no root hairs. From the time the food reserves are exhausted until the second root system is established, the plant is in difficulty and growth may stop, sometimes for several years. Best results are secured from the larger seeds. Naik reports the occurrence of polyembryony, with 21 extra seedlings from 384 seeds, in one case. This is not important, however, as all the embryos are vegetative and there is little, if any, variation among plants.

Plump seed should be sown soon after extraction, although Winters and Rodiguez-Colon (1953) report that it retains its viability at room temperature for four weeks or, if stored in moist charcoal dust or peat moss, about twice that time. Temperatures as low as 50° F. resulted in death. Seed stored in the fruit for a week to a month germinated only after several months, whereas fresh seed germinated in about two weeks.

The root system is weak and deep, making transplanting difficult. Cuttings and budding are said to be fairly successful, and Naik (1949 a) reports almost 100% success in side-grafting, but the plants failed to grow well in the orchard. Inarching on seedlings of *G. tinctoria* about 4 years old seemed promising. Gonzalez and Anoos (1951) tested 13 species of *Garcinia* and found only *G. kydia*, *G. venulosa*, and *G. morella* compatible with the mangosteen.

The young trees should be planted in the orchard not later than two years after the seed is sown, according to Naik (1949) who says the spacing should be not less than 28 ft. and preferably 35. Shade is necessary, at least during the first summer. He recommends the same irrigation as for citrus, and no pruning except the removal of dead branches. Heavy applications of organic manure seem necessary. As the flowers are borne on shoots more than two years old, pruning may seriously reduce the crop. The trees are very slow in coming into bearing. Hume says that in Ceylon they may begin in 8 or 9 years after planting, but that more frequently it is 10 to 20 years.

No serious insect pest is known in India, although leaf-eating caterpillars may require hand picking. The only disease of any importance is a physiological one, called gamboge.

In Madras the main crop matures from August to October, and another, generally lighter, crop from April to June. Khan (1946 a) reports a five-year average at the Kallar and Burliar stations of from 18 to 620 fruits per tree, averaging, 220, while Naik(1949) gives a higher yield, with 240 fruits in the monsoon and 160 in the earlier crop at Kallar, and a still higher yield at Burliar, 1,000 feet higher. Better production seems to be secured in other countries, for Hume (1947) indicates that good trees yield from 500 to 1,500 fruits most years. A record crop at the Kallar and Burliar stations in 1952-53 of 1,075 fruits per tree is reported (Anon., 1953 b). This resulted in a net income per acre of Rs. 3,540, compared with an average for 10 years of Rs. 700. These figures are on the actual receipts, but it is said that the fruit could have been sold at higher prices.

The ripe fruit may be kept about a week at room temperature, or for six or seven weeks at 35 to 41°F., according to Siddappa and Bhatia (1954 d). They found the pulp was about 32% of the fruit, and that nearly 75% of the pulp was extractable juice. This contained 16.5% sugar and 0·52% acid. They report the canning of segments and the making of moderately good squash and the making of jelly from the rind. However, until production is very greatly increased, there would seem to be no occasion for preservation.

Three other species, *G. tinctoria*, *G. cambogia*, and *G. indica*, all yielding edible fruit of inferior quality, are found in South India.

The Durian

Many people live where durians are available for years without ever tasting one, while their neighbours regard them as the most delicious of fruits. Even the enthusiasts admit that the odour of the fruit is not only strong but very unpleasant. It is said that this odour can be eliminated by keeping the pulp in coconut 'milk' overnight. Some varieties, or perhaps related species, in Borneo are reported to be without the odour. The trees grow as much as 90 ft. tall and the fruits, weighing 4-8 lb. each, have a hard shell armed with numerous short, pointed protuberances. As they fall to the ground when ripe they are dangerous to anyone passing under the trees. Although there is a slight resemblance between the durian and the jackfruit, they are unrelated. The durian is *Durio zibethinus*, of the family Bombacaceae. It is probably indigenous to Borneo, but is common in tropical southeast Asia.

The durian prefers a warm, humid atmosphere and rich soil with plenty of moisture, so the area in India in which it thrives is strictly limited. Naik (1949) says there are probably not more than 100 trees in this country. Some extension of the culture of this fruit may be expected if enough people learn to appreciate their rich flavour. They are commonly grown from seed, but Wilson (1954) says that budded trees are now being planted in Malaya. Inarching is successful in South India, according to Khan and Rao (1952), but the grafts have to remain attached to the parent tree for many months, so a more satisfactory method is needed. In some countries seedlings are said to come into bearing at the age of five years, but in South India they take from 9 to 21 years. Naik (1949) suggests that they be planted 30-40 ft. apart.

In India bearing trees ordinarily produce 40-50 fruits each, but Wilson (1954) says that even allowing for some sterile trees, the average production is about 100 fruits. The fruit is allowed to fall to the ground and is then picked up for use or sale. Trees 60 years old continue to bear. Mathur and Srivastava say that the optimum temperature for storage is 39-42°F., at which they may be kept 30-55 days.

The Langsat

The langsat, *Lansium domesticum*, of the family Meliaceae, is another excellent Malayan fruit, the culture of which in India may be extended. Naik reports only stray trees at Burliar, producing about 30 lb. each of very good fruit each year. There are also trees at Kallar. Srivastava and Mathur (1955) report that the best storage temperature is 52-55° F.

The Carambola

The carambola is another fruit which seems to be used more extensively by the Chinese than by Indians, although it grows in both countries. It is said to be a native of the Moluccas, or of the Malayan region, but has been grown in India for many centuries. Botanically it is *Averrhoa carambola*, of the family Oxalidaceae, which is combined by some botanists with the Geraniaceae.

As far as climate is concerned, the carambola can be grown throughout most of India where there is very little frost, although it is said that young trees may be damaged by cool weather above the freezing point. It is said to prefer a warm, moist climate, and probably produces better under such conditions. While a rich soil produces more rapid growth and better crops, the tree has been successfully grown on soils ranging from sand to clay. While it is scarcely a commercial crop in any part of India, a few fruits do reach the market. Naik (1949) says that it is grown in gardens all over the plains of South India, though it thrives best in moist situations along the west coast and the lower slopes of the hills.

Propagation has been almost entirely by seed, with the expected result that there is a great deal of variation in the types grown. The vegetative propagation of the better types is therefore desirable. Naik says that layering and inarching are easy and should be used. Both methods were used at Kallar in January with complete success. Shield budding has been used in the Philippines, and the Forkert method in Java, and bark grafting has been used. In budding, bud wood should be fairly mature, smooth, and purplish with the leaves still attached. Seedlings of the same species, at least a year old, are desirable as rootstock.

The tree is rather erect, and reaches a height of about 30 feet under favourable conditions. A distance of about 20 feet between trees is recommended by Naik and others, but very limited experience at Allahabad suggests that on good soil anything less than 30 feet is inadequate. Little is known about the best methods of culture. Pruning seems not to be required to shape the tree, which is naturally symmetrical, but some thinning out is probably desirable. The inner branches keep drying, and may well be removed.

While there are no well known clonal varieties, two types, sweet and sour, are generally recognized. The sour type seems to be mainly grown in India, while China claims some very good sweet forms. Lewis and others (1954) report 3·83% sugar, mainly glucose, and 0·22% acid, mainly oxalic, in a variety they call sweet, while the one they call sour actually contained more sugar, 4·60%, but 0·51% acid. Firminger's Manual refers to a sweet form smaller and deep green even when ripe, in contrast with the rich, translucent yellow of the ordinary type, without acidity, but of very inferior flavour.

Under tropical conditions, the carambola may flower and ripen fruit in every month and Naik (1949) reports ripe fruit in large quantities throughout the year, with peaks in January-February and September-October. In northern India the fruit seems to be borne mainly in the cold weather and spring. The flowers are borne profusely in the rainy season and winter, but under some conditions little fruit sets until after the rains. There is some evidence that cross-pollination is an advantage, and it may be necessary in order to secure good crops. Naik reports yields of 100 to 250 lb. per tree each year. The fruit, specially of the sweet type, is eaten out of hand, and in China is well esteemed. Haiek (1952) states that it is rich in ascorbic acid, and in such minerals as potassium, calcium, magnesium, and phosphorus.

The juice is used in a refreshing drink. Jam, jelly and preserves are made, though some find that the pulp becomes tough when cooked, and others that cooking imparts an unpleasant, bitter flavour. Naik (1949) reports these uses, and also the manufacture of pickles, and the use of the fruit as a substitute for the tamarind in the preparation of various foods. The acid pulp is also used in removing stains from linen and in shining brass.

One other member of the genus is also grown, *Averrhoa bilimbi.* Because of the shape of the fruit, which is about an inch in diameter and two or three inches long and only obscurely angular, it is sometimes called the cucumber tree. 'Bilimbing' and 'bilimbi' are other names. The tree is more tropical than the carambola, and the fruit is too sour to be eaten fresh, but is pickled, stewed with sugar, or preserved. Propagation and culture are similar to those for the carambola.

Chapter XXIV

OTHER SUBTROPICAL FRUITS

The Jujube

The jujube (*ber, bor*) is one of the most common wild fruit trees in India, and it is cultivated to a considerable extent. Statistics are lacking for much of the country, but it is estimated that there are about 6,000 acres in Bihar and about 2,220 acres in Baroda. Dutta (1954) estimates enough trees around homes in Assam to amount to about 1,200 acres. About 600 acres have been reported in Uttar Pradesh. Basha (1952) refers to more than 500 acres of budded jujubes near a village in Kurnool district, South India. Gokhale (1944) states that in the village of Bina, near Kamptee, there are from 40,000 to 42,000 budded plants, which would amount to about 800 acres. This industry is said to have started when a Moslem cultivator won an *inam* by presenting fruits from a budded plant to Raja Raghoji Bhonsle II. Naik (1949) says that a few years ago there were more than 500 acres of superior varieties in Madras, but that because of damage by fruits flies, the area has been decreasing. Most of the seedling trees bear small fruits of poor quality, but there are a number of superior varieties. These are very popular, but sell at low prices, and are considered a 'poor man's fruit'.

The classification of the jujubes is confused, and this has led to much confusion about the nature and culture of the fruit. One type of jujube has been grown in China for at least 4,000 years, and is considered one of the five most important fruits in that country. There are said to be some 400 varieties of it, some of them seedless. This Chinese jujube is a small, upright tree with glabrous bright green leaves. It is deciduous and is said to start growth late enough in the spring to avoid danger of frost. The tree can stand temperatures as low as 13° F. It flowers in the spring and the fruit ripens in the autumn. There seems to be agreement in calling this fruit *Ziziphus jujuba*, of the family Rhamnaceae. The Indian jujube differs in many ways. The tree is spreading, and the branches are almost vine-like. The leaves are a darker green and are densely tomentose on the under side. The flowers are borne in the autumn and the fruit ripens in the winter or early spring. If the tree is deciduous at all, it is in the hot weather after the crop has been harvested. It can stand much less frost than the Chinese jujube. In spite of these differences, most Indian authorities refer to this also as *Z. jujuba*. Foreign authors generally classify the Indian jujube as *Z. mauritiana*, but are likely to add that there seems to be little difference between the two species. This species is said by Morton and Morton (1946) to be indigenous to the area stretching from India to southwestern China and Malaya. Synonyms for

Z. jujuba are *Z. vulgaris* and *Z. sativa.* It is possible that some of these names are sometimes applied to a third species. The incorrect spelling *zizyphus* has been used by many botanists.

An explanation of the confused nomenclature is given by Chatterjee and Randhawa (1952), who state that Lamarck called the Indian jujube *Z. jujuba* after that name had been applied by Miller to the Chinese species. Lamarck also used the name of *Z. mauritiana* for the Indian species.

Chinese jujubes are said to have reached Rome toward the end of the reign of Augustus (63 B. C. to A. D. 14), from Syria, and they have become fairly common in the Mediterranean region. Oppenheimer (1947) says they have grown wild in Israel for hundreds of years, but that it is not known whether they are truly wild or have escaped from cultivation. About 100 acres are cultivated, with about 400 trees per acre, and the dried fruits are sold locally and exported. The Indian species was introduced in 1939, grew well but set little fruit all of which dropped before maturity because badly infested by the fruit fly. The trees were discarded as a menace to the adjacent trees of *Z. jujuba.* The Chinese jujube is reported by Everinoff (1945) to thrive in the south of France, but there it does not flower until June or July, compared with March or April in Israel. Samsurin (1947) refers to the same species near Samarkand, and says that the leaves contain a glucoside which temporarily inhibits the capacity of one who chews them to taste sweetness. Both species have been introduced into the United States, where the Chinese jujube is preferred except in the warmest part of Florida. Jujubes are grown to a slight extent in other subtropical countries, but nowhere else do they have the importance they enjoy in China or even India.

Other species grow wild in this country, one *Z. rotundifolia* (*nummularia*), being a common weed which is controlled with difficulty. Others are *Z. oenoplia*, *Z. rugosa*, and *Z. xylocarnus.* These are all possible rootstocks for the jujube.

Seedling trees constitute the bulk of the jujubes grown in India, and bear very large crops of small fruits, 5 to 10 thousand per tree per annum being common. Vegetative propagation of superior varieties is the most important step in improving the industry. The statement is sometimes made that budding the jujube is difficult, but this seems to apply only to the Chinese type, which is said to be propagated by grafting, root cuttings, or suckers. Fortunately, Indian jujubes are fairly readily budded. Ring budding has been used for a long time. Vagholkar (1916) reports that this method gave up to 60% success in top-working wild plants. Shield budding seems to be at least as satisfactory, and is easier, especially if the bud wood has to be transported for some distance, so that it dries out enough to prevent the bark from slipping easily. It is considered best to plant seed where the plants are desired, and to bud in place, as the plants do not stand transplanting very well. Gokhale (1944) states that transplanting is impossible unless the seedling is raised in a pot, which is not desirable, and recommends planting two seeds at a place, and shield budding the better one at the age of about 18 months. Such plants bear in the second or third year. The seed is slow in germinating unless the seed coat is cracked, filed, or treated with acid.

Seedling jujubes are commonly used as rootstocks, but the *jharberi, Z. rotundifolia,* is also reported to be satisfactory, and others are being tried. Several experiments involving the testing of rootstocks as well as of scion varieties are being conducted in different States.

Considerable progress has been made in top-working seedling trees growing wild or in gardens or along fields in several parts of the country. In Gujarat (Anon., 1927) success was reported on wild bushes of the species *Z. rotundifolia* as well as trees of the ordinary jujube, though the former produced only bushes of the good varieties to which they were budded. The plants were headed back to a foot above the ground in February or March and the budding was done about two months later.

While top-working is thus not difficult and results in the production of fruit of good quality from trees which were formerly almost worthless, it must be recognized that an uncultivated plant on poor soil which may bear a fairly large number of small sour fruits, may not be able to produce many large sweet ones. In some cases the crops following top-working have been disappointing.

There is considerable question as to the best spacing for jujubes, but 40 ft. is not too much if the trees are to be allowed to spread to their maximum size. In Gujarat they are planted about half that far apart, and even closer planting, especially if dwarfing rootstocks are used, with heavy pruning to prevent crowding, may prove economical. It is not likely to be profitable to cultivate trees even approaching in size one reported by Watt (1889) which was 80 ft. high, with a girth 5 ft. from the ground of more than 16 ft.

Almost any agricultural soil seems suitable for the jujube, which can withstand moderate amounts of alkali and some water-logging. In Gujarat, where the jujube is given better care than in most places, Cheema and others (1954) say that 40-60 lb. of farmyard manure is given to each tree. Barakzai (1920) and Gokhale (1944) also recommend annual manuring, and this will probably be profitable in any jujube orchard. There is more question about the application of 2-4 lb. of salt per tree, which is commonly done in some places. Irrigation while the fruit is developing is also desirable, although some fruit will be produced without it. The value of cultivation is not clear. Popenoe quotes Meyer to the effect that this is the one tree which the Chinese do not cultivate, as it does just as well without tillage. Cheema and others (1954) say that no regular cultivation is practised in the Deccan or Konkan, but that in Gujarat the orchards are ploughed in September.

Pruning is highly desirable. Growth is vigorous, and the long, slender branches bend badly or break under the heavy loads of fruit which they begin to bear at a very early age. It is therefore necessary to form a strong framework, which involves heading back the branches. Some thinning out is also necessary to avoid crowding. The trees can stand very heavy annual pruning and still bear heavy crops. Gokhale (1944) considers that in order to get a profitable crop, it is necessary to prune the trees annually, removing all growth less than half or three-quarters of an inch in diameter. This heavy pruning may be g just after harvest, and another lighter pruning shortly before flow commences. Cheema and others (1954) consider it sufficient to prune once in two years, the small shoots being reduced to stubs. On the other hand, they say that trees on *jharberi* rootstock may be pruned back to the base each year in April-May. New shoots grow which bear the following winter.

While named varieties are not well established, superior trees have been selected in various parts of the country and propagated by budding. The great advantage of these over the seedling trees is commonly recognized. Dutta (1954) has described six varieties in Assam, one of which may be the *jharberi*. Another he thinks to be *Z. jujuba*, but as it is described as recumbent, with leaves indistinctively tomentose, and with fruit which is ripe in January-February like that of the other varieties, this seems most improbable. Cheema and others (1954) refer to a seedless variety which originated near Surat, from which much budwood has been distributed. It has small round fruits.

The most serious pest of the jujube in India is the fruit fly, *Carpomyia vesuviana*, which was recorded here as early as 1892. It occurs all over India and in the Mediterranean countries, being limited to the genus *Ziziphus*. Batra (1953 a) says that the first brood of flies lasts from about August 20 to late October, the second from the end of January to the middle of March, while the third starts the middle of April, but most of this brood dies. The eggs are laid when the fruits of the large varieties are 1.3-2 CM. long. They are laid beneath the surface of the fruit and hatch in 2-3 days. The maggots feed on the pulp for 9-12 days, emerge, fall to the ground and pupate in the top three inches of the soil. Pupation lasts about 12 days except in the case of the last brood, when it lasts until the next season. There is great difference in the attractiveness to the fly of the different varieties and types and the early, large, and sweet fruits are most attacked. Cherian and Sundaram (1941) state that in some trees as few as 2% of the fruits are infested while on neighbouring trees every fruit is attacked. Sometimes 80% of the fruits in an orchard are ruined. This is the only factor preventing a profit from growing jujubes in some places.

A number of measures have been tried against the fruit fly, including boiling or burying the infested fruits, digging or raking the soil under the trees in May or June, and poisoned baits. None of these has proved very effective. Batra (1953 a) has recommended spraying after the middle of October with 0·1% chlordane or BHC. Basha (1952) reports an experiment with BHC and DDT. A randomized experiment was unsatisfactory because the BHC acted as a repellant and reduced infestation in all of the plots. When applied to separate gardens, 0·1% DDT reduced the infestation from 73·1% in the control plot to 18·8% and 0·05% BHC reduced infestation from 71·8% to 12·8%. While BHC thus seemed slightly more effective, it leaves an odour on the fruit, so DDT was preferred. It is also recommended by Ramchandran (1951). Another fruit fly, *Dacus ferrugineus*, has been reported by Batra (1953 a) on the jujube in Delhi in April and Basha (1952) mentions *D. correctus*.

Another fruit borer, the caterpillar of *Meridarchis scyrodes*, causes less, but still important, damage in South India. Basha (1952) found neither DDT nor BHC as effective as against the fruit fly, though BHC reduced the infestation from 10·7% in the control to 4·5%. He lists other pests of the jujube as a hairy caterpillar, *Thiacidas postica;* the orange hairstreak, *Tarucus theophrastus;* the leaf weavils, *Myllocerus transmarinus* and *Xanthochelus superciliosus;* and several plant bugs. Chowdhury and Majid (1954) mention the larvae of a moth, *Porthmologa paraclina* which feeds on the leaves under a silken covering. They recommend hand picking or a preventive treatment with DDT or BHC. The bark-eating caterpillars are also serious pests and, because of the thorny nature of the tree are less easily treated than on most of the trees they attack.

Powdery mildew, caused by a species of *Oidiopsis* seems to be the only serious disease of the jujube in India. It is reported by Mehta (1950) as being particularly severe in the western districts of Uttar Pradesh, where it causes a brown discoloration and shedding of the young fruits. He suggested that the mycelium may carry over in the new shoots that arise in February. In one case an application of sulphur dust in December gave good control, but at Jeolikote lime-sulphur has seemed more effective. At the latter station, attacks by *Mitterellia ziziphina* and a species of *Cercospora* have also been reported.

Most jujubes are regular and heavy bearers, but few accurate figures of the yield are available. Naik (1949) says that the best variety in South India yields about 175 lb. per tree per annum, of fruits running about 30 to the pound. Another variety, second in flavour, is larger, averaging 20 to the pound. Ram (1941) reports that at Lyallpur 58 trees, planted 10 ft. apart as a windbreak and heavily pruned, yielded about 115 lb. per tree. Gokhale (1944) estimates about 80 to 120 lb. per tree in Madhya Pradesh. He estimates the value of the crop at only Rs. 240 to Rs. 290 per acre. Ullah and Khan (1954) state that at Lyallpur the income from 1949 to 1954 ran from Rs. 9 to Rs. 27 per plant or Rs. 432 to Rs. 1,332 per acre.

In India almost the entire crop is eaten fresh. Stahl (1935) reports Indian jujubes in Florida with a sugar content of 10-13%, while Ullah and Khan (1954) report total soluble solids in the Punjab as 12-18·7%. They report from about 50 to 67 mg. of ascorbic acid per 100 g. of pulp, while Riaz-ur-rahman and others (1954) report from 45·2 to 150·8 mg., also in the Punjab. It is said that the ascorbic acid is lost very rapidly in storage at any temperature. The Chinese species seem to contain much more of both sugar and ascorbic acid.

Candied jujubes are considered excellent and have been made successfully in the Punjab (Anon., 1939). In Burma the fruits are dried and made into jam or powdered and mixed with molasses or jaggery, or the powdered fruit is made into a drink. Morton and Morton (1946) say that the unripe fruits of the Indian jujube make an excellent jelly, but experiments at Allahabad have yielded only a sticky syrup unless some other fruit was added. Reed (1946) says that by adding the proper amount of pectin and acid to this fruit or by mixing it with other fruits, a good jelly can be made which retains a fairly large amount of ascorbic acid.

The Loquat

The rose family contains many important fruits of the temperate zone, but the only subtropical fruit of importance in this family is the loquat,

Eriobotrya japonica. This fruit is probably a native of central China, but it has long been grown in Japan and is highly developed and largely grown in both countries. Japan is said to produce about 10,000 tons annually, while the production in China is probably greater. The loquat is now known throughout the subtropics, and is grown commercially in the Mediterranean region, Australia, South Africa, South America, and the United States, as well as in India. One of the Government reports on marketing (Anon., 1950) estimates that there are 1,760 acres in Uttar Pradesh, 554 in the Punjab (including the West Punjab), 325 in Delhi, and a total of 3,086 in India. The Wealth of India, however, suggests that there are about 2,000 acres each in Uttar Pradesh and the Punjab, and adds that there are small areas in Assam, Bombay, and the hills of South India.

Although the loquat is evergreen, the tree is very hardy. Some branches are likely to be killed at about 15° F. but mature trees can withstand temperatures as low as 0° for a short time without great damage. This makes it possible to grow the tree as an ornamental in the milder part of the temperate zone. On the other hand, the tree can stand very great heat, and may be grown in the tropics. But it does not fruit well in the tropics, and flowers and fruits are subject to severe damage when there is more than 10° of frost. Commercial production is thus limited to subtropical areas. Gammie and Patwardhan (1921) report that in Bombay the trees bear well but the fruit is smaller than in northern India and is not highly regarded. In Madras, according to Naik (1949) the loquat is grown mainly as an ornamental tree, propagated from seed and bearing poor crops of sour fruits. C. P. Singh (1940) states that in warmer countries the loquat does better when planted with tall trees which provide some shade.

The loquat thrives on a wide variety of soils, in some places seeming to do best on a light sandy loam, in others on a heavier soil. Good drainage is generally considered essential, but Oppenheimer (1947) says that a medium heavy soil, even with imperfect drainage, is to be preferred to a very light soil.

Various methods of propagation are used. Seeds grow readily unless they have been allowed to dry out, but seedling trees vary greatly, and should not be used. Bajpai (1949) reports the occurrence of polyembryony in the loquat, which suggests that it might be possible to avoid variation in seedlings by careful selection among them. Cuttings are possible, but difficult, whereas layering is comparatively easy and satisfactory. S. N. Singh and Sharma (1954) report only 20% of untreated air-layers rooting within 18 weeks, whereas 3% NAA induced rooting of 80-100% within 6 weeks. Other hormones were less effective. However, graftage is probably to be preferred Chhonkar (1954) found both budding and grafting in Uttar Pradesh better in February than in July and budding better than grafting in both seasons. Shield budding, using buds from three-month-old branches, in January and February, is reported by C. P. Singh (1940) to give 90% success, while budding in September and October was less successful. Ring budding can also be used. In India the form of grafting ordinarily used is inarching, which does not give as desirable results as budding, but in other countries other types of grafting give good results. Many other members of the family can be used as rootstock, including the apple and pear, and the genera *Crataegus*, *Sorbus*, and *Mespilus*. Under most conditions, however, seedling loquats make the best rootstock and they are used in this country. The quince is also a very satisfactory stock in other countries, producing a more or less dwarfed tree, but on the plains of Uttar Pradesh it has proved entirely unsuccessful, according to C. P. Singh (1940).

Where conditions are favourable and no effort is made to dwarf the trees, they may well be planted about 30 feet apart. In Uttar Pradesh 25 feet seems to be enough, and where the quince root is used, still closer planting is common. Some reduction in size is possible by suitable pruning even on loquat roots.

As the ripe fruit is very delicate, and requires careful handling, a low, flat tree is an advantage. The Japanese are said to produce trees of this shape by training and pruning, and this might prove desirable in other parts of the world. Japanese authorities also recommend heading back about half of the growth of the current season in the autumn. As the flowers are borne on this growth in the winter, such treatment results in a reduction of the number of fruits, and a consequent improvement in the size and quality of the fruits which are produced. It also assures an adequate amount of shoot growth the next year. The trees assume a satisfactory shape without pruning, and the amount of pruning which is desirable probably depends on its effect on bearing which is considered below.

While little experimental work has been done, it is generally recognized that the loquat tends to exhaust the soil, and that fairly generous manuring is necessary. Farmyard manure is commonly used and C. P. Singh (1940) recommends 200 lb. for a mature tree. Green manuring during the rainy season is also desirable. Large amounts of potassium are removed in the fruit, according to M. P. Singh (1952) who suggests that the manurial programme should be planned to meet this need.

As the fruit matures during the dry season, irrigation is necessary. Ordinarily it should begin as soon as the fruit has set and continue until the rainy season.

In most countries the loquat flowers in the late autumn or winter, but in India flowering begins in July or August and may continue until January. Muramasu and Shiraki (1948) found flower bud differentiation to take place from the middle of July until the middle of August, 90 to 110 days before the flowers opened. Bajpai (1949) reports that at Kanpur shoots were observed to start growth in March or April, sometimes in continuation from the previous July or August, and to bear inflorescences in July, August, and less commonly in September, with flowers opening from August to December. Shoots starting early in July bore inflorescences in October which opened in December and January. The number of inflorescences observed was 84 in July, 41 in August, 16 in September, and 60 in October. No viable pollen was produced in August and September, so the flowers opening then fell. Pollen was produced in October, and with hand pollination gave a good set, but with open pollination the set was unsatisfactory, perhaps because there were few bees or other insects present at that time. He considers the bee the most important agent of pollination. Bees were abundant in December and January, when about 17 to 19% of the flowers set, which is considered satisfactory. Flowers bagged in December set little fruit, indicating little self-fertility. Bajpai (1952) found that when cross-pollinated, Golden Yellow and Pale Yellow set 18·5% and 20%, in contrast to 1·4% when both were self-pollinated. U. P. Singh (1956) also found Golden Yellow self-sterile, while Pale Yellow, California Advance, and Tanaka when selfed set 17-22%. Tanaka caused a set of only 12·5% in Golden Yellow and Pale Yellow of only 16·6% in Tanaka, but all other combinations proved satisfactory, California Advance being the best pollinator. Others have found that the fruit set in October and November is most important as under some conditions that set in December and January may not develop well because of the hot weather which comes on before they are ripe. If a large number of flowers are produced early in the season, there may be few later, and a poor crop of fruit. Pruning and other cultural operations should therefore be planned to encourage mid-season flowering.

In a later report, Bajpai (1951) reports that removing the July inflorescences in July was found to cause shoots to arise which flowered in the second flush. Normally, inflorescences were found to arise from the terminal portion of the current season's growth, and to contain from 18 to 200 flowers each. Purely floral inflorescences, or those with one vegetative shoot, did not abort, but mixed inflorescences with two vegetative shoots generally did, and those with more than two always did.

Still better results are reported by Bajpai (1953) from removing about two inches from the ends of the branches by the end of May. Four trees of the Pale Yellow variety were so pruned and produced an average of 114 vegetative shoots from July to October, compared with 45 on unpruned trees. The pruned trees produced no panicle before November, while the unpruned ones produced 59 on the average. The yield of the pruned trees averaged almost 59 lb. and that of the unpruned ones about 15 lb.

In addition to the thinning of branches, thinning of the fruits is practised in Japan, and may be desirable elsewhere if fruit of large size is demanded. Hodgson and Moore (1943) report that the increase in size is roughly proportional to the severity of the thinning. Thinning may be of individual flowers, of flower clusters, or of fruits, and is effective in avoiding the tendency of the trees to produce a large crop of small fruits one year, followed by a small crop of larger fruit. Fruit size was found to be determined largely by the number and weight of fruits in the preceding crop and the leaf area per fruit in the current crop.

Many excellent varieties are grown in Japan and China, and in other countries. A number of varieties have been originated in this country which seem adapted to the climate. The fruits vary from pale yellow to orange, and the number of seeds from one to five or even more. The size and flavour also vary considerably. C. P. Singh (1940) recommends the following varieties for Uttar Pradesh : Golden Yellow, Improved Golden Yellow, and Thames Pride (ripening from the middle of March); Pale Yellow, Large Pale Yellow, and Large Agra (ripening from the end of March); and California Advance and Tanaka (ripening from the middle of April).

In India the loquat seems to be free from serious pests and diseases. Near Jeolikote the stem-brown diseasé, which is a major disease of apples, causes some damage. It is caused by *Botryosphaeria ribis*. Die-back is caused by a species of *Macrophoma* and may be controlled by pruning the branches a foot below visible damage and covering the wounds with Chevastelon solution (a mixture of 6% solutions of copper sulphate and potassium dichromate) or Chaubattia paste (2 oz. red lead, 2 oz. copper carbonate, and 2·5 oz. lanolin).

The fruit ripens late in the spring when conditions favour rapid spoiling. As it is necessary to allow it to become fairly ripe on the tree in order to be of good quality, and as it is thin-skinned and easily damaged, very careful handling is necessary. The clusters of fruit should be cut or clipped by hand, ladders being used where necessary. The fruit should be graded and packed in shallow baskets or boxes, and marketed promptly. Bajpai (1949) reports the yield of seven trees of the Golden Yellow variety at Kanpur varying from 28 to 41·8 lb. with an average of 33·2, whereas Oppenheimer in Israel suggests that 33 to 44 lb. per tree is a reasonable yield in Israel, with a maximum of about 66 lb. Most of the fruit is eaten fresh. The ripe fruit contains about 8 to 13% sugar, 0·5 to 1·75% acid, and 0·3 to 0·5% pectin.

An excellent jelly is made from slightly unripe fruit or, as suggested from Mysore (Anon., 1955 a), from fully ripe fruit which is cooked after removing the seeds, with 10 g. of citric acid per pound of fruit. To each cup of juice, half to three-fourths of a cup of sugar is added, and it is cooked until the boiling point is about 222° F.

Two other species bear edible fruits, according to the Wealth of India, *E. angusitssima*, an evergreen shrub found at elevations of 4,500-5,500 ft. in Assam, and *E. dubia*, a small tree occurring slightly higher in the eastern Himalayas.

The Pomegranate

Grown all over India, from Kashmir to Madras, the pomegranate is nowhere of much commercial importance. Its popularity is due in part to the ornamental character of the tree, especially when bearing bright red flowers, as it is much of the year. It is thought to be indigenous to the region of Iran where it was first cultivated in about 2,000 B. C., according to Evreinoff (1949), but it spread to the Mediterranean countries at a very early date. The Romans received it from Carthage, whence the name of the genus, *Punica*. Some botanists place it in the family Lythraceae, but because of the peculiar type of fruit, called a balausta, most authorities make it the only genus in the family Punicaceae. There are only three or four species, of which the common edible pomegranate is *P. granatum*.

The pomegranate is of considerable importance in the Mediterranean countries, where about 5,000 acres are grown in Spain. Evreinoff (1949) says that Morocco, with 670,000 trees, is the largest producer. There are a few hundred acres in California, and scattered plantings in other places where the climate is suitable. Gammie and Patwardhan (1929) reported 1,451 acres in Bombay, more than half in Poona district, and by 1937 this had increased to 2,088, but the acreage fell again immediately, and in 1948 was only 1,243. About 250 acres are grown in Uttar Pradesh. Naik (1949) reports only about 100 acres in South India, although the pomegranate succeeds in all parts, up to an elevation of about 6,000 feet. Assam may have 50 acres.

Although pomegranates of high quality can be grown only where there is a cool winter and a dry summer, the tree grows under a wide range of climatic conditions. It can stand considerable frost, but is injured by temperatures below about 12° F. Where the winter is cool, the tree is deciduous, but on the plains of India it is evergreen or partially deciduous. It does well under desert conditions. It is very drouth-resistant, but does not bear well without irrigation. On the other hand, it will flourish on land too wet for many crops.

As regards soil requirements, it is not particular, though it is thought that a heavy loam is favourable to the production of fruit of high quality. It is more tolerant of alkali than most fruit trees.

Cuttings are almost universally used for propagation in other countries, as they root readily and seedlings vary widely and are unsatisfactory. Mature wood is cut into pieces about 9 to 12 inches long which are planted so that not more than one-third of the cutting is exposed, and in some places the entire cuttings is lightly covered. Barakzai (1920) says that the top is covered with cowdung to avoid drying. Layering may be used, and grafting has been tried in an attempt to induce imported varieties to do well at Poona but the local rootstock seems to be of no advantage. Cuttings are ready for planting in the orchard after a year or two. In India, seedlings are ordinarily grown, and Desai (1950) claims that the fine quality for which the fruits of Dholka in Ahmedabad district is famous is maintained by taking seeds only from choice fruits.

When pomegranates are planted in orchard form, they should probably be planted from 15 to 20 ft. apart, but closer planting is common. Barakzai (1920) reports that they are planted 12 ft. apart, and Gadgil and Gadgil (1933) say that around Poona they are planted at the rate of 400 per acre, which would mean about 10½ ft. apart. Desai (1950) says that at Dholka two seedlings about one year old are planted in a pit, the pits being 18 to 20 ft. apart. In some places the trees are placed close together as a hedge around the orchard.

The value of manuring is recognized, and Cheema and others (1954) say that at planting each tree is given about 40 lb. of farmyard manure mixed with ashes and that 3-6 baskets of old manure are given annually at the beginning of the monsoon. Desai (1950) indicates that much heavier manuring is done in Dholka, where 60-80 lb. of manure is mixed in the pit at the time of planting. After bearing begins in about two years, the soil is removed about once a month to a depth of 6·8 in. in a circle with a radius of 5 ft. around each tree, within which 60-80 lb. of manure is added.

Irrigation is said to be needed in Bombay only during May and June, and to supplement the rains if they are inadequate during the rainy season.

The plant may be left unpruned, pruned to bush form with three or four main stems rising from the ground, or pruned to a single stem which is generally allowed to form a rather low head. The plants are left unpruned when an impenetrable hedge is desired. If either the bush or tree form is used, it is necessary to remove the suckers which continually arise from the roots, trunk, and main branches, especially during the first few years. Aside from that the only pruning which seems desirable is the shortening of long slender branches, some thinning out when the plant becomes too thick, and the removal of very low branches.

While flowers are borne throughout the year, the number during the rainy season is large. Cheema and others (1954) say that in Bombay most growers treat the plants to favour flowering at that time by exposing the roots in April, applying manure, and renewing irrigation in May. The fruits from the rainy-season flowers ripen in October-December. Some growers use a similar treatment in winter to encourage the *ambe bahar* which results in fruits ripe in summer when the demand is greater although the quality is worse.

There are many types and varieties, some much better than others. A white-flowered type is known, but is of very poor quality. There are also ornamental types with double flowers, which are largely sterile, and are not grown for fruit. All varieties produce some sterile flowers. The fruit varies from a pale yellow to purple, and the juicy pulp in the arils from almost colourless to bloodred. The darker coloured fruits are more attractive, but not necessarily of better quality. The quality depends largely on the amounts of sugar and acid present in the juice. Sugar varies from about 12 to 16%, and acid from 1·5 to 2·5% in good varieties grown in arid regions. In humid areas, both are likely to be less. Siddappa and Bhatia (1954 c) report only 8·93% reducing sugar and 0·18% sucrose. There is also much variation in the seeds, some being soft enough to be eaten, and some large and hard. Barakzai (1920) names 12 varieties commonly grown. At Kodur, according to Naik (1949) the most promising varieties are Paper Shell, Spanish Ruby, Musket Red, and Vellodu. Cheema and others (1954) say that some varieties of the type grown in the Deccan have been selected at the Ganeshkhind garden, but they recognize that neither local selections nor imported varieties produce fruit in India of as high quality as the best in other countries.

The most serious pest is the pomegranate butterfly, *Virochola isocrates*, which lays its eggs on the flower or young fruit. On hatching, the caterpillar enters the fruit and ruins it. Damage may be prevented by bagging the flowers or young fruits after wiping them to make sure there are no eggs present. This is reported to be an economical method in Bombay (Anon., 1927 a) but obviously involves much labour and it has the disadvantage of lessening the colour of the rind. Clipping the calyx cup after the petals fall and spraying with calcium arsenate has been recommended in Madras (Naik, 1949). Lime sulphur is somewhat effective, according to Lal (1958), who found parathion, BHC, and DDT useless. Narayanan (1954) states that dusting two or three times a month with a mixture of 9 lb. Paris green, 5 lb. lime, 15 lb. talc, and 4 oz. flour, which is enough for 40 trees, proved effective in Delhi. He also suggests burying infested fruit and catching the butterflies.

In the valleys of Kumaun another caterpillar, *Epijarbus ancus*, does considerable damage of a similar nature. Unfortunately this also is called the pomegranate butterfly. It has four generations on the pomegranate and three on the horse chestnut. While spraying with DDT has some effect, no satisfactory treatment is known. The bark-eating caterpillars also do considerable damage, and Cheema and others (1954) mention a species of *Aleurodes*. Pigs, porcupines, squirrels, and birds also cause serious damage.

A rot of the fruit following butterfly attack in Bombay is said to be caused by *Phomopsis versoniana*, and a species of this genus is reported by Mehta (1951) to cause an almost total loss of the fruits on unsprayed trees in Bulandshahr district. Spraying with cuprous oxide checked the disease to a considerable extent. Leaf and fruit spots, caused by species of *Cercospora* and *Gloeosporium* and controlled by spraying with Bordeaux mixture, are reported from Madras. A fruit rot in Bombay is said to be controlled by the same spray. Hingorani and Mehta (1953) report a bacterial leaf spot observed at Delhi which caused some shedding of the leaves.

The yield in Bombay is said to be 70-200 fruits per tree per annum, up to half of which may crack before mature enough to have good quality. The cause of the cracking is not understood, but fluctuations in the soil moisture are thought to increase it. Early harvesting in order to avoid cracking is one of the causes of the poor quality of Indian pomegranates. The fruit should be clipped from the tree when ripe, and its quality improves on storing. This may last several months in a cool dry place, or six months in cold storage.

Pomegranates are used very largely as a dessert fruit. The juice makes a delicious drink, but as the rind and carpellary membranes contain tannin, it is difficult to extract the juice without getting more tannin into it than is pleasant. This can be avoided by allowing the fruit to shrivel before crushing, or by adding gelatin to absorb the tannin. Siddappa (1943) found that when the whole fruit was cut and pressed, the juice contained 0·175% tannin, but when the grains were separated and pressed, an operation involving considerable loss, the tannin in the juice was only 0·120%. In one good variety the juice was 40·1% of the entire fruit, and total solids varied from 17·3 to 18·5% of the juice, acids running from 0·81 to 1·23% as citric acid. He produced bottled juice of satisfactory quality by heating it to 175-180° F., cooling it quickly and after allowing it to stand overnight, decanting or filtering it. After filling the bottles, they may be pasteurized at 175-180° F. for 30 minutes. Or the juice may be preserved by using sodium benzoate. He also reports a successful syrup made by adding sugar and acid, and a product known as 'anar rub' with fairly good keeping qualities, made by concentrating the juice with added sugar until it has a total-solids content of 75-80%. At pre-war prices, a bottle of juice cost about 7 annas to prepare and sold for 8 to 10 annas. The rind, which is used in tanning, and the seeds which are dried and used in cooking, are by-products. An attractive jelly is also made.

The Phalsa

As has been seen, the phalsa is probably a native of India, although not mentioned in the earliest literature. It is grown in many parts of the country, but nowhere attains very great importance. While it is quite popular, it is not likely to be grown on a large scale because it does not keep well, and has to be marketed locally. There seems to be an opportunity for increased production near cities. If the bottling of phalsa juice or syrup is developed on any large scale, this will justify a corresponding increase in production.

The only members of the family *Tiliaceae* which yield edible fruits are in the genus *Grewia*. Of these the most important is the phalsa (sometimes spelled falsa) *G. asiatica*. Another species, *G. sapida*, is mentioned in Firminger's Manual, while Wester (1935) records three other species, one of them a tree of medium to large size, all producing edible fruits, but none cultivated in the Philippines.

Seedlings are most commonly grown, the seed being planted when the crop is harvested in May, or in the rainy season. According to Mehra (1932), the seedlings are ready to transplant the following January or February. It may be well to wait until the rainy season, and the plants may be kept in the nursery for another year or two. Firminger's Manual states that the phalsa is easily propagated by cuttings during the rainy season, but in the Punjab (Anon., 1934 c) this was found difficult. In the Philippines it is said that budding is successful, using mature, brownish, petioled bud wood.

As ordinarily grown, the plants may be placed about 10 ft. apart, or on poor soil, somewhat closer together. The phalsa is not particular regarding soil, but is more productive on rich soil and responds to manuring. The application of 20 lb. of farmyard manure to each plant at the beginning of February is advocated in the Punjab. It is drouth-resistant, and is sometimes grown without irrigation after the plants are established, but in order to get satisfactory crops in northern India it is necessary to irrigate, especially during the period of January to May when growth takes place and the fruit is borne. Irrigation is said to be unnecessary in Madras.

Pruning is a very important operation in growing phalsa, and in North India is ordinarily done annually. It is frequently the practice to prune the plants practically to the level of the ground, and in some places the process is completed by burning the stalks on top of the pruned plant. Such severe treatment is undesirable. L. Singh and S. Singh (1938) have shown that pruning at a height of 3½ to 4 ft. gave a greater number of shoots and a much higher yield than pruning at 1½ to 2 ft. or at just above the ground. Unpruned bushes were found to yield less fruit per acre and gradually to lose vigour. The size of the fruit was in inverse proportion to the yield, but the smaller fruit gave juice of a higher specific gravity. Similar results, as far as yields are concerned, have been obtained at Allahabad. Naik, on the other hand, says that in the South, where the phalsa is a relatively new introduction, it is not pruned to a bush form, and the plants are set 10 to 15 ft. apart.

The phalsa is deciduous, but is slow in losing its leaves in regions of mild winters. Pruning is done when the plants are about to lose their leaves, in the middle of winter, and new growth starts almost immediately. If pruning is done early in December, there is danger of the new growth being killed by frost, but recovery seems to be complete. On the other hand, early pruning and growth does not seem to result in earlier ripening of the fruit. Pruning may therefore be done at the time of greatest convenience, during December or January. The long stems which are removed may be used for supporting garden crops, such as peas, or may be made into strong baskets.

The bark-eating caterpillar seems to be the only serious pest of the phalsa, but it may attack the plants in large numbers. The direct damage may not be great, but the phalsa may be a source of infection for other plants. This is one disadvantage in using phalsa as an intercrop between larger trees when they are young, a purpose for which it is otherwise quite suitable. Galls are formed at the apices of the growing shoots by a blackish caterpillar, according to Lal (1950).

A severe leafspot disease has been observed on the phalsa at Kanpur and elsewhere in Uttar Pradesh by Srivastava and Mehta (1951). It is caused by a fungus described by them as *Cercospora grewiae.*

The plants begin to bear a year or two after planting, and the fruit ripens in the hot weather. The fruits are small, and ripen gradually, so that on one plant only a few are ready to pick on one day. This means going over the plants very frequently. The expense of harvesting is thus comparatively large. The fruit does not keep well, and must be sold within twenty-four hours of picking. Both of these facts favour the selling of the crop to a contractor, who uses his children or other low-paid workers for harvesting and marketing. Even so, the crop is quite profitable. Barakzai (1920) reported a yield of 20 to 25 lb. per plant. In the Punjab (Anon. 1934 c) also, the yield is put at an average of 20 lb. for four-year-old plants, and the price is given as three annas a seer, which amounts to more than Rs. 800 an acre. Naik also reports an average yield of 20 to 25 lb. per plant, but this would mean less per acre because of the greater distance between plants.

The fruit is used very largely in making a refreshing drink. Methods of preserving the juice and of making a syrup from it have been worked out in the Punjab (Anon., 1934 d). Directions for the preparation of squash are given by M. Khan (1951). He recommends extracting the juice cold, and then adding water to the pomace, heating to 160° F. and extracting again. The two extractions are mixed, sugar of half the weight of the fruit is added, and the squash is bottled and pasteurized for 30 minutes at 175-180° F. Or it may be preserved by adding 0·1% sodium benzoate before bottling. For home use he recommends that the fruit be crushed and strained. To each pound, 1 oz. of the extract 'kiora' is added, and the juice is placed in bottles filled with sugar and these are sealed.

The Avocado

A fruit of great importance in tropical America, where it is indigenous, the cultivation of which should be extended in India, is the avocado. It differs from most fruits in that it is neither sweet nor juicy. It has a high oil content, at least 15% in one leading variety, and also a high protein content. In tropical America it is a staple food and, along with bread, makes a satisfactory meal, while in other countries it is used in salads. Before it is largely used in India, the people will have to be taught to eat it, but there is no reason this cannot be done. In view of the need for more protein and fat in the average diet in this country and the fact that the avocado grows well in some parts, a persistent effort to increase its production and use seems wise.

In other countries where it has spread, the avocado is increasingly popular, as it is also in England. Malan and Nan der Meulen (1954), in a well-illustrated article, estimate that there are about 58,000 acres in the United States, 9,000 in Cuba, 8,000 in South Africa where the acreage is increasing rapidly, and 600 in Hawaii.

Three races of avocadoes are recognized, and have sometimes been classified in two or three species of the genus *Persea* of the Laurel family. At present the preferred classification, according to Hodgson (1950) who gives a complete account of the fruit and its classification, is that which makes the West Indian and Guatemalan races *P. americana*, and the Mexican race variety *drymifolia* of that species.

All races are more tender to frost than the citrus fruits and they cannot stand the hot dry summers of much of northern India. The West Indian race is the most promising, and does well on the plains and low hills of South India. The Guatemalan race does better at somewhat higher elevations, and it is doubtful if the Mexican race will thrive in India.

The avocado was introduced at Bangalore in 1819, according to Gowda (1952), but is still grown only as scattered trees in that area. Eleven varieties, foreign and local, are said to grow well and their cultivation can be extended as the market justifies. A few trees are found in Madras, mainly in the low hills. Five varieties were brought from Ceylon to Poona in 1941, of which only two set fruit there. One of these, known as the Purple, is of the West Indian race, and the other, the Green, is probably Guatemalan. Experience with these led Gandhi (1952 b) to state that, 'Excepting for some arid tracts of Bombay State where extremes of temperature prevail, the avocado will easily grow everywhere, particularly where the rainfall ranges from 30 to 75 inches during the monsoon.'

Vegetative propagation is desirable, and Gowda (1952) recommends shield budding. Gandhi (1952 b) found Forkert budding and side grafting possible, inarching easier, but layering most satisfactory as the plants grew faster and formed more shapely trees. He recommends layering branches in pots, in the monsoon, detaching them after six months and keeping them in the same pots until they are planted in the next monsoon. Gandhi (1952 b) and Rangacharlu (1951) both recommend spacing the trees 25-30 ft. apart. Little pruning seems desirable, but ordinary cultivation, irrigation, and manuring should be provided.

Bearing starts when the trees are about five years old. Both varieties in Bombay flower in January, but the Purple matures in June-July and the Green in August-September. Rangacharlu (1951) says that the trees at Kallar and Burliar yield 100-200 fruits each annually, and those near Madras 150-200. Gowda estimates only 50-60 in the large-fruited varieties and 200-300 in those with medium fruits. There is considerable tendency toward alternate bearing in the avocado, and this is said to be stronger in the Green than in the Purple.

The Bael and The Wood Apple

Although belonging to different genera of the family Rutaceae, the bael and the wood apple or elephant apple have much in common. Both grow wild in this country and are considered indigenous. Both are found in gardens, but neither is grown systematically. As commonly grown, both form rather slender, tall trees, and if planted in orchards may be placed about 30 to 35 feet apart. Both have fruits with very hard rinds, the bael being somewhat larger than the wood apple. The bael is *Aegle marmelos* while the wood apple is *Limonia acidissima* [Feronia *limonia* (*elephantum*)]. Both grow on poor soil, and the bael is said to thrive on either swampy or dry soil, and to tolerate alkaline soils. It is also said to be not greatly injured by temperatures as low as 20° F.

Both trees are ordinarily propagated from seed, although root cuttings or layers are said to be successful. In the case of the bael, neither is satisfactory. L. B. Singh (1954 c) reports 80% success in budding in June, using budwood about a month old, from the only flush of the year. The rootstocks were two-year-old seedlings. In transplanting these after budding, one out of eight died. Budding in March and September was almost a complete failure. Fairchild (1943) states that the bael can be grafted on a number of related plants : *Afraegle gabonensis, A. chevlieri, A. paniculata,* and *Swinglea glutinosa.*

Bael seed may be sown in June or July and the seedlings planted a year later. Fruiting bogins in five years and full bearing is reached in 10, according to Choudhri (1953). The trees are hardy and are given little attention. Patel and others (1953) report an infection of the leaves, fruits, twigs, and thorns by *Xanthomonas bilvae*, which is also capable of infecting the sour lime and the wood apple.

Named varieties are not grown, but there is much variation in the bael and it is desirable that superior varieties be vegetatively propagated. Choudhri (1953) reports a yield of about 5-6 md. per tree, made ap of 300-400 small fruits or 200 large ones. The pulp is not of an attractive consistency, but is eaten by many and is regarded as of value in preventing or treating dysentery. It contains about as much ascorbic acid as the sweet orange.

A stiff jelly can be made from the wood apple, but the flavour is somewhat harsh, so it is seldom used alone, but more frequently mixed with such fruits as the guava. Bhat (1944), however, speaks of the jelly as having an exceedingly agreeable flavour. He mentions syrup and chutney as other possible products. He refers to two types of wood apple, one with fruit larger and sweeter than the other, and states that the ripe pulp contains 2·3% acid and 7·25% sugars, but fails to mention whether this is the sweet or sour type.

The Cape Gooseberry

The cape gooseberry, *Physalis peruviana*, of the Solonaceae, is commonly grown as an annual on the plains of northern India and as a perennial in the hills of the South. It will not stand much frost and in the Punjab must be given protection in the winter, according to Phillip and Khan (1952). They recommend planting the seedlings in September or October on heavily manured ridges,

1·5-3 ft. wide. Harvesting then begins about the middle of April. In Uttar Pradesh seed should be sown from May until early July and the seedlings set out when not more than 9 in. high. The land should be well drained, for the plants are very sensitive to standing water, and well manured. The application of 200 md. of farmyard manure per acre before planting is recommended (Anon., 1955 b). Irrigation and weeding are required. The crop is harvested in February and March and a good yield is given as 150-250 md. per acre, worth Rs. 4-5 a maund. Perhaps the price is higher in the Punjab where only about 9 md. per acre are expected.

Where the cape gooseberry is grown as a perennial, vegetative propagation is desirable. Kuppuswami (1954 a) reports that the yield of seedling plants at Coonoor ranged from none up to 227 fruits per plant. Layering gave 80% success in an experiment reported by Ramasomayazulu (1954) while only 20% of the softwood cuttings grew. This author recommends spacing the plants 2 ft. apart in rows 2·5 ft. apart, in July, which brings the harvest in February-April. He recommends applying 10 tons of manure per acre and periodic hoeing. He reports an average yield in the Araku valley at an elevation of 3,000 ft. of about 250 fruits per plant; more than 15,000 lb. per acre have been harvested. Costs are given as about Rs. 855 per acre, and as the fruit is worth about 4 annas a pound, a net profit of Rs. 2,895 per acre seems possible. He recommends keeping the plants only two years, but Naik (1949) says that it is customary to keep them about four years at Coonoor where yields of more than 30,000 lb. per acre have been reported.

The fruit is eaten fresh or made into an excellent jam. It is said to be unusually rich in vitamin P (the bioflavonoids).

The Carissas

The karanda, *Carissa carandas*, has been mentioned as a hedge plant, and it is thus that it is most commonly found, but it may also be grown as a shrub or small tree. Even as a hedge plant, it bears heavily unless very severely pruned. It is commonly grown from seed, but the seedlings are slow in growth, and ordinarily not ready to set out until about two years old. Cuttings are very difficult to grow, although said to be possible. Inarching also seems to be possible but improved clones have not been propagated. Etiolation with ring wiring was reported as successful in Malaya. Once established, the plant is very hardy and thrives without irrigation or other care.

The fruit is used for pickles and preserves, and is one of the best fruits for jelly grown on the plains. The flowers appear in the spring, and some of the earliest develop into fruits which ripen early in the rainy season. Most of the small fruits, however, make practically no growth during the dry summer, and ripen at about the end of the rainy season. There are two types commonly grown, one with fruit which becomes a dark purple, almost black, while that of the other is pink and white, giving it a more attractive appearance.

Two diseases of the karanda have been reported. Lal and Singh (1953) state that anthracnose, caused by *Colletotricum inamadarii*, is widely spread in

Uttar Pradesh. The fungus enters through thorn wounds in the leaves and produces spots which may result in the premature death of the leaves. Nema (1953) isolated *Oospora citri aurantii* from decaying fruits in the market at Nagpur.

At least one other species is grown to a limited extent in India, and may become more important. For this species, *C. grandiflora*, a number of names are used, but Schroeder (1945) says that 'African carissa' is preferred to 'Natal plum', 'carissa', 'amutungula', or 'governor's thorn'. In India the name 'Natal plum' is more commonly used. This is a smaller shrub with leaves of a deeper green, bifurcate thorns, much larger flowers and somewhat larger fruits which turn dark red when they ripen. As the common name indicates, the species is indigenous to South Africa, while the karanda is Indian. The Natal plum is very ornamental, as during most of the year it presents white flowers and red fruits against a dark green background. But this habit of bearing throughout the year is a disadvantage from the point of view of harvesting the fruit. Several plants may be necessary in order to get enough fruit at one time to be useful. Seedlings vary greatly in productivity and in the quality of fruit. Firminger made the statement that the Natal plum is more productive when grafted on the karanda. Miller and Bazore (1945) say that the Natal plum is a better source of ascorbic acid than an average orange, and that it makes a good jelly. Another species, *C. brownii*, from Australia, is said to be more resistant to frost, and to bear a fruit about the size of that of the karanda and of good quality. Naik (1949) mentions two other species found in South India, with edible fruit, *C. spinarum* and *C. pancinervia*.

Irregular bearing occurs in some varieties of *C. grandiflora*, with a tendency to shy bearing when they are planted alone, according to Schroeder (1951). He divides the species into two groups, one with short-styled pistils and functional anthers, and the other in which the styles are long and the anthers small and without pollen. He observed a distinct benefit from cross-pollination in almost all cases, even when both varieties produce pollen. He found few insect visitors to the flowers, although night hawk moths and thrips are said to pollinate the flowers in South Africa.

There is again some confusion in the botanical nomenclature of the genus, which has also been called *Arduina*, and belongs to the family Apocynaceae. There are about 30 species several of which grow wild in this country, including *C. congesta* and *C. diffusa*. *C. spinarum* is used by some authors for *C. diffusa* but was used by Linnaeus for another species.

Sturrock divides *C. carandas* into two botanical varieties, *amara*, the karanda, and *dulcis*, the perunkila. The former seems to be the ordinary darkfruited karanda while the latter is said to have sweeter fruit, dark brown or rusty black with cream-coloured flesh.

The Date

The date may have been the first tree to be cultivated, and some regard it is the most important of all trees. Its history may go back to 7,000 B. C. in Iraq which has always been the most important centre of production. It is an important crop in West Pakistan, but is not now grown commercially in India, although attempts are being made to grow it. There seems to be a good prospect of success in the Punjab, the desert areas, and perhaps in South India.

The commercial date is *Phoenix dactylifera*. The wild date, *P. sylvestris*, has fruit which is edible but of very inferior quality. Its value is as a source of sugar. Ramchandran (1950) estimates that there are 50 million palms, other than the coconut, in India and that under favourable conditions each one should produce about 25 lb. of crude sugar. Many of these are of the wild date. This has long been an important industry, and has recently received much attention.

Much of India would be suitable for date growing except for one factor—rain during the ripening season. Much heat is required for the production of dates of good quality, and this is present in this country. Moderate frost causes little damage, and this is not a limiting factor here. But the fruit ripens during the monsoon season and it is only in the very dry areas that good fruit can be produced. In some of these the limiting factor is the lack of irrigation water, which is needed in large amounts. Almost any deep soil will do, even if it is too alkali for most crops.

Vegetative propagation is very important, not only because of genetic variation but because about half of the seedlings are staminate, whereas 3-5% will provide sufficient pollen. The only type of vegetative propagation possible is the use of offshoots which appear at the base of young palms. These may be removed and planted when weighing as little as 2 lb. or as much as 800. While closer planting is common, under most circumstances a spacing of 25-35 ft. seems desirable.

The value of tillage and manuring is generally recognized, but irrigation is perhaps more important. About seven acre feet per annum seems desirable, but the ideal situation is that in which the permanent water table is within reach of the roots or that along the lower Shat-at-Arab where the tide backs the water up into the gardens twice a day throughout the year.

Artificial pollination has been practised since it was discovered by the Assyrians three or four thousand years ago. The most common method of assisting pollination has been the tying of a few strands of male flowers into the female spadix. In recent years many growers have begun to collect the pollen and blow it into the female flower cluster. The old belief that the pollen affects the fruit has been confirmed by modern science. This is known as metaxenia. Pollen from different varieties results in fruits of different sizes, but the most important effect is on the time of maturity. By proper selection of the pollen the time of ripening may be hastened by about two months.

If left to themselves, palms will bear from 5 to 30 bunches, but if more than about 12 are allowed to remain the fruit will be small and the crop the next year poor. It is the practice to pollinate only as many bunches as desired and to remove part of the strands from those which are pollinated and shorten each strand.

No very serious disease of the palm seems to be known in India or Pakistan, but insect pests cause considerable damage. These include borers, the most important being the larva of a weevil, *Rynchophorus ferrugineus*, and scale insects.

The date may be used long before it is fully ripe, and in areas where there is danger of rain this is often reduced by early harvesting. The best varieties may repay the additional cost of picking each fruit separately at its prime, but most dates are harvested by the bunch. The fresh, fully ripe date is a very choice fruit, but without cold storage will ferment within a few days. The great bulk of the crop is dried, mainly in the sun. The yield varies greatly, but trees properly spaced and cared for should average well over 100 lb. a year. Yields of 500 lb. are fairly common. The dried dates contain about 70% carbohydrates, mostly sugars, 2% protein, and 2·5% fat. Most of the dates in international commerce are of the soft or semi-soft type (*khajur*) but in the countries in which they are largely grown the dry or bread date (*chhuhara*) is also important.

The Genus Flacourtia

There is much confusion regarding the group of minor fruits in the genus *Flacourtia*. Most authorities place the genus in the family Flacourtiaceae, but Grant and Williams (1936) put it in the Bixineae and Firminger's Manual includes it there and in the Rubiaceae. The species best known in India is *F. jangomas* (*cataphracta*), the paniala, a native of India or Malaya. But Grant and Williams use the name paniala for *F. inermis*, another Malayan species, generally known as the lovi-lovi, louvi or tomi-tomi. The ramontchi, governors' plum, or Madagascar plum, *F. indica* (*ramontchi*), variously said to be indigenous to southern Asia, Madagascar, or Africa, is sometimes considered the same as *F. sepiaria*, which Firminger gives only as an ornamental. Chatterjee and Randhawa (1952) use the term *baichi* for both *F. indica* and *F. jangomas*.

Difference of opinion is also expressed concerning the relative quality of the different species. Each species seems to have its own champions, apparently because of the great variation among the plants, which have been grown almost exclusively from seed. Apparently in each species there are some seedlings which produce comparatively sweet fruits and others the fruit of which is too sour to be eaten fresh. There seems, therefore, to be need that the best varieties of each be propagated by vegetative means, and tried out under different conditions so that the best may be selected for each locality.

Several methods of vegetative propagation are available. The paniala may be inarched or budded on seedlings of the same species. Budding, grafting and the use of layers and cuttings are reported successful on other species, and suckers are said to be used in the case of one species, *F. rukam*. Vegetative propagation is particularly desirable because the genus is dioecious except for *F. inermis*, and there are more staminate plants among seedlings than is necessary.

The different species vary somewhat in size and appearance, but are small to medium trees, with a spreading, bushy style of growth. In Ceylon and Java it is recommended that they be planted at least 40 ft. apart, but in this country less distance is commonly allowed. All except *F. inermis* are thorny and some, such as *F. indica*, are quite ornamental, with glistening green leaves. Some pruning is required to keep the plants from becoming too dense. The plants are somewhat drouth-resistant, but should be irrigated while the fruit is being developed, unless there is rain.

The fruit is about half an inch to an inch in diameter and red or dark purple. Some of the better types are sweet enough to be eaten raw. The paniala is said to be greatly improved by rolling it between the palms before eating. Even the sour types may be eaten stewed and are said to make excellent jams and jellies. Hartley (1950) states that in Penang the trees of *F. inermis* yield from 81 to 576 lb. a year of fruit that is too sour and astringent to be eaten raw, but which is used in pickles, jam, and jelly.

In this family is also the Ceylon gooseberry, *Dovyalis hebecarpa* (*Aberia gardneri*), a small tree with fruits which are pickled or preserved.

Mulberry

The mulberry is primarily a plant of the temperate rather than of the tropical or subtropical zones, but some species do fairly well in warm regions, and are grown over a large part of India but for fruit only to a small extent. Commercially, the mulberry is of importance mainly as forage for silkworms, and Naik (1949) reports 70,000 acres in Mysore, 20,000 in Kollegal taluk, and 500 in the rest of Madras, all for this purpose. The fruit is edible, but is highly perishable and seldom reaches the market. There are a number of species of the genus *Morus* and the family Moraceae which is sometimes included in the Urticaceae. There is much confusion regarding the species and varieties in India. At the Sericultural Research Station at Dum Dum, 110 types have been collected for study, according to Datta (1940, 1941). There the interest is primarily in fodder for silkworms. The type formerly called *M. indica is* now considered part of *M. alba*, the white-fruited species mainly used for silkworms in Europe and Asia, which is indigenous to China where it was mentioned as early as 2690 B. C. The fruit of *M. alba* is also used, but the most important species for fruit is the black mulberry, *M. nigra*, which is less hardy to cold. Some types grow into large trees, while others are vigorous bushes.

Although mulberries may be propagated from seed, it is preferable to use cuttings, which root readily. Hormones may be used to encourage rooting. Shield and ring budding and inarching may also be used. They do well on various types of soil, and seem to require no special care. Sturrock (1940) points out that in the warm climate of Florida the mulberry fruit tends to be smaller than in cooler regions, and that the fruit is better after comparatively cold winters. He suggests that proper pruning before the fruiting season causes vigorous growth and the production of larger fruits. The climate may account for the low yield which Naik (1949) reports in Madras, 7 to 15 lb. per unpruned tree. These trees are not manured, but for fodder for silkworms the plants are regularly manured, and are pruned annually from the second year. They are planted at the rate of 4,000 an acre.

The fruit is eaten fresh or stewed, or made into juice. In Europe it is also used for wine. J. Singh (1952) reports the preparation of attractive jam by adding 3 lb. of sugar and half a tola of citric acid to 5 lb. of fruit. Sturrock quotes an analysis by the United States Department of Agriculture showing about 9% sugar and 0·95% acid, as an average.

The Olive

The olive is one of the most important subtropical fruits, ranking next to the grape in acreage in the world. The industry is almost entirely confined to the Mediterranean basin, although there are some 26,000 acres of olives in California. Trees have been grown in various parts of India since about 1800, but have been unproductive, for while the tree grows well in a tropical climate, chilling is required to stimulate flower bud differentiation. Hartmann (1953) states that in California a mean temperature in January below 50° F. is required for commercial production. The tree withstands at least 10 degrees of frost except when in flower, and also very high temperatures. It enjoys a dry climate and is drouth-resistant. It has been tried in the Punjab, Pakistan, and may succeed on the Indian side of the border or in the lower valleys of the Himalayas.

The cultivated olive, *Olea europaea*, of the family Oleaceae, is thought to be native to the Mediterranean region, where it has been cultivated from very early times. The species *O. cuspidata* grows in large numbers in the lower Himalayas, and in Pakistan has been tried as a rootstock for the olive.

The olive differs from most fruits in that it is oily, not sweet, and in its fresh state, extremely bitter. Both green and ripe olives are pickled by several rather complicated processes and the products are very nutritious food. The taste for them is generally acquired, however. Large amounts of olive oil are expressed, as in Europe this is considered one of the best cooking and salad oils.

The Passion Fruit

Several species of *Passiflora* are grown for their edible fruits as well as for their interesting and ornamental flowers. They are placed in the family Passifloraceae, which is closely related to the Caricaceae. The purple passion fruit or granadilla, *P. edulis*, is an important crop in Australia and New Zealand, and thrives and bears heavily in Coonoor and elsewhere from 3,000 to 6,000 ft. above sea-level in South India. It needs a mild climate and is injured by more than a couple of degrees of frost, but on the plains it sets no fruit. It is grown from seed or, preferably, stem cuttings, and seems to require little irrigation or manuring. The plants are set out about 10 by 15 ft. apart, according to Naik (1949), and are trained on trellises, fences, or pergolas.

Fruiting commences in the second year and reaches its maximum in about the sixth year, when each vine bears 12-15 lb. Pruthi and Lal (1955 a, b) apparently have closer planting in mind when they give the yield per acre as 10,000 lb. Each fruit weighs about an ounce and is juicy inside a rather hard rind. The juice contains about 12·4% sugar and 3·5% acid, according to these authors, and when sweetened and diluted makes a drink which compares well with other fruit juices. It is a good source of ascorbic acid and carotine. It may be preserved with potassium metabisulphite. The rind contains a good amount of pectin for making jelly, and other products are also made. The fresh fruit stands transport well.

The yellow-fruited variety, *P. edulis* var. *flavicarpa*, does better than the purple at low altitudes in the tropics and on the plains of South India, according to Muthuswamy (1954), begins a year from planting to produce abundant crops of fruits of better flavour than that of the purple variety. Propagation and culture are similar to those given the purple variety. Buell (1955) recommends planting the vines 12 ft. apart along a trellis with wires 3, 5, and 7 ft. from the ground, and training them to a single stem as high as the upper wire. Laterals are trained in both directions on the upper wires, while the lower wire is used to support the fruit. Trellises may be 8 ft. apart. He found that pruning the tertiary branches which hang down from the wires to two nodes gave significantly better results than other methods or no pruning. In South India the vines have mostly been kept unpruned, but it is recognized that pruning might be advantageous.

The Persimmon or Kaki

Several species of the genus *Diospyros* bear edible fruit, and some also produce ebony, the black tropical hardwood for which the family, the Ebenaceae, is famed. Commercially, the value of the wood far exceeds that of the fruit, but nevertheless, one species ranks as one of the most important fruits in Japan and China. This is the persimmon, kaki, kaki-persimmon, keg fig, or date plum, *D. kaki*, which is also grown commercially in the United States, and to a very limited extent in India. Another species, *D. tomentosa*, the *tendu*, grows wild in India north of the Godaveri river and from Bengal to the Punjab. The fruit is eaten, and the heartwood is called a type of ebony and is used for making small articles such as picture frames. This and *D. melanoxylon*, the Coromandel ebony, also with edible fruit, are said by Naik (1949) to occur wild in South India. Biswas (1944) refers to an 'Indian persimmon' *D. embryopteris*, the fruit of which is said to contain about 50% pectin which might prove a good sizing material for textiles. The mabolo or velvet apple, *D. discolor*, is more tropical, and is grown in the Philippines, Malaya, Ceylon, South India, Bihar, and Assam although the fruit is only of fair quality. The lotus persimmon or date plum, *D. lotus* which is of importance as a rootstock for *D. kaki*, is found wild in the Punjab, according to Chatterjee and Randhawa (1952). The fruit is only a third to a half inch in diameter but contains about 11% sugar and may be eaten fresh or dried, according to the Wealth of India, which mentions at least four other species with edible fruit.

The persimmon is a fruit of excellent quality, and under favourable conditions produces heavy crops. It prefers a mild climate. It is deciduous and flowers late in the spring, so can stand a good deal of cold. It is reported to tolerate temperatures as low as 0° F. in its native land, China. On the other hand, it does not require as cool winters as do many deciduous trees. But high summer temperature, especially with low humidity, is likely to cause the shedding of the young fruit, the scorching of leaves, and the blackening of the fruit. The persimmon can be grown in the hills and in the mild areas near them. Khan (1940) reports that it thrives and bears profusely at Jamalpur in the Punjab, where the temperature does not ordinarily exceed 100° F. and the annual rainfall is about 50 in. but that the quality of the fruit is not excellent. It is said to do well in Kashmir and to be well liked, but little grown because of the difficulty of propagation, no suitable rootstock having been secured. It does fairly well at Coonoor but has not been tried sufficiently in other parts of South India to justify a statement as to the possibilities of its culture there. More work is needed to determine the areas where it can be grown commercially. The public will need to be educated as to how to use the fruit, but it should be possible to create a profitable market for as much as can be produced in the country. Intercropping with some larger tree which provides some shade and protection from wind, is a good practice.

Various types of soils have proved suitable to the persimmon, as long as drainage is good. On shallow soils the trees remain smaller and come into bearing sooner than on deep soils. The soil need not be very rich, but better crops are secured where plenty of nitrogen is available, and there is no evidence of damage from excessive fertility.

Many excellent varieties exist, and may be propagated by whip grafting or by budding. Seedlings of the same species are commonly used in Japan but in China the lotus persimmon, *D. lotus*, which is hardier, is preferred. An American species, *D. virginiana*, is sometimes used where drainage is poor. Hodgson (1940) found that the Japanese variety Hachiya, which is a favourite in California, is invigorated by *D. lotus*, and this results in an excessive shedding of immature fruits. Later Schroeder (1947 b) reports that during two years this combination produced more flowers but less than half as many fruits as the same variety on *D. kaki* rootstock. He found that a satisfactory crop results if 4 to 5% of the flowers mature fruits, but in these years less than 2% did so on *D. lotus*. On *D. virginiana* the crop was unsatisfactory because the trees were small and the bloom scarce. On the whole, *D. kaki* seems the most satisfactory rootstock in California, with a wider range of compatibility than either of the others.

Propagation is a problem at Coonoor as well as in Kashmir, as none of the varieties which have been grown there produce seed. Rao and others (1952) reported some success with inarching on *D. lotus*, which was considered promising, and *D. molli*, but no success with budding. It would seem desirable to import a variety with staminate flowers so that seed and seedlings of the kaki might be produced.

The persimmon is either monoecious or dioecious. Some trees bear only staminate flowers, and are of no commercial value. Some bear only pistillate while some always bear both kinds. Then there are some which always bear pistillate flowers, and in some years staminate also, while others are generally monoecious, but sometimes bear only staminate flowers. Commercially the purely pistillate type is the most important. Many of the best varieties develop seedless fruits without pollination. Morettini (1948) found it possible to increase the yield of pistillate varieties by hand pollination, but hesitated to advocate the planting of pollinators because of the danger of excessive cropping and alternate bearing.

Pollination influences the amount of fruit fall in the early summer, but Kadiura (1944) points out that in some varieties there is another drop in late summer, which is independent of pollination. This is influenced by blossom thinning, ringing, and nitrogen fertilization, and he concludes that the chief cause of this late drop is competition for food materials between new growth and the fruit. If pollination is needed, a monoecious variety may be grown for this purpose. In some varieties the flesh is light-coloured when seedless, but dark when seedy.

The trees should be planted 15 to 30 ft. apart, according to the variety and the fertility of the soil. Water requirements are moderate. There is danger of the trees breaking, so it would be desirable to develop strong frameworks, but this seems difficult to accomplish. There is a tendency toward alternate bearing, especially in older trees, and in Japan and China the fruit is thinned when there is a heavy crop. The fruit is borne on the growth of the previous season and in order to reduce the crop in the year following a light crop, many of the shoots are removed in the autumn. Hodgson and Schroeder (1947) found that out of 25 varieties studied, 23 clearly exhibited a tendency to alternate bearing, but this seems more marked in some than others. Most of the trees started alternate bearing with the first large crop borne. Naik (1949) reports that at Coonoor light pruning has increased the crop.

Most varieties contain tannin and are astringent until fully ripe and soft. As they cannot be kept long, or handled except very gently, at this stage, they are generally marketed while firm. Persons attempting to eat them at this stage decide they do not like them. Astringency has long been removed in China and Japan by such methods as immersion in lime water and enclosing in recently emptied wine tubs. Ethylene treatment also removes astringency and leaves the fruit firm. About 1930 four varieties were imported from Japan and planted at Coonoor, of which the Dai Dai Maru and an unnamed variety are considered more promising than the Tananashi and Hyakume. All are astringent which has interfered with their introduction to the market. Rao (1945 a) found little satisfaction in any of the methods used to remove the astringency : pricking with a needle, piercing with a knife, incense, hot water, and lime water. By chance it was noticed that persimmons stored with Kieffer pears quickly lost their astringency. Late Nayar and Shetty (1949) found that similar results could be secured with tomatoes, mangosteens, passion fruit, cape gooseberries, or more slowly, with bananas. The treated fruit lost its astringency in 3 to 5 days, the untreated in about 21 days, with much decay if the fruit was at all bruised. It is known that ripening fruit gives off ethylene and other gases which probably bring about the change in the persimmons. There are some varieties which never are astringent, and which may be eaten while quite firm, but in all cases the quality is better after the fruit is soft.

The ripe fruit is two or three inches in diameter, from yellow to tomato-red and with a smooth thin skin. It is very sweet, with a sugar content ranging from 14 to 18% in good varieties. It is mainly eaten as dessert fruit, but is also used in cooking. In China the fruits are exposed and allowed to freeze, in which condition they keep very well, and both there and in Japan they are frequently dried.

Analyses in the Wealth of India show only 10·66% sugar in the Tananashi, but indicate that the persimmon is a good source of minerals and carotene.

The Genus Phyllanthus

Two fruits which occur wild in India, and are indigenous here or elsewhere in southern Asia, are species of the genus *Phyllanthus*, of the family Euphorbiaceae. One of these, *P. emblica*, (*Emblic officinalis*) is commonly known as *aonla* (or some variation of this name) or, in South India, *nelli*, rather than by its English names, emblica, Indian gooseberry, and myrobalan. The latter name is unsatisfactory as it is also used for the fruits of certain species of *Terminalia*, used for tanning, and for *Prunus cerasifera*, used as a rootstock in temperate countries. The other species, *P. acidus* (*distichus*) is known as the Otaheite gooseberry or star gooseberry. In both species, the leaves are small and are arranged in two rows along small branches, come of which are deciduous. These branches thus resemble pinnately-compound leaves. As the fruits are also borne on these branches, in the case of the *aonla*, the plant appears to bear flowers on its leaves, giving rise to the name of the genus, which means 'leaf-flower'. Naik (1949) also mentions a third species, *P. fischeri*, found in the forests of South India, which bears fruits suitable for pickling.

Inarching seems less satisfactory than budding, according to L. B. Singh (1952) who was able to detach 50 to 60% of the grafts successfully, but these plants were so weak that only about half of them survived. Budding in early June in Saharanpur gave a 'take' of 70%, and within two months the shoots were 3 ft. long.

Success in top working seedling trees 4, 8, and 15 years old is also reported by L. B. Singh (1953). They were headed four feet from the ground in March and the vigorous shoots which grew were shield budded in June, using buds from very young shoots. After two months, the shoots which came from the buds were thinned to six on the oldest tree and four each on the others. After a year these shoots averaged 50 in. in length on the youngest tree and 90 in. on the oldest.

Both *P. emblica* and *P. acidus* are occasionally planted in gardens, but are not grown commercially to any extent, there being about 120 acres of *aonla* in Uttar Pradesh. Little is known as to the best soil or cultural methods. Superior types of the *aonla*, with comparatively large fruit are known, and should be vegetatively propagated. The wild trees are commonly seen in the lower Himalayas, as well as in forests on the plains, and up to 4,500 ft. above sea-level in the southern mountains.

The *aonla* flowers in the late spring and the fruit ripens in the winter, in northern India while, in some parts of Madras, it flowers in July and again, lightly, in February. Patel and Kulkarni (1953) report a heavy infestation of the aphid, *Ceriaphis emblica* at Poona and Anand in 1949.

The Otaheite gooseberry produces two crops, one in April or May and the other at the end of the rainy season. At Kodur, however, some fruits are found throughout the year, with the greatest number in January. In both species the fruit is too sour to be eaten raw, but is esteemed for making pickles, preserves, or candy. The fruits of the Otaheite gooseberry, sliced and cooked with plenty of sugar, are said by Morton and Morton (1946) to turn a rich ruby red and to be delicious. They also say that with enough sugar and enough cooking, they yield a fine tangy jelly.

The *aonla* is one of richest natural sources of vitamin C. Jain and Lal (1954) found 747 mg. per 100 g. of pulp. They also report 5·02% of tannins which are useful in that they protect the ascorbic acid from oxidation. Srinivasan (1944) reports somewhat less ascorbic acid, 540 to 720 mg. K. G. Naik and others (1951) found 588 mg. in Gujarat. Rao (1954) says that an attack of scurvy in the Indian army in Rajputana in 1837 was successfully treated with an extract of the dried fruits. The fruits was also used in treating the disease in the Hissar famine of 1939-40.

Most of the ascorbic acid is lost in the ordinary method of pickling, but much can be retained by putting the fruit in boiling water for a few minutes and then in a heavy salt solution. A powder made by mincing the fresh fruit, drying it rapidly in the sun, and then powdering it, may contain from 10 to 16 mg. of vitamin C. per g., and the amount may be increased considerably by refinements of the process. The powder has been used as a source of vitamin C for soliders and others unable to secure a normal diet. Jain and Lal (1954) extracted about 90% of the ascorbic acid after steaming the fruit for 15 minutes at 15 lb. pressure. The extract can be used to fortify other products, but is astringent and slightly bitter. Steeping the fruit for a week in 2% brine removes most of the astringency and almost a third of the ascorbic acid. The extract can be preserved with potassium metabisulphite or by adding 7·5 lb. of sugar to 8·5 lb. of the extract.

The Tree Tomato

As the name indicates, the tree tomato, *Cyphomandra betacea*, belongs to the family Solonaceae. It thrives at elevations of 3,000 to 7,000 ft. in South India and produces large crops, according to Khan and Krishnaswamy (1952) and is also grown in the hills of Assam. Trees grew well in the winter and flowered at Allahabad, but died in the summer heat. It is a short, ornamental tree which is common in gardens but is seldom found in orchards. It is commonly grown from seed, but the quality of the fruit varies greatly and vegetative propagation is highly desirable. Khan and Krishnaswamy (1952) secured the maximum rooting of hard-wood cuttings, 72% in November and failed completely only in January and February.

In the Nilgiris a variety with dark purplish fruits is preferred to the more common type with yellow or tomato-coloured fruits, but there is no named variety. The trees begin to bear in about two years and from the third to about the 10th year yield about 40 lb. per annum. The fruit is eaten raw or stewed with sugar and is highly esteemed by many.

Chapter XXV

THE TEMPERATE FRUITS

The fruits which are of such great importance in the temperate zones of the world can be grown only in limited areas of India. These areas are mainly in and near the Himalayas and in some of them fruit growing is an important industry. Difficulty in transporting the fruit to the market has prevented the growing of fruit on much land which is well adapted to it. With improved facilities for shipping, the industry will probably continue to expand.

At the western end of the Himalayas, Kashmir has about 18,400 acres of fruit, all temperate, according to L. Singh and Singh (1939). The main fruits are apples, walnuts, apricots, pears, cherries, plums, peaches, and quinces. Some types of fruits have been grown there for centuries, but the modern industry was greatly encouraged by the introduction of many varieties from France and other foreign countries by M. Pychard, the Frenchman who was Director of Agriculture from about 1910 to 1920. Some trees had been imported a little earlier, for it is said that the San Jose scale was introduced on nursery plants from France in about 1906. The State has been actively encouraging the development of the industry, particularly with reference to the control of San Jose scale and the provision of cheap and reliable nursery stock. That the plants supplied in large numbers were cheap cannot be denied, for at first they were given free, in 1946 at one anna each, and in 1947 at 4 annas each, which was said to cover the cost of production. Possibly, however, more money might have been spent to secure more reliable plants, with more satisfaction to the growers. That the industry is fairly profitable is indicated by the reported sale of the crop of 24,000 trees in 1946 for Rs. 1,67,000. There were four canning factories in operation in 1947, but because of the high cost of sugar and tins, and of transporting the product to the markets on the plains, competition with foreign products was very severe.

The Kulu valley, between Kashmir and Simla in the Punjab hills, is famous for apples, but the area is probably not much more than 200 acres. The valley is about 35 miles long, and the elevation ranges from about 3,500 to 8,000 ft. Of 45,972 acres under cultivation, most of which would be well suited to fruit growing, only 223 acres are actually in fruit, according to Mahngar (1946). Fruit was first planted there by Europeans about 1870, and some of the best and largest orchards were started by Europeans. The fruit from these orchards is mainly sold directly to consumers, at a large profit, while the small producer sells at low rates to a contractor or one of the big growers. Transportation to the plains is expensive. A large part of the crop is shipped by parcel post, 13,573 parcels of about 10 lb. each having been mailed from July to November, 1945, while several hundred maunds were shipped by railway out-agent. This system of marketing seems to encourage the growing of many varieties, for Mahngar lists as the chief commercial varieties, 21 apples, 11 pears, 9 plums, 6 cherries, 6 persimmons, and 4 walnuts. This means an average of about 4 acres per variety.

In the interior of the Simla hills a small area is suitable, and some fruit has been grown there for about 100 years. There was little development, according to Kalra (1947) until S. C. Stokes imported trees from the United States in 1917-18. More rapid progress came after the agricultural department started work in 1934. Ten years later there were 146 acres in Kotgarh *ilaka*, and another 40 acres in other parts of what was British India, out of a total of 9,667 acres under cultivation, much of which is well suited to fruit. About three-fourths of the area under fruit is under apples, but pear, cherry, apricot, plum, and peach trees are also grown, and in the lower areas some citrus and other subtropicals. In spite of the difficulty of transport into Simla, which cost Rs 3 per case of apples in 1940 and Rs. 9 in 1944, the industry is profitable, for the fruit sold for an average price of Rs. 14 in 1940 and Rs. 36 in 1944. In 1944 the average price of the fruit sold to contractors on the trees was about Rs. 1,400 per acre. It was expected that profits would be less, but continue satisfactory for at least 20 years. In the mountainous parts of Patiala State there is some suitable land, and efforts to develop a fruit industry there have been started. An extensive variety trial has been carried out, and Varma (1949 b) states that it has been proved that in this area there is room for planting a million fruit trees on the edges of terraces, where they will help prevent erosion, and in other places where they will not occupy land now used for other crops. About 10,000 trees had already been distributed.

An industry of considerable importance exists in the Kumaun hills and elsewhere in Uttar Pradesh. Various estimates of the area under temperate fruits have been made, varying from 2,468 acres in 1940 to about 8,000 in 1953. About 70% of this seems to be used for apples, and there are smaller acreages of peaches, plums, apricots, cherries, and pears. The Fruit Experiment Station at Chaubattia is investigating problems connected with temperate fruits, and encouraging the development of the industry on proper lines.

All of these mountain areas have certain problems in common. One is that of transport to market which remains expensive in most places although the extension of motorable roads is helping. Another is that of erosion. Varma (1949 b) estimates that about 2,000 acres of land has gone out of cultivation in Patiala in the last 25 years because of this. But he says that if orchards are planted on terraces with a reverse slope and proper drains, and green manure is grown during the monsoon season, very little erosion takes place. He mentions an apple orchard at Chail still in good condition after 50 years. Stone walls are not considered necessary there. In Kumaun many of the orchards are terraced, but with a slight down-hill slope, and it is estimated that about 600 acres of orchard land has been ruined for any sort of cultivation. Efforts are being made at Chaubattia to discover practicable methods of reclaiming such land. Hail is a serious hazard in many places, and Varma (1946, 1949 b) considers this the worst problem in Patiala, where some damage had occurred every year for ten years. He considers the second most severe handicap the long rainy season which delays maturity, decreases the sweetness of the fruit, and increases the damage done by disease and pests. The third problem was that of insect control, although damage had been severe in only two out of 10 years. He also points out the danger of frost damage in October-November and March unless there is good air-drainage. He considers it unwise to have low-growing trees of hedges at the lower edge of an orchard.

Outside the Himalayan range, but at fairly high elevations, temperate fruits are grown in the submontane areas of the Punjab and U. P. and in Assam, where it is estimated there are about 300 acres of plums, peaches, pears, and apples. For the most part, the fruits grown are those which stand warm summers and have a low requirement for winter cold.

Attempts to grow temperate fruits in the low hills of Madhya Pradesh have not been very successful. M. P. Singh (1949) relates the history of an effort made in 1922 when many varieties of pears, apricots, plums, peaches, and figs were imported from Australia and planted at Chhindwara, at an elevation of 2,240 ft. Many of the trees grew well, but did not bear satisfactorily, and in 1928 some of the trees were moved to Pachmarhi which has an elevation of 3,300 ft. The peach and plum trees have survived, but do not produce well. At least one persimmon has also survived. Strawberries and raspberries did well, but have been abandoned for lack of a market. Singh considers the heavy summer rains the greatest obstacle to the growing of temperate fruits in Madhya Pradesh, but high summer temperatures and insufficient cool weather in winter also interfere, while hail and frost are also hazards.

In the hills of South India, particularly in the Nilgiris above 4,000 ft. and around Bangalore, at elevations of 2,500 to 3,000 ft., temperate fruits are grown with some success. Apples at Coonoor have not done well because of the lack of sufficient chilling weather for the varieties grown. Naik (1949) estimates about 1,060 acres of pears, apples, and plums in South India, with smaller acreages of other temperate fruits. Some types are occasionally grown in the warmer parts of the country, but are generally not commercially successful. Bihar reports 120 acres of pears.

When Rao (1946) estimated that temperate fruits occupied 26,800 acres and produced about 81,000 tons each year, he was including a considerable acreage in what is now West Pakistan. Nevertheless, it would seem that the acreage in India alone must be approximately what Rao estimated for the undivided country.

Most of the temperate fruits, including all except the walnut which are of any importance in India, belong to the great family Rosaceae, and to about five of its hundred genera. In this large and important family it is not surprising that there has been and remains some disagreement as to classification and nomenclature, but the following names are generally accepted. The most important fruit in the group is undoubtedly the apple, *Malus sylvestris* (*malus*). The apple has commonly been included with the pear in the genus *Pyrus*, and had been called *P. malus*. Even excluding the apples, there are more than 30 species of *Pyrus*, divided into two groups. The Oriental pears are usually characterized by deciduous calyxes, non-fleshy pedicels, and the shape of an apple, while the Occidental pears usually have persistent calyxes, and fleshy pedicels, and are pyriform. *P. communis*, the common European pear, is undoubtedly of more importance than all the other species put together. One other western species is cultivated, *P. nivalis*. Formerly *P. sinensis* was considered to cover all of the cultivated pears of eastern Asia, but according to Lee (1948) these are now put into three species : *P. pyrifolia* (*serotina*), the sand pear; *P. bretschneideri*, the Chinese white pear; and *P. ussuriensis*, the Ussurian pear. Of these, only the first is grown in central and southern China, where there are hundreds of named varieties. The *nashpati*, which flourishes in the submontane districts, is classified by Chatterjee and Randhawa (1952) as *P. pyrifolia* var. *culta*.

The quince is *Cydonia oblonga* (*vulgaris*). The Japanese and Chinese quinces, which are grown in cold regions primarily for their flowers, belong to the related genus *Chaenomeles*.

The genus *Prunus* is a large one, and is sometimes divided into several genera. The important plums are of two types, *P. domestica*, the European, and *P. salicina*, the Japanese. The Bokhara plum, which has been called *P. bokharensis*, is listed by Naik (1949) under *P. salicina*, but according to Rashid (1949) it is a variety or type of *P. domestica*. It has also been suggested that it may belong to the *P. cerasifera* group. The apricot is *P. armeniaca*. The almond is *P. amygdalus* (*communis*) and the peach *P. persica*, and these two are sometimes separated into the genus *Amygdalus*. There are two types of cherry, the sweet, *P. avium and* the sour, *P. cerasues*. Many other species yield more or less edible fruit.

In Europe and America the brambles are cultivated to a considerable extent. They include the black and red raspberries, *Rubus occidentalis* and *idaeus;* and *R. flagellaris* and *R. allegheniensis*, forms of which are called blackberries and dewberries. The loganberry was long suspected of being a blackberry-raspberry cross, but for years all attempts to cross these species failed, but finally by using parents with the right number of chromosomes, crosses were made, more of which closely resemble the loganberry. Waldo and Darrow (1948) describe this work and conclude that the loganberry is such a cross. It had previously been classified as *R. loganobaccus*. Some other hybrids are of considerable importance in the United States. Some of these have been introduced into India. There are wild species in the Himalayas, and Joshi (1943) speaks of the possibility of improving the yellow-fruited *hinsalu*, *R. ellipticus* and the dark-fruited *kalahinsalu*, *R. lasiocarpus*. The latter is said by Gammie and Patwardhan (1929) to be cultivated at Mahabaleshwar and to grow wild in the Western Ghats. Firminger's Manual lists two species, *R. rosaefolius*, the Mauritius raspberry, and *R. albescens*, the Mysore raspberry. Both can be grown on the plains as well as in the hills, and the latter is said to be of good quality.

The strawberry is of more importance, and is cultivated to a limited extent on the plains as well as in the hills. Small wild strawberries occur in the Himalayas and in serveral other parts of the world, and some of them are more tasty than the much larger cultivated species. Darrow (1949) states that the cultivated varieties are all octaploid, and that into them have entered three octaploid species, *Fragaria virginiana*, *F. ovalis*, and *F. chiloensis*, which in turn may have originated from the diploid *F. vesca*, and perhaps other diploid species. He suggests that the less striking flavour of the large cultivated strawberries is due to their origin from diploids of less flavour than the best, and points out that one breeder has already bred the desirable fragrance of *F. vesca* into cultivated varieties.

The Apple

The apple is believed to have originated in Europe or the temperate region of western Asia, although the related species known as crab-apples are indigenous in northern Asia, Europe, and America. Wild forms of *Malus sylvestris* are also called crab-apples. It is not known when the apple was introduced into the cooler parts of India, but Mundy mentioned it as being scarce in Agra in 1632 (Temple 1914). In Firminger's time attempts were being made to grow apples in various parts of India, and good fruits were reported in Bihar. Experience, however, has discouraged the growing of apples on the plains, although Barakzai (1920) reports a very small but apparently profitable industry at one place in Sind, where crab-apples are grown primarily for the making of preserves, or for use as vegetables. Few apples are grown commercially in India below an elevation of about 5,000 ft. The main exception is about 60 acres at below 3,000 ft. near Bangalore, and a total of about 10 acres above 4,000 feet in the Nilgiris and other Madras hills.

Apples are ordinarily propagated by budding or grafting, as seedlings are entirely unsatisfactory, and rootage is very difficult in most varieties. Seedling root-stocks are most commonly used, and in some countries types are available which are known to produce satisfactory trees, and to vary only slightly. In Sind and around Bangalore suckers arising from the roots of mature plants are used. A great deal of work has been done on the vegetative propagation of stocks at the East Malling Research Station and the John Innes Horticultural Institution in England, separately and, more recently, in a joint effort. The rootstock varieties produced bear such numbers as Malling IX, Merton 778, and MM 101. Most of the recent ones are resistant to the woolly aphis, according to Preston (1955).

Many of these types have been grown in other countries, including India. R. S. Singh (1941) reports tentatively on trials of these and other stocks at Chaubattia, naming six as appearing promising. One of these is a species growing wild in Kumaun. Khan (1955) reports on work done in 1937-41 in the Kulu valley, where *Pyrus baccata* had been exclusively used in spite of the fact that it is highly susceptible to the wooly aphis. Merton stocks 778, 779, 789, and 793 were found to be resistant. The aphis was unable to breed on them, but when the apple was grafted on them, some of the resistance was lost. The quince and three wild species, *Cotoneaster bracillaris*, *Pyrus pashia*, and one tentatively called *P. communis* var. *shiara*, were found immune except that the aphids can live on the quince after grafting. Only *C. bracillaris* imparted considerable resistance to the scions. The quince dwarfed the scions and they had not flowered at the age of three years, when the others had produced fruit. The growth and fruiting on the others was as good as on *P. baccata*, and the quality was considered better. The improved flavour might result from comparative freedom from aphid damage. In a trial at Coonoor, Merton 778 and 779 seem most promising with the variety Rome Beauty.

On the basis of these trials, it would seem desirable to select the most suitable rootstock for each district, preferably one which can be propagated by mound or trench layering as is the case with the English rootstocks. U. N. Rao (1947), however, states that any apple available is used in Kumaon, while local wild varieties are used in Kashmir and the Kulu valley, and because of its resistance to the wooly aphis, the variety Northern Spy in Bangalore. Naik (1949) says that in Madras the most promising rootstocks are the Merton series.

Equally good trees can be produced by budding and grafting, and both are commonly used. Shield budding is the form used, while various types of grafting are practised. U. N. Rao (1947) states that shield budding is universal except in the Nilgiris, where it gives only about 50% success, compared with nearly 100% achieved with whip grafting. But grafting is also used in Kashmir and to a considerable extent in Kumaun. Singh (1941) prefers budding in September, with or without the wood, to grafting in March, which in turn is better than budding in May. Tongue grafting is the form most commonly used in Kumaun. Bajwa and others (1955) report on the basis of trees only three years old that root grafting seems to be successful in Kulu.

The size to which an apple tree will grow, and therefore the distance to be allowed between trees, depends on the variety, the rootstock, the soil, and the climate. In Europe, dwarf trees are frequently grown, while in America large trees are common, and are planted from 20 to 50 ft. apart. In India most of the trees are rather small, even when not purposely dwarfed, and it is probably sufficient in most cases to allow 20 to 25 ft., as recommended by Burns (1939). This is about the distance commonly allowed in Kashmir. With more vigorous rootstocks and scions, more space may be justified. On the other hand, in South India dwarf trees are grown, and are planted 10 to 15 ft. apart. Apples and other deciduous fruits are planted while dormant, from November until the middle of February.

Apples are grown on many kinds of soil. In Kashmir they do very well on deep, organic loams, and it is said that they do not require manuring. The soils of Kulu are light loams. Das (1947) says that in Kumaun apples do best on brown or reddish brown loams at least four feet deep, with a surface layer of six inches to a foot of organic matter. In Mysore, where the trees are small and short-lived, they are sometimes planted where there is not more than two feet of soil above an impervious layer.

Where apples are planted on level ground, they may be cultivated in much the same way as other trees, but in India many of them are on land which slopes so steeply that clean cultivation would result in excessive erosion. Frequently the land is more or less distinctly terraced, and the use of animals in cultivation is difficult or impossible. Under such conditions, it is probably wise to leave most of the soil in sod or weeds or some cover crop, but to dig around the trees so as to prevent the growth of weeds during the summer. Irrigation may be necessary for the first year or two, and available water is a good insurance against drought throughout the life of the orchard, but in this country and elsewhere, most apples depend on rainfall. Burns (1939) recommends mulching with leaves or grass to preserve moisture as well as to provide organic matter. He also advises the use of five baskets of manure in each hole at the time of planting, and Firminger's Manual suggests an annual dressing of a ton of farmyard manure with 400 pounds of bone-meal and 800 pounds of wood ashes per acre. This amount of manure is seldom available, and experiments are necessary to show what kinds and amounts of fertilizer are required. Experiments at Chaubattia seem to indicate that the application of superphosphate significantly increases growth and yield on some rootstocks while neither nitrogen nor potash has any marked effect. However, Das (1947) recommends 10 cartloads of farmyard manure or compost per acre per annum. On micacious soils, which are poorer than those derived from slates, he advises that this be supplemented with bone-meal and superphosphate. If the soil is acid, he suggests liming it once in five years.

Pruning the apple presents a very complicated problem. The best solution depends on an intelligent understanding of the variety, the environment, and the demands of the market. R. S. Singh (1937) states that the open-centre type of framework is the only one used extensively in India, and although he says that most of the growers are ignorant of the principles of pruning he seems satisfied that this type is best. In sections of Europe where the trees are commonly kept small, and where there is not much sunshine, it is frequently preferred. In some other countries it has been found entirely unsatisfactory, resulting in too small a tree or in excessive splitting of the branches. In Kashmir the open-centre type of tree is preferred, with the lowest branch 4 or 5 feet from the ground in order to avoid damage from cattle. Naik (1949) states that in the South trees in commercial orchards are trained to the modified leader form although in home gardens they are sometimes grown on cordons or as espaliers.

Apples bear mostly on very short, slow-growing branches known as spurs, although some varieties produce a good deal of fruit on the twig growth of the previous season. This fact needs to be borne in mind in pruning bearing trees. Pruning which removes spurs is a very effective method of reducing the number of fruits. R. S. Singh (1937) outlines and recommends a method of pruning by which the leading branches are cut back from a third to a half of their length, the most vigorous ones receiving the least severe treatment. This encourages the buds at the base of the branch to form spurs, while those near the tip develop into shoots. One or more of the stronger shoots is allowed to take the lead, while weaker shoots are cut back to a length of three or four inches in the hope that they will form spurs. This calls for careful and laborious pruning each winter. Again it must be remembered that different varieties grow and react to pruning in different ways, and must be studied separately. Where labour is expensive, less detailed pruning is done. In some cases good results can be had by removing a few of the larger branches each year. This may be necessary where annual heading back is practised, in order to keep the tree open so that light can reach the fruit. If the open-centre type of framework is used, considerable pruning is likely to be necessary to keep the centre open.

Actually, in most parts of India pruning is frequently neglected, and it is suggested that in regions subject to hail, after the scaffold branches have been formed, pruning may be reduced to a minimum so that there is some crowding, and the long branches hang down so that the foliage offers more protection to the fruit.

Frequently such heavy crops of apples set that in order to secure satisfactory size and to avoid breakage of limbs, thinning is necessary. U. N. Rao (1947) says that this is standard practice in the Himalayan regions. He refers to work at Chaubattia which indicates that early varieties should be thinned a month after full bloom, while the time may be extended by 10 days with later varieties. The early varieties should be thinned to leave one fruit to 30 leaves, and the others, one to 25.

Apple growing around Bangalore differs in several respects from that in the Himalayas. Apples were introduced there and in the Nilgiri hills in 1820, according to Javaraya (1943) who states that an outbreak of woolly aphis about 1897 destroyed practically all the trees. The industry has revived since 1908, on Northern Spy rootstock, which is resistant to the aphis. No matter how the trees are treated, they are dwarfed, and can be planted 15 or 20 ft. apart. The extreme crowding practised by some growers, who put trees 5 or 6 ft. apart, according to Aiyangar and Aiyangar (1930) is unwise. Two crops a year are borne. The peculiar behaviour of the tree is probably due to the very mild climatic conditions; at very few other places in the world are apples and mangoes grown commercially in the same orchard. Root pruning is practised in January or February and in August or September, and the leaves which do not fall are stripped off. Spurs are kept at least six inches apart, and the fruit is thinned to one or two on a spur, and tied to a strong shoot for support. The yield is from 4 to 12 dozen per tree, giving a net income from the 5th to the 10th year, of Rs. 800 an acre per annum. Collar or root rot ordinarily makes it unprofitable to keep the trees more than 12 years. In order to protect the trees from collar rot, the most serious disease, burnt clay collars about a foot and a half in diameter are placed around the trunk, and the earth inside these is replaced with sand. The roots are also washed with Bordeaux mixture.

Hundreds of varieties of the apple are grown in the world and R. S. Singh (1942) recommends ten for India. He also describes and recommends desirable varieties of other fruits. The most popular variety in Kashmir is the Ambri, which is thought to have been introduced from Central Asia. It bears well and its sweet taste makes it appeal to the Indian market. Most European varieties are more tart, and these are largely grown in all the other producing areas. At Bangalore the Rome Beauty, a variety of only fair quality, seems to be about the only one which succeeds. U. N. Rao (1947) lists 28 varieties, mostly from

Great Britain and the United States, which are grown to some extent. Naik (1949) describes eight promising varieties selected out of about 30 tested at Coonoor, mainly varieties introduced from Australia. As many varieties are self-sterile, care must be taken to plant inter-fertile varieties if any self-sterile variety is included in a planting. Naik states that of the promising varieties at Coonoor only the Irish Peach does not need cross-pollination. Varma (1949 b) gives much information on self-sterile varieties and pollinizers for apples, pears, and plums.

Apples may be stored in good condition longer than most fruits, and in temperate climates are regularly kept through the winter and, with cold storage, well into the following summer. Much research work has been done on preventing the various types of decay and breakdown which occur. In India the bulk of the crop is marketed in a comparatively short season, but R. S. Singh (1943) has reported on storage experiments in Kumaun. There the main crop ripens about a month before that of Kashmir, which floods the market from October through December. Most of the crop is sold during this season, with comparatively little profit, and it would seem desirable to store much of the crop until after December. Of 20 varieties tried, seven kept through January with no special precautions, but only one of these, the Rome Beauty, meets the market requirements. One of the best dessert apples is the Delicious, and it was found possible to keep this in good condition through January by picking it at maturity, wrapping it in paper impregnated with linseed oil or packing it in peat. Wrapping was cheaper, costing about one rupee for a bushel of apples. Small fruits kept better than large ones. Best results were secured by packing the fruit in crates and placing them on racks in a masonry godown with top and bottom ventilators open at night and closed during the day with the floor sprinkled to keep the humidity moae than 90%. In the cold storage experiments at Poona, it was found that the Ambri from Kashmir and the Delicious from Chaubattia kept satisfactorily for eight months at 32 or 35° F.

Pests and Diseases of the Apple

Presumably not less than 500 species of insects attack the apple, of which about 40 have been recorded in India, according to Isaac and Renjhen (1946). Some of the most important of these are comparatively recent introductions, and there is still danger of their spread to areas now free. The codling (codlin) moth, *Laspereysia* (*Cydia, Carpocapsa*) *pomonella* causes great damage to apples, pears, and other fruits in many countries. The egg is laid on the very young fruit and the larva enters and develops inside the fruit, which is then called 'wormy'. The codling moth has not been reported in India but has long been a serious pest in Afghanistan, and was doubtless introduced from there to Baluchistan, where it was first reported in 1935. It was found in the North-West Frontier Province in 1937, and there is danger that it may spread to India. Care should be taken to prevent this, or to eliminate the pest immediately if it is introduced.

The San Jose scale, *Quadraspidiotus* (*Aspidiotus, Aonidiella*) *perniciosus*, was introduced into Kashmir in about 1910, where it threatened to wipe out the fruit industry. It is a very serious pest in the Kulu valley, and Karla (1946) estimates the loss in Kotgarh, including the cost of spraying, at about Rs. 4,000 a year. It has been reported from the hills all over India (Rao 1948 a, b) and is said to be serious in South India. The name is pronounced 'San Hosay'. A thorough report on this important pest is given by Pruthi and Rao (1951), who state that it has been found in practically all parts of India where temperate fruits are grown. They list many of the nearly 200 species of host plants, and describe the life history of the scale. They also give detailed reports of many methods which have been and are being used to control it. Since 1932 the spraying of all orchards in Kashmir has been compulsory, and about 750,000 trees were being sprayed annually, according to Fotidar (1941). The spray used contains diesel oil, fish oil, and rosin and kills practically all scale insects on the trees. This and lime-sulphur, which has been used effectively in other countries, are recommended in the Punjab (Anon.). In Kumaun dinitro cresol with Euphyton (a mineral oil) have proved superior to diesel oil emulsion and lime sulphur. It is important that efforts be made to prevent the spread of the scale particularly on nursery stock. Another scale insect, *Icerya purchasi*, is said by Naik (1949) to attack the apple and other trees in South India, while Rao (1948) mentions four others.

The wooly aphis, *Eriosoma lanigerum*, is another introduced pest. The first mention of it in India was in 1889 at Coonoor, according to Lal and Singh (1947). It was observed in Kumaun and in the Simla hills about 1909 but may have been present for a long time. It apparently occurs wherever apples are grown in India. In Kashmir and Assam sexual forms occur as they do in other countries, where the elm is frequently an alternative host, but in Kumaun and the Punjab it occurs only on the apple and is viviparous, parthenogenic, and multi-brooded. It is active from March to the middle of December especially in May and June and at the end of the season. Winged aphids appear in July and August and accelerate the spread of the pest, but migration also takes place practically throughout the season. The health of the trees is affected, and the fruit borne by infested trees is of poor quality.

It is particularly serious and difficult to control because it attacks the roots as well as the aerial parts of the plant. Rahman and Khan (1941 a, b) recommend spraying with rosin soap to control the aerial forms, and the use of paradichlorobenzene in trenches four inches deep, covered with earth, to kill those on the roots. Isaac and Renjhen (1946) for the aerial forms prefer spraying in summer with nicotine sulphate and soft soap, and in winter with 4 lb. of mohwa oil, 1 lb. 5 oz. of caustic soda, 6 lb. rosin, 4 lb water, and 1¼ lb. of tobacco boiled in 6 lb. of water. They also emphasize the importance of making sure that nursery. stock is free from the pest before planting. They favour the fumigation of the roots with paradichlorobenzene, but R. N. Singh (1942) found that any fumigation which killed the aphids also damaged the roots. More modern insecticides, parathion, malathon, metacide, toxaphene, and xanthone, have been found effective in the United States, where the use of DDT against codling moths has resulted in a large. increase in the numbers of aphids present in the orchards.

To protect nursery stock, chlordane in the furrow before planting or BHC on the surface of the soil near one-year-old plants has proved effective. BHC as a dormant or summer spray has also been effective, but the summer spray taints the fruit unless the form with 99% of the gamma isomer is used. DDT kills the parasite, *Aphelinus mali*, but not the aphids.

Biological control of this pest is of considerable importance, but there is much difference of opinion, perhaps based on the different functioning of the insects in different areas. *Aphelinus mali* was introduced into the Kulu valley in 1937 and is well established there and in the Simla hills. It seems to provide fairly effective control in those places. In Kumaun, however, R. N. Singh (1942) states that it cannot establish itself in nature because the lady-bird beetle, *Coccinella septempunctata*, keeps the aphids under control for the greater part of the summer. He suggests that it may be possible to use the parasite to some extent by breeding it in a cage in each orchard. Rao (1945b) states that in the Nilgiris also this parasite does not seem promising. *Coccinella septumpunctata* is one of several lady-bird beetles which attack the woolly aphis, but it is the only one of much importance. It has been largely effective at Chaubattia, at least through June, according to Lal and Singh (1945). There it also feeds on aphids on two wild grasses, *Andriopogon partusus* and *A. assimilis*, but in Ramgarh, where these grasses are less common, it is not so successful. In order to encourage the beetles, it has been suggested that these grasses be planted.

Resistant rootstocks have long been used in South India, and consitute a promising method of dealing with the aphids on the roots. Rao (1945 b) reports that several of the rootstocks used in South India are immune and others more or less resistant. Several varieties are also immune, but none of these is of any commercial importance thus far in the main apple growing regions of the country. As has been seen, resistance to the woolly aphis is an important consideration in choosing rootstocks in the North also.

A pest of great importance in Kumaun, and a potential danger in other fruitgrowing districts, is the apple root borer, *Lophosternus* (*Dorysthenes*) *hugelii*. R. N. Singh (1941) states that in Almora and Naini Tal districts about 40% of the trees in portions of every orchard are attacked. Very few of the attacked trees bear normal crops, and many, especially of the young trees, die. The borer is said to be very serious in Abbottabad also, and has been recorded from all parts of the hills of northern India, up to an elevation of about 7,000 feet, but not as a pest. It is found on the dead roots of oaks and occasionally on other wild plants and fruit trees. The adult beetles emerge, mate and lay eggs at the beginning of the monsoon, and the eggs hatch in less than a month. Those of the grubs which happen to find roots nearly an inch in diameter or larger feed on them and sever the root. After finishing one root, they wander about and may find another. After three and a half years they pupate. Although the eggs are laid in the ground, they are not destroyed by cultivation. Sharma and Singh (1940) state the powdered paradichlorobenzene applied three inches below the surface at the rate of 1 oz. per linear foot kills young grubs within six inches.

Other insect pests are of comparatively minor importance, but may at times cause serious damage. Thus Rahman and Kalra (1944) report on a hairy caterpillar, *Lymantria obfuscata,* which sometimes infests a fourth of the trees in the Simla hills, completely defoliating many of them. Another hairy caterpillar, *Euproctis signata,* is reported by Janjua (1947) as causing serious damage to the apple and other fruits in Baluchistan, Kashmir, and Murree. The May-beetle or June-bug, *Mimastra cyanura,* is said by Varma (1949 b) to have defoliated 26 trees in one day in the Patiala hills. The most common defoliating beetle at Chaubattia is said to be *Lachnosterna longipennis.* For this and other beetles 0·5% D D T seems slightly superior to a weaker solution or lead arsenate. A stem borer, *Aprioni cinerea,* is said by Rahman (1944) to be a very destructive pest. Isaac and Renjhen (1946) refer to the bud moth, *Spilonota ocellana,* and the fruit tree roller, *Cacoecea sarcostega.* Sharma and Singh (1940) deal with the tent caterpillar, *Cilisocampa indica,* a stem and shoot borer, *Zeuzera sp.*, and several other minor pests. Chowdhury and Majid (1954) mention considerable damage in the Khasi and Jaintia hills of Assam caused by the shoot borer, *Alcides mali,* the stem borer, *Linda nigroscutata,* and the fruit borers, *Dyscerus fletcheri* and *D. malignus.* All of these may be controlled by collecting the beetles and the destruction of the affected twigs or fruits. The bug, *Helopeltis antonii,* is reported by Puttarudriah and Appanna (1955) to be becoming common on apples as well as guavas and grapes around Bangalore, where it damages the young fruits.

Of a number of serious diseases of the apple, the stem-black disease seems to be the worst in India. It is by far the most destructive in Kumaun, where it is said by Dey and Singh (1939) to be found in every orchard. More than 60% of the trees are affected. It is caused by the fungus *Coniothecium chomatosporum.* The disease was reported by Kheswalla (1936) as being prevalent throughout Baluchistan, and causing great damage. He called it the blister disease. It occurs in the other sections of northern India and in other countries. The fungus enters through pruning wounds and, according to Kheswalla, through the lenticels. It extends down the branch, turning the tissue jet black, causing cankers, and eventually killing the branch. Control depends on the removal of the diseased branches, and Kheswalla also recommends spraying twice in the spring with lime-sulphur. Dey and Singh found that painting pruning wounds with a paste containing two ounces each of red lead and copper carbonate and 100 c.c. of raw linseed oil was 92% effective in preventing infection.

The disease second in severity in Kumaun is stem-grown, caused by *Botryosphaeria ribis.* This also ordinarily enters through pruning wounds, and can be effectively controlled by protecting wounds with the same sort of paste, although U. B. Singh (1942) reports lanolin to be better than linseed oil for the purpose. The disease appears in April and is most virulent by the middle of May. A type of die-back is caused, with a loosening and browning of the bark.

Pink disease, caused by *Pellicularia* (*Corticium*) *salmonicolor,* and collar-rot caused by species of *Rosellinia* are also serious in Kumaun. Pink disease attacks many kinds of trees, especially in warm moist climates, and has been mentioned on oranges in Madhya Pradesh. According to U. B. Singh (1943), it causes considerable damage to the apple and pear in some Kumaun orchards, and was once recorded on the apricot. It is worst where drainage is poor and the trees are crowded. Control measures are very similar to those recommended for stem-black and stem-brown, and should include the removal of any wild trees in the neighbourhood which may be infected. A leaf-spot disease caused by *Phyllosticta pirini* is reported by U. R. Singh (1944 b) which lasts from June until the leaves fall, being most virulent in August. It interferes with growth and may cause premature leaf-fall, but may be controlled by one spray of 2-10-40 Bordeaux at the open cluster or petal-fall stage. In winter all the leaves should be collected and burned.

A brown rot caused by *Sclerotinia fructigena* causes heavy losses of both apples and pears in the Punjab, according to Hafiz (1946). It over-winters on mummies which should be burned or buried, and as dormant mycelium in cankers, which should be removed in the summer. If necessary, the trees may be sprayed with 4-4-50 Bordeaux at the pink bud and calyx stages, and again two weeks later. In South India, Naik (1949) refers to mildew, caused by a species of *Oidium*, pink disease, and a collar rot caused by an unidentified fungus formerly thought to be *Sclerotium rolfsii*. Powdery mildew, caused by *Sphaerotheca leucotricha*, has been reported causing damage to the leaves and twigs, especially of young trees, at Chaubattia. It can be controlled by dusting with sulphur in the spring.

A number of diseases of the apple fruit occur. The fungus *Leptothyrium pomi* causes two types of symptom resulting in the common names sootyblotch and fly-speck. In Kumaun it appears on light-coloured late varieties, by the time of harvest, and develops during storage. The sooty material can be easily removed, but small black specks remain. Only the appearance of the fruit is damaged. U. B. Singh (1941 a) reports effective control by spraying with lime-sulphur or colloidal sulphur, but as the cost was about 12 annas a plant he considered this prohibitive. Thinning the fruits was found to reduce the incidence of the disease without greatly decreasing the weight of the crop. Washing the fruit in a 5% solution of bleaching powder or a 3% solution of sodium chlorate removed the blotch and prevented much increase of specks during storage.

The most common rot of apples all over the world is the soft rot or blue mould, caused by *Penicillium expansum*. The decayed section of the fruit is soft with a light brown watery appearance, and gives off a characteristic odour. The disease has been reported in Kumaun by U. B. Singh (1941 b). As the mould is very common, spores are almost certain to get on the fruit. They can enter only through injuries, so it becomes very important to handle the fruit carefully, and to discard before packing fruit with any injury to the skin. Bose and Mehta (1951) report that an attack of *Phytophthora cactorum* caused many apples to rot on the trees at Chaubattia one year. Chowdhury and Majid (1954) state that in Assam bitter rot, caused by *Glomerella cingulata*, may be controlled by regular, frequent spraying with 4-4-50 Bordeaux. They also mention two physiological troubles of apples in storage, Jonathan spot and bitter pit.

Lichens on apple trees are reported to cause some damage in Kumaun by smothering dormant buds. It is reported that they may be controlled for five years by spraying in mid-winter with 3 lb. of caustic soda in 20 gal. of water. Weed-killers have also been used to control lichens, but with less success.

Other Fruits

It is estimated that in 1941-42 there were more than 6,000 acres of pears (Anon., 1950), of which perhaps 3,400 acres are now in India. This includes more than 1,000 acres each in Kashmir and the Punjab, 710 acres in Madras and perhaps 100 acres in Bihar. The pear is very similar to the apple in its cultural requirements. The tree is more erect and does not require as much space as the more vigorous apples. The fruit is borne on spurs, and pruning is very similar to that given the apple. Some of the choicest varieties, particularly those grown in France, are considered among the most delicious fruits of the world. The Bartlett or Williams is a variety of excellent commercial quality, and bears well under a variety of conditions. It is fairly commonly grown in India. These European varieties are harvested while still firm, but become mellow and very juicy when ripe. The Indian types vary a good deal in quality, and none compares well with the best of Europe, but they have the advantage of growing in the submontane areas. L. Singh and Hamid (1941) recommend the Kashmiri nakh for these warmer regions. This has been identified in Kashmir as the Winter Nelis, a European variety. This identification is very questionable, but the variety is certainly superior to the *nashpati* which never becomes mellow but will grow in areas too warm for the better varieties, and which is extensively grown in these regions.

Pears are the most widely grown temperate fruit in South India and do best at elevations of from 5,500 to 7,000 feet, according to Naik (1949). He says that in 1942-43 the estimated acreage was 557 of 'country' pears and 153 of 'English'. The former is an introduced type which has become semi-wild, produces heavy crops of gritty fruit, and is largely used as rootstock. It is probably *P. pyrifolia*. The only promising commercial variety is the Kieffer which is a variety which originated in America, probably as a hybrid between the European and Oriental types. The yield is given as 2·8 tons per acre, much lower than that of the 'country' pear, but the quality is much better, although not so good as that of three varieties sometimes found in gardens. In Kumaun a wild species, *P. pashia*, is commonly used as a rootstock, while in Shillong, according to Woodford (1948), *P. khasiana* has long been used, and it and *P. baccata* are both successful.

Some of the insect pests and diseases which attack the apple are also found on the pear. There was severe outbreak of a fruit fly, *Chaetodacus ferrugineus*, in the Punjab hills in 1945, according to Varma (1946, 1949 b). In some orchards all of the pears and peaches were damaged, with less injury to grapes and apricots, and very little to apples. Sharma and Singh (1940) mention some damage from the pear leaf tortrix, *Acrolita raevana*, which can be controlled, if necessary, by spraying with lead arsenate. In the Kumaun the most serious diseases are stem blister, caused by *Haplosporella mali;* stem canker, caused by *Molochaetia mali;* and fire blight, caused by a *Erwinia amylovora*. The last is a very destructive disease in the United States and is responsible for the growing of hybrids with the sand pear which are more resistant than the common pear. As has been seen in Chapter X, very encouraging results in controlling fire blight have been secured by the use of antibiotic drugs. Prasad (1938) has reported a severe rotting of pears in the Delhi market caused by a wound parasite closely resembling *Aspergillus japonicus*.

The pear does not stand shipping and storage at relatively high temperatures as well as does the apple, and as it ripens at a time when the weather on the plains is hot, marketing is a problem. L. Singh and Hamid (1941) suggest that Bartlett pears be harvested when they show a resistance of 16 to 18 lb. on a special pressure gauge, at which stage the skin is light green with a yellow tinge and the lenticels have turned brown. A little later L. Singh and Lal (1944) found it best to pick this variety at 13 or 14 lb. pressure. Fruit so picked may be stored 20 to 35 days at 40° F., or 4 or 5 months at 32°, but some breakdown occurs.

The quince is a fruit grown only to a slight extent in any part of the world and not grown commercially in India, except in Kashmir, where there are about, 90 acres. It is grown primarily because of the supposed medicinal value of the seeds. The fruit is not palatable raw, but makes excellent jelly and preserves. Few people in India know how to use it, so there is almost no market for the fruit. The trees are small, and may be planted 15 ft. apart.

Many varieties of plums are grown in the world, some 1,500 varieties of *P. domestica* being listed as grown in the State of New York alone. Some of these, and of the other species, are very fine fruits. The plum is not of great importance in northern India, however, although there may be about 500 acres of them there. The varieties grown, mainly in the submontane tracts, are mostly small and of rather poor quality. There seems to be about 150 or 200 acres in South India, mainly at elevations between 4,500 and 5,500 feet in the Nilgiris. Naik (1949) mentions 10 good varieties, all of the species *Prunus salicina*, with the possible exception of the Alu Bokhara. Attempts to grow plums in the warmer districts have failed. Twelve varieties were planted at the Government Gardens, Agra, without success. They may be grown from cuttings or be budded or grafted. Dikshit (1953 a, b) says that while inferior varieties root easily, the Early Round, Howe, and Kelsey are difficult. Dipping the cuttings in 30 ppm of indolebutyric acid gave satisfactory results except with the Kelsey, with which 40 ppm or 10 ppm of NAA was slightly better but still gave only 25% success. In South India shield budding on peach or plum root-stocks is common. In some countries the myrobalan plum, *P. cerasifera*, has been found to be the most suitable rootstock.

It is said that the plums do better in the submontane tracts if planted close together, for protection against the wind, and Burns (1939) recommends planting them 16 to 18 ft. apart. Naik (1949) recommends spacing of from 12 to 20 ft. according to the vigour of the variety. Plentiful irrigation is necessary in the submontane areas. Fruit is borne on small spurs and on branches of the previous season's growth. Little pruning is necessary except as some may be needed to keep the trees growing vigorously. In the Nilgiris considerable pruning is done, and the open-centre tree is preferred.

Many varieties are self-sterile, and as inter-sterility is also common, much care is necessary in choosing varieties, and the keeping of bees in the orchard is frequently a very valuable practice. Kuppuswami (1954 b) deals with the pollination problem in the Nilgiris, where the early varieties are self-fertile and the late varieties are largely self-sterile. The Hale, a mid-season variety, is fairly self-fertile and a good polliniser for the late varieties, into which it may be budded. Certain combinations of the late varieties are also satisfactory. Plums, like other deciduous trees normally flower in the spring and the fruit ripens in summer, but Saptarishi and Azariah (1952) report that of four varieties planted in 1941, Rubio and Hale developed stray fruits in the winter of 1950-51 and bore about 300 fruits per tree in the next winter. In the case of one prolific variety, the Rubio, in the Nilgiris, thinning to leave an inch or two between fruits increased the size from 50 to 76%.

The shoot borer, *Sphenoptera lafertei*, is a serious pest of the plum and other species of *Prunus* in northern India, according to Batra and Renjhen (1946, 1950). It kills branches and sometimes trees, especially young ones. Good drainage and manuring are recommended to counter the damage, and the use of oil as an ovicide or of a stomach poison to kill the adult beetles before oviposition may help, but the only effective control is said to be the removal and burning of the infested trees. A fruit-fly, *Dacus incisus*, and the San Jose scale are mentioned by Naik as pests of the plum. Lal (1950) states that in Uttar Pradesh also plums are sometimes attacked severely by an unidentified fruit-fly.

The ripe fruit is very perishable, and must be marketed promptly. Plums are used in making excellent jam and other products. Siddappa and others (1950) found several varieties suitable for canning.

The apricots also do not enjoy a position of much importance in this country except in Kashmir, which grows more than 1,000 acres. Trees of an inferior sort are found growing semi-wild near many Himalayan villages, but seem to be valued mainly for the seeds, the kernels of which are eaten like almonds and are crushed for oil. The seeds of some types contain hydrocyanic acid and are inedible, but these also yield oil and a cake which is burned, but according to Das (1945) could better be used as manure as it contains 6·7% nitrogen, 1·49% phosphate (P_2O_5), and 1·09% potash (K_2O). He states that the kernel is about 20% of the pit, and yields 40 to 45% oil, which is used as fuel and in cooking, in toilet creams, and in 'certain pharmaceutical preparations'. Small quantities of imported varieties are grown in Kashmir and other hill stations, for the local trade. The apricot has not succeeded in South India. Self-sterility is not nearly as common as with most species of *Prunus*, according to Schultz (1948). The fresh fruit does not keep well, and in countries where the apricot is grown on a large scale, much of the crop is dried or canned or made into jam. The tree is more spreading than the plum, and at least 20 ft. should be allowed between plants. Pruning similar to that given the plum is considered satisfactory.

Of the temperate fruits, the peach will probably succeed in the warmest climate, and it is grown to a limited extent on the plains as well as in the sub-montane areas and in the hills. It is said (Anon., 1950) that there are about 1,500 acres of peaches near Amritsar in the Punjab. In Uttar Pradesh the peach is probably second to the apple in acreage, but a very poor second. Under such climatic conditions as those of Allahabad, the trees grow fairly well, and some varieties bear well, but the fruit is of poor quality. The flat or peen-to peach may prove more successful under such conditions. By crossing the varieties which bear well where the winters are as warm as in Allahabad with superior varieties from cooler areas, it may be possible to breed better varieties for the plains. Naik (1949) states that the peach is grown from the plains of South India to high elevations, but that it is not grown commercially on the plains, and thrives best between 4,500 and 6,000 ft. above sea-level. Even in the hills it is rarely grown in orchards.

Peaches are generally propagated by budding on seedling peach rootstock. The fresh seeds do not germinate easily, but are generally sown in October and germinate the following spring. They are sometimes kept in moist sand until January or February, and then planted out. They are ready for budding in April and May, or in September. About a year can be saved by carefully cracking the seed before sowing it, according to L. B. Singh and Singh (1956). They recommend budding in April or May on the plains of U. P. and in September or October in the hills. Gupta (1942) recommends ring budding but shield budding is also satisfactory. Shetty (1950) reports that two varieties at Coonoor did better on peach seedlings 20 months old than on those either 8 or 32 months old. The trees are ready to be set out in the winter when the bud is a year or a year and a half old. The distance commonly used between trees is about 18 ft. The trees are generally trained to a rather low head, and so pruned as to allow plenty of light to enter the tree. As the fruit is borne on the growth of the previous year, bearing trees have to be pruned in a different way from that used with the apple. If the trees are left unpruned or the branches are only lightly tipped, the bearing growth will soon be at the end of long branches, with the result that the fruit is small and hard to harvest, and the trees are likely to break. Either all shoots of the last year should be cut back severely each year, or some branches should be removed entirely.

Peaches are not long-lived and while under some conditions they will bear for 20 years or more, under others they die in 10 or 12 years, and Gupta (1942) indicates that in Uttar Pradesh the commercial life is not more than 15 years. Naik (1949) says they are seldom remunerative for more than 20 years. Bearing begins, however, at the age of two or three years. As in the case of the plum, some varieties may produce a winter crop in addition to the normal summer crop in the hills of South India (Saptarishi and Alwa, 1953). A yield of 1½—2 md. per tree is considered satisfactory. Sun-scald does considerable damage to the peach and other drupes in parts of Kumaun, according to U. B. Singh (1944 a) and may reduce the life of the trees. Low-headed trees are less damaged than those with high heads, and all damage may be avoided by tying straw all around the main trunk of each tree.

Peaches have been classified into five races : the peen to, honey or South China, Spanish, North China, and Persian. Of these the first two are more suited to warm climates. Peaches are either clingstone or freestone, depending on whether the flesh separates easily from the seed. Clingstone varieties are suitable for canning, but for use fresh freestones are preferred. However, the only commercially satisfactory varieties in South India are clingstones. For the plains of U. P., L. B. Singh and Singh (1956) recommend the Sharbati, a clingstone, but describe 23 other varieties they consider suitable. They recommend Alexander for the hills and describe three other good varieties. Shah and Azeez (1949) found that total sugar and sucrose increase during a ripening period of 9 days whether on the tree or in packed boxes, while invert sugar also increases in the packed fruit but decreases on the tree. They conclude that it is satisfactory to pick fruit for consumption within six days when it has 4% total sugar, although this seems like a very low figure. At Poona it was found that one variety could be kept for four weeks at 32 to 35° F.

A number of insects attack the peach. One of the most serious is the aphid which causes leaf-curl, *Anuraphis helichrysi*, which damages the plum also in Uttar Pradesh, according to Lal and Siddiqi (1952). The leaves curl and become yellowish green, while those attacked by the leaf-curl fungus are generally red or pink. The only alternate host observed above 5,000 ft. elevation in Kumaun is the golden rod, *Erigeron canadensis*, but at Chaubattia its eradication was only partly successful in controlling the aphid, although the aphid is found on the peach only from November to May. Lower in the hills the alternate host is *Ageratum conyzoides*. There other aphids are included as pests of the peach by Batra (1953 b). He recommends spraying with a mixture of tobacco decoction, soap, washing soda, and resin. At Jeolikote diesel oil emulsion, lime sulphur, and DDT were found about equally effective as ovicides, and DDT was found effective against the nymphs of the lead-curl aphid.

A borer attacks the trunk of the tree, according to Gupta (1942), and may be controlled by sprinkling paradichlorobenzene around the base of the tree and piling up the soil around it in October. Another borer kills buds and twigs, and for this he recommends spraying just after the petals fall with arsenate of lead and lime-sulphur. At least eight different scale insects, including the San Jose, have been reported on the peach in India. Sharma and Singh (1940) mention a species of *Lecanium* and one of *Diaspis*, which should be guarded against on nursery stock. *Eulecanium coryli* and *Pseudolecaspis pentagona* are also reported in Kumaun. Infested trees may be sprayed during winter with lime-sulphur or fish-oil rosin soap. The attack of fruit flies in the Punjab hills has been mentioned, and Naik (1949) mentions fruit-flies in the South also.

Probably the most common disease of the peach is the leaf-curl, which occurs all the way from Baluchistan to South India. It is caused by the fungus *Taphrina* (*Exoascus*). *deformans*. Hafiz (1947) recommends the removal of the leaves before the spores are formed and spraying just before the buds swell in the spring with lime-sulphur or 5-5-50 Bordeaux, preferably with the addition of 4 lb. of rosin, 2 lb. of washing soda, and 2 gal. of water. Chowdhury and Majid (1954) state that the disease may be reduced considerably by carefully timed and applied 4-4-50 Bordeaux sprays in the autumn and again just before the buds open. Varma (1949 b) had better success by controlling the aphids, mites, and scales which carry the disease, with contact insecticides. L. B. Singh and Singh (1956) refer to powder mildew, caused by *Sphaeortheca pannsao;* scab, caused by *Cladosporium carpophilum;* blossom wilt and twig blight, caused by *Sclerotinia laxa;* rust, caused by *Puccinia pruno-spinosae;* shot hole disease caused by *Clasterosporium carrpophilum;* and a bacterial gummosis. Naik (1949) also mentions rust, caused by a species of *Puccinia*, in South India.

The nectarine is a smooth-skinned peach, somewhat smaller than most peaches, and with a richer flavour. Nectarines may come from peach seeds, and peaches from nectarine seeds, or either may originate as a bud mutation from the other. Nectarines are of little commercial importance.

The almond is in some ways very similar to the peach, but the pericarp which is the edible flesh of the peach is, in the almond, hard and generally considered inedible. The kernel of the seed is the part commonly eaten. Almonds are among the principal crops of Kashmir. The tree will grow under a fairly wide range of soil and climatic conditions, but tends to bear very light crops unless conditions are just right. Most varieties are self-sterile, so it is necessary to plant more than one variety in a place. The so-called paper-shell varieties are most popular. Some selection of varieties has been done in Kashmir, but there are still far too many trees of inferior quality there. Pests reported are black and green peach aphids, controlled by rosin-fish oil spay; almond scale, controlled by lime-sulphur with nicotine; and three borers which can be controlled only by removing the infested branches.

Cherries are grown on nearly 500 acres in Kashmir, and to a cretain extent in other temperate regions, there being about 45 acres in Uttar Pradesh. The sweet cherry is the one grown, and it is eaten almost entirely as a fresh fruit. The sour cherry is used only in cooking. Cherries should be given about the same distance between trees as apples. The tree may well be headed low in order to decrease the danger of sunburn on the trunk. The fruit is borne on small spurs on the year-old wood, and also on the shoots. Very little pruning is ordinarily practised except what is necessary to keep the head fairly open, and to prevent the tree from becoming so tall that harvesting is very difficult. In old trees some 'renewal' pruning may be desirable, to force out bearing wood close to the main branches. Most cherries are self-sterile, and many of the best varieties are also inter-sterile. It thus becomes necessary to plant a few trees of poor varieties in order to provide pollination. Lewis and Crow (1954) have pointed out the possibility of inducing self-fertility by damaging the incompatibility genes by X-radiation. They state that 10% of the progeny of self-sterile cherries, after treatment and incompatible pollination are fully self-fertile, and from these individuals can be selected for quality. The same technique has been successfully applied to apples and pears.

The brambles are very little cultivated in India, but Burns (1939) suggests using them as hedges, and their cultivation may be increased. Some of them bear fruit of excellent quality, and while it does not keep well, it can be made into very good jam. Wild fruits are plucked and used fresh or made into jam. Blackberries have been introduced at Coonoor and Bangalore and according to Naik (1949) bear as many as 352 berries per vine, running about 90 to the pound. The prospect of increasing the cultivation of Blackberries and raspberries in the hills of South India is stressed by Rao and Rangacharlu (1951), who state that both kinds do well at elevations of 5,000 to 7,000 ft. They say that at Coonoor the yield of raspberries is about 3,000 lb. per acre, while blackberries produce 6—10,000 lb. Some of the hybrids now grown extensively in the United States might prove desirable there and elsewhere in India. Propagation is by means of suckers, root cuttings, and rooted tips of canes. The plants are set out a few feet apart in rows. After bearing, old canes are cut out, and in some cases it is desirable to thin out the suckers.

The possibility of increasing the size of blackberries, and possibly other berries, by hormone treatment is reported by Zielinski and others (1954). By spraying one variety with 50 ppm of para-chlorophenoxyacetic acid about 14 days after pollination and repeating this twice at 10-day intervals, at half the concentration, they increased the size 21·6%, while adding 50 ppm of beta-naph-thoxyacetic acid gave an increase of 24%. The number and size of the drupelets and the size of the receptacle were all increased.

The strawberry is a much more important fruit than the brambles, and about 200 acres are grown commercially in and near the hills of northern India, and about 60 acres at such hill stations as Mahabaleshwar in Bombay and Coonoor in the South. Naik (1949) says that strawberries are grown above 4,000 ft. and particularly between 5,000 and 7,000 ft. elevation. An edible wild species, *Fragaria nilgherrensis,* of no market value, grows above 6,000 ft. high in the Nilgiris. The extent of the industry is limited by climatic conditions and by the local market, as the fruit is very perishable, and can be shipped only under refrigeration. It is possible to produce ripe berries in the warmer districts of the northern plains, but only with great care and at expense which prevents commercial success. Strawberries are grown for market in the Meerut, Muzaffarnagar, and Saharanpur districts of Uttar Pradesh, and the Jullundur and Gurdaspur districts of the Punjab, as well as in the hills. Yields, however, are smaller than in some other countries, and the price comparatively high. The uncertainties both in raising and in marketing the crop discourage growing it on a large scale.

Land for strawberries should be thoroughly cultivated and manured. Any good garden soil is satisfactory. Propagation is commonly by means of runners, which are shoots which come out from the parent plant and root at alternate nodes. They should be taken only from vigorous healthy plants of the desired types, and it is best to restrict the number of runners on a plant to from 4 to 8. Naik (1949), however, reports that a small trial at Coonoor showed that 'splits' were preferable to runners, as a larger percentage of them grew and they commenced flowering in 75 days while the runners took 135. In the South, planting may be done in March or in July or August. In Uttar Pradesh Swarup (1933) recommends planting in October plants from runners which developed in the rainy season, while in the Punjab (Anon) it is considered better to plant in January and February on the plains and in March and April in the hills. The plants are placed about a foot apart in rows two or three feet apart. The crop is borne in the spring, and in India it is thought that the best crop is produced the first year. Thorough but shallow cultivation is required, and it is well to remove all runners until the end of the bearing season. Naik says that heavy manuring is necessary in order to get a good crop, and recommends 25 cartloads of well-rotted cattle manure per acre. Fairly frequent irrigation is required as the roots go not more than two feet deep. Swarup (1933) says that during the bearing season the plants should be irrigated every third or fourth day, and as he is writing about their growth on the plains, this may be of value mainly in decreasing the temperature. The importance of maintaining the supply of moisture to the plants by frequent irrigation is also emphasized by Randhawa and Singh (1951). Swarup considers about five years the useful life of the plant, while in the Punjab it is suggested that plants two or three years old be ploughed under, and in the South the plants are generally removed after the second crop. In the hotter areas it may be necessary to grow new plants every year.

Only one insect pest of the strawberry seems to be of importance in India, the flea beetle, *Haltica caerulescens*, which damages the plants in Kumaun. The damage may be decreased by spraying with 0·25% DDT emulsion or other insecticides. Leaf-spot diseases in Kumaun are caused by *Dendrophoma obscurons*, *Diplocarpon earliana*, *Pestalotiopsis fragariae*, and a species of *Gloeosporium*. Several fungicides have reduced the damage, but none has been found satisfactory.

The berries should not be picked until fully ripe and red, and as they have no protecting skin, great care is necessary to protect them from birds and squirrels. In order to avoid damaging them by handling more than once, they are generally picked directly into small baskets, holding not more than a pound each, in which they are marketed. To keep the berries clean, straw is sometimes worked in among the plants in early spring. Zielinski and Garren (1952) found it possible to increase the size of the berries by nearly a third by spraying them when half grown with 50 ppm of beta-naphthozyacetic acid. In addition to being used fresh, the berries are preserved in several ways. Strawberry jam is considered one of the best, but because of the relatively high price of the fruit, is more expensive than most jam.

Walnuts occupy more land in Kashmir than any other fruit except the apple, and are found to a smaller extent in other areas of the Himalayas. They have not done well in the hills of South India. The common walnut, *Juglans regia*, is considered indigenous to the region from Persia to Kashmir, and the walnuts growing in the region of Kashmir have been placed in four species. Those cultivated in Kashmir fall into eight groups which seem to come true from seed. Most of the walnuts grown in this country are seedlings, and many of them are growing semi-wild, or scattered in fields. Some very large and majestic trees are growing along the Ganga river not far below its source. These and some others have thick-shelled nuts of very little value, but there are many trees, especially in Kashmir, which bear nuts of good quality. In other countries walnuts are grafted or budded, and are planted in orchards. Attempts at budding and grafting in Kashmir have not yet succeeded, although all other fruit trees are propagated in those ways. They should be planted at least 50 ft. apart. As the nuts are comparatively light, will keep for months at ordinary temperatures, and are not subject to bruising, they have distinct advantages for those sections of the hills where transportation to market is a problem.

The walnut weevil, *Alcides porrecterostris*, does considerable damage in parts of the Himalayas, including the Kulu valley, according to Husain and Khan (1949). While the adults attack various parts of the tree, the principal damage is done by the grubs which destroy the nuts. These authors suggest spraying the trees with 6-18-50 Bordeaux mixture as a repellent and the destruction of all nuts which fall prematurely and of infested ones at the time of harvest.

Another member of the family Juglandaceae is the pecan, *Carya illinoensis* (*Pecan*). This is a native of the United States, and requires more heat than the walnut. It therefore seems promising for the submontane, and perhaps for the plains, regions of this country. It is reported to do well at Palampur in the Kangra valley, and a few trees are found in other places in the lower Himalayas Chestnuts are grown to a very limited extent in the hills, and more could be grown if the market justified this. There are two common types, the European, *Castanea sativa*, and the Japanese, *C. crenata*, of the family Fagaceae. The trees are large and ornamental.

BIBLIOGRAPHY

Aala, F. T. 1953. Effect of hand pollination on the production of Siamese pummelo. *Phil. J. Agr.* **18** : 101-3.

Abbot, C. E. 1935. Blossom bud differentiation in citrus trees. *Amer. J. Bot.* **22** : 476-85.

Abbot, O. D. 1931. General properties of some tropical and sub-tropical fruits of Florida. *Fla Agr. Exp. Sta. Bul.* 237.

Abraham, E. V. 1953. A pest of new importance on pineapple in Wynad area of Madras State—the mealy bug, *Pseudococcus brevipes* Cockerell. *S. Ind. Hort.* **1** : 99-104.

Abul Fazl. Ain-i-Akbari (Ayeen Akbery).

Adsuar, J. 1946. Transmission of papaya bunchy top by a leaf hopper of the genus *Empoasca*. *Science* **103** : 316.

Agharkar, S. P. and Roy, N. 1951. On the origin and distribution of cultivated mangoes, *Ind. J. Genetics* and *Plant Breed.* **11** : 48. (Synopsis only).

Agnew, G. W. J. 1946. Papaw latex production in Queensland. *Qd. Agr. J.* **63** : 74-80. 1951. The papaw. *ibid.* **73** : 197-211.

Agrawal, L. N. 1947. Studies in the bearing habit of sweet-lime (*Citrus limettioides Tanaka*). Unpublished thesis.

Ahmad, M. N. and Ullah, M. H. 1950. Two new varieties of Sangtra orange—Kinnow mandarin and Feutrell's Early. *Punjab Fruit J.* **14** : 1-38.

Ahmed, M. S. 1936 a. Pollination and selection in *Anona squamosa* and *A. cherimolia*. *Ministry Agr. Egypt Hort. Section Bul.* 157.

1936 *b*. The anonas in Egypt. *Ministry Agr. Egypt Hort. Section Booklet* 14.

Ahmed, S. and Khan, M. 1950. Fruit bud differentiation studies in sour lime (*Citrus aurantifolia*) in the Punjab. *Punjab Fruit J.* **14** : 13-9.

1951. The time of fruit bud formation in grapefruit. *ibid.* **15** : 18-23.

Aiyangar, N. S. and Aiyangar, B. S. 1930. Apple cultivation around Bangalore. *Poona Agr. Col. Mag.* **22** : 160-71.

Aiyar, K. S. P. 1943. On three caterpillars destructive to mango flowers. *Ind. J. Ent.* **5** : 53-7.

Akamine, E. K. and Arisumi, T. 1953. Control of post-harvest storage decay of fruits of papaya (*Carica papaya L.*) with special reference to the effect of hot water. *Proc. Amer. Soc. Hort. Sci.* **61** : 270-4.

Aldrich, D. G. and Coony, J. J. 1951. A response of lemon trees to phosphate fertilization. *Calif. Citrogr.* **36** : 93, ff.

Aldrich, D. G. and Taylor, O. C. 1954. Nitrogen fertilizer practices in California citrus orchards. *Calif. Citrogr.* **39** : 144, ff.

Ali, A. M. 1941. Nagari oranges—their past and present. *Madras Agr. J.* **29** : 347-50.

Allen, R. G. 1934. Citrus cultivation. *U. P Dept. Agr. Fruit Ser. Bul.* 6.

1935. Modern mango cultivation. *U. P. Dept. Agr. Fruit Ser. Bul.* 13.

Alvarez-Garcie, L. A. and Lopez-Matos, L. 1954. Influence of root-knot nematodes on the decline in vigour of the Red Spanish Variety of pineapple in Puerto Rico. *J. Agr. Univ. Puerto Rico* **38** : 61-72.

Anantanarayanan, K. P. and Subramanian, T. R. 1955. A note on the unusual occurrence of the mango leaf-weevil (*Rhynchaenus mangiferae*, Mshll:), at Coimbatore. *Madras Agr. J.* **42** : 373-6.

Anantanarayanan, K. P. and Venugopal, S. 1952. A short note on the *Eugenia leaf caterpillar, Carea subtilis* Wlk. *J. Bombay Nat. Hist. Soc.* **50** : 418-21.

1954. Pests of *Eugenia jambolana* in Coimbatore (South India). *S. Ind. Hort.* **1** : 137-40.

1955. Notes on a new pest, *Lepidogma sp.* (Pyralidae) on *Eugenia jambolana* in Coimbatore. *Ind. J. Ent.* **17** : 183-5.

Anderssen, F. G. 1937. Citrus manuring—its effect on cropping and on the composition and keeping quality of the orange. *J. Pom. Hort. Sci.* **15** : 117-59.

Anderssen, F. G. and Bathurst, A. C. 1938. Nitrogen and phosphorus in oranges. *Fmg. S. Afr.* 349-52.

Anonymous. 1919. Plantain stalks as fodder for cattle in famine years. *Bombay Dept. Agr. Leaflet.* 1.

1926. Work of the Ganeshkhind Botanical Gardens and Modi Bag Garden for the years 1921-25. *Bombay Dept. Agr. Bul.* 133.

1927. *a.* Economic method of controlling the pomegranate caterpillar. *Bombay Dept. Agr. Leaflet* 23.

1927 b. Royal Commission on Indian Agriculture, Evidence **9** : 20.

1927 *C.* The budding of wild *bor* trees in Gujarat. *Bombay Dept. Agr. Leaflet* 24.

1928. Home canning of fruits. *Bombay Dept. Agr. Leaflet* 4.

1930. Mango hoppers and mildew and their control. *Bombay Dept. Agr. Leaflet* 6.

1931. Loranthus. *Bombay Dept. Agr. Leaflet* 4.

1932. Investigations on the standardization of citrus trees by propagation methods. *Imp. Bur. Fruit Prod. Tech. Com.* 3.

1933 *a.* Some insecticides, fungicides and appliances. *Bombay Dept. Agr. Leaflet* 3.

1933 *b.* A way for improving the keeping quality of plantains. *Bombay Dept. Agr. Leaflet* 6.

1934 *a.* Annual report on agricultural research in Arizona. *Arizona Agr. Exp. Sta.*

1934 *b.* Budding and topworking of *ber* trees (*Ziziphus jujubee*). *Punjab Dept. Agr. Leaflet* 95.

1934 *c.* Cultivation of falsa (*Grewia asiatica*). *Punjab Dept Agr. Leaflet* 114.

1934 *d*. Preparation of phalsa syrup and juice. *Punjab Dept. Agr. Leaflet* 115.

1935. Report of the committee on the improvement in the marketing of fruit and vegetables in the town of Bombay, 1934. Govt. Central Press, Bombay.

1937 *a*. Annual report of the Fruit Research Station, at Kodur for the year 1936-37, in Report of the Madras agricultural station for 1936-37, pp. 727-67.

1937 *b*. Common salt and its use as manure in Konkan. *Bombay Dept. Agr. Leaflet* 3.

1938. Export of mangoes to England in 1937. *Bombay Dept. Agr. Leaflet* 3.

1939. Candying "bers" (jujubee). *Punjab Dept. Agr. Leaflet* 58.

1940 *a*. Agricultural Produce (Grading and marketing) Act, 1937 with rules made prior to 31st August, 1940. Govt. of India Press.

1940 *b*. Report on the marketing of grapes in India and Burma. *Govt. Ind. Marketing Ser*. 20.

1941 *a*. Grape vine cultivation. *U. P. Dept. Agr. Fruit Ser. Bul.* 23.

1941 *b*. Selection of banana suckers. *Qd. Agr. J.* **54** : 312.

1941 *c*. Useful hints for fruit growers in the Bombay Province. *Bombay Dpt. Agr. Leaflet.* 3.

1942. Crop and season report. Punjab Govt.

1943 *a*. Report on the marketing of citrus fruits in India. *Govt. Ind. Marketing Ser.* 43.

1943 *b*. U. P. agricultural pocket-book for 1943. Dept. Agr., United Provinces.

1944 *a*. Report on the work of the agricultural stations in Madras Presidency for 1942-3. Govt. Press, Madras.

1944 *b*. Cold and gas storage of fruits and vegetables in Bombay. *Bombay Dept. Agr. Leaflet* 2.

1945 *a*. Report on the marketing of bananas in India. *Govt. Ind. Marketing Ser.* 49.

1945 *b*. The cashew industry. *Eastern Economist* **4** : 768-9.

1946. The answer was—a lemon. *The Grower* (Australia), reprinted in *Calif. Citrogr.* **32** : 163.

1947. Cold and gas storage of fruits and vegetables. *Bombay Dept. Agr. Leaflet* 1.

1948. Fruit industry in the India Union. *Ind. Fmg.* **9** : 275-7.

1950. Marketing of some important stone, pome and small fruits and pineapples in India. *Govt. Ind. Marketing Ser.* 62.

1953 *a*. Progress and profits in bananas, demonstrated at Duranbah experimental plot. *Agr. Gaz. N. S. Wales* **64** : 351-3.

1953 *b*. Mangosteen—a remunerative fruit crop for South India. *Madras Agr. J.* **40** : 510.

1954 *a*. Notes on current investigations, agronomy. Pineapples. *Malay. Agr. J.* 37 : 235-6.

1954 *b*. Hatha. *Ind. Food Packer* **8** (9) : 13.

1954 *c*. Jaman seed as cattle food. *Ind. Fmg.* **4** (3) : 10-1.

1954 *d*. Why mandarin orchards deteriorate. *ibid.* **4** (3) : 12-3, 15.

1954 *e*. Preparation and preservation of jackfruit nectar. *Leaflet* 39, fruit and *Vegetable Preparation Ser., Cent. Food Tech. Res. Inst., Mysore.*

1954 *f*. Canning of sapota segments. *Bul. Cent. Food Tech. Res. Inst., Mysore* **3** : 252-3.

1955 *a*. Preparation and preservation of loquat jelly. *ibid.* **4** : 40.

1955 *b*. Cape gooseberry (*Physalis Peruviana Linn*). *Agr. and An. Husb. U. P.* **5** (9) : 26-9.

Control of peach scale insect. *U. P. Dept. Agr. Leaflet.* 125.

Cultivation of strawberries. *Punjab Dept. Agr. Leaflet* 61.

Manuring oranges. *Punjab Dept. Agr. Leaflet* 109.

Protection of fruit trees from frost. *Punjab Dept. Agr. Leaflet* 81.

Report of the Fruit Research Station, Kodur for 1939-40. *Madras Dept. Agr.*

San Jose scale. *Punjab Dept. Agr. Leaflet* 88.

The mango hoppers and their control. *Punjab Dept. Agr. Leaflet* 32.

Ansari, A. R. 1947. Bourbon scale in the Punjab. *Punjab fruit J.* **11** : 175-7.

Ansari, M. A. R. 1945. *Dichoecrocis punctiferalis* Gn. as a pest of guava. *Ind. J. Ent.* **7** : 241.

Appanna, M. and Maheswaruah, B. M. 1954. The grape flea beetle, *Scelodonta strigicollis* Moths. and its control. *Mysore Agr. J.* **30** : 107-11.

Argles, G. K. 1937. A review of the literature on stock-scion incompatibility in fruit trees, with particular reference to pome and stone fruits. *Imp. Bur. Fruit Prod. Tech. Com.* 9.

Asthana, R. B. and Nayak, J. P. 1947. Survey of the incidence of *Indarbela quadrinotata* WLK on oranges in the Central Provinces and Berar. *Nagpur Agr. Col. Mag.* **22** : 14-21.

Asthana, R. P. 1947. Bacterial root-rot of citrus. *Nagpur Agr. Col. Mag.* **21** : 77-99.

Auguste, A. 1954. (Study on the fruiting of Clementines.) *Fruits et Prim.* **24** : 182-91.

Aykroyd, W. R. 1951. The nutritive value of Indian foods and the planning of satisfactory diets. Fourth edition, revised by V. N. Patwardhan and S. Ranganathan. Govt. of India Press, New Delhi.

Ayyar, T. V. R. 1940. Handbook of economic entomology for South India, Govt. Press Madras.

1943. Notes on some fruit sucking moths of the Deccan. *Ind. J. Ent.* **5** : 29-13.

B., P. I. 1949. Cold storage facilities increase. *Ind. Fmg.* **10** : 464.

Badami, V. K. 1941. Bael as a source of hardy stock for oranges. *Proc. 28th Ind. Sci. Cong.*, p. 255.

Baier, W. E. 1955. The citrus health team—bioflavonoids and vitamin C. *Calif. Citrogr.* **40** : 207, 227-8.

Baillon, A. F., Holmes, E., and Lewis, A. H. 1933. The composition and nutrient uptake of the banana plant, with special reference to the Canaries. *Trop. Agriculture* **10** : 139-44.

Bain, F. M. 1941. Mineral deficiencies in citrus. *Proc. Agr. Soc. Trin. Tob.* **41** : 657-9, ff.

1949. Citrus and climate. *Calif. Citrogr.* **34** : 382, ff.

Bajpai, P. N. 1947. Vegetative propagation of tropical and sub-tropical fruits. *Cawnpore Agr. Col. Students' Mag.* **7** : 25-33.

1949. Studies on the bearing habits of the loquat—'*Eriobotrya japonica*' Lindle. *ibid.* **9** : 26-7.

1951. Vegetative growth and blossom biology in the loquat. *Allahabad Farmer* **25** : 199-208.

1952. Sterility in loquat. *Sci. and Cult.* **18** : 88-9.

1953. Effect of "pinching-off" shoots on the yield of the loquat (*Eriobotrya japonica*). *Kanpur Agr. Col. J.* **13** (1) : 58-9.

Bajpai, P. N. and Chand, N. 1955. Waterless gootee in Kagzi lime with ordinary plastic sheet. *Kanpur Agr. Col. J* **14** (1) : 8.

Bajpai, R. N. 1955. A simple method of controlling fruit piercing moths (*Othries fullonica* Linn. and *O. materna* Linn.). *Sci* and *Cult.* **20** : 387.

Bajwa, B. S. 1953. Review of fruit industry in the Punjab—planting and economics of a 25-acre orchard. *Ind. J. Hort.* **10** : 67-73.

Bajwa, B. S. and Chhabra, P. 1946. Quick production of 'Khatti' stock for budding of citrus plants. *Punjab Fruit J.* **10** : 101-3.

Bajwa, B. S. and Jawanda, J. S. 1952. Cultivation of papaya in the Punjab. *Punjab Farmer* **4** : 204-7, 232.

1953. Present status of the mango growing industry of the Punjab and suggestions for its improvement. *ibid.* **5** (2) : 4-9. 12

1954. Intercropping orchards in the Punjab. *Ind. J. Hort.* **11** : 13-5.

Bajwa, B. S. and Kaura, N. R. 1951. Windbreaks for orchards. *Punjab Farmer* **3** : 114-6.

1952. Manuring citrus trees. *Ind. J. Hort*: **9** (1) : 29-32.

Bajwa, B. S., Kaura, N. R., and Chhada, T. R. 1955. Comparative vigour of apple trees of Baldwin variety produced by grafting on apple roots, seedlings and suckers. *Ind. J. Hort.* **12** : 29-31.

Bajwa, B. S. and Musahib-ud-din. 1946. The present status of mango industry in the Punjab. *Punjab Fruit J.* **10** : 1-7.

Bajwa, B. S. and Ram, A. 1943. Sunburn of Malta and Sangtra oranges. *Ind. Fmg.* **4** : 182-3.

1946. Budding of mango seedlings in situ. A brief resume of work done during the years 1943-45. *Punjab Fruit J.* **10**: 10-3.

Bajwa, B. S. and Singh, B. 1945. Citrus rootstock trials in the Punjab. *ibid.* **9** : 103-6.

Bajwa, B. S. and Thapar, A. R. 1949. Present status of fruit industry in East Punjab. *E. Punjab Farmer* **1** : 6-13.

Baker, R. E. D. 1938. Notes on the control of mango anthracnose (Colletotrichum gloeosporioides). *Trop. Agriculture* **15** : 12-4.

Balakrishnamurti, D. and Jogiraju, G. 1932. Graft mango gardens—how to start and maintain them. *Madras Dept. Agr. Bul.* 24.

Banerjee, B. N. and Rao, G. R. 1933. Cold storage of mangoes. *Proc. 20th Ind. Sci. Cong.* p 69.

Banerji, S. and Chatterji, N. C. 1051. *Altica* (*Haltica*) *coerulea*, oliver, as a flower feeding beetle of mango. *Sci. and Cult.* **17** : 179-80.

(Banerji, S. K. and Ramdas, L. A.) 1946. Weather and the Indian farmer. Govt. of India Press, Simla.

Baptista, B. A. 1944. The fruit piercing moth (*Otheris fullonica L.*) with special reference to its economic importance. *Ind. J. Ent.* **6** : 1-13.

Barakzai, M. U. F. 1918. First report on fruit culture as practised round about Tharushah (Sind) in Nawabshah District. *Bombay Dept. Agr. Bul.* 88.

1920. Fruit culture as practised near Shikarpur, Sind. *Bombay Dept. Agr. Bul.* 98.

Barnard, C. 1949. Temperatures for citrs. *Citrus News*, Australia, quoted in *Calif. Citrogr.* 34 : 182-4.

Barnell, H. R. 1940. The banana in relation to human nutrition. *Trop. Agriculture* **17** : 143-6.

Barnes, H. 1937. The papaw. *Qd. Agr. J.* **59** : 207-13.

Barret, O. W. 1928. The tropical crops. Macmillan Co., New York.

Bartholomew, E. T. and Sinclair, W. B. 1947. Bud selection and granulation. *Calif. citrogr.* **32** : 94, ff.

Basha, J. M. G. 1952. Experiments on the control of the fruit borers of the jujube (*Zizyphus spp.*), *Carpomyia vesuviana* Costa and *Meridarchis scyrodes Meyr.* in South India *Ind. J. Ent.* **14** : 229.-38.

Basu, G. 1954. Preservation of Fazli mango. *Ind. Food Packer* **8** (4) : 15-7.

Basu, S. K. 1911. Report on the banana diseases of Chinsurah. *Quart. J. Dept. Agr. Bengal* **4**.

Batchelor, L. D. 1933. Fertilizing citrus trees. *Calif. Citrogr.* **18** : 266, 298.

1948 *a*. Fertilization : principles and methods. Chapter 7 of The citrus industry. Vol. 11. Univ. of Calif. Press, Berkeley and Los Angeles.

1948 *b*. Cover crops and manures. Chapter 8 of the citrus industry, Vol. 11. Univ. of Calif. Press, Berkeley and Los Angeles.

Batchelor, L. D. and Bitters, W. P. 1952. Two promising rootstocks for citrus in California. *Calif. Citrogr.* **37** : 390, ff.

Batchelor, L. D. and Cameron, J. W. 1950. Nucellar seedling strains in citrus. *ibid.* **35** : 454, ff.

Batchelor, L. D. and Parker, E. R. 1934. Progress report on citrus station experiments. *ibid.* **19** : 174.

Bathurst, A. C. 1943. New method for estimating the fertilizer requirements of citrus trees. *Fmg. S. Afr.* **18** : 323-7.

Batjer, L. P. 1943. Harvest sprays for the control of fruit drop . *U. S. Dept. Agr. Circ.* 685.

Batjer, L. P., Siegelman, H. W., Rogers, B. L., and Gerhardt, F. 1954. Results of four years' tests of the effects of 2,4,5-trichlorophenoxypropionic acid on maturity and fruit drop of apples in the Northwest. *Proc. Amer. Soc. Hort. Sci.* **64** : 215-21.

Batjer, L. P. and Uota, M. 1951. Effect of 2,4,5,-trichlorophenoxypropionic acid sprays on fruit set of pears and apples. *ibid.* **58** : 33-6.

Batra, H. N. 1952 *a*. Occurrence of three banana pests at Delhi. *Ind. J. Ent.* **14** : 60.

1952 *b*. A record of fig midge at Delhi. *ibid.* **14** : 60.

1953 *a*. Biology and control of *Dacus diversus* Coquillett and *Carpomiya vesuviana* Costa and important notes on other fruit flies in India. *Ind. J. Agr. Sci.* 23 : 87-112.

1953 *b*. Aphids infesting peach and their control. *Ind. J. Ent.* **15** : 45-51.

Batra, H. N. and Renjhen, P. L. 1946. Some observations on the bionomics and control of peach shoot borer in North-West Frontier Province. *Ind. Fmg.* 7 : 127-8.

1950. Preliminary observations on the biology of the Bupestred borer (Sphenoptera lafertei Thompson) of certain fruit trees in north-west India. *Ind. J. Ent.* **12** : 159-65.

Beal, S. (translator). 1884. Buddhist records of the western world, from the Chinese of Hiuen Tsiang. Trubner & Co., London.

Beattie, J. M. 1952. A summary of three years' work with foliage applications of urea. *Proc. Ohio St. Hort. Soc.*, pp. 86-91.

Bennet, C. W. and Costa, A. S. 1949. Tristeza disease of citrus. *J. Agr. Res.* **78** : 207-37.

Benson, N. R. 1953. Nutritional sprays for fruit trees. *Proc. Ann. Mtg. Wash. St. Hort. Ass.* **49** : 160-5.

Benton, R. J., Bowman, F. T., Fraser, Lilian, and Kebby, R. G. 1953. The significance of *Poncirus trifoliata* for citrus rootstock problems. *Rpt.* 13*th Internat. Hort. Cong.*, 1952, pp. 1235-40.

Berger, E. W. 1935. The destructor scale. How to control it. *Fla. Agr. Exp. Sta. Bul.* 473.

Berwick, E. J. H. 1940. Mangoes in Krian. *Malay. Agr. J.* **28** : 517-24.

Beyers, E. 1955. Effect of fertilizers on composition of grape leaves, with special reference to magnesium deficiency. *U. S. Afr. Dept. Agr. Sci. Bul.* 353 (*Fruit Res. Tech. Ser.* 37).

Bhat, S. S. 1929. Jamburi (*Citrus medica var. limonum*), the stock variety for citrus trees. Poona *Agr. Col. Mag.* **21** : 114-7.

1934. The development of santra bud on jamburi stock. *Agr. and Livestock Jnl.* **4** : 624.

1943. Economic utilization of Indian limes. Sadhana Press, Raopura, Baroda.

1944. The wood apple. *Ind. Fmg.* **5** : 17-8.

1945. The die-back disease of citrus trees. *ibid.* **6** : 250-3.

Bhattacharya, S. C. 1950. Correspondence.

Bhattacharya, S. C. and Dutta, S. 1945. A manurial trial with Khasi orange trees in Assam. *Ind. J. Hort.* 3 : 30-7.

1949 *a.* The cultivation of oranges and allied fruits in Assam. *Assam Dept. Agr. Fruit Ser. No.* 5.

1949 *b.* A cultural experiment with Khasi orange (*Citrus reticulata*) trees in Assam. *Ind. J. Hort.* **6** : 6-10.

1951. Citrus varieties in Assam. *Ind. J. Genetics and Plant Breed* **11** : 57-62.

1952. A preliminary observation on rootstocks for citrus in Assam. *Ind. J. Hort.* **9** (3) 1-11.

Bhattia, B. S., Siddappa, G. S. and Lal, G. 1955. Composition and nutritive value of jackfruit. *Ind. J. Agr. Sci.* **25** : 303-6.

Bhutiani, R. C. 1946. Vitamin contents of the mango. *Punjab Fruit J.* **10** : 112-5.

Biale, J. B. 1953. Storage of lemons in controlled atmosphere. *Calif. Citrogr.* **38** : 427, ff.

Bijhouwer, A. P. C. 1937. Flowering and fruiting habits of the mango. H. Veenman & Zonen. Wageningen.

Bioletti, F. T. 1922. Pruning young olive orchards. *Calif. Agr. Exp. Sta. Bul.* 348.

Biswas, H. G. 1944. Pectin in fruits of the Indian persimmon (*D. embryopteris* Pers.). *Sci. and Cult.* **9** : 501.

Bitancourt, A. A. 1944. A test for the early identification of the "tristeza" disease of citrus. *O. Biologico* **10** : 169-75.

Bitters, W. P. and Batchelor, L. D. 1953. Gummosis resistance of Troyer citrange. *Calif. Citrogr.* **38** : 192, 200.

Black, M. H. 1953. The problem of prolonged rest in deciduous fruit trees. *Rpt. 13th Internat. Hort. Cong.*, pp. 1122-31.

Blackford, F. W. 1941. The establishment of a home-made cuprous oxide mixture as a citrus fungicide in southern Queensland. *Qd. Agr. J.* **56** : 4-33.

Blommaert, K. L. J. 1953. Effect of growth-substance sprays on the ripening of peaches—tests with 2,4, 5-trichloro-phenoxy-acetic acid (2, 4, 5-T) on Early Dawn, Peregrine, and Elbertas. *Fmg. S. Afr.* **28** : 207-9.

Blommaert, K. L. J and Meynhardt, J. T. 1955. Preliminary experiments with hormone sprays as a substitute for girdling of Zante currants. *Fmg.* **S.** *Afr.* **30** : 367-8, 376.

Blondeau, R. and Crane, J. C. 1950. Further studies on the chemical induction of parthenocarpy in the Calimyrna fig. *Plant Physiol.* **25** : 158-68.

Bonavia, E. 1885. The future of the date palm in India (*Phoenix dactylifera*). Thacker, Spink & Co., Calcutta.

1890. The cultivated oranges and lemons, etc., of India and Ceylon. W. H. Allen & Co., London.

Bonner, J. and Liverman, J. 1953. Hormonal control of flower differentiation. Chapter 14 of Growth and differntiation in plants, edited by W. E. Loomis. Iowa State College Press.

Borja, V. and Bautista, B. 1932. Mango investigations in Muntinluda, Rizal. *Phil. J. Agr.* **3** : 111-43.

Bose, A. N. and Basu, G. 1953. Extension of storage life of Fazli mango by coating with paraffin. *Sci. and Cult.* **19** : 263-4.

. 1955. Lye peeling of Fazli mango (*Mangifera indica L.*). *ibid.* **20** : 448.

Bose, A. N. and Dutt, J. M. 1952. Dehydration of mango pulps. *Ind. Food Pacer* **6**(4) : 12, 33.

Bose, S. K. 1953a. Powdery mildew of mango in Kumaun and its control *Proc. 40th. Ind. Sci. Cong.*, P. 78.

1953 b. An entomogenous fungus on citrus whitefly, *Dzaleurodes citri* Asmm. *ibid.* p. 79.

Bose, S. K. and Mehta, P. R. 1951. Some hitherto unrecorded diseases of Kumaun and Garhwal region of Uttar Pradesh. *Plant Protection Bul.* **3** : 46-8.

Bould, C. 1955. Chelated iron compounds for the correction of lime-induced chlorosis in fruit. *Nature* 175 : 90-1.

Boyce, A. M. 1948. Insects and mites and their control. Chapter 14 in The citrus industry, Vol. II, Univ. of Calif. Press, Berkeley and Los Angeles.

Boyes, W. W. 1955. Effect of polyethylene (polythene) wrappers on the keeping quality of apricots, peaches and plums. *Fmg. S. Afr.* **30** : 13-9.

Bracciolini, P. 1857. The travels of Nicolo Conti in the East. India in the fifteenth century. Edited by R. H. Major. Hakluyt Society, London.

Bradley, M. V. and Crane, J. C. 1955. The effect of 2, 4, 5-trichlorophenoxyacetic acid on cell size and endopolyploidy in parenchyma of apricot fruits. *Amer. J. Bot.* **42** : 273-81.

Brahmachari, K. 1938. On the bionomics of the bagworm (*Kophene cuprea M.*) on banana *J. Bombay Nat. Hist. Soc.* **40** : 56-61.

Bregger, J. T. and Brown, G. F. 1945. Conserving soil and moisture in orchards and vineyards. *U. S. Dept. Agr. Farmers' Bul.* 1970.

Bretschneider, E. History of European botanical studies in China. Press of the Imperial Russian Academy of Sciences.

Brooks, F. A., Rhoades, D. G., and Schultz, H. B. 1950. Frost protection for citrus. *Calif. Agr.* **4** (9) : 11, ff.

Brooks, F. A. Kelly, C. F., Rhoades, D. G., and Schultz, H. B. 1951. Heat transfer in citrus groves. *ibid.* **5** (8) : 5, 14-5.

Brown, W. R. 1920. The orange : a trial of stocks at Peshawar. *Pusa Agr. Res. Bul.* 93.

Brusca, J. N. and Haas, A. R. C. 1955. Zinc effect in citrus and avocado. *Calif. Citrogr.* **40** : 384-5.

Bruton, W. News from the East Indies, or a voyage to Bengalla.

Buchanan, F. 1807. A journey from Madras through the countries of Mysore, Canara and Malabar. W. Bulmer and Co., London.

Buell, E. P. 1955. Training and pruning the passion vine. *Trop. Agriculturist* **111** : 18-27.

Bunell, A. C. and Tiele, P. A. (editors). 1885. The voyage of John Hughrn van Linschoten to the East Indies, from the English translation of 1598. Hakluyt Society, London.

Burkill, I. H. A dictionary of the economic products of the Malay Peninsula.

Burns, J. G. 1939. Notes on fruit culture in the hills. *U. P. Dept. Agr. Fruit Ser. Bul.* 10.

Burns, W. (editor, 7th. edition). 1930. Firminger's manual of gardening for India. Thacker, Spink and Co., Calcutta.

Burns, W. and Dani, P. G. 1920. Some facts and figures regarding banana cultivation. *Agr. J. Ind.* **15** : 386-92.

Burns, W. and Joshi, P. G. 1920. The drying of bananas. *ibid.* **15** : 166-73.

Burns, W. and Prayag, S. H. 1920. The book of the mango. *Bombay Dept. Agr. Bul.* 103.

Cain, J. C. 1953. The absorption and distribution of mineral nutrients in apple trees as affected by nutrient supply. *Proc. Amer. Soe. Hort. Sci.* **62** : 53-66.

Calavan, E. C., White, F. A., Schneider, H., and Wallace, J. M. 1951. Collapse and decline of lemŏn trees. *Calif. Citrogr.* **37** : 46, ff.

Cameron, J. W. and Soost, R. K. 1952. Size, shape, and fruit characters of orchard trees of citrus propagated from young nucellar-seedling lines and parental old lines. *Proc. Amer. Soc. Hort. Sci.* **60** : 255-64.

Camp, A. F. 1954. The citrus industry of Japan. *Calif. Citrogr.* **39** : 282-6.

Camp, A. F. and Fudge, B. R. 1939. Some symptoms of citrus malnutrition in Florida. *Fla. Agr. Exp. Sta. Bul.* 335.

Camp, A. F. and others 1949. Symptoms of citrus malnutrition. Chapter 9 in Hunger signs in crops, edited by G. Hambridge. Revised edition. *Amer. Soc. Agron. and Nat. Fert. Asso.*, Washington.

Campos, M. 1943. Vitamin content of Brazilian foods. *Nature* **151** : 584.

Cann, H. J. 1952. Bunchy top disease of bananas "at all time low" in N. S. W. *Agr. Gaz. N. S. W.* **63** : 73-6.

Capoor, S. P. and Varma, P. M. 1948. A mosaic disease of Carica *papaya* L. in the Bombay province. *Cur. Sci.* **17** : 265-6.

Caprio, J. M., Harding, R. B., and Jennings, R. F. 1954. Effect of temperature on orange size and yield. *Calif. Citrogr.* **40** : 47, 76-80.

Casson, S. 1939. Light from the East. *Atlantic Monthly* **163** : 685, ff.

Chakrabarti,. S. 1943. What's doing in all-India. Assam. *Ind. Fmg.* **4** : 318.

Chakravorti, A. K. 1951. Origin of cultivated bananas of South East Asia. *Ind. J. Genetics* and *Plant Breed.* **11** : 34-46.

Chandler, W. H. 1925. Fruit growing. Houghton Mifflin Co., Boston.

1950. Evergreen orchards. Lea and Febiger, Philadelphia.

1954. Cold resistance in horticultural plants : a review. *Proc. Amer. Soc. Hort. Sci.* **64** : 552-72.

Chandler, W. H. and others. 1937. Chilling requirements for opening of buds on deciduous and some other plants in California. *Calif. Agr. Exp. Sta. Bul.* 611.

Chandra, A. (translator and editor). Charaka-samhita. Calcutta.

Chapman, H. D. 1949. Tentative leaf analysis standards. *Calif. Citrogr.* **34** : 518.

1951. Reasons for the high nitrogen requirements of citrus in California. *Calif. Citrogr.* **36** : 223, ff.

1953. Studies on the nutrition of citrus. *Rpt.* 13*th*. *Internat. Hort. Cong.*, 1952, Pp. 1241-56.

1954. Citrus observations in Brazil. *Calif. Citrogr.* **39** : 390-2.

Chapman, H. D. and Brown, S. M. 1942. Some fungal infections in citrus in relation to nutrients. *Soil Sci.* **34** : 303-12.

Chapman, H. D., Brown, S. M., and Liebig, G. F. 1943. Some effects on citrus fruit quality of nitrogen, phosphorus and potassium. *Calif. Citrogr.* **28** : 198, ff.

Chapman, H. D., Brown, S. M., and Rayner, D. S. 1945. Nautrient deficiencies in citrus. *ibid.* **30** : 162-3, ff.

Chapman, H. D. and Fullmer, F. 1951. The potassium and phosphorus question. *ibid.* **36** : 178, ff.

Chapman, H. D. and Harding, R. B. 1955. What is happening to our citrus soils *ibid.* **40** : 207, 222-6.

Chapman, H. D. and Rayner, D. S. 1951. Effect of various maintained levels of phosphate on the growth, yield, composition, and quality of Washington Navel oranges. *Hilgardia* **20** : 325-58.

Charavanapavan, C. 1945. Studies in the preparation, properties, and assay of commercial papain. *Trop. Agriculturist* **101** : 72-6.

Chatterjee, D. 1948. Botanical nomenclature of the shaddock or pomelo. *Nature* **161** : 770.

Chatterjee, D. and Randhawa, G. S. 1952. Standardized names of cultivated plants in India. I. Fruits. *Ind. J. Hort.* **9** (2) : 24-36.

Chattopadhyay, S. B. and Sen Gupta, S. K. 1954. Studies on wilt of guava (*Pasidium guajava L.*) in West Bengal. *Proc.* 41*st*. *Ind. Sci. Cong.*, pp. 126-6.

1955. Studies on wilt of *Psidium guajava L.*, in West Bengal. *Ind. J. Hort.* **12** : 76-9.

Chaturvedi, P. L. 1950-51. Biology and control of fruit sucking moths of citrus in the Uttar Pradesh. *Agr. and An. Hus. U. P.* **1** (6, 7) : 21-3.

1954. Annual report of the scheme for controlling some serious pests attacking fruits and fruit trees grown in the plains of Uttar Pradesh, 1952-53. Supdt., Printing and Stationery, U. P. Allahabad.

Cheema, G. S. 1926. The fig industry in Asia Minor. *Bombay Dept. Agr. Bul.* 131.

1933. The marketing of fruits and vegetables in Bombay. Supdt., Govt. Printing and Stationery, Bombay.

Cheema, G. S., Bhat, S. S., and Naik, K. C. 1954. Commercial fruits of India with special reference to Western India. Macmillan & Co.

Cheema, G. S. and Dani, P. G. 1928. Economic value of fruit farming in Western India. *Bombay Dept. Agr. But.* 153.

1930. Papaya cultivation in the Bombay Presidency (excluding Sind). *Bombay Dept. Agr. Bul.* 162.

Cheema, G. S. and Deshmukh, G. B. 1927. Culture of guava and its improvement of selection in Western India. *Bombay Dept. Agr. Bul.* 148.

Cheema, G. S. and Gandhi, S. R. 1926. Refrigeration as a means of preserving mangoes and other tropical fruits. *Agr. J. Ind.* **21** : 403-5.

Cheema, G. S. and Karmarkar, D. V. 1939. The cold storage of fruits and vegetables. *Imp. Council Agr. Res. Misc. Bul.* 23.

Cheema, G. S., Karmarkar, D. V., and Joshi, B. M. 1937. The cold storage of Nagpur oranges (*Citrus aurantium*). *Ind. J. Agr. Sci.* **7** : 168-75.

1939. Investigations on the cold storage of mangoes. *Imp. Council Agr. Res. Misc. Bul.* **21**. See also *Ind. J. Agr. Sci.* **20** : 259-325. 1950.

Cheesman, E. E. 1949. Banana research at I. C. T. A. *Trop. Agriculture* **26** : 78-84.

Chellappa, T. 1954. New finds. In the mango, a souvenir, pp. 103-7. Dept. Agr. Hyderabad.

Chen, W. C. C. 1954. Studies on the absorption of nitrogen by citrus from foliar applications of urea. *Mem. Col. Agr. Nat. Taiwan Univ.* **3** (3) : 43-63.

Cherian, M. C. 1942. Our present position with regard to the control of fruit pests. *Madras Agr. J.* **30** : 14-7.

Cherian, M. C. and Anantanarayanan, K. P. 1942. Bionomics and control of *Nephoteryx eugraphella* Rag.—a pest of sapota. *ibid.* **30** : 409-11.

1943. The mango shoot-webber—*Orthaga exvinacea* Hmpsn. *ibid.* 31: 3213.

Cherian, M. C. and Ramchandran, S. 1942. *Thevetia nerifolia* Juss.—a new indigenous vegetable insecticide. *ibid.* **30** : 260-4.

Cherian, M. C. and Sundaram, C. V. 1941. The ber fruit fly—*Carpomyia vesuviana* A. Costa and its control. *Proc. 20th. Ind. Sci. Cong.*, p. 191.

Chhonkar, V. S. 1954. Comparative studies on budding and grafting in *loquat, Eriobotrya Japonica* Lind. *Agra Univ. J. Res. Sci.* **3** : 159-69.

Chiddarwar, P. P. 1955. A powdery mildew on *Carica papaya L. Cur. Sci.* **24** : 239.

Childers, N. F. (editor). 1955. Mineral nutrition of fruit crops. Rutgers University.

Childs, J. F. L. and Hrnciar, G. 1949. A method of maintaining viability of citrus seeds in storage. *Proc. Fla. St. Hort. Soc. for* 1948 pp. 64-9.

Chona, B. L. 1933. Preliminary investigations on the diseases of bananas occurring in the Punjab and their method of control. *Ind. J. Agr. Sci.* **3** : 673-87.

Chopra, N. N. 1941. Utilization of inferior grades of citrus fruit. *Ind. Fmg.* **2** : 408-12.

Choudhri, B. L. 1953. Belva or Bel (*A. marmelos*). *ibid.* **3** (8) : 10-1.

Choudhury, H. 1936. Diseases of citrus in the Punjab. *Ind. J. Agr. Sci.* **6** : 72-109.

Choudhury, S. D., Bhattacharya, S. C., and Dutta, S. 1947 *a*. Valencia orange holds out a promise in Assam. *Ind. Fmg.* **8** : 454-6.

1947 *b*. Cultivation of Assam lemon. *ibid.* **8** : 554-6.

Chowdhury, S. 1944. A leaf spot of *Carica papaya* L. caused by a new species of *Phyllosticta*. *Ind. J. Agr. Sci.* **14** : 395-8.

1945 *a*. *Ceratosmella* disease of pineapple. *ibid.* **15** : 135-9.

1945 *b*. Heart or stem-rot pineapple. *ibid.* **15** : 139-40.

1946. Wilt of pineapple in Assam. *Cur. Sci.* **15** : 82.

1947 *a*. Pineapple culture in Assam. *Ind. Fmg.* **8** : 187-90.

1947 *b*. A *Clomerella* rot of *nuna*. *Cur Sci.* **16** : 384.

1949. Some studies in the *Rhizopus* rot of jackfruit *J. Ind. Bot. Soc.* **28** : 42-50.

1950 *a*. A fruit rot of papaya (*Carica papaya L.*) caused by *Assochyta Caricae* Pat. *Trans. Brit. Mycol. Soc.* **33** : 317-22.

1950 *b*. Foam disease of citrus in Assam. *Cur. Sci.* **19** : 62-3.

1951 *a*. Gummosis of citrus in Assam. *Sci. and Cult.* **16** : 570-1.

1951 *b*. Felt disease of citrus in Assam *ibid.* **17** : 264-5.

1951 *c*. Citrus canker in Assam. *Plant Protection Bul.* **3** (3) : 78-9.

1952. Some observations on citrus canker in Assam. *Sci.* & *Cult.* **18** : 246-8.

1953. Further observations on foam disease of citrus. *ibid.* **18** : 343-5.

1954 *a*. Deficiency diseases of citrus in Assam, India. *FAO Plant protection Bul.* **2** : 151-3.

1954 *b*. Control of citrus trunk borer. *Sci. and Cult.* **19** : 457-9.

1955 *a*. Citrus scab in Assam and its control. *ibid.* **20** : 391-3.

1955 *b*. Citrus sooty moulds in Assam. *ibid.* **21** : 164-5.

1955 *c*. Citrus melanose in Assam and its control. *ibid.* **21** : 323-5.

Chowdhury, S. and Dutta, S. 1950. Vein-splitting, a boron deficiency disease of citrus in Assam. *ibid.* **15** : 358-9.

Chowdhury S. and Majid, S. 1954. Handbook of plant protection. Dept. Agr., Assam.

Christopher, E. P. 1941. The Bordeaux formula in horticultural research. *Proc. Amer. Soc. Hort. Sci.* **38** : 153-6.

Clark, F., Friend, B., and Bunk, M. C. 1947. Nutritive value of the per capita food supply, 1909-1945. *U. S. Dept. Agr. Misc. Publ.* 619

Clausen, C. P. 1931. Two citrus leaf miners of the Far East. *U. S. Dept. Agr. Tech. Bul.* 252.

1933. The citrus insects of tropical Asia. *U. S. Dept. Agr. Circ.* 266.

Claypool, L. L. and Allen, F. W. 1947. Modified atmosphere in relation to the transportation of deciduous fruits. *Proc. Amer. Soc. Hort. Sci.* **49** : 92-8.

Claypool, L. L. and Osbeck, S. 1952. Some influences of temperature and carbon dioxide on the respiration and storage life of the Mission fig. *ibid.* **60** : 226-30.

Clements, J. R. and Pentzer, W. T. 1950. Growth and ripening response of figs to olive oil and other materials. *ibid.* **55** : 172-6.

Coit, J. E. 1945. The ubiquitous guava. *Calif. Citrogr.* **30** : 408-9.

Collins, J. L. 1951. Notes on the origin, history and genetic nature of the Cayenne pine-apple. *Pacific Sci.* **5** : 8-17.

Condit, I. J. 1933. Fig culture in California. *Calif. Agr. Ext. Service Circ.* 77.

1941. Fig. characteristics useful in the identification of varieties. *Hilgardia* **14** : 1-68.

1947. The fig. Chronica Botanica Co., Waltham, Mass., U. S. A.

1950. Fig characteristics as affected by climate. *Proc, Amer. Soc. Hort. Sci.* **55** : 114-8.

1955. Fig varieties : a monograph. *Hilgardia* **23** : 323-509, plus 28 plates.

Connor, Jane. 1955. Effect of cultural practices on the manganese status of soil and citrus trees under irrigation. *Australian J. Agr. Res.* **5** (1) : 31-8.

Conover, R. A. and Ruehle, G. D. 1949. A study of diseases of avocado and mango and development of control measures. *Annual Report Fla. Agr. Exp. Sta. for* 1948-49, p. 253.

Cooper, W. C. and Knowlton, K. R. 1940. The effect of synthetic growth substances on the rooting of subtropical fruit plants. *Proc. Amer. Soc. Hort. Sci.* **37** : 1093-8.

Cooper, W. C. and Peynado, A. 1955. Boron accumulation in citrus as influenced by rootstocks. *Proc. 9th. Ann. Rio. Grande Valley Hort. Inst.*, pp. 86-94.

Cooper, W. C. and Stoutmyer, V. T. 1945. Suggestions for the use of growth substances in the vegetative propagation of tropical plants. *Trop. Agriculture* **22** : 21-31.

Costa, A. S., Grant, T. J., and Moreira, S. 1955. Behavior of various citrus rootstock-scion combinations following inoculation with mild and severe strains of triste za virus. *Proc. Fla. St. Hort. Soc. for* 1954, pp. 26-30.

Courtenay, C. E. 1947. The reconstruction of the Malayan canned pineapple industry. I. The pre-war industry and the problem of post-war reconstruction. *Malay. Agr. J.* **30** : 183-90.

Coville, P. V. 1921. The lychee (*Litchi chinesis*) a mycorhizal plant. Appendix to the lychee and longan, by G. W. Groff. Canton Christian College and Orange Judd Co., New York.

Cowart, F. F. 1942. The effect of magnesium deficiency in grapefruit trees upon the composition of the fruit. *Proc. Amer. Soc. Hort. Sci.* 40 : 161-4.

Crane, J. C. 1952 a. Growth-regulator specificity in relation to ovary wall development in the fig. *Science* **115** : 238-9.

1952 *b*. Ovary-wall development as influenced by growth-regulators inducing parthenocarpy in the Calimyrna fig. *Bot. Gaz.* **114** : 102-7.

1953. Further responses of the apricot to 2, 4, 5-trichlorophenoxyacetic acid application. *Proc. Amer. Soc. Hort. Sci.* **61** : 163-74.

1954 *a*. Responses of the Royal apricot to 2, 4-dichlorophenoxyacetic acid application. *ibid.* **63** : 189-93.

1954 *b*. Frost resistance and reduction of drop of injured apricot fruits affected by 2, 4, 5-trichlorophenoxyacetic acid. *ibid.* **64** : 225-31.

1954 *c*. The effectiveness of 2, 4, 5-trichlorophenoxyacetic acid in reducing drop and promoting growth of frosted apricot fruits. *Science* **119** : 383-5.

1955. Preharvest drop, size and maturity of apricots as affected by 2, 4, 5-trichlorophenoxyacetic acid. *Proc. Amer. Soc. Hort. Sci.* **65** : 75-84.

Grane, J. C. and Baker, R. E. 1953. Growth comparisons of the fruits and fruitlets of figs and strawberries. *ibid.* **62** : 257-60.

Crane, J. C. and Blondeau, R. 1949. The use of growth regulating chemicals to induce parthenocarpic fruit in the Calimyrna fig. *Plant Physiol.* **24** : 44-54.

1949 *b*. Controlled growth of fig fruits by synthetic hormone application. *Proc. Amer. Soc. Hort. Sci.* **54** : 102-8.

1951. Hormone-induced parthenocarpy in the Calimyrna fig and a comparison of parthenocarpic and caprified syconia. *Plant Physiol.* **26** : 136-45.

Crang, A. and Sturdy, M. 1947. The keeping quality of chutneys. *Annual report, Long Ashton Res. Sta.* 1946, pp. 153-5.

Crawford, D. L. 1937. Hawaii's crop parade. Advertiser Publishing Co., Honolulu.

Crous, P. A. 1940. The reduction of acidity in Valencias by the use of arsenical sprays. *Citrus Grower No.* 82, pp. 1, 315, 317.

1947. Reduction of acidity in Valencias. *Citrus Grower*, No. 156, pp. 8-9.

Crowe, A. D., Ricketson, C. L., and Smith, G. R. 1954. Nutrient sprays for apples. *Annual Report, Nova Scotia Fruit Grs. Ass.*, pp. 109, 111-4.

Cruess, W. V. 1938. Commercial fruit and vegetable products. Second edition. McGraw-Hill Book Co.

1943. Investigations in vegetable dehydration. *Proc. Amer. Soc. Hort. Sci.* **42** : 487-92.

Cruess, W. V. and others. 1945. Experiments with guavas. *Fruit Prod. J.* **24** : 263-6, ff.

Cuille, J. 1953. (Insecticidal treatment of banana plantations against the banana borer (*Cosmopolites sordidus*) *Fruits d'Outre Mer* **8** : 490-6.

Damodaran, M. and Srinivasan, M. 1935. Ascorbic acid (Vitamin C) in some Indian plant materials. *Proc. Ind. Acad. Sci., Sec. B.* **2** : 377-87.

Darling, M. L. 1930. Rusticus loquitor. Oxford Univ. Press.

Darrow, G. W. 1949. Polyploidy in fruit improvement. *Proc. Amer. Soc. Hort. Sci.* **54** : 523-32.

Das, D. P., Siddappa, G. S., and Lal, G. 1954. Effect of extraction of papain on the pectin content of raw papaya. *Bul. Cent. Food Tech. Res. Inst., Mysore* **3** : 300-1.

Das, N. B. and Banerjee, R. M. 1952. Utilization of mango seed kernel as a source of starch. *Sci. & Cult.* **17** : 339-40.

Das, N. K. 1947. Soils in relation to fruit culture in Kumaun hills. *Ind. fmg.* **8** : 344-5.

1948. What's doing in all-India. Assam. *ibid.* **9** : 120-1.

Das, P. M. 1937. The Punjab "ber" trees. *Punjab fruit J.* **1** : 52-4.

Das, S. 1945. Apricot seed cake as a nitrogenous manure. *Ind. J. Agr. Sci.* **15** : 30-6.

Dasarathy, T. B. 1951. The guava (*Psidium guajava*). *Madras Agr. J.* **38** : 521-7.

Dastur, J. F. 1915. A rot of bananas. *Agr. J. Ind.* **10** : 278-84.

1916. Spraying for ripe-rot of the plantain fruit. *ibid.* **11** : 142-9.

1941. Pink disease of orange trees in the Central Provinces. *Ind. J. Agr. Sci.* **11** : 892-901.

1946. Notes on *Corticium alba* Dast. And *C. salmonicolor B.* and Br. *Cur. Sci.* **15** : 192-3.

Datta, R. M. 1940, 1941. The mulberry. *Mod. Rev.* **68** : 74-9; **69** : 182-8.

Davidson, O. W. 1949. Nutrient-deficiency sypmptoms in deciduous fruits. In Hunger signs in crops, edited by G. Hambridge. Revised edition. Amer. Soc. Agron. and Nat. Fert. Asso., Washington.

Davies, H. J. 1918. Notes on oranges and lemons. *U. P. Dept. Agr. Bul.* 38.

Davison, R. M. 1952. Control of preharvest drop of Washington Navel Oranges. *N. Z. J. Sci.* and *Technol. Ser. A.* 34 (4) : 306-12.

Day, B. E. 1955. Urea herbicides for citrus weed control. *Calif. Citrogr.* 40 : 398, 408-14.

De Jong, W. H. 1934 *a*. The smudging of mangoes. *Landbouw.* **9** : 514-8.

1934 *b*. Rootstocks for mango and citrus. *ibid.* **9** : 556-8.

De la Cruz, E., Jr. and gonzalez, L. G. 1953. The graft affinity of the fig. *Ficus Carica,* with some of its congeners. *Phil. Agriculturist* **37** : 119-29.

Dermen, H. 1954. Colchiploidy in grapes. *J. Hered.* **45** : 159-72.

Desai, R. 1950. Pomegranate cultivation in Dholka. *Dharwar Agr. Col. Mag.* **4** : 14-21.

Deszyck, E. J. 1953. Physiological studies. Effect of lead arsenate in relation to borax sprays in Marsh grapefruit. *Annual Report Fla. Agr. Exp. Sta. for* 1952-53. pp. 182-3.

Deszyck, E. J. Retiz, H. J., and Sites, J. W. 1954. Basic copper arsenate—a new material for grapefruit maturity sprays. *Citrus Mag.* 16 : 15-7.

De Tar, J. E., Griggs, W. H., and Crane, J. C. 1950. The effects of growth-regulating chemicals applied during the bloom period on the subsequent set of Bartlett pears. *Proc. Amer. Hort. Sci.* **55** : 137-9.

Devarajan, M. R. 1946. Powdery mildew of oranges in Coorg. *Ind. Fmg.* **7** : 303-4.

DeWolfe, T. A., Klotz, L. J., Moore, P. W., and Hashimoto, S. 1954. Effect of mulches on citrus orchards. *Calif. Citrogr.* **39** : 422, 436-7.

Dey, P. K. 1934. Two common diseases of citrus trees in the United Provinces. *U. P. Dept. Agr. Fruit. Ser. Bul.* 7.

Dey, P. K. and Singh, U. B. 1939. The stem-black disease of apple in Kumaun. *Ind. J. Agr. Sci.* **9** : 703-10.

Dhareshwar, S. R. 1950. Trench cultivation of pineapple. *Dharwar Agr. Col. Mag.* **4** : 9-11.

1952. Response of the Basrai banana to different manures under Deccan conditions. *Rural India* **15** : 193-5.

Dhillon, A. S. and Singh, L. 1949 *a*. The efficiency of cane and trunk ringing on grapevines. *Proc. Amer. Soc. Hort. Sci.* **53** : 259-62.

1949 *b*. The influence of thinning and ringing on the cropping and quality of grapes and the vigor of grapevines. *ibid.* **53** : 263-8.

Dhopeshwarkar, G. A. and Magar, N. G. 1954. Nutritive value of canned foodstuffs : Part 1—Effect of canning procedures on vitamin C content of fruits and vegetables. *J. Sci. and Indus Res.* **13** : 849-52.

Dias, D. P., Jain, N. L., and Lal, G. 1955. Investigations on the canning of bananas. *Trop. Agriculturist* **111** : 37-41.

Dickson R. C., Flock, R. A., and Johnson, M. M. 1951. An insect vector of the citrus quick decline disease. *Calif. Citrogr.* **36** : 135, ff.

Dikshit, N. N. 1953 *a*. Propagation of three varieties (Horti.) of *Prunus* species by stem cuttings. *Cur. Sci.* **22** : 47-8.

1953 *b*. Studies in the propagation of plum, horti. Variety Kelsey (*Prunus salicina* Lindl) by stem cuttings. *Sci.* and *Cult.* **18** : 496.

Division of Food Preservation, C. S. I. R., Australia. 1943. The nutritive value of tropical fruits in Australia. *Food Press. Quart.* **3** : 45-50.

Doidge, E. M. 1938. The successful eradication of citrus canker in South Africa. *Fmg. S. Afr.* **13** : 450.

Dorasami, L. S. 1951. *Ficus palmata* as a stock for fig. *Mysore Agr. J.* **27** : 83-5.

Drury, H. 1858. Useful plants of India. Madras. Army, Madras.

DuCharme, E. P. and Knorr, L. C. 1953. Comments on methods of minimizing tristeza damage. *Proc. Fla. St. Hort. Soc. for* 1952, pp. 57-62.

Du Preez, D. 1943. Hints on guava culture. *Fmg. S. Afr.* **18** : 388.

1954. Propagation of guavas. *ibid.* **29** : 297-9.

Dutta, S. 1952. Some bananas of Assam. *Ind. J. Hort.* **9** (3) : 26-35.

1953. Some guavas of Assam. *ibid.* **10** : 137-9.

1954. Jujubes of Assam. *ibid.* **11** : 53-6.

Dutta, S. and Bhattacharya, S. C. 1951. A new citrus species of Assam. *ibid.* **8**(3) : 1-5.

Dutta, S. C. and Biswas, S. C. 1942. Vinegar from sugarcane and fruit juices. *Ind. Fmg.* **3** : 527-30.

Eastwood, H. W. 1945. Pineapple growing. *Agr. Gaz. N. S. W.* **57** : 235-8.

Eden, R. 1577. The history of trauayle in the West and East Indies. Richard Iugge, London.

Edgerton, L. J. and Hoffman, M. B. 1955. Effect of N-1-napthyl phthalamic acid on fruit set of peaches. *Science* **121** : 467-8.

Eggert, R. and Kardos, L. T. 1954. Further results on the absorption of phosphorus by apple trees. *Proc. Amer. Soc. Hort. Sci.* **64** : 47-51.

El-Tomi, A. L. 1954. Effect of cross-pollination on fruit setting in Washington Navel orange. *Citrus Ind.* **35** (8) : 5-6.

Erickson, L. C. and Brannaman, B. L. 1950. Sprays to increase size of lemons. *Calif. Citrogr.* **35** : 392-3.

Erickson, L. C., Brannaman, B. L., and Hield, H. Z. 1952. Response of Delicious and Rome Beauty apples to preharvest spray of 2, 4, 5-trichlorophenoxypropionic acid in southern California. *Proc. Amer. Soc. Hort. Sci.* **60** : 160-4.

Evans, H. R. 1952. Pineapple propagation. *E. Afr. Agr. J.* **17** : 179-82.

Everett, P. 1947. The white sapote. A little known sub-tropical fruit which can be grown in citrus districts. *N. Z. Agr.* **74** : 470.

Evreinoff, V. A. 1949. (The pomegranate.) *Fruits d'Outre Mer.* **4** : 161-70.

Fahmy, I. 1952. Grafting studies on macadamia and sapedilla in relation to carbohydrates, using pre-girdled scions. *Proc. Fla. St. Hort. Soc.* **65** : 140-3.

Fairchild, D. 1913. The grafted papaya as an annual fruit tree. *U. S. Dept. Agr. Bur. Plant Ind. Circ.* 19.

Farrag, E. E. 1955. Thinning of grapes with naphthalene acetic acid, *Trop. Agriculture* **32** : 147-9.

Farrall, A. W., Sheldon, W. H., and Hansen, C. 1946. Protection of crops from frost damage through the use of radiant energy. *Quart. Bul. Mich. Agr. Exp. Sta.* **29** : 53-63.

Fawcett, H. S. 1936. Citrus diseases and their control. 2nd edition. McGraw-Hill Book Co.

1948. Biological control of citrus insects by parasitic fungi and bacteria. Chapter 13 of the Citrus industry, Vol. 11. Univ. Calif. Press, Berkeley and Los Angeles.

Fawcett, H. S. and Klotz, L. J. 1948. Diseases and their control. Chapter 11 of The Citrus industry, Vol. II. Univ. Calif. Press, Berkeley and Los Angeles.

Fawcett, H. S. and others. 1946. A progress report on quick decline studies. *Calif. Citrogr.* **31** : 198, ff.

Fawcett, H. S. and Wallace, J. M. 1946. Evidence of the virus nature of citrus quick decline. *ibid.* **32** : 50, 88-9.

Feilden, G. S. and Garner, R. J. 1936. Vegetative propagation of tropical and subtropical fruits. *Imp. Bur. Fruit Prod. Tech. Com.* 7.

Fellers, C. R. 1936. The effect of processing on vitamins in fruits and vegetables—a review. *Mass. Agr. Exp. Sta. Bul.* 338.

Fennell, J. J. 1945. The tropical grape. *Sci. Monthly* **61** : 465-8.

Finch, A. H. and McGeorge, W. T. 1940. Studies on grapefruit fertilization in Arizona. *Proc. Amer. Soc. Hort. Sci.* **37** : 62-7.

1945. Fruiting and physiological responses of Marsh grapefruit trees to fertilization. *Ariz. Agr. Exp. Sta. Tech. Bul.* 105.

Fisher, E., Boynton, D., and Skodvin, K. 1948. Nitrogen fertilization of the McIntosh apple with leaf sprays of urea. *Proc. Amer. Soc. Hort. Sci.* **51** : 23-32.

Flory, W. S., Jr. and Moore, R. C. 1947. An early post-blossom thinning agent for York apples. *ibid.* **49** : 33-4.

Ford, H. W. 1954. The influence of rootstock and tree age on root distribution in citrus. *ibid.* **63** : 137-42.

Fork, H. W., Stewart, I., and Leonard, C. D. 1954. The effect of iron chelate on root development of citrus. *ibid.* **63** : 81-7.

Fotidar, M. R. 1941. The San Jose scale and its control in Kashmir. *Ind. Fmg.* **2** : 242-50.

Fraser, L. 1942 *a.* Citrus decline in the Murrumbidgee Irrigation Area. *Agr. Gaz. N. S. W.* **53** : 415-9.

1942 *b.* Phytophthora root rot of citrus. *J. Aust. Inst. Agr. Sci.* **8** : 101-5.

1952. Seedling yellows, and unreported virus disease of citrus. *Agr. Gaz. N. S. W* **63** : 125-31.

Fraser, S. 1924. American fruits. Orange Judd Publishing Co., New York.

Freeman, H. J. 1936. Date culture in Queensland. *Qd. Agr. J.* **45** : 376-96, 487—501; **46** : 392-406.

Frost, H. B. 1938. Nucellar embryony and juvenile characters in clonal varieties of citrus. *J. Hered.* **29** : 423-32.

Fryer, J. 1909. East India and Persia (being nine years' travels, 1672-1681). Hakluyt Society, London.

Furr, J. R., Reece, P. C., and Hrnciar, G. 1945. Nitrogen absorption of ringed orange trees in sand culture. *Proc. Amer. Soc. Hort. Sci.* **46** : 51-4.

Gadgil, D. R. and Gadgil, V. R. 1933. A survey of the marketing of fruit in Poona. *Gokhale Inst. Politics and Econ.* Pub. 3.

Galang, G. A. and Agati, J. A. 1936. A progress report on the influence of heat and smoke on the development of Carabao mango buds (*Mangifera indica L.*) *Phil J. Agr.* **7** : 245-59.

Gandhi, S. R. 1924. Investigations in fig culture and treatment. *Bombay Dept. Agr. Bul.* 117.

1928. Grape culture in western India. *Bombay Dept. Agr. Bul.* 156.

1942. Recent advances in horticultural practices. *Poona Agr. Col. Mag.* **34** : 86-99.

1947. Factors governing stature and fruiting habit of papaya. *Ind. J. Hort.* **5** : 45-50.

1949. Pineapple culture in Western India. *Poona Agr. Col. Mag.* 40(3) : 33-9.

1950 *a.* Effect of buttress grafting on growth and development of orchard trees. Reprinted from *Poona Agr. Col. Mag.*

1950 *b.* Correspondence.

1952 *a.* Banana culture in Western India. *Poona Agr. Col. Mag.* **42** : 180-209.

1952 *b.* The avocado. *Bombay Dept. Agr. Bul.* 188.

1956 *a.* Bombay bananas, their history, botany and nomenclature. *Poona Agr. Col. Mag.* **40** : 27-64.

1956 *b.* Grape culture in India. *Ind. Coun. Agr. Res. Farm Bul.* 12.

Gane, R. 1952. Pilot plant experiments on the refrigerated gas storage of Gros Michel bananas. *Trop. Agriculture.* **29** : 150-5.

Gangopadhyaya, R. 1932. Agriculture and agriculturists in ancient India. N. C. Mukherjee & Co., Serampur.

Gangolly, S. R. and Singh, D. 1950. Distribution of the mango (*Mangifera Indica L.*) and its varieties. *Ind. J. Hort.* **7** : 7-16.

Gardner, F. E. 1932. The vegetative propagation of plants. *Md. Agr. Exp. Sta. Bul.* 335.

Gardner, V. R., Bradford, F. C., and Hooker, H. D. 1927. Orcharding. McGraw-Hill Book Co., New York.

Garg, D. N. 1951. Some new diseases of economic plants in Uttar Pradesh. *Agr. and An. Hus. U. P.* **1**(9) : 12-4.

Garg, M. L. 1954 a. Mango grafting made easy and cheap. *Ind. J. Hort.* **11** : 145-6.

1954 b. Mango propagation by means of marcotting or air layering. *ibid.* **11** : 147-8.

Garner, R. J. Propagation by cuttings and layers. Recent work and its application with special reference to pome and stone fruits. *Imp. Bul. Hor.* and *Plant. Crops. Tech. Com.* 14.

Ginsburg. L. 1953. Cold-storage tests to determine shipping temperatures for pineapples. *Fmg. S. Afr.* **28** : 85-91.

Glover, P. M. 1935. An account of the occurrence of *Chyrsomphalus ourantii* Mask and *Lacifera lacca* Ferr on grapefruit in Ranchi District. *J. Bombay Nat. Hist. Soc.* **38** : 151.

Gokhale, A. V. and Kanitkat, U. K. 1951. Fruit drop of Alphonso mango and its control. *Proc.* 38*th Ind. Sci. Cong.*, p. 151.

Gokhale, V. V. 1944. The cultivation of grafted ber (*Zizyphus jujube*). *Nagpur Agr. Col. Mag.* **18** : 17-20

Golberg, L. and Levy, L. 1941. Vitamin C content of fresh, canned, dried guavas. *Nature* **148** : 286.

Gole, H. V. 1943. The bearing grape vines. *Ind. Fmg.* **4** : 617-9.

Goodman, R. N. 1954. Development of methods for use of antibiotics to control fireblight (*Erwinia amylovora*). *Res. Bul. Mo. Agr. Exp. Sta.* 540.

Gonzalez, L. G. and Anoos, Q. A. 1951. The Growth and behaviour of mangosteen and its graft-affinity with some relatives. *Phil. Agr'st.* **35** : 379-85.

Gonzalez, L. G. and Fabella, E. L. 1952. Inter-generic graft affinity of the chico. *ibid.* **35** : 402-7.

Gonzalez, L. G. and Feliciano, P. A., Jr. 1954. The blooming and fruiting habits of the Ponderosa chico. *ibid.* **37** : 384-98.

Goswami, K. N. 1954. Performance of sapodilla (chiku Kali- patti) on various rootstocks. *Bansilal Amritlal Agr. Col. Mag.* **7** (1) : 6-7.

Gowda, M. C. M. 1952. The cultivation of the avocado pear in Mysore State. *Mysore Agr. J.* **28** : 1-7.

Graham, J. A. 1839. A catalogue of the plants growing in Bombay and its vicinity. Govt. Press, Bombay, for the Agri-Horticultural Society of western India.

Grant, J. W. and Williams, A. N. P. 1936. Burma fruits and their cultivation. *Burma Dept. Agr. Bul.* 30.

Grant, T. J., Costa, A. S., and Moreira, S. 1950. 1951. Tristeza disease of citrus in Brazil. *Calif. Citrogr.* **35** : 135; **36** : 310, ff.

Grant, T. J. and Schneider, H. 1953. Initial evidence of the presence of tristeza, or quick decline, of citrus in Florida. *Phytopath.* 43 : 51-2.

Grey, E. (translator and editor). 1890. The voyage of Francois Pyrard. Hakluyt Society, London.

1892. The travels of Pietro Della Valle in India. Hakluyt Society, London.

Griessen, A. E. P. 1924. Upper India hedges. *U. P. Dept. Agr. Bul.* 30.

Griggs, W. H., Iwakiri, B. T., and DeTar, J. E. 1954. The effect of 2,4, 5-trichlorophenoxypropionic acid applied during the bloom period on the fruit of several pear varieties, and on the shape, size, stem length, seed content, and storage of Bartlett pears. *Proc. Amer. Soc. Hort. Sci.* **58** : 37-45.

Grist, D. H. 1935. Derris (tuba root). *Malay. J. Agr.* **23** : 477-82.

Groff, G. W. 1921. The lychee and lungan. Canton Christian Col. and orange Judd Co., New York.

Gross, R. A. and Simmonds, N. W. 1954. Mutations in the Cavendish banana group. *Trop. Agriculture* **31** : 131-2.

Groszmann, H. M. 1950. Hormones and flowering in pineapple. *Qd. Agr.* **70** : 88-9.

Grove, W. R. 1946. Plastic aids Chinese plant propagation method. *Fla. Grower* **55** : 5, 26.

Guest, P. L. and Chapman, H. D. 1944. Some effects of pH on the growth of citrus in sand and solution cultures. *Soil Sci.* **58** : 455-65.

Gupta, M. 1955. Fazli : the colossus of Indian mangoes. *Amrita Bazar Patrika*, July 17.

Gupta, R. L. 1953. Distribution of *Apsylla cistellata* Buck (Psyllidae : Homoptera) causing bud-galls in mango in Uttar Pradesh. *Ind. J. Ent.* **15** : 378-9.

1954. Life-history of *Tonica zizyphi* Stn.—the citrus leaf roller. *ibid.* **16** : 20-3.

1955. The *life cycle and seasonal history of chikoo-moth* (*Nephopteryx eugraphella* Rag. *ibid.* **17** : 326-36.

Gupta, S. N. D. and others 1950. Necrosis of the mango fruit. *Cur. Sci.* **19** : 153.

Gustafson, F. G. 1942. Parthenocarpy : natural and artificial. *Bot. Rev.* **8** : 599-654.

Guthrie, J. D. 1941. Sprays that break the rest period of peach buds. *Cont. Boyce Thompson Inst.* **12** : 45-7.

Haas, A. R. C. 1936. Phosphorus deficiency in citrus. *Soil Sci.* **42** : 93-105.

1939. Growth of citrus and walnut trees as affected by pH. *Calif. Citrogr.* **24** : 351, ff. 388, ff; 430, ff.

1940. Relation of pH to growth in citrus. *Plant Phys.* **15** : 377-407.

1947. Growth stimulation in Valencia orange trees on sour orange rootstock by means of aluminum citrate. *Calif. Citrogr.* **32** : 185, 198-9.

1948 a. Magnesium deficiency and its effect on citrus. *ibid* **33** : 134, ff.

1948 b. Symptoms of low potassium in leaves of citrus orchards. *ibid* **33** : 520, ff.

1948 c. Potassium, calcium, and magnesium content in citrus flowers collected from trees on various rootstocks. *Proc. Amer. Soc. Hort. Sci.* **52** : 7-10.

1950. Fertilizer distribution and citrus tree growth *Calif. Citrogr.* **35** : 136, ff.

1951. Growth-response of lemon and orange to phosphate. *ibid.* **36** : 137, ff.

Hass, A. R. C. and Brusca, J. N. 1954 a. 2. 4-D treatment of avocado plants. *Yearb. Calif. Avocado Soc.* 38 : 165-70.

1954 b. 2, 4-D treatment of citrus seed. *Calif. Agr.* **8** (2) 8 : 8, 12.

Haertl, E. J. 1955. New horizons in the application of chelation to agriculture. *Down to Earh* **11** : 6-9.

Hafiz, A. 1946. Brown rot of stone and pome fruits. *Punjab Fruit. J.* **10** : 145-6.

1947. Peach leaf curl. *ibid.* **11** : 178-80.

1950. Powdery mildew of apple. *ibid.* **14** : 26-7.

Haiek, I. 1952. (Contribution to the bromatological shady of Averrhoa carambola). An. *Fac. Farm. e Odoutol. Univ. Sao Paula.* **10** : 125-33.

Haigh, J. C. 1946. The improvement of papaw by selection. II. *Trop. Agriculturist* **102** : 17-22.

Halma, F. F. 1931. The propagation of citrus by cuttings. *Hilgardia* **10** : 137-57.

1943. Rootstock influence on the composition of Valencia orange fruit. *Proc. Amer. Soc. Hort. Sci.* **42** : 349-52.

1947. Own-rooted and budded lemon trees. *ibid.* **50** : 172-6.

Hamilton, R. A. 1954. Growth studies of papaya plants on a tropical soil with a compacted subsoil. *ibid.* **64** : 111-6.

Hamner, C. L. and Rai, G. S. 1953. Plastic for plants. *Ind. J. Hort.* **10** : 74-7.

Harding, P. L. 1945. Effect of lead arsenate sprays on the seasonal changes in Florida grapefruit. *Proc. Fla. St. Hort. Soc., pp.* 161-9.

1953. Effects of oil-emulsion and parathion sprays on composition of early oranges. *Proc. Amer. Soc. Hort. Sci.* **61** : 281-5.

Harding, R. B. 1951. High yielding orange orchards. *Calif. Agr.* **5** (9) 12, 14.

Harding, R. B. Chapman, H. D., and Whiting, F. L. 1954. Size fluctuations of Valencia oranges in major California citrus districts, 1932 to 1952. indicate significance of climate as a casue of small-sized fruit. *Proc. Amer. Soc. Hort. Sci.* **64** : 128-38.

Harkness, R. W. 1951. Laboratory tests of mango maturity. Mango studies, pp. 133-6. Florida Mango Forum.

Harkness, R. W. and Cobin, M. 1951. Haden mango maturity observations during 1950. *ibid. pp.* 141-6.

Harris, W. B. 1950. Growth responses with chlorophenoxyacetic acid in Smyrna figs. *J. Australian Inst. Agr. Sci* **16** : 71-2.

Hartless, A. C. 1913. The flowering of the mango. *Agr. J. Ind.* **8** : 90.

1914. Mango crops and some factors influencing them *ibid.* **9** : 140-59.

Hartley, C. W. S. 1950. *Flacourtia inermis*—rokam masam. *Malay. Agr. J.* **33** : 93-7.

Hartmann, H. T. 1953. Effect of winter chilling on fruitfulness and vegetative growth in the olive. *Proc. Amer. Soc. Hort. Sci.* **62** : 184-90.

Hayes, W. B. 1943. Pruning the guava. *Ind. J. Hort.* **1** : 120-5.

1945 The citrus industry in Sikkim. *ibid.* **3** : 49-55.

Hayward, W. 1942. Guava proved vitamin king. *Fla Grower* **50** : 12.

Head, W. 1932. The papaya or papeeta—its cultivation in the United Provinces. *U. P. Dept. Agr. Bul.* **60.**

Hemphill, D. D. 1954. Spray thinning apples. *Amer. Fruit Gr.* **74** (2) : 36-9.

Hensill, G. S. 1950. The "newer" organic insecticides. *Calif. Citrogr.* **35** : 321, ff.

Hill, A. G. G. and Campbell, G. K. G. 1949. Prolonged dormancy of deciduous fruit trees in warm climates. *Emp. J. Exp. Agr.* **17** : 259-64.

Hingorani, M. K. and Mehta, P. R. 1953. Bacterial leaf spot of pomegranate. *Ind. Phytopath.* **5** : 55-6.

Hinrich, H. and Cross, F. B. 1943. The relationship of compact subsoil to root distribution in peach trees. *Proc. Amer. Soc. Hort. Sci.* **42** : 33-8.

Hoagland, D. R. 1941. Water culture experiments on molybdenum and copper deficiencies in fruit trees. *ibid.* **38** : 8-12.

Hodgson, R. W. 1934. Resistance to low winter temperatures of subtropical fruit plants. *ibid.* **30** : 349-54.

1935. Further observations on frost injury to subtropical fruit plants. *ibid.* **32** : 227-9.

1940. Rootstocks for the oriental persimmon. *ibid.* **37** : 338-9.

1950. The avocado—a gift from the middle Americas. *Econ. Bot.* **4** : 253-93.

1954. Citriculture in Egypt. *Calif. Citrogr.* **39** : 143, ff.

1955. Origin of citrus fruits grown in California. *ibid.* **40** : 118, 132-46.

Hodgson, R. W. and Cameron, S. H. 1938. Effects of reproduction by nucellar embryony on clonal characteristics in citrus. *J. Hered.* **29** : 417-9.

Hodgson, R. W. and Moore, P. W. 1943. Fruit thinning experiments with the loquat. *Proc. Amer. Soc. Hort. Sci* **42** : 187-92.

Hodgson, R. W. and Schroeder, C. A. 1947. On the bearing behaviour of the kaki persimmon (*Diospyros kaki*). *ibid.* **50** : 145-8.

Hodgson, R. W., Schroeder, C. A., and Wright A. H. 1950. Comparative resistance to low winter termperatures of subtropical and tropical plants. *ibid.* **56** : 49-64.

Hoffmeyr, J. D. J. 1936. Inheritance in the papaya. Progeny studies of selected parents. *Fmg. S. Afr.* **11** : 107, ff.

1941. The use of colchicine in horticulture, with special reference to *Carica papaya ibid.* **16** : 311. ff.

Holmes-Smith, E. 1911. Notes on a tour in the fruit, spice and paddy growing tracts of North Kanara, Bombay Presidency. *Agr. J. Ind.* **6** : 377-91.

Horn, C. L. 1943. The frequency of polyembryony in twenty varieties of mango. *Proc. Amer. Soc. Hort. Sci.* **42** : 318-20.

Hough, W. S. and Mason, A. F. 1951. Spraying, dusting and fumigation of plants. Macmillan & Co.

Howard, A. 1906. First report on the fruit experiments at Pusa. *Pusa Agr. Res. Inst. Bul.* 4.

1910. Second report on the fruit experiments at Pusa. *Pusa Agr. Res. Inst. Bul.* 16.

1925. The effect of grass on trees. *Agr. J. Ind.* **20** : 285-317.

Howard, A. and Howard, G. L. C. 1918. Some improvements in the packing and transport of fruits in India. *ibid.* **8** : 245-66.

1920. The improvement of fruit packing in India. *ibid.* **15** : 51-4.

Hu, C. C. 1934. (The history and distribution of citrus fruits in China.) (English summary.) *Univ. Nanking Col. Agr. & For. Bul.* 31, *n.s.*

Huberty, M. R. and Richards, S. J. 1954. Irrigation experiments with Navel oranges at Riverside. *Citrus Leaves* **34** (8) : 6-7.

Hughes, W. A. and Lister, C. A. 1953. Lime dieback in the Gold Coast, a virus disease of the lime, *Citrus aurantifolia* (Christmann) Swingle. *J. Hort. Sci.* **28** : 131-40.

Hume, E. P. 1947. Difficulties in mangosteen culture. *Trop. Agriculture* **24** : 32-6.

Hume, E. P. and Cobin, M. 1946. Relation of seed size to germination and early growth of mangosteen. *Proc. Amer. Soc. Hort. Sci.* **48** : 298-302.

Hume, H. H. 1926. The cultivation of citrus fruits. Macmillan Co., New York.

Hume, H. H. and Miller, H. K. 1904. Pineapple culture, II. Varieties. *Fla. Agr. Exp. Sta. Bul.* 70.

Husain, M. A. and Khan, A. W. 1940. Bionomics and control of the fig-tree borer, *Batocera rufomaculata* De Geer (Colepotera : Lamiidae). *Ind. J. Agr. Sci.* 10 : 945-59.

1949. Binomics and control of the walnut weevil (*Alcides porrectirostris* Mshll.) (Alcidinae : Colepotera). *Ind J. Ent.* **11** : 77-82.

Ibrahim, S. 1943. A study of guava cultivation in the Circars. *Madras Agr. J.* **31** : 279-82.

Imam, S. I. Kitabul asmar. Paisa Akhbar Press, Lahore.

Innes, R. F. 1946. Fertilizer experiments on grapefruit in Jamaica. *Trop. Agriculture* **23** : 131-3.

Isaac, P. V. and Renjhen, P. L. 1946. Controlling pests of apple trees and fruits. *Ind. Fmg.* **7** : 446-9.

Ives, E. 1773. A voyage from England to India in the year MDCCLIV. Edward & Charles Dilly, London.

Iyengar M. L. N., Anandaramiah, M. R., and Sharma, M. D. 1954. Grapes are not sour *Mysore Agi. J.* **30** : 159-65.

Iyengar, N. V. R. and Kale, G. T. 1951. Cashew-nut industry in India. *Bul. Cent. Food Tech. Res. Inst. Mysore* **1** (6) : 197-202.

Jacob, K. C. 1934. South Indian bananas. *Madras Agr. J.* **22** : 41-57.

1942 *a.* Bananas of Mysore State. *ibid.* **30** : 37-44.

1942 *b.* Bananas in Travancore State. *ibid.* **30** : 277-87.

1948. A new banana for India. *Ind. Fmg.* **9** : 297.

1952. Madras bananas. Government Press, Madras.

Jain, A. C. 1950. Anthracnose rot of immature plantain fruits in Madhya Pradesh. *Nagpur Agr. Col. Mag.* **25** : 35-7.

Jain, N. L., Bhattia, B. S., Anand, J. C., and Lal, G. 1951. Cashew apple products. *J. Sci. Res.* **10A** : 209-10.

Jain, N. L., Das, D. P., and Lal, G. 1952. Cashew apple processing—a new industry. *Bul. Cent. Food. Tech. Res. Inst. Mysore* **1**(11) : 34-44.

Jain, N. L. and Lal, G. 1954. Studies on the preparation of amla syrup. *Bul. Cent. Food. Tech. Res. Inst. Mysore* **3** : 297-300.

Jain, S. S. 1956. A preliminary note on the inactivation of *Fusarium oxysporum F. psidii* in guava plants by chemotherapeutic treatment. (under publication.)

Janaki Amal, E. K. 1953. A new interspecific citrus hybrid. *Cur. Sci.* **22** : 178-9.

Janjua, N. A. 1947. The biology of the hairy caterpillar (*Euprocits signata Blanchard*) in Baluchistan. *Ind. J. Ent.* **9** . 159-65.

Janjua, N. A., Mustafa, A. M., and Samuel, C. K. 1943. On the biology and control of codling moth (*Cydia pomonella* Linn.) in Baluchistan. *Ind. J. Agr. Sci.* **13** : 113-28.

Javaraya, H. C. 1943. Bi-annual cropping of apple in Bangalore. *Ind. J. Hort.* **1** : 31-4.

Jeffery, C. W. 1949. Dinitro-cresol for controlling delayed foliation *Fmg. S. Afr.* **24** : 431-6.

Johar, D. S. and Anand, J. C. 1952. Nature and prevention of spoilagein amla preserves. *Ind. Food Packer* **6** (11) : 9-11.

Johar, D. S. and Lewis, Y. S. 1955. Pectin for jams and jellies from tamarind pulp. *Ind. Food. Packer* **9** (4) : 28-9.

Johnson, M. O. 1935. The pineapple. Paradise of the Pacific Press, Honolulu.

Johnston, D. P. 1934. Results of manurial experiments conducted by the Punjab Agricultural Department over a period of twenty years. *Punjab Seasonal Notes* **12** : 50.

Johnston, J. C. 1953. Irrigation in alternate middles. *Calif. Citrogr.* **38** : 338-351.

Jones, W. W., Bitters, W. P., and Finch, A. H. 1944. The relation of nitrogen absorption to nitrogen content of fruit and leaves in citrus. *Proc. Amer. Soc. Hort. Sci.* **45** : 1-4.

Jones, W. W. and Cree, C. B. 1953. Fertilizer placement for citrus. *Calif. Citrogr.* **38** : 363.

1954. Effect of time of harvest on yield, size, and grade of Valencia oranges. *Proc. Amer. Soc. Hort. Sci.* **64** : 139-45.

Jones, W. W. and Embleton, T. W. 1954. Urea sprays for oranges. *Calif. Citrogr.* **39** : 252.

Jones, W. W., Embleton, T. W., and Goodall, G. E. 1955. Urea : source of citrus nitrogen. *ibid.* **41** : 4.

Jones, W. W. and Parker, E. R. 1947. Ascorbic acid—nitrogen relations in Navel orange juice, as affected by fertilizer applications. *Proc. Amer. Soc. Hort. Sci.* **50** : 195-8.

1949 *a*. Effects of nitrogen, phosphorus, and potassium fertilizers and of organic materials on the composition of Washington Navel orange juice. *ibid.* **53** : 91-102.

1949 *b*. Application of urea to foliage of orange trees. *Calif. Citrogr.* **34** : 463.

Jones, W. W. and Steinacker, M. L. 1953. Leaf sprays of urea as a source of nitrogen for citrus leaves. *ibid.* **38** : 84-107.

Jones, W. W., Van Horn, C. W., and Finch, A. H. 1945. The influence of nitrogen nutrition of the tree upon the ascorbic acid content and other chemical and physical characteristics of grapefruit. *Ariz. Agr. Exp. Sta. Tech. Bul.* 106.

Joshi, A. C. 1943. Exploration of the wild forms in relation to the improvement of the fruit trees. *Ind. J. Hort.* **1** : 77-84.

1946. A palm suitable for cultivation in India, *Bactris utilis* Benth. Hook. *Ind. Fmg.* **7** : 237-9.

Kadiura, M. 1944. Studies on physiological dropping of fruits in the Japanese persimmon. *Dept. Agr. Com. Okitsu Hort. Exp. Sta. Res. Bul.* 19.

Kaikini, N. S. 1955. The cashew-nut (Kaju). *The Farmer* **6** (6) : 53-4.

Kains, M. G. and Mcquesten, L. M. 1944. Propagation of plants. Orange Judd, New York.

Kalra, A. N. '946. Future of San Jose scale in India. *Punjab Fruit J.* **10** : 75-8.

1947. Fruit Industry in the Simla Hills. *Ibid.* **11** : 222-8.

Kalyankar, G. D., Krishnaswamy, P. R., and Sreenivasaya, M. 1952. Papyrographic characterisation and estimation of organic acids in plants. *Cur. Sci.* **21** : 220-2.

Kamal, M. 1953. Leaf blight of *Blighia sapida*, akee. *Proc. 40th. Ind. Sci. Cong.*, p. 75.

Kamat, M. N. and Patel, M. K. 1951. Notes on two important plant diseases in Bombay State. *Plant Protection Bul.* **3** (1) : 16.

Kamat, V. N., Pandya, H. G. and Narayana, N. 1952. Ascorbic acid (vitamin C) contents of the fruits and vegetables of the Poona market. *Poona Agr. Col. Mag.* **42** : 266-70.

Kamath, M. G. 1955. Baramati farmer turns grape king. *Ind. Fmg.* **5** (6) : 6-8.

Kannan, K. K. 1928. The large citrus borer of South India. *Mysore Dept. Agr. Entom. Ser. Bul.* 8.

Karmarkar, D. V. and Joshi, B. M. 1940 *a.* Cold storage of Indian fruits. *Ind. Fmg.* **1** : 173-7.

1940 *b.* The relation of the size of fruit to the loss of weight in storage. *Ind. J. Agr. Sci.* **10** : 1021-9.

1942. Investigations on the cold storage of Nagpur oranges. *Imp. Coun. Agr. Res. Misc. Bul.* 49.

Katyal, S. L. 1949. Effects of intermediate stem-piece and its physiological application, particularly in temperate zone fruits. *Ind. J. Hort.* **6** : 36-44.

Kearney, T. H. 1908. Dry land olive cultivation in northern Africa. *U. S. Dept. Agr. Bur. Plant Ind. Bul.* 8.

Kehar, N. D. and Chanda, R. 1946. Mango-seed kernel—a new source of food. *Cur. Sci.* **15** : 48.

Kelkar, G. M. 1953. A note on banana fibre. *Rural Ind.* **16** : 154-5.

Kenworthy, A. L. 1947. A spray mixture useful to thin apples after bloom. *Proc. Amer. Soc. Hort. Sci.* **49** : 35-6.

Kessler, K. L. and Allison, J. R. 1948. Use of growth regulators on lemons in storage. *Calif. Citrogr.* **34** : 24-5, 28.

Khan, A. A. 1945. Manuring the Nagpur santra orange. *Nagpur Agr. Col. Mag.* **20** : 37-9.

1949. Fruit-growing industry in Pakistan. *Agr. Pakistan* **1** (1) : 36-8.

Khan, G. S. 1949. Effect of rootstock on Valencia orange. *W. Punjab. Fruit J.* **13** : 3-6.

Khan, K. A. W. 1955. Studies on stocks immune to wooly aphis of apple (*Erisoma lanigerum* Hausm.) *Punjab Fruit J.* **19** : 28-35.

Khan, K. F. 1925. Propagation of seedless breadfruit. *Ind. J. Hort.* **3** : 44.

1946 *a.* Crop yields in mangosteen (*Garcinia mangostana*) as influenced by seasonal conditions. *ibid.* **4** : 39-42.

1946 *b.* Clones of jack-fruit (*Artocarpus integrifolia*). *ibid.* **4** : 46-7.

Khan, K. F. and Krishnaswamy, A. R. 1952. A note on the propagation of the tree-tomato (*Cyphomandra betacea* Sendt.) by stem cuttings. *ibid.* **9** (3) : 49.

Khan, K. F. and Rao, I. K. S. 1952. A note on the vegetative propagation of the durian (*Durio zibethinus L.*) by inarching. *ibid.* **9** (3) : 49.

1953. A note on the vegetative propagation and clonal performance in custard-apple (*Annona squamosa L.*) *ibid.* **10** : 140-4.

Khan, K. M. A. 1941. Drying of fruits and vegetables. *Ind. Fmg.* **2** : 461-4.

Khan, M. 1951. Preparation of falsa squash. *Punjab Fruit J.* **15** : 9.

Khan, M. and Haq. I. 1954. Nomenclature of citrus species in the Punjab. *Punjab Fruit. J.* **18** : 41-5.

Khan, M. and Mazhar, H. 1954. Preserving Punjab kumquats. *ibid.* **18** : 23-5.

Khan, M. A. 1940. Japanese fruit or persimmon (*Diospyros Kaki*). *ibid.* **4** : 846-7.

Khare, J. L. 1923. Ber (*Zizyphus jujuba*) fruit and its fly pest. *Pusa Agr. Res. Inst. Bul.* 143.

Kheswalla, K. F. 1936. Fruit diseases in Baluchistan. *Agr. and Livestock Ind.* **6** : 204-15.

Kimball, M. H., Wallace, A., and Mueller, R. T. 1950. Changes in soil and citrus root characteristics with non-tillage. *Calif. Citrogr.* **35** : 409, 432-3.

King, G., Sakanashi, H., and Song, E. 1951. High powder from papaya. *Ind. Food. Packer* **5** (12) : 31.

"Kissan". 1942. Estate farming in India, V.—the Indian Mildura Fruit Farms, Ltd. *Ind. Fmg.* **3** : 361-3.

Klotz, L. J. 1936. Nitrogen trichloride and other gas fungicides. *Hilgardia* **10** : 27-52.

Koyamu, K. 1951. A preliminary note on the germination of papaya seeds. *Madras Agr. J.* **38** : 348-9.

Kraus, E. J. 1954. The significance of growth regulators in agricultural practice. *Proc. Amer. Soc. Hort. Sci.* **63** : 529-46.

Kraus, E. J. and Kraybill, H. R. 1918. Vegetation and reproduction with special reference to the tomato. *Ore. Agr. Exp. Bul.* 149.

Kriel, K. T. 1943. Breaking the 'rest period' of deciduous trees. *Fmg. S. Afr.* **18** : 321-2.

Krug, C. A. and Bacchi, O. 1943. Triploid varieties of citrus. *J. Hered.* **34** : 277-83.

Kulkarni, H. L. and Patel, R. C. 1953 *a*. Blister leaf-galls of mango and their control. *Cur. Sci.* **22** : 48.

1953 *b*. Seasonal emergence of mango leaf-gall insects in Gujerat (Bombay). *Proc. 40th. Ind. Sci. Cong.*, p. 199.

Kulkarni, L. B. 1911 *a*. The cultivation of guavas near Poona, Dharwar and Limbgaon. *Bombay Dept. Agr. Bul.* 40.

1911 *b*. The drying of plantains at Agashi. *Agr. J. Ind.* **6** : 289-91.

1915. Variation in the flowers of the papaya. *Poona Agr. Col. Mag.* **7** : 102-12.

Kumar, L. S. S. 1944. Flowering plants which attack economic crops. III. Loranthus. *Ind. Fmg.* 5 : 460-2.

1946. Correspondence.

Kumar, L. S. S. and Abraham, A. 1943. The papaya, its botany, culture, and uses. Reprinted from *J. Bombay Nat. His. Soc.*, pp. 5.

Kumar, L. S. S., Abraham, A., and Srinivasan, V. K. 1945. The cytology of *Carica papaya* Linn. *Ind. J. Agr. Sci.* **15** : 242-53.

Kumar, L. S. S. and Ranade, S. G. 1952. Autotriploidy in guava (*Pisidium guajava, Linn.*) *Cur. Sci.* **21** : 75-6.

Kumar, V. 1951. Studies in *Carica papaya* Linn., I. Preliminary observations on the relation of sex to the pre-flowering growth of papaya seedlings and external characters of seeds. *Ind. J. Hort.* 8(1) : 26-34.

1952. Studies in *Carica papaya Linn.* II. Sex expression in some varieties. III. Economics of papaya cultivation and fruit utilization with special reference to the production of papain. *ibid* **9** (1) : 20-8; (3) : 36-48.

Kuperberg, J. 1954. Rooting guava (*Psidiun guajava L., c.* Supreme) stem cuttings in a hydroponic mist-type plant propagator. *Proc. Fla. St. Hort. Soc. for* 1953, pp. 220-3.

Kuppuswami, B. S. 1954 *a.* A note on the vegetative propagation of cape gooseberry (*Physalis pervuviana* Linn.) by shoot cuttings. *S. Ind. Hort.* **2** : 24.

1954 *b.* Studies in plum pollination on the Nilgiris. *ibid.* **2** : 14-6.

Lal, A. and Singh, R. P. 1953. Anthracnose disease of *Carissa carandus* Linn. caused by *Collectotrichum inamdarii. J. Ind. Bot. Soc.* **32** (1, 2) : 54-63.

Lal, G. 1944. Studies in the preservation of fruit juices. IV. Vitamin C (ascorbic acid) content of citrus fruit squashes. *Ind. J. Agr. Sci.* **14** : 171-80.

Lal, G. and Jain, N. L. 1947 *a.* Canning trials on fruits. *ibid.* **17** : 187-95.

1947 *b.* Utilization of Coorg oranges. *Ind. Fmg.* **8** : 623-7.

1948. Sugar requirements in candying fruits and peels. *ibid.* **9** : 187-90.

1951. Canning of oranges. *Ind. J. Hort.* **8** (2) : 1-10.

Lal, G. and Pruthi, J. S. 1955. Ascorbic acid retention in pineapple products *ibid.* **12** : 137-41.

Lal, G., Tandon, G. L., and Pruthi, J. S. 1952. Pilot plant trials on the processing of canned mangoes and mango squash. Reprinted from *Chemical age series* 6.

Lal, K. (translator and editor). 1907, 1911, 1916. Sushruta Samhita. Calcutta.

Lal, K. B. 1949, 1953. Annual reports on the scheme for investigations on some serious insect pests attacking fruits and fruit trees grown in the plains of Uttar Pradesh, 1948-49 and 1951-52.

1950. Insect pests of fruit trees grown in the plains of Uttar Pradesh. *Agr. & An. Hus. U. P.* **1**(3) : 46—57; (4) : 30-45.

Lal, K. B. and Singh, R. N. 1945. Control of woolly aphis by *Coccinella septumpunctata* Linn. *Ind. Fmg.* **6** : 24-5.

1947. Seasonal history and field ecology of woolly aphis in the Kumaun hills. *Ind. J. Agr. Sci.* **17** : 211-8.

Lal, K. B. and Siddiqi, Z. A. 1952. Biology of the peach leaf curling aphis on the Kumaun hills. *Ind. J. Ent.* **14** : 191-6.

Lambourne, J. 1935. The etioloation shoot method of fruit propagation. *Malay. Agr. J.* **23** : 514-27.

LaRue, R. G. and Rounds, M. B. 1948. Planning and planting the orchard. Chapter 5 of the citrus industry, Vol. II. Univ. of Calif. Press, Berkeley and Los Angeles.

Latif, A. and Qayyum, A. 1950. The use of synthetic insecticide (Guesarol 550) against mango hopper. *Punjab Fruit J.* **14** (49) : 6-7.

Latif, A. and Yunus, C. M. 1950. Observations on the relationship between citrus leaf-miner (*Phyllocnistis citrella* Stn.) and citrus canker *Pseudomonos citri* Hasse).. *Ind. J.* **12** : 27-9.

1951. Food plants of citrus leaf-miner (*Phyllocnistis citrella Stn.*) in the Punjab. *Bul. Ent. Res.* **42** : 311-6.

Laufer, B. 1919. Sino-Iranica. Chinese contributions to the history of civilization in ancient Iran, with special reference to the history of cultivated plants and products. *Field Mus. Nat. Hist. Pub.* 201, *Anthrop. Ser.* 15, No. 3.

Lee, S. H. 1948. A taxonomic survey of the Oriental pears. *Proc. Amer. Soc. Hort. Sci.* **51** : 152-6.

Leley, V. K., Narayana, N., and Daji, J. A. 1943. Biochemical studies in the growth and ripening of the Alphonse mango. *Ind. J. Agr Sci* **13** : 291-9.

Leme, J., Jr. 1951. (Vitamin C content of some native and exotic fruits of Brazil.) *Rev. Agr. Piracicaba* **26**. 319-30.

Leonard, C. D. and Stewart, I. 1953. An available source of iron for plants. *Proc. Amer. Soc. Hort. Sci.* **62** : 103-10.

1954. Chelated iron as a corrective for lime-induced chlorosis in citrus. *Proc. Fla. St. Hort. Soc. for* 1953, pp. 179-84.

Le Riche, E. J. H. 1946. Guava varieties in South Africa. *Fmg. S. Afr.* **21** : 9-12.

1951. Chemical changes during the development of some guava varieties. *Dept. Agr. U. S. Afr. Sci. Bul.* 286 (*Fruit Res. Tech. Ser.* 21).

Lewis, D. 1946. Chemical control of fruit formation. *J. Pom. Hort. Sci.* **22** : 175-83.

Lewis, D. and Crowe, L. K. 1954. The induction of self-fertility in tree fruits. *J. Hort. Sci.* **29** : 220-5.

Lewis, T. and Woodward, E. F. 1950. Papain, the valuable latex of a delicious tropical fruit *Econ. Bot.* **4** : 192-4.

Leyden, J. and Erskin, W. (translators). 1826. Memoirs of Baber. Longman, Rees, Orme, Brown, and Green, London.

Li, L. Y. and Li, C. S. 1949. An improved method of air-layering lychee trees. (Chinese with English summary). *Fukien Agr. J.* **11** : 1-6.

Lilleland, O., Brown, J. G., and Conrad, J. P. 1942. The phosphate nutrition of fruit trees. III. Comparison of fruit tree and field crop responses on a phosphate deficient soil. *Proc. Amer. Soc. Hort. Sci.* **40** : 1-7.

Liu, S. Y. 1954. Studies of *Litchi chinensis*. *Diss. Abstr.* **14** : 1018-9.

Lombard, T. A. 1950 a. Eucalyptus windbreaks vs. lemon production. *Calif. Citrogr.* **35** : 301.

1950 b. Nitrogen needs of tilled vs. non-tilled soils in citrus. *ibid.* 35 : 437.

Longley, R. P. 1954. Fruit thinning and its effect in promoting annual bearing in apples. *Annual report, Nova Scotia Fruit Grs. Ass.*, pp. 147-50.

Lorenz, A. J. 1939. Dietetic history of lemon. *Calif. Citrogr.* **40** : 122, ff.

Luckwill, L. C. 1953. The mechanism of fruit drop in pome fruits and its control by synthetic growth substances. *Rpt.* 13*th*. *Internat. Hort. Cong.* 1952, pp. 273-9.

Lulla, B. S. and Johar, D. S. 1954. Organic acids in bananas. *Cur. Sci.* **23** : 362.

1955. Chromatographic analysis of sugars in banana. *ibid.* **24** : 92-3.

Lushington, A. W. 1910. The genus *Citrus*. *Ind. For.* **36** : 323-53.

Luthra, J. C. and Sattar, A. 1942. The citrus canker and its control in the Punjab. *Punjab Fruit. J.* **6** : 1179-82.

Lynch, S. J. and Nelson, R. 1950, 1951. Mango budding. Additional notes on mango budding. *Proc. Fla. St. Hort. Soc. for* 1949, and *for* 1950.

Macmillan, H. F. 1936. Tropical planting and gardening. Macmillan Co., New York.

Magness, J. R. 1935. Status of soil moisture research. *Proc. Amer. Soc. Hort. Sci.* **32** : 651-61.

Mahngar, B. S. 1946. Fruit industry in the Kulu valley. *Punjab Fruit J.* **10** : 123-6.

Malan, E. F. 1953. The production of papaws. *Fmg. S. Afr.* **28** : 257-62, 274.

1954. Pineapple production in South Africa. *ibid.* **29** : 175-80; 201-5, 212.

Malan, E. F. and Van der Meulen, A. 1954. Avocado culture in South Africa. *ibid.* **29** : 309-15.

Malik, A. R. 1936. Correspondence.

Mallik, P. C. 1951. Inducing flowering in mango by ringing the bark. *Ind. J. Hort.* **8** (1) : 1-10.

1953-54 a. Life-history and characteristics of the new mango "Prova sankar" *Proc. Bihar Acad. Agr. Sci.* **2, 3** : 125-7.

1953-54 b. A note on biochemical investigations in connection with fruit-bud differentiation in mango (*Mangifera indica Linn.*). *ibid.* **2,** 3 : 141-5.

Mallik, P. C. and Choudhury, B. 1955. Detection of root-knot nematoed (*Heterodera sachachtie* Schmidt) at Sabour, Bihar *Sci, and Cult.* **21** : 213-4.

Mallik, P. C. and De, B. N. 1952. Manures and manuring of the mango and economics of mango culture. *Ind. J. Agr. Sci* **22** : 151-66.

Mallik, P. C. and Singh, T. S. N. 1952. Studies for ensuring maximum number of fruit-producing population of papaya by various methods. *Proc. Bihar Acad. Agr. Sci.* **1**(1) : 25-36.

Mandlekar, M. R., Purohit, R. K., and Thosar, V. B. 1951. Dehydrated Mango pulp. *J. Sci. Ind. Res.* **10** : 342.

Manucci, N. (translated by W. Irvine). 1907. Storia do Mogor or Mogul India—1653-1708. John Murray, London.

Marloth, R. H. 1947 a. The mango in South Africa. III (a) Production and marketing, (b) Diseases and pests. *Fmg. S. Afr.* **22** : 609-19.

1947 b. The litchi in South Africa. I. varieties and propagation. II. Cultural practices and marketing *ibid.* **22** : 823-30; 863-70.

1954 Citrus and subtropical fruit research. *ibid.* **29** : 87-90, 104.

1955 Citrus and subtropical fruit research. *ibid.* **30** : 160-5.

Marsh, G. L. and Cameron, S. H. 1950. A rootstock—Navel bitterness relationship. *Calif. Citrogr.* **35** : 458, ff.

Marsh, R. S. and Taylor, C. F. 1947. Observed residual effects on apples of 2, 4-D in central spray system. *Proc. Amer. Soc. Hort. Sci.* **49** : 59-62.

Marth, P. C. 1953. Advances in the use of growth-regulating substances on deciduous fruits. *Rpt.* 13*th. Internat. Hort. Cong.*, 1952, pp. 240-9.

Martin, J. P., Bitters, W. P., and Ervin, J. O. 1955. Influence of soil factors on trifoliate seedlings. *Calif. Citrogr.* **40** : 199, 201.

Martin, W. R. 1940. Some effects of cultural practices upon the composition, yield and quality of Marsh grapefruit in Arizona. *Proc. Amer. Soc. Hort. Sci.* **37** : 68-75.

Martorell, L. F. and Adsuar, J. 1952. Insects associated with papaya virus diseases in the Antilles and Florida. *J. Econ. Entom.* **45** : 863-9.

Marudarajan, D. 1949. Deficiencies of minor elements responsible for diseases of crop plants in this province. *Madras Agr. J.* **36** : 488-93.

Mathur, P. B. and Singh, K. K. 1954. Technical aid to cold storage industry in India. In technical aid to food industries, p. 143. Central Food Technological Research Institute, Mysore.

Mathur, P. B. Singh, K. K., and Kapur, N. S. 1953 a. Cold storage of mangoes. *Ind. J. Agr. Sci.* **23** : 65-77.

1953 b. Refrigerated preservation of seedling mangoes. *Ind. Food Packer* **7** (4) : 7-11.

Mathur, P. B. and Srivastava, H. C. 1954. Preliminary experiments on the cold storage of durian (*Durio zibethinus, Murr.*) *Bul. Cent. Food Tech. Res. Inst. Mysore* **3** : 199-200.

May, D. W. 1929. Report of the Porto Rico Agricultural Experiment Station.

McClean, A. P. D. and Van der Plank, J. E. 1955. The role of seedling yellows and stem pitting in tristeza of citrus. *Phytopath.* **45** : 222-4.

McCormick, A. C. 1933. Control of biennial bearing in apples. *Proc. Amer. Soc. Hort. Sci.* **30** : 326.

McCready, R. M. and Owens. H. S. 1954. Pectin—a product of citrus waste. *Econ. Bot.* **8** : 29-47.

McKee, R. K. 1940. Experiments on the control of mango anthracnose by spraying. *Trop. Agriculture* **17** : 115-7.

Mehra, I. D. 1932. The cultivation of falsa. *Punjab Seasonal Notes* **10** : 27-30.

Mehta, G. D. and Kulkarni, L. B. 1912. A note on germination of papaya seeds. *Poona Agr. Col. Mag.* **4** : 89.

Mehta, P. R. 1950. Some new diseases of plants of economic importance in Uttar Pradesh. *Plant Prot. Bul., New Delhi* **2** (3) 50-1.

1951. Observations on new and known diseases of crop plants in Uttar Pradesh. *ibid.* **3**(1) : 7-12.

Mehta, P. R. and Bose, S. K. 1947. A leaf-spot disease of fig (*Ficus carica* L.) caused by *Cylindrocladium scoparium* Morg. *Ind. J. Agr. Sci.* **17** : 219-21.

Mehta, P. R. and Gupta, S. L. 1951. Eradication of *Cuscuta reflexa,* Roxb. by weedicides. *Agr. and An., Hus. U. P.* **2**(3) : 26-8.

Mehta, V. A. 1954. Recent advances in the development of food industries in India. In Technical aid to food industries. Central Food Technological Research Institute, Mysore.

Mendiola, N. B., Capinpin, J. M., and Mercado, T. M. 1951. Pineapple breeding in the Philippines, 1922-41. *Phil. J. Agr.* **16** : 51-84.

Menenghini, M. 1946. (The nature and transmission of the tristeza disease of citrus.) *O. Biologico* **12** : 285-7.

1948. (Experiments on transmission of the tristeza disease of citrus by the black orange aphid, *Aphis tavaresi*). *ibid.* **14** : 115-8.

Metcalf, R. L. 1954. Systemics may change pest control methods. *Calif. Citrogr.* **39** : 266, 276.

Miege, 1948. (A hormone trial against pre-harvest drop of fruit of the Clementine orange.) *C. R. Acad. Agr. Fr.* **34** : 302-6.

Miller, C. D. and Bazore, K. 1945. Fruits of Hawaii. *Hawaii Agr.Exp. Sta. Bul.* **96**.

Miller, E. V. 1946. Physiology of citrus fruits in storage. *Bot. Rev.* **12** : 393-423.

Miller, E. V. and Marsteller, R. L. 1953. The effect of parachlorophenoxyacetic acid on physiological breakdown of fruits of the pineapple (*Ananas comosus* L. Merr). *Food Res.* **18** : 421-5.

Miller, E. V. and Winston, J. R. 1941. Seasonal changes in the carotenoid pigments in the juice of Florida oranges. *Proc. Amer. Soc. Hort. Sci.* **38** : 219-21.

Milsum, J. N. 1935. Cube or braiani root. *Malay. Agr. J.* **23** : 426-7.

Mishra, J. N. and Jha, A. 1955. Mosaic of papaya (*Carica papaya* L.) in Bihar. *Proc. Bihar Acad. Agr. Sci.* **4** : 102-3.

Misra, S. C. 1912. Litchi leaf curl. *Agr. J. Ind.* **7** : 286-93.

Mitchel, J. H. 1950. Banana plantation management. *Qd. Agr. J.* **70** : 255-61.

Mitchel, P. and Cannon, R. C. 1953. The pineapple. *ibid.* **77** : 125-38.

Mitra, P. 1945. The moth *Taragama siva* Lefroy, as a pest of guava tree (*Psidium guava*). *Cur. Sci.* **14** : 209.

Mitra, S. K. 1926. Canning and preserving. Thacker, Spink and Co., Calcutta.

Moore, P. 1946. Grass roots views on non cultivation. *Calif. Citrogr.* **31** : 200, 218.

Moosad, C. R. 1953. Cashewnut—its production, Processing and marketing. *Madras Agr. J.* **40** : 537-43.

Monselise, S. P. and Heymann-Herschberg, L. 1953. Influence of exposure and age on dry matter content, area and mineral composition of Shamouti orange leaves. *Proc. Amer. Soc. Hort. Sci.* **62** : 67-74.

Morettini, A. 1948. (The effect of pollination on fruit fall in the kaki.) *Riv. Orto frutt. Ital.* **32** : 4-13.

Moris, A. A. 1937. Annual report of the Mazoe Citrus Experiment Station for 1936, pp. 109-53.

1938. Some observations on the effects of borax treatment in the control of "hard fruit" in citrus. *J. Pom. Hort. Sci.* **16** : 167-81.

Morris, W. D. 1941. A clean bill of health for apples. *Hygeia* **9** : 964, ff.

Morton, K. and Morton, J. 1946. Fifty tropical fruits of Nassau. Text House, Coral Gables, Florida.

Mukherjee, J. N. 1949. Trace element deficiencies in citrus. *Sci. and Cult.* **15** : 235-7.

Mukherjee, S. K. 1948. The varieties of the mango (*Mangifera indica* L.) and their classification. *Bul. Bot. Soc. Bengal* **2** : 101-33.

1949- The mango and its relatives. *Sci. and Cult.* **15** : 5-9.

1950 a. Wild mangoes of India. *ibid.* **15** : 469-71.

1950 b. Origin of the genus *Mangifera.*

1951. The origin of the mango. *Ind. J. Genetics and Plant Breed.* **11** : 49-56.

1953 *a.* Origin, distribution and phytogenetic affinity of the species of *Mangifera* Linn. *J. Linn. Soc. of London* **55** : 65-83.

1953 *b.* The mango—its botany, cultivation, uses and future imporvement, especially as observed in India. *Econ. Bot.* **7** : 130-62.

1953 *c.* Cytology of some Malayan *Mangifera. Proc. 40th. Ind. Sci. Cong.* pp. 134-5.

Munsell, H. E. 1946. Ascorbic acid content of the mango in relation to variety. *Food Res.* **11** : 95-8.

Murasu, H. and Shiraki, T. 1948. (The time of flower bud differentiation in loquats). *J. Hort. Asso. Japan* **17** : 1/2 : 100-10.

Murneek, A. E. 1941. Vitamin B_1 vs. organic matter for plant growth. *Proc. Amer. Soc. Hort. Sci.* **38** : 715-7.

1954. The embryo and endosperm in relation to fruit development, with special reference to the apple, *Malus sylvestris. ibid.* **64** : 573-82.

Murneek, A. E. and Wittwe, S. H. 1948. Some factors affecting ascorbic acid content of apples. *ibid.* **51** : 97-102.

Musahib-ud-din. 1946. A note on fruit bud differentiation in mangoes in the Punjab. *Punjab Fruit J.* **10** : 30-1.

Musahib-ud-din and Dinsa, H. S. 1946. The floral-count and fruit-set studies in some North Indian mangoes. *ibid.* **10** : 35-42.

Mustard, Margaret J 1951. Preservation of mangoes by freezing. Mango studies, pp. 111-3. Florida Mango Forum.

Mustard, Margaret J. and Lynch, S. J. 1945. Effect of some factors upon the ascorbic acid content of some Florida-grown mangoes. *Fla. Agr. Exp. Sta. Bul.* 406.

Muthuswamy, S. 1954. A passion fruit for the plains. *Madras Agr. J.* **41** : 384-7.

Nagpal, R. L. 1954. Summary of technical report (1953-54) and programme of work (1954-55) of the research activities of the horticultural section. Bombay.

Naidu, N. A. 1955 a. Preliminary studies on the occurrence of self-sterility in the Italian, Nepali Oblong and Lucknow Seedless lemons, *Citrus limon* (Linn.) Burn. *Andhra Agr. J.* **2** : 236-40.

1955 b. Autonomic parthenocarpy in some lemon varieties. *ibid.* **2** : 259-60.

Naidu, N. B. and Salctore, S. A. 1954. Studies on *Annona squamosa* (*sitaphal*) seed. III. Production and collection In Hyderabad. *Ind. J. Agr. Sci.* **24** : 253-9.

Naik, K. C. 1939. Some citrus nursery technique trials at the Fruit Research Station, Anantarajupet, Madras Presidency. *ibid.* **9** : 651-73.

1940 a. A study of the pre-orchard life of certain rootstocks for *Chinee* orange (*Citrus sinensis* Osbeck) and acid lime (*C. aurantifolia* (*Christm*) *Swingle* at Kodur. *ibid.* **10** : 601-39.

1940 b. Orchard efficiency analysis in mangoes (*Mangifera indica* Linn.) and oranges (*Citrus sinensis* Osbeck). *Madras Agr. J.* **28** : 99-109.

1941. Studies on the propagation of the mango, *Mangifera indica*, L. *Ind. J. Agr. Sci.* **11**: 736-68.

1943. Dehydrated banana products and their food value. *Madras Agr. J.* **31** : 342-6.

1944. Rootstock for acid (sour) lime (*Citrus aurantifolia* Swingle). *Ind. J. Hort.* **2** : 44.

1946. Banana fibre investigations. *ibid.* **3** : 14-28.

1947 a. Mango propagation methods at Fruit Research Station, Kodur. *Ind. Fmg.* **8** : 22-5.

1947 b. Mango research in Madras. *Punjab Fruit J.* **11** : 22-5.

1947 c. South Indian mangoes. *Madras Agr. Dept. Bul.* 24, 2nd. edition.

1948 a. Improvement of the mango, *Mangifera indica* L., by selection and hybridization. *Ind. J. Agr. Sci.* **18** : 35-41.

1948 b. Rootstocks for acid lime [*Citrus aurantifolia* (Christm) Swingle]. *ibid.* **18** : 137-46.

1948 c. Vegetative propagational methods and their relation to tree performance in the mango. *ibid.* **18** : 147-56.

1949. South Indian fruits and their culture. P. Varadachary and Co., Madras.

Naik, K. C. and Gangolly, S. R. 1950. A monograph on classification and nomenclature of South Indian mangoes. Govt. Press, Madras.

Naik, K. C. and Sugurappa, S. 1943. Grading of Sathgudi oranges. *Ind. Fmg.* **4** : 243-6.

Naik, K. G., Shah, C. C., and Pandeya, H. G. 1951. Ascorbic acid content of some common fruits and vegetables available in Gujrat. I. *J. Univ. Bombay* **19** (N. S. part 5) : 51-8.

Nair, K. R. R. 1925. Bananas in Travancore. *Poona Agr. Col. Mag.* **17** : 26-8.

Nair, T. G. and Sundararaj, D. 1950. Production of broad-leaved suckers in bananas. *Madras Agr. J.* **37** : 385-7.

Naithani, S. P. and Chandra, V. 1954. Systematic study of some locally grown guavas, *Psidium guajava* Linn., of Allahabad. *Sci. and Cult.* **20** : 133-5.

Nakata, S. 1953. Girdling as a means to induce flower-bud initiation in litchi. *Hawaii Agr. Exp. Sta. Prog. Notes* **95** : 1-4.

Nambiar, K. P. P. 1954. Note on the performance of sapota (*Achras zapota*) on three rootstocks at the Agricultural Research Station, Taliparamba. *S. Ind. Hort.* **2** : 62.

Nand, D. 1955. Colour of young leaves as a means of identifying mango varieties. *Kanpur Agr. Col. J.* **14**(1) : 15-9.

Nandi, H. K. Bhattacharya, S. C., and Dutt, S. 1943. Nursery behaviour of five indigenous citrus rootstock varieties with Khasi orange as scion in Assam. *Ind. J. Agr. Sci.* **13** : 489-93.

1945. Investigations on some fundamental aspects of citrus propagation in Assam. *ibid.* **15** : 191-200.

Narasimham, B. 1949. Influence of sex and parentage on the improvement of the papaya. *Ind. J. Hort.* **6** : 22-9.

Narasimhan, M. J. 1954. Malformation of panicles in mango incited by a species of *Eriophyes*. *Cur. Sci.* **23** : 297-8.

Narayanan, E. S. 1954. The anar-butterfly, *Virachola isocrates* Fabr. *Ind. Fmg.* **4** : 8.

Narayanarao, D. 1955. Studies on quality grading standards for Chini orange. *Andhra Agr. J.* **2** : 15-29.

Nauriyal, J. P. 1952. Self-incompatibility in pumelo (*Citrus maxima* Merr.) *Cur. Sci* **21** : 347.

1954. The banana (*Musa paradisaca* L.) and its culture. *Agr. and An. Hus. U. P.* **5** (1) : 4-7.

1955. A study of premature fruit drop in citrus. *Ind. J. Hort.* **12** : 39-52.

Nayar, T. G. 1953. Manurial experiments with the Poovan banana (I) *Ind. J. Agr. Sci.* **23** : 283-8.

1954. Banana. Madras Agriculture Department.

Nayar, T. G. and Bakthavathsalu, C. M. 1955. Cavendish bananas—their culture and systematic status. *Ind. J. Hort.* **12** : 22-8.

Nayar, T. G. and Shetty, K. M. 1949. A note on curing of persimmons (*Diospyros kaki* L. F.) (A further report). *ibid.* **6** : 30-5.

Nelson, R. O. 1954. High humidity treatment for air layers of lychee. *Proc. Fla. St. Hort. Soc. for* 1953. pp. 198-9.

1955 a. Propagation of guavas by graftage. *ibid. for* 1954, pp. 228-31.

1955 b. Notes on lychee grafting. *ibid.*, pp. 231-3.

Nema, K. G. 1953. A fruit-rot of *Carissa carandus* Linn, *Sci. and Cult.* **18** : 337.

Nirody, B. S. 1923. Investigations in avocado breeding. *Rpt. Calif. Avocado Ass.* (1922-23), p. 65.

Nirvan, R. S. 1953 a. Control of papaya foot rot. *Ind. Phytopath.* **6** : 47-8.

1953 b. 'Bunchy top' of young mango seedlings. *Sci. and Cult.* **18** : 335-6.

Oberholzer, P. C. J. 1947. The bitter-seville rootstock problem. *Fmg. S. Afr.* **22** : 489-95.

1953. Degeneration of our citrus clones. *ibid.* **28** : 173-4.

Ochse, J. J. 1931. Fruits and fruit culture in the Dutch East Indies. G. Kolff & Co., Batavia.

1953. Observations on rooting lychee cuttings. *Proc. Fla. St. Hort. Soc. for* 1952, pp. 168-7.

Olsen, E. O. and Sleeth, B. 1954. Tristeza virus carried by some Meyer lemon trees in South Texas. *Proc. 8th Ann., Rio Grande Hort. Inst.*, pp. 84-8.

Oppenheimer, C. 1947. The acclimatization of new tropical and subtropical fruit trees in Palestine. *Agr. Res. Sta. Rehovot Bul.* 44.

Oppenheimer, C. and Gottreich, M. 1954. Studies on growth and development of the dwarf banana in the coastal plain of Israel. II. Comparative value of follow-suckers from young and old rhizomes. III. Comparative value, as planting material, of suckers from young and old rhizomes. *Ktavim* **5**(1) : 45-52 and 53-5.

Oppenheimer, H. R. 1953. Water requirements and irrigation of citrus groves. *Rpt. 8th. Internat. Hort. Cong.*, 1952. pp. 1267-74.

Ordonyo, A. V. 1951. Artificial production of parthenocarpic fruits. *Phil. Agr'st* **35** : 115-29.

Orillos, M. O. 1954. The effects of different methods of budding citrus on the development of the scion. *Araneta* **1** (2) : 27-45.

Oxenham, B. L. and Sturgess, O. W. 1953. Citrus virus diseases in Queensland. *Qd. Agr., J* **76** : 68-75.

Paddy Specialist and Government Agricultural Chemist. 1944. A review of the manurial experiments on the agricultural crops of the Madras Presidency for the decennial period 1930-40. *Madras Agr. J.* **32** : 3-10.

Pal, B. P. 1951. Dried litchis. *Ind. Fmg.* (N. S.) **1**(3) : 13.

Pal, N. L., Chatterjee, U. N., and Ranjan, S. 1937. Effects of gases from brick-kilns on mango crops. *Proc. 24th. Ind. Sci. Cong.*, pp. 270-1.

Paranjpye, H. P. 1937. The cultivation of oranges and allied fruits in the Bombay Presidency. *Bombay Dept. Agr. Bul.* 19, revised.

Parker, E. R. 1934. Some effects of thinning orange fruits. *Calif. Agr. Exp. Sta. Bul.* 576.

1935. Experiments on mottle leaf by spraying with zinc compounds. *Calif. Citrogr.* **20** : 90, ff.

Parker, E. R. and Southwick, R. W. 1941. Manganese deficiency in citrus *Proc. Amer. Soc. Hort. Sci.* **39** : 51-8.

Parsai, P. S. 1952. Top working inferior type of mango trees to superior varieties. *Nagpur Agr. Col. Mag.* **26** : 1-3.

1954. Mango-new propagation methods. In the mango, a souvenir, pp. 64-7. Dept. of Agr., Hyderabad.

Parsons, T. H. 1932. Fruit cultivation in Ceylon with cultural details. *Trop. Agriculturist* **79.**

Patel, G. A. and Hadli, S. N. 1953. Experiments with some new insecticides for the control of mango hoppers (*Idiocerus atkinsoni* Leth). *Ind. J. Ent.* **15** : 107-14.

Patel, G. A. and Kulkarni, H. L. 1953. *Cerciaphis emblica* Sp. Nov. (Family Aphididae)—a new aphis pest on *Emblica officinalis. J. Bombay Nat. Hist. Soc.* **51** : 435-8.

Patel, G. A. and Patel, H. K. 1952. Control of termites as pests of fruit trees. *Proc. Zool. Soc. Bengal* **5** : 133-40.

1953. Seasonal incidence of termite injury in the northern parts of Bombay State. *Ind. J. Ent.* **15** : 376-8.

Patel, J. S. 1949. What's doing in all-India. Bihar. *Ind. Fmg.* **10.** 212-3.

Patel, M. K., Allayyanavaramath, S. B. and Kulkarni, Y. S. 1953. Bacterial shot-hole and fruit canker of *Aegle marmelos* Correa. *Cur. Sci.* **22** : 216-7.

Patel, M. K., Kamat, M. N. and Hingorani, G. M. 1950. *Pestalotia psidii* on guava. *Ind. phytopath.* **3** : 165-76.

Patel, M. K., Kulkarni, Y. S., and Moniz, L. 1948. *Pseudomonas mangiferae,* pathogenic on mango. *ibid.* **1** : 147-52.

Patel, M. K., Moniz, L., and Kulkarni, Y. S. 1948. A new bacterial disease of *Mangifera indica* L. *Cur. Sci.* **17** : 189-90.

Patel, M. K. and Pandhye, Y. A. 1948. Bacterial soft rot of mango in *Bombay. Ind. Phytopath.* **1** : 127-8.

Patel, M. S. and Kale, M. N. 1938. The production of lime oil and calcium citrate in the province of Bombay. *Bombay Dept. Ind. Bul.* 11.

Patwardhan, G. B. 1919. Grape-vine pruning in India. *Poona Agr. Col. Mag.* **10** : 139-48.

Patwardhan, G. B. and Deshmukh, G. B. 1931. A handbook of horticultural practices. G. B. Patwardhan, Poona.

Patwardhan, V. G. 1928. Jackfruit as famine food. *Poona Agr. Col. Mag.* **20** : 87-90.

Penman, F. 1949. Boron poisoning in citrus. *J. Dept. Agr. Vict.* **47** : 181-9.

Pennant, T. 1798. The view of Hindoostan. London.

Pennock, W. 1949. Field response of Red Spanish pineapples to nitrogen, calcium, iron, and soil pH. *J. Agr. Univ. Puerto Rico* **33** : 1-26.

Perez, V. M. 1949. (A hormone that hastens fruiting of pineapples.) *Suleo Tico* **1** : 465-7.

Petrucci, V. E. and Crane, J. C. 1950. Fruit bud initiation and differentiation in the fig. *Proc. Amer. Soc. Hort. Sci.* **56** : 86-92.

Phatak, B. R. 1934. Fruit culture. *Nagpur Agr. Col. Mag.* **8** : 135-44.

Phillip, A. G. and Khan, M. A. 1952. Trials on the cultivation of cape gooseberry (*Physalis peruviana*). *Punjab Fruit J.* **15** : 17.

Pickering, S. U. 1911. The effect of grass on trees. *Woburn Exp. Fruit Farm Rpt.* 13.

Pomeroy, C. S. and Aldrich, W. W. 1943. Set of citrus fruits in relation to applications of certain growth substances. *Proc. Amer. Soc. Hort. Sci.* **42** : 146-8.

Pope, W. T. 1929. Mango culture in Hawaii. *Hawaii Agr. Exp. Sta. Bul.* 58.

1930. Papaya culture in Hawaii. *Hawaii Agr. Exp. Sta. Bul.* 61.

Popenoe, W 1920. Manual of tropical and subtropical fruits. Macmillan Co., New York.

1941. The Mango : a study in systematic pomology. *Trop. Agriculture* **18** : 23-5.

1953. The development of tropical pomology. *Rpt. 13th. Internat. Hort. Cong.* 1952, pp. 1210-7.

Powell, H. C. 1930. The culture of the orange and allied fruits. Central News Agency, Ltd., South Africa.

Praloran, J. C. 1954. (Studies on attempts to induce bearing in the Clementine orange by double ringing.) *Fruits et Prim.* **24** : 138-46.

Prasad, H. H. 1938. A note on soft rot of pears caused by a species of *Aspergillus*. *Ind. J. Agr. Sci.* **8** : 549-51.

Prasad, M. 1936. Economics of guava growing and marketing in Allahabad and environs. *Allahabad Farmer* **10** : 122-32, 153-9.

Prasad, N., Mehta P. R., and Lal, S. B. 1952. Fusarium wilt of guava (*Psidium guyava L.*) in Uttar Pradesh, India. *Nature* 169 : 753.

Prest, R. L. 1935. Pruning of citrus trees in Queensland. *Qd. Agr. J.* **44** : 760-77.

1947. Citrus pruning. *ibid.* **64** : 208-11.

1955 *a*. The custard-apple. *ibid.* **80** : 17-20.

1955 *b*. Unfruitfulness in papaya. *ibid.* **81** : 144-8.

Preston, A. P. 1955. Apple rootstock studies. *J. Hort. Sci.* **30** : 25-33.

Principal, Harcourt Butler Technological Institute. 1932. Production of papain from the fruit of the papaya tree (*Carica papaya*). *Agr. and Livestock Ind.* **2** : 471-9.

Proebsting, E. L. and Warner, R. M. 1954. The effect of fertilizers on yield, quality and leaf composition of figs. *Proc. Amer. Soc. Hort. Sci.* **63** : 10-8.

Provan, J. L. 1933. Root stocks for citrus trees. *Vict. Dept. Agr. J.* **31** : 266-70.

Pruthi, H. S. 1938. The distribution, status, and biology of codling moth (*Cydia pomonella L.*) in Baluchistan with notes on some other insects infesting apples. *Ind. J. Agr. Sci.* **8** : 499-519.

1950. A foreign insect menace to Indian citrus industry checked. *Ind. Fmg.* **11** : 5-6.

Pruthi, H. S. and Mani, M. S. 1945. Our knowledge of the insect and mite pests of citrus in India and their control. *Imp. Counc. Agr. Res. Sci. Monogr.* 16.

Pruthi, H. S. and Rao, V. P. 1951. San Jose scale in India. *Tech. pub.* **3**, Directorate of Plant Protection, Quarantine and Storage, Ministry of Agr., Govt. of India, New Delhi.

Pruthi, J. S. and Lal, G. 1955 *a*. Passion fruit processing—a new promising line in fruit technology. *Ind. Food. Packer* **9** (4) : 13-8.

1955 *b*. Studies on the nutritive value and utilization of purple passion fruits (*Passiflora edulis* Sims.) *Ind. J. Hort.* **12** : 34-7.

Puttarudraiah, M. 1952. Blister disease "kajji" of guava fruits (*Psidium guava*). *Mysore Agr. J.* **28** : 7-13.

Puttarudraiah, M. and Appanna, M. 1955. Two new hosts of *Helopeltis antonii* signoret in Mysore. *Ind. J. Ent.* **17** : 391-2.

Quaile, H. J. 1938. Insects of citrus and other subtropical fruits. Comstock Publishing Co., Ithaca, N. Y.

Rahman, K. A. 1941. Preliminary observations on the use of nicotine sulphate against citrus *Psylla*. *Proc.* 28*th*. *Ind. Sci. Cong.*, p. 192.

1944. Insect pests of fruit trees. *Ind. Fmg.* **5** : 463-6.

1946. Important insect pests of the mango and how to combat them. *Punjab Fruit J.* **10** : 52-6.

Rahman, K. A. and Ansari, A. R. 1941. Scale insects of the Punjab and North-West Frontier Province usually mistaken for San Jose scale. *Ind. J. Agr. Sci.* **11** : 816-30.

Rahman, K. A. and Kalra, A. N. 1944. Apple hairy caterpillar in the Simla hills. *Ind. Fmg.* **5** : 312-4.

Rahman, K. A. and Khan, A. W. 1941 a. Biology and control of woolly aphis, *Erisoma lanigerum* Hausm (Aphididae : Rhynchota) in the Punjab. *Ind. J. Agr. Sci.* **11** : 265-78.

1941 *b*. Observations on *Aphelinus mali* held in the Punjab. *ibid.* **11** : 446-50.

Rahman, K. A. and Latif, M. A. 1941. Habits and behaviour of the giant mealy bug (*Drosicha stebbingi*). *Proc.* 28*th*. *Ind. Sci. Cong.*, p. 192.

1944. Description, bionomics and control of the giant mealy bug, *Drosichu stebbingi*, Green (*Homoptera* : *Coccidae*). *Bul. Ent. Res.* **35** : 197-209.

Rahman, K. A. and Singh, S. 1943. Honey-bee in the service of the fruit grower. *Punjab Fruit J.* **9** : 1328-30.

Rahman, K. A. and Yunus, M. 1945. The citrus leaf miner. *Ind. Fmg.* **6** : 221.

Rai, J. N. 1956. Stylar end rot of the guava fruit (*Psidium guayava* Linn.) *Proc. Ind. Acad. Sci. Sec. B* **43** : 55-61.

Raina, J. L. 1944. What's doing in all-India. Kashmir. *Ind. Fmg.* **5** : 379-80.

Raisinghani, G. S. 1945. Spring rains and mango fruit crops in Sind. *ibid.* **6** : 341.

Rajen, M. R. D. and Aiyappa, K. M. 1944. Leaf-fall and fruit rot disease of oranges. *ibid.* **2** : 512-3.

Rakshpal, R. 1945. Citrus sucking moths and their control. *ibid.* **6** : 441-3.

Ram, A. 1941. Ber (*Ziziphus jujubee*) crop, 1940. *Punjab Fruit J.* **5** : 898.

Ramachandran, G. 1950. The romance of palm *gur*. *Ind. Fmg.* **11** : 368-70.

Ramchandran, S. 1951. Plant protection work in Madras during 1948-50. *Plant Protection Bul.* **3** : 61-8.

1954. Insect pests of oranges in the Madras State. Madras Agr. Dept.

Ramakrishnan, T. S. 1954. Common diseases of citrus in Madras State. Madras Agr. Dept.

Ramakrishnan, T. S. and Sundaram, N. V. 1955. Grapevine diseases and their control. *Madras Agr. J.* **42** : 108-15.

Ramamoothy, B. and Desai, S. V. 1946. Preliminary studies of the nutritional diseases of plants and their spectographic diagnosis. *Ind. J. Sci.* **16** : 103-11.

Raman, K. R. 1949. Methods of inducing seedlessness in fruits. *Ind. J. Hort.* **6** : 11-5.

Ramasarma, C. B. and Banerjee, B. N. 1941. Studies on the vitamin content of mangoes. *Proc. 20th. Ind. Sci. Cong.*, p. 123.

Ramasomayazulu, M. V. 1953. A promising guava (Lucknow No. 49) for the Agency tracts of the Andhra State. *Ind. J. Hort.* **10** : 154-6.

1954. Cape gooseberry (*Physalis peruviana L.*)—a promising bush fruit for the Agency tracts of the Andhra State *S. Ind. Hort.* **1** : 145-7.

Ramdas, L. A. 1940. Cold waves and frosts. *Ind. Fmg.* **1** : 531-3.

Randhawa, G. S. and Singh, D. 1951. Strawberry culture in India. *Ind. J. Hort.* **8**(4) : 49-53.

Randhawa, G. S. and Dinsa, H. S. 1947 *a*. Quality of Valencia oranges as affected by aspect, exposure, and height of tree. *Proc. Amer. Soc. Hort. Sci.* **50** : 161-4.

1947 *b*. Time of blossom-bud differentiation in citrus. *ibid.* **50** : 165-71.

Randhawa, M. S. 1949. A giant mango tree. *Ind. Fmg.* **10** : 257-8.

Rangacharlu, V. S. 1951. Avocado pear. *Ind. Fmg.* (N. S.) **1**(4) : 11-2.

1952. Peculiarities of viticultural practices in Madurai district. *Madras Agr. J.* **39** : 558-63.

1954. Guava, the "apple of the tropics." *Andhra Agr. J.* **1** : 105-9.

1955. Mango rootstock investigations at the fruit research station, Kodur (South India). *ibid.* **2** : 182-6.

Rangacharlu, V. S. and Rao, I. K. S. 1952. "Oleification" of fig and its effect on fruit maturity. *Sci. and Cult.* **18** : 244-5.

Rangacharlu, V. S and Rao, K. S. 1951. Note on a new type of quick yielding jacktree. *Madras Agr. J.* **38** : 488-90.

Rangacharlu, V. S. and Venkatarao, M. 1954. Culture of Sathgudi and other tight-skinned sweet oranges. *Andhra Agr. J.* **1** : 164-8.

Ranjan, S. and Jha, V. R. 1940. The effect of ethylene and sulphurdioxide on the fruits of *Mangifera indica. Proc. Ind. Acad. Sci.* **11** : 267-88.

Rao, A. N. and Rangacharlu, V. S. 1951. Two new berry fruits—blackberry and raspberry (*Rubus spp.*) for the hill ranges of South India. *Madras Agr. J.* **38** : 553-5.

Rao, A. S. 1954. The Indian gooseberries. *S. Ind. Hort.* **1** : 121-4.

Rao, C. B. 1944. Fig (*Ficus carica*) pollination. *Ind. J. Hort.* **2** : 44-5.

1954 *a*. The importance of fruit-growing and allied industries in the Andhra State. *Andhra Agr. J.* **1** : 152-6.

1954 *b*. Promising mangoes of Andhra. In The mango, a souvenir, pp. 53-60. Dept. Agr. Hyderabad.

Rao, C. B., Rangacharlu, V. S., and Sundararao, Y. R. 1954. Budlings and seedlings of acid lime. *Andhra Agr. J.* **1** : 171-2.

Rao, C. B. and Sundararao, Y. R. 1954. A note on a new promising citrus fruit—lemon (*Citrus limonia* Linn.). *ibid* **1** : 169-70.

Rao, M. 1941. Culture of oranges at Kodur. *Madras Agr. J.* **29** : 429-34.

Rao, P. G. 1951. Control of plant diseases in the northern region of the Madras State in the year 1949-50. *Plant Protection Bul.* **3**(1) : 21-2.

Rao, P. R. B., Balakrishnan, S., and Rajagopalan, R. 1952. Influence of freezing on the volume of juice extracted and ascorbic acid content of certain fruits. *Cur. Sci.* **21** : 337-8.

Rao, U. N. 1945 *a*. Curing the persimmon (*Diospyros kaki*). *Ind. J. Hort.* **3** : 8-13.

1945 *b*. Woolly aphis resistant apples on the Nilgiris. *ibid.* **3** : 44-5.

1947. Regional peculiarities in apple production. *ibid.* **5** : 8-17.

Rao, U. N., Rangacharlu, V. S., and Kuppuswamy, B. S. 1952. Effect of linseed oil spray on the growth and yield of apple trees on the Nilgiris. *ibid.* **9**(4) : 59-63.

Rao, U. N., Rangacharlu, V. S. Kuppuswamy, B. S., and Krishnaswami, A. R. 1952. Vegetative propagation trials with the persimmon (*Diospyros kaki* Linn.). *ibid.* **9**(4) : 1-6.

Rao, U. N. and Rao, V. N. M. 1953. Cashewnut—a dollar earning crop of India. *Ind. Fmg.* **3**(4) : 12-3.

Rao, V. K. R. V. 1946. The food statistics of India. Govt. of India Press, New Delhi.

Rao, V. P. 1948. The spread of San Jose scale—*Quadraspidotus perniciosus* Comstock—in India. *Ind. J. Ent.* **10** : 41-4.

Rao, V. P. and Chatterjee, S. N. 1948. The San Jose scale and other scale insects usually mistaken therefor in India. *ibid.* **10** : 5-29.

Rao, V. T. 1953. The mango hopper problem in Madras State. *S. Ind. Hort.* **1**(1) : 25-8.

Rashid, M. A. 1949. History of introduction of some of the deciduous fruit plants in the North-West Frontier Province. *W. Punjab Fruit J.* **13** : 13-5.

Reece, P. C., Furr, J. R., and Cooper, W. C. 1946. The inhibiting effect of the terminal bud on flower formation in the axillary buds of the Haden mango. *Amer. J. Bot.* **33** : 209-10.

Reece, P. C. and Horanic, G. E. 1952. Some varietal responses of Florida oranges to pre-harvest sprays. *Proc. Fla. St. Hort. Soc.* **65** : 88-92.

Reed, H. M. 1946. A note on the ascorbic acid content of the jujube. *Fruit Prod. J.* **26** : 71.

Rege, N. D. and Devadatta, S. C. 1943. Vitamins, minerals, carbohydrates and proteins in fruits. *Cur. Sci.* **12** : 20-1.

Reinecke, O. S. H. 1936. Environment and its influence upon deciduous fruit production. *J. Pom. Hort. Sci.* **14** : 164-74.

Reuther, W., Gardner, F. E., Smith, P. F., and Roy, W. R. 1949. Phosphate fertilizer trials with oranges in Florida. 1. Effects on yield, growth, and leaf and soil composition. *Proc. Amer. Soc. Hort. Sci.* **53** : 71-84.

Reuther, W. and Smith, P. F., 1953. Effects of high copper content of sandy soil on growth of citrus seedlings. *Soil Sci.* **75** : 219-24.

Reynolds, P. K. 1927. The banana. Houghton Mifflin Co., Boston and New York.

Riaz-ur-rahman, Ahmad, S., and Khan, M. 1954. Some studies on the qualities of Punjab guavas (*Psidium, Guajava*). *Punjab Fruit J.* **18** : 64-9.

Riaz-ur-rahman, Rashid, M. A., and Khan, M. 1954. Ascorbic acid in *ber* varieties in the Punjab. Abstracts of papers presented at a symposium on fruit and vegetable preservation, October, 1954.

Richards, A. V. 1938. Studies on stock-scion interaction in citrus. I. *Trop. Agriculturist* **19** : 2-24.

1940. Influence of rootstocks on quality of citrus fruit. *ibid.* **94** : 354-61.

1945. Stock-scion influence in citrus. *ibid.* **101** : 61-71.

1948. The influence of root-stocks on budgrafted citrus. *ibid.* **104** : 182-9.

1950. A note on the cultivation of Singapore jak. *ibid.* **105** : 12-3.

1952. The mango (*Mangifera indica L.*). *ibid.* **108** : 121-4.

1954. A new citrus rootstock. *ibid.* **110** : 292.

1955. Correspondence.

Rivnay, E. 1954. The Mediterranean fruit fly, *Ceratitis capitata* Woed. Studies in toxicants, mass migration and control in Israel. *Ktavim* **4** : 3-38.

Robinson, R. H. 1935. Sprays, their preparation and use. *Ore. Agr. Exp. Sta. Bul.* 336.

Robinson, T. R. 1951. The mango on the Florida west coast. Mango studies, pp. 21-3. Florida Mango Forum.

Roddis, L. H. 1953. James Lind—his place in medical history. *Calif. Citrogr.* **38** : 312.

Rodriguez, F. L. 1954. (Seedless annona.) *Rev. Agric.* (Cuba) **37** (2) : 83-5.

Rogers, A. (translator). 1909, 1914. Tuzuk-i-Jahangir. Asiatic Society, London.

Rogers, B. L. and Batjer, L. P. 1954. Effects of 2.4. 5-T on size, maturity, and drop of apricots. *Proc. Wash. St. Hort. Ass.*, pp. 81-2.

Roistacher, C. N., Eaks, I. L., and Klotz, L. J. 1955. Ammonia gas to control blue-green mold decay of citrus fruits. *Plant Dis. Reptr.* **39** : 202-5.

Rose, D. H. Wright, R. C., and Whiteman, T. M. 1941. The commercial storage of fruits, vegetables and florists' stocks. *U. S. Dept. Agr. Circ.* 278.

Roxburgh, W. 1824. Flora indica. Serampore.

Roy, R. S. 1950 *a*. Horticultural development as an important side industry to agriculture in Bihar. *Bihar Agr. Col. Mag.* **2** : 4-14.

1950 *b*. Correspondence.

1950 *c*. The cultivation of the banana in Bihar *Ind. Fmg.* **11** : 179-82.

1952. A consolidated report of the Fruit Research Scheme, Bihar from 2nd April, 1934 to 31st March, 1951. Supdt., Government Printing, Bihar, Patna.

Roy, R. S. and Ahmed, S. F. 1951. Description of Bihar guava varieties. *Ind. J. Hort.* **8**(3) : 22-3.

Roy, R. S. and De, B. N. 1950. Control of litchi mite. *Ind. J. Hort.* **7**(1) : 16.

Roy, R. S., Mallick, P. C., and De, B. N. 1951. Manuring of the mango (*Mangifera indica* Linn.). *Proc. Amer. Soc. Hort. Sci.* **57** : 9-16.

Roy, R. S. and Ram, K. B. 1951. Control of mango hopper in Bihar. *Proc. 39th. Ind. Sci. Cong.*, pp. 305-6.

Roy, R. S. and Sharma, C. 1951. Chromosome studies in Bihar bananas. *Ind. J. Gen. and Plant Breed.* **11** : 211-4.

1952. Diseases and pests of bananas and their control. *In J. Hort.* 9 (4) : 39-52.

Roy, R. S. and Singh, D. R. 1952. Utilization of unripe mango fruit. *Ind. Food Packer* **6** (4) : 31-3.

Roy, S. K. 1953. Embryology of *Eugenia jambos L. Cur Sci.* **22** : 249-50.

Royle, J. F. 1839. Illustrations of the botany of the Himalayan mountains. Wm. H. Allen and Co., London.

Ruehle, G. D. 1948. The common guava—a neglected fruit with a promising future. *Econ. Bot.* **2** : 306-25.

Ruehle, G. D. and Lynch, S. J. 1948. Mango cross-pollination. *Fla. Grower.*

S., A. E. 1949. Radiant heat for citrus. *Calif. Citrogr.* **35** : 75.

S., G. C., 1949. Note on a simple method of plant propagation by cuttings. *Trop. Agriculture* **36** : **4**.

Sahasrabuddhe, D. L. 1934. Experiments in manuring crops in the Bombay Presidency, 1896-1931. Dept. Agr. Bombay.

Sambamurty, K. and Ramalingam, V. 1954 *a*. Preliminary studies in blossom biology of the jack (*Artocarpus heterophyllus* Lam) and pollination effect. *Ind. J. Hort.* **11** ; 25-9.

1954 *b*. A note on hybridisation in the sapota (*Achras zapota L.*). *ibid.* **11** : 57-60.

Samisch, R. M. 1945. The use of dinitrocresol mineral oil sprays for the control of prolonged rest in apple orchards. *J. Pom. Hort. Sci.* **21** : 164-79.

Samsurin, A. A. 1947. (The "anti-sweetness" effect of *Zizyphus* leaves.) *Prioda* No. 1, p. 96.

Sane, V. 1935. A note on pineapple. *U. P. Dept. Agr. Fruit Ser. Bul.* 9.

Sankaram, A. 1942. Cultivation and marketing of papaya in the West Godavari district. *Madras Agr. J.* **30** : 247-55.

Saptarishi, K. and Alwa, K. R. 1953. Off-season peaches at the agricultural research station, Nanjanad. *ibid.* **40** : 548.

Saptarishi, K. and Azariah, M. D. 1952. Off-season bearing in plums, an unusual phenomenon at the agricultural research station, Nanjanad. *ibid.* **39** : 455.

Sarma, K. 1952. The Loranthus parasite as a pest of citrus trees in Assam. *Ind. J. Hort.* **9**(2) : 18-21.

Sato, K., Ishihara, M., and Harada, R. 1954. Studies on foliar sprays of phosphates for fruit trees. I. (Japanese, English summary). *J. Hort. Ass. Japan* **23** : 159-64.

Sattar, A. and Malik, S. A. 1939. Some studies on anthracnose of mango caused by *Glomerella cingulata* Stonem (S. and V. S.) (*Colletotrichum gloeosporioides* Penz) in the Punjab. *Ind. J. Agr. Sci.* **9** : 511-21.

Sax, K. 1954. Stock and scion relationship in graft incompatibility. *Proc. Amer. Soc. Hort. Sci.* **64** : 156-8.

Sayed, I. A. 1939. The development of the cashew-nut industry in India. *Agr. and Livestock Ind.* **9** : 26-41.

1942. Developing mango canning in western India. *Ind. Fmg.* **3** : 129-32.

1951. Extension of the cashew-nut cultivation and development of the cashew-nut industry in the Bombay State *Poona Agr. Col. Mag.* **41** : 237-47.

Schomer, H. A., Gerhardt, F., and Sainsbury, G. F. 1954. Polyethylene box liners for pears and apples. *Proc. Wash. St. Hort. Ass. pp.* 193-8.

Schroeder, C. A. 1943. Hand pollination studies on the cherimoya. *Proc. Amer. Soc. Hort. Sci.* **43** : 39-41.

1945. The nomenclature of certain subtropical fruits. *Yearb. Calif. Avocardo Soc., pp.* 36-40.

1947 *a.* Pollen requirements of the feijoa. *Proc. Amer. Soc. Hort. Sci.* **49** : 161-2.

1947 *b.* Rootstock influence on fruit set in the Hachiya persimmon. *ibid.* **50** : 149-50.

1951. Heterostyly and sterility in *Carissa grandi flora. ibid.* **57** : 419-22.

Schultz, J. H. 1948. Self-incompatibility in apricots. *ibid.* **51** : 171-4.

Sen, A. C. 1955. Control of mealy-bug pest in Bihar. *Ind. J. Ent.* **17** : 129-32.

Sen, A. C. and Prasad, D. 1953. Pests of bananas in Bihar. *Ind. J. Hort.* **9**(4) : 240-6.

1954. Experiments with the new synthetic insecticides for the control of the mango hopper in Bihar. *Ind. J. Ent.* **16** : 234-46.

Sen, H. D. 1931. A study of the extraction of papain, the active digestive principle from papaya. *J. Agr. Sci.* **21** : 209-19.

Sen, P. K. 1939, 1941 *a*, 1942 *a*. Annual reports of the Fruit Research Station, Sabour, Bihar, for 1938-39, 1939-40, and 1940-41. Supdt., Govt. Printing, Bihar, Patna.

1941 *b*. 'Black-tip' of the mango. *Sci. and Cult.* **7** : 56.

1941 *c*. Effect of indole-butyric and three other acids on rooting of *Litchi* Cuttings. *Proc.* 28*th*. *Ind. Sci. Cong.*, p. 262.

1942 *b*. Further studies on 'black-tip' of the mango. *Sci. and Cult.* **8** : 91-2.

1942 *c*. Production of flowers on rootstock stems on mango grafts in the nursery. *Ind. J. Agr. Sci.* **12** : 523-4.

1943 *a*. Black-tip disease of the mango. *ibid.* **13** : 300-33.

1943 *b*. The bearing problem of the mango and how to control it. *Ind. J. Hort.* **1** : 48-71.

1944. Irregular bearing of mango. *Ind. Fmg.* **5** : 408-11.

1945. On the flowering on rootstock stem of mango grafts at nursery stage. *Ind. J. Hort.* **3** : 92-5.

1946. You can get a full crop of mangoes every year. *Punjab Fruit J.* **10** : 31-4.

Sen, P. K., Ganguly, B. D. and Mallik, P. C. 1945. A note on a leaf-curl disease of the papaya (*Carica papaya* Linn.). *Ind. J. Hort.* **3** : 38-40.

Sen, P. K. and Mallik, P. C. 1940. The embryo of the Indian mangoes (*Mangi fera indica* Linn.). *Ind. J. Agr. Sci.* **10** : 750-60.

1941. The time of differentiation of the flower-bud of the mango. *ibid.* **11** : 74-81.

1945. Effect of smudging on the mango. *Proc.* 32*nd*. *Ind. Sci. Cong.*, pp. 81-2.

1947. Effects of smudging on mango. *Ind. J. Hort.* **5** : 29-34.

Sen, P. K., Mallik, P. C., and Ganguly, B. D., 1946. Hybridization of the mango. *ibid.* **4** : 4-15.

Sen, P. K. and Roy, P. K. 1945. Mineral nutrition of the mango. *Proc.* 32*nd*. *Ind. Sci. Cong.*, p. 23.

Sen, P. K., Roy, P. K., and De, B. N. 1947. Hunger signs in mango. *Ind. J. Hort.* **5** : 35-44.

Sen, P. K. and Verma, B. S. 1954. Studies on the die-back disease in guava (*Psidium guajava L.*). A survey of the incidence of the disease in Jhargram area (West Bengal). *Proc.* 41*st*. *Ind. Sci. Cong.*, p. 258.

Sen-Gupta, J. C. and Chattopadhaya, S. K. 1954. Hormones and rooting in intact plants and cuttings. *Cur. Sci.* **23** : 294-5.

Serr, E. F. and Forde, H. I. 1952. Sprays for control of pre-harvest drop of Peerless almonds. *Proc. Amer. Soc. Hort. Sci.* **60** : 193-6.

Shah, M. I. and Azeez, N. A. 1949. Studies in the sugar acid relationship and other physical and chemical developments in peach fruit ripened on tree as compared to that seasoned in the packed boxes of woodwool. *W. Punjab Fruit J.* **12** : 22-5.

Shah, R. 1946. An effective and inexpensive method for the control of stem-borers in fruit trees with special reference to *Santra* trees in C. P. and Berar. *Cur. Sci.* **15** : 135.

Shamel, A. D. and Pomeroy, C. S. 1934. Girdling Valencia orange trees. *Calif. Citrogr.* **19** : 176.

1936. Report on a girdling test with Washington Navel orange trees. *ibid.* **21** : 320, 343.

1937. Bud selection in citrus and other fruit trees. *ibid.* **23** : 24, ff.

1944. Effect of girdling on the performance of Washington Navel orange trees. *Proc. Amer. Soc. Hort. Sci.* **44** : 80-4.

Sharma, B. B. 1953. Studies in the diseases of *Mangifera indica* Linn. *Proc. 40th. Ind. Sci. Cong.*, pp. 70-1.

Sharma, H. N. and Singh, B. N. 1940. Insect pests of fruit trees in Kumaun and their control. *U. P. Dept. Agr. Bul.* 21.

Shaw, J. G. 1955. Poison-lure sprays for Mexican fruit fly. *Calif. Citrogr.* **40** : 188-92.

Shear, C. B., Crane, H. L., and Myers, A. T. 1946. Nutrient-element balance : a fundamental concept in plant nutrition. *Proc. Amer. Soc. Hort. Sci.* **47** : 239-48.

Shetty, K. M. 1950. Observations on the 'bud take and scion growth of peach trees as influenced by rootstocks'. *Madras Agr. J.* **37** : 126-8.

Shmueli, E. 1953. Irrigation studies in the Jordon Valley. I. Physiological activity of banana in relation to soil moisture. *Bul. Res. Coun. Israel* **3**: 228-47.

Shrivastava, K. P. 1931. The cultivation of oranges in the C. P. and Berar. *C. P. and Berar Dept. Agr. Bul.* 19.

Shunmukhasundaram, R. and Naidu, D. K. 1941. Some promising fruit products of South India. *Madras Agr. J.* **39** : 351-5.

Siddappa, G. S. 1942. Ripening changes in some important varieties of grapes. *Ind. J. Agr.* **12** : 499-522.

1943. Pomegranate juice. *Ind. Fmg.* **4** : 196-8.

1949. Economics of fruit preservation as a cottage industry. *Madras Agr. J.* **36** : 69-81.

1951. Utilization of jackfruit and orange. *Ind. Coffee.* **15** : 130-2.

1952 a. Cost of a small-scale production of canned mangoes. *Madras Agr. J.* 39 : 7-12.

1952 b. Quality standards for South Indian citrus fruits. *Ind. J. Hort.* **9** (4) : 7-24.

Siddappa, G. S and Bhatia, B. S. 1952. Preparation of Jelly from jackfruit rind. *Bul. Cent. Food. Tech. Res. Inst. Mysore* **2**(3) : 70-2.

1954 a. Tender green mangoes as a source of vitamin *C. Ind. J. Hort.* **11** : 104-11.

1954 b. A comparative study of the composition and bitterness of loose jacket oranges grown in India. *J. Sci. Industr. Res.* **13B** : 148-50.

1954 c. The identification of sugars in fruits by paper chromatography. *Ind. J. Hort.* **11** : 19-23.

1954 d. Preservation of mangosteen (*Garcinia mangostana*). *Bul. Cent. Food. Tech. Res. Ist. Mysore.* **3** : 296-7.

Siddappa, G. S. and Ishaq, M. 1950. Canning grapes in Baluchistan. *Ind. J. Agr. Sci.* **20** : 101-6.

Siddappa, G. S., Ishaq, M., and Chugtai, I. D. 1950. Canning of peaches and plums in Baluchistan. *ibid.* **20** : 149-63.

Simmonds, N. W. 1946. The relative yields of bananas and potatoes. *Trop. Agriculture* **23** : 226-8.

1954 a. Varietal identification in the Cavendish group of bananas. *J. Hort. Sci.* **29** : 81-8.

1954 b. A survey of the Cavendish group of bananas. *Trop. Agriculture* **31** : 126-30.

Simmonds, N. W. and Simmonds, F. J. 1953. Experiments on the banana borer, *Consmopolites sordidus* in Trinidad, B. W. I. *ibid.* **30** : 216-23.

Singh, B. 1945. Propagation of citrus trees. *Punjab Fruit J.* **9** : 196-9.

Singh, B. and Paharia, K. D. 1952. Damping off of papaya (*Carica papaya* L.) seedlings. *Sci. and Cult.* **17** : 477-9.

Singh, B. N. and Dutt, S. 1941. Studies on the formation of jellies from some Indian fruits. *Ind. J. Agr. Sci.* **11** : 1006-21.

Singh, C. P. 1940. The loquat. *U. P. Dept. Agr. Fruit Ser. Bul.* **19**.

Singh, D. and Nijhawan, S. D. 1944. A critical study of the effect of soil mulch on conservation of soil moisture. *Ind. J. Agr. Sci.* **14** : 124-37.

Singh, G. P. 1954. Some aspects of marketing mangoes in Bihar. *Rur. India* **17** : 160-3.

Singh, H. 1945. Some useful wild plants of the Delhi province. *Ind. J. Agr. Sci.* **15** : 297-308.

Singh, J. 1949. What's doing in all-India. East Punjab. *Ind. Fmg.* **10** : 32-4.

1952. Preparation of jam from mulberry. *Punjab Farmer* **4** : 275, 278.

Singh, K. 1949. On the anatomy of the fourth instar larva (pre-pupal stage) of the jaman whitefly, *Dialeurodes eugeniae* (*Markel*) (Homoptera, Aleurodidae). *Ind. J. Ent.* **11** : 25-46.

Singh, K. and Singh, S. 1947. Citrus propagation studies. *Ind. J. Agr. Sci.* **17** : 34-54.

Singh, K. K. 1951. Prospects of the cold storage industry in India. *Bul. Cent. Food. Tech. Res. Inst. Mysore* **1** (**2**) : 21-5.

1954. Rootstock effect on fruit quality of Malta orange (*Citrus sinensis* Osbeck). *Ind. J. Agr. Sci.* **24** : 1-22.

Singh, K. K., Kapur, N. S., and Mathur, P. B. 1953. Cold storage of 'Totapuri' (Bangalora) mangoes. *Bul. Cent. Food. Tech. Res. Inst. Mysore* **2** : 149-51.

1954. Further studies on the cold storage of mangoes. *Ind. J. Agr. Sci.* **24** : 137-48.

Singh, K. K. and Mathur, P. B. 1952. Ripening of mangoes at controlled temperatures. *Bul. Cent. Food. Tech. Res. Inst. Mysore* **2** : 14-6.

1953 a. Cold storage of Cavendish variety of banana. *ibid.* **2** : 307.

1953 b. Studies in the cold storage of cashew apples. *Ind. J. Hort.* **10** : 115-21.

1954 a. Cold storage of guavas. *ibid.* **11** : 1-5.

1954 b. A note on investigations on the cold storage and freezing of jack-fruit. *ibid.* **11** : 149.

1954 c. A note on the cold storage of sapotas (*Achras sapota*). *Ind. J. Agr. Sci.* **24** : 149-50.

Singh, K. K. and Singh, S. 1948. The development of red colour in Blood Red malta orange (*C. sinensis Osbeck*). *ibid.* **18** : 157-65.

Singh, L. 1932. Improvement of fruit industry through bud selection. *Punjab Seasonal Notes* **10** . 39-41.

1934. Root pruning of oranges (santras). *ibid.* **12** : 24-5.

1940. Top-working of 'bers', wild olives and other inferior fruit varieties. *Punjab Fruit J.* **4** : 634.

Singh, L., Bajwa, B. S., and Ram, L. A. 1940. Grapes. *ibid.* **4** : 667-74.

Singh, L. and Hamid, A. 1941. The cold storage of pears (Bartlett) in the Punjab. *Ind. J. Agr. Sci.* **11** : 769-77.

1942. The cold storage of fruits in the Punjab. I. Citrus fruits : Malta (*Citrus sinensis*) and Sangtra (*C. nobilis*). *ibid.* **12** : 757-78.

Singh, L. and Khan, A. A. 1939. Relation of growth to bearing in mangoes. *ibid.* **9** : 835-67.

1942. Factors responsible for intensity of red colour in Blood red oranges. *Punjab Fruit J.* **6** : 1121-3.

1943 a. Mango budding in situ. *Ind. Fmg.* **4** : 199-200.

1943 b. How to prolong the life of mango bud-wood. *Punjab Fruit J.* **7** : 1264-5.

1946. Deblossoming in relation to biennial bearing of the mango. *ibid.* **10** : 22-39.

Singh, L. and Lal, G. 1941. Drying of vegetables. *Ind. Fmg.* **2** : 308-16.

1944. Studies in the preservation of fruits and vegetables. Effect of maturity of William's pear (Kulu Valley, Punjab) on their canning quality. *Ind. J. Agr. Sci.* **14** : 167-71.

Singh, L., Lal, G., Sadassivan, T. S., and Jain, N. L. 1951. Some studies in the preservation of fruits and vegetables. *ibid.* **21** : 137-53.

Singh, L. and Singh, B. 1939. The Kashmir fruit industry. Punjab Fruit Development Board.

Singh, L., Singh, B., and Khan, A. A. 1941. Citrus manuring. I. Fertilizer experiment with sweet orange (Malta) growing on rough lemon. *Ind. J. Agr. Sci.* **11** : 778-94.

Singh, L., Singh, B., Khan, A. A., and Ram, A. 1940. Citrus fruits. *Punjab Fruit J.* **4** : 648-61.

Singh, L. and Singh S. 1938. Pruning fruit trees—the effect of dormant pruning on cropping and vegetative vigour of phalsa (*Grewia asiatica*). *Ind. J. Agr. Sci.* **8** : 319-30.

1940. The distinguishing characters and behaviour of some grapevine varieties introduced at Lyallpur in the Punjab. *Ibid.* **10** : 552-98.

1942 a. Citrus rootstock trials in the Punjab. I. The vigour of young trees of sweet orange, mandarin, and grapefruit as influenced by different rootstocks. *ibid.* **12** : 381-99.

1942 b. Grapevine varieties at Lyallpur. *Ind. Fmg.* **3** : 372-5.

1944. Citrus rootstock trials in the Punjab. II. The influence of different rootstocks on the vigour of Blood red oranges. *Ind. J. Agr. Sci.* **14** : 95-100.

Singh, L. B. 1948. Studies on biennial bearing. II. A review of the literature. III. Growth studies in "on" and "off" year trees. IV. Bud-rubbing, blossom thinning, and defoliation as possible control measures. *J. Hort. Sci.* **24** : 45-65, 123-48, 159-77.

1951 a. Air layering of litchi without soil or water *Cur. Sci.* **20** : 102.

1951 b. Propagating jackfruit, *Artocarpus integrifolia*, by air-layering with hormones. *ibid.* **20** : 102-3.

1952 a. A new technique for propagating aonla (*Phyllanthus emblica*). *Sci. and Cult.* **17** : 345-6.

1952 b. Preliminary trial on top working *ber* (*Zizyphus mauritiana* Lam.) in Uttar Pradesh. *Ind. J. Hort.* **9**(1) : 16-9.

1954 a. Annual report of the Plain Fruit Research Scheme, Uttar Pradesh, for the year July 1, 1953 to June 30, 1954.

1954 b. Propagation of mango by air-layering for root stocks. *Proc. Amer. Soc. Hort. Sci.* **63** : 128 30.

1954 c. Propagating bael (*Aegle marmelos*) vegetatively. *Sci. and Cult.* **19** : 405-6.

Singh, L. B. and Dikshit, N. N. 1952. Studies in introducing earliness in maturity of grapes (*Vitis vinifera* Linn.). I. Effect of early pruning on the growth of vines and maturity of fruits. *Ind. J. Hort.* **9**(3) : 20-5.

Singh, L. B. and Nauriyal, J. P. 1953. A preliminary study in cover cropping citrus orchards. *ibid.* **10** : 44-8

Singh, L. B. and Singh, R. L. 1955. Mango orcharding. *Agr. and An. Hus. U. P.* **6**(1) : 3-26.

1956. Peach Special Number. *ibid.* **6**(8) : 3-28.

Singh L. B. and R. N. 1955. Studies in nucellar seedling of some common rootstocks for citrus. *Ind. J. Hort.* **12** : 53-7. See also *Sci. and Cult.* **20** : 347-8.

Singh, L. B. and Singh, U. P. 1954. The litchi. Supdt. Printing and Stationery, U. P., Allahabad.

Singh, M. B. R. 1949. Papain. *Ind. Fmg.* **10** : 472.

Singh, M. P. 1948. The budding of kagzi nimboo, sweet lime and the mango. *Nagpur Agr. Col. Mag.* **22** : 144-7.

1949. Can the hill fruits be grown in the Central Provinces ? *Ind. J. Hort.* **6** (3, 4) : 16-21.

1951 a. Grade and quality of the chikoo fruit. *ibid* **8**(1) : 11-7.

1951 b. Preliminary growth rate studies of chikoo fruit. *ibid.* **8**(3) : 17-21.

1952. Mineral composition of fruits of the litchi (*Litchi chinensis* Sonn.) and loquat (*Eriobotrya japonica* Lindl.). *ibid.* **9** (4) : 53-8.

1953. Iron deficiency in citrus plants and its control. *ibid.* **10** : 56-8.

1954. An improved marcot box for the aerial propagation of fruits. *ibid.* **11** : 89-93.

Singh, M. P. and Kunte, Y. N. 1949. Composition of juice from Santra halves. *ibid.* **6** (2) : 11-9.

Singh, M. P. and Singh, R. P. 1953. Studies on dying-back in citrus. *ibid.* **10** : 1-8.

Singh, R. N. 1941. The life history, biology and ecology of the apple root-borer (*Lophosternus hugelii* Redtembach) in Kumaun. *Ind. J. Agr. Sci.* **11** : 902-5.

1942. Control of woolly aphis (*Erisoma lanigerum* Hausmann) by spraying and other methods. *ibid.* **12** : 588-602.

1954 a. Hybridization and mango improvement. *Ind. J. Hort.* **11** : 16-8.

1954 b. Studies in floral biology and subsequent development of fruits in the mango (*Mangifera indica* L.) varieties *Dasheri and Langra. ibid.* **11** : 69-88.

1955. Further studies in colchicine induced polyploidy in papaya (*Carica papaya* Linn.). *ibid.* **12** : 63-71.

Singh, R. S. 1937. *Pruning of deciduous fruit trees. U. P. Dept Agr. Fruit Ser. Bul.* 18.

1941. Propagation of the apple in Kumaun. *Ind. Fmg.* **2** : 242-50.

1942. Fruit tree varieties for the hills. *ibid.* **3** : 581-4.

1943. Storage of apples in Kumaun. *ibid.* **4** : 74-6.

Singh, R. S. and Gupta, A. P. 1950-51. Export trial of U. P. mangoes to United Kingdom in 1950. *Agr. and An. Hus. U. P.* **1** (6,7) : 6-11.

Singh, R. S. and Singh, L. B. 1952. Cultivation of papaya and papain extraction. *Bur. Agr. Inf. U. P. Tech. Bul.* No. 10.

Singh, R. S. and Sinha, R. P. 1954. The fruit drop in grapefruit (*Citrus paradisi*) due to *Colletotrichum gloeosporioides. Sci. and Cult.* **20** : 41-3.

Singh, Sham. 1940. Ringing and root-pruning of non-bearing Sangtra trees in the Punjab. *Punjab Fruit J.* **4** : 808-10.

1951. The nomenclature and distinctive characters of some citrus root-stocks tried in the Punjab. *Ind. J. Agr. Sci.* **21** : 1-9.

Singh, Sham and Nagpal, R. L. 1947. Citrus rootstock trials in the Punjab. III. The influence of different rootstocks on the vigour and cropping of Marsh seedless grapefruit. *ibid.* **17** : 117-27.

1954. Rootstock trials in the Punjab. IV. The influence of different rootstocks on the vigour and cropping of Malta orange. *ibid.* **24** : 73-109.

Singh, Sirdar 1953. Activities of insect pollinators and orchard planning. *Ind. J. Hort.* **10** : 125-32.

Singh, S. M. 1950 a. *Rhynchaenus mangiferae*, a serious mango pest in the Uttar Pradesh. *Cur. Sci.* **23** : 270-1.

1954 b. A note on serious damage to mango crop by *Lymantria mathura* Moore, in Doon Valley. *Ind. J. Hort.* **11** : 150.

1954 c. Studies on *Apsylla cistellata* Buckton causing mango galls in India. *J. Econ. Entom.* **47** : 563-4.

Singh, S. N. 1950. Effect of some hormones on the rootage of *Psidium guajava* L. *Sci* and *Cult.* **16** : 198-202.

1955 a. Studies on rootage of fruit plants in relation to hormones. IV. *Artocarpus heterophyllus* Lam. *ibid.* **20** : 393-5.

1955 b. Studies on rootage of fruit plants in relation to hormones. V. Citrus fruits. *ibid.* **21** : 206-8.

Singh, S. N., Fozdar, B. S., and Singh, M. 1949. Vegetative reproduction of jackfruit. *Allahabad Farmer* **23** : 93-7.

Singh, S. N. and Sharma, M. K. 1954. Studies on the effects of some hormones on the rootage of *Eriobotrya japonica* Lindl. var. Golden Yellow. *Sci. and Cult.* **19** : 508-9.

Singh, S. N. and Singh, S. P. 1952. Studies on the storage and longevity of pollens of some fruits and vegetables. I. *Agr. and An. Hus. U. P.* **2** (9) : 3-11.

Singh, S. N. and Teotia, S. S. 1951. Effect of some hormones on the rootage of mango. *Sci. and Cult.* **17** : 207-10.

Singh, S. N. and Tomar, B. S. 1949. Bearing habits of kaghzi lime. *Ind. Fmg.* **10** : 532-40.

Singh, U. B. 1941 a. Sooty-blotch and fly-speck of apple in Kumaun. *Ind. J. Agr. Sci.* **11** : 597-602.

1941 b. The soft-rot of apple fruit in Kumaun. *ibid.* **11** : 902-5.

1942. Stem-brown disease of apple in Kumaun. *ibid.* **12** : 368-80.

1943. The pink disease of apple in Kumaun. *ibid.* **13** : 528-30.

1944 a. Control of sun-scald of peach trees in Kumaun. *Ind. Fmg.* **5** : 73.

1944 b. Leaf-spot disease of apple in Kumaun. *ibid.* **5** : 566-7.

Singh, U. B. and Garg, D. N. 1949. Powdery mildew of the mango in the United Provinces. *Agr. Col. Students' Mag., Kanpur* **9** : 15.

Singh, U. P. 1955. A study of varietal incompatibility in loquat (*Eriobotrya japonica* Lindl.). *Ind. J. Hort.* **12** : 115-6.

Sinha, A. C. and Mullik, P. C. 1950. A study of premature drops in oranges in Bihar. *Ind. J. Agr. Sci.* **20** : 347-57.

Smith, G. E. P., Kinnison, A. F. and Carns, A. G. 1931. Irrigation investigations in young grapefruit orchards on the Yuma Mesa. *Ariz. Agr. Exp. Sta. Tech. Bul.* 37.

Smith, H. S. 1948. Biological control of insect pests. Chapter 12 of The citrus industry, Vol. II. Univ. of Calif. Press, Perkeley and Los Angeles.

Smith, P. F., Reuther, W., and Gardner, F. E. 1949. Phosphate fertilizer trials with oranges in Florida. II. Effect on some fruit qualities. *Proc. Amer. Soc. Hort. Sci.* 53 : 85-90.

Smith, P. F., Reuther, W. and Specht, A. W. 1949. The influence of root-stock on the mineral composition of Valencia orange leaves. *Plant Physiol.* **24** : 455-61.

Smith, P. F. and Scudder, G. K. 1952. Some studies of mineral deficiency symptoms in mango. *Proc. Fla. St. Hort. Soc. for* 1951, pp. 243-8.

Smith, W. S. 1934. The guava. *U. P. Dept. Agr. Fruit Ser. Bul.* 8.

1940. The fig in rural areas. *U. P. Dept. Agr. Fruit. Ser. Bul.* 20.

Smock, R. M. Edgerton, L. J., and Hoffman, M. B. 1952. Inhibition of the ripening effect of certain auxins on apples with maleic hydrazide. *Proc. Amer. Soc. Hort. Sci.* **60** : 184-92.

Sodhi, G. S. and Batra, A. L. 1950. Use of power-driven sprayer in the control of mange hopper in the Punjab. *Ind. Fmg.* **11** : 158-61.

Sokolskaya, V. P. 1940. (Parthenocarpy as a result of pistil removal in flowers of citrus species). *Proc. Lenin Acad. Agr. Sci.* Nos. 23, 24, pp. 12-6.

Sontakay, K. R. 1943. Lemon butterfly and its control. *Ind. Fmg.* **4** : 456-7.

1945 a. The bark-eating borer of orange. *ibid.* **6** : 74-5.

1945 b. Biology and control of *Indarbela quadrinotata* (Wlk.), a pest of orange. *Proc. 32nd. Ind. Sci. Cong.*, p. 106.

Sontakay, K. R. and Gupta R. L. 1945. Seasonal incidence of *Phyllocnistis citrella* Stt., the citrus leaf miner *ibid.*, p. 106.

Sonwalkar, M. S. 1951 A study of jackfruit seeds. *Ind. J. Hort.* **8** (2) 27-30.

Soost, R K. and Cameron, J. W. 1954. Production of hybrids by the use of stored trifoliate orange pollen. *Proc. Amer. Soc Hort. Sci.* **63** : 234-8.

Spencer, J. L. and Kennard, W. C. 1955. Studies on mango (*Mangifera indica* L.) fruit set in Puerto Rico. *Trop. Agriculture.* **32** : 323-30.

Srivastava, H. C. and Mathur, P. B. 1954. Semi-commercial trial on the cold storage of Coorg oranges. *Bul Cent. Food. Tech. Res. Inst. Mysore* **3** : 248-50.

1955. Studies in the cold storage of langsats. *J. Sci. Food and Agr.* **6** : 511-3.

Srivastava, H. C. and Mehta, P. L. 1951. A new species of *Cercospora* on *Grewia asiatica* Linn. *Ind. Phytopath.* **4** : 67-70.

Srivastava, H. C. and Singh, B. 1954. Seedling trouble in citrus beds and their control. *Sci. and Cult.* **20** : 93-5.

Stahl, A. L., 1953. Composition of miscellaneous tropical and sub-tropical Florida fruits. *Fla. Agr. Exp. Sta. Bul.* 283.

Stephens, S. E. 1935. The litchi. *Qd. Agr. J.* **44** : 191-4.

1936. The sugar apple. *ibid.* **40** : 100-2.

1955. The litchi. *ibid.* **81** : 19-20.

Stevenson, S. A. 1947 a. The technique of budding in citrus. *Nagpur Agr. Col. Mag.* **21** : 60-6.

1947 b. The effect of season on the growth in citrus. *Punjab Fruit J.* **11** : 245-52.

1948. Girth in relation to budding in citrus. *Nagpur Agr. Col. Mag.* **22** : 186-90.

Stewart, I. and Leonard, C. D. 1952 a. Possible cau es and control of iron chlorosis. *Calif. Citrogr.* **37** : 427, 444-5.

1952 b. Molybdenum deficiency in Florida citrus. *Nature* **170** : 714-5.

1953. Correction of molybdenum deficiency in Florida citrus. *Proc. Amer. Soc. Hort. Sci.* **62** : 111-5.

1955. Chelated metals for growing plants. Chapter 16 of Mineral nutrition of fruit crops, edited by N. F. childers. Rutgers University.

Stewart, W. S. 1953. Effects of growth regulator sprays on set, size, abscission, and storage of citrus fruits. *Rpt.* 13*th. Internat. Hort. Cong.* 1952, pp. 1281-91.

Stewart, W. S. and Hield, H. Z. 1954. Sprays to increase size of fruit. *Calif. Citrogr.* **39** : 261, 263.

Stewart, W. S., Hield, H. Z., and Brannaman, B. L. 1952. Effects of 2, 4-D and related substances on fruit-drop, yield, size and quality of Valencia oranges. *Hilgardia* **21** : 301-29.

Stewart, W. S., Palmer, P. E., and Hield, H. Z. 1952. Packing house experiments on the use of 2, 4-dichlorophenoxyacetic acid and 2, 4, 5-trichlorophenoxacetic acid to increase storage life of lemons. *Proc. Amer. Soc. Hort. Sci.* **59** : 327-34.

Stewart, W. S. and Parker, E. R. 1954. The effects of 2, 4-D and related substances on fruit-drop, yield, size, and quality of grapefruit. *Hilgardia* **22** : 623-41.

Storey, W. B. 1937. The primary flower types of papayas and the fruit types that develop from them. *Proc. Amer. Soc. Hort. Sci.* **35** : 80-2.

1953. Genetics of the papaya. *J. Hered.* **44** : 70-8.

Sturrock, D. 1940. Tropical fruits for southern Florida and Cuba and their uses. Arnold Arboretum of Harvard University, Jamaica Plain, Mass.

Subbayya, J. 1954. The purpose and effects of mechanical tillage in the culture of orchard crops. *S. Ind. Hort.* **2** : 23-51.

Subramaniam, V. K. 1954, 1955. Control of the fluted scale in peninsular India. *Ind. J. Ent.* **16** : 391-515 and **17** : 103-20.

Sulaiman, M. 1954. Citrus die-back—its cause and control in Hyderabad State. *Proc.* 41*st Ind. Sci. Cong.*, p. 126.

Sultan, M. R. 1935. Hints on fruit growing. *Hyderabad Farmer* **5** : 58-60.

Sundararaj, D. D. 1952. Cultivation of bananas for leaves in Tanjore district. *Madras Agr. J.* **19** : 13-5.

(Sundays River Research Station). 1944. Research work in the Sundays River valley. *Citrus Grower* No. 121, pp. 1-3.

Suryanarayana, K. 1951. An economic survey of the production and marketing of mangoes in Visakhapatnam district. *Madras Agr. J.* **38** : 476-87.

Susainathan, B. 1924. The fruit moth problem in the northern Circars. *Agr. J. Ind.* **19** : 402-4.

Swarup, S. R. 1933. The strawberry : its cultivation and economic possibilities in the United Provinces. *U. P. Dept. Agr. Fruit Ser. Bul.* 5.

Swingle, C. F. 1947. The Peruvian cooking papaya, *Carica monoca*, a promising new fruit and vegetable for the United States corn belt. *Proc. Amer. Soc. Hort. Sci.* **47** : 137-8.

Swingle, W. T. 1943. The botany of citrus and its wild relatives of the orange sub-family (family Rutaceae, sub-family Aurantioideae). Chapter 4 of The Citrus Industry, Vol. 1. Univ. of Calif. Press, Berkeley and Los Angeles.

1948. Nucellar bud seedlings. *Calif. Citrogr.* **34** : 54, 66-7.

Syamal, N. B. and Patel, G. I. 1953. A wild species of grape in India. *Proc. Amer. Soc. Hort. Sci.* **62** : 228-30.

Tainter, M. L. and others. 1951. Papain. *Annals N. Y. Acad. Sci.* **54** : 143-296.

Talbert, T. J. 1935. How poisonous is spray residue ? *Proc. Amer. Soc. Hort. Sci.* **32** : 170-4.

Tanaka, T. 1937 *a*. Citrus fruits of India. *Allahabad Farmer* **11** : 2, ff.

1937 *b*. Further revision of Rutaceae-Aurantioideae of India and Ceylon. *J. Ind. Bot. Soc.* **16** : 227-40.

1954. Species problem in citrus. Japanese Society for the Promotion of Science, Ueno, Tokyo.

Tandon, D. N. 1941. Citrus psylla situation and what citrus growers should do. *Punjab Fruit. J.* **5** : 896-7.

Tandon, R. N. and Agarwala, R. K. 1954. Pathological studies of *Gloeo-Sporium psidii* causing die-back of guavas. *Proc. Ind. Acad. Sci. Sec. B* **40** : (4) 102-9.

Tandon, R. N. Sisodia, U. S., and Bilgrami, K. S. 1955. Pathological studies of *Pestalotia mangiferae*. *Proc. Ind. Acad. Sci. Sec B* **42** : 219-25.

Tarr, L. W., Baker, G. L., and Myers, P. B. 1923 to 1929. Fruit jellies. *Del. Agr. Exp. Sta. Bul.* 134, 136, 142, 144, 149, 160.

Taylor, C. A. 1941. Irrigation problems in citrus orchards. *U. S. Dept. Agr. Farmers' Bul.* 1876.

Temple, R. C. (editor). 1914. The travels of Peter Mundy in Europe and Asia, 1608 1667. Hakluyt Society, London.

Terry, E. 1777. A voyage to East-India (reprinted from the edition of 1665). London.

Texido, G. G. and Alvarez, J. L. P. 1954. (Seedless sapodilla). *Rev. Agr.* (Cuba) **37** (2) : 81-2.

Thakurta, A. G. and Dutt, B. K. 1941. Vegetative propagation of mango from gootes (marcotte) and cuttings by treatment with high concentration auxin. *Cur. Sci.* **10** : 297.

Thompson, A. R. 1914. Composition of Hawaiian fruits and nuts. *Hawaii Agr. Exp. Sta. Ann. Rpt., pp.* 62-73.

Thorold, C. A. 1949. Manurial experiments with papaw (*Carica papaya*). *Trop. Agriculture* **26** : 120-32.

Titus, J. S. and Boynton, D. 1953. The relationship between soil analysis and leaf analysis in eighty New York McIntosh apple orchards. *Proc. Amer. Soc. Hort. Sci.* **61** : 6-26.

Tolkowsky, S. 1930. The history of the cultivation of citrus fruits in Palestine. *Pal. Dept. Agr. and For. Agr. Leaflet* 22.

1938. Hesperides. John Bale, Sons and Curnow, London.

Toxopeus, H. J. 1936. Stock-scion incompatibility in citrus and its causes. *J. Pom. Hort. Sci.* **14** : 360-4.

Traub, H. P. and Marshall, L. C. 1936. Rooting of papaya cuttings. *Proc. Amer. Soc. Hort. Sci.* **34** : 291-4.

Trehan, K. N., Talgeri, G. M., and Dhareshwar. S. R. 1949. Control of "redants" (*Oecophylla smaragdina Fab.*). *Proc. Ind. Acad. Sci. Sec. B.* **30** : 338-42.

Trehan, K. N., Wagle, P. V., Bagal, S. R., and Talgeri, G. M. 1947. Biology and control of *Scelodonta strigicollis* Mots. (Chrysomelidae : Coleoptera). *Ind. J. Ent.* **9** : 93-107.

Tripathi R. D. 1954. 'Bunchy top' and 'malformation' diseases of the mango. *Ind. J. Hort.* **11** : 122-4.

Tukey, H. B. 1938. Stock and scion terminology. *Proc. Amer. Soc. Hort. Sci.* **35** : 378-82.

Tukey, H. B. and Hamner, C. L. 1949. Form and composition of cherry fruits (*Prunus avium* and *P. cerasus*) following fall applications of 2, 4-dichlorophenoxyacetic acid and napthalene acetic acid. *ibid.* **54** 95-101.

Ullah, H. 1954. The differentiation of flower bud of the peach (*Prunus persica*) in the Punjab. *Punjab Fruit J.* **18** : 34-41.

Ullah, H. and Khan, M. 1954. Some aspects of jujube (*Zizyphus jujuba ber*) cultivation in the Punjab. *Punjab Fruit J.* **18** : 16-20.

Ulvi, A. M. 1940. Mango budding. *Ind. Fmg.* **1** : 222-5.

Uppal, B. N. 1936. A serious disease of guava in Bombay. *Int. Bul. plant Protect.* **10** : 99 M. 68.

Uppal, B. N., Cheema, G. S., and Kamat, M. N. 1930. Powdery mildew of the grape and its control in Bombay. *Bombay Dept. Agr. Bul.* 163.

Uppal, B. N. and Kamat, M. N. 1936. Gummosis of citrus in Bombay. *Ind. J. Agr. Sci.* **6** : 803-22.

Uppal, B. N. and Wagle, P. V. 1944. Control of mango hoppers in Bombay province. *Ind. Fmg.* **5** : 401-3.

Vagholkar, P. B. 1916. Notes on the propagation of *bor* trees in East Khandesh. *Poona Agr. Col. Mag.* **8** : 124.

Vaheeduddin, S. 1954. Mango diseases. In The Mango, a souvenir, pp. 82-5. Dept. Agr., Hyderabad.

1955. Rust on grapefruit. *Cur. Sci.* **24** : 345.

Vaidyanathan, M. 1934. Analysis of manurial experiments in India. Govt. of India.

Van der Merwe, A. J. 1952-53. Nitrogen nutrition of citrus in nitrate and ammonium forms. *U. S. Afr. Dept. Agr. Sci. Bul.* 229.

Van der Merwe, D. P. 1944. Variations in vitamin C content in guavas. *Clin. Proceed.* **3** : 441-4.

Van der Meulen, A. 1954. Why and how mangoes are budded. *Fmg. S. Afr.* **29** : 209-12.

Van der Plank, J. E. and Turner, F. A. S. 1936. Are our sour oranges due to lack of phosphorus ? *Fmg. S. Afr.* 59-60.

Van Horn, C. W. 1941. Delayed foliation of pecan trees. *Proc. Amer. Soc. Hort. Sci.* **39** : 87-94.

Van Overbeek, J. 1946. Control of flower formation and fruit size in the pineapple. *Bot. Gaz.* **108** : 64-73.

Van Overbeek, J. and others, 1946. Plant physiology. In *Ann. Rpt. Inst. Trop. Agr. Puerto Rico., Mayaguez*, 1945-46, *pp.* 5-18.

Varadarajan, B. S. and Subramanian, C. K. 1953. Mandarin oranges in Coorg. *Ind. J. Hort.* **10** : 89-97.

Varghese, M. K. 1945. Bunchy top disease of plantains. *Ind. Fmg.* **6** : 239-40.

Varma, S. R. 1946. Importance of alpine fruits and the role that Patiala State plays in their culture. *Punjab Fruit J.* **10** : 134-6.

1947 *a.* A decade of performance of seven leading varieties of American grapes in Patiala hill territories. *ibid.* **11** : 233-5.

1947 *b.*, 1949 *a.* Glimpses into the fruit culture of ancient India. *Ind. J. Hort.* **5** : 1-7; **6** : 31-4.

1949 *b.* The synopsis of the biggest selective trials of the age in the Patiala State hills. B. S. Press, Patiala.

Vasudeva, R. S. and Raychaudhury, S. P. 1954. Guava disease in Pushkar valley and its control. *Ind. Phytopath.* **7** : 78-81.

Veeraraghavan, R. 1945. Side-grafting in mangoes. *Ind. J. Hort.* **3** : 45.

Venkatakrishnia, N. S. 1947. Pseudostem rot of plantains (*Musa sapientum* Linn.). *Mysore Agr. J.* **25** : 66-70.

1952. *Glomerella psidii* (Del.) Sheld. and *Pestalotia psidii* Pat. associated with a cankerous disease of guava. *Proc. Ind. Acad. Sci. sec. B.* **36** : 129-34.

1954. *Pestalotiopsis psidii on Psidium guava. Cur. Sci.* **23** : 164-5.

Venkataramani, K. S. 1949. On the occurrence of *Musa balbisiana* Colla., in S. India and its importance in banana breeding. *Madras Agr. J.* **36** : 552-4.

Venkataratnam, L. 1949. Hormone induced set and parthenocarpy in mango (*Mangifera indica L.*) *Cur. Sci.* **18** : 409.

1953. Horticultural wealth of Hyderabad. *Ind. J. Hort.* **10** : 149-53.

1954. The thirteenth annual report of the Hyderabad Fruit Research Scheme for the year 1953-54. Hyderabad Dept. Agr.

1955. Fourteenth annual report of the Hyderabad Fruit Research Scheme for the year 1954-55. Hyderabad Dept. Agr.

Venkataratnam, L., Farooqi, M. M., and Chellappa, T. 1952. The Anab-e-shahi grapevine and its culture in Hyderabad State. *Ind. J. Hort.* **9**(3) : 12-5.

Venkitasubban, C. S. 1948. A campaign on Nendrum plantation in Cochin. *Ind. Fmg.* **9** : 113-5.

Verma, G. S. 1950. Tip pulp of the mango fruit. *Cur. Sci.* **19** : 246.

Verma, G. S. and Kamal, M. 1951. Rot of *Mangifera indica* Linn. Caused by *Aspergillus*. *ibid.* **20** : 68-9.

Vestal, E. F. 1947. Further observations on weather and plant disease at Allahabad. *Allahabad Farmer* **21** : 79-84.

Von Loesecke, H. W. 1949. Bananas. Interscience Publishers, New York and London.

Vyas, N. D. 1938. The litchi, *U. P. Dept. Agr. Fruit Ser. Bul.* 12.

Vyvyan, M. C. 1946. Experiments with growth substance sprays for reduction of pre-harvest drop of fruit. *J. Pom. Hort. Sci.* **22** : 11-37.

Wagle, P. V. 1928. Ringing and notching experiments with the mango. *Agr. J. Ind.* **23** : 287-9.

1931. The bearing of the Alphonso mango in the Konkan and some methods of regulating the same. *Agr. and Livestock Ind.* **1** : 286-90.

Wahhab, A. and Zamir-ud-din. 1954. Retention of vitamin C in citrus juices. *Punjab Fruit J.* **18** : 8-17.

Waldo, G. F. and Darrow, G. W. 1948. Origin of the Logan and Mammoth blackberries. *J. Hered.* **39** : 99-107.

Walker, D. R. 1955. Foliar and soil applications of nitrogen to sour cherry and magnesium to apple trees. *Diss. Abst.* **15** : 188.

Wallace, A., Kimball, M. H., Mueller, R. T., and Welch, H. V. 1952. Influence of nitrogen fertilizers on the soil in the coastal zone of southern California. *Proc. Amer. Soc. Hort. Sci.* **59** : 22-30.

Wallace, A., North, C. P., and Frolich. E. 1953. Intoractions of rootstock, soil pH, and nitrogen on the growth and mineral composition of small lemon trees in a glasshouse. *ibid.* **62** : 75-8.

Wallace, A., North, C. P., Mueller, R. T., and Hemaidan, N. 1953. Chelating agents as a means of supplying micronutrients to woody plants in alkaline and calcareous soils. *ibid.* **62** : 116-8.

Wallace, J. M. and Darke, R. J. 1955. Tristeza virus in Meyer lemon. *Calif. Citrogr.* **40** : 84, 95-6.

Wallace, T. and Hewitt, E. J. 1946. Studies in iron deficiency in crops. I. Problems of iron deficiency and interrelationships of mineral elements in iron nutrition. *J. Pom. Hort. Sci.* **22** : 153-61.

Wallschlaeger, F. O. 1933. Cost of producing citrus continues to show decline. *Calif. Citrogr.* **18** : 12.

Walters, E. A. 1932. Plant propagation. *Trop. Agriculture* **9** : 35-9.

Walters, T. 1904. On Yuan Chwang's travels in India. Royal Asiatic Society, London.

Wander, I. W. 1954. Sources contributing to subsoil acidity in Florida citrus groves. *Proc. Amer. Soc. Hort. Sci.* **64**: 105-10.

Wardlaw, C. W. and Leonard, F. R. 1936. Storage of West Indian mangoes. *Trin. Low Temp: Res. Sta: Mem.* 3.

Wardlaw, C. W. and McGuire, L. P. Bananas. The behaviour and diseases of bananas in storage and transport. Empire Marketing Board.

Watt, G. 1889. Dictionary of the economic products of India. Govt. of India.

1908. The Commercial products of India. John Murray, London.

Weathers, L. G., Calavan, E. C., Wallace, J. M., and Christiansen, D. W. 1955. Troyer citrange with Eureka tops. *Calif. Citrogr.* **40** : 427-30.

Weaver, R. J. 1952. Response of Black Corinth grapes to applications of 4-chlorophenoxyacetic acid. *Bot. Gaz.* **114** : 107-13.

1953. Further studies on effects of 4-chlorophenoxyacetic acid on development of Thompson Seedless and Black Corinth grapes. *Proc. Amer. Soc. Hort. Sci.* **61** : 135-43.

Webber, H. J. 1932. Variation in citrus seedlings and their relation to rootstock selection. *Hilgardia* **7** : 1-79.

1939. When did the sweet orange reach Europe ? *Calif. Citrogr.* **23** : 451, ff.

1942. Extending guava production in California. *Proc. Amer. Soc. Hort. Sci.* **41** : 228-33.

1943 *a*. The "tristeza" disease of sour-orange rootstock. *ibid.* **43** : 160-8

1943 *b*. Cultivated varieties of citrus. Chapter 5 of The citrus industry, Vol. I. Univ. of Calif. Press, Berkeley and Los Angeles.

1943 *c*. The commercial citrus regions of the world. Chapter 3 of The citrus industry, Vol. I Univ. of Calif. Press, Berkeley and Los Angeles.

1944. The vitamin C content of guavas. *Proc. Amer. Soc. Hort. Sci.* **45**: 87-94.

Weinberger, J. H. 1940. Studies on the use of certain dinitrophenol compounds to break the rest period in peach trees. *ibid.* **37** : 353-8.

West, E. S. and Barnard, C. 1953. The alternation of heavy and light crops in the Valencia Late orange. *J. Coun. Sci. Ind. Res. Australia* **8** : 93-100.

Wester, P. J. 1913. Citriculture in the Philippines. *Phil. Bur. Agr. Bul.* 27.

1917. A contribution to the history of the mango in Florida. *Phil. Agr. Rev.* **10** (2). Reprinted in Mango studies, pp. 9-11. 1951. Florida Mango Forum.

1922. A descriptive list of mango varieties in India. *Phil. Bur. Agr. Bul.* 36.

1925. The food plants of the Philippines. *Phil. Bur. Agr. Bul.* 39.

White, D. G. 1953. Promotion of red color of apples. II. Effects of preharvest sprays of certain chemicals in multiple combinations. *Proc. Amer. Soc. Hort. Sci.* **61** : 180-4.

Wilkins, E. G. 1942. Mango kernels as food. *Ind. Fmg.* **2** : 636-7.

Williams, C. H. B. and Choong, P. A. C. 1944. Guava yields in British Guiana. *Trop. Agriculture* **21** : 67-8.

Williams, J. M. 1926. The expansion of rural life. Alfred A. Knopf.

Wilson, T. B. 1954. The marketing of durian fruit from Parit District, Perak. *Malay Agr. J.*, **37** : 211-7.

Winters, H. F. and Rodriguez-Colon, F. 1953. Storage of mangosteen seed. *Proc. Amer. Soc. Hort. Sci.* **61** : 340-6.

Woglum, R. S. 1949. History of fumigation in California. *Calif. Citrogr.* **35** : 46, ff.

Woglum, R. S., Plummer, C. C., and Shaw, J. G. 1949. Insecticides for citrus blackfly. *ibid.* **34** : 146, ff.

Woodford, R. C. 1948. Annual report of the Department of Agriculture, Assam, for the year ending 31st. March, 1946, pp. 25-7.

Young, T. W. 1951. Investigations of the unfruitfulness of the Haden Mango in Florida. Mango studies, pp. 26-9. Florida Mango Forum.

Zanini, E. 1950. (The use of growth substances to reduce crop failure and fruit drop in citrus.) *Fruits et Prim.* **20** : 269-74.

Zielinski, Q. B. and Garren, R., Jr. 1952. Effects of beta-naphthoxyacetic acid on fruit size in the Marshall strawberry. *Bot. Gaz.* **114** : 134-9...

Zielinski, Q. B., Garren, R., Jr., and Annen, C. J. 1954. Effects of para-chlorophenoxyacetic acid and beta-naphthoxyacetic acid on increasing fruit size in Thornless Evergreen blackberries. *Proc. Amer. Soc. Hort. Sci.* **63** : 182-8.

Zimmerman, P. W. and Hitchcock, A. E. 1946. The relation between age of stem tissue and the capacity to form roots. *J. Gerontol.* **1** : 27-32.

INDEX

A

B

M

N

O

P